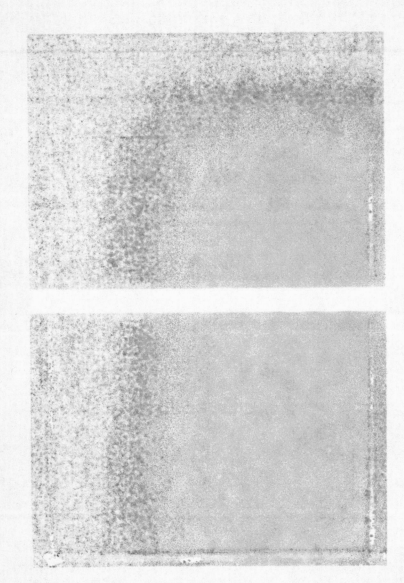

ENGLISH RECUSANT LITERATURE
1558–1640

Selected and Edited by
D. M. ROGERS

Volume 345

Sacra Institutio Baptizandi
1604

GIOVANNI PIETRO MAFFEI
Fuga Saeculi
1632

Sacra Institutio Baptizandi
1604

The Scolar Press
1977

ISBN 0 85967 384 7

Published and printed in Great Britain by
The Scolar Press Limited, 59-61 East Parade,
Ilkley, Yorkshire and
39 Great Russell Street,
London WC1

NOTE

The following works are reproduced (original size) with permission:

1) *Sacra institutio baptizandi*, 1604, from a copy in the library of Heythrop College, by permission of the Librarian.
References: Allison and Rogers 718; not in STC (but see STC 16158).

2) Giovanni Pietro Maffei, *Fuga saeculi*, 1632, from a copy in the library of Heythrop College, by permission of the Librarian.
References: Allison and Rogers 490; STC 17181.

SACRA INSTITVTIO BAPTIZANDI: MATRIMONIVM CELEBRANDI: INFIRMOS VNGENDI: MORTVOS SEPELIENDI: AC ALII NONNVLLI RITVS ECCLESIASTICI: iuxta vsum insignis Ecclesiæ Sarisburiensis.

MAT. VLT.

Data est mihi omnis potestas in cœlo, & in terra, Euntes ergo docete omnes gentes: baptizantes eos in nomine Patris, & Filij, & Spiritus sancti: docentes eos seruare omnia quæcunque mandaui vobis.

Conc. Trid. sess. 7. Can. 13. de Sacr. in genere.

Si quis dixerit, receptos, & approbatos Ecclesiæ catholicæ ritus, in solemni Sacramentorum administratione adhiberi consuetos, aut contemni, aut sine peccato a ministris pro libito omitti, aut in alios per quemcunque Ecclesiarum pastorem mutari posse; anathema sit.

DVACI,
Excudebat LAVRENTIVS KELLAM,
Typog. Iurat. M. DC. IIII.
Permissu Superiorum.

ORDO AD CATECHVMENVM FACIENDVM.

Mprimis deferatur infans ad valuas Eccleſiæ, & inquirat Sacerdos ab obſtetrice, vtrum ſit infans maſculus an fœmina. Deinde. Si infans fuerit baptizatus domi: & quo nomine vocari debeat. Licet enim baptizatus fuerit domi propter periculum mortis : tamen totum habeat ſubſequens ſeruitium, præter immerſionem aquæ, & quo nomine debet vocari. Maſculus autem ſtatuatur a dextris Sacerdotis, fœmina verò à ſiniſtris.

His quæſitis faciat ſignum crucis cum pollice in fronte infantis, ita dicens:

Signum Saluatoris Domini noſtri Ieſu Chriſti in frontem tuam pono. Et poſtea in pectore ita dicens:

Signum Saluatoris Domini noſtri Ieſu Chriſti in pectus tuum pono.

Deinde tenens manum dexterã super caput infantis dicat.

℣. Dominus vobiscum. ℟. Et cum spiritu tuo.

Oremus.

OMnipotens sempiterne Deus, pater Domini nostri Iesu Christi, respicere dignare super hunc famulum tuum (vel hanc famulam tuam.)

Hic inquirat Sacerdos nomen infantis, & respondeant patrini.

N. quem (vel quam) ad rudimẽta fidei vocare dignatus es: omnem cæcitatem cordis ab eo (vel ea) expelle, disrumpe omnes laqueos Satanę, quibus fuerit colligatus (vel colligata) Aperi ei Domine ianuam pietatis tuæ, vt signo sapientiæ tuæ imbutus (vel imbuta) omnium cupiditatum fœtoribus careat, & ad suauem odorem præceptorum tuorum lætus (vel læta) tibi in Ecclesia tua deseruiat, & proficiat de die in diem, vt idoneus (vel idonea) efficiatur accedere ad gratiam Baptismi tui, percepta medecina. Per eundem Christum Dominum nostrum. Amen.

Deinde dicatur oratio sine Dominus vobiscum.

Oremus.

PReces nostras quæsumus Domine clementer exaudi, & hunc electum tuum (vel hanc electam tuam)

Hic patrini & matrinæ nominent puerum.

N. Crucis dominicæ, (cuius impressione,

Hic faciat Sacerdos crucem in fronte infantis,

eum (vel eam) signamus) virtute custodi, vt magnitudinis gloriæ tuæ rudimenta seruans, per custodiam mandatorum

rum ad nouæ regenerationis gloriam peruenire mereatur. Per Christum Dominum nostrum. Amen.

Oremus.

DEus qui humani generis ita es conditor, vt sis etiam reformator: propitiare populis adoptiuis, & nouo testamento sobolem nouæ prolis ascribe, vt filij promissionis, quod non potuerunt assequi per naturam, gaudeant se recepisse per gratiam. Per Dominum nostrum Iesum Christum filium tuum, qui tecum. Amen.

Exorcismus salis. sine Oremus.

EXorcizo te creatura salis, in nomine Dei Patris omnipotentis, & in charitate Domini nostri Iesu Christi, & in virtute Spiritus sancti. Exorcizo te per Deum ✠ viuum, per Deum ✠ verum, per Deum ✠ sanctum, per Deum qui te ad tutelam humani generis procreauit, & populo venienti ad credulitatem, per seruos suos consecrari præcepit, vt in nomine sanctæ Trinitatis efficiaris salutare sacramentum, ad effugandum inimicum. Proinde rogamus te Domine Deus noster vt hanc

Hic respiciat Sacerdos sal,

creaturam salis, sanctificado sancti ✠ fices, benedicendo bene ✠ dicas, vt fiat omnibus accipientibus perfecta medecina permanens in visceribus eorum, virtute eiusdem Domini nostri Iesu Christi, qui venturus est iudicare viuos & mortuos & sæculum per ignem. ℟. Amen.

Iterum interroget Sacerdos nomen pueri, & ponat de ipso sale in ore eius dicens.

N. Accipe ſal ſapientiæ, vt propitiatus ſit tibi Deus in vitam æternam. Amen.

Poſtea dicat Sacerdos ſuper maſculum vel fœminam.

℣. Dominus vobiſcum. ℟. Et cum ſpiritu tuo.

Oremus.

DEus patrum noſtrorũ, Deus vniuerſæ conditor creaturæ, te ſupplices exoramus vt hunc famulũ tuũ [vel hanc famulam tuam] N. reſpicere digneris propitius, & hoc primum pabulum ſalis guſtantem, non diutius eſurire permittas, quo minus cibo repleatur cœleſti, quatenus ſit ſemper Domine ſpiritu feruens, ſpe gaudens, tuo nomini ſeruiens, & perduc eum [vel eam] ad nouæ regenerationis lauacrum, vt cum fidelibus tuis promiſſionum tuarum æterna præmia conſequi mereatur. Per Dominum noſtrum Ieſum Chriſtum, &c. Amen.

Sequatur Oratio ſuper maſculum tantum, ſine Dominus vobiſcum ſed cum Oremus. Si fuerit fæmina, verte ad pag. 9.

Oremus.

M. DEus Abraham, Deus Iſaac, Deus Iacob, Deus qui Moyſi famulo tuo in monte Sinai apparuiſti, & filios Iſrael de terra Ægipti eduxiſti, deputans eis Angelum pietatis tuæ, qui cuſtodiret eos die ac nocte: te quæſumus Domine, vt mittere digneris Angelum tuum de cœlis, qui ſimiliter cuſtodiat hunc famulum tuum N. & perducat eum ad gratiam Baptiſmi tui. Sine per Chriſt.

Adiuratio ſuper maſculum, ſine Dominus vobiſcum, & ſine

& sine oremus, Sacerdote dicente.

Ergo maledicte diabole recognosce sententiam tuam, & da honorem Deo viuo & vero, da honorem Iesu Christo Filio eius & Spiritui Sancto, & recede ab hoc famulo Dei N. quia istum sibi Deus & Dominus noster Iesus Christus ad suam sanctam gratiã & benedictionem, fontemq; Baptismatis dono Spiritus Sancti vocare dignatus est.

Hic faciat Sacerdos signum crucis in fronte infantis cum pollice suo, ita dicens:

Et hoc signum sanctæ Cru ✠ cis, quod nos fronti eius imponimus, tu maledicte diabole, nunquam audeas violare. Per eum qui venturus est iudicare viuos & mortuos & sæculum per ignem. ℟. Amen.

Hæc sequens oratio dicitur super masculum tantum, sine Dominus vobiscum, & sine oremus.

DEus immortale præsidium omnium postulantium, liberatio supplicum, pax rogantium, vita credentium, resurrectio mortuorum, te inuoco super hunc famulum tuum N. qui Baptismi tui donum petens, æternam consequi gratiam spirituali regeneratione desiderat. Accipe eum Domine, & qui dignatus es dicere, petite & accipietis, quærite & inuenietis, pulsate & aperietur vobis, petenti præmium porrige, & ianuam pande pulsanti, vt æternam cælestis lauacri benedictionem consequutus, promissa tui muneris regna percipiat. Qui viuis & regnas cum Deo Patre in vnitate Spiritus Sancti Deus, per omnia sæcula sæculorum ℟. Amen.

Adiuratio

Adiuratio super masculum tantum, sine Dominus vobiscum, & sinè Oremus, hoc modo.

AVdi maledicte Satana aduiratus per nomen æterni Dei Saluatoris nostri Filij eius, cum tua victus inuidia tremens, geménsque discede, nihil tibi sit commune cum seruo Dei N. iam cælestia cogitanti, renunciaturo tibi, atque sæculo tuo, & beatæ immortalitati victuro. Da igitur honorem aduenienti Spiritui Sancto, qui ex summa cæli arce descendens, perturbatis fraudibus tuis, diuino fonte purgatum pectus (id est sanctificatum Deo templum & habitaculum) perficiat, vt ab omnibus penitus noxijs præteritorum criminum liberatus, hic seruus Dei, gratias perenni Deo referat semper, & benedicat nomen eius sanctum in sæcula sæculorum. Amen.

Exorcismus super masculum tantum, sine oremus.

EXorcizo te immunde spiritus in nomine Dei Patris ✠, & Filij ✠, & Spiritus sancti ✠, vt exeas & recedas ab hoc famulo Dei (respice) N. Ipse enim tibi imperat maledicte, damnate, atque damnande, qui pedibus super mare ambulauit, & Petro mergēti dexteram porrexit.

Sequatur aduratio.

ERgo maledicte diabole recognosce sententiam tuam, & da honorem Deo viuo & vero, da honorem Iesu Christo filio eius, & Spiritui sancto, & recede ab hoc famulo Dei N. quia istum sibi Deus & Dominus noster Iesus Christus ad suam sanctam gratiam & benedictionem fontemque Baptismatis dono Spiritus Sancti vocare dignatus

gnatus est. Et hoc signum sanctæ cru ✠ cis Hic faciat Sacerdos signum crucis in fronte infantis cum pollice. quod nos fronti eius imponimus, tu maledicte diabole nunquam audeas violare. Per eum qui venturus est iudicare viuos & mortuos & sæculum per ignem. ℟. Amen.

Verte ad paginam. 11.

Hæc sequens oratio dicatur super fæminam tantum, sine Dominus vobiscum, & sine Oremus.

DEus cæli, Deus terræ, Deus Angelorum, Deus Archangelorum, Deus Patriarcharum, Deus Prophetarum, Deus Apostolorum, Deus Martyrum, Deus Confessorum, Deus Virginum, Deus omnium benè viuentiũ, Deus cui omnis lingua confitetur, & omne genu flectitur, cælestium, terrestrium, & infernorum, te inuoco Domine super hanc famulam tuam (respice) N. & perducere eam digneris ad gratiam Baptismi tui.

Sequatur adiuratio super fæminam.

ERgo maledicte diabole recognosce sententiam tuam, & da honorem Deo viuo & vero, da honorem Iesu Christo Filio eius, & Spiritui Sancto, & recede ab hac famula Dei N. quia istam sibi Deus & Dominus noster Iesus Christus ad suam sanctam gratiam & benedictionẽ, fontemque Baptismatis dono Spiritus Sancti vocare dignatus est. Et hoc signum sanctæ cru ✠ cis Hic faciat Sacerdos signum crucis in fronte infantis cum pollice, quod nos fronti eius damus, tu maledicte diabole nunquam audeas violare. Per eum qui venturus est iudicare viuos & mortuos, & sæculum per ignem. ℞. Amen.

Item super fæminam tantum, dicitur sequens oratio, sine Dominus vobiscum, & sine Oremus.

DEus Abraham, Deus Isaac, & Deus Iacob, Deus qui Tribus Israel de Ægiptiaca seruitute liberasti, & per Moysen famulum tuum, de custodia mandatorũ tuorum in deserto monuisti, & Susannam de falso crimine liberasti: te supplex deprecor Domine, vt liberes hanc famulam tuam [respice] N. & perducere eam digneris ad gratiam Baptismi tui.

Sequatur adiuratio.

ERgo maledicte diabole recognosce sententiam tuã, & da honorẽ Deo viuo & vero, da honorẽ Iesu Christo Filio eius, & Spiritui Sancto, & recede ab hac famula Dei N. quia istam sibi Deus, & Dominus noster Iesus Christus, ad suam sanctam gratiam & benedictionem, fontémque Baptismatis dono Spiritus Sancti vocare dignatus est. Et hoc signum sanctæ cru ✠ cis, Hic faciat Sacerdos signum crucis in fronte infantis cum pollice suo, quod nos fronti eius damus, tu maledicte diabole nunquam audeas violare. Per eum qui venturus est iudicare viuos & mortuos, & sæculum per ignem. ℞. Amen.

Exorcismus super fæminam tantum, sine Dominus vobiscum, & sine Oremus.

EXorcizo te immunde spiritus, per Pa ✠ trem, & Fi ✠ lium, & Spiritum ✠ Sanctum, vt exeas & recedas ab hac famula Dei [respice] N. Ipse enim tibi imperat marat maledicte damnate, atque damnande, qui cæco nato oculos aperuit, & quatriduanum Lazarum de monumẽto suscitauit. Sequatur adiuratio.

Ergo maledicte &c. vt supra,

Exinde tam super masculos quam super fæminas dicantur orationes sequentes, sine Dominus vobiscum, & sine Oremus.

Hic facit Sacerdos crucem cum pollice in fronte infantis, tenensque manum super caput eius, dicat.

ÆTernam ac iustissimam pietatẽ tuam deprecor Domine, sãcte Pater omnipotẽs, æterne Deus, Auctor luminis & veritatis: respice super hunc famulũ tuum (vel hãc famulam tuam [respice] N. vt digneris illum (vel illã) illuminare lumine intelligentiæ tuæ. Munda eum (vel eã) & sancti ✠ fica, da ei scientiam veram, vt dignus (vel digna) efficiatur accedere ad gratiam Baptismi tui: teneat firmam spem, consilium rectum, doctrinam sanctam, vt aptus (vel apta) sit ad percipiendam gratiam Baptismi tui. Per Christum Dominum nostrum. ℟. Amen.

Sequatur Exorcismus, sine Oremus.

NEc te latet Satana, imminere tibi pœnas, imminere tibi tormẽta, imminere tibi diem iudicij, diem supplicij sempiterni: diem qui venturus est velut clibanus ardens: in quo tibi atque vniuersis angelis tuis æternus superueniet interitus. Et ideo pro tua nequitia, damnate atque damnande, da honorem Deo viuo & vero, da honorem Iesu Christo Filio eius, da honorem Spiritui Sancto

Paracléto, in cuius nomine atque virtute præcipio tibi, quicunque es spiritus immunde, vt exeas & recedas ab hoc famulo [vel ab hac famula] Dei (respice) N. quem [vel quam] hodie idem Deus & Dominus noster Iesus Christus ad suam sanctam gratiam & benedictionem, fontemque Baptismatis vocare dignatus est: vt fiat eius templum per aquam regenerationis, in remissionem omnium peccatorum suorum: In nomine eiusdem Domini nostri Iesu Christi, qui venturus est iudicare viuos & mortuos, & sæculum per ignem. ℟. Amen.

His dictis dicat Sacerdos.

Dominus vobiscum, ℟. Et cum spiritu tuo.

Sequentia sancti Euangelij secundum Mattheum.

℟. Gloria tibi Domine.

IN illo tempore, Oblati sunt Iesu paruuli, vt manus eis imponeret & oraret. Discipuli autem increpabant eos. Iesus vero ait eis: Sinite paruulos, & nolite eos prohibere ad me venire, talium est enim regnum cœlorum. Et cum imposuisset eis manus, abijt inde. ℟. Laus tibi Christe.

Deinde spuat Sacerdos in sinistra manu, & tangat aures & nares infantis cum pollice suo dextero de sputo, dicens ad aurem dexteram. Epheta quod est adaperire. Ad nares, In odorem suauitatis, Ad aurem sinistram, Tu autem effugare diabole, appropinquabit enim iudicium Dei.

Postea dicat Sacerdos compatribus, & commatribus, vna cum omnibus circumstantibus, vt sequitur.

GOdfathers and Godmothers, and al that be here present, ſay in the vvorship of God, and our B. Ladie and of the tvvelue Apoſtles: a Pater noſter, & Aue Maria: and Credo in Deum: that vve may ſo miniſter this bleſſed Sacrament, that it may be to the pleaſure of almightie God, and confuſion of our ghoſtlie enimie, & ſaluation of the ſoule of this childe.

Eadem etiam ipſe Sacerdos dicat, cunctis audientibus, modeſte & diſtincte.

PAter noſter, qui es in cœlis: ſanctificetur nomen tuũ: adueniat regnum tuum: fiat voluntas tua, ſicut in cœlo & in terra: panem noſtrum quotidianũ da nobis hodie: & dimitte nobis debita noſtra, ſicut & nos dimittimus debitoribus noſtris: & ne nos inducas in tentationem: ſed libera nos a malo. Amen.

AVe Maria, gratia plena, Dominus tecum: benedicta tu in mulieribus, & benedictus fructus ventris tui Ieſus. Sancta Maria mater Dei, ora pro nobis peccatoribus, nunc & in hora mortis noſtræ. Amen.

CRedo in Deum patrem omnipotentem, creatorem cœli & terræ: & in Ieſum Chriſtum Filium eius vnicũ Dominum noſtrum: qui conceptus eſt de Spiritu Sancto, natus ex Maria virgine: paſſus ſub Pontio Pilato, crucifixus, mortuus, & ſepultus, deſcendit ad inferos: tertia die reſurrexit a mortuis: aſcendit ad cœlos, ſedet ad dexteram Dei patris omnipotentis: inde venturus eſt iudicare viuos & mortuos: Credo in Spiritum Sanctum: ſanctam Eccleſiam Catholicam, ſanctorum communionem: remiſſionem peccatorum: carnis reſurrectionem: vitam æternam. Amen.

His dictis faciat Sacerdos ſignum crucis in manu dextera infantis, interrogato eius nomine, ita dicens.

N. Trado tibi ſignaculum Domini noſtri Ieſu Chriſti in manu tua dextera, vt te ſignes, & te de aduerſa parte repellas, & in fide Catholica permaneas, & habeas vitam æternam, & viuas in ſæcula ſæculorum. Amen.

Poſtea benedicat Sacerdos infantem ſic:

Benedictio Dei Patris omnipotentis, & ✠ Filij, & Spiritus Sancti, deſcendat ſuper te, & maneat ſemper.
℟. Amen.

Poſtea introducat Catechumenum per manum dexteram in Eccleſiam, interrogato nomine eius, dicens.

N. Ingredere in Templum Dei, vt habeas vitam æternam, & viuas in ſæcula ſæculorum. Amen.

BENE-

BENEDICTIO FONTIS.

QVando fuerit Fons mundãdus, & de pura aqua renouandus, (quod ſæpe debet fieri propter aquæ corruptionem) tunc dicatur ſequens Litania, & benedicatur fons modo ſequẽti. Et nota quod aqua Baptiſmatis non debet tranſmutari propter honorem alicuius potentis, niſi fuerit corrupta. Nota etiam quod aqua benedicta Fontium, in vigilia Paſchæ & Pentecoſtes, non aſpergatur per Eccleſiam, ſed aliqua alia aqua benedicta more ſolito, ſicut in alijs Dominicis diebus. Memorialiter retinendum eſt quod aqua benedicta circa Fontes eſt aſpergenda, ſed non aqua Fõtium, ſiue Chriſmate fuerit ſanctificata, ſiue non. Quoniam in Decretis originalibus ſanctorum Patrum Clementis, & Paſcaſij Paparum, inuenitur, quod aqua Fontium non eſt aqua aſperſionis, ſed Baptiſmatis, & purgationis. Vnde caueat vnuſquiſque Sacerdos, ne illâ aquâ tãgat, niſi quos baptizat: quia non eſt opus vt baptizati iterum baptizentur. Ceſſet ergo ſtulta preſumptionis aſperſio, tã in vigilia Paſchatis & Pentecoſtes, quam in omnibus alijs diebus, quia per Eccleſiam Romanam cunctis chriſtianis ſub pena Excommunicationis maioris eſt inhibita.

SEQVVNTVR LITANIÆ.

Kyrie eleiſon.
Chriſte eleiſon.
Kyrie eleiſon.
Chriſte audi nos.
Pater de cœlis Deus, Miſerere nobis.
Fili redemptor mundi Deus, Miſerere nobis.
Spiritus Sancte Deus, Miſerere nobis.

Sancta Trinitas vnus Deus,
Miſerere nobis.
Sancta Maria, ora pro no.
Sancta Dei genetrix, ora.
Sancta virgo virginũ, ora.
Sancte Michael, ora.
Sancte Gabriel, ora.
Sancte Raphael, ora.
Omnes ſancti Angeli & Archangeli Dei, orate.
Omnes ſancti beatorũ ſpiritum ordines orate.
Sancte Ioannes Baptiſta, ora pro nobis.
Omnes ſancti Patriarchæ & Prophetæ, orate.
Sancte Petre, ora.
Sancte Paule, ora.
Sancte Andræa, ora.
Sancte Ioannes, ora.
Sancte Iacobe, ora.
Sancte Thoma, ora.
Sancte Philippe, ora.
Sancte Iacobe, ora.
Sancte Matthæe, ora.
Sancte Bartholomæe, ora.
Sancte Simon, ora.

Sancte Thadæe, ora.
Sancte Matthia, ora.
Sancte Barnaba, ora.
Sancte Marce, ora.
Sancte Luca, ora.
Omnes ſancti Apoſtoli & Euangeliſtæ, orate.
Omnes ſancti Diſcipuli & Innocentes, orate.
Sancte Stephane, ora.
Sancte Line, ora.
Sancte Clete, ora.
Sancte Clemens, ora.
Sancte Fabiane, ora.
Sancte Sebaſtiane, ora.
Sancte Albane, ora.
Sancte Coſma, ora.
Sancte Damiane, ora.
Sancte Prime, ora.
Sancte Fæliciane, ora.
Sancte Dioniſi cum ſocijs tuis. orate.
Sancte Victor cum ſocijs tuis, orate.
Omnes ſancti Martyres, orate pro nobis.
Sancte Silueſter, ora.

Sancte

Sancte Leo, ora.
Sancte Hieronime, ora.
Sancte Augustine, ora.
Sancte Isidore, ora.
Sancte Iuliane, ora.
Sancte Gildarde, ora.
Sancte Medarde, ora.
Sancte Albine, ora.
Sancte Eusebi, ora.
Sancte Suithune, ora.
Sancte Berine, ora.
Omnes sancti Confessores, orate pro nobis.
Omnes sancti Monachi, & Eremitæ, orate.
Sancta Maria Magdalena, ora pro nobis.
Sancta Maria Ægiptiaca, ora pro nobis.
Sancta Margareta, ora.
Sancta Scholastica, ora.
Sancta Petronella, ora.
Sancta Genouefa, ora.
Sancta Praxedes, ora.
Sancta Sotheris, ora.
Sancta Prisca, ora.
Sancta Thecla, ora.
Sancta Afra, ora.
Sancta Editha, ora.
Omnes sanctæ Virgines, orate pro nobis.
Omnes Sancti, & Sanctæ, Dei, orate pro nobis.

His ita completis, accedat Sacerdos ad Fontium consecrationem, quæ semper dicatur sine cantu, nisi tantum in vigilia Paschæ & Pentecostes. Tunc enim cantata secunda Litania, incipiat Sacerdos ad hunc locum cantare modesta voce.

℣. Dominus vobiscum. ℟. Et cum spiritu tuo.

Oremus.

OMnipotens sempiterne Deus, adesto magnæ pietatis tuæ mysterijs, adesto sacramentis: & ad recreandos nouos populos, quos tibi fons Baptismatis parturit,

 spiritum

ſpiritum adoptionis emitte: vt quod noſtræ humanitatis gerendum eſt miniſterio, tuæ virtutis impleatur effectu. Per Dominum noſtrum Ieſum Chriſtum Filium tuum, qui tecum viuit & regnat in vnitate Spiritus Sancti Deus, per omnia ſæcula ſæculorum. ℟. Amen.

Dominus vobiſcum. ℟. Et cum ſpiritu tuo.

Surſum corda ℟. Habemus ad Dominum.

Gratias agamus Domino Deo noſtro. ℟. Dignum & iuſtum eſt.

Vere dignum & iuſtum eſt, æquum & ſalutare: nos tibi ſemper & vbique gratias agere, Domine ſancte, Pater omnipotens æterne Deus. Qui inuiſibili potentia, ſacramentorum tuorum mirabiliter operaris effectum. Et licet nos tantis myſterijs exequendis ſimus indigni: tu tamen gratiæ tuæ dona non deſerens, etiam ad noſtras preces aures tuæ pietatis inclines. Deus cuius Spiritus ſuper aquas inter ipſa mundi primordia ferebatur: vt iam tunc virtutem ſanctificationis aquarum natura conciperet. Deus qui nocentis mundi crimina per aquas abluens, regenerationis ſpeciem in ipſa diluuij effuſione ſignaſti: vt vnius eiuſdemq; elementi myſterio, & finis eſſet vitijs, & origo virtutibus. Reſpice quæſumus Domine in faciem Eccleſiæ tuæ, & multiplica in ea regenerationes tuas, qui gratiæ tuæ affluentis impetu lætificas ciuitatem tuam, fontemq; Baptiſmatis aperis, toto orbe terrarum gentibus inuocandis: vt tuæ majeſtatis imperio, ſumat vnigeniti tui gratiam de Spiritu Sancto.

Hic

Hic Sacerdos diuidat aquam manu sua dextera in modum crucis sic dicens:

Qui hanc aquam regenerandis hominibus præparatam, arcana sui luminis admistione fæcundet: vt sanctificatione concepta, ab immaculato diuini fontis vtero, innouã, renata creaturam, progenies cœlestis emergat. Et quos aut sexus in corpore, aut ætas discernit in tempore, omnes in vnam pariat gratia mater infantiam. Procul ergo hinc iubẽte te Domine omnis spiritus immundus abscedat: procul tota nequitia diabolicæ fraudis absistat. Nihil hic loci habeat contrariæ virtutis admistio: non insidiando circumuolet, non latendo surrepat, non inficiendo corrumpat. Sit hæc sancta & innocens creatura, libera ab omni impugnatoris incursu, & totius nequitiæ purgata discessu. Sit fons viuus, aqua regenerans, vnda purificans: vt omnes hoc lauacro salutifero diluendi, operante in eis Spiritu Sancto, perfectæ purgationis indulgentiam cõsequantur. Vnde bene ✠ dico te creatura aquæ: per Deum ✠ viuum: per Deum ✠ verum: per Deum ✠ sanctum: per Deum qui te in principio, verbo separauit ab arida: cuius Spiritus super te ferebatur. Qui te de paradiso manare fecit, & in quatuor fluminibus totam terram rigare præcepit.

Hic eijciat Sacerdos aquam de fonte per quatuor partes, cum manu dextera in modum crucis.

Qui te in deserto amaram, suauitate indita fecit esse potabilem, & sitienti populo de petra produxit. Bene ✠ dico te per Iesum Christum Filium eius vnicum Dominũ nostrum: qui te in Cana Galileæ signo admirabili, sua potentia conuertit in vinum. Qui pedibus super te ambulauit, & a Ioanne in Iordane in te baptizatus est. Qui te vna cum sanguine de latere suo produxit, & Discipulis iussit vt credentes baptizarentur in te dicens: Ite, docete omnes gentes, baptizantes eos in nomine Pa ✠ tris, & Fi ✠ lij, & Spiritus ✠ Sancti. Hæc nobis præcepta seruantibus, tu Deus omnipotens, clemens adesto: tu benignus aspira.

Hic aspiret Sacerdos ter in fontem, in modum crucis: deinde dicat sic:

Tu has simplices aquas tuo ore benedicito: vt præter naturalem emundationem, quam lauandis possunt adhibere corporibus, sint etiam purificandis mentibus efficaces.

Hic stillet Sacerdos de Cereo in fontem in modum crucis: postea dicat:

Descendat in hanc plenitudinem fontis, virtus Spiritus Sancti, totamq; huius aquæ substantiam regenerandi fæcundet effectu.

Hic diuidat Sacerdos aquam cum Cereo in fonte, in modum crucis dicens:

Hic omnium peccatorum maculæ deleantur: hic natura ad imaginem tuam condita, & ad honorem sui reformata principij, cunctis vetustatis squaloribus emundetur.

Hic tollat Sacerdos Cereum de aqua, & tradat Clerico, a quo ibidem contra fontes teneatur, donec finiatur tota præfatio.

Vt om-

Vt omnis homo hoc Sacramentum regenerationis ingressus, in veræ innocentiæ nouam infantiam renascatur. Per Dominum nostrum Iesum Christum Filium tuum: qui tecum viuit & regnat in vnitate eiusdem Spiritus Sancti Deus, per omnia sæcula sæculorum. ℟. Amen.

Non procedatur vlterius in hoc officio in vigilia Paschæ & Pentecostes, nisi aliquis sit baptizandus: vt postea patebit.

Nota quod in vigilia Paschæ, & Pentecostes consecratis fontibus non infundetur Oleum neque Chrisma, nisi adsint aliqui qui debeant baptizari, sed linteamine mundo cooperiantur, & vsque ad Completorium Paschæ vel Pentecostes reseruentur: vt si forte his diebus aliquis baptizandus aduenerit (fæcundatis & sanctificatis fontibus tunc Olei & Chrismatis infusione) baptizetur.

Post hæc mittat Sacerdos Oleum sanctum cum ipsa billione, quæ est in vase eius, in aquam, signum crucis faciens & dicens:

Coniunctio Olei Vnctionis, & aquæ Baptismatis: In nomine Patris, & Filij, & Spiritus Sancti. Amen.

Simili modo mittat Chrisma dicens:

Fœcũdetur, & sanctificetur fons iste, hoc salutifero Chrismate salutis: In nomine Patris, & Filij, & Spiritus Sancti. Amen.

Postea mittat simul Oleum cum Chrismate modo supradicto dicens:

Coniunctio Chrismatis sanctificationis, & Olei Vnctionis, & aquæ Baptismatis: In nomine Patris, & Filij, & Spiritus

ritus Sancti. Amen.

Ritus Baptizandi.

Tunc portetur infans ad fontes ab his qui eum ſuſcepturi ſunt ad Baptiſmum: ipſiſque eundem puerum ſuper fontes inter manus tenentibus, ponat Sacerdos manum dexteram ſuper eum, & interrogato eius nomine, reſpondeat qui eum tenet,

N. Item Sacerdos dicat.

N. Abrenuncias Satanæ?

Reſpondeant compatrini & commatrinæ.

Abrenuncio. Item Sacerdos.

Et omnibus operibus eius? ℞. Abrenuncio.

Item Sacerdos.

Et omnibus pompis eius? ℞. Abrenuncio.

Poſtea tangat Sacerdos pectus infantis, & inter ſcapulas de oleo ſancto, crucem faciens cum pollice dicens.

N. Et ego lineo te ſuper pectus oleo ſalutis, & inter ſcapulas, in Chriſto Ieſu Domino noſtro, vt habeas vitam æternam & viuas in ſæcula ſæculorum. Amen.

Deindè interrogato nomine eius, reſpondeant. N.

Item Sacerdos:

N. Credis in Deum patrem omnipotentem creatorem cæli & terræ?

Reſpondeant; Credo. Item Sacerdos.

Credis & in Ieſum Chriſtum Filium eius vnicum Dominum noſtrum, natum & paſſum? Reſpondeant; Credo.

Item Sacerdos.

Credis

Credis & in Spiritum Sanctum: Sanctam Eccleſiam Catholicam, Sanctorum cõmunionem: Remiſſionem peccatorum: carnis reſurrectionem, & vitam æternam poſt mortem: Reſpondeant, Credo.

Tunc Sacerdos dicat:

N. Quid petis? Reſpondeant, Baptiſmum. Itẽ Sacerdos. Vis Baptizari? Reſpondeant, Volo.

Deindè accipiat Sacerdos infantem per latera in manibus ſuis, & interrogato nomine eius, baptizet eum ſub trina immerſione, ſanctam Trinitatem inuocando, ita dicens.

N. Et ego Baptizo te in nomine Patris,

Et mergat eum ſemel verſa facie ad aquilonem, & capite verſus orientem.

& Filij, Iterum mergat ſemel, verſa facie ad meridiem. & Spiritus Sancti. Amen.

Et mergat tertio recta facie verſus aquam.

Tunc patrini accipientes infantem de manibus Sacerdotis leuent eum de fonte. Vt autem ſurrexit a fonte, accipiat Sacerdos de Chriſmate cum pollice ſuo, dicens:

Dominus vobiſcum ℟. Et cum ſpiritu tuo.

Oremus.

Deus omnipotens, Pater Domini noſtri Ieſu Chriſti, qui te regenerauit ex aqua & Spiritu Sancto, quique dedit tibi remiſſionem omnium peccatorum tuorum,

Hic lineat infantem de ipſo Chriſmate cum pollice in

vertice

vertice in modum crucis, dicens:

Ipſe te liniat Chriſmate ſalutis in eodem Filio ſuo Domino noſtro Ieſu Chriſto in vitam æternam.

Poſtea induatur infans veſte Chriſmali, Sacerdote interrogante nomen eius & dicente ſic:

N. Accipe veſtem candidam, ſanctam, & immaculatam: quam perferas ante tribunal Domini noſtri Ieſu Chriſti, vt habeas vitam æternam, & viuas in ſæcula ſæculorum. Amen.

Licitum eſt autem pannum Chriſmalem ſecundo linire Chriſmate, & ſuper alium baptizatum immittere: tamen ad communes vſus non debet pannus ille aſſumi, ſed ad Eccleſiam reportari & in vſus Eccleſiæ reſeruari.

Deinde quæſito nomine ponat Cereum ardentem in manu infantis dicens:

N. Accipe lampadem ardentem & irreprehenſibilem, cuſtodi Baptiſmum tuum, ſerua mandata: vt cum venerit Dominus ad nuptias, poſſis ei occurrere vna cum Sanctis in aula cœleſti: vt habeas vitam æternam, & viuas in ſæcula ſæculorum. Amen.

Si Epiſcopus adeſt ſtatim eum confirmari oportet, & poſtea communicari ſi ætas eius id depoſcat, Sacerdote dicente:

Corpus Domini noſtri Ieſu Chriſti, cuſtodiat corpus tuũ & animam tuam in vitam æternam. Amen.

Si infans ſit, iniungatur patri & matri, vt conſeruent puerum ab igne

igne & aqua, & omnibus alijs periculis, vſque ad ætatem ſeptem annorum: & ſi ipſi non faciant, patrini & matrinæ tenentur. Item compatribus & commatribus iniungatur, vt doceant infantem Pater noſter, Aue Maria, & Credo in Deum, vel doceri faciat: & Quod Chriſmate deferat ad Eccleſiam; & quod confirmetur infans quam cito Epiſcopus aduenerit, circa eas partes per ſeptem miliaria. hoc modo.

GOdfathers, & Godmothers of this childe, we charge you, that you charge the father & mother to keepe it from fire and water, and other perils, to the age of ſeauen yeares; and that you teach, or ſee it be taught the Pater noſter, Aue Maria, and Credo: according to the law of holie Church, and with conuenient ſpeede to be confirmed, of my Lord of the Dioceſe, or his deputie; and that the mother bring againe the chriſome at her purification. And wash your hands ere you depart the Church.

Deindé dicatur hoc ſequens Euangelium ſuper infantem (ſi placuerit), quia ſecundum Doctores maxime valet pro morbo caduco.

℣. Dominus vobiſcum ℟. Et cum ſpiritu tuo.
Sequentia ſancti Euangelij ſecundum Marcum.
℟. Gloria tibi Domine.

IN illo tempore: Reſpondens vnus de turba dixit ad Ieſum, Magiſter, attuli filium meum ad te habentem ſpiritum mutum: qui vbicunque eum apprehenderit, allidit illum, & ſpumat, & ſtridet dentibus, & areſcit: &

dixi diſcipulis tuis vt eijcerent illum, & non potuerunt. Qui reſpondens eis, dixit: O generatio in credula, quamdiu apud vos ero? quamdiu vos patiar? afferte illum ad me. Et attulerunt eum. Et cum vidiſſet eum, ſtatim ſpiritus conturbauit illum: & eliſus in terram, volutabatur ſpumans. Et interrogauit patrem eius. Quantum temporis eſt ex quo ei hoc accidit: At ille ait. Ab infantia. Et frequenter eum in ignem & in aquas miſit vt eum perderet. Sed ſi quid potes, adiuua nos miſertus noſtri. Ieſus autem ait illi. Si potes credere, omnia poſſibilia ſunt credenti. Et continuo exclamans pater pueri cum lachrymis aiebat. Credo, domine: adiuua incredulitatem meam. Et cum videret Ieſus concurrentem turbam, comminatus eſt ſpiritu immundo dicens illi. Surde & mute ſpiritus, ego tibi precipio exi ab eo: & amplius ne introeas in eum. Et clamans & multum diſcerpens eum, exijt ab eo. Et factus eſt ſicut mortuus, ita vt multi dicerent: Quia mortuus eſt. Ieſus autem tenens manum eius, eleuauit eum, & ſurrexit. Et cum introiſſet in domum, diſcipuli eius ſecretò interrogabant eum: Quare nos non potuimus eijcere eum? Et dixit illis: Hoc genus in nullo poteſt exire, niſi in oratione, & ieiunio.

Et poſtea dicatur hoc Euangelium ſequens, ſub forma prædicta, videlicet. Secundum Ioannem.

IN principio erat verbum, & verbum erat apud Deum, & Deus erat verbũ. Hoc erat in principio apud Deum. Omnia per ipſum facta ſunt: & ſinè ipſo factum eſt nihil, quod

quod factum eſt, in ipſo vita erat, & vita erat lux hominum: & lux in tenebris lucet, & tenebræ eum non comprehenderunt. Fuit homo miſſus à Deo, cui nomen erat Ioannes. Hic venit in teſtimonium vt teſtimonium perhiberet de lumine, vt omnes crederent per illum. Non erat ille lux, ſed vt teſtimonium perhiberet de lumine. Erat lux vera, quæ illuminat omnem hominem venientem in hunc mundum. In mundo erat, & mundus per ipſum factus eſt, & mundus eum non cognouit. In propria venit, & ſui eum non receperunt. Quotquot autem receperunt eum, dedit eis poteſtatem filios Dei fieri, his, qui credunt in nomine eius, qui non ex ſanguinibus, neque ex voluntate carnis, neque ex voluntate viri, ſed ex Deo nati ſunt. Et verbum caro factum eſt, & habitauit in nobis: & vidimus gloriam eius, gloriam quaſi vnigeniti a patre plenum gratiæ, & veritatis.

Notandum eſt quod quilibet Sacerdos parochialis debet parochiauis ſuis formam baptizandi in aqua pura, naturali, & recenti, & non in alio liquore, frequenter in diebus Dominicis exponere: Vt ſi neceſſitas emergat, ſciant paruulos in forma Eccleſiæ baptizare, proferendo formam verborum Baptiſmi in lingua materna diſtinctè, & apertè, & ſolum vnica voce nullo modo iterando verba illa rite ſemel prolata, vel ſimilia ſuper eundem: ſed ſine aliqua additione, ſubtractione, interruptione, verbi pro verbo poſitione, mutatione, corruptione, ſeu tranſpoſitione ſic dicendo:

I Chriſten thee N. in the name of the Father, and of the Sonne, and of the holy Ghoſt. Amen.

Vel in lingua latina ſic.

Ego baptizo te N In nomine Patris, & Filij, & Spiritus Sancti Amen. Aquam ſuper paruulum ſpargendo, vel in aquam mergendo ter vel ſaltem ſemel.

Et ſi puer fuerit baptizatus, ſecundum illam formam, caueat ſibi vnuſquiſque, ne iterum eundem baptizat: Sed ſi huiuſmodi paruuli conualeſcãt deferantur ad eccleſiam, & dicãtur ſuper eos Exorciſmi & Catechiſmi cum Vnctionibus & omnibus alijs ſupradictis præter immerſionem aquæ & formam baptiſmi, quæ omnino ſunt omittenda: videlicet: Quid petis & ab hinc vſque ad illum locum quo Sacerdos debeat paruulum Chriſmate linire. Et ideo ſi laicus baptizauerit puerum, antequam deferatur ad Eccleſiam interroget Sacerdos diligenter quid dixerit, & quid fecerit: & ſi inuenerit laicum diſcretè & debito modo baptizaſſe, & formam verborum Baptiſmi vt ſupra in ſuo idiomate integre protuliſſe, approbet factum, & non rebaptizet eum. Si vero dubitet rationabiliter Sacerdos vtrum infans ad baptizandum ſibi oblatus prius in forma debita fuerit baptizatus vel non: debet omnia perſicere cum eo ſicut cum alio quem conſtat ſibi non baptizatum, præterquam quod verba ſacramentalia eſſentialia proferre debeat ſub conditione hoc modo dicendo.

N. Si baptizatus es, ego non rebaptizo te: ſed ſi nondum baptizatus es, ego baptizo te, in nomine Patris, & Filij, & Spiritus Sancti. Amen.

Sub aſperſione vel immerſione vt ſupra.

Et eſt

Et eſt obſeruandum tam de Baptiſmate quam de Cōfirmatione, quod quandocunque dubitatur, ſine dubitatione conferantur, quia non dicitur iteratum quod neſcitur fuiſſe collatum. Et ideo ſub forma prædicta baptizantur infantes expoſiti, de quorum Baptiſmo probabiliter dubitatur, ſiue inueniantur cum ſale, ſiue ſine ſale.

Notandum eſt etiam quod ſi infans ſit in periculo mortis, tunc primo introducatur ad fontem, & poſtea baptizetur incipiendo ad hunc locum. Quid petis. Et ſi poſt Baptiſmum vixerit habeat totum reſiduum ſeruitium ſupradictum.

Hoc autem in quolibet Sacramento obſeruetur, quod quandocunque periculum videtur imminere, ſemper incipiatur ad ſubſtantiam illius Sacramenti, & poſtea reſiduum compleatur ſi poterit.

Non licet aliquem baptizare in aula, camera, vel aliquo loco priuato, ſed duntaxat in Eccleſijs in quibus ſunt fontes ad hoc ſpecialiter ordinati, niſi fuerit filius Regis, vel Principis, aut talis neceſsitas emerſerit, propter quam ad Eccleſiam acceſſus abſq; periculo haberi non poteſt.

Presbyter autem ſi poterit ſemper habeat fontem lapideum, integram, & honeſtam, ad bapizandum: Si autem nequiuerit, habeat vas conueniens ad baptiſmum, quod alijs vſibus nullatenus deputetur, nec extra Eccleſiam deportetur.

Solemnis Baptiſmus celebrari ſolet in Sabbato ſancto Paſchæ, & in vigilia Pentecoſtes: & ideo pueri nati infra octo dies ante Paſcha, vel infra octo dies ante Pentecoſten, debent reſeruari ad baptizandum in Sabbato ſancto Paſchæ, vel in vigilia Pen-

tecoſtes, ſi commode, & ſine periculo valeant reſeruari. Ita quod tempore medio inter natiuitatem puerorum & huius Baptiſmi perfectum recipiant Catechiſmum, ſolaque diebus prædictis Baptiſmi (conſecratis fontibus) immerſio ſit facienda.

Alij autem qui alijs anni temporibus nati extiterint, incontinenter cum nati fuerint, propter mortale periculum (quod ſæpe pueris imminet improuiſum) baptizentur.

Veruntamen in Sabbato ſancto Paſchæ, & in vigilia Pentecoſtes peracta conſecratione fontium non infundatur oleum neque Chriſma, nec vlterius in officio Baptiſmi procedatur, niſi forte aliquis adſit baptizandus: ſed linteamine mundo cooperiantur, & vſque ad cõpletoriũ Paſchæ & Pentecoſtes reſeruentur, vt ſi fortè his diebus aliquis baptizãdus aduenerit: fœcundatis & ſanctificatis fontibus Olei & Chriſmatis infuſione baptizetur. Et nota quod de aqua ſanctificata in fonte Baptiſmati in Sabbato ſancto Paſchæ, & in vigilia Pentecoſtes, nunquam debet populus aſpergi nec poſt aquæ Chriſmationem nec antè.

Non licet laico vel mulieri aliquem baptizare niſi in articulo neceſsitatis. Si vero vir & mulier adeſſent vti immineret neceſſitatis articulus baptizandi puerum, & non eſſet alius miniſter ad hoc magis idoneus preſens, vir baptizet & non mulier, niſi fortè mulier benè ſciret verba ſacramentalia & non vir, vel aliud impedimentum ſubeſſet.

Similiter pater vel mater non debet proprium filium de ſacro fonte leuare, nec baptizare, niſi in extremæ neceſſitatis articulo: tunc enim bene poſſunt ſine præiudicio copulæ coniugalis ipſum baptizare, niſi fuerit aliquis alius præſens qui hoc facere ſciret & vellet.

Preterea

Preterea vir & vxor non debent ſimul leuare puerum alterius de ſacro fonte.

Nulli religioſi debent admitti in patrinos, quod etiam de Monialibus obſeruandum eſt.

Viri autem & mulieres qui ſuſcipiūt pueros de Baptiſmo, cōſtituuntur eorum fideiuſſores apud Deum: & ideo frequēter debēt eos admonere cum adulti fuerint, ſeu diſciplinæ capaces, vt caſtitatem cuſtodiant, iuſtitiam diligant, charitatem teneant & ante omnia orationē Dominicalem, ſalutationē Angelicam, Symbolum fidei & ſignaculo ſanctæ crucis ſe ſignare, eos docere tenētur.

Vndè non debent recipi in patrinos, nec admittantur niſi qui ſciunt prædicta: quia patrini debent inſtruere filios ſuos ſpirituales in fide, quod facere non poſſunt niſi ipſimet in fide prius inſtructi ſint.

Si baptizandus non poterit loqui, vel quia paruulus, vel quia mutus, vel quia ægrotans, aut aliundè impotens, tunc debent patrini pro eis reſpondere ad omnes interrogationes in Baptiſmo. Si autem loqui poterit, tunc pro ſeipſo reſpondeat, ad ſingulas interrogationes, niſi ad interrogationem ſui nominis tantum, ad quas ſemper patrini ſui reſpondeant pro eo.

Qui ſuſcipiunt pueros de ſacro fonte non debent eos tenere coram Epiſcopo in Confirmatione niſi cogente neceſſitate.

Non plures quam vnus vir, & vna mulier debent accedere ad ſuſcipiendum paruulum de ſacro fonte: vnde plures ad hoc ſimul accedentes peccant faciendo contra prohibitionem canonis, niſi alia fuerit conſuetudo approbata: tamen vltra tres amplius ad hoc nullatenus recipiantur.

Mone-

Monendi ſunt etiam laici quod paruuli ſui confirmati, tertia die poſt confirmationem deportentur ad Eccleſiam: & frontes eorum per manus Sacerdotis propter Chriſmatis reuerentiam in Baptiſterio abluantur, & ligaturæ eorum tunc igne comburantur.

Item nullus debet admitti ad Sacramentum Corporis et Sanguinis Chriſti Ieſu, extra mortis articulum, niſi fuerit confirmatus, vel à receptione ſacramenti Confirmationis fuerit rationabiliter impeditus.

Non debet Sacerdos parochialis eſſe ſine Chriſmate: ſed debet quilibet Sacerdos parochialis ſuo Epiſcopo, non ab alio, in propria perſona ſua, vel per alium Sacerdotem, Diaconum, vel Subdiaconum Chriſma petere ſingulis annis ante Paſcha.

Sacerdos qui de veteri Chriſmate vngit baptizatum, niſi in articulo neceſſitatis, deponendus eſt: & ideo debet omni die cœnæ Domini in nouum Chriſma ab Epiſcopo confici, & vetus remoueri, & concremari.

Item tam ſacrum Oleum quam Chriſma, ſub fideli cuſtodia claui adhibita debent obſeruari, ne ad illa poßit manus temeraria extendi ad aliqua nefaria exercenda.

Nota quod tempore interdicti generalis, licitè poſſunt conferri Baptiſmus & Confirmatio tam adulti: quam paruulis, ſed non cum pulſatis Campanis, neque alta voce.

ORDO

ORDO AD PVRIFICANDAM MVLIEREM

Post partum antè ostium Ecclesiæ.

Primo Sacerdos & ministri eius dicant Psalmos sequentes. Psal. 120.

LEuaui oculos meos in montes: vnde veniet auxilium mihi.

Auxilium meum a Domino: qui fecit cœlum & terram.

Non det in commotionem pedem tuum: neque dormitet qui custodit te.

Ecce non dormitabit neq; dormiet: qui custodit Israel.

Dominus custodit te, Dominus protectio tua: super manum dexteram tuam.

Per diem sol non vret te: neque luna per noctem.

Dominus custodit te ab omni malo: custodiat animam tuam Dominus.

Dominus custodiat introitum tuum, & exitum tuum: ex hoc nunc, & vsque in sæculum.

Gloria Patri & Filio, &c. Sicut erat, &c.

Psal. 127.

BEati omnes qui timent Dominum: qui ambulant in vijs eius.

Labores manuum tuarum quia manducabis: beatus es, & bene tibi erit.

Vxor tua sicut vitis abundans: in lateribus domus tuæ.

F ilij tui ſicut nouellæ oliuarum: in circuitu menſæ tuæ.
E cce ſic benedicetur homo: qui timet Dominum.
B enedicat tibi Dominus ex Sion: & videas bona Hieruſalem omnibus diebus vitæ tuæ.
E t videas filios filiorum tuorum, pacem ſuper Iſrael.
G loria patri, & Filio, &c. Sequatur.
K yrie eleiſon, C hriſte eleiſon, K yrie eleiſon. P ater noſter. E t ne nos inducas in tentationem. ℟. S ed libera nos à malo. ℣. D omine ſaluam fac ancillam tuam. ℟. D eus meus ſperantem in te. ℣. E ſto ei Domine turris fortitudinis. ℟. A facie inimici. ℣. D omine exaudi orationẽ meam. ℟. E t clamor meus ad te veniat. ℣. D ominus vobiſcum. ℟. E t cum ſpiritu tuo.

O remus

DEus qui hanc famulam tuam de pariendi periculo liberaſti, & eam in ſeruitio tuo deuotam eſſe feciſti: concede vt temporali curſu fideliter peracto, ſub alis miſericordiæ tuæ vitam perpetuam & quietam conſequatur. Per Chriſtum Dominum noſtrum. A men.

Tunc aſpergatur mulier aqua benedicta. Deinde inducat eam Sacerdos per manum dexteram in Eccleſiam, dicens.

I ngredere in templum Dei vt habeas vitam æternam, & viuas in ſæcula ſæculorum. A men.

N ota quod mulieres poſt prolem emiſſam, quandocunque Eccleſiam intrare voluerint acturæ gratias, purificari poſſunt, & nulla proindè peccati mole grauantur: nec Eccleſiarum aditus eſt tus est eis denegandus, ne pœna illis conuerti videatur in culpam. Si tamen ex veneratione voluerint aliquandiu abstinere, deuotionem earum non credimus improbandam. De purificatione post partum, cap. vnico.

ORDO AD FACIENDVM SPONSALIA. siue Matrimonium.

IN primis statuantur vir & mulier ante ostium Ecclesiæ coram Deo, Sacerdote & populo, vir a dextris mulieris, & mulier a sinistris viri.

Et sciendum est quod licet omni tempore possint contrahi Sponsalia & etiam Matrimonium, quod fit priuatim solo consensu, tamen traditio vxorum, & nuptiarum solemnitas certis temporibus fieri prohibentur: videlicet ab Aduentu Domini vsque ad octauam Epiphaniæ, & à Septuagesima vsque ad octauam Paschæ, & à Dominica ante Ascensionem Domini, vsque ad octauam Pentecostes. In die tamen octaua Epiphaniæ licitè possunt nuptiæ celebrari, quia non inuenitur prohibitum, quamuis in Octauis Paschæ hoc facere non liceat. Similiter in Dominica proxima post festum Pentecostes licitè celebrantur nuptiæ, quia dies Pentecostes octauam diem non habet.

Tunc interroget Sacerdos Banna dicens in lingua materna sub hac forma.

Ecce conuenimus huc fratres coram Deo, Angelis, & omnibus Sanctis eius in facie Ecclesiæ, ad coniungẽdum duo corpora, ſcilicet huius viri, & huius mulieris, Hic reſpiciat Sacerdos perſonas, vt amodò ſint vna caro, & ſi duæ animæ, in fide, & in lege Dei, ad promerendam ſimul vitam æternam, quicquid antè hoc fecerint. Admoneo igitur vos omnes, vt ſi quis ex vobis aliquid dicere ſciat, quare iſti adoleſcentes legitimè contrahere non poſſint, modo confiteatur.

Eadem admonitio fiat ad virum, & ad mulierem, vt ſi quid ab illis occultè actum fuerit, vel ſi quid deuouerint, vel alio modo de ſe nouerint, quarè legitime contrahere non poſſunt, tunc confiteantur.

Si vero aliquis impedimentum aliquod proponere voluerit, & ad hoc probandum cautionem præſtiterit, differantur Sponſalia, quouſque rei veritas cognoſcatur. Si verò nullus impedimentum proponere voluerit, interroget Sacerdos dotem mulieris, videlicet arras ſponſales: & dicuntur arræ annuli vel pecuniæ, vel aliæ res dandæ ſponſæ per ſponſum. Quæ datio ſubarratio dicitur, quando fit per annuli dationem, & tunc vulgariter deſponſatio vocatur.

Non fidabit Sacerdos, nec conſentiet ad fidationem inter virum & mulierem, ante tertium dictum bonnorum. Debet enim Sacerdos banna in facie Eccleſiæ infra Miſſarum ſolemnia, cum maior populi adfuerit multitudo, per tres dies ſolennes, & diſiunctos, interrogare: ita vt inter vnumquemq; diem ſolennem cadat ad minus vna dies.

Debet etiam Sacerdos terminum præfigere competentem, infra quem qui voluerit & valuerit, legittimũ opponat impedimentum: &

tum: & si contrahentes diuersarum sint parochiarum, tunc in vtraque Ecclesia parochiarum illarum sunt Banna interrogāda. Si autem vnius & eiusdem sint parochiæ, tunc tantum in Ecclesia illius parochiæ banna interrogentur.

Sacerdos vero qui contractibus matrimonialibus antè trinam solennem interrogationem bannorum, vt prædictum est, præsumpserit interesse, pœnam suspensionis ab officio per triennium incurrit.

Similiter Sacerdos parochialis qui Matrimonia clandestina, in parochia sua prohibere contempserit, ab officio per triennium debet suspendi, & grauius est puniendus si culpæ qualitas id requirat. Prohibentur autem clādestina Matrimonia duplici ratione: videlicet, ne sub specie Matrimonij committatur fornicatio, & ne Matrimonialiter coniuncti iniustè separentur. Sæpe enim in Matrimonio occulto alter coniugum mutat propositum, & dimittit alterum probationibus destitutum, & sine remedio restitutionis. Et ideo prohibeant Sacerdotes frequenter parochianos suos, ne dent sibi fidem mutuò, sed coram publicis & honestis personis ad hoc constitutis.

Quisquis etiam Sacerdos, seu sæcularis, seu regularis extiterit, qui solemnizationem Matrimonij extra Ecclesiam parochialem, vel capellam habentem iura parochiæ, sibi ab antiquo competentia, absque Diocæsani loci licentia speciali, celebrare præsumpserit, aut celebrationi interesse, ipso facto per annum integrum ab officio est suspensus.

Postea dicat Sacerdos ad virum cunctis audientibu in lingua materna sic.

N. vis habere hanc mulierem in sponsam, & eam dilige-re, honorare, tenere, & custodire sanam & infirmam, sicut sponsus debet sponsam, & omnes alias propter eam dimittere, & illi soli adhærere quamdiu vita vtriusque vestrum durauerit?

Respondeat vir. Volo.

Item dicat Sacerdos ad mulierem hoc modo.

N. vis habere hunc virum in sponsum & ei obedire, & seruire, & eum diligere, honorare, ac custodire sanum & infirmum, sicut sponsa debet sponsum, & omnes alios propter eum dimittere, & illi soli adhærere quamdiu vita vtriusque vestrum durauerit?

Respondeat mulier. Volo.

Deinde detur fæmina a patre suo, vel ab amicis eius Quod si puella sit, discoopertam habeat manum, si vidua tectam. Vir eam recipiat in Dei fide & sua seruandam, sicut vouit coram Sacerdote, & teneat eam per manũ suam dexteram in manu sua dextera, & sic det fidem mulieri per verba de presenti ita dicens, docente Sacerdote.

I N. take thee N. to my wedded wife, to haue & to hold, from this day forward, for better, for worse, for richer, for poorer, in sicknesse and in health, til death vs depart, if holie Church wil it permit, and therto I plight thee my troth. Manum retrahendo.

Deinde dicat mulier docente Sacerdote.

I N

I N. take thee N. to my wedded husband, to haue and to hold, from this day forward, for better, for worſe, for richer, for poorer, in ſickneſſe & in health, to be bonnair and buxom, in bed and at boord til death vs depart, if holy Church vvil it permit, and therto I plight thee my troth. Manum retrahendo.

Meeke
Obedient

Deinde ponat vir aurum, argentum, & annulum ſuper ſcutam, vel librum, & quærat Sacerdos ſi annulus antea fuerit benedictus, vel non? Si dicatur quod non, tunc benedicat Sacerdos annulum hoc modo.

D ominus vobiſcum ℟. E t cum ſpiritu tuo.

O remus.

C Reator & conſeruator humani generis, dator gratiæ ſpiritualis, largitor æternæ ſalutis, tu Domine mitte benedictionem tuam ſuper hunc annulum, [reſpice] vt quæ illum geſtauerit ſit armata virtute cæleſtis defenſionis, & proficiat illi ad æternam ſalutem. Per Chriſtum Dominum noſtrum. A men.

O remus.

B Ene ✠ dic Domine hunc annulum [reſpice] quem nos in tuo ſancto nomine benedicimus, vt quæcunque eum portauerit in tua pace conſiſtat, & in tua voluntate permaneat, & in tuo amore viuat, & creſcat, & ſeneſcat, & multiplicetur in longitudinem dierum. Per Dominum noſtrum Ieſum Chriſtum. A men.

Tunc aſpergatur aqua benedicta ſuper annulum.

Si autem antea fuerit annulus ille benedictus, tunc ſta-

tim po

tim postquam vir posuerit annulum super librum, accipiens Sacerdos annulum tradat ipsum viro: quem vir accipiat manu sua dextera, cum tribus principalioribus digitis & manu sua sinistra tenens dexteram sponsæ, docente Sacerdote dicat:

With this ring I thee wed, this gold and siluer I thee giue, and with my bodie I thee worshippe, & with al my wordly goodes I thee endew.

Tunc inserat sponsus annulum pollici sponsæ dicens: In nomine Patris. Deinde secundo digito, dicens:
& Filij. Deinde tertio digito, dicens:
& Spiritus Sancti. Deinde quarto digito, dicens:
Amen. Ibique dimittat annulum. Quia in medico est quædam vena procedens vsque ad cor, & in sonoritate argenti designatur interna dilectio, quæ semper inter eos debet esse recens.

Deinde inclinatis eorum capitibus, dicat Sacerdos benedictionem super eos.

Benedicti ✠ sitis a Domino, qui fecit mundum ex nihilo. Amen.

Postea dicatur Psalmus sequens. Psal. 67.

MAnda Deus virtuti tuæ: confirma hoc Deus quod operatus es in nobis.

A Templo tuo in Hierusalem: tibi offerent reges munera.

Increpa feras arundinis, congregatio taurorum in vaccis populorum: vt excludāt eos qui probati sunt argento.

Gloria Patri, & Filio, &c.

Kyrie

Kyrie eleiſon, Chriſte eleiſon, Kyrie eleiſon. Pater noſter. ℣. Et ne nos inducas in tentationem. ℟. Sed libera nos a malo. ℣. Benedicamus Patrem, & Filium, cum ſancto Spiritu. ℟. Laudemus & ſuperexaltemus eum in ſæcula. ℣. Laudemus Dominum quem laudant Angeli. ℟. Quem Cherubin & Seraphin, Sanctus, Sanctus, Sanctus, proclamant. ℣. Domine exaudi orationem meam ℟. Et clamor meus ad te veniat. ℣. Dominus vobiſcum. ℟. Et cum ſpiritu tuo.

Oremus.

DEus Abraham, Deus Iſaac, Deus Iacob ſit vobiſcum: & ipſe vos coniungat, & impleat benedictionem ſuam in vobis. Qui viuit & regnat Deus, per omnia ſæcula ſæculorum. Amen.

Alia oratio cum Oremus.

BEne ✠ dicat vos Deus pater, cuſtodiat vos Ieſus Chriſtus, illuminet vos Spiritus Sanctus. Oſtendat Dominus faciem ſuam in vobis & miſereatur veſtri. Conuertat Dominus vultum ſuum ad vos, & det vobis pacem, impleatque vos omni benedictione ſpirituali in remiſſionem omnium peccatorum veſtrorum, vt habeatis vitam æternam, & viuatis in ſæcula ſæculorum. Amen.

Hic intrent Eccleſiam vſque ad gradum altaris, & Sacerdos in eundo cum ſuis miniſtris dicat hunc pſalmum ſequentem. Pſal. 127.

BEati omnes qui timent Dominum: qui ambulant in vijs eius.

Labores manuum tuarum quia manducabis: beatus es, & bene tibi erit.

Vxor tua ſicut vitis abundans: in lateribus domus tuæ.

Filij tui ſicut nouellæ oliuarum: in circuitu menſæ tuæ.

Ecce ſic benedicetur homo: qui timet Dominum.

Benedicat tibi Dominus ex Sion: & videos bona Hieruſalem omnibus diebus vitæ tuæ.

Et videas filios filiorum tuorum: pacem ſuper Iſrael.

Gloria Patri, & Filio, &c.

Kyrie eleiſon, Chriſte eleiſon, Kyrie eleiſon.

Tunc proſtratis ſponſo & ſponſa ante gradum altari roget Sacerdos circumſtantes orare pro eis dicendo:

Pater noſter. ℣. Et ne nos inducas in tentationen ℟. Sed libera nos à malo. ℣. Saluum fac ſeruum tui & ancillā tuam. ℟. Deus meus ſperantes in te. ℣. Mitt eis Domine auxilium de ſancto. ℟. Et de Sion tuere eos ℣. Eſto ei Domine turris fortitudinis. ℟. A facie inimici. ℣. Domine exaudi orationem meam. ℟. Et clamo meus ad te veniat. ℣. Dominus vobiſcum. ℟. Et cun ſpiritu tuo.

Oremus.

BEne ✠ dicat vos Dominus ex Sion, vt videatis qua bona ſunt Hieruſalem omnibus diebus vitæ veſtræ: & videatis filios filiorum veſtrorum, & pacem ſuper Iſrael Per Chriſtum Dominum noſtrum. Amen.

Oremus.

DEus Abraham, Deus Iſaac, Deus Iacob, bene ✠ di adoleſcentes iſtos, & ſemina ſemen vitæ æternæ ir mentibu nentibus eorum: vt quicquid pro vtilitate ſua dedicerêt, hoc facere cupiant. Per Ieſum Chriſtum filium tuum recuperatorem hominum, qui tecum viuit & regnat in vnitate Spiritus Sancti Deus per omnia ſæcula ſæculorum. Amen.

Oremus.

RESpice Domine de cælis, & bene ✠ dic conuentionem iſtam. Et ſicut miſiſti ſanctum Angelum tuum Raphaelem ad Tobiam & Saram filiam Raguelis: ita digneris Domine mittere bene ✠ dictionẽ tuam ſuper iſtos adoleſcentes, vt in tua voluntate permaneant, & in tua ſecuritate perſiſtant, & in amore tuo viuant & ſeneſcant: vt digni atque pacifici fiant & multiplicentur in longitudinem dierum. Per Chriſtum Dominum noſtrum. Amen.

Oremus.

RESpice Domine propitius ſuper hunc famulũ tuum [reſpice] & ſuper hanc famulam tuam [reſpice] vt in nomine tuo bene ✠ dictionem cæleſtem accipiant, & filios filiorum ſuorum & filiarũ ſuarum vſque ad tertiam & quartam progeniem incolumes videant, & in tua voluntate perſeuerent, & in futuro ad cæleſtia regna perueniant. Per Chriſtum Dominum noſtrum. Amen.

Oremus.

OMnipotens ſempiterne Deus, qui primos parentes noſtros Adam & Euam ſua virtute creauit, & in ſua ſanctificatione copulauit, ipſe corda & corpora veſtra ſanctificet & bene ✠ dicat, atque in ſocietate & amore veræ dilectionis coniungat. Per Chriſtũ Dominũ noſtrũ. Amẽ.

Deinde benedicat eos dicens, Oremus.

BEne✠dicat vos Deus omnipotẽs omni bene ✠ dictione cælesti, efficiatq; vos dignos in conspectu suo superabundet in vobis diuitias gratiæ suæ, & erudiat vos in verbo veritatis, vt ei corpore pariter & mente complacere valeatis. Per Dominum nostrum Iesum Christum &c. Amen.

Finitis orationibus quæ dicebantur super eos prostratos ad gradum altaris, & introductis illis in presbyterium (scilicet inter chorum & altare) ex parte Ecclesiæ australi, & statuta muliere a dextris viri (videlicet inter ipsum & altare) incipiatur Missa.

Nota quod ordo thuris benedicti nunquam datur in Ecclesi sponso & sponsæ. Inde est quod oblato thure benedicto super altare, si descendat thuribulus ad clericos, vel ad laicos, aliud thu est apponendum & hominibus offerendum.

Post Sanctus, prosternant se sponsus & sponsa in oratione ad gradum altaris, extenso super eos pallio, quod teneant quatuor clerici per quatuor cornua, in superpelliceis: nisi alter eorum prius fuerit desponsatus & benedictus, quia tunc non habeatur pallium super eos, nec dicatur Sacramentalis benedictio, vt postea patebit.

Deinde dicto, Per omnia sæcula sæculorum, Amen, post Pater noster, antequam dicatur: Pax Domini sit semper vobiscum, facta fractione Eucharistiæ more solito, dimissaque hostia in tribus fractionibus super patenam: dicat Sacerdos conuersus ad illos, orationes sequentes, illis in-

terim

terim genu flectentibus sub pallio, Sacerdote sic dicente.

℣. Dominus vobiscum. ℟. Et cum spiritu tuo.

Oremus.

PRopitiare Domine supplicationibus nostris, & institutis tuis quibus propagationem humani generis ordinasti benignus assiste: vt quod te auctore coniungitur, te auxiliante seruetur. Per Christum Dominum nostrum. Amen.

Oremus.

DEus qui potestate virtutis tuæ de nihilo cuncta fecisti, quique dispositis vniuersitatis exordijs, homini ad imaginem Dei facto, ideo inseperabile mulieris adiutorium condidisti, vt fœmineo corpori de virili dares carne principium, docens quod ex vno placuisset institui, nunquam liceret disiungi.

Hic incipit benedictio sacramentalis.

Deus qui tam excellenti mysterio coniugalem copulam consecrasti, vt Christi & Ecclesiæ sacramentum præsignares in fœdere nuptiarum.

Hic finitur benedictio sacramentalis.

Deus per quem mulier iungitur viro, & societas principaliter ordinata, ea benedictione ✠ donatur, quæ sola nec per originalis peccati pænam nec per diluuij est ablata sententiam. Respice propitius super hanc famulam tuam, quæ maritali iungenda consortio, se tua expetit protectione muniri. Sit in ea iugum dilectionis & pacis: fidelis & casta nubat in Christo, imitatrixq; sanctarum permaneat fœminarum. Sit amabilis vt Rachel viro

 suo

ſuo. Sapiens, vt Rebecca. Longæua & fidelis, vt Sara. Nihil in ea ex actibus ſuis ille auctor præuaricationis vſurpet. Nexa fidei, mandatiſque permaneat, vni thoro vincta. Contractus illicitos fugiat, muniatque infirmitatem ſuam robore diſciplinæ. Sit verecundiæ grauis, pudore venerabilis, doctrinis cæleſtibus erudita. Sit fæcunda in ſobole, ſit probata & innocens. Et ad optatam perueniat ſenectutem, & videat filios filiorum ſuorum vſque in tertiam & quartam progeniem. Et ad beatorum requiem, atque ad cœleſtia regna perueniat. Per Dominum noſtrum Ieſum Chriſtum, &c. Amen.

Notandum quod hæc clauſula: Deus qui tam excellenti myſterio. vſque, Deus per quem mulier iungitur viro: non dicatur in ſecundis nuptijs. Vir enim aut mulier ad bigamiam tranſiens, non debet iterum a Sacerdote benedici, quia cum alia vice benedicti ſint, eorum benedictio non debet iterari, quia caro benedicta trahit ad ſe carnem non benedictam.

Notandum eſt autem quod inhibitum eſt per capitulum extra, de ſecundis nuptijs, ne benedictio detur in ſecundis nuptijs, quod etiam teſtatur beatus Ambroſius qui ait. Primæ nuptiæ à Domino ſunt conſtitutæ, ſecundæ vero permiſſæ. Primæ nuptiæ ſub omni benedictione celebrantur, ſecundæ vero carent omni benedictione. Sed quia plures benedictiones ſunt in nuptijs celebrādis (ſcilicet in introitum Eccleſiæ, & ſuper pallium, & poſt Miſſam, & ſuper thorum in ſero) dubium eſſe poteſt quæ benedictio in ſecundis nuptijs ſit iteranda & quæ non. Sciendum eſt. quod in hac oratione quæ ſic incipit: Deus qui poteſtate virtutis

tuæ

tuæ de nihilo cuncta fecisti &c. tres sunt benedictiones ibidem quæ idem habent principium, scilicet: Deus. Media autem est omittenda, scilicet ista: Deus qui tam excellenti mysterio coniugalem copulam consecrasti. vsque, Deus per quem mulier iungitur viro, & societas principaliter ordinata &c. Quia in ista benedictione agitur de vnitate Christi & Ecclesiæ, quæ figuratur in primo Matrimonio, non autem in secundo. Vnde Apostolus ad Corinthios ait. Erunt duo in carne vna. Et hoc notatur in cap. Extra, de Bigamis & cap. Debitum & si vir vnius vxoris. Et hoc pro primo matrimonio, sed qui adhæret pluribus dissoluit vnitatem, vel fœdus vnitatis, & ideo illa benedictio quæ agit de vnitate, (scilicet: Deus qui tam excellēti mysterio &c.) non dicetur in secundis nuptijs. Et hoc est verum tam in viro bigamo, quam in muliere vidua, quia caro benedicti trahit ad se carnem non benedictam. Sed omnes aliæ benedictiones siue orationes debent dici indifferentur, secundum curiam Romanam, secundum Hostiensem, & Thomam Aquinatem, & Morandū Doctorem. Et quæstio ista discussa erat, & determinata in sacro palatio Romæ, & translata in Angliam per Magistrum Joannem Haysted anno Domini 1321. Et causa discussionis erat, quia multitudo Sacerdotum tunc temporis ad sedem Apostolicam conuolarunt causa obtinendi absolutionis beneficium pro benedictionibus in secundis nuptijs indiscrete collatis. Jdeo super hoc statuitur constitutio noua, quæ sic incipit.

Concertatio in antiquæ finem imponere cupientes presenti declaramus edicto, quod licet vir vel mulier ad bigamiam vel ad secundas nuptias trāsierint benedici non debent

bent cum fuerint alias benedicti: quod si forsan alter eorum vel ambo essent ad secundas nuptias transeuntes & in primus nuptijs benedicti non fuerint, danda est eis benedictio in secundis nuptijs. Sane volentes antiquam rigorem temperare, concedimus quod presbyter qui secundas nuptias benedixerit scienter, ad sedem Apostolicam ex hoc venire minimè teneatur: sed a pæna suspensionis hoc casu a iure indicta, per suos possunt Diocæsanos absolui. Si qui vero iuxta opinionem quorundam hactenus se non reputat suspensos ordines quoslibet, seu quæuis beneficia receperint, Diocæsani eorum a pæna suspensionis prædicta ipsos absoluere, ac super executione ordinum, & retentione beneficiorum huiusmodi cum eis valeant licitè dispensare.

Hic quæri potest quare secundæ nuptiæ non benedicantur? Ad hoc dico quod secundum Matrimonium quamuis in se consideratum sit perfectum Sacramentum, tamen in ordine ad primum Sacramentum consideratum, aliquem habet defectum Sacramenti, quia non habet plenam significationem, cum non sit vna caro, sicut est in matrimonio Christi & Ecclesiæ, & ratione huius defectus benedictio a secundis nuptijs subtrahitur. Sed hoc est intelligendum quando secundæ nuptiæ sunt secundæ ex parte viri & ex parte mulieris tantum. Si enim virgo contrahat cum illo qui habuit aliam vxorem nihilominus nuptiæ benedicuntur. Saluatur & aliquo modo significatio in ordine ad primas nuptias, quia Episcopus & si vnam Ecclesiam habeat sponsam, habet tamen plures personas desponsatas in vna Ecclesia. Sed anima non

potest

potest esse sponsa alterius quam Christi, quia cum demor e fornicatur, nec est matrimonium spirituale. Et propter hoc quando mulier secundo nubit, nuptiæ non benedicuntur propter defectum Sacramenti.

Post hæc vertat se Sacerdos ad altare & dicat Pax Domini & Agnus Dei.

Tunc amoto pallio surgant ambo sponsus & sponsa, & accipiat sponsus pacem a Sacerdote, & ferat sponsæ osculans eam & nenminem alium nec ipse, nec ipsa: sed statim Diaconus vel clericus a presbytero pacem accipiens, ferat alijs sicut solitum est.

Post Missam benedicatur panis & vinum, vel aliud quid potabile in vasculo, & gustent in nomine Domini, Sacerdote dicente. ℣. Dominus vobiscum. ℟. Et cum spiritu tuo. Oremus.

BEne ✠ dic Domine panem istum, & hunc potum, & hoc vasculum sicut benedixisti quinque panes in deserto, & sex hydrias in Cana Galileæ: vt sint sani & sobrij, atque immaculati omnes gustantes ex eis, Saluator mundi. Qui viuis & regnas cum Deo Patre in vnitate Spiritus Sancti Deus, per omnia sæcula sæculorum. Amen.

Nocte vero sequenti cum sponsus & sponsa ad lectum peruenerint accedat Sacerdos & benedicat thalamum dicens. ℣. Dominus vobiscum. ℟. Et cum spiritu tuo. Oremus.

BEne ✠ dic Domine thalamum istum, & omnes habitantes in eo: vt in tua pace consistant, & in tua voluntate permaneant, & in amore tuo viuant, & senescant, & multiplicentur in longitudinem dierum. Per Dominũ nostrum Iesum Christum. A men.

Item benedictio super lectum ℣. D ominus vobiscum ℟. E t cum spiritu tuo. O remus.

B Ene ✠ dic Domine hoc cubiculum [respice] qui non dormis, neque dormitas. Qui custodis Israel, custodi famulos tuos in hoc lecto quiescentes ab omnibus phantasmaticis dæmonum illusionibus. Custodi eos vigilantes, vt in præceptis tuis meditẽtur dormientes, & te per soporem sentiant, vt hic & vbique defensionis tui muniãtur auxilio. Per Dominum nostrum. A men.

Deinde fiat benedictio super eos in lecto tantum cum O remus.

B Ene ✠ dicat Deus corpora vestra, & animas vestras: & det super vos benedictionem, sicut benedixit Abraham, Isaac, & Iacob. A men.

Alia benedictio. O remus.

M Anus Domini sit super vos, mittatq; Angelum suum sanctum qui custodiat vos omnibus diebus vitæ vestræ. A men.

Alia benedictio, O remus.

B Ene ✠ dicat vos Pater, Filius, & Spiritus Sanctus, qui trinus est in numero & vnus in numine. A men.

ORDO

ORDO AD VISITANDVM INFIRMVM.

IN primis induat se Sacerdos superpelliceo cum stola, & in eundo dicat cum suis ministris septem psalmos pænitentiales, cum **Gloria Patri** & cum Antiphona. **Ne reminiscaris.** Quæ in fine repetatur hoc modo.

Ne reminiscaris, Domine, delicta nostra, vel parentum nostrorum, neque vindictam sumas de peccatis nostris. Parce Domine, parce famulo tuo (vel famulæ tuæ) quem (vel quam) redemisti præcioso sanguine tuo, & ne in æternum irascaris ei.

Et cum intrauerit domum dicat.

Pax huic domui, & omnibus habitantibus in ea, pax ingredientibus, & egredientibus.

Et sciendum est, quod quando infirmus debet iniungi, offerenda est ei imago crucifixi, & ante conspectum eius statuenda, vt redemptorem suum in imagine crucifixi adoret, & passionis eius quam pro peccatorum salute sustinuit recordetur.

Deinde aspergat infirmum aqua benedicta, & statim sequatur.

Kyrie eleison. Christe eleison. Kyrie eleison. Pater noster. ℣. Et ne nos inducas in tentationem. ℟. Sed libera nos a malo. ℣. Saluum fac seruum tuum (vel) ancillam tuam) ℟. Deus meus sperantem in te. ℣. Mitte ei

Domine auxilium de sancto. ℟. Et de Sion tuere eum, [vel eā] ℣. Nihil proficiat inimicus in eo [vel ea] ℟. Et filius iniquitatis non opponat nocere ei. ℣. Esto ei Domine turris fortitudinis. ℟. A facie inimici. ℣. Domine exaudi orationem meam. ℟. Et clamor meus ad te veniat. ℣. Dominus vobiscum. ℟. Et cum spiritu tuo.

Oremus

DEus qui beatum Petrum Apostolum tuum misisti ad Tabitham famulam tuam, vt eius præcibus suscitaretur ad vitam: exaudi nos quæsumus, vt hunc famulum tuum (vel hanc famulam tuam) N. quem (vel quam) in nomine tuo visitat nostra fragilitas, exorata medecinæ tuæ medela citius sanitati restituat. Per Christum Dominum nostrum. Amen.

Oremus.

OMnipotens sempiterne Deus, qui subuenis in periculis, & necessitate laborantibus, & flagella clementer temporas: te Domine supplices exoramus, vt per visitationem tuam sanctam erigas hunc famulum tuum (vel hanc famulam tuam) N. ex hac ægrotatione qua tenetur, & præsentes eum Ecclesiæ tuæ sanctæ incolumem, ad laudem & gloriam nominis tui. Per Christum Dominum nostrum. Amen.

Oremus.

EXaudi nos omnipotens & misericors Deus, & visitationem tuam conferre digneris super hunc famulum tuum (vel hanc famulam tuam) N. quem (vel quam) diuersa vexat infirmitas. Visita eum (vel eā) Domine, sicut visitare dignatus est socrum Petri, puerum Centurionis, & To-

& Tobiam, & Saram per sanctum Angelum tuum Raphaelem. Restitue in eo (vel ea) Domine pristinam sanitatem, vt mereatur in atrio domus tuæ dicere: castigans, castigauit me Dominus, & morti non tradidit me Saluator mundi. Qui cum Deo Patre, & Spiritu Sancto viuis & regnas Deus per omnia sæcula sæculorum. Amen.

Oremus.

DEus qui famulo tuo Ezechiæ ter quinos annos ad vitam donasti: ita & hunc famulũ tuum (vel hanc famulam tuam) N. a lecto ægritudinis, tua potentia erigas ad salutem. Per Christum Dominum nostrum. Amen.

Oremus.

REspice quæsumus Domine famulum tuum (vel famulam tuam) N. in infirmitate sui corporis laborã-tem: & animam refoue quam creasti, vt castigationibus emendata, continuò se sentiat, tua medecina saluatam. Per Christum Dominum nostrum. Amen.

Oremus.

DEus qui facturæ tuæ pio semper dominaris affectu, inclina aurem tuam supplicationibus nostris, & famulum tuum (vel famulam tuam) N. ex aduersa valetudine sui corporis laborantem, placatus respice, & visita in salutari tuo, ac cælestis ei gratiæ præsta medecinam. Per Christum Dominum nostrum. Amen.

Oremus.

VIrtutum cælestium Deus, qui ab humanis corporibus omnem languorem, & omnem infirmitatem

 præcepti

præcepti tui potestate depellis : adesto propitius huic famulo tuo (vel famulæ tuæ) N. vt fugatis infirmitatibus, & viribus receptis, nomen sanctum tuum instaurata protinus sanitate benedicat. Per Christum Dominum nostrum. Amen.

Oremus.

DOmine sancte, pater omnipotens, æternæ Deus, qui fragilitatem conditionis humanæ, infusa virtutis tuæ dignatione confirmas, vt salutaribus remedijs pietatis tuæ corpora nostra, & membra vegetentur : super hunc famulum tuum (vel famulam tuam) N. propitius intẽde, vt omni necessitate corporeæ infirmitatis exclusa, gratia in eo (vel ea) pristinæ sanitatis perfecta reparetur. Per Christum Dominum nostrum. Amen.

Oremus.

REspice Domine de cælo, & vide & visita hunc famulum tuum (vel hanc famulam tuam) N. & benedic eum (vel eam) sicut benedicere dignatus es, Abraham, Isaac, & Iacob. Respice super eum (vel eam) Domine oculis misericordiæ tuæ, & reple eum (vel eã) omni gaudio, & lætitia & timore tuo. Expelle ab eo (vel ea) omnes inimici insidias, & mitte Angelum pacis qui eum (vel eam) custodiat, & domum istam in pace perpetua. Per Dominum nostrum. Amen.

Deinde priusquam vngatur infirmus, aut communicetur, exhortetur eum Sacerdos hoc modo.

FRater charissime, gratias age omnipotenti Deo pro vniuersis beneficijs suis, patiẽter & benigne suscipiens infir-

infirmitatẽ corporis, quã tibi Deus immisit: nam si ipsam humiliter sine murmure toleraueris, inferet animæ tuæ maximum præmium, & salutem. Et frater charissime quia viam vniuersæ carnis ingressurus es, esto firmus in fide: qui enim non est firmus in fide, infidelis est, & sine fide impossible est placere Deo. Et ideo si saluus esse volueris, ante omnia opus est vt teneas Catholicam fidem, quam nisi integram, inuiolatamque seruaueris, absque dubio in æternum peribis.

Deinde bonum & valdè expediens est vt Sacerdos exprimat infirmò quatuordecem articulos fidei: quorum septem primi ad mysterium Trinitatis, & septem alij ad Christi humanitatem pertinent: vt si fortè prius in aliquo ipsorum errauerit, titubauerit, vel dubius fuerit, ante mortem dum adhuc spiritus vinctus est carni ad fidem solidam reducatur. Et potest Sacerdos dicere sic.

FIdes autem Catholica hæc est frater. 1 Credere in vnũ Deum, hoc est in vnitatem diuinæ essentiæ, in trium personarum indiuisibile Trinitate. 2 Patrem ingenitẽ esse Deum. 3 Vnigenitum Dei Filium, esse Deum per omnia coæqualem Patri. 4 Spiritum Sanctum, non genitum, non factum, non creatum, sed a Patre & Filio pariter procedentem, esse Deum Patri Filioque consubstantialem, etiam & æqualem. 5 Creationem cæli & terra, id est, omnis visibilis & inuisibilis creaturæ a tota indiuisibili Trinitate. 6 Sanctificationem Ecclesiæ per Spiritum Sanctũ, & gratiæ sacramenta, ac cætera omnia in quibus communicet nicat Ecclesia Christiana: In quo intelligitur, quod Ecclesia Catholica cum suis Sacramentis & legibus, per Spiritum Sanctum regulata, omni homini (quantumcunque facinoroso peccatori) sufficit ad salutem, & quod extra Ecclesiam Catholicam non sit salus. 7 Consummatione Ecclesiæ per gloriam sempiternam, in anima & carne veraciter suscitanda: & per huius oppositum intelligitur æterna damnatio reproborum. Si vis ergo saluus esse frater, ita de mysterio Trinitatis sentias.

Deinde exprimat ei Sacerdos alios septem articulos ad Christi humanitatem pertinentes, hoc modo.

Similiter (frater charissime) necessarium est ad æternam salutem, vt credas, & confitearis Domini nostri Iesu Christi Incarnationẽ, seu veram carnis assumptionem per Spiritum Sanctum ex sola virgine gloriosa. 2 Veram incarnati Dei natiuitatem ex virgine incorrupta. 3 Veram Christi passionem & mortem sub tyrannide Pilatĩ. 4 Veram Christi descensionem ad inferos in anima ad spoliatorem tartari, quiescente corpore eius in sepulchro. 5 Veram Christi Dei tertia die a morte resurrectionem. 6 Veram ipsius ad cælos ascensionem. 7 Ipsius venturi ad iudicium certissimam expectationem. Hæc est fides catholica (frater) quam nisi fideliter, firmiterque credideris, sicut sancta mater Ecclesia credit, saluus esse non poteris.

Et si infirmus laicus, vel simpliciter literatus fuerit, tunc potest Sacerdos articulos fidei in generali ab eo inquirere sub hac forma.

Charis

CHarissime frater, credis Patrem, & Filium, & Spititũ Sanctum, esse tres personas, & vnũ Deum, & ipsam enedictam, atque indiuisibilem Trinitatem creasse omia creata visibilia, & inuisibilia. Et solum Filium, de piritu Sancto conceptum, incarnatum fuisse ex Maria rgine, passum & mortuũ pro nobis in cruce, sub Pontio ilato, sepultum descendisse ad inferna, die tertia resurxisse a mortuis, ad cœlos ascendisse, iterumque venturũ l iudicandos viuos & mortuos, omnesque homines tunc corpore & anima resurrecturos, bona & mala secũdum ierita sua recepturos, & remissionem peccatorum per acramentorum Ecclesiæ perceptionem, & Sanctorum ommunionem: id est omnes homines in charitate exientes, esse participes omnium bonorũ gratiæ, quæ fiunt Ecclesia, & omnes qui communicant cum iustis hic in ratia, cõmunicaturos cum eis in gloria. Deinde responeat infirmus. Credo firmiter in omnibus, sicut sancta iater credit Ecclesia, protestando coram Deo, & omniius sanctis continuè hoc esse meam veram & firmam inntionem, quomodocunque aliquis spiritus malignus iemoriam meam aliter fortè in futuro solicitauerit perirbare.

Deinde dicat Sacerdos.

CHarissime frater, quia sine charitate, nihil proderit tibi fides, testante Apostolo, qui dicit: Si habuero mnem fidem ita vt mõtes transferam, charitatem autem on habuero, nihil sum: ideo opportet te deligere Doinum Deum tuum super omnia ex toto corde tuo, &

ex tota anima tua, & proximum tuum propter Deum ſicut teipſum. Nam ſine huiuſmodi charitate nulla fid valet. Exerce igitur charitatis opera dum vales: & ſi mul tibi affuerit, abundanter tribue, ſi autem exiguum illu impartire ſtude. Et ante omnia ſi quem iniuſtè læſeri ſatisfacias ſi valeas, ſi autem non valeas, expedit vt ab e veniam humiliter poſtules. Dimitte debitoribus tuis, illis qui in te peccauerunt, vt Deus tibi dimittat. Odiēt te diligas, pro malis bona retribuas. Dimittite (inquit Saluator) & dimittetur vobis. Spem etiam firmam, & bo fiduciam (frater) opportet te habere in Deo, & in miſericordia eius. Et ſi occurrerit cogitatui tuo multitudo peccatorum tuorum, dole: ſed nullo modo deſperes. Im cogita quoniam (vt teſtatur ſcriptura) miſericordia ei ſuper omnia opera eius, & illi ſoli proprium eſt miſere ſemper & parcere, & quia ſecundum altitudinem cœli terra corroberauit miſericordiam ſuam ſuper timentes ſ Spera igitur in Deo, & fac bonitatem, quoniam ſperan tem in Domino miſericordia circundabit. Qui ſperāt i Domino habebunt fortitudinem, & aſſument pennas aquilæ, volabunt & non deficient. Volabūt enim a tenebris ad lumen, a carcere ad regnum, a miſeria præſenti a gloriam ſempiternam.

Deindè ſtabilito ſic infirmo in fide, charitate, & ſpe dicat ei Sacerdos.

CHariſſime frater ſi velis ad viſionem Dei peruenir opportet omnino quod ſis mundus in mente, & pu

rus i

us in conscientia. Ait enim Christus in Euangalio: Beati mundo corde, quoniam ipsi Deum videbunt. Si ergo vis mundum cor & conscientiam sanam habere, peccata tua niuersa cōfitere: ore enim confessio fit ad salutem, vt ait postolus. Et quia fortè ante hac aut per obliuionem, aut erecundiæ confusionem, aliqua peccata tua, vel eorum ircumstantias aggrauantes omisisti, truncasti, abscondi- i, vel minus confessus fuisti: ideo iam resume ab initio, confitere. Quoniam in proximo est, vt viam vniuersæ arnis ingressurus sis, & tunc amplius cōfiteri non poteris. Dic ergo vni, peccata tua, vt Deus coram multis milib⁹ in ie iudicij ea tegat. Si autem tu hic ea tegas & abscōdas, in mnium conspectu ad tui confusionem in die iudicij de- udabuntur. Recogita ergo omnes annos tuos in amari- dine animæ tuæ, & non sit tibi solicitudo de aliqua cre- tura, vel rebus mundanis: sed omnem solicitudinem tu- m proijce in Deum, & noli esse immemor salutis animæ uæ. Multum tempus in vanum transegisti, nunc vna ho- a tibi fortè tantum superest in hac vita, & ideo hanc ex- ende totaliter in vtilitatem & commodum animæ tuæ. urge (frater) de lacu miseriæ, et de luto peccati per con- essionem. Grandis enim tibi restat via. Surge euge vt lotus achrimis cōtritionis comedere valeas panē vitæ, hoc est, acramentum Corporis Christi, quod erit tibi in via hac ua gradieris robur & fulcimētum: & ambulabis per Dei ratiam in fortitudine cibi illius vsque ad montem Dei. Quod tibi cōcedat omniū fidelium Redēptor Dei Filius, esus Christus, Amen.

Deinde audita integra confessione infirmi, & factis in terrogationibus quæ expediunt, iniungat Sacerdos in firmo, quod si quid alieni iniustè habuerit, vel si quem iniustè læserit, seu damnificauerit, reddat & satisfacia si valeat: si non valeat, veniam humiliter postulet. At tamen non iniungat ei Sacerdos aliquam pænitētiam sed dicat ei benigniter hoc modo.

FRater tu tot, & talia peccata commisisti, pro quibu si tu esses sanus talem pænitētiam deberes agere vsqu ad tale tempus (innotescendo ei illam pænitentiam in sp ciali) sed quia infirmus es, & forté vita tua ad hoc pera gendum extendi non valebit, ideo non iniungo tibi al quam pænitētiam. Volo tamen, quod (si forte decesseris facias talem Eleemosinam, vel ad minus iniungas amic vel executorib⁹ tuis, ipsam facere ex parte tua, pro ipsa pæ nitentia. (assignando ipsam Eleemosinam in speciali) S autem conualueris, pænitentiam quam tibi notificaui ac impleas, vel iterum humiliter redeas ad confessionem, v mihi, vel alteri qui tibi absolutionis beneficiū in hac par te de iure conferre valeat & debeat. Et concedo tibi quo omnes indulgentiæ quorumcunque Prælatorum tibi cō cessæ, seu qualitercunque concedendæ, eorumque be nedictiones, omnes aquæ benedictæ aspersiones, deuot pectoris tui tunsiones, cordis tui cōtritiones, ista cōfessio & omnes aliæ confessiones tuæ deuotæ, omnia ieiuni abstinentiæ, eleemosinæ, vigiliæ, disciplinæ, oratione peregrinationes, & omnia alia bona quæ fecisti, vel facie

& om

& omnia mala quæ pro Deo vel iniuste sustinuisti, vel sustinebis, passio Saluatoris domini nostri Iesu Christi, meritaq; beatæ & gloriosæ virginis Mariæ & omnium aliorum sanctorum, necnon suffragia totius sanctæ Ecclesiæ catholicæ, cedant tibi in remissionem istorũ, & omnium aliorum peccatorũ tuorum, in augmẽtationem meritorũ, & consecutionem præmiorum æternorum. Amen.

Deinde dicat Sacerdos. Misereatur tui &c. Et postea eum absoluat ab omnibus peccatis suis dicendo.

Dominus noster Iesus Christus &c.

Notandum est quod licet Sacerdos possit de facto absoluere infirmum in articulo mortis ab omnibus peccatis suis, tamen si aliquis casus occurrat in Confessione a quo ipse Sacerdos eum alias de iure absoluere non posset, inungendum est infirmo, quod cum conualuerit præsentet se illi ad confitendum, qui eum de iure, vel consuetudine in hac parte absoluere debeat, recepturus eius mandata, & satisfacturus: nam alias reincidit in eandem sententiam quam prius sustinuit.

Deinde dicat Sacerdos orationem sequentem.

℣. Dominus vobiscum. ℟. Et cum spiritu tuo.

Oremus.

PRætende Domine huic famulo tuo [vel famulæ tuæ] dexteram cœlestis auxilij: vt te toto corde perquirat, & quæ digne postulat assequatur. Per Christum Dominũ nostrum Amen.

Sequatur.

BEne ✠ dictio Dei Patris omnipotẽtis, & Filij, & Spiritus Sancti, super te descendat, & maneat semper. Amen.

Deinde infirmus osculetur crucem, & Sacerdotem, & postea omnes alios per ordinem: & interim dicat Sacerdos morosius.

℣. Dominus vobiscum. ℟. Et cum spiritu tuo.

Oremus.

DEus misericors, Deus clemens, qui secundum multitudinem miserationum tuarum, peccata pænitentium deles, & præteritorum criminũ culpas, venia remissionis euacuas: respice super hunc famulum tuum [vel hanc famulam tuam] N. sibi remissionem omnium peccatorum suorum tota cordis cotritione poscentẽ. Renoua in eo (vel ea) pijssime Pater quicquid diabolica fraude violatum est, & vnitati corporis Ecclesiæ tuæ mẽbrum infirmum (peccatorum percepta remissione) restitue. Miserere Domine gemituum eius, miserere lachrimarum, miserere tribulationum atque dolorum: & non habẽtem fiduciam nisi in tua misericordia, ad sacramentum reconciliationis admitte. Per Christum Dominum nostrum. Amen.

Oremus.

DA nobis quæsumus Domine, vt sicut publicani precibus, & confessione placatus es, ita & huic famulo tuo (vel famulæ tuæ) N. beingnus aspires: vt in confessione flebili permanens, misericordiam tuam celeriter consequatur, sacrisque altaribus restitutus (vel restituta) rursus diuino famulatui mancipetur. Per Christum Dominum nostrum. Amen.

Abso-

Abſolutio.

ABſoluimus te N. vice beati Petri Apoſtolorum principis, cui Dominus poteſtatem ligandi, atque ſoluẽdi dedit, & quantum ad te pertinet accuſatio, & ad nos remiſſio, ſit tibi omnipotens Deus vita & ſalus, & omnium peccatorum tuorum pius indultor. Qui viuit & regnat cum Deo Patre in vnitate Spiritus Sancti Deus per omnia ſæcula ſæculorum. Amen.

DE EXTREMA VNCTIONE.

PRiuſquam vngatur infirmus incipiat Sacerdos Antiphonam. Saluator mundi. Deinde dicatur pſal. 70.

IN te Domine ſperaui, non confundar in æternum: in iuſtitia tua libera me, & eripe me.

Inclina ad me aurem tuam: & ſalua me.

Eſto mihi in Deum protectorem, & in locum munitum: vt ſaluum me facias.

Quoniam firmamentũ meum. & refugium meum es tu.

Deus meus eripe me de manu peccatoris, & de manu contra legem agentis & iniqui.

Quoniam tu es patientia mea Domine: Domine ſpes mea a iuuentute mea.

In te confirmatus ſum ex vtero: de ventre matris meæ tu

es proes protector meus.

In te cantatio mea ſemper: tanquam prodigium factus ſum multis & tu adiutor fortis.

Repleatur os meum laude,& cantem gloriam tuam: tota die magnitudinem tuam.

Ne proijcias me in tempore ſenectutis: cum defecerit virtus mea, ne derelinquas me.

Quia dixerunt inimici mei mihi: & qui cuſtodiebant animam meam, concilium fecerunt in vnum.

Dicentes, Deus dereliquit eum: perſequimini, & comprehendite eum, quia non eſt qui eripiat.

Deus ne elongeris a me: Deus meus in auxilium meum reſpice.

Confundantur, & deficiant detrahētes animæ meæ: operiantur confuſione,& pudore, qui quærunt mala mihi.

Ego autem ſemper ſperabo: & adijciam ſuper omnem laudem tuam.

Os meum annunciabit iuſtitiam tuam: tota die ſalutare tuum.

Quoniam non cognoui literaturam, introibo in potentias Domini: Domine memorabor iuſtitiæ tuæ ſolius.

Deus docuiſti me a iuuentute mea: & vſque nunc pronunciabo mirabilia tua.

Et vſque in ſenectam,& ſenium:Deus ne derelinquas me.

Donec annunciem brachium tuum: generationi omni quæ ventura eſt.

Potentiam tuam, & iuſtitiam tuam Deus vſque in altiſſima, quæ ma, quæ fecisti magnalia: Deus quis similis tibi.

Quantas ostendisti mihi tribulationes multas, & malas, & conuersus viuificasti me: & de abyssis terræ iterum reduxisti me.

Multiplicasti magnificentiam tuam: & conuersus consolatus es me.

Nam & ego confitebor tibi in vasis psalmi veritatẽ tuam Deus: psallam tibi in cythara sanctus Israel.

Exultabunt labia mea cum cantauero tibi: & anima mea quam redemisti.

Sed & lingua mea tota die meditabitur iustitiam tuam: cum cõfusi & reueriti fuerint, qui quærunt mala mihi.

Gloria patri. &c. Finito psalmo dicatur Antiphona.

Saluator mundi salua nos, qui per crucem, & sanguinem tuum redemisti nos: auxiliare nobis te deprecamur Deus noster.

Tunc dicat Sacerdos. ℣. Dominus vobiscum.

℟. Et cum spiritu tuo. Oremus.

OMnipotens sempiterne Deus, qui per beatum Iacobum Apostolum tuum, loquutus es, dicens: Infirmatur quis in vobis? inducat Presbyteros Ecclesiæ, & orẽt super eũ, vngẽtes eum Oleo, in nomine Domini: & oratio fidei saluabit infirmum, & alleuiabit eum Dominus, & si in peccatis sit, remittentur ei: Dignare per manus nostras hunc famulum tuum (vel hanc famulam tuam) N infirmum (vel infirmam) de oleo sanctificato vngere, & virtute benedictionis tuæ saluti pristinæ restituere: vt quod exterius per minysterium nostrum efficitur, hoc interius spiritualiter tua diuina virtus, ac inuisibiliter tua malagmata operentur. Per Dominum nostrum Iesum. &c. Amen.

Tunc Sacerdos accedens ad infirmum incipiat psalmũ sequentem, quem chorus vel clericus totum prosequatur; & sic fiat de cæteris psalmis sequentibus.

Psal. 12.

VSquequo Domine obliuisceris me in finem? vsquequo auertis faciem tuam a me?

Quandiu ponam consilia in anima mea? dolorẽ in corde meo per diem.

Vsquequo exaltabitur inimicus meus super me? respice, & exaudi me Domine Deus meus.

Illumina oculos meos ne vnquam obdormiam in morte: nequando dicat inimicus meus, præualui aduersus eũ.

Qui tribulant me, exultabunt si motus fuero: ego autem in misericordia tua speraui.

Exultabit cor meum in salutari tuo, cantabo Domino qui bona tribuit mihi: Et psallam nomini Domini altissimi.

Gloria Patri, & Filio, & Spiritui Sancto, &c.

Dum dicitur prædictus psalmus a choro, vel clerico, accipiat interim Sacerdos oleum infirmorum super pollicem dexterum, & sic cum illo pollice tangat infirmum cum oleo, signum sanctæ crucis faciens, super vtrumque oculũ incipiẽdo ad dexterũ, & dicat Sacerdos hoc modo.

Per

Per istam vnctionem,& suam pijssimam misericordiam, indulgeat tibi Dominus quidquid peccasti per visum.

℞. Amen. Sequatur psalmus. Psal.29.

Exaltabo te Domine, quoniam suscepisti me: nec delectasti inimicos meos super me.

Domine Deus meus clamaui ad te: & sanasti me.

Domine eduxisti ab inferno animam meam: saluasti me a descendentibus in lacum.

Psallite Domino sancti eius:& confitemini memoriæ sanctitatis eius.

Quoniã ira in indignatione eius:& vita in voluntate eius.

Ad vesperam demorabitur fletus: & ad matutinũ lætitia.

Ego auté dixi in abũdantia mea:non mouebor in æternũ.

Domine in volũtate tua: præstitisti decori meo virtutem.

Auertisti faciem tuam a me: & factus sum conturbatus.

Ad te Domine clamabo: & ad Deum meum deprecabor.

Quæ vtilitas in sanguine meo: dum descendo in corruptionem.

Nunquid confitebitur tibi puluis, aut annunciabit veritatem tuam?

Audiuit Dominus, & misertus est mei: Dominus factus est adiutor meus.

Conuertisti plãctum meum in gaudium mihi: conscidisti saccum meum,& circundedisti me lætitia.

Vt cantet tibi gloria mea, & non compungar: Domine Deus meus in æternum confitebor tibi.

Gloria Patri, &c.

Deinde ſuper aures dicens.

Per iſtam vnctionem, & ſuam pijſſimam miſericordiam, indulgeat tibi Dominus quicquid peccaſti per auditum. ℟. Amen. Sequatur Pſalmus. pſal. 42.

IVdica me Deus, & diſcerne cauſam meam de gente nõ ſancta: ab homine iniquo & doloſo erue me.

Quia tu es Deus fortitudo mea: quare me repuliſti, & quare triſtis incedo dum affligit me inimicus?

Emitte lucem tuam & veritatem tuã: ipſa me deduxerũt, & adduxerunt in montem ſanctum tuum, & in tabernacula tua.

Et introibo ad altare Dei: ad Deum qui lætificat iuuentutem meam.

Confitibor tibi in cythara Deus, Deus meus: quare triſtis es anima mea, & quare conturbas me?

Spera in Deo, quoniam adhuc confitebor illi: ſalutare vultus mei, & Deus meus.

Gloria Patri, &c. Deinde ſuper labia dicens.

Per iſtam vnctionem, & ſuam pijſſimam miſericordiam, indulgeat tibi Dominus quicquid peccaſti per guſtum, & illicita verba. ℟. Amen. Sequitur Pſalmus. pſal. 53.

DEus in nomine tuo ſaluum me fac: & in virtute tua iudica me.

Deus exaudi orationem meam: auribus percipe verba oris mei.

Quoniam alieni inſurrexerunt aduerſum me: & fortes quæſierunt animam meam: & non propoſuerunt Deum

Deum ante conspectum suum.

Ecce enim Deus adiuuat me: & Dominus susceptor est amimæ meæ.

Auerte mala inimicis meis:& in veritate tua disperde illos.

Voluntarie sacrificabo tibi: & confitebor nomini tuo Domine quoniam bonum est.

Quoniam ex omni tribulatione eripuisti me: & super inimicos meos despexit oculus meus.

Gloria Patri. &c. Deinde super nares dicens.

Per istam vnctionem, & suam pissimam misericordiam, indulgeat tibi Dominus, quicquid peccasti per odoratum, &c. Amen. Sequitur Psalmus. psal. 69.

Deus in adiutorium meum intende. Domine ad adiuuandum me festina.

Confundantur, & reuereantur: qui quærunt animam meam.

Auertantur retrorsum, & erubescant: qui volunt mihi mala.

Auertantur statim erubescentes: qui dicunt mihi, euge, euge.

Exultent, & lætentur in te omnes qui quærunt te: & dicant semper, magnificetur Dominus, qui diligunt salutare tuum.

Ego vero egenus, & pauper sum: Deus adiuua me.

Adiutor meus, & liberator meus es tu: Domine ne moreris.

Gloria Patri, &c.

Manus Sacerdotis infirmi debent inungi in partibu exterioribus: nam Episcopus liniebat in partibus interioribus. Manus vero cuiuscunque alterius infirmi deben inungi interius.

Deinde super manus ita dicens.

P er istam vnctionem, & suam pijssimam misericordiam indulgeat tibi Dominus, quicquid peccasti per tactum.

℞. Amen. Sequatur Psalmus. psal 85

I Nclina Domine aurem tuam, & exaudi me: quoniam inops & pauper sum ego.

C ustodi animam meam, quoniam sanctus sum: saluum fac seruum tuum Deus meus sperantem in te.

M iserere mei Domine, quoniam ad te clamaui tota die lætifica animam serui tui, quoniam ad te Domine animam meam leuaui.

Q uoniam tu Domine suauis & mitis: Et multæ misericordiæ omnibus inuocantibus te.

A uribus percipe Domine orationem meam: & intend voci deprecationis meæ.

I n die tribulationis meæ clamaui ad te: quia exaudisti me

N on est similis tui in dijs Domine: & non est secundum opera tua.

O mnes gentes quascunque fecisti venient, & adorabun coram te Domine: & glorificabunt nomen tuum.

Q uoniam magnus es tu, & faciens mirabilia: tu es Deus solus.

D educ me Domine in via tua, & ingrediar in veritate tua

late

lætetur cor meum, vt timeat nomen tuum.

Confitebor tibi Domine Deus meus in toto corde meo: & glorificabo nomen tuum in æternum.

Quia misericordia tua magna est super me: & eruisti animam meam ex inferno inferiori.

Deus iniqui insurrexerunt super me, & synagoga potentium quæsierunt animam meam: & non proposuerunt te in conspectu suo.

Et tu Domine Deus miserator & misericors: patiens & multæ misericordiæ & verax.

Respice in me & miserere mei, da imperium tuum puero tuo: & saluum fac filium ancillæ tuæ.

Fac mecum signum in bonum, & videant qui oderunt me, & confundantur: quoniam tu Domine adiuuisti me, & consolatus es me.

Gloria Patri, &c.

Deinde super pedes ita dicens.

Per istam vnctionem & suam pijssimam misericordiam, indulgeat tibi Dominus quicquid peccasti per incessum pedum. ℞. Amen.

Sequatur Psalmus. psal. 87.

Domine Deus salutis meæ: in die clamaui & nocte coram te.

Intret in conspectu tuo oratio mea: inclina aurem tuam ad precem meam.

Quia repleta est malis anima mea: & vita mea inferno appropinquauit.

Æstima-

Æstimatus sum cum descẽdentibus in lacum: factus sum sicut homo sine adiutorio, inter mortuos liber.

Sicut vulnerati dormientes in sepulchris quorum non e memor amplius: Et ipsi de manu tua repulsi sunt.

Posuerunt me in lacu inferiori: in tenebris & in vmbra mortis.

Super me confirmatus est furor tuus: Et omnes fluctu tuos induxisti super me.

Longè fecisti notos meos a me: posuerunt me abomina tionem sibi.

Traditus sum, & non egrediebar: oculi mei languerun præ inopia.

Clamaui ad te Domine tota die: expandi ad te manu meas.

Nunquid mortuis facies mirabilia: aut medici suscitabũt Et confitebuntur tibi;

Nunquid narrabit aliquis in sepulchro misericordian tuam: Et veritatem tuam in perditione.

Nunquid cognoscentur in tenebris mirabilia tua: & iusti tia tua in terra obliuionis.

Et ego ad te Domine clamaui: Et mane oratio mea præ ueniet te.

Vt quid Domine repellis orationem meam: auertis fa ciem tuam a me?

Pauper sum ego, Et in laboribus a iuuentute mea: exalta tus autem humiliatus sum & conturbatur.

In me transierint iræ tuæ: Et terrores tui cõturbauerũt me

Circun

ircundederunt me sicut aquæ: tota die circundederunt ıe simul.

longasti a me amicum, & proximum: & notos meos a ıiseria.

loria Patri & Filio, & Spiritui Sancto, &c.

Deinde in dorso inter lumbos maris, vel super vmbilicum mulieris, ita dicens.

er istam vnctionem & suam pijssimam misericordiam, ıdulgeat tibi Dominus, quicquid peccasti per illicitas coitationes, & per ardorem libidinis. ℟. Amen.

Tunc erigens se Sacerdos lauet manus suas, cum sale & aqua, in vase quo stuppæ olei ponuntur: quæ igne crementur, vel in cœmiterio fodiantur.

Postea dicat Sacerdos super infirmum benedictionem, hoc modo.

n nomine Patris, & Filij, & Spiritus Sancti, sit tibi hæc lei vnctio, ad purificationem mentis & corporis, & ad ıunimen & defensionem, contra iacula immundorum iirituum. ℟. Amen.

Sequatur Psalmus. 140.

DOmine clamaui ad te, exaudi me: intende voci meæ cum clamauero ad te.

irigatur oratio mea sicut incensum in conspectu tuo: eleuatio manuum mearum sacrificium vespertinum.

one Domine custodiam ori meo: & ostium circunstantiæ labijs meis.

Jon declines cor meum in verba malitiæ: ad excusandas

excuſationes in peccatis.

Cum hominibus operantibus iniquitatem: & non con municabo cum electis eorum.

Corripiet me iuſtus in miſericordia, & increpabit me: leum autem peccatoris non impiuguet caput meum.

Quoniam adhuc & oratio mea in beneplacitis eorum:al ſorpti ſunt iuncti petræ iudices eorum.

Audient verba mea, quoniam potuerunt: ſicut craſſitud terræ erupta eſt ſuper terram.

Diſſipata ſunt oſſa noſtra ſecus infernum, quia ad te Do mine, Domine oculi mei: in te ſperaui non aufer animam meam.

Cuſtodi me a laqueo, quem ſtatuerunt mihi: & a ſcan dalis operantium iniquitatem.

Cadent in retiaculo eius peccatores: ſingulariter ſumeg donec tranſeam.

Gloria Patri &c.

Deinde dicat Sacerdos.

℣. Dominus vobiſcum. ℟. Et cum ſpiritu tuo.

Oremus.

DOmine Deus ſaluator noſter, qui es vera ſalus & m dicina, a quo omnis ſanitas & omne medicament venit, quique nos Apoſtoli tui Iacobi documento iuſtr xiſti, vt languentes olei liquore orantes tangeremus: r ſpice propitius ſuper hunc ſamulum tuum (vel hanc f mulam tuam) N. & quem (vel quam) languor cruci ad exitum, & virium defectus protrahit ad occaſum, m

de

la gratiæ tuæ ſaluti reſtituat caſtigatum (vel caſtigatã) xtingue in eo (vel ea) clementiſſime Deus omnium feium æſtus, dolorum ſtimulos, & cunctorum languom cruciatus. Viſcerum quoque & ſecretorum, interna edicina, atque medullarum diſcrimina ſana. Conpagum iam & artuũ dele cicatrices veteres, & acerbas compee paſſiones. Reformetur in eo (vel ea) carnis & ſanguis, quam creaſti perfecta materies: ſicque illum (vel illam) giter tua cuſtodiat pietas, vt nec ad corruptionem aliiando ſanitas, nec ad perditionem perducat infirmitas. ed fiat illi hæc ſacra olei perunctio, cita morbi præſentis languoris expulſio, & peccatorum omnium exoptata miſſio. Per te Saluaror mundi. Qui cum Deo Patre, & iritu Sancto viuis & regnas Deus, per omnia ſæcula ſælorum. Amen.

De communicando Infirmo,

Acta vnctione vt prædictum eſt, expedit, vt Sacerdos ante communionem inquirat ab infirmo an aliia alia peccata ibi ad memoriam occurrant, de quibus on erat confeſſus: nam poſſet eſſe quòd per preces & detas orationes Sacerdotis ſiue aliorum, Deus cor infirmi uſtraret & daret ei gratiam veriùs & plenùis confitendi. Et poſtea interroget eum Sacerdos, ſi recognoſcat coris & ſanguinem Domini noſtri Ieſu Chriſti, ſic dicendo:

FRater, credis quod Sacramentum quod tractatur i Altari sub forma panis, est verum corpus, & sangu Domini nostri Iesu Christi?

Respondeat infirmus, Credo.

Deinde communicetur infirmus, nisi prius commun catus fuerit: & nisi de vomitu, vel alia irreuerentia prob bilitei timeatur: in quo casu, dicat Sacerdos infirmo.

Frater in hoc casu sufficit tibi vera fides, & bona volunta tantum crede, & manducasti.

Sacerdos vero in infirmis communicandis stola ir duetur. Et cum Sanctum Sacramentum administra dicat,

Corpus Domini nostri Iesu Christi custodiat corpus tu & animam tuam, in vitam æternam. Amen.

Deinde dicat Sacerdos sine Dominus vobiscum, se cum Oremus, orationem sequentem, quę non dicatur n si tantum, quando infirmus communicatur.

Oremus.

DOmine sancte pater omnipotens æternæ Deus, t fideliter deprecamur, vt accipienti huic fratri nostr (vel sorori nostræ) N sacrosanctum corpus & sanguiner filii tui Domini nostri Iesu Christi, tam corporis quar animæ sit salus. Amen.

Deinde sequatur Psalmus. 145.

LAuda anima mea Dominum, laudabo Dominum i vita mea: psallam Deo meo quandiu fuero.

Nolite confidere in principibus: in filijs hominum, i quibu

quibus non eſt ſalus.

Exibit ſpiritus eius, & reuertetur in terram ſuam: in illa die peribunt omnes cogitationes eorum.

Beatus cuius Deus Iacob adiutor eius, ſpes eius in Domino Deo ipſius: qui fecit cælum & terram, mare, & omnia quæ in eis ſunt.

Qui cuſtodit veritatem in ſæculum, facit iudicium iniuriam patientibus: dat eſcam eſurientibus.

Dominus ſoluit compeditos: Dominus illuminat cæcos.

Dominus erigit eliſos: Dominus diligit iuſtos.

Dominus cuſtodit aduenas, pupillum & viduam ſuſcipiet: & vias peccatorum diſperdet.

Regnabit Dominus in ſæcula, Deus tuus ex Sion: in generatione, & generationem.

Gloria Patri & Filio, & Spiritui Sancto, &c.

Quo finito dicat Sacerdos; Oremus.

DEus qui peccatores, & ſcelerum onere vulneratos, Sacerdotibus tuis oſtendere iuſſiſti, Deus qui diſci-ulis tuis manus ſuper infirmos, vt benè haberent impo-nere præcepiſti, Deus qui per Apoſtolorum manus infir-mos ſacro oleo vngere, & pro eis orare docuiſti, Deus qui per impoſitionem manuum Sacerdotum, cum ſancti nominis tui inuocatione, peccata relaxare voluiſti: exaudi orationes noſtras, & da huic famulo tuo (vel famulæ tuæ) N. infirmitatis noxa oppreſſo (vel oppreſſæ) per hoc ſacroſanctum myſterum, quod nos indignos famulos tuos ngere voluiſti, remiſſionem omniū peccatorum: quatenus hanc ſacrati olei vnctionem, corporis & ſanguinis tui ſuſceptionem, atq; manus noſtræ impoſitionem, cuncta e facinora Spiritus Sancti gratia relaxentur, ſanitas animæ & corporis reſtituatur, vt non ei plus noceat conſcientiæ reatus ad pænam, quam indulgentia tuæ pietatis ad emendationem proſit & veniam. Te concedente Saluator mundi, qui viuis & regnas cum Deo Patre in vnitate eiuſdem &c. Amen.

Deinde benedicat Sacerdos infirmum dicens.

BEne ✠ dicat te Pater qui in principio cuncta creauit. ℟. Amen.

Et ſic reſpondeatur ad ſingulas benedictiones.

Sanet te Dei Filius. ℟. Amen. Illuminet te Spiritus ſãctus ℟. Amen. Corpus tuum cuſtodiat. ℟. Amen. Animam tuam ſaluet. ℟ Amen. Cor tuum irradiet. R. Amen. Senſum tuum dirigat, & ad ſupernam patriam te perducat qui in Trinitate perfecta, viuit & regnat Deus, per omnia ſæcula ſæculorum. Amen.

Alia benedictio.

BEne ✠ dicat te Deus cæli Reſp. Amen. Adiuuet te Deus Chriſtus filius Dei. Reſp. Amen. Corpus tuum in ſuo ſancto ſeruitio cuſtodiri & cõſeruari faciat. Reſp. Amen. Mentem tuam illuminet. Reſp. Amen Senſum tuum cuſtodiat. Reſp. Amen. Gratiam ſuam ad profectum animæ tuæ in te augeat. Reſp. Amen. Ab omni malo te liberet. Reſp. Amen Omnia peccata tua deleat. Reſp. Amen. Dextera ſua te defendat.

Reſp.

Resp. Amẽ. Qui sanctos suos semper adiuuat, ipse te ad-
iuuare & cõseruare dignetur. Qui viuit & regnat Deus per
omnia sæcula sæculorũ. Resp. Amen. Alia benedictio.

BEne ✠ dicat te Deus Pater qui in principio cuncta
creauit ℟. Amen.

Bene ✠ dicat te Dei filius qui de supernis sedibus pro
nobis saluandis descendit, & crucem subire non recusauit.
℟. Amen. Bene ✠ dicat te Spiritus Sanctus, qui in si-
militudine columbæ in flumine Iordanis, in Christo re-
quieuit. ℟. Amen. Ipseque te in Trinitate sanctificet
quem omnes gentes venturum expectant ad iudicium,
Qui cum Deo Patre & eodem Spiritu Sancto viuit & regnat in sæcula sæculorum. Resp. Amen.

Finito hoc officio conuenienter dici poterunt ab infirmo languente in extremis si placeat, orationes subscriptæ
vel earum aliquæ, videlicet. Psalmus. 50.

MIserere mei Deus &c. Item psal 53. Deus in
nomine tuo saluũ me fac &c. pag. 68. Item versus.
Suscipe me Domine secũdum eloquium tuum & viuam:
& non confundas me ab expectatione mea. Et. Quæ est
expectatio mea: nonne Dominus?

Vel sic, Domine Iesu Christe suscipe spiritum meum.

Item, Deus propitius esto mihi peccatori.

Item, ℣. In manus tuas Domine commendo spiritum
meum: redemisti me Domine Deus veritatis. Item versus.
Delicta iuuẽtutis meæ: & ignorantias meas ne memineris
Domine. Item ℣. Ab occultis meis munda me: &
ab alienis

ab alienis parce seruo tuo. Item ℣. Ne proijcias me Domine in tempore senectutis: cum defecerit virtus mea ne derelinquas me.

Sciendum est autem quod non licet alicui ministrare Sacramentum Vnctionis extremæ nisi tantum Sacerdoti. Vnde si aliquis non Sacerdos attentaret hoc facere, nihil faceret collatio.

Loca vero vngenda sunt supradicta, & non alia, nisi in mutilatis, in quibus debent inungi loca magis propinqua.

Et notãdum est quod si Sacerdos, iam aliquibus partibus inunctis, alijs restantibus ad vngendum defecerit, partes inunctæ non sunt iteratò vngendæ, sed quæ restant partes vngendæ, per alium Sacerdotem compleantur.

Potest Sacerdos vno clerico præsente infirmum inungere, & etiam sinè clerico in necessitatis articulo.

Moneant frequenter Sacerdotes parochianos suos, quod omnes quatuordecim annorum & amplius, se exhibeant ad Sacramentum Vnctionis extremæ suscipiendum, quando mortis metus imminet.

Doceant etiam eos, quod hoc Sacramentum licitè potest itirari sinè aliqua sui iniuria, vndè quoties homo cõualuerit, & noua infirmitas iterato superuenerit, ex qua fuerit metus mortis, potest idem homo in vnaquaque huiusmodi infirmtate inungi. In eadem quoque infirmitate hoc Sacramentum iterari potest, nam in ægritudine diuturna debet fieri quando videtur deducere ad mortem. Et si illum articulum euadat & eadem infirmitate durãte postea ad statum similẽ reducatur, iterũ potest inungi: quia alius est infirmitatis status, licet sit eadem infirmitas. Et si qu...

po-

post hoc Sacramentum conualuerit, mihilominus ad opus coniugale & ad omne opus honestum licite poterit reuerti.

Hoc Sacramentum non est conferendum euntibus ad bellum, vel ad duellum, peregrinis, aut nauigantibus, vel his qui statim occidendi sunt.

Similiter pueri, frænetici, furiosi, & alij, huiusmodi alienationem mentis patientes, eo quod debitam discretionem deuotionis & veræ pænitentiæ non habeant, ad hoc Sacramentum non admittantur; nisi forte ipsi frænetici, furiosi vel amentes in sana mente constituti, hoc Sacramentū petierint, vel alias ante huiusmodi passionem, seu mentis alienationem de sua salute fuerint soliciti, tunc nihilominus consulitur hoc Sacramentum eis fiducialiter ministrandum. In constit. Lambeth p. c. vlt.

Nota quod tempore interdicti, non debet conferri Sacramentum Vnctionis extremæ, nec alia Sacramenta exceptis Baptismo, Confirmatione, pænitentia, & viatico, existentibus in articulo mortis tantum conferendis.

Commendatio Animæ in articulo mortis.

CVm anima in exitu seu dissolutione corporis visa fuerit laborare, percutiatur tabula minutè & acriter, & tunc omnes clerici cum summa velocitate accurrant, & dicant;

Credo in vnum Deum; Patrem omnipotentem factorem

rem cœli & terræ, visibilium omnium & inuisibilium. Et in vnum Dominum Iesum Christum, Filium Dei vnigenitum, Et ex Patre natum ante omnia sæcula, Deum de Deo, lumen de lumine, Deum verum de Deo vero. Genitum non factum, consubstantialem Patri: per quem omnia facta sunt. Qui propter nos homines, & propter nostram salutem descendit de cælis.

Et incarnatus est de Spiritu sancto ex Maria vigine: Et homo factus est.

Crucifixus etiam pro nobis sub Pontio Pilato, passus & sepultus est. Et resurrexit tertia die secundum Scripturas. Et ascendit in cœlum: sedet ad dexteram Patris. Et iterum venturus est cum gloria iudicare viuos & mortuos: cuius regni non erit finis. Et in Spiritum sanctum Dominum & viuificantem: qui ex Patre Filioq; procedit. Qui cum Patre & Filio simul adoratur & conglorificatur: qui locutus est per Prophetas. Et vnam sanctam Catholicam & Apostolicam Ecclesiam. Confiteor vnum baptisma in remissionem peccatorum. Et expecto resurrectionem mortuorum. Et vitam venturi sæculi. Amen.

Deindè dicant septem Psalmos pænitentiales cum Gloria Patri Quibus dictis, subiungatur hoc capitulũ.

Parce Domine parce famulo tuo quem redimere dignatus es præcioso sanguine tuo, nè in æternum irascaris ei.

Hoc captilum dicatur tribus vicibus tam a Sacerdote

quam

quam a toto conuentu, ita tamen quod Sacerdos prius dicat, quam conuentus repetat.

Deindé dicatur ſequens Litania ſine nota hoc modo.

Pater de cælis Deus, miſerere animæ famuli tui, (vel famulæ tuæ.)

Fili redemptor mundi Deus, miſerere animæ famuli tui.

Spiritus Sancte Deus, miſerere animæ famuli tui.

Sancta Trinitas vnus Deus, miſerere animæ famuli tui.

Sancte Sanctorum Deus, miſerere, &c.

Qui es trinus & vnus Deus, miſerere.

Sancta Maria, intercede pro anima eius.

Sancta Dei genitrix, inter.

Sancta virgo virginum, int.

Sancte Michael, intercede.

Sancte Gabriel, intercede.

Sancte Raphael, intercede.

Omnes ſancti Angeli & Archangeli, intercedite pro anima eius.

Omnes ſancti beatorum ſpirituũ ordines, intercedite.

Sancte Ioannes Baptiſta, intercede pro anima eius.

Omnes ſancti Patriarchæ & prophetæ, intercedite.

Sancte Petre, intercede.

Sancte Paule, intercede.

Sancte Andræa, intercede

Sancte Mathæe, intercede.

Sancte Thoma, intercede.

Sancte Iacobe, intercede.

Sancte Ioannes, intercede

Sancte Philippe, intercede.

Sancte Iacobe, intercede.

Sancte Bartholomeæ, int.

Sancte Simon, intercede.

Sancte Iuda, intercede.

Sancte Mathia, intercede.

Sancte Marce, intercede.

Sancte Luca, intercede.

Sancte Barnaba, intercede.

Omnes ſancti Apoſtoli & Euan-

Euangelistæ, intercedite.

Omnes sancti discipuli Domini & Innocentes, int.

Sancte Stephane, interce.

Sancte Line, intercede.

Sancte Clete, intercede.

Sancte Clemens, intercede.

Sancte Corneli, intercede.

Sancte Laurenti, intercede.

Sancte Sixte, intercede.

Sancte Vincenti, intercede.

Sancte Georgi, intercede.

Sancte Fabiane, intercede.

Sancte Sebastiane, interce.

Sancte Albane, intercede.

Sancte Edmunde, interce.

Sancte Blasi, intercede.

Sancte Dionisi, cum sociis tuis, intercedite pro anima eius.

Sancte Eustachi cum sociis tuis, intercedite.

Sancte Geruasi, intercede

Sancte Protasi, intercede.

Sancte Cosma, intercede.

Sancte Damiane, intercede

Sancti Ioannes & Paule, intercedite pro anima eius.

Sancti Crispine & Crispiniane, intercedite.

Omnes sancti Martyres, intercedite pro anima eius.

Sancte Benedicte, interce.

Sancte Siluester, intercede.

Sancte Nicolae, intercede.

Sancte Martine, intercede.

Sancte Hilari, intercede.

Sancte Ambrosi, intercede

Sancte Hieronime, interce.

Sancte Augustine, interce.

Sancte Berine, intercede.

Sancte Swithune, inter.

Sancte Æthelvvolde, int.

Sancte Dunstone, interce.

Sancte Cuthberte, interce.

Sancte Leonarde, interce

Sancte Ægidi, intercede.

Omnes sancti Confessores intercedite pro anima eius.

Omnes sancti Monachi & Eremitæ, intercedite

Sancta Maria Magdalena interce-

intercede.
Sancta Maria Egiptiaca, intercede.
Sancta Fælicitas, intercede.
Sancta Perpetua, intercede.
Sancta Cecilia, intercede.
Sancta Lucia, intercede.
Sancta Agatha, intercede.
Sancta Agnes, intercede.
Sancta Fides, intercede.
Sancta Catharina, interce.
Sancta Scholaſtica, inter.
Sancta Iuliana, intercede.
Sancta Margarita, interce.
Sancta Anaſtaſia, intercede
Sancta Petronilla, interce.
Sancta Editha, intercede.
Sancta Brigida, intercede.
Omnes ſanctæ Virgines, intercedite.
Omnes Sancti, intercedite.
Propitius eſto, parce & dimitte ei omnia peccata ſua Domine.
Ab omni malo, libera & defende animã eius Domine.
Ab hoſte iniquo, libera & defende animam eius Domine.
Ab inſidiis & laqueis Diaboli, libera.
Ab incurſu malignorum ſpirituum, libera & def.
A timore inimicorum, lib.
Ab ira tua, libera.
A damnatione perpetua, libera.
A pænis inferni, libera
A periculo mortis, libera.
A pondere peccatorum, libera.
Per immenſam pietatem tuam, libera & defende animam eius Domine.
Per myſterium ſanctæ Incarnationis tuæ, libera.
Per ſanctam circuncisionẽ tuam. libera
Per ſanctam apparitionem tuam, libera
Per Baptiſmum tuũ, libera.
Per Ieiunium tuum, libera.
Per paſſionem & crucem tuam

tuam, libera. & defende animam eius Domine.

Per pijssimam mortem tuā libera.

Per gloriosam resurrectionem tuam libera& defēde animā eius Domine.

Per admirabilem ascensionem tuam, libera

Per aduentum sancti Spiritus paracleti. libera

Per intercessionem omniū Sanctorum tuorū, libera & defende auimam eius Domine.

In die iudicii, libera & defende animam eius Domine.

Peccatores, te rogamus audi nos.

Vt animam famuli tui (vel famulæ tuæ de principibus tenebrarum, & de locis pænarum liberare digneris, Te rogamus audi nos.

Vt eam ab inferorum cruciatibus liberare digneris, Te rogamus.

Vt cuncta eius peccata obliuioni perpetuæ tradere digneris, Te rogamus.

Vt ei omnes lubricæ temeritatis offensas dimittere digneris, Te rogamus.

Vt delicta iuuentutis eius & ignorantias non reminiscaris, Te rogamus.

Vt quicquid vitiorum fallente diabolo, & propria iniquitate, atque fragilitate contraxit, clementer indulgere digneris, Te rogamus.

Vt eum in pacis ac lucis regione constituere digneris, Te rogamus.

Vt ei gaudium & exultationem in regno tuo, cum sancti

ctis & electis tuis donare digneris, Te rogamus audi.
t nos exaudire digneris, Te rogamus.
ili Dei, Te rogamus audi nos.
gnus Dei qui tolis peccata mundi, Miſerere animæ eius.
hriſte Ieſu, Miſerere animæ eius.
gnus Dei qui tollis peccata mũdi, Dona ei pacem, æter-
amque felicitatem, & gloriam ſempiternan. A men.
roficiſcere anima Chiſtiana de hoc mundo, in nomine
Dei Patris omnipotentis qui te creauit: A men. I n no-
nine Ieſu Chriſti Filij eius qui pro te paſſus eſt. A men.
n nomine Spiritus ſancti qui in te infuſus eſt. A men I n
omine A ngelorum & A rchangelorum. A men. I n no-
nine Thronorum & Dominationum. A men. I n nomi-
e Principatuũ & Poteſtatum & omnium cæleſtium vir-
utũ. A men. I n nomine Cherubin & Seraphin: A men.
n nomine patriarcharum & prophetarum A men. I n
omine A poſtolorũ & Martyrum. A men. I n nomine
piſcoporũ & Confeſſorum. A men. I n nomine Sacer-
otum & Leuitarum, & omnium Eccleſiæ graduum.
men. I n nomine Monachorum & Anachoretarum.
men. I n nomine Virginum & fidelium viduarum,
Iodie in pace locus tuus fiat, & habitatio tua in cæleſti
Iieruſalem, Amen. O remus.
Vſcipe itaque Domine ſeruum tuum in bonum &
lucidum habitaculum tuum. A men. L ibera Domine
nimam ſerui tui ex omnibus periculis infernorum & de
ocis pænarum & de omnibus doloribus tribulationum.
. A men. Libera

Libera Domine animam serui tui, sicut liberasti Enoch & Eliam de morte communi ℟. Amen.

Libera Domine animam serui tui, sicut liberasti Lot de Sodomis, & de flamina ignis. ℟. Amen.

Libera Domine animam serui tui, sicut liberasti Isaac de manu patris sui Abrahæ. ℟. Amen.

Libera Domine animam serui tui, sicut liberasti Moysen de manu Pharaonis. ℟. Amen.

Libera Domine animam serui tui, sicut liberasti Iob de passionibus suis. ℟. Amen.

Libera Domine animam serui tui, sicut liberasti Dauid de manu Goliæ, & de manu Saul regis ℟. Amen.

Libera Domine animam serui tui, sicut liberasti Daniel de lacu leonum. ℟ Amen.

Libera Domine animam serui tui, sicut liberasti tres pueros de camino ignis ardentis. ℟. Amen.

Libera Domine animam serui tui, sicut liberasti Susann de falso crimine ℟. Amen.

Libera Domine animam serui tui, sicut liberasti Petrum & Paulum de vinculis. Resp. Amen.

Sicut liberasti sanctos seruos tuos de tormẽtis, sic liberare dignaris animam serui tui de gehennæ incendijs, & ab omnibus angustijs Resp. A

Sequatur Commendatio animarum quæ habetur infra pag. 106. & dicatur in camera vel in aula siue nota iuxta corpus defuncti & omnia subsequentia similiter vsque ad processionem, ad hominem mortuum suscipiendum.

Po:

Post commendationem sequatur.

Resp. Subuenite Sancti Dei, occurrite Angeli Domini suscipientes animam eius: ✶ Offerentes eam in conspectu Altissimi. ℣. Suscipiat te Christus qui vocauit te, & in sinum Abrahæ Angeli deducant te. Offerentes.

Sequatur oratio, sine Dominus vobiscum & sine Oremus.

Tibi Domine commendamus animam famuli tui (vel famulæ tuæ) N. vt defunctus (vel defuncta) sæculo tibi viuat: & quæ per fragilitatem mundanæ conuersationis peccata admisit, tu venia misericordissimiæ pietatis absterge. Per Christum Dominum nostrum. Amen.

Oremus.

Misericordiam tuam Domine sancte, Pater omnipotens, æterne Deus, pietatis affectu rogare pro alijs cogimur, qui pro nostris supplicare peccatis nequaquam sufficimus: tamen de tua confisi gratuita pietate & inolita benignitate clementiam tuam deposcimus, vt animam famuli tui (vel famulæ tuæ) N. ad te reuertentem cum pietate suscipias. Adsit ei Angelus Testamenti tui Michael, & per manus Sanctorum Angelorum tuorum in sinu Abrahæ Patriarchæ tui, eam collocare digneris: quatenus liberata de principib⁹ tenebrarum, & de locis pænarum, nullus iam primæuæ natiuitatis, vel ignorantiæ, aut propriæ iniquitatis seu fragilitatis cõfundatur erroribus: sed potius agnoscatur a tuis, & sanctæ beatitudinis requie perfruatur, atq; cum magni iudicij dies aduenerit, inter Sanctos & electos tuos aggregata, gloria manifestæ contemplationis tu: perpetuò satietur. Per Christum Dominum nostrum Amen.

Antiph. Suscipiat te Christus qui vocauit te, & in sinum Abrahæ Angeli deducant te. Psal. 113.

IN exitu Israel de Ægipto: &c. Totus Psalmus dicitu sed sine Gloria Patri. Vt inferius in officio sepultura pag. Quo finito dicat Sacerdos.

Dominus vobiscum. ℟. Et cum spiritu tuo.

Oremus.

OMnipotens sempiterne Deus, qui humano corpo animam ad similitudinem tuam inspirare dignatu es: dum te iubente puluis in puluerem reuertitur, tu ima ginem tuam cum Sanctis & electis tuis, æternis sedibu præcipias sociari, eamque ad te reuertentem, de Ægip partibus, blandè leniterque suscipias, & Angelos tuo sanctos ei obuiam mittas, viamque illi iustitiæ demonstr & portas gloriæ illi aperi. Repelle quæsum⁹ ab eo (vel ea omnes principes tenebrarũ, & agnosce depositum fidel quod tuum est. Suscipe Domine creaturam tuam non e dijs alienis creatam, sed a te solo Deo viuo & vero: qu non est ali⁹ Deus præter te Domine, & non est secũdur opera tua. Lætifica clementissime Pater animam serui tu (vel ancillæ tuæ) N. & clarifica eam in multitudine mise ricordiæ tuæ. Ne memineris quæsumus iniquitatum eiu antiquarum, & ebriatum quas suscitauit furor mali desi derij: licet enim peccerit, tamen te non negauit, sed sign

fide

idei insignitus (vel insignita) te qui omnia & eum (vel eam) inter omnia fecisti, fideliter adorauit. Qui viuis & egnas Deus, per omnia sæcula sæculorum. Amen.

Antiph. Chorus Angelorum. Psalmus 114.

Dilexi quoniam exaudiet. pag. 96. Item Psal. 115.

Credidi propter quod. pag 96. Item Psal. 116.

Laudate Dominum omnes gentes: laudate eum omnes populi.

Quoniam confirmata est super nos misericordia eius: & veritas Domini manet in æternum. Item Psal. 117.

Confitemini Domino quoniam bonus. pag. Item Psal. 118.

eati immaculati in via pag. 79. Sine Gloria Patri.

Finitis Psalmis incipiatur Antiphona.

Chorus Angelorum te suscipiat, & in sinu Abrahæ collocet, vt cum Lazaro quondam paupere æternam habeas requiem. Qua finita dicat Sacerdos.

Oremus.

DIri vulneris nouitate percussi, & quodammodo cordibus sauciati, misericordiam tuam mundi Redẽptor, flebilibus vocibus imploramus: vt chari nostri (vel charæ nostræ) N. animam ad tuam clementiam (qui fons s pietatis, reuertentem blande leniterque suscipias: & si quas illa ex carnali commercio contraxit maculas, tu Deus olita bonitate clementer deleas, piè indulgeas, obliuioni n perpetuum tradas, atque hanc laudem tibi cum cæteris redditura m, & ad corpus proprium quandoque reuersuram,

ram, Sanctorum tuorum cætib⁹ aggregari præcipias. Qui cum Deo Patre & Spiritu sancto viuis & regnas in sæcula sæculorum. Amen.

Hic roget Sacerdos astantes orare pro eo: ita dicens.

Pro anima N. & pro animabus omnium fidelium defunctorum, Pater noster. ℣. Et ne nos inducas in tentationem. ℟. Sed libera nos a malo.

℣. Requiem æternam dona ei Domine. ℟. Et lux perpetua luceat ei. ℣. A porta inferi. ℟. Erue Domine animam eius. ℣. Non intres in iudicium cum seruo tuo (vel ancilla tua) Domine. ℟. Quia non iustificabitur in conspectu tuo omnis viuens. ℣. Dominus vobiscum. ℟. Et cum spiritu tuo.

Oremus.

Partem beatæ resurrectionis obtineat, vitamque æternam mereatur habere in cœlis. Per te saluator mundi qui cum Patre & Spiritu Sancto viuis & regnas Deus, per omnia sæcula sæculorum. Amen.

Oremus.

Deus cui soli competit medicinā præstare post mortem: tribue quæsumus, vt anima famuli tui (vel famulæ tuæ) N terrenis exuta contagijs, in tuæ redemptionis parte numeretur.

Oratio.

Absolue quæsumus animam famuli tui (vel famulæ tuæ) N & animas omnium fidelium defunctorum ab omni vinculo delictorum: vt in resurrectionis gloria inter Sanctos & electos tuos resuscitati respirēt. Per Christum Dominum nostrum. Amen.

OFFI

OFFICIVM SEPVLTVRÆ.

DEinde si corpus regis inuncti fuerit, qui migrauit ex hoc sæculo, primum a suis cubicularijs corpus eiusdem aqua calida siue tepida lauetur. Deinde balsamo cum aromatibis vngatur per totum, & postea in panno linieo cerato inuoluatur: ita tamē quod facies & barba illius tantum pateant, & circa manus & digitos ipsius, dictus pannus ceratus ita sit dispositus, vt quilibet digitus cum police vtriusque manus singulatim insuatur per se, ac si manus eius chyrothecis lineis essent coopertæ. Deindè corpus induatur tunica vsque ad talos longa, & desuper pallio regali adornetur. Barba verò ipsius decenter componatur super pectus illius: & postmodum caput cum facie ipsius sudario serico cooperiatur: ac deinde corona regia aut diadema capiti eiusdem apponatur. Posteà induantur manus eius Chyrothecis, cum aurefragijs ornatis, & in medio digito dexteræ manus supponatur anulus aureus aut deauratus, & in dextera manu sua pola rotunda deaurata, in qua virga deaurata sit fixa, a manu ipsius vsque ad pectus protensa, in cuius virgæ summitate sit signum dominicæ crucis, quæ supra pectus eiusdem principis honestè debet collocari. In sinistra vero manu sceptrum deauratū habeat vsque ad aurem sinistram decenter protensum: ac postremò tibiæ & pedes ipsius caligis sericis & sandalijs induantur. Deinde dictus princeps ita adornatus cum regni sui Pontificibus & Magnatibus, cum omni reuerentia & exequijs regalibus honestissime tradatur sepulturæ.

Si vero corpus alterius fuerit, tunc tãtum lauetur corpus aqu. tepida, vel calida, si placeat: & postea linteamine mundo honest inuoluatur, & in pheretro locetur. Clericis interim dicẽtibu Vesperas de die & de sancta Maria & postea Vigilias mortu orum.

Quibus dictis dicant sine nota Psalmos sequentes.

Psal. 5.

VErba mea auribus percipe Domine: intellige clamo rem meum.

Intende voci orationis meæ: Rex meus, & Deus meus.

Quoniam ad te orabo Domine: mane exaudies vocen meam.

Manè astabo tibi, & videbo: quoniam non Deus volen iniquitatem tu es.

Neque habitabit iuxta te malignus: neque permanebun iniusti ante oculos tuos.

Odisti omnes qui operantur iniquitatem: perdes omne qui loquuntur mendacium.

Virum sanguinum & dolosum abominabitur Dominus ego autem in multitudin misericordiæ tuæ

Itroibo in domum tuam: adorabo ad templum sanctun tuum, in timore tuo.

Domine deduc me in iustitia tua propter inimicos meos dirige in conspectu tuo viam meam.

Quoniam non est in ore eorum veritas: cor eorũ vanun est.

Sepulchrum patens est guttur eorum: linguis suis dolos agebant

agebant, iudica illos Deus.

Decidant a cogitationibꝰ ſuis, ſecundum multitudinem impietatum eorum expelle eos: quoniam irritauerunt te Domine.

Et lætentur omnes qui ſperant in te: in æternum exultabunt, & habitabis in eis.

Et gloriabuntur in te omnes qui diligunt nomen tuum: quoniam tu benedices iuſtos

Domine vt ſcuto bonæ voluntatis tuæ: coronaſti nos.

Pſal. 6.

Domine, ne in furore tuo arguas me: neque in ira tua corripias me.

Miſerere mei Domine, quoniam infirmus ſum: ſana me Domine, quoniam conturbata ſunt oſſa mea.

Et anima mea turbata eſt valdè: ſed tu Dñe vſquequò?

Conuertere Domine, & eripe animam meam: ſaluum me fac propter miſericordiam tuam.

Quoniam non eſt in morte qui memor ſit tui: in inferno autem quis confitebitur tibi?

Laboraui in gemitu meo, lauabo per ſingulas noctes lectum meum: lachrimis meis ſtratum meum rigabo.

Turbatus eſt a furore oculus meus: inueteraui inter omnes inimicos meos.

Diſcedite a me omnes qui operamini iniquitatem: quoniam exaudiuit Dominus vocem fletus mei.

Exaudiuit Dominus deprecationem meam: Dominus orationem meam ſuſcepit.

Erube-

E rubeſcant & conturbentur vehementer omnes inimic
mei: conuertantur, & erubeſcant valdè velociter.

Pſalmus. 114.

DIlexi, quoniam exaudiet Dominus: vocem oratio
nis meæ.

Quia inclinauit aurem ſuam mihi: in diebus meis inuo
cabo.

Circundederunt me dolores mortis: & pericula infern
inuenerunt me.

Tribulationem & dolorem inueni: & nomen Domin
inuocaui.

O Domine, libera animam meam, miſericors Dominu
& iuſtus: & Deus noſter miſeretur.

Cuſtodiens paruulos Dominus: humiliatus ſum, & libe
rauit me.

Conuertere anima mea in requiem tuam: quia Dominu
benefecit tibi.

Quia eripuit animam meam de morte: oculos meos
lacrymis, pedes meos à lapſu.

Placebo Domino: in regione viuorum. Pſal. 115.

CRedidi propter quod locutus ſum: ego autem humi
liatus ſum nimis.

Ego dixi in exceſſu meo: omnis homo mendax.

Quid retribuam Dño: pro omnibus quæ retribuit mih

Calicem ſalutaris accipiam: & nomen Domini inuocabo

Vota mea Domino reddam coram omni populo eius
præcioſa in conſpectu Domini, mors ſanctorum eius.

O Domin

O Domine quia ego ſeruus tuus: ego ſeruus tuus, & filius ancillæ.

Dirupiſti vincula mea, tibi ſacrificabo hoſtiam laudis: & nomen Domini inuocabo.

Vota mea Domino reddam in conſpectu omnis populi eius: in atrijs domus Domini, in medio tui Hieruſalem.

De profundis clamaui. pag. 66. Pſal. 141.

Pſal. 129.

VOce mea ad Dominum clamaui: voce mea ad Dominum deprecatus ſum.

Effundo in conſpectu eius orationem meam: & tribulationem meam antè ipſum pronuncio.

In deficiendo ex me ſpiritum meum: & tu cognouiſti ſemitas meas.

In via hac qua ambulabam: abſconderunt ſuperbi laqueam mihi.

Conſiderabam ad dexteram, & videbam: & non erat qui cognoſceret me.

Perijt fuga a me: & non eſt qui requirat animam meam.

Clamaui ad te Domine: dixi, tu es ſpes mea, portio mea in terra viuentium.

Intende ad deprecationem meam: quia humiliatus ſum nimis.

Libera me a perſequentibus me: quia confortati ſunt ſuper me.

Educ de cuſtodia animam meam, ad confitendum nomini tuo: me expectant iuſti donec retribuas mihi.

N Qui-

Quibus finitis dicatur Antiphona.

Requiem æternam dona eis Domine: & lux perpetua luceat eis. Kyrie eleiſon. Chriſte eleiſon. Kyrie eleiſon. Pater noſter. ℣. Et ne nos inducas in tentationem. ℟. Sed libera nos a malo. ℣. Requiem æternam dona eis Domine. ℟. Et lux perpetua luceat eis. ℣. A porta inferi. ℟. Erue Domine animas eorum. ℣. Non intres in iudicium cum ſeruo tuo (vel ancilla tua) Domine ℟. Quia non iuſtificabitur in conſpectu tuo omnis viuens:

℣. Dominus vobiſcum. ℟. Et cum ſpiritu tuo.

Oremus.

SVſcipe Domine animam famuli tui (vel famulæ tuæ) N. ad te reuertentem, veſte quoque cœleſti indue eam & laua eam ſancto fonte vitæ æternæ: vt inter gaudentes gaudeat, & inter ſapientes ſapiat & inter Martyres coronata incedat, & inter Patriarchas & Prophetas proficiat, & inter Apoſtolos Chriſtum ſequi ſtudeat, & inter Angelos & Archangelos claritatem Dei videat, & inter paradiſi rutilos lapides gaudium Dei poſſideat, notitiamque myſteriorum Dei agnoſcat, & inter Cherubin & Seraphin claritatem Dei videat, & inter viginti quatuor ſeniores cãtica canticorum audiat, & inter lauãtes ſtolas ſuas in fonte luminis veſtem lauet, & inter pulſantes, portas cœleſtis Hieruſalem apertas reperiat, & inter vidẽtes Deum faciẽ ad faciẽ videat, & inter cantãtes canticum nouum cantet & inter audiẽtes, cœleſtem ſonum audiat. Per Dominum noſtrum Ieſum Chriſtum. &c. Amen.

Ali

Alia Oratio.

SVſcipe Dñe animam famuli tui (vel famulæ tuæ) N. quam de ergaſtulo huius ſæculi vocare dignatus es , & ibera eam de principibus tenebrarũ, & de locis pœnarum t abſoluta omni vinculo peccatorum , quietis ac lucis ternæ beatitudine perfruatur , & inter ſanctos & electos uos in reſurrectionis gloria reſuſcitari mereatur. Qui cum Deo Patre & Spiritu Sancto viuis & regnas Deus per omia ſæcula ſæculorum. A men.

nima eius & animæ omnium fidelium defunctorum er miſericordiam Dei requieſcant in pace. A men.

Deinde deportetur corpus ad Eccleſiam, ibidem vel in cœmiterio humandum. Quando vero deportari debet corpus defuncti ad Eccleſiam, inprimis ſumat Sacerdos ſpiculam & aſpergat aquam benedictam ſuper corpus examine, interim dicendo pſalmum ſequentem.

Pſal. 129.

DE profundis clamaui ad te Domine : Domine exaudi vocem meam.

iant aures tuæ intendẽtes : in vocem deprecationis meæ.

i iniquitates obſeruaueris Domine : Dñe quis ſuſtinebit?

Quia apud te propitiatio eſt: & propter legem tuam ſuſtinui te Domine.

uſtinuit anima mea in verbo eius: ſperauit anima mea in Domino.

cuſtodia matutina vſque ad noctem : ſperet Iſrael in Domino.

Quia apud Dominum misericordia. & copiosa apud eum redemptio.

Et ipse redimet Israel: ex omnibus iniquitatibus eius.

Requiem æternam dona eis Domine. & lux perpetua luceat eis. Quo dicto sequatur.

Kyrie eleison. Christe eleison. Kyrie eleison. Pater noster. ℣. Et ne nos inducas in tentationem. ℟. Sed libera nos a malo. ℣. Requiem æternā dona eis Domine. ℟. Et lux perpetua luceat eis. ℣. A porta inferi. ℟. Erue Domine animas eorum. ℣. Credo videre bona Domini Resp. In terra viuentium. ℣. Dominus vobiscum. ℟. Et cum spiritu tuo. Oremus.

INclina Domine aurem tuam ad preces nostras, quibus misericordiam tuam supplices deprecemur ut animam famuli tui (vel famulæ tuæ) N. quam de hoc sæculo migrare iussisti, in pacis ac lucis regione constituas, & sanctorum tuorum iubeas esse consortem.

Fidelium Deus omnium conditor & redemptor, animabus omnium fidelium defunctorum: remissionem cunctorum tribue peccatorum: vt indulgentiam quam semper optauerunt pijs supplicationibus consequantur. Qui cum Deo Patre & Spiritu Sancto viuis & regnas in sæcula sæculorum. Amen. Requiescant in pace. Amen.

Si vero fuerit corpus mortuum cum processione sepeliendum, tunc eodem modo ordinetur processio sicut in simplicibus Dominicis, præterquam quod in hac processione Sacerdos & Ministri eius in albis, cum

amicti

amictibus induti incedant, chorus autem in cappis nigris quotidie. Et cum ad locum destinatum peruenerit processio cadauer ipsum Sacerdos aqua benedicta aspergat, & postea thurificet interim dicendo psalmum De profundis vt supra dictum est.

Deinde in redeundo dum deportatur corpus ad Ecclesiam, cantetur sequens Antiphona cantore incipiente.

Antiphona.

Subuenite sancti Dei, occurrite Angeli Domini, suscipientes animam eius, offerentes eam in conspectu altissimi. ℣. Suscipiat te Christus qui vocauit te, & in sinum Abrahæ Angeli deducant te.

Repetitur antiphona. Subuenite.

Deinde dicatur Psalmus De profundis vt supra pag. 99. Et post vnumquemq; versum repetatur Antip. & postea si necesse fuerit dicatur eodem ordine psalmus In exitu Israel. Require post in officio sepulture pag. Deindé in introitu cæmiterij vel citius inchoetur Respon. sequens.

Libera me Domine de morte æterna in die illa tremenda: Quando cæli mouendi sunt & terra, dum veneris iudicare sæculum per ignem.

℣. Dies illa dies iræ calammitatis & miseriæ, dies magna & amara valde. Quando cæli.

Nunquam autem portetur corpus alicuius defuncti circa cæmiteriũ, sed directè in Ecclesiam: & si corpus Canonici vel alteri⁹ magnatis fuerit, in chorum deferatur, sin autem alterius, extra chorũ in Eeclesia post orationẽ relinquatur.

 In in-

In introitu Ecclesiæ dicitur hæc antiphona cantore incipiente. Antiphona.

In Paradisum deducãt te Angeli in suum cõuentum, suscipiant te Martires & perducãt te in ciuitatem sanctam Hierusalem. vers. Requiem æternam dona eis Domine, & lux perpetua luceat eis. Repetatur antiph. In paradisum. Qua finita sequatur: Kyrie eleison. Christe eleison. Kyrie eleison.

Deinde aspergat Sacerdos aqua benedicta corpus defuncti, & thurificet, rogans astantes orare pro anima defuncti, ita dicens.

Pro anima N & pro animabus omnium fidelium defunctorum. Pater noster. ℣. Et ne nos inducas in tentationem. ℟. Sed libera nos a malo. ℣. A porta inferi. ℟. Erue Domine animas eorum. ℣. Non intres in iudicium cum seruo tuo Domine. ℟. Quia non iustificabitur in cõspectu tuo omnis viuens.

vers. Dominus vobiscum. Res. Et cum spiritu tuo.

Oremus.

SVscipe Domine seruum tuum (vel ancillam tuam) in bonum habitaculum, & da ei requiem in regno cœlestis Hierusalem: vt in sinu Abrahæ Patriarchæ tui collocatus (vel collocata) resurrectionis diem præstoletur, & inter resurgentes ad gloriam resurgat, & cum benedictis ad dexteram Dei venientibus veniat, & cum possidentibus vitam æternã possideat. Per Christum Dominum nostrum. Amen.

Anim

nima eius & animæ omnium fidelium defunctorum er Dei misericordiam in pace requiescant. Amen.

Deindè dicantur solemniter vigiliæ mortuorum & posteà completorium de die more solito.

Vbi vero in die sepulturæ deportatur corpus ad Ecclesiam, tunc immediatè post prædictam orationem Suscipe Domine, dicatur Commendatio Animarum solenniter vt infra & finito psalmo, **Domine probasti me,** statim incipiatur Missa pro defūctis. Deinde exeat Sacerdos cum stola & aqua benedicta ad locum vbi sepeliendus est mortuus, & signo crucis signet locum, & postea aspergat aqua benedicta. Deinde accipiat Sacerdos fossorium vel aliud instrumētum & aperiat terram in modum crucis ad longitudinem & latitudinem corporis defuncti dicens.

perite mihi portas iustitiæ, & ingressus in eas confiteor Domino: hæc porta Domini iusti intrabunt in eam.

Notandum est vero quod quandocunque per totum annum Missa pro corpore præsenti, anniuersario, vel trigintali cuiuscūue in choro vel in capitulo fuerit celebranda, vbi Missa ibi iam commendatio animarum statim post primam ante missam pitularem pro defunctis a toto choro cum nota dicatur, incipite antiphonam aliquo de superiori gradu. Ita tamen quod si in e sepulturæ deportetur corpus ad Ecclesiā, tunc finita oratione; ulcipe Domine animam serui tui. *statim sequitur commentio animarum eodem modo & ordine, sicut post deportationem rporis ad Ecclesiam, supra dictum est. Præterea omni die per totam*

totam quadrageſſimam quando de feria agitur, ſtatim poſt pr mam antè Miſſam capitularem dicatur in choro commendat animarum, viſi in craſtino feſtorum duplicium, & hoc ſinè no quando Dirige *ſiuè nota præceſſerit. Et ſciendum eſt quod quar docunqne dicatur Commendatio animarum, ſemper dicatur ſ dendo vſque ad antiphonam poſt Laudes dicendam.*

Commendatio animarum.

Antiph. Requiem æternam. Pſal. 118.

BEati immaculati in via: qui ambulant in lege Do mini.

Beati qui ſcrutantur teſtimonia eius: in toto corde exqu runt eum.

Non enim qui operantur iniquitatem: in vijs eius amb lauerunt.

Tu mandaſti mandata tua: cuſtodiri nimis.

Vtinam dirigantur viæ meæ: ad cuſtodiendas iuſtific tiones tuas.

Tunc non confundar: cum perſpexero in omnibus ma datis tuis.

Confitebor tibi in directione cordis: in eo quod did iudicia iuſtitiæ tuæ.

Iuſtificationes tuas cuſtodiã: non me derelinquas vſqu quaque.

In quo corrigit adoleſcentior viam ſuam? in cuſtodie do ſermones tuos.

In to

In toto corde meo exquiſiui te: ne repellas me a mandatis tuis.

In corde meo abſcondi eloquia tua: vt non peccem tibi.

Benedictus es Domine: doce me iuſtificationes tuas

In labijs meis pronunciaui: omnia iudicia oris tui.

In via teſtimoniorum tuorum delectatus ſum: ſicut in omnibus diuitijs.

In mandatis tuis exercebcr: & conſiderabo vias tuas.

In iuſtificationibus tuis meditabor: non obliuiſcar ſermones tuos.

Retribue ſeruo tuo, viuifica me: & cuſtodiam ſermones tuos.

Reuela oculos meos: & conſiderabo mirabilia de lege tua.

Incola ego ſum in terra: non abſcõdas a me mandata tua.

Concupiuit anima mea deſiderare iuſtificationes tuas: in omni tempore.

Increpaſti ſuperbos: maledicti qui declinant a mandatis tuis.

Aufer a me opprobrium & contemptum: quia teſtimonia tua exquiſiui.

Etenim ſederunt principes, & aduerſum me loquebantur: ſeruus autem tuus exercebatur in iuſtificationibus tuis.

Nam & teſtimonia tua meditatio mea eſt: conſilium meum iuſtificationes tuæ.

Adhæſit pauimento anima mea: viuifica me ſecundum verbum tuum.

Vias meas enunciaui, & exaudiſti me: doce me iuſtificationes tuas.

Viam iuſtificationum tuarum inſtrue me : & exerceb
in mirabilibus tuis.

Dormitauit anima mea præ tædio : confirma me in ver
bis tuis.

Viam iniquitatis amoue a me, & de lege tua miſerer
mei.

Viam veritatis elegi: iudicia tua non ſum oblitus.

Adhæſi teſtimonijs tuis Domine: noli me confundere.

Viam mandatorum tuorum cucurri : cum dilataſti co
meum.

LEgem pone mihi Domine viam iuſtificationum tua
rum, & exquiram eam ſemper.

Da mihi intellectum, & ſcrutabor legem tuam : & cu
ſtodiam illam in toto corde meo.

Deduc me in ſemita mandatorum tuorum : quia ipſan
volui.

Inclina cor meum in teſtimonia tua : & non in auari
tiam.

Auerte oculos meos ne videant vanitatem: in via tua vi
uifica me.

Salue ſeruo tuo eloquium tuum: in timore tuo.

Amputa opprobrium meum quod ſuſpicatus ſum ; qui
iudicia tua iucunda.

Ecce concupiui mandata tua : in æquitate tua viui
fica me.

Et veniat ſuper me miſericordia tua Domine : ſalutar
tuum ſecundum eloquium tuum.

Et reſ

Et respondebo exprobantibus mihi verbum: quia speraui in sermonibus tuis.

Et ne auferas de ore meo verbum veritatis vsquequaque: quia in iudicijs tuis supersperaui.

Et custodiam legem tuam semper: in sæculum, & in sæculum sæculi.

Et ambulabam in latitudine: quia mãdata tua exquisiui.

Et loquebar de testimonijs tuis in conspectu regum: & non confundebor.

Et meditabor in mandatis tuis: quæ dilexi.

Et leuaui manus meas ad mandata tua quæ dilexi: & exercebor in iustificationibus tuis.

MEmor esto verbi tui seruo tuo: in quo mihi spem dedisti.

Hæc me consolata est in humlitate mea: quia eloquium tuum viuificauit me.

Superbi iniquè agebant vsquequaque: a lege autem tua non declinaui.

Memor fui iudiciorum tuorum a sæculo Domine: & consolatus sum.

Defectio tenuit me pro peccatoribus derelinquentibus legem tuam.

Cantabiles erant iustificationes tuæ: in loco peregrationis meæ.

Memor fui nocte nominis tui Domine: & custodiui legem tuam.

Hæc facta est mihi: quia iustificationes tuas exquisiui.

P ortio mea Domine: dixi custodire legem tuam.

D eprecatus sum faciem tuam in toto corde meo: miserere mei secundum eloquium tuum.

C ogitaui vias meas: & cõuerti pedes meos in testimonia tua.

P aratus sum, & non sum turbatus: vt custodiam mandata tua.

F unes peccatorum circumplexi sunt me: & legem tuam non sum oblitus.

M edia nocte surgebam ad confitendum tibi: super iudicia iustificationis tuæ.

P articeps ego sum omnium timentium te: & custodientium mandata tua.

M isericordia tua Domine plena est terra: iustificationes tuas doce me.

B Onitatem fecisti cum seruo tuo Domine, secundum verbum tuum.

B onitatem, & disciplinam, & scientiam doce me; quia mandatis tuis credidi,

P riusquam humiliarer ego deliqui: propterea eloquium tuum custodiui.

B on⁹ es tu: & in bonitate tua doce me iustificationes tuas

M ultiplicata est super me iniquitas superborum: ego autem in toto corde meo scrutabor mandata tua.

C oagulatum est sicut lac cor eorum: ego vero legem tuam meditatus sum.

B onum mihi quia humiliasti me: vt discam iustificationes tuas.

B onum

Bonum mihi lex oris tui: ſuper millia auri & argenti.

Manus tuæ fecerunt me, & plaſmauerunt me: da mihi intellectum vt diſcam mandata tua.

Qui timent te videbunt me, & lætabuntur: quia in verba tua ſuperſperaui.

Cognoui Domine quia æquitas iudicia tua: & in veritate tua humiliaſti me.

Fiat miſericordia tua vt conſoletur me: ſecundum eloquium tuum ſeruo tuo.

Veniant mihi miſerationes tuæ, & viuam: quia lex tua meditatio mea eſt.

Confundantur ſuperbi, quia iniuſtè iniquitatem fecerunt in me: ego autem exercebor in mandatis tuis.

Conuertantur mihi timentes te: & qui nouerunt teſtimonia tua.

Fiat cor meum immaculatum in iuſtificationibus tuis: vt non confundar.

DEfecit in ſalutare tuum anima mea: & in verbum tuum ſuperſperaui.

Defecerunt oculi mei in eloquium tuum: dicentes quando consolaberis me.

Quia factus ſum ſicut vter in pruina: iuſtificationes tuas non ſum oblitus.

Quot ſunt dies ſerui tui? quando facies de peſequentibus me iudicium?

Narrauerunt mihi iniqui fabulationes: ſed non vt lex tua.

Omnia mādata tua veritas: iniqui perſequuti ſunt me, adiuua me.

Paulominus consummauerunt me in terra: ego autem non dereliqui mandata tua.

Secundum misericordiam tuam viuifica me: & custodiam testimonia oris tui.

In æternum Domine: verbum tuum permanet in cælo.

In generatione, & generationem veritas tua: fundasti terram & permanet.

Ordinatione tua perseuerat dies: quoniam omnia seruiunt tibi.

Nisi quod lex tua meditatio mea est: tunc fortè perijssem in humiltate mea.

In æternum non obliuscar iustificationes tuas: quia in ipsis viuificasti me.

Tuus sum ego, saluum me fac: quoniam iustificationes tuas equisiui.

Me expectauerunt peccatores vt perderent me: testimonia tua intellexi.

Omnis consummationis vidi finem: latum mandatum tuum nimis.

QVomodo dilexi legem tuam Domine: tota die meditatio mea est.

Super inimicos meos prudentem me fecisti mandato tuo quia in æternum mihi est.

Super omnes docentes me intellexi: quia testimonia tua meditatio mea est.

Super senes intellexi: quia mandata tua quæsiui.

Ab omni via mala prohibui pedes meos: vt custodiam verba tua.

A iu

A iudicijs tuis non declinaui: quia tu legem posuisti mihi.

Quam dulcia faucibus meis eloquia tua: super mel ori meo.

A mandatis tuis intellexi: propterea odiui omnem viam iniquitatis.

Lucerna pedibus meis verbum tuum: & lumen semitis meis

Iuraui & statui: custodire iudicia iustitiæ tuæ.

Humiliatus sum vsquequaque: Domine viuifica me secundum verbum tuum.

Voluntaria oris mei beneplacita fac Domine: & iudicia tua doce me.

Anima mea in manibus meis semper: & legem tuam non sum oblitus.

Posuerunt peccatores laqueum mihi: & de mandatis tuis non erraui.

Hæreditate acquisiui testimomonia tua in æternum: quia exultatio cordis mei sunt.

Inclinaui cor meum ad faciendas iustificationes tuas in æternum propter retributionem.

INiquos odio habui: & legem tuam dilexi.

Adiutor & susceptor meus es tu; & in verbum tuum supersperaui.

Declinate a me maligni: & scrutabor mandata Dei mei.

Suscipe me secundum eloquium tuum, & viuam, & non confundas me ab expectatione mea.

Adiuua

Adiuua me, & saluus ero : & meditabor in iustificationibus tuis semper.

Spreuisti omnes discedentes a iudicijs tuis : quia iniusta cogitatio eorum.

Præuaricantes reputaui omnes peccatores terræ : ideò dilexi testimonia tua.

Confige timore tuo carnes meas: iudicijs enim tuis timui

Feci iudicium & iustitiam : non tradas me calumniantibus me.

Suscipe seruum tuum in bonum : non calumnientur me susperbi.

Oculi mei defecerunt in salutare tuum : & in eloquium iustitiæ tuæ.

Fac cum seruo tuo secundum misericordiam tuam : & iustificationes tuas doce me.

Seruus tuus sum ego, da mihi intellectum : vt sciam testimonia tua.

Tempus faciendi Domine : dissipauerunt legem tuam.

Ideo dilexi mandata tua : super aurum & topazion.

Propterea ad omnia mandata tua dirigebar: omnem viam iniquam odio habui.

Mirabilia testimonia tua Domine : ideo scrutata est ea anima mea.

Declaratio seruorum tuorum illuminat : & intellectum dat paruulis

Os meum aperui, & attraxi spiritum quia mandata tua desiderabam.

Aspic

ſpice in me, & miſerere mei: ſecundum iudicium diligentium nomen tuum.

reſſus meos dirige ſecundum eloquium tuum: & non dominetur mei omnis iniuſtitia.

edime me a calumnijs hominum: vt cuſtodiam mandata tua.

aciem tuam illumina ſuper ſeruum tuum: & doce me iuſtificationes tuas.

xitus aquarum deduxerunt oculi mei: quoniam non cuſtodierunt legem tuam.

uſtus es Domine: & rectum iudicium tuum.

andaſti iuſtitiam teſtimonia tua: & veritatem tuam nimis.

abeſcere me fecit zelus meus: quia obliti ſunt verba tua inimici mei.

gnitum eloquium tuum vehementer: & ſeruus tuus dilexit illud.

doleſcentulus ſum ego, & contemptus: iuſtificationes tuas non ſum oblitus.

uſtitia tua iuſtitia in æternum: & lux tua veritas.

ribulatio & anguſtia iuuenerunt me: mandata tua meditatio mea eſt.

quitas teſtimonia tua in æternum: intellectum da mihi & viuam.

Lamaui in toto corde meo, exaudi me domine: iuſtificationes tuas requiram.

lamaui ad te, ſaluum me fac: vt cuſtodiam mandata tua.

Præueni in maturitate, & clamaui: quia in verba tua su perſperaui.

Præuenerunt oculi mei ad te diluculò: vt meditarer elo quia tua.

Vocem meam audi, ſecundum miſericordiam tuam Do mine &: ſecundum iudicium tuum viuifica me.

Appropinquauerunt perſequentes me iniquitati: a leg autem tua longè facti ſunt.

Propé es tu Domine: & omnes viæ tuæ veritas.

Initio cognoui de teſtimonijs tuis: quia in æternum fun daſti ea.

Vide humilitatem meam, & eripe me: quia legem tuam non ſum oblitus.

Iudica iudicium meum, & redime me: propter eloquium tuum viuifica me.

Longé a peccatoribus ſalus: quia iuſtificationes tuas no exquiſierunt

Miſericordiæ tuæ multæ Domine: ſecundum iudicium tuum viuifica me.

Multi qui perſequuntur me, & tribulant me: a teſtimonij tuis non declinaui.

Vidi præuaricantes, & tabeſcebam: quia eloquia tua no cuſtodierunt.

Vide quoniam mandata tua dilexi Domine: in miſericor dia tua viuifica me.

Principium verborum tuorum veritas: in æternum om nia iudicia iuſtitiæ tuæ.

Princi

PRincipes perſequuti ſunt me gratis: & a verbis tuis formidauit cor meum.

ætabor ego ſuper eloquia tua: ſicut qui inuenit ſpolia multa.

niquitatem odio habuiret, abominatus ſum: legem autem tuam dilexi.

epties in die laudem dixi ſuper iudicia iuſtitiæ tuæ.

ax multa diligentibus legem tuam: & non eſt illis ſcandalum.

xpectabam ſalutare tuum Domine: & mandata tua dilexi.

uſtodiuit anima mea teſtimonia tua: & dilexit ea vehementer.

eruaui mandata tua, & teſtimonia tua: quia omnes viæ meæ in conſpectu tuo.

ppropinquet deprecatio mea in conſpectu tuo Domine: iuxta eloquium tuum da mihi intellectum.

ntret poſtulatio mea in conſpectu tuo: ſecundum eloquium tuum eripe me.

ructabunt labia mea hymnum: cum doceris me iuſtifitiones tuas.

ronunciabit lingua mea eloquium tuum: quia omnia mandata tua æquitas.

iat manus tua vt ſaluet me: quoniam mandata tua elegi.

oncupiui ſalutare tuum Domine: & lex tua meditatio mea eſt.

iuet anima mea; & laudabit te: iudicia tua adiuuabũt me.

Erraui sicut ouis quæ perijt, quære seruum tuum: qui mandata tua non sum oblitus.

Finitis Psalmis repetatur antiphona.

Requiem æternam dona eis Domine: & lux perpetua luceat eis. Kyrie eleison. Christe eleison. Kyrie eleisor

Deinde dicatur. **Pater noster.** Et sinè pronunciation (**Et ne nos inducas**) sequatur sinè nota iste psalmus. 13

Domine probasti me &c. habetur infra **pag.**

Deinde sine interuallo incipiatur Missa pro defunctis, Sacerdote interim exeunte ad locum sepulchri signandum (si corp⁹ præsens affuerit) vt supra dictum es. Tamen quandocunque sigillatim extra conuentum dicitur commendatio animarum, tunc immediate po psalmum **Domine probasti,** sequatur.

℣. Requiem æternam dona eis Domine. ℟. Et lux perpetua luceat eis. ℣. A porta inferi. ℟. Erue Domine animas eorum. ℣. Credo videre bona Domini. ℟. In terr viuentium. ℣. Dominus vobiscum. ℟. Et cum spiritu tuo.

Oremus.

Tibi Domine commendamus animas famulorum, famularumque tuarum: vt defuncti sæculo tibi viuan & quæ per fragilitatem mundanæ conuersationis pecca admiserunt, tu venia misericordissimæ pietatis absterg Per Christum Dominum nostrum. Amen.

Nunquam dicatur alia commendatio in Ecclesia Sar sburiensi siue corpus præsens fuerit, siue non.

Rit

Ritus sepeliendi Mortuos.

POst Missam accedat Sacerdos ad caput defuncti alba indutus absque cappa serica, & duo clerici de secunda orma, ad caput defuncti stantes incipiat tribus vicibus ntiphonam sequentem quam chorus singulis vicibus otam prosequatur vsque in finem.

Antiph. **Circundederunt me gemitus mortis, dolores inerni circundederunt me.**

Deinde post tertiam repetitionem sequatur.

Kyrie eleison. Christe eleison. Kyrie eleison.

Non dicatur pater noster nec Dominus vobiscum, neque Oremus sed tantum oratio, sacerdote dicente modesta voce, videlicet sine nota.

Non intres in iudicium cum seruo tuo (vel seruula tua) Domine, quoniã nullus apud te iustificabitur homo, nisi er te omnium peccatorum tribuatur remissio: non ergo um (vel eã) tua quæsumus iudicialis sententia premat, quẽ vel quam) tibi vera supplicatio fidei Christianæ commenlat: sed gratia tua illi succurrente mereatur euadere iudiium vltionis qui (vel quæ) dum viueret insignitus (vel nsignita) est signaculo sanctæ Trinitatis. In qua viuis & egnas Deus per omnia sæcula sæculorum Amen.

Eodem modo dicuntur orationes sequentes. Deinde incipiat cantor.

℞. Qui Lazarum resuscitasti a monumento fœtidum: Tu eis Domine dona requiem & locum indulgentiæ.

 ℣. Qui

℣. Qui venturus es iudicare viuos & mortuos, & sæculum per ignem. Tu eis.

Et percantetur a choro cum suo versu, & interim Sacerdos cum Thuribulo circumeundo corpus illud incenset. Smiliter fiat in Respōlorijs sequentibus. Deinde dicitur. Kyrie eleison. Christi eleison. Kyrieeleison. Siné pater noster, & siné Dominus vobiscum sed tantum cum Oremus

DEus cui omnia viuunt, cui non pereunt moriēdo corpora nostra, sed mutantur in melius te supplices deprecamur, vt quicquid famulus tuus (vel famula tua) vitiorum tuæ voluntati contrarium, fallente diabolo, & propria iniquitate atque fragilitate contraxit, tu pius & misericors abluas indulgendo, eiusque animam suscipi iubeas, per manus sanctorum Angelorum tuorum deducēdam in sinum Patriarcharum tuorum, Abrahæ scilicet amici tui, & Isaac electi tui, atque Iacob dilecti tui quo aufugit dolor & tristitia, atque suspirium fidelium quoque animæ fælici iucūditate lætantur; & in nouissimo magni iudicij die inter Sanctos & electos tuos eam facias perpetuæ gloriæ tuæ percipere portionem, quam oculus non vidit, nec aures audiuit, & in cor hominis non ascendit, quam præparasti diligentibus te. Per Christum Dominum nostrum. Amen.

℟. Heu mihi Dn̄e quia peccaui nimis in vita mea; quid faciam miser? vbi fugiam, nisi ad te Deus meus? miserere mei, * Dum veneris in nouissimo die. ℣. Anima mea tu-

bat

ata est valdé, sed tu Domine succure ei. Dum veneris.

Et percantetur a choro cum suo versu, & interim incensetur corpus vt supra. Deinde sequatur. Kyrie eleison. Christe eleison. Kyrie eleison.

Sine Pater noster, & sine Dominus vobiscum, sed tantum cum. Oremus.

Ac quæsumus Domine hanc cum seruulo tuo defuncto (vel seruula tua defuncta) misericordiam: vt ctorum suorum in pœnis non recipiat vicem: qui (vel uæ) tuā in votis tenuit voluntatem :& quia hic illum (vel lam) vera fides iunxit fidelium turmis, illic eum (vel am) tua miseratio societ angelicis choris. Per christum ominum nostrum. Amen.

Deinde incipiat cantor Responsorium.

ibera me Domine de morte æterna in illa tremenda uando cæli mouendi sunt & terra * Dum veneris iudiare sæculum per ignem. ℣. Dies illa, dies iræ calamitis & miseriæ, dies magna & amara valdé. Dum veneris iudicare.

Et percantetur a choro cum vno versu tantum, scilicet Dies illa vt supra, & interim incensetur corpus a Sacerdote semel circumeundo, & postea aspergatur aqua benedicta: deinde sequatur.

Kyrie eleison. Christe eleison. Kyrie eleison.

Deinde roget Sacerdos circumstantes orare pro anima defuncti dicens

ro anima N. & pro animabus omnium fidelium defunctorum.

ctorum. Pater noster ℣. Et ne nos inducas in tentationem. ℟. Sed libera nos a malo.
℣. Non intres in iudicium cum seruo tuo (vel seruu.
tua) Domine. ℟. Quia non iustificabitur in conspect
tuo omnis viuens.
℣. A porta inferi ℟. Erue Domine animas eorum.
V. Credo videre bona Domini. ℟. In terra viuentium.
V. Domine exaudi orationem meam. Resp. Et clamo
meus ad te veniat.
V. Dominus vobiscum. Resp. Et cum spiritu tuo.

Oremus

INclina Domine aurem tuam ad preces nostras quibu
misericordiam tuam supplices deprecamur: vt animam
famuli tui (vel famulæ tuæ) quam de hoc sæculo migra
iussisti, in pacis ac lucis regione constituas, & Sanctorum
tuorum iubeas esse consortem. Per christum Dominum
nostrum. Amen.

Hic deportetur corpus ad sepulchrum cantore incipient
Antiph. In paradisum. Psal. 123.

IN exitu Israel de Ægipto: domus Iacob de populo bar-
baro.
Facta est Iudæa sanctificatio eius: Israel potestas eius.
Mare vidit, & fugit: Iordanus conuersus est retrorsum.
Montes exultauerunt vt arietes: & colles sicut ag-
ouium.

Qu

Quid eſt tibi mare quod fugiſti? & tu Iordanis quia conuerſus es retrorſum.

Montes exultaſtis ſicut arietes: & colles ſicut agni ouium.

A facie Domini mota eſt terra: a facie Dei Iacob.

Qui conuertit petram in ſtagna aquarum: & rupes in fontes aquarum.

Non nobis Domine, non nobis: ſed nomini tuo da gloriam.

Super miſericordia tua, & veritate tua: nequando dicant gentes vbi eſt Deus eorum?

Deus autem noſter in cœlo: omnia quæcunque voluit fecit.

Simulachra gẽtium argentum, & aurum: opera manuum hominum.

Os habent, & non loquentur: oculos habent & non videbunt.

Aures habent & non audient: nares habent & non odorabunt.

Manus habent, & non palpabunt, pedes habent, & non ambulabunt: non clamabunt in gutture ſuo.

Similles illis fiant qui faciunt ea: & omnes qui confidunt in eis.

Domus Iſrael ſperauit in Domino: adiutor eorum & protector eorum eſt.

Domus Aaron ſperauit in Domino: adiutor eorum & protector eorum eſt.

Q ui timent Dominum ſperauerunt in Domino : adiutc eorum & protector eorum eſt.

D ominus memor fuit noſtri : & benedixit nobis.

B enedixit domui Iſrael : benedixit domui Aaron.

B enedixit omnibus qui timent Dominum : puſillis cu maioribus.

A dijciat Dominus ſuper vos : ſuper vos, & ſuper filic veſtros.

B enedicti vos a Domino : qui fecit cælum & terram,

C ælum cæli Dño : terram autem dedit filijs hominun

N on mortui laudabunt te Domine : neque omnes qı deſcendunt in infernum.

S ed nos qui viuimus, benedicimus Domino : ex ho nunc & vſque in ſæculum.

Alius pſalmus ſi tantum reſtat iter, ſcilicet pſal. 24.

A d te Domine leuaui animam meam. Habetur in Bre uiario feria tertia ad primam.

Finito pſalmo vel pſalmis dicatur iſte verſus.

R equiem æternam dona eis Domine : & lux perpetua lu ceat eis.

Deinde repetatur Antiphona.

I n paradiſum deducant te Angeli, in ſuum conuentu ſuſcipiat te Martires, & perducant te in ciuitatem ſanctar Hieruſalem.

Quibus dictis dicat Sacerdos ſine Dominus vobiſcur ſed tantum cum. Oremus. Humili voce.

Pi.

PIæ recordationis affectu (fratres charissimi) commemorationem faciamus chari nostri quem (vel charæ nostræ quam) Dominus noster de tentationibus huius sæculi assumpsit. Obsecremus misericordiam Dei nostri, vt ipse ei tribuere dignetur placitam & quietam mansionem, & remittat ei omnes libricæ temeritatis offensas: vt concessa sibi venia plenæ indulgentiæ quicquid in hoc sæculo proprio vel alieno reatu deliquit, totam ineffabili pietate & benignitate sua deleat, & abstergat. Per Christum Dominum nostrum. Amen.

Alia oratio cum. Oremus.

TE Domine sancte, Pater omnipotens, æterne Deus, suppliciter deprecamur pro spiritu fratris nostri, quem (vel sororis nostræ quam) a voraginibus huius sæculi accersiri iussisti: vt digneris Domine dare ei lucidum locum refrigerij & quietis: Liceat ei transire portas inferorum & pænas tenebrarum, maneatque in mansionibus sanctorum, & in luce sancta quam olim Abrahæ promisisti & semini eius. Nullam læsionem sentiat spiritus eius; sed cum magnus ille dies resurrectionis aduenerit, resuscitare eum (vel eam) digneris vna cum sanctis & electis tuis, deleasque eius omnia delicta atque peccata vsque ad nouissimum quadrantem, tecumque immortalitatis tuæ vitam & regnum consequatur æternum. Per Christum Dominum nostrum. Amen.

Finitis orationibus aperiatur sepulchrum, cantore incipiente. Antiph. Aperite. psal. 117.

Confitemini Domino quoniam bonus: quoniam in sæculum misericordia eius.

Dicat nunc Israel quoniam bonus: quoniam in sæculum miserecordia eius.

Dicat nunc domus Aaron: quoniam in sæculum misericordia eius.

Dicant nunc qui timent Dominum: quoniam in sæculum misericordia eius.

De tribulatione inuocaui Dominum: & exaudiuit me in latitudine Dominus.

Dominus mihi adiutor: non timebo quid faciat mihi homo.

Dominus mihi adiutor: & ego despiciam inimicos meos.

Bonum est confidere in Domino: quam confidere in homine

Bonum est sperare in Domino: quam sperare in principibus.

Omnes gentes circuierunt me: & in nomine Domini quia vltus sum in eos.

Circundantes circundederunt me: & in nomine Domini quia vltus sum in eos.

Circundederunt me sicut apes, & exarserunt sicut ignis inspinis: & in nomine Domini, quia vltus sum in eos.

Impulsus, euersus sum vt caderem: & Dñus suscepit me.

Fortitudo mea, & laus mea Dominus: & factus est mihi in salutem.

Vox exultationis, & salutis: in tabernaculis iustorum.

Dexter

Dextera Domini fecit virtutem, dextera Domini exaltauit me: dextera Domini fecit virtutem.

Non moriar, ſed viuam: & narrabo opera Domini.

Caſtigans caſtigauit me Dominus: & morti non tradidit me.

Aperite mihi portas iuſtitiæ, ingreſſus in eas, confitebor Domino: hæc porta Domini, iuſti intrabunt in eam.

Confitebor tibi, quoniam exaudiſti me: & factus es mihi in ſalutem.

Lapidem quẽm reprobauerunt ædificantes: hic factus eſt in caput Anguli.

A Domino factum eſt iſtud: & eſt mirabile in oculis noſtris.

Hæc dies quam fecit Dñus: exultemus & lætemur in ea.

O Domine ſaluum me fac, o Domine benè proſperare, benedictus qui venit in nomine Domini.

Benediximus vobis de domo Domini: Deus Dominus, & illuxit nobis.

Conſtitui te diem ſolennem in cõdenſis: vſque ad cornu Altaris.

Deus meus es tu, & confitebor tibi: Deus meus es tu, & exaltabo te.

Confitebor tibi, quoniam exaudiſti me: & factus es mihi in ſalutem.

Confitemini Domino quoniam bon⁹: quoniam in ſæculum miſericordia eius.

Finito pſalmo dicatur Antiphona.

A perite mihi portas iustitiæ, & ingressus in eas confitebor Domino: hæc porta Domini iusti intrabunt in eam

Qua dicta dicat Sacerdos. Oremus.

OBsecramus misericordiam tuam omnipotens æterne Deus qui hominem ad imaginē tuam creare dignatus es: vt animā famuli tui (vel famulæ tuæ) N. quam hodierna die rebus humanis eximi, & ad te accersiri iussisti blandè & misericorditer suscipias. Non ei dominentur vmbræ mortis, nec tegat eam chaos & caligo tenebrarum sed exuta omnium criminum labe, in sinu Abrahæ collocata, locum refrigerij se adeptam esse gaudeat: vt cum dies iudicij aduenerit, cum sanctis & electis tuis, eam resuscitari iubeas. Per Christum. Dominū nostrum Amen

Alia oratio cum Oremus.

DEus qui iustis supplicationibus semper præsto es qui pia vota dignaris intueri, da famulo tuo (vel famulæ tuæ) N. cuius depositioni hodiè officia humanitati exhibemus, cum sanctis atque fidelibus tuis beati muneri portionem. Per christum Dominum nostrum. Amen.

Deinde dicatur Benedictio sepulchri. sine Oremus hoc modo.

ROgamus te Domine sancte, pater omnipotens, æterne Deus: vt bene✠dicere & sancti✠ficare digneris hoc sepulchrum, & corpus in eo collocandum: vt sit remedium salutare in eo quiescenti, & redēptio animæ eius, atque tutela, & munimen contra sæua iacula inimici Per christum Dominum nostrum. Amen.

Alia

Alia benedictio Tumuli.

. Adiutorium nostrum in nomine Domini. ℟. Qui
ecit cælum & terram.

ene ✠ dic Domine locum sepulchri huius, sicut bene-
ixisti sepulchra Abrahæ, Isaac, & Iacob.

. Ostende nobis Domine misericordiam tuam. ℟. Et
lutare tuum da nobis. Oremus.

DEus qui fundasti terra, & formasti cœlos, qui omnia
syderibus instituta fixisti, qui captum laqueis mortis
ominem lauacri ablutione reparas: qui sepultos Abrahã,
aac, & Iacob in spelunca duplici, in libro vitæ, ac to-
us gloriæ principes aduotasti benedicendos: ita bene ✠
icere digneris hunc famulum tuum (vel hanc famulam
uam, vt eum (vel eam) requiescere facias, & in sinu A-
rahæ collocare digneris: qui Dominum nostrum Iesum
hristum filium tuum, deuictis laqueis infernorum re-
rgere, & in se credentium suorum membra resuscitare
ssisti. Qui uenturus est iudicare viuos & mortuos &
eculum per ignem. ℟. Amen.

Oremus.

REspice Domine super hanc fabricam sepulturæ, &
descendat in eam Spiritus tuus, vt te iubente sit ei in
oc loco quieta dormitio, & tempore iudicij cum omni-
us sanctis sit vera resurrectio, te præstante Domino no-
ro, qui in Trinitate perfecta viuis & regnas per cuncta
ecula sæculorum. ℟. Amen.

Hic

Hic aspergatur aqua benedicta super sepulchrum, & incensetur sepulchrum. Finitis orationibus ponatur corpus in sepulchro cantore incipiente Antipho.

Ingrediar. Psal. 41.

QVemadmodum desiderat ceruus ad fontes aquarũ ita desiderat anima mea ad Deus.

Sitiuit anima mea ad Deum fontem viuum: quando veniam, & apparebo ante faciem Dei?

Fuerunt mihi lachrimæ meæ panes die ac nocte: dum dicitur mihi quotidie, vbi est Deus tuus?

Hæc recordatus sum, & effudi in me animam meam quoniam transibo in locum tabernaculi admirabil. vsque ad domum Dei.

In voce exultationis, & confessionis: sonus epulantis.

Quare tristis es anima mea? & quare conturbas me.

Spera in Deo, quoniam adhuc confitebor illi: salutar vultus mei, & Deus meus.

Ad meipsum anima mea cõturbata est: propterea memo ero tui, de terra iordanis, & Hermonij a monte modico

Abyssus abyssum inuocat: in voce cataractarum tuarum

Omnia excelsa tua, & fluctus tui: super me trãsierunt.

In die mandauit Dominus misericordiam suam: & nocte canticum eius.

Apud me oratio Deo vitæ meæ: dicam Deo, Susceptor meus es.

Quarè oblitus es mei? & quarè contristatus incedo, dum affligit me inimicus?

D um

um confringuntur ossa mea: exprobauerunt mihi qui tribulant me inimici mei.

um dicunt mihi per singulos dies, Vbi est Deus tuus? quarè tristis es anima mea, & quarè conturbas me?

pera in Deo, quoniam adhuc confitebor illi: salutare vultus mei & Deus meus.

Finito psalmo repetatur Antiphona.

ngrediar in locum tabernaculi admirabilis vsque ad domum Dei.

Qua dicta dicat Sacerdos Orationem hoc modo.

O Remus (fratres Charissimi) pro spiritu chari nostri (vel charæ nostræ) N. quem Dominus de laqueo uius sæculi liberare dignatus est, cuius corpusculum hoie sepulturæ traditur, vt eum (vel eam) pietas Domini 1 sinu Abrahæ collocare dignetur, vt cum magni iudicij ies aduenerit inter Sanctos & electos suos eum (vel eam) 1 parte dextera collocandum (vel collacandam) resusitari faciat. Qui viuit & regnat Deus per omnia sæcula æculorum. ℟. Amen.

Alia oratio cum Oremus.

D Eus qui humanarum animarum æternus amator es: animã famuli tui (vel famulæ tuæ) N quam vera dũ 1 corpore maneret tenuit fides, ab omni cruciatu inferoum redde extorrem: vt segregata ab infernalibus claustris, anctorũ tuorum mereatur adunari consortijs. Per Chritum Dominum nostrum. ℟. Amen.

Finitis orationibus claudatur sepulchrum ponente prius

R Sacer-

Sacerdote absolutionem super pectus defuncti si- dicendo.

DOminus Iesus Christus qui beato Petro Apostolo suo, cæterisque discipulis suis licentiam dedit ligandi atque soluendi, ipse te N. absoluat ab omni vinculo delictorum: & in quantum meæ fragilitati permittitur, precor sis absolutus ((vel absoluta) ante tribunal eiusdem Domini nostri Iesu Christi, habeasque vitam æternam, & viuas in secula seculorum. ℟. Amen.

Hic aspergatur Tumulus aqua benedicta, & incensetur cantore incipience.

Antipho. Hæc requies mea. Psal 131.

MEmento Domine Dauid: & omnis mansuetudinis eius.

Sicut iurauit Domino: vota vouit Deo Iacob.

Si introiero in tabernaculum domus meæ: si ascendero in lectum strati mei.

Si dedero somnum oculis meis: & palpebris meis dormitationem.

Et requiem temporibus meis, donec inueniam locum Domino: tabernaculum Deo Iacob.

Ecce audiuim⁹ eã in Ephrata: inuenimus eã in cãpis siluæ.

Introibimus in tabernaculum eius: adorabim⁹ in loco vbi steterunt pedes eius.

Surge Dñe in requiem tuã: tu & arca sanctificationis tuæ.

Sacerdotes tui induantur iustitiam: & sancti tui exultent.

Propter Dauid seruũ tuum: non auertas faciem Christi tui.

Iuraui

urauit Dominus Dauid veritatem & non frustrabitur eum: de fructu ventris tui ponam super sedem tuam.

i custodierint filij tui testamẽtum meum: & testimonia tua hæc quæ docebo eos.

t filij eorum vsque in sæculum: sedebunt super sedem tuam.

Quoniam elegit Dominus Sion: elegit eam in habitationem sibi.

I æc requies mea in sæculum sæculi: hic habitabo quoniam elegi eam.

iduam eius benedicens benedicam: pauperes eius saturabo panibus.

acerdotes eius iuduam salutari: & sancti eius exultatione exultabunt.

lluc producã cornu Dauid: paraui lucernã Christo meo.

nimicos eius induam confusione: super ipsum autem efflorebit sanctificatio mea.

Finito psalmo sequatur Antitph.

I æc requies mea in sæculum sæculi: hic habitabo quonin elegi eam. Qua dicta dicat Sacerdos orationem, cum

O remus.

DEus apud quem spiritus mortuorum viuunt & in quo electorũ animæ deposito carnis onere, plena fælicite lætãtur: presta supplicãtib⁹ nobis, vt anima famuli tui vel famulæ tuæ) N. quæ temporali per corpus visionis ui⁹ luminis caruit visu, æternæ illi⁹ lucis solatio potiatur. on eam tormẽtum mortis attingat, nec dolor horrẽdę vi

 sionis

ſionis afficiat: non pœnalis timor excruciet, non reoru
peſſima catena conſtringat, ſed conceſſa ſibi venia om
nium delictorum, optatæ quietis conſequatur gaudia re
promiſſa. Per Chriſtum Dominum noſtrum. ℟. Amen

Alia oratio cum Oremus.

TV Domine Deus omnipotens, precibus noſtris au
pietatis accõmodare digneris, tu miſeris opem fera
& miſericodiam largiaris, & ſpiritum famuli tui (vel fa
mulæ tuæ) N. vinculis corporalibus liberatum in pace
Sanctorũ tuorum recipias, vt locum pœnalem & gehenn
ignem, in regionem viuentium tranſlatus, euadat. P
Chriſtum Dominum noſtrum. Amen.

Finitis orationibus executor officij terram ſuper corp
ad modum crucis ponat, & corpus thurificet & aq
benedicta aſpergat. Et dum ſequens pſalmus canit
corpus omnino cooperiatur, cantore incipiente. A
tiphona. De terra plaſmaſti me. Pſal. 138.

DOmine probaſti me, & cognouiſti me: tu cognoui
ſeſſionem meam, & reſurrectionem meam.

Intellexiſti cogitationes meas de longé: ſemitam meam
funiculum meum inueſtigaſti.

Et omnes vias meas præuidiſti: quia non eſt ſermo in li
gua mea.

Ecce Domine tu cognouiſti omnia nouiſſima, & ant
qua: tu formaſti me, & poſuiſti ſuper me manum tuã

Mirabilis facta eſt ſcientia tua ex me: cõfortata eſt, & nc
potero ad eam.

Qu

Quo ibo a ſpiritu tuo? aut quo a facie tua fugiam?

Si aſcendero in cœlum, tu illic es: ſi deſcendero in infernum ades.

Si ſumpſero pennas meas diluculo: & habitauero in extremis maris.

Etenim illuc manus tua deducet me: & tenebit me dextera tua.

Et dixi, forſitan tenebræ conculcabunt me: & vox illuminatio mea in delicijs meis.

Quia tenebræ non obſcurabuntur a te, & nox ſicut dies illuminabitur: ſicut tenebræ eius, ita & lumen eius.

Quia tu poſſediſti renes meos: ſuſcepiſti me de vtero matris meæ.

Confitebor tibi, quia terribiliter magnificatus es: mirabilia opera tua, & anima mea cognoſcet nimis.

Non eſt occultatum os meum a te, quod feciſti in occulto: & ſubſtantia mea in inferioribus terræ.

Imperferctum meum viderunt oculi tui, & in libro tuo omnes ſcribentur: dies formabuntur & nemo in eis.

Mihi autem nimis honorificati ſunt amici tui Deus: nimis confortatus eſt principatus eorum.

Dinumerabo eos, & ſuper arenam multiplicabuntur: exurrexi, & adhuc ſum tecum.

Si occideris Deus peccatores: viri ſanguinum declinate a me.

Quia dicitis in cogatione: accipient in vanitate ciuitates ſuas.

Nonné qui oderunt te Domine, oderam: & super inimi cos tuos tabelcebam?

Perfecto odio oderam illos: & inimici facti sunt mihi.

Proba me Deus, & scito cor meum: interroga me, & agnosce semitas meas.

Et vide si via iniquitatis in me est: & deduc me in via æter na.

Finito Psalmo tota dicatur Antiphona.

De terra plasmasti me, & carnem induisti me redempto meus Domine, resuscita me in nouissimo die.

Qua dicta dicat Sacerdos sine Dñs vobisc. & sine Oremu

Commendo animam tuam Deo patri omnipotenti, ter ram terræ, cinerem cineri, puluerem pulueri, In nom ne Patris, & Filij; & Spiritus Sancti. Amen.

Deindé dicat Sacerdos hanc orationem, sine Oremus.

TEmeritatis quidem est Domine, vt homo hominem mortalis mortalem, cinis cinerem tibi Domino De nostro audeat commendare: sed quia terra suscipit terram & puluis conuertitur in puluerem, donec omnis caro i suam redigatur originem; inde tuam Deus pijssime pat lachrymabiliter quæsumus pietatem, vt huius famuli tu (vel famulæ tuæ) N. animâ quam creasti de huius mun voragine cœnolenta ad patriam ducas, Abrahæ amici tu sinu recipias, & refrigerij rore perfundas. Sit ab æstuant gehennæ truci incendio segregata, & beatæ requiei (t donante) coniuncta. Et si quæ illi sunt Domine dign cruciatibus culpæ, tu eas gratia tuæ mitissimæ lenitatis in dulge, ne peccati vicem, sed indulgentiæ tuæ piam senti

bon

onitatem. Cumque finito mundi termino ſupremum anctis illuxerit regnum, nouus (vel noua) homo Sanctorum omnium cætibus aggregatus (velaggregata) cum ectis tuis reſurgat in parte dextra coronandus (velcoronanda) Per Chriſtum Dominum noſtrum. ℟. Amen.

Alia oratio. Oremus

DEus vitæ dator, & humanorum corporum reparator qui te a peccatoribus exorari voluiſti; exaudi preces uas ſpeciali deuotione pro anima famuli tui (velfamulæ iæ) N. tibi lachrymabiliter fundimus: vt liberare eam inferorum cruciatibus, & collocare eam inter agmina anctorum tuorum digneris: veſte quoque cœleſti, & ola immortalitatis iudui, & paradiſi amœnitate confoeri iubeas. Per Chriſtum Dominum noſtrum. Amen.

Finita oratione incipiat cantor Antiphona.

Omnis ſpiritus. Pſal 148.

Audate Dominum de cœlis: laudate eum in excelſis.

Laudate eum omnes Angeli eius: laudate eum omnes virtutes eius.

audate eum ſol & luna: laudate eum omnes ſtellæ & lumen.

audate eum cœli cœlorum: & aquæ quæ ſuper cœlos ſunt, laudent nomen Domini.

uia ipſe dixit, & facta ſunt: ipſe mandauit, & creata ſunt.

tatuit ea in æternum, & in ſæculum ſæculi: præceptum poſuit & non præteribit.

L audate Dominum de terra: dracones, & omnes abyssi.

I gnis, grando, nix, glacies, spiritus procellarum: quæ fa-ciunt verbum eius.

M ontes & omnes colles: ligna fructifera, & omnes cedr

B estiæ, & vniuersa pecora: serpẽtes, & volucres pennat

R eges terræ, & omnes populi: principes, & omnes iud-ces terræ.

I uuenes, & virgines, senes cum iunioribus laudent no-men Domini: quia exaltatum est nomen eius solius.

C onfessio eius super cœlum & terram: & exaltauit corn populi sui.

H ymnus omnibus sanctis eius filijs Israel: populo appro-pinquanti sibi.

Psal. 149.

C Antate Domino canticum nouum: laus in Eccles Sanctorum.

L ætetur Israel in eo, qui fecit eum: & filiæ Sion exulte in rege suo.

L audent nomen eius in choro: in tympano & psalteri psallant ei.

Q uia beneplacitum est Domino in populo suo: & exa-tauit mansuetos in salutem.

E xultabunt sancti in gloria: lætabuntur in cubilib suis.

E xultationes Dei in gutture eorum: & gladij ancipites manibus eorum.

A d faciendam vindictam in nationibus: & increpati-nes in populis.

A-da

Ad alligandos reges eorum in compedibus: & nobiles eorum in manicis ferreis.

Vt faciant in eis iudicium conscriptum: gloria hæc est omnibus Sanctis eius Psal. 150.

Laudate Dominum in Sanctis eius: laudate eum in firmamento virtutis eius.

Laudate eum in virtutibus eius: laudate eum secundum multitudinem magnitudinis eius.

Laudate eum in sono tubæ: laudate eum in psalterio & cythara.

Laudate eum in tympano & choro: laudate eum in chordis & organo.

Laudate eum in cymbalis benesonantibus, laudate eum in cymbalis iubilationis: omnis spiritus laudet Dñum.

Finitis psalmis dicatur Antiph scilicet.

Omnis spiritus laudet Dominum.

Qua dicta dicat Sacerdos, sine Dominus vobiscum & sine Oremus

DEbitum humani corporis sepeliendi officium fideliũ more complentes, Deum cui omnia viuunt fideliter deprecamur: vt hoc corp⁹ chari nostri (vel charæ nostræ) a nostra infirmitate sepultum, in ordine Sanctorum suorum resuscitet, & eius spiritum Sanctis ac fidelibus aggregari iubeat, cum quibus inenarrabili gloria & perenni felicitate perfrui mereatur. Per Dominũ nostrum Iesum Christũ Filium eius, qui cum eo viuit & regnat in vnitate Spirit⁹ Sancti Deus. Per oñia sæcula sæculorũ. ℟. Amen.

Finita oratione incipiat Sacerdos Antiphonam & intonetur canticum Benedictus, & cantetur solenniter sicut ad matutinum. Antiph. Ego sum.

Canticum Zachariæ.

BEnedictus Dominus Deus Israel: quia visitauit & fec redemptionem plebis suæ.

Et erexit cornu salutis nobis: in domo Dauid pueri su

Sicut locutus est per os Sanctorum: qui a sæculo sunt pro phetarum eius.

Salutem ex inimicis nostris: & de manu omnium q cderunt nos.

Ad faciendam misericordiam cum patribus nostris: memorari testamenti sui sancti.

Iusiurandum quod iurauit ad Abraham patrem nostri daturum se nobis.

Vt siné timore de manu inimicorum nostrorum libera seruiamus illi.

In sanctitate & iustitia corá ipso: omnib⁹ diebus nostı

Et tu puer propheta altissimi vocaberis: præibis eni anté faciem Domini parare vias eius.

Ad dandam scientiam salutis plebi eius: in remissione peccatorum eorum.

Per viscera misericordiæ Dei nostri: in quibus visitau nos oriens ex alto.

Illuminare his qui in tenebris, & in vmbra mortis seden ad dirigendos pedes nostros in viam pacis.

Finito cantico, tota dicatur Antiphona.

E g

go ſum reſurrectio & vita qui credit in me etiam ſi
ıortuus fuerit, viuet, & omnis qui viuit & credit in me
on moriatur in æternum.

Qua dicta ſequatur hoc modo.

yrie eleiſon. Chriſte eleiſon. Kyrie eleiſon.

Hic roget Sacerdos circumſtantes orare pro anima defuncti dicens.

ro anima N. & pro animabus omnium fidelium de-
ınctorum; Pater noſter.

Deindè dicat Sacerdos.

. Et ne nos inducas in tentationem. ℟. Sed libera
os a malo.

. Requiem æternam dona eis Domine. ℟. Et lux per-
etua luceat eis.

. A porta inferi. ℟. Erue Domine animas eorum.

. Credo videre bona Domini. ℟. In terra viuentium.

. Non intres in iudicium cum ſeruo tuo Dñe.

. Quia non iuſtificabitur in cõſpectu tuo omnis viuens.

. Domine exaudi orationem meam. ℟. Et clamor
ıeus ad te veniat.

. Dominus vobiſcum. ℟. Et cum ſpiritu tuo.

Oremus.

DEus origo pietatis, pater miſericordiarum, ſolamen triſtium, indultor criminum, de cuius munere venit mne quod bonum eſt, & procedit, reſpice propitius ıpplicum preces: Et quamuis propria nos reputet indigos conſcientia, te dignum noſtris flecti petitionibus:

pulſamus tamen quantulumcunque conceditur aures tu pietatis. Nam ſi omittim⁹ in vtraque veremur eſſe rei: quoniam & te præcipis a peccatoribus exorari, noſtroque (& ſi non merito) hoc agendum te præſtante tribuitur miniſterio. Ergo te Dñe Sancte, Pater omnipotens, ætern Deus, qui vnicum Filium tuum Dominum noſtrum Ieſum Chriſtum incarnari de virgine conſtituiſti, quo vetuſtum ſolueret proprio cruore peccatum, & vitam redderc mundo, ipſo opitulante animam fratris noſtri (vel ſorori noſtræ) N. ab ergaſtulo cœnolentæ materiæ exemptã al omnibus piaculis quæſumus abſoluas. Nullas patiatur inſidias occurſantium dæmonum, propter quã miſiſti ad ter ras vnigenitum Filium tuum. Libera & abſolue eam a tetr voragine inferni, quam redemiſti præcioſo ſanguine vnigeniti Filij tui. Libera & abſolue eam ab æſtuantis gehẽn truci incendio, collocans in paradiſi amœnitate. Non ſentiat pijſſime Pater quod calet in flammis, quod ſtridet i pœnis, & quod horret in tenebris: ſed munificentiæ tu munere præuenta mereatur euadere iudicium vltionis, & beatæ requiei ac lucis æternæ fælicitate perfrui. Per eundem Chriſtum Dominum noſtrum. Amen.

Alia oratio cum. Oremus.

TIbi Domine commendamus animam famuli tu (vel famulæ tuæ) N. vt defunctus (vel defuncta ſæculo tibi viuat, & quæ per fragilitatem mundanæ conuerſationis peccata admiſit, tu venia miſericordiſſimæ pietatis abſterge. Per Chriſtum Dominũ noſtrum Amen

H

His dictis dicatur Pſalmus. 50.

MIſerere mei Deus: ſecundum magnam miſericordiam tuam.

t ſecundum multitudinem miſerationum tuarum: dele iniquitatem meam.

mplius laua me ab iniquitate mea: & a peccato meo munda me.

uoniam iniquitatem meam ego cognoſco: & peccatum meum contra me eſt ſemper.

ibi ſoli peccaui & malum coram te feci: vt iuſtificeris in ſermonibus tuis, & vincas cum iudicaris.

cce enim in iniquitatibus conceptus ſum: & in peccatis concepit me mater mea.

cce enim veritatem dilexiſti: incerta & occulta ſapientiæ tuæ manifeſtaſti mihi.

ſperges me Domine hyſſopo, & mundabor: lauabis me, & ſuper niuem dealbabor.

uditui meo dabis gaudium, & lætitiam: & exultabunt oſſa humiliata.

uerte faciem tuam a peccatis meis: & omnes iniquitates meas dele.

or mundum crea in me Deus: & ſpiritum rectum innoua in viſceribus meis.

e proijcias me a facie tua: & Spiritum Sanctum tuum ne auferas a me.

edde mihi lætitiam ſalutaris tui: & ſpiritu principali confirma me.

Docebo iniquos vias tuas: & impij ad te conuertentur.

Libera me de sanguinibus Deus, Deus salutis meæ: & exaltabit lingua mea iustitiam tuam.

Domine labia mea aperies: & os meum annunciabit laudem tuam.

Quoniam si voluisses, sacrificium dedissem vtique: holocaustis non delectaberis.

Sacrificium Deo spiritus contribulatus: cor contritum & humiliatum Deus non despicies.

Benignè fac Domine in bona voluntate tua Sion: vt ædificentur muri Hierusalem.

Tunc acceptabis Sacrificium iustitiæ, oblationes & holocausta: tunc imponent super altare tuum vitulos.

Antiph. Requiem æternam dona eis Domine: & lux perpetua luceat eis.

Qua dicta dicat Sacerdos in auditu omnium.

Pater noster, Pro anima eius, & pro animabus quorum ossa in hoc cœmiterio vel in alijs requiescunt, & pro animabus omnium fidelium defunctorum.

Deindè dicat Sacerdos,

vers. Et ne nos inducas intentationem. ℟. Sed libera nos a malo.

℣. A prota inferi. Resp. Erue Domine animas eorum.

℣. Ne tradas bestijs animas confitentium tibi. Resp. Et animas pauperum tuorum ne obliuiscaris in finem.

℣. Dominus vobiscum. Resp. Et cum spiritu tuo.

Ore-

Oremus.

DEus cuius miseratione animæ fidelium requiescunt, animab⁹ famulorum, famularumque tuarum, hic & bique in Christo quiescentium, da propitius suorum veiam peccatorum, vt a cūctis reatibus absoluti, tecum sine ne lætentur. Per Christū Dominū nostrum. ℟. Amen.

Postea reuertentes clerici de tumulo dicant septem psalmos pœnitentiales, vel psalmum, De profundis pag. 99. cum Antiphona. Requiem æternam.

Sequatur.

yrie eleison. Christe eleison. Kyrie eleisō. Pater nost.

rs. Et ne nos inducas in tentationem. Resp. Sed libe- nos a malo.

A porta inferi. Resp. Erue Domine animas eorum.

rs. Anima eius in bonis demoretur. Resp. Et semen eius æreditet terram.

rs. Credo videre bona Domini. Resp. In terra viuenum.

rs. Non intres in iudicium cum seruo tuo (vel ancilla a) Dñe. Resp. Quia non iustificabitur in conspectu o omnis viuens.

rs. Dominus vobiscum. Resp. Et cum spiritu tuo.

Oremus.

Atisfaciat tibi Domine Deus noster pro anima famuli tui (vel famulæ tuæ) N. fratris nostri (vel sororis ostræ) sanctæ Dei genitricis semperque virginis Mariæ, Sanctissimi Apostoli tui Petri, omniumque Sanctorum tuorum

tuorum oratio, & presentis familiæ tuæ humilis & deuot:
supplicatio: vt peccatorum omnium veniam quam Fil
tui Domini nostri Iesu Christi prætioso sanguine rede
misti. Qui tecum viuit & regnat in vnitate Spiritus Sanct
Deus, Per omnia sæcula sęculorum. Resp. A men.

In fine omnium dimissa voce dicatur sic.

A nima eius, & animæ omnium fidelium defunctorun
per Dei misericordiam requiescant in pace, A men.

BENEDICTIONES AB EPISCOPIS ET SVFFRAganeis faciendæ.

Et primo Confirmatio puerorum.

In primis dicat Episcopus.

vers. A diutorium nostrum in nomine Domini. Resp
Q ui fecit cœlum & terram.

vers. S it nomen Domini benedictum. Resp. E x ho
nunc & vsque in sæculum.

vers. Dominus vobiscum. Resp. E t cum spiritu tuo.

O remus.

O Mnipotens sempiterne Deus, qui regenerare digna
tus es hos famulos tuos (vel has famulas tuas) e
aqua & Spiritu Sancto, quique dedisti eis remissioner
omnium peccatorum: immitte in eos septiformem S pir:
tum Sanctum paraclitū de cœlis. Resp. A men.

S pir

piritum ſapientiæ & intellectus. R. A men.
piritum ſcientiæ & pietatis. R. A men.
piritum conſilij ✠ & fortitudinis. ℟. A men.
t imple eos (vel eas) ſpiritu timoris Dñi ✠ ℟. A men.
t conſigna eos (vel eas) ſigno ſanctæ crucis ✠ con-
irma eos (vel eas) Chriſmate ſalutis in vitam propitia-
us æternam. ℟. Amen.

Et tunc Epiſcopus petat nomen, & vngat pollicem Chriſmate, & faciat infronte pueri crucem, dicens.

onſigno te N. ſigno crucis ✠ & confirmo te Chriſ-
nate ſalutis In nomine Patris, & Filij ✠, & Spiritus
anċti A men. Pax tibi. Oremus.

D Eus qui Apoſtolis tuis Sanctum dediſti Spiritum; quique per eos, eorum ſucceſſoribus, cæteriſque fi-
lelibus tradendum eſſe voluiſti: reſpice propitius ad noſtræ
umilitatis famulatum, & præſta, vt horum corda quo-
um frontes ſacroſancto Chriſtmate deliniuimus, & ſi-
;no ſanctæ crucis conſignauimus, idem Spiritus Sanctus
duenïens, templum gloriæ ſuæ dignantér inhabitando
erficiat. Per Dominum noſtrum Ieſum Chriſtum Filiũ
uum, qui tecum viuit & regnat in vnitate euiſdem Spiri-
us Sancti Deus per omnia ſæcula ſæculorum. ℟. A men.
cce ſic benedicetur omnis homo qui timet Dominum.
enedicat vos Dominus ex Sion: vt videatis bona Hieruſalem omnibus diebus veſtris.
enedicat vos Omnipotens Deus, Pa ✠ ter, & Fi ✠ lius,
Spiritus ✠ Sanctus. ℟. A men.

Benedictio indumentorum Sacerdotalium.

℣. Adiutorium nostrum in nomine Domini.

℟. Qui fecit cœlum & terram.

℣. Dominus vobiscum. ℟. Et cum spiritu tuo.

Ista in omnibus benedictionibus primo dicantur.

Oremus.

OMnipotens sempiterne Deus qui per Moysen famu lum tuum Pontificalia seu Sacerdotalia, ac Leuitic vestimenta, ad explendum ministerium eorum in conspe ctu tuo, & ad decorum tui nominis fieri decreuisti: adest propitius inuocationibus nostris & hæc indumenta de super irrigata gratia tua, ingenti benedictione per nostr. humilitatis seruitutem purifi ✠ care, bene ✠ dicere, & conse ✠ crare digneris: vt diuinis cultibus & sacris myste rijs apta, & bene ✠ dicta existant; hisque sacris vestibu Pontifices, Sacerdotes, seu Leuitæ tui induti, ab omni bus impulsionibus malignorum spirituum muniti ac de fensi esse mereantur, omnisque eis vtentes tuis mysteri aptos & condignos seruire, atque in his placidè in hærer & deuote perseuerare tribue. Per Dominum nostrum Iesum Christum. ℟. Amen.

Oremus Alia

DEus inuictæ virtutis auctor, & omnium rerum crea tor ac sanctificator, intende propitius: vt hæc indu méta Sacerdotalis & Leuiticæ gloriæ ministris tuis fruéda

tu

uo ore proprio bene ✠ dicere, & sancti ✠ ficare & onse ✠ crare digneris: omnesque eis vtentes, tuis mysteijs aptos, & tibi in eis deuotè & amicabiliter seruientes, ratos effici concedas. Per Dominum. ℟. Amen.

Et aspergat ea Episcop⁹ aqua benedicta: & idem faciat in benedictione cuiuslibet specialis indumenti.

Benedictio specialis cuiuslibet indumenti.

. Adiutorium. &c.

Oremus.

DEus omnipotens bonarum virtutum dator & omnium benedictionum largus infusor, te supplices oramus, vt manibus nostris opem tuæ benedictionis fundas: vt hunc amictum (vel albam, vel cinctorium, l manipulum, vel dalmaticam, vel casulā, vel pluuiale) uino cultui præparatum, virtute Sancti Spirit⁹ bene ✠ cere, & sancti ✠ ficare, atque conse ✠ crare digneris, omnibus eo vtentibus gratiam sacri mysterij tui beninus concede, vt in conspectu tuo sancti & immaculati, que irreprehensibiles appareant & auxilium misericoræ tuæ acquirant. Per Dominum nostrum. ℟. Amē.

Benedictio Amictus. Oremus.

BEne ✠ dic Domine quæsumus omnipotens Deus amictum istum tam Leuitici quam Sacerdotalis offij; & concede propitius, vt quicunque eum capiti suo nposuerit, benedictionem tuam accipiat, sitque in fide lidus, & sanctitatis grauedine fundatus. Per Dominum ostrum Iesum Christum. Resp. Amen.

Benedictio Albæ Oremus.

DEus inuictæ virtutis auctor, & omnium rerum crea-tor & sanctificator, intende propitius, vt albam Le-uiticæ ac Sacerdotalis gloriæ tuo ore proprio bene ✠ di-cere, sancti ✠ ficare, atque conse ✠ crare digneris: om-nesque ea vtentes tuis mysterijs aptos, & tibi in ea deuo-& a micabiliter seruiẽtes, gratos effici concedas. Per Chri-stum Dominum nostrum ℟. Amen.

Benedictio Cinguli. Oremus.

OMnipotens sempiterne Deus, qui Aaron & filijs su-Sacerdotali ministerio cingulo cum baltheo in r-nibus stringi iussisti: adesto supplicationibus nostris, omnes tuæ sanctæ operationis ministri hac zona iustiti-circumsepti, renes lumbosque sancta pudicitia præci-gere satagant, atque præualeant, quaten⁹ nec vento elati-nis, nec frigore iniquitatis tabescant, sed magis ac mag-te opitulante confirmari & corroborari ad tibi placi-queant. Per Christum Dominum nostrum. Amen.

Benedictio Manipuli Oremus.

EXaudi nos Domine Sancte, pater omnipotens, æter-Deus: vt hunc manipulum sacri mysterij vsui præp-ratum, bene ✠ dicere, sancti ✠ ficare, atque conse ✠ crare digneris. Per Christum Dominũ nostrum. Ame-

Benedictio Stolæ Oremus.

DEus qui Stolis, predicatoribus collum & pectus m-niri iussisti, exaudi nos propitius, vt quicunque tu-rum Sacerdotum huic stolæ colla subiecerint, quicqu-

cor

corde credunt boni, proferant, & quod verbis edocuerint, factis adimplere festinent. Per Dominum nostrum Iesum Christum Resp. Amen.

Benedictio Stolæ, & Manipuli simul. Oremus.

DOmine Iesu Christe fili Dei viui, qui pius & misericors, ore tuo sancto & benedicto dixisti; Venite ad me omnes qui laboratis, & onerati estis, & ego reficiam vos, & inuenietis requiem animabus vestris. Iugum enim meum suaue est, & onus meum leue; Stolam istam & manipulum istum, quem famuli tui Sacerdotes & Leuitæ ad ostendendum se seruituti tuæ mancipatos gestaturi sunt, bene ✠ dicere, sancti ✠ ficare, atque conse ✠ crare digneris, quatenus eis vtentes iugum tuum suaue & onus tuum leue sentiant, & animabus suis requiem inueniant sempiternam. Per te saluator mundi rex gloriæ. Qui viuis & regnas cum Deo patre in vnitate Spiritus Sancti Deus per omnia sæcula sæculorum. ℟. Amen.

Benedictio Casulæ. Oremus.

DEus fons pietatis & iustitiæ, qui tui operis ministros ad extremum vestimentorum suorum casula, cuius munimento interius omnia tegerentur, vestiri sanxisti: concede precibus nostris virtutem & bene ✠ dictionem gratiæ tuæ; vt omnis hac casula induti, enumeratis interius omnium virtutum ornamentis, vinculum perfectæ charitatis super omnia habeant & conseruent, quo perficere valeant Sacrificiũ tibi gratum pro viuis & mortuis, & quæ adipisci desiderant, deuota mente implere valeant:

præstante Domino nostro Iesu Christo Qui tecum viuit & regnat Deus Per. Resp. Amen.

Benedictio mapparum seu linteaminum Altaris.

Oremus.

EXaudi preces nostras Domine: & hæc linteamina sacri Altaris vsui præparata, bene ✠ dicere, & sancti ✠ ficare digneris Per Dominum nostrum. Resp. Amen.

Oremus.

DOmine Deus omnipotens qui Moysen famulum tuum per quadraginta dies ornamenta, & linteamina facere docuisti, quæ etiam Maria texuit in vsum Tabernaculi fœderis, bene ✠ dicere sancti ✠ ficare, & conse ✠ crare digneris hæc linteamina, ad tegendum & inuoluendum Altare gloriosissimi Filij Domini nostri Iesu Christi. Qui tecum viuit & regnat in vnitate Spiritus Sancti Deus per omnia sæcula sæculorum. Amen.

Benedictio Patenæ.

OReemus (fratres dilectissimi) vt diuinæ gratiæ benedictio conse ✠ cret, & sancti ✠ ficet hanc patenam ad confringendum in ea corpus Domini nostri Iesu Christi, qui crucis passionem sustinuit pro salute omnium nostrum. Qui viuit & regnat cum Deo patre in vnitate Resp. Amen.

Oratio.

OMnipotens sempiterne Deus, qui legalium iustitutor es hostiarum, quique inter eas conspersam simlaginem deferri in patenis aureis & argenties ad Altare tuum iussisti: bene ✠ dicere, sancti ✠ ficare, atque con secr

:ra ✠ re digneris hanc patenam in administrationem
ıcharistiæ Iesu Christi Filii tui, qui pro nostrum omi-
m salute seipsum tibi Deo Patri in crucis patibulo ele-
: immolari. Qui tecum viuit. Resp. A men.

Hic faciat Episcopus crucem cum pollice de ~~oleo san-~~
~~cto~~ chrismate, super patenam, & mox liniat totam superficiem cũ
ipso pollice decens:

Onse ✠ crare, & sancti ✠ ficare dignare Domine
patenam istam, per istam vnctionem, & nostram san-
ım benedictioné, in Christo Iesu Dño nostro. Qui te-
m viuit. ℞. A men.

Præfatio ad Calicem.

Remus (dilectissimi fratris) vt Deus & Dominus
noster calicem istum in vsum sui ministerii conse-
ındum, cœlestis gratiæ inspiratione sanctificet: & eum
habendam plenitudinem diuini amoris accomodet.
r Dominum nostrum IesumChristum. Resp. A men.

Benedictio Calicis.

Ignare Domine Deus noster calicem istum bene ✠
dicere, in vsum ministerii tui pia deuotione forma-
m : & sanctificatione perfundere, qua Melchisedec
nuli tui sacratum vas vel calicem perfudisti; & quod
e vel metallo effici non potest Altaribus tuis dignum,
t tua benedictione sanctificatum. Per Christum Donum nostrum. Resp. A men.

Hic faciat crucem de Chrismate a labio eius in labium
cum pollice, & mox liniat & perungat calicem totum
intra dicens.

C onse-

COnsecra ✠ re, & sancti ✠ ficare dignare Domi calicem istum per istam sanctam vnctionem, & n stram benedictionem, in Christo Iesu Domino nostr Qui tecum viuit. Resp. Amen.

Actiones nostras quæsum⁹ Domine aspirando præu ni, & adiuuãdo prosequere; vt cuncta nostra oper tio a te semper incipiat, & per te cœpta finiatur. Per D minum nostrum Iesum Christum. Resp. Amen.

Oremus.

OMnipotens sempiterne Deus manibus nostris qu sumus opem tuæ benedictionis infunde: & per n stram benedictionẽ hoc vasculum cum patena sancti ✠ ficetur, & corporis & sanguinis Domini nostri Iesu Chr nouum sepulchrum Sancti Spiritus gratia perficiatur. P eundem. &c. In vnitate eiusdem Spiritus. Resp. Am

Vasa sacra & alia ornamenta Ecclesiæ in generali ben dicantur hoc modo.

verſ. Adiutorium nostrum. Dominus vobiscum.

Oremus.

EXaudi Domine preces nostras clementissime pater hæc purificanda vasa & ornamẽta, sacri Altaris atq Ecclesiæ tuæ sacræ mysterij vsui præparata, bene ✠ cere, & sancti ✠ ficare, digneris. Per Dominum nostru Iesum Christum. Resp. Amen.

Oremus.

OMnipotens & misericors Deus, qui ab initio vt & necessaria hominibus creasti, Templaque ma hor ominum facta nomini tuo sancto dicari, tuæque ha bitaonis loca vocare voluisti: quique per famulũ tuum Moy n vestimẽta Pontificalia, & Sacerdotalia, & Leuitica, & ia quæque diuersi generis ornamenta ad cultum & decom tabernaculi & Altaris tui fieri decreuisti: exaudi proitius preces nostras, & omnia hæc diuersarum specierum rnamenta in vsum Basilicæ tuæ vel Altaris, ad honorem gloriam tuã præparata, purifica ✠ re, bene ✠ dicere ncti ✠ ficare, atque conse ✠ crare digneris: vt diuinis ltibus sacrisque mysterijs apta & benedicta existant, atq; onfectionibus corporis & sanguinis Domini nostri Iesu hristi dignis parentur famulatibus. Qui tecum. Resp. Amen. Et aspergatur aqua benedicta.

Benedictio Librorum.

diutorium Dominus vobiscum.

Oremus.

DEscendat Domine virtus Spiritus Sancti super hunc librum, qui eum mundando puri ✠ ficet & bene ✠ dicat atque sancti ✠ ficet, & omnium in eo legenum clementer corda illuminet, & verum intellectum ibuat; sed & intelligendo tua præcepta conseruare & nplere secundum voluntatem tuam bonis operibus oncedat. Per Dominum nostrum. In vnitate eiusdem. . Amen. Et aspergatur aqua benedicta.

Benedictio Thuribuli.

. Adiutorium nostrum. ℟. Qui fecit celum &c.

. Dominus vobiscum. ℟. Et cum spiritu tuo.

Oremus.

DOmine Deus qui dum Filios Israel in deserto mur-
murantes ob rebellem suam audaciam dudum va-
staret incendium, Aaron Sacerdotem tuum orantem, a
repleto igne Altaris thuribulo tibi incensum ponenter
exaudire, eosque de incendio liberare dignatus es: bene ✠
dic quæsumus Domine Thuribulum hoc, & præsta, v
quoties in eo thus adolebitur, votum populi tui bon
odoris efficias. Per Dominum nostrum Iesum Christum.

℟. Amen.

Benedictio Incensi. Oremus.

DOmine Deus omnipotens, cui astat exercitus Angelorum cum tremore, quorum seruitium spirituale e
igneum esse cognoscitur: dignare respicere, bene ✠ d
cere, & sancti ✠ ficare hanc creaturam incensi, vt omne
languores, cunctæque insidiæ inimici odorem eius sent
entes effugiant, & separentur a plasmate tuo quod prætios
sanguine redimisti, vt nunquam lædantur a morsu antiqu
serpentis. Per Dominum nostrum. Amen.

Benedictio Corporalis.

℣. Adiutorium nostrum in nomine Domini.

Resp. Qui fecit cœlum & terram.

℣. Dominus vobiscum. Resp. Et cum spiritu tuo.

Oremus

CLementissime Deus, cuius inenarrabilis est virtus
cuius mysteria arcana miraculis celebrantur: tribu
quæsumus, vt hoc linteamen tuæ propitiationis bene ✠

dictioni

ictione sanctificetur, & ad consecrandum super illud corus Dei & Domini nostri Iesu Christi filij tui, dignum fficiatur. Per eundem. Resp. Amen.

Oremus.

DEus qui pro humani generis saluatione verbum caro factus es, & habitare totus in nobis non dedignatus : quique traditori tuo perfido osculum pium dedisti, dũ ro vita omnium pius mactari voluisti, atque sindone lineo exto te inuolui permisisti: Respice propitius ad vota nostra ui tua fideliter charismata amplecti cupimus. Quæsumus Dñe sancti ✠ ficare, bene ✠ dicere, & conse ✠ crare digeris hoc corporale in vsum Altaris tui, ad cõsecrãdum suer illud siue ad tegendum, inuoluenduuque Sacrosantum Corpus & Sanguinem tuum Domine Iesu Christe, ignisque pareat famulatibus, vt quicquid sacro ritu super oc immolabitur, sicut Melchisedec oblatum placeat ibi holocaustum. Et obtineat per hoc præmium, quicunue obtulerit votum. Te quoque humiliter rogamus ac etimus, vt hoc corporale tuæ sanctificationis vbertate, er Sancti Spiritus gratiam purifices & sanctifices, qui te ro nobis omnibus offerre Sacrificium uoluisti. Et præsta, t super hoc sint tibi libamina accepta, sint grata, sint inguia, & Spiritus Sancti rore perfusa. Saluator mundi, ui viuis & regnas cum Deo Patre in vnitate eiusdem. ℟. Amen

Oremus.

DEus qui dignè tibi seruientium, nos imitare desideras famulatũ, respice propitius ad humilitatis nostræ seruitutem, & hoc corporale nomini tuo dedicatum, seruitutis tuæ vsibus præparatum, cœlestis virtutis benedictione sancti✠fica, puri✠fica, & conse✠cra. Quatenus super illud Spiritus Sanctus tuus descendat: qui & oblationes populi tui benedicat, & corda siue corpora sumentium benignus reficiat. Per Dominum nostrum Iesum Christum Filium tuum, qui tecum viuit & regnat in vnitate eiusdem Spiritus. ℟. Amen.

Benedictio Precariorum.

℣. Adiutorium nostrum. Dominus vobiscum.

Oremus.

DEus omnium benedictionum largus infusor, & omnis bonæ actionis inspirator: qui omnia tabernaculi fœderis ornamẽta ad deuotionẽ populi, tuo ore proprio fieri præcepisti: te humili prece deposcimus vt hæc oracula siue precaria sanctiatis effigiem prætendentia, & ad deuotè orandam beatissimam virginem Mariam Dei genitricem adaptata, & ad psallendum eiusdem Sanctissimæ virginis psalterium confecta & præparata, illa benedictione perfundas & benedi✠cas, qua olim per manus Sacerdotum vtensilia tabernaculi perfudisti. Et concede vt quicunque in his oraculis siue precarijs ipsam gloriosissimam virginem suppliciter honorare studuerint, aut in his quocunque in loco coram sua imagine preces effundere decreuerint, aut eius patrocinium postulauerint: illius precibus & obtentu gratiam, & gloriam

cononsummato vitæ præsentis termino obtineant, & tuæ ropitiationis indulgentiam consequantur. Per Dominum nostrum Iesum Christum. ℟. Amen.

Oremus.

SOlus & ineffabilis, & incomprehensibilis creator, omnipotens Deus, cuius verbo & potestate cuncta sunt reata, cuius dono percepimus quæ ad vitæ remedia possidemus; te supplices obnixis precibus deprecamur, vt de ede maiestatis tuæ hæc oracula siue precaria fidelium famulorũ tuorũ sanctitati conuenientia, tua bene✠dictioe & cœlesti sancti✠ficatione perundere digneris, quatenus beneplacitum munus in his orantium accipias. Sintque hæc oracula siue precaria, in conspectu tuæ clementiæ ibenter accepta, sicut Abel alumni tui, vel sicut Melchisedec munera tibi placuerunt oblata, qui in his Beatissimã Dei genitricem Mariam suis Sanctis nititur decorare obsequijs, Filius eius Dñs noster Iesus Christ⁹ magna pro parus recompenset; deuotionem eius accipiat; peccata dimittat; fide eum repleat; indulgentia foueat; misericordia rotegat: aduersa destruat: prospera cõcedat. Habeat in ho æculo bonæ actionis documẽtũ, charitatis studiũ; sancti moris affectum: & in futuro cum Sãctis Angelis gaudium dipiscatur perpetuum. Per eundem Dominum nostrum. Resp. Amen. Deinde aspergantur aqua benedicta.

Benedictio ad omnia quæcunque volueris.

℣. Adiutorium nostrum. Resp. Dominus vobiscum.

Oremus

Oremus.

BEne ✠ dic Domine creaturam istam N. vt sit remedium salutare generi humano, & præsta per inuocationem sanctissimi nominis tui, vt quicũque ex ea sumpserit, corporis sanitatem & animæ tutelam percipiat. Per Dominum nostrum. ℟. Amen.

Incipit modus ad signum siue Campanam benedicendam.

IMprimis præsbiter indutus super pelliceo & stola, & cruce præcedente cum clero & populo congregato dum metallum decurrit pro campana facienda incipit Hymmũm: **Veni creator Spiritus**: cum versu & collecta de S. Spiritu. Quando vero completa est incipit **Te Deum laudamus**: & omnes clerici vna voce debent cantare. Et in fine: **Da pacem.**

℣. A Domino factum est istud. ℟. Et est mirabile.

℣. Dominus vobiscum. ℟. Et cum spiritu tuo.

Oremus.

ACtiones nostras quæsumus Domine aspirando præueni & adiuuando prosequere: vt cuncta nostra oratio & operatio a te semper incipiat, & per te cœpta finiatur. Per Christum. ℟. Amen.

Quando volunt pendere, possunt; sed primitus benedicitur & consecratur in modum qui sequitur.

Benedictio aquæ.

℣. Adiutorium nostrum in nomine Domini.

℟. Qui fecit cœlum & terram.

℣. Si

℣. Sit nomen Domini benedictum. ℟. Ex hoc, nunc, & vsque in sæculum.

Oremus.

BEne ✠ dic Domine hanc aquā benedictione cœlesti; & assistat super eam virtus Spiritus Sancti, vt cum hoc vasculum ad inuitandos filios Ecclesiæ præparatum in ea fuerit tinctum, vbicunque sonuerit eius tintinabulum, longè recedat virtus inimicorum, vmbra phantasmatum, incursio turbinum, percussio fulminum, læsio tonitruū, calamitas tempestatum, omnisque spiritus procellarum. Et cum clangorem illius audierint filij Christianorum, crescat in eis deuotionis augmentum: vt festinantes ad piæ matris gremium, cantent tibi in Ecclesia Sanctorum, deferentes in sono tubæ præconium, modulationem per psalterium, exultationem per organum, suauitatem per cymbalum, gentes inuitare valeant in Templum Sanctum tuum suis obsequijs, & precibus exercitum Angelorum. Per Dominum nostrum Iesum Christum, in vnitate eiusdem. ℟. Amen.

Postea debent cantari hi sex psalmi

Lauda anima mea Dominum Psal. 145.

Laudate Dominum quoniam bonus Psal. 146.

Lauda Hierusalem Dominum. Psal. 147.

Laudate Dominum de cœlis psal 148.

Cantate Domino canticum nouum: laus eius. Psal. 149.

Laudate Dominum in Sanctis eius. Psal. 150.

Et dum cantatur debet Sacerdos lauare clocam de supradicta

pradicta aqua benedicta cum oleo benedicto, & sale benedicto, quod benedicitur sicut in die Dominico.

Deindé dicit orationem sequentem.

DEus qui per beatum Moysen legiferum tubas argen-
teas fieri præcepisti, quas dum Leuitæ Sacrificij tempore clangerent, sonitu dulcedinis populus monitus a-
adorandum te fieret præparatus, quarum clangore horta-
tus ad bellum tela prosterneret aduersarium: præsta vt ho-
vasculum tuæ Ecclesiæ præparatum sanctificetur a Spiritu Sancto: vt per illius tactum fideles inuitentur ad præmium. Et cum melodia illius auribus insonuerit populorum, crescat in eis deuotio fidei, procul pellantur omne
insidiæ inimici. Fragor grandinum, procella turbinum
impetus tempestatum temperentur. Infesta tonitrua, ven-
torũ flagra fiant salubriter ac inodoraté suspensa.proste-
nas aereas potestates dextera tuæ virtutis, vt hoc audient
tintinabulũ, tremiscant & fugiant ante sanctæ crucis ve-
illum. per Dominum nostrum Iesum Christum Filium
tuum qui tecum viuit & regnat in vnitate eiusdem. Res
Amen.

Tunc debet eam extergere linteo dicendo hunc
psalmum. Ex Psal. 28.

VOx Domini super aquas, Deus maiestatis intonuit
Dominus super aquas multas.

Vox Domini in virtute: vox Domini in magnificentia.

Vox Domini confringentis cedros: & confringet Dom-
nus cedros Libani.

Et con

t comminuet eas tanquam vitulum Libani : & dilectus quemadmodum filius vnicornium.

ox Domini intercidentis flammam ignis, vox Domini concutientis desertum : & commouebit Dominus desertum Cades.

ox Domini præparantis ceruos, & reuelabit cōdensa : & in Templo eius omnes dicent gloriam.

ominus diluuium inhabitare facit : & sedebit Dominus Rex in æternum.

omin⁹ virtutem populo suo dabit: Dominus benedicet populo suo in pace.

loria patri. Sicut erat.

Post hæc tangere eam debet de Chrismate, foris septies, & intus quater, dicendo.

Oremus.

O Mnipotens sempiterne Deus, qui ante arcam fœderis per clangorem tubarum muros lapideos quibus duersantium cingebatur exercitus cadere fecisti : tu hoc ntinabulum cœlesti benedictione perfunde : vt ante nitum eius longius effugentur ignita iacula inimici, rcussio fulminum, impetus lapidum, læsio tempestam, vt ad interrogationem propheticam ; Quid est tibi are quod fugisti? suis motibus cum Iordanico retroacto iendo respondeat : A facie Domini commota est terra : acie Dei Iacob. Qui conuertit solidam petrā in stagna quæ, & rupem in fontes aquarum. Non ergò nobis Doine non nobis : sed nomini tuo da gloriam. Super mi-

 sericor-

sericordia tua & veritate tua. Vt cum præsens vasculur
(sicut reliqua Altaris vasa) sacro chrismate tangitur & vr
gitur oleo sancto, quicũque ad sonitum eius conuenerin
ab omnibus inimicorũ tentationibus liberi, semper fid
catholicæ documenta sectentur. Per Dominum nostrun

Resp. Amen.

Tunc ponit in incensario ignem & thimiama, & thu & myrrham, erigẽdo clocam supra incensarium vt tc tum illum fumum colligat, dicendo hanc antipho nam.

DEus in sancto via tua: quis Deus magnus sicut De noster.

Ex Psalmo 76.

VIderunt te aquæ, Deus, viderunt te aquæ: & timu runt, & turbatæ sunt abyssi.

Multitudo sonitus aquarum: vocem dederunt nubes.

Etenim sagittæ tuæ transeunt: vox tonitrui tui in rota.

Illuxerunt coruscationes tuæ orbi terræ: commota e & contremuit terra.

In mari via tua, & semitæ tuæ in aquis multis: & vestig tua non cognoscentur.

Deduxisti sicut oues populum tuum: in manu Moysi Aaron.

Gloria patri. Sicut erat. Postea dicit.

℣. Domine exaudi orationem meam. ℟. Et clam meus ad te veniat. ℣. Dominus vobiscum. ℟. Et cu spiritu tuo.

O

Oremus.

O Mnipotens dominator Chriſte, qui ſecundum aſ-ſumptionem carnis dormiente in naui, oborta tem-eſtas maria conturbauit, & protenus excitato & impe-.nte diſſiluit : tu neceſſitatibus populi tui benignus ſuc-ırre. Tu hoc tintinabulum Sancti Spiritus rore perfunde, : ante ſonitum illius ſemper fugiat inimicus, inuitetur l fidem populus Chriſtianus, hoſtilis terreatur exerci-ıs, confortetur in Domino per eum populus euocatus, que ſicut Dauidica cythara delectatus, deſuper deſcen-ıt Spiritus Sanctus. Atque vt Samuele agnum mactante holocauſtum tuum, rex æterni imperij fragore aura-ım turbam repulit aduerſantem : ita dum huius vaſculi ›nitus tranſit per nubila, Eccleſiæ conuentum manus ruet Angelica fruges credentium, & mentes, & corpora luet protectio ſempiterna. Qui viuis & regnas cum Deo atre in vnitate eiuſdem &c. ℟. Amen.

Deinde aſpergatur aqua benedicta, & totus populus preſens. Et imponatur illi nomen per Sacerdotem, apponendo manus ſupra, & ſimul imponunt Patrini & matrinæ. qui etiam, poſt præſbiterum, nominant eã, cooperiendo clocam linteis.

Benedictio enſis noui militis fiat hoc modo.

Interim genuflectente ipſo milite coram Altari. Primo dicat Sacerdos ſine nota.

. Dominus vobiſcum. ℟. Et cum ſpiritu tuo.

Oremus.

DEus cunctorum in te ſperantium protector, adeſt ſupplicationibus noſtris: & concede huic famul tuo qui ſincero corde gladio ſe primo nititur præcinger militari, vt in omnibus galea tuæ virtutis ſit protectus & ſicut Dauid & Iudith contra gẽtis ſuæ hoſtes fortitud nis potentiam & victoriam tribuiſti: ita tuo auxilio mu nitus contra hoſtium ſuorum ſæuitiam victor vbiqu exiſtat, & ad ſanctæ Eccleſiæ tutelam proficiat. Per Do minũ noſtrũ. ℟. Amen. Alia oratio, cum Oremus.

DEus qui trinos gradus hoſtium poſt lapſum Adæ i toto orbe terrarum conſtituiſti: quo minus pleb tua fidelis immunis ab omni impetu nequitiæ ſecura & quieta permaneret: adeſto ſupplicationibus noſtris, & hunc enſem (reſpice) quem inuocatione tui Sanctiſſim nominis benedicimus, benedi ✠ cere dignare, vt famu lus tuus cui eum te largiente concedimus & accingimu Hic ſuccingat Sacerdos militem enſe. ſic eo vtatur, qua tenus hoſtes Eccleſiæ inſidiantes reprimat, & ſeipſum a omni inimico tua protectione potenter defendat. Pe Chriſtum Dominum noſtrum. ℟. Amen.

Deindè aſpergat Sacerdos militem enſe ſuccinctum aqua benedicta & recedat miles in nomine Domini.

Benedictio carnium in die Paſchæ.

℣. Dominus vobiſcum. ℟. Et cum ſpiritu tuo.

Oremus.

DEus cœli terræque dominator, qui das eſcam omn carni & imples omne animal benedictione: bene✠ dic ic & sancti ✠ fica hanc creaturam carnis: nobis dona ıa sumentibus, animæ & corporis sanitatem concedas. er Christum. ℟. Amen.

Alia oratio. Oremus.

DEus qui vniuersæ carnis es conditor, qui Noe & filijs suis de mundis & immundis animalibus præcepta edisti, quique sicut olera herbarum humano generi quarupedia mũda edere permisisti, & qui agnum in Ægipto Ioysi & populo tuo in vigilia Paschæ comedere præceısti in figuram agni Domini nostri Iesu Christi, cuius ınguine omnia primogenita tibi de mundo redemisti; : nocte illa omne primogenitum in Ægipto percutere ræcepisti, seruans populum tuum agni sanguine præotatum. Dignare Domine Deus omnipotens bene ✠ icere & sancti ✠ ficare has carnes: vt quicunque de poulo tuo fideli ex illis comederint, omnium benedictione œlesti & gratia tua saturati repleantur in bonitate. Per uem hæc omnia Domine condita sunt & ab initio creta, Saluator mundi. Qui viuis & regnas cum eodem Filio ıo in vnitate Spiritus Sancti, Deus per omnia sæcula sæulorum ℟. Amen.

Hic aspergatur aqua benedicta super carnes.

Benedictio carnis, casei, butyri, ouorum, siue pastillarum in pascha. ℣. Dominus vobiscum. ℟. Et ım spiritu tuo. Oremus.

DOmine Deus omnipotens, qui fecisti & creasti cuncta viuentibus tuæ largitatis alimoniam, humanum-

 que ge-

genus ſpiritualibus eſcis ac poculis tuorum præcepto rum, terreniſque ſubſtantijs tuorum donorum indeſiner ter reficis: te omnipotentem Deum obnixè petimus, v hæc dona tua carnis, caſei, butyri, vel ouorum, ſiue cuiu cunque alterius cibi, quem tu ipſe creaſti & nobis do naſti, perpetua claraque benignitate ſancti ✠ ficare a bene ✠ dicere digneris. Veſcentibus ex eis largam tu benedictionis ſanitatem in viſceribus eorum clemente colloca, & præſentis vitæ ſoſpitatem, & futuræ beatitud nem miſericorditer indulge. Per Dominum noſtrum.

℟. Amen.

Deindé aſpergat Sacerdos aquam benedictam.

Benedictio ſeminis.

℣. Dominus vobiſcum. Reſp. Et cum ſpiritu tuo.

Oremus.

OMnipotens ſempiterne Deus creator generis hu mani, ſuppliciter tuam clementiam exoramus: v hoc ſemen, quod in tuo ſancto nomine ſaturi ſumus i agris noſtris, cœleſti benedictione bene ✠ dicere & mul tiplicare, atque ad maturitatem perducere digneris: vt pe vniuerſum orbem terrarum collaudetur dextera tua. Pe Dominum. Reſp. Amen.

Deindé aſpergatur aqua benedicta ſuper ſemen.

Benedictio pomorum in die S. Iacobi. ℣. Domin vobiſcum. ℟. Et cum ſpiritu tuo. Oremus.

DOmine Sancte, pater omnipotens, æterne Deus, qu ad infirmi mundi ornatum, die tertia lignum po

miſerun

iferum facere fructum primo præcepisti, quique ama-
m vetiti pomi saporem, antiqui serpentis suasu, a patri-
is nostris gustatum, vnigeniti Filij tui Domini nostri
su Christi passione salutari, non sentire posteros filios
r Baptismum voluisti, a quo sanitas & omne medica-
entum venit: quæsumus inenarrabilem pietatem tuam
hunc nouorum pomorum fructum, tuo conspectui
olatum bene ✠ dicere, & sancti ✠ ficare digneris; qua-
nus Sancti Apostoli tui Iacobi, & Martyris tui Christo-
iori (quorum hodie festa celebramus) omniumque
nctorum tuorum meritis ac precibus, quicunque fide-
s tui cum gratiarum actione ex eo gustauerint, sanita-
m mentis & corporis operante in eis Spiritu Sancto per-
pere mereantur. Per eundem Dominum nostrum Ie-
m Christum Filium tuum, qui tecum viuit & regnat in
iitate eiusdem. Resp. Amen.

Item benedictio pomorum.

Dominus vobiscum. Resp. Et cum spiritu tuo.

Oremus.

TE deprecamur omnipotens Deus, vt bene ✠ dicas
hunc fructum nouorum pomorum; vt qui esu ar-
oris lethalis, & pomo in primo parente iusta funeris sen-
ntia mulctati sumus, per illustrationem vnici Filij tui re-
mptoris, Dei ac Domini nostri Iesu Christi, & Spiritus
ncti benedictione sanctificata sint omnia atque bene-
cta: depulsisque primi facinoris intentatoris insidijs,
lubriter ex huius diei anniuersaria solemnitate diuersis
terris

terris edenda germina sumamus. Per eundem Dominu nostrum in vnitate eiusdem. Resp. Amen.

Deinde Sacerdos aspergat ea aqua benedicta.

Benedictio ad omnia quæcunque volueris.

℣. Domin⁹ vobiscum.. Resp. Et cum spiritu tuo.

O remus.

CReator & conseruator humani generis, dator grati spiritualis, largitor æternæ salutis: tu Domine mit Spiritum Sanctum tuum supra hanc creaturam N. vt a mata virtute cœlestis defensionis, quicunque ex ea gust uerint, proficiant illis ad salutem, & tam corporis qua animæ recipiant sanitatem. Per Dominum nostrum I sum Christum Filium tuum, qui tecum viuit & regnat vnitate eiusdem. Resp. Amen.

Hic aspergatur aqua benedicta.

Benedictiones quarundum aliarum rerum reperiunt in fine Missalis Romani.

FINIS.

Laus Deo, Virginiq; matri,
& S. Osmundo.

ANNOTATIONES IN PRECEDENTEM SACRAM INSTITVTIONEM.

Ex quibus Christianus lector & venerandam nonnullorum Ecclesiæ Catholicę Rituum antiquitatem percipiet, & aliqua obscuriùs in Manuali Sarisburiensi tradita, elucidata reperiet.

In ordinem faciendi Catechumenum Annotationes.

In *primis deferatur infans, &c.* Pag. *3.*) Sacerdos Sacramentum Baptismi administraturus, induatur superpellicco & stola. Parentur cærea candela, sal, oleum Catechumenorum, sanctum Chrisma, linteũ chrismale, & si benedicẽdus sit fõs, Cære⁹ paschalis.

Ibid. *quo nomine vocari debeat*) Impositionis nomi-s in Baptismate meminerunt Dionysius Areopagita, lib. de Hie-rchia Eccles. cap. de Baptismo: Dionysius Alex. apud Eusebium ɔ. *7.* hist. cap. 20. & alij. Nomen alicuius Sancti semper impo-endum est baptizando. Chrisost. homil. 20. in Genes. Concil, Nicæn. I. secundum editionem Turriani, can. 30. Constitutiones rouinciales Angliæ, titulo de Baptis. cap. Circa.

Ibid. *licet enim baptizatus fuerit domi, &c.*) Si infans antea fuerit aptizatus quæ in orationibus, adiurationibus, seu exorcismis in-ra præscriptis, de dono seu gratia Baptismi dicuntur, ad vberiorem ratiæ aut doni effectum, tota vita reliqua, percipiendum, a baptizante referantur. Quomodo etiam frequens ibi memorata Satanæ iectio, fuga, aut exitus referenda sunt ad perfectiorem eius pau-atim eiectionem, ac pleniorem purgationem. Refert enim S. Augustinus de nuptiis & concupis. cap. 33. regenerationis gratiam quę er sacrum lauacrum datur, vsque in finem vitæ, cuncta mala sanare purgare.

Ibid. *Signum saluatoris, &c.)* De hac cæremonia Dionysius Are pag. de Hierarch. eccles. cap. de Baptis. Basilius lib. de Spiri Sancto, cap. 27. August. to. 4. lib. de catechizandis rudibus, cap. 2 tom. 8. in psal 30. conc. 3. in psal. 36. conc. 2. & in psal. 141. to. lib. 1. confess. cap. 11. tom. 9. de Symbolo ad catechumenos, ca 1. & alibi. De consecrat. dist. 4. cap. Postea.

Pag. 4, *Deinde tenens manum dexteram super caput, &c.)* De hac m. nuum impositione Dionysius de Hierarch. ecclesiast. cap. de Ba tismo. Concilium Carthag. 4. can. 85. Cyprian. in *Actis* Conci Carthag. August. to. 7. lib. 2. de peccatorum meritis & remiss. ca 26. Christus etiam ipse paruulis manus imposuit, Math. 19. v. 15.

Ibid. *Omnipotens sempiterne Deus, &c.)* Orationes olim dictæ su super Catechumenum. vt testatur Dionysius de Hierarch. eccle cap. de Baptis. August. tom. 9. de Symbolo ad Cathecum. lib. . cap. 1. & alii Patres.

Ibid. *Et respondeant patrini)* de patrinis mentionem facit Diony Areopag. loc. cit. August. tom. 10. ser. 116. de tempore, lib. 1. c peccatorum meritis & remiss. cap. 34. Tertullian. lib. de Baptism

Pag. 6. *Accipe sal, &c.)* De consecrat. dist. 4. cap. Ex hinc, & ca Sal. Concilium Carthag. 3. can. 5. Orig. homil. 6. super Ezechie August. tom. 1. lib. 1. Confes. cap. 12.

Pag. 7. *Ergo maledicte Diabole &c.)* De huiusmodi exorcismis an Baptismum, vide de consecrat. d. 4. cap. Sicut nostis. Dionys. c Eccles. Hierarcih cap. de Baptismo Cyrillum Cathechesi 2. myst gogica, Nazianz. orat. in sanctum lauacrum, Ambros. lib. 1. de S cramentis cap 5. Leonem 1. epist. 4. cap. 7. August. lib. de fide operibus cap. 6. lib. 2. de nuptiis & concupisc. cap. 20. & 29. to. . in psal. 41. & alibi. Chrisost. homil de Adam & Eua.

Pag. 12. *Deinde spuat Sacerdos, &c.)* De hac re Ambrosius lib. 1. c Sacramentis cap. 1. & de ijs qui initiantur mysterijs cap. 1. De co secrat. dist. 4. cap. postea tanguntur. Simile quid factum a Salu tore vide Marci. 7. v. 33. & 34. Ioan. 9. v. 6.

Pag. 9. *Trado tibi signaculum &c.)* Christiani signo crucis olim et se sign signabant. Tertull. lib de corona militis. Nazianz.orat. 1. in Iuanum, Hieron. epist. 22. ad Eustochium, & in cap. 9. Czechielis, hrisost. homil. 55. in Matth. item in demonstratione quod Chrius sit Deus. Origen. homil. 8. in diuersos euangelij locos, Athaas. in vita beati Antonij, Ignatius in epist. ad Philipp. Augvst. to. in Ioan. tract, 36to. 5. de ciuitate Dei, lib. 22, cap. 13 &c.

Annotationes in benedictionem Fontis.

Pag. 15. *Benedictio Fontis)* Fontem benedicendum asserunt Dioys. Areopag. de Eccles. Hie rarch. cap. de Baptismo. Cyprianus pist. 70. ad Ianuarium, Basil. de Spiritu Sancto cap. 27. August. to. contra Iulianum, lib. 4. cap. 8. item Tract. 118. in Ioann. Ambros. b. 1. de Sacramentis cap. 5, vide epist, Paschasij ad Leonem ter epistolas, Leonis, epist. 65.

Ibid, *Nota quod aqua benedicta fontium in vigilia &c,* Secundum um Romanæ Ecclesiæ stat m ante Olei Catchumenorum & hrismatis infusionem (vt videre licet in Missali Romano) præribitur aquæ benedictæ fõtium aspersio. Quare illa inhibitio Ecesiæ Romanæ de qua hic sermo est, intelligenda est de aspersione ius aquæ post talem Olei & Chrismatis infusionem. Attamen in nglia seruanda est consuetudo loci, vt omnino aqua fontium on aspergatur.

Pag. 20 *De Cæreo &c.* Prudentius in hymno de Cæreo Paschali,

Pag, 21, *Post hæc mittat Sacerdos Oleum sanctum,* scilicet Chatecuenorum siue Baptismi. De hac trina cõiunctione Olei Baptismi, cri Chrismatis & aquæ baptismatis, Dionysius Areop. de Eccles. Iierar, cap. de Baptismo, vide etiam dist, 11 can, Ecclsiasticarum

Annotationes in ritum Baptizandi.

Pag 11 *Abrenuncias satana,* De his abrenunciationibus Diosius loc. cit. Tertullian. lib. de Spectaculis cap. 1. Cyrillus cachesi. 1. Cyprian. de duplici martyrio. Origin. homil. 12 in Nueros, Basilius de Spiritu Sancto cap. 27. August. tom. 2. epist.

105, ad Sixtum, tom.9. de Symbolo, lib, 2, cap. 1, & alibi. De con secrat. dist. 4, cap. Primum interrogetur, & cap. Prima igitur.

Ibid. *Et ego lineo te*, De hac vnctione Chrysost. homil. 6. i cap. 2. ad Coloss. Iustinus martyr quæst. 207. Ambros. lib. 2. d Sacramentis cap. 2. Cyrillus catechesi 2, August. serm. 206. de te pore, to. 9. in Euangel Ioan, Tract. 44. vide eunden tom. 9. d vita christiana, cap. 1, to 4, quæst, Euang, lib. 2. cap. 40. De con secrat. dist. 4. cap. Deinde a Sacerdote.

Ibid. *Credis in Deum patrem &c.*, De his interrogationibu vide Dionysuum Areopagitam lib. de Ecclesiast. Hierarch. ca de Baptis. Cyrillum catechef. 1. & 2. Cyprian. lib. 1. epist. 12. & epist. 70. ad Ianuarium, Origen. homil. 5. in Numeros, Hilar. ca 15. in Math. August. lib. 8. confes. cap. 2. De consecrat. dist. 4. ca Prima igitur.

Pag 23. *Quid petis*, Meminit huius interrogationis Dionysius loc citato.

Ibid. *Sub trina immersione*, Huius etiam trinæ immersionis mem nit Dionysius ibid. Tertull. lib. de corona militis, Cyrillus Cate chesi 2. Basilius de Spiritu Sancto cap. 27. Chrisost. homil. 24. i Ioann. August. tom. 10. ser. 91. & 201. de tempore, vide, De conse crat. dist. 4. cap. Postquam vos.

Ibid. *Hic lineat infantem de ipso Chrismate*, De hac Vnctione Iust nus quæst. 107. Ambros. lib. 2. de Sacramentis cap. 7. & lib. 3. ca. Cyrillus catechesi 3. August. to. 10. serm. 206. de tempore, Hiero contra Luciferianos. Innocentius 1. epist. 1. cap. 3. De consecra dist. 4. cap Presbiteris. cap. Postquam. cap. Accepisti, & cap. Eme sisti.

Pag, 24 *Accipe vestem candidam* De consecrat. dist. 4. cap. Post Bap tismum, Dionysius de Hierarch. Eccles. cap. de Baptis. Ambro de ijs qui mysterijs initiantur, cap. 17. Cyrillus catechesi 4.

Ibid. *Licitum est autem &c.* De consecrat. dist. 4. cap. Si qu Voluerit.

Ibid. *Accipe lampadem ardentem*. vide Gregor. Nazianz. ora tion one in sanctum lauacrum. August. in Psal. 65.

Pag. 27. *Notandum quod quilibet Sacerdos, &c.* Ex constitutio-busOthonis &Othoboni,titulo de Baptismo. Ad plenioremin-telligentiam huius Canonis sciendum est, quod dum fœtus est in ero materno inclusus, non potest baptizari, si uero caput emer-it, & timeatur periculum mortis, baptizetur etiam non cognito xu, & postea natus non rebaptizabitur etiam sub conditione. Se-us tamen si pedem aut manum emiserit extra vtèrum matris, quia nc membrum illud baptizabitur, & postea natus, est iterato ptizandus sub conditione. Si mater mortua fuerit extrahatur etus & baptizetur. Vide his de rebus, de consecrat. dist. 4. cap. ui in maternis, & constitut. Edmundi, cap. Si mulier. Hinc enim antiqua Ecclesiæ Anglicanæ constitutione, mulieres dum pa-unt tenentur semper habere aquam paratam, ad infantem si opus ierit baptizandum.

Pag. 28. *Et si puer fuerit baptizatus, &c.* prouĩciales constitut. Angl. .3. titulo de Baptis. cap. Baptisterium, & cap. Circa.

Ibid. *Et ideo si laicus, &c.* constitut. prouinciales Angliæ lib. 1. tit, Sacram. item. cap, Quod, & lib, 3. titulo de Baptismo, cap. Bap-terium. De consecrat. dist, 4, cap, Hi de quibus,

Ibid, *Si vero dubitet rationabiliter, &c.* Leo 1, epist, 92, cap, 15, de nsecrat, dist, 4, cap, Placuit, De Baptismo & eius effectu, cap, De uibus, cõstitut, prouinc, Angliæ, lib, 3, tit, de baptismo, cap, Circa.

Pag, 26, *Et est obseruandum, &c.* De consecrat, dist, 5. cap, Paruu-s, Concilium Oxoniense, cap, de Baptismo.

Ibid, *Præsbyter autem, &c,* De consecrat, dist, 4, cap, Omnis Pres-yter, Constitut, Angliæ lib, 3, tit, de Baptismo cap, Baptisterium.

Ibid, *Solemnis Baptismus, &c,* Siricius in Decretali cap, 2. Leo 1, ist, 4 & 80, Gelasius epist, 1 cap, 12 Constitut. prouincial. Angliæ .3 titulo de Baptismo cap, Quod.

Pag. 30. *Alij autem qui alijs anni temporibus, &c,* Constitut, prouinc, Angliæ ibid.

Ibid *Similiter pater & mater &c*). De cognatione spirituali cap.

 Si vir

Si vir. Non debent hi proprium filium de sacro fonte leuare, etiamsi immineat mortis periculum, quia tunc non est opus patrino.

Pag. 31 *Praeterea vir & vxor &c.*) Hoc modó licitum est, ex concilio Tridentino sess. 24. de reformatione Matrimonij. cap. 2.

Ibid. *Nulli religiosi &c.)* De consecrat. dist. 4 cap. Non licet.

Ibid. *Viri autem & mulieres &c.*) De consecrat. dist. 4. cap. Vos autem omnia; vide August. ser. 119. de peccatorum meritis & remiss. lib. 1. cap. 14.

Ibid *Vnde non debent recipi &c.*) Praeter hos ab hoc munere arcendi sunt manifesti Daeretici, Infideles, Iudei, non baptizati, vsurarij, aut alias perditae famae homines. Vide de consacrat. dist. 4 cap. Vos.

Ibid. *Qui suscipiunt pueros, &c.)* De consecrat. dist. 4. cap. in Catechismo.

Ibid. *Non plures quam vnus vir, &c.*) De consecrat. dist. 4. cap Non plures, Constitut. Angliae lib. 3. titulo de Baptismo, cap. Baptisterium, in concilio Trident, sess. 24. de reformat. cap. 2. definitur ab vno tantum siue viro siue muliere, vel ad summum ab vno & vna baptizatum de fonte suscipiendum.

Pag. 32. *Monendi sunt etiam laici, &c.* Cōstitutiones Angliae lib. 1 tit. de sacra Vnctione, cap. Sacerdotes.

Ibid. *Item nullus debet, &c.* constitut. prouinc. Angliae lib. 1. titulo de sacra Vnctione cap. 1 Confirmationis.

Ibid. *Non debet Sacerdos parochialis, &c.* De consecrat. dist. 4. cap Presbyteri, vide concil. Carthag. 2. can. 3. tertium cap. 36. & quart can, 36. Constitut. Angliae tit. de Vnctione cap. Cum sacri.

Ibid. *Sacerdos qui de veteri, &c.* De consec. dist. 4. cap. Si qu

Ibid, *Et ideo debet &c,* Concilium Nicaenum 1 secundum editionem Turriani can, 69, Fabian, Papa epist, 2 Cyprian de Vnction Chrismatis & alijs Sacramentis,

Ibid, *Item tam sacrum oleum quam Chrisma, &c,* Constitut, Angli lib, 3 titulo de custodia, &c, cap, Fontes, & cap, Statuimus,

Annotationes in ordinem purificandæ mulieris post partum.

Mulier ad purificationem accedens, caput habeat secundum ntiquam Angliæ consuetudinem, coopertum velo albo, in manu ortet candelam accensam, & sit media inter duas matronas.

Pag.34. *Nota quod mulieres,&c*, De purificat. post partum cap. nico, Distinct,5,cap. Si mulier,

Annotationes in ordinem faciendi sponsalia.

Nomen sponsalium hic sæpenumero pro Matrimonio ipso umitur, non in stricta significatione, qua promissionem tantum Matrimonij contrahendi significat.

Matrimonium esse Sacramentum docet Apost, ad Ephes 5.v, 2.August. tract,15, in Ioan, lib. 9,de Genesi ad literam cap. 7, lib, e fide & operibus cap,7, de bono cõiugali cap,7, 8, 15, 17, 18, 24, 5, de sancta virginitate cap, 2, Leo 1 epist, 92, ad Rust, cap. 4, hrysost, homil. 20, in epist, ad Ephes, Ambros, lib 1, de Abraham ap, 7, &c

Hortandi sunt vt anteqam contrahant, vel saltem triduo anté matrimonij consummationem, sua peccata confiteantur, & ad nctissimum Eucharistiæ Sacramentum pié accedant, Concil, Trident, sess 24 de refor. Matrimonii. cap. 1.

Pag, 35, *Et sciendum est quod licet &c.* A Dominica 1 Aduentus vsque in diem Epiphaniæ, & à feria 4 Cinerum, vsque adctauam Paschæ inclusiue, solemnitates nuptiarum prohibentur, liis temporibus permittuntur, Concilium Trident, ibid.

Pag 36, *Interroget Sacerdos dotem mulieris &c.* Hæc subarratio t post Matrimonium contractum, quando a sponso datur sponsæ nulus, aurum, & argentum.

Ibid. *Non fidabit Sacerdos &c.* constitut.prouincial. Angliæ lib 4, itul, de sponsalibus cap. Matrimonium, & titulo, de clandestina

 desponsat

desponsat, cap , Quia. De his clandestinis contractibus hæc pastorale Mechliniense ex concilio Tridentino: Irritum est Matrimonium quod contrahitur aliter quam præsente proprio Parocho vel alio Sacerdote, de ipsius, aut, de Ordinarij licentia, & duobus aut tribus testibus. Conc. Trident, sess, 24, de reform. Matrimoni cap, 1. Est autem proprius parochus(secundum definitionem cõgregationis eiusdẽ cõcil, sub Pio V & Gregorio xiii) qui adesse debet is in cuius Parochia matrimoniũ celebratur, siue viri siue mulieris Sed hæ cõstitutiones quia nondum in Anglia publicatæ sunt, suum robur in illa non habent. De denuciationibus seu bannis idem fere in eodem concilio decernitur, quod in hoc canone præscribitur.

Ibid. *Debet etiam Sacerdos terminum præfigere &c,* De clandestina desponsat. cap. Cum inhibitio.

Ibid. *Sacerdos vero &c* Constitut. Angliæ lib. 4, titulo de Sponsalibus cap, Matrimonium, & titulo de clandestina desponsatione cap, Quia,

Pag 37. *Similiter Sacerdos &c* constit. Angliæ lib 4, titulo de Sponsalib, cap, Matrimonium, & de clandestina desponsat, cap. Sanè

Ibid, *Quisquis etiam Sacerdos &c.* constitut. prouinc. Angl. lib 4, titulo de Sponsalibus, cap, Matrimonium, & titulo de clandestina desponsatione, cap. Quia, & cap, Humana. Vide concilium Tridentium sess, 24, cap, 1, de matrimonij reformat.

Pag, 39, *to be bonnair,* Bonnair verbum gallicum est, idem significans quod latine mitis, humanus, vel animo lenis. Hinc in manuscripto quodam antiquo anglico codice, mansuetudo qua est octauus fructus Spiritus Sancti dicitur bonnernesse. Idem significat verbum, debonnair, quod nondum est obsoletum. Eo enim vtitur inter cæteros Chaucerus.

Ibid, *and buxom,* Buxom idem est, quod latinè obediens. Id colligitur etiam ex manuscripto quodam antiquo Anglico codice, in quo inobediens mandatis, dicitur Vnbuxom to God and his hests. Itẽ in manuscripto codice cui titulus est; cursor of the worl Auctor ita Deum metricé alloquitur:

Shev

hevv thy selfe to vs.
VVe to thee haue benne vnbus.
Ie feared not(inquit Stanihurst, in descriptione Hyberniæ) such
'as his buxomnes. *A*libi. *E*quus indomitus dicitur an vnbuxom
orse. Denique, liber qui inscribitur, Hortus vocabulorum, verbũ
ıtinum(Cermas) vertit anglicé bovv able and buxom. Idem igi-
ır est bonnair and buxom, quod meeke and obedient.
Pag. *40. VVith this ring et c.)* Anuli oblationis qua Matrimoniũ
ı Ecclesia confirmatur, velaminis, & benedictionis sacerdotalis
ıemineı unt Nicolaus Papa can. Nostrates, ante annos *700*. Isi-
orus lib .*2*. de officijs cap. 19, ante annos plus minus 900.
Ibid. *Quia in medico est quædam vena &c.*) Decret. *30* quæst.
. cap. Fæminæ.
Pag. 44. *Incipiat missa.)* Sacrificij Altaris in Ecclesia pro nouis
ıonsis oblati mentionem facit Tertull. lib 2. ad vxorem. Missa dici
otest ea quæ in Romano Missali habetur, pro Sponso & Sponsa.
Ibid. *Extenso super eos pallio &c.*) De hoc pallio seu velamine
.mbrosius epist. *70*. ad Vigilium. Indé etiam nuptias dictas esse
ıterpretatur .lib 1. de Abraham cap. vlt. quod velo obnubetur
ıonsa.
ag. *46. Propitiare Domine &c.)* De benedictione Sacerdotali nouis
ıonsis adhibenda, agit Siricius Papa(qui floruit ante annos 1200.)
pist. 1. cap *4*. Innocentius 1. epist, *2*. cap 6. Concilium carthag.
. cui interfuit August. cap. 13. *A*mbros. epist. 70. ad Vigiliũ
Pag 31. *Notãdũ quod hæc clausula &c.)* Quæ hic dicũtur de bene-
ictione secundarum nuptiarum non adeó sunt perspicua. Ex illis
ɔr té hic breuis canon colligı potest. *B*enedictio Sacramenta-
s quæ continetur illis verbis(Deus qui tam excellenti &c.) non
atur in secundis nuptijs. Tunc autem nuptiæ dicuntur secundæ
t non benedicantur, quando vnus siue vir, siue fæmina, vel ambo
.ıerunt anteà benedicti. Licet enim alter eorum vel ambo antea
ıatrimonio iuncti fuerint, si tamẽ in primis nuptijs neuter fuerit
enedictus, danda est eis benedictio sacramentalis, in secundis
b 2 nuptijs.

nuptijs. Verbi gratia, Petrus adolescens nūquam benedictus, duci in vxorem Annam viduam, iam ante benedictam: vel e contra non benedicuntur hæ nuptiæ. Moritur Anna & Petrus ducit i vxorem Elizabetham virginem non benedictam, benedicūtur h nuptiæ, quia neuter eorum fuit aliquando benedictus. Scio ex cō suetudine & præscripto nonuullarum Ecclesiarum, semper bene dici nuptias si mulier non fuerit antea benedicta: attamen verb ipsa, vt mihi videtur, contrarium sonant, & consuetudo etian antiqua Ecclesiæ nostræ (vt accepi a quodā reuerendo viro, qui tē pore Reginæ Mariæ parochiam admistrauit) non consentit. Vid aliqua hac de re, pag. 44.

Annotationes in ordinem visitandi infirmum.

Si eodem tempore communicandus sit infirmus & simul vngen dus, administraturus superpelliceum & stolam iuduat cum plu uiali, accipiat pixidem cum hostia & oleum infirmorum, coope riat pixidem velo, quod ab humeris dependeat. Inter eundum fieri potest ferant quatuor viri baldachinum supra Sacramentum Custos superpellicio indutus lumen in lanterna & campanulan præferat, cæteris comitibus viris piis sequentibus & lumem etian si voluerint ferentibus ad quos conuocandos non erit abs re si pa rochus vtatur signo campanæ. Sacerdos hoc modo domū egro petat, & inter eundum caueat ne vagos oculos huc illuc leuite conijciat, sed timidé potius ac grauiter ambulet, cælestéque illun quem manibus gestat thesaurum fidé portet, & linguam & mentem precando exerceat, quoad in ægrotātis cubiculum intro ducatur. Hæc ex consuetudine Romana & pastorali Mechlniensi

Si solum communicādus sit infirmus eodem modo procedatu tantum Sacerdos non sumat secum oleum infirmorum. Si sit ante inunctus & in illa visitatione vsus sit Sacerdos toto sequenti or dine, omittantur in secunda visitatione infra scriptæ exhortatio nes, & dictis orationibus quæ illas præcedunt, commonicetur in firmus, vt prescribitur pag 51 Si non sit antea inunctus nihil ex se

quen

uenti ordine visitandi infirmum omittatur.

Eodem modo si infirmus qui antea cōmunicauit sit vngendus, ımat secum Sacerdos tantum oleum infirmorum, & indutus su-ːrpelliceo & stola reuerenter ab Ecclesia progrediatur, conco-itantibus amicis & custode sine lumine & campana. Et si paro-ıus cum eum communicauit, fecerit totum quod in sequenti 'dıne visitandi infirmum prescribitur, in extrema Vnctione o-ittuntur dictæ exhortationes & confessio. Inquirat tamen Sa-ːrdos vtrum aliquo delicto conscientia eius grauetur, & si intel-xerit eum velle confiteri, annuat. Quo facto accedat ad Vnctio-ːm.

Si denique neque vngendus neque cōmunicādus sit infirmus, rochus eum visitās non vtatur superpellicio, neque stola, dicere men potest super eum ōnes, vel aliquas ex infra prescriptis ora-ınibus.

Pag. *51*. *Pax huic domni &c.)* Math. 10. v. 12.

Ibid. *Offerendı est ei imago crucifixi &c)* Huius ceremoniæ eminit August. to. *9* de visitatione infirmorum, lib. *2*. cap. *3*.

Pag *55*. *Fides autem catholica &c.* Constitutiones Angliæ lib 1. p. de summa Trinitate ex Concilio de Lambeth.

Pag *59*. *Dic ergo vni peccata tua &c.* Confessionis necessitas col-itur ex Math. *18* v. 18. Ioan 20 v. 23. Act *19*. v. *18*. Asseritur ab rigine homil *2*. in Leuit. & homil. 1 & 2. in psal. 37. Chrysost lib 33 Sacerdotio, homil 30. in Genesin, hom. 10. in Math. Nyssen. at. in eos qui alios acerbius iudicant, Clemens epist. 1. ad fra-ːm Domini, Dionysius Areopagita epist. 8. ad Demòphilum ːrtullian; lib de pænitent. Cyprian. epist. *10* ad Præsbyteros & iaconos, lib 3. epist 14. epist 55. ad Cornelium, tract. vel serm. lapsis, Pacianus in parænesi ad penitentiam. Hieron in Cap. 10. :clesiastę, Basilius quæst. 288. in regulis breuioribus, quest. *229*. mpendio explicata: epist. 3. canon. ad Amphilochium. August mil. *41*. & *49*. ex lib *50* homil. Ibid. homil. 50. cap 10, 11 & 16. *2*. de visitat. infirmorum cap *4*. Leo *1*. epist. *91*. ad Theodorum, &c. epist. 86. ad Episcopos per Campaniam.

Pag 60. *Attamen non iniungat illi Sacerdos aliquam pænitentiam.* Id est, non iuiungat illi pœnitentiam conformem pro peccati nisi conditione si conualescat. Aliqua enim pænitentia siue sit ora tio, siue ieiunium, siue eleemosina semper iniungenda est.

Pag 61. *Notandum est quod licet &c.*) De reseruatione quorunc casuum, vide concilium Carthag. 2. cap 3. & 4. Carth. 3. caj 32. & 33.

Annotationes in ordinem administrnadi Sacra. mentum extremæ Vnctionis.

De hac Vnctione S. Iacobus Apostolus in epist. cap. 5. v. 1 August tom. 9 de visitat infirmorum, lib. 2. cap. 4 & de rectitudi catholicæ conuersationis. to. 10. ser. 215. de tempore. Conciliu Nicænum primum, iuxta editionem Turriani, can. 69. Oı gines hom. 2. in Leuiticum. Concilium Cabilonense. 2. caj 48. Innocentius 1. epist. ad Decentium, cap. 8. lib 1. Decretali cap. Vnico, de sacra Vnctione, Chrysost. lib. 3. de Sacerdot. caj 6. Innocentuis 3, cap. Cum venisset, Extra. de sacra Vnction Concilium Florentinum in doctrina de Sacramentis &c.

Pag. 63. *Priusquam vngatur infirmus*) Ante administratione huius Sacramenti parentur, linum stuppa vel lana, ad ter gendu sacrũ oleum a membris inunctis: & sal & aqua, siue panis & aq (sicut Romæ fit) ad lauandas manus peracta Vnctione.

Pag. 67. *Per istam Vnctionem &c.*) Vide concilium Trident. s 14. in doctrina de Sacramento extremæ Vnctionis, cap. 1. & Facta Vnctione tergat Sacerdos administrans Sacramentum, v alius Sacerdos presens, locum inunctum lino, stuppa, vel lana.

Pag. 63. *Deinde in dorso &c.*) Cõmunior opinio (inquit Card B larminus cap. 1. de Vnctione) quam sequitur S. Thomas est, qu ad essentiam Sacramenti extremæ Vnctionis solum pertineat V ctio quinque sensuũ &: sané ratio honestatis in Feminis id post

lare vid

are videtur, vt renes non vngantur, multo minus vmbelicus. Ex præscripto enim Sacerdotalis Romani, mulieres vngendæ sunt n renibus: secundum Pastorale Mechliniense in pectore.

Pap 57. *Facti Vnctione &c.*) Si infirmus non sit communicandus (quod semper secundum vsum Srisburiensem fit post Vnctionem) benedicere eum potest Sacerdos vt infra, pag. sequenti, & post eum breui consolationis verbo confortatum, & aqua benedicta aspersum, abscedete in pace.

Pag. 76. *Deinde communicetur infirmus &c.*) Infirmi olim in Primatiua Ecclesia in articulo mortis Eucharistiam sumere solebant. Dionysius Alexandri. epist. ad Fabium apud Eusebum, lib. . hist. cap. 36. Concilium Nicænum 1. can. 12. Paulinus in vita S. Anbrosij, Chrysost. lib. 6. de Sacerdotio. Vide Gregor. homil 40. in Euang. Concilium Arelatense 2. can. 12. Aurelianse 3. can. 24.

Pag. 80, *Sciendum est autem &c.* De sacra Vnctione cap. Vnico, de verborum significatione, cap. Quæ sunt.

Ibid. *Loca vero vugenda &c.*) In morbis contagiosis, & peste grassante, vt periculum vitetur, sufficit perungi sensus organum magis ad Vnctionem expositum, siue detectum, dicendo. Per istam Vnctionem & suam pijssimam misericordiam, iudulgeat tibi Dominus, quicquid peccasti per visum, auditum, gustum, odoratum, tactum, & gressum. Et tunc preces quæ præmittendæ & subiungende forent poterunt in Ecclesia coram venerabili sacramēto deuoté legi. Hæc ex pastorali Mechliniensi.

Ibid. *Potest Sacerdos &c.*) De verborum significatione cap. Quæ sunt.

Ibid. *Moneant frequenter Sacerdotes &c.* Constitut. prouinciales Anglie, titulo de sacra Vnctione, cap. Cum magna.

Ibid. *Doceant etiam eos, quod &c,*) Secundum constitutiones prouinciales Anglie, hoc Sacramentum conferri debet ejdem semel tantum in anno. Vide lib. 1. titul. de Sacramentis iterandis. cap. Sacramentum.

Ibid. *Et si quis post hoc Sacramentum &c.*) Constitut. Anglie lib. 1 itulo de sacra Vnctione cap. Cum magna.

Pag. *81. Similiter pueri, frænetici. &c.* De freneticis & furiosis ho decernitur in constitut. prouinc. Anglie. titul. de Sacramentis ite randis, cap. Ignorantia. & in constit. Lambeth cap. vltimo.

Annotationes in officium sepulturæ.

Pag. 94, *Tunc tantum lauetur corpus &c.* Antiquus est iste ritus vide Act. 9. v. 37. Gregor. lib. 3. Dialog. cap. 18. & lib. 4. cap 16. &. 17.

Ibid. *Et postea vigilias mortuorum.*) Intellige de vigilijs mortuo rum pro defunctis in genere, quæ singulis diebus (excepto tēpor paschali & aliis quibusdam festis) secundum vsum Satum dice bantur. De vigiliis mortuorum pro defuncto sepeliendo, vide pag. 103.

Pag. *99. Deinde deportetur corpus ad Ecclesiam.*) Corpora christia norum pie in Domino morientium, cum honore & multitudine comitantium, cum hymnorum & psalmorum cantu, olim ad loca sepulturæ delata sunt. Cerei etiam in eorum funeribus accensi, v apparet ex Nazianz. orat. 2. in Iulianum & orat. in funere Cæsari fratris, Dionysio Areopagita de Ecclesiast. Hierarch. cap. 7. Pon tio in actis passionis S. Cypriani. Sulpitio in vita S. Martii Nysseno orat in funere Meletii, & epist ad Olimpiadem de obitu sororis, Euseb in funere Constantini lib. 4. eius vite. cap. 65. 6 Hieron. in funere Paulæ, in vita. S. Pauli Eremite, & S. Fabiolæ Athanas. apud Damascenum lib. de mortuorū suffragiis Chryso homil. 14 in Epist. 1. ad Timoth, homil. 4. in epist 70. ad po pulum Antiochenum. Theodoreto lib. 5. hist. cap. 36. Lege Ge nes. cap. 50. Luc 7. Act. 8. August. to 5. lib. 21. 1. de Ciuitate Dei cap. 13.

Ibidem, vel in cæmiterio humandum.) De sepultura i locis sacris fieri solita, vide Ambros. lib. 1. de Abraham, cap. 9 Hieron. locis citatis, Gtegor. lib. 3. August. lib. de cura pro mo tu is cap.1.4.5.18. Chryſoſt.homil.*26*.in Epiſt *2*. ad Cornich. Euſeb. ›. *4*. de vita Conſtantini cap. *65*. & *66*. Maximum ſerm. in na- ›tali SS. Octauij, Aduentoris, & Solutoris.

Pag.100 *Sacerdos & miniſtri eius in Albis cum Amictibus &c.)* Id eſt ›e pluuialibus, attamen Sacerdos ſuper albam ſtola ex more in- ›atur. Ibid. In cappis) id eſt pluuialibus.

Pag. 103. *Deinde dicantur ſolenniter vigiliæ mortuorum.)* Pro de- nctis orandum eſſe conſtat Ex *2*. Machab. cap. 12. Auguſt. lib. . de Ciuit. Dei, cap. *24*. lib. de cura pro mortuis gerenda, cap. *1*. ›. De verbis Apoſtoli ſer. 34. vel ſecundum alios *32*. Dionyſio ›reopagita in lib. de Eccleſiaſt. Hierarchia cap. 7. Chryſ. homil. in epiſt. ad Philipp. homil. *41*. in priorem Epiſt. ad Corinth. ›mil. *69*. ad populum, Cyprian. epiſt. *66*. ad plebem & clerum ›rnitanorum & alijs.

Ibid. *Vbi vero in die ſepulturæ &c.)* Secundum antiquam Angliæ ›nſuetudinem (vt ex his rubricis liquidó apparet) nullius de- ncti corpus ſepiliendũ eſt, niſi pro anima eius prius oblato Miſſæ ›crificio. Si igitur corpus defũcti poſt veſperas deferatur ad Eccle- m, ibi inſepultum relinquendum eſt, vſque in diem ſequentem, tunc Miſſa prius pro anima celebrata, ſepeliendum. Si vero ali- ›ando contigerit, corpus defuncti matutino tẽpore, ante Miſſam ›ferri ad Eccleſiam, obſeruanda eſt rubrica de qua modo agitur. ›ic ordo non ſep liendi, niſi prius dicta Miſſa præſcribitur in ›ſtolali Mechlinienſi.

Plura de hac re vide, in Annotatione ſequente.

Pag. 116. *Deinde ſine interuallo incipiatur Miſſa.)* Sacrificij altaris ›o defunctis offerri ſoliti, meminit Tertullian. lib de corona mili- ›, Cyprian. epiſt. *66*. ad plebem & clerum Furnitanorum lib. 1. ›ſt. *9*. Auguſt. lib. de hæreſibus. hæreſi. *53*, lib. *9*. Confeſſ. ›p. 12. de verbis Apoſtoli ſer, *32*. to 5. de ciuit Dei lib. 20. cap. *9*. 6. de ſancta virginitate, cap. *45*. &c. Cõcilium Carthag. ca. *79*. ›nbroſ. Orat. de obitu Valentiniani. Diei anniuerſariæ meminit ›am Tertull. loc. citat. & in lib. de Monogamia, Nazianz. orat.

Cæſarium fratrem. Hieron. epiſt. *27*, Ambroſ. in orat de obitu Theodoſij. Vide Chryſ. homil. *3*. in epiſt. ad Philip. homil. *69*. a populum, & homil. *41*. in priorem ad Corinth.

Pag. *129*. *Finitis orationibus clauditur ſepulchrum*) Id eſt, præparen ſe Sacerdos & miniſtri ad claudendum ſepulchrum. Nam clauditur infra, pag. *132*.

Annotationes in Confirmationem puerorum.

De hoc Sacramento vide Act. 8. Auguſt. lib. *2*. contra litera Petiliani. cap. 104. lib. 5. de Baptiſmo contra Donatiſtas, cap, *19* & *20*. Tract. *6* in epiſt. Ioan. in pſal. *141*. &c. Concilium Elibertinum, can. *38* Laodicenum, can. *48*. Tarraconenſe, cap *6*. Cypriar epiſt. 70. ad Ianuarium, epiſt. ad Iubaianum. & lib. de Vnctione Chriſmatis, & aliis Sacramentis. Hieron. aduerſus Luciferianos Ambroſ, de his qui myſterijs initiantur, cap, *7*, lib, 1, de Spiritu Sancto, cap *6*. lib. *3*, de Sacramentis, cap. *2*. Dionyſium Areopagitam lib. de Eccleſiaſt Hierarch, cap. *2*, & 4. Origen. hom. *9*, in Leuit. cyrillum catach. *3*. &c.

Pag. 145. *Conſigno te N. ſigno crucis &c*) Cõcilium Florentinum in doctrina de Sacramentis. Vide *2*. Corinth. 1. v. 22. Epheſ. 4. v 30. Ambroſ. de his qui myſterijs initiantur cap. 7. & lib. 1. de Spiritu Sancto, cap. *6*.

Poſt conſignationem frontis ſacro Chriſmate, frons faſcia mũda, ob reuerentiam eiuſdem ſacri Chriſmatis, tegatur. Quam cõfirmati triduo geſtent. Vide plura hac de re, pag. *32*.

FINIS.

INDEX EORVM QVÆ IN HOC LIBRO CONTINENTVR.

Hæc sacra Institutio baptizandi, & alia quædam, sacramenta & ritus ecclesiasticos administrandi, antiqua, pia, ac Catholica est. Subiuncta quoque annotationes doctæ sunt & vtiles, Actum Duaci die 5. Iulij 1604.

Georgius Coluenerius. S. Theol. Licent. & Professor, ac librorũ in Academia Duacena, Visitator.

GIOVANNI PIETRO MAFFEI

Fuga Saeculi

1632

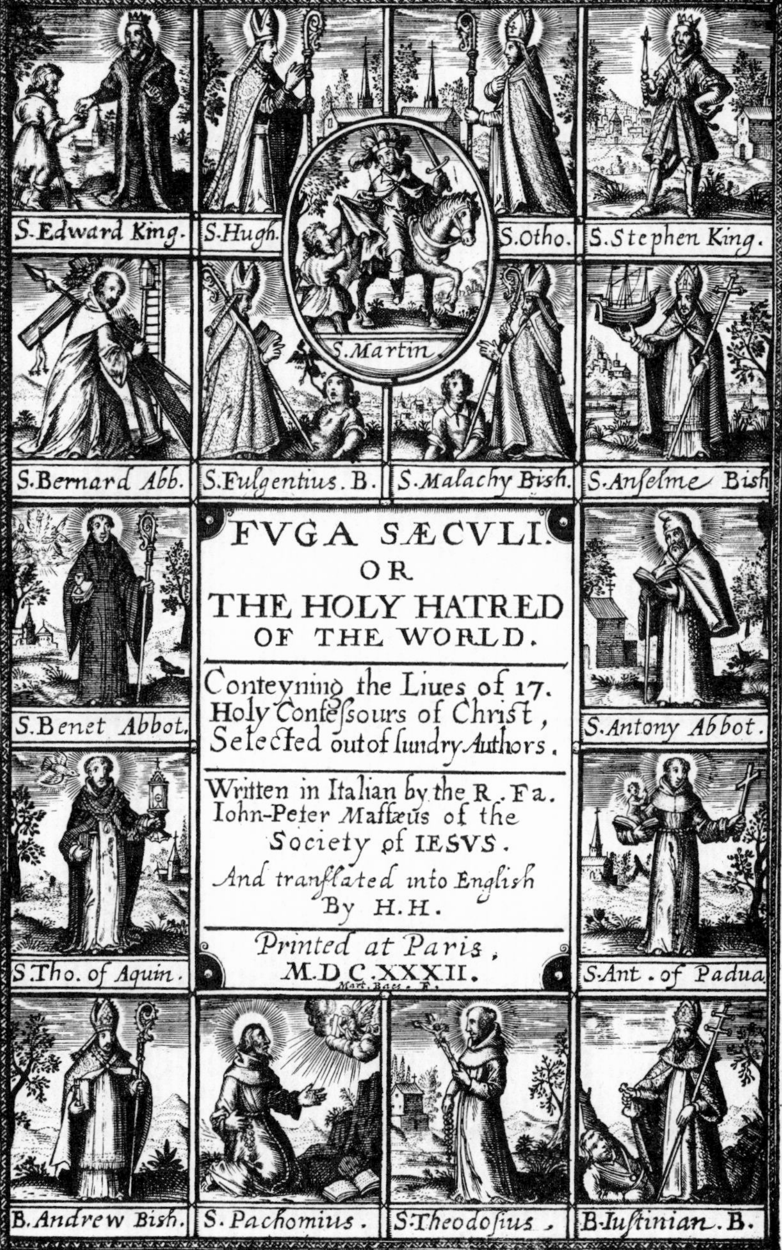

FVGA SÆCVLI. OR THE HOLY HATRED OF THE WORLD.

Conteyning the Liues of 17. Holy Confessours of Christ, Selected out of sundry Authors.

Written in Italian by the R. Fa. Iohn-Peter Maffæus of the Society of IESVS.

And translated into English By H. H.

Printed at Paris, M.D.C.XXXII.

TO THE NOBLE AND MOST VVORTHY KNIGHT SYR B. B.

SYR.

THE Emperour TIBERIVS vvas of opinion, by vvearing a *Laurell-vvreath* on his Brovv, no disastrous Lightning could touch his Person.

And I, as ſecure and confident, vnder the couert of your Noble Patronage, feare no malignant blaſt of Obloquie, or breath of thoſe, that shall ſeeke to ſoile the *Mirrour* of my ſincere *Intention*, in my louing Seruice to my *Countrey*. Which made me thus preſume, to erect your *Name*, as a *Laurell-branch*; that euery one beholding it, vvho knovves your excellent Dotes, and Faculties in this kind, may make more fauourable reflections on the Worke.

I forbeare to alleadge many *Motiues*, (as the manner is) vvhich I had for this dedication: It is inough, that your *VVorth* and *Merit* claymes it as due: This the *Tuſcan Genius* ſecondes; *Maffæus* himſelfe requeſts; my *Obligations* vrge; and *Neceſſity* importunes. Your free and Generous aſſent onely remaines. To obtaine vvhich, I appeale to your Noble *Diſpoſition*, and *Goodneſſe*, apt to communicate it ſelfe.

And therefore to go about to extort this *Fauour*, vvere iniurious to your Bounty, vvhich

vvhich flovves like a Torrent; and ouer-flovving al obſtacles that might deterre me, makes the paſſage cleare. So that I, vievving the BROOKE, like NARCISSVS (though I ſavv nothing before, but my *Unvvorthy-neſſe*) behold my ſelfe, as you haue enabled, and encouraged me, reſolute to publish theſe my ſmall *Labours*.

Vouchſafe then (SYR) to shrovvd them vnder the *Laurell* of your Protection: Whereby you shall patronize Holy, and Glorious CONFESSOVRS, and oblige Me further, to be

Your most deuoted

to commaund.

H. H.

THE AVTHOVR TO THE *PIOVS READER.*

*I*N *things vvhich at first sight are vvont to bee considered in any VVorke vvhatsoeuer, it seemes the* Intention *of the Authour, and* Trace, *or* Method *are the principall. VVhence I, to giue a breife accompt of eyther, say first;*

My End *in this vvorke to haue been, to make a choyce of* Liues, *not led so much in Solitude, as in Community; and of Examples also, not so miraculous, or stupendious, as vertuous, and (vvith diuine Grace) not vneasy to bee*

imitated.

imitated.

Next, in the manner of proceeding I haue taken lycence to cut of al superfluityes, to reduce scattered Narrations to the order of Tymes, *or* Kinds; *and finally to modify those passages, vvhich transferring the thoughts to things dishonest or hurtfull (as somtymes it happens) the chaster* Eares, *or more delicate* Consciences, *in some manner, come to be offended: But yet is all endeauoured in such sort: as the substance and truth of the Historyes remayne (vvhat possible) entire, sincere, and vncorrupted.*

Such in summe, my designe in this present vvriting hath beene: VVhich if, in so great an infinity of Bookes, it proue not to be superfluous or vnprofitable; the vvhole Glory therof shall be ovving to our Lord: *And vvhen the* Effect *likevvise, shall not ansvvere the* Desire, *at least the* Good-Will, *I trust, shall be had in reguard.*

THE

THE TRANSLATOVR TO THE *ENGLISH READER*.

COVRTEOVS READER,

Behold I put *Maffæus* into your Hands, no leſſe *Serious*, then *Delightfull*, *Pious* then *Elegant*, *Simple* then *Admirable*; whoſe *Pleaſure* yet takes not away the *Grauity*, whoſe *Quaintneſſe* the *Piety*, nor *Induſtry* the *Simplicity*; as being *Graue* without *Seuerity*, *Fluent* without *Superfluity*, *Terſe* without *Affectation*, and full of the *Ornament* he shuns.

And I preſent him to YOV, thus clad, and

reueſted

reuested in our English *VVeedes*, that he might now walke as familiar amongst VS, as in his natiue Vulgar he hath done: As properly *Ours*, as *Theirs* from whence he came. Since, besides that Examples and Liues of SAINTS are vniuersall, and cōmon to the whole Church, some of these are found to be of our *Nation*.

Wherein I suppose, that such as are acquainted with the *Genius* of his neater stile, will rather challenge me for attempting it at all; then wonder I should fall so short, if they but consider how hard it is, to frame a perfect *Copy*, of so rare and genuine a *Prototype*.

Yet take it, *Gentle Reader*, as it is, from him, who holds it a lesse ill the while to blush therat, then the glory of such *SAINTS* should be vnknowne amongst VS.

THE

THE PREFACE TO THE ENSVING TREATISE

Of the Holy Hatred of the VVorld.

MAN is a *Spheare*, his Soule th' *Intelligence*;
Grace is the *Sun* that ſends his light from hence:
Vertues the *Starres*, that gliſtring deck this frame
And with their rayes giue luſtre to the ſame;
Whoſe Lights ſtill fixt, which like th' immortall ſourſe
Maintaine a conſtant gyre, a ſettled courſe.
The Worlds Contempt, *Canopus* like, doth keepe
The higheſt point, moſt ſeuered from the deepe
And earthly Center: T'is the Starre that brought
The Eaſterne Sages to the Light they ſought;
Which through the Heau'ns as it his courſe did run,
Aurora-like forſhewd the following *Sunne*.
T'is that, which did th' *Iſaacian* ſquadrons garde,
And to the promis'd *Land* their way prepar'd;
And while we floate vpon theſe daungerous waues,
The *Cynoſura* that vs wandring ſaues.

THE PREFACE.

Within the Land, which that myſterious floud
Fattens with his blacke ſlime, and fruitfull mud,
The *Crocodile* (*Niles* Pirate) euer ſtriues
Of their delicious combes to ſpoile the hiues:
This to effect, he takes a thouſand guiles,
And ſummons all his ſlights, and all his wiles.
But vſe is made of that Antipathie
That is betweene the Saffron-floure, and hee;
Which planted round doth giue aſſur'd redreſſe,
And counter-mands his luſt, and greedineſſe.
This *Crocodile*, is mans inueterate Foe,
Th'Apoſtate Prince of darkneſſe, that doth goe
Euer about to ſpoile th'increaſe of Grace,
And in our ſouls Gods Image to deface.
Senſuall Delights, Pleaſures, Deſires to be
Great in the World, the Philters are that he
Doth vſe in this deſigne. The Worlds Diſdaine
The Moly is, that ſaues our ſoules from baine;
The Saffron-floure, that driues his force away,
And guards vs ſafe, that els might be his pray.
For if the Eye, cleare and vnblemiſhed,
Void of all preiudice, accuſtomed
In their owne colours obiects to deſcry,
To know Appearance from pure Verity,
Would take a right ſuruey of what's below,
The *Spheare* and *Center* of true Bliſſe to know;
And not (as thoſe Aſtronomers, who take
Great heights by Inſtruments vnequall) make
Vnpardonable errors: So the Senſe
Fore-taken, blinding the Intelligence
(Void of proportion) ſhould preſume to raigne
A Handmaid o're the Miſtreſſe; or to gaine
So great preheminence, as Iudge to be

Of

Of perfect Blisse, or true Felicitie:
Then as in Landskipp's, where we thinke appeare
Disioyned farre parts that indeed are neare,
Little things great: Or as that hellish art
By altering the *Medium*, doth impart
Chimera's to the Senses, and doth make
Th'astonisht Powers for Truth Impostures take:
We should discerne the glossed Alchimy
Of our allurements; and the vanity
Of worldly pleasures; and vndoubting know
Our ioyes are dreames, how euer faire in show.
 Wee are but In-mates heere, and entertain'd
As if no Denizens, or rather chayn'd
In golden fetters; When first Life began,
A darkesome prison clos'd vp wretched man:
Whence if we rightly come, we fall vpon
An ominous precipitation.
So witty's ruine, so importunate
Vpon mankind; so seemeth angry Fate
To enuy vs the least conceipt of ioy,
As all things doe conspire to our annoy.
The Elements, that so much disagree,
Band against vs, their common Enemie:
Yea, that which, void of substance, Essence takes
From that first motion which all motions makes,
Time, measure of our ioyes, is tedious growne,
And not by pleasures, but afflictions knowne;
Whome Tyrant-like we would deceiue, and bend
(Only to shun, what least we wish) to end:
Yet, as if Sorrowes we might not enioy,
Or as the Fates did enuy our annoy,
So as they would not grant vs Time for woe,
Our Time's contracted, as Tymes larger grow;

And their increaſe doth haſten to their waine,
Hopeleſſe to bring them to their ſpring againe.
For in the worlds firſt infancy, when man
Æquall wellnigh vnto the *Spheares*, began
His being, then was abſolute, and he
Enfranchized to Immortality:
But forfaiting this ſtate, though Death could claime
And challenge part in him; yet the ſtrong fraime,
And firme connexion of his parts, did cauſe
A laſting vnion, and a during pauſe.
Th'immortall *Starres*, and *Man* then ſeemd to ſtriue,
Ioint-tennants to the world, who ſhould ſuruiue.
Now *Time*, hath Time abridg'd, our Life's a breath.
Which ſcarcely drawne, is ſtopped ſtraight by death.
The world's in a Conſumption, not as then
We ſeeme mankind, nor the ſame ſonnes of men;
And ſeiz'd as with an *Hecticke*, ſeemes to dance
His ſickly motions, led with diſcordance.
Behold how thoſe, which as they moue, do giue
By ſympathie, to moue, to breath, to liue:
The golden *Spheares* are in their motions chang'd,
And from their former courſes ſeeme eſtrang'd.
The liuely Spring, the Summer we behold
Like thoſe weake children, who are borne of old
And ſap-leſſe Parents, quite degenerate,
Void of their ancient ſtrength, their vigorous ſtate.
In vaine we ſeeke the ſtations of the Sun,
And falſely thinke the wandring Planets run
Their wonted courſes: *Southward* ſtill they flye
And leaue our Clime ſtain'd with Impietie.
So when our Proto-martyrs Holy gore,
Guiltleſſe it ſelf, made guiltie *Verlam's* ſhore,
The ſiluer *Thames* recall'd his ancient floud,

And

And left the ſoile diſtain'd with ſacred bloud.
Diſtracted Nature, ſeemeth to haue loſt
Coherence, with a thouſand Monſters croſt,
A thouſand Prodigies; Proportion's gone,
Strength is decay'd, loſt is Connexion.
Sometimes ſtrang *Starres* affright th'amazed skie,
The ayre oft thunders, it not knowing why.
More ſtrange Coniunctions do the Heau'ns infeſt,
And bloudy *Comets* rayſe a worſer creſt.
Winter yields Flowers, the luſty *Ramme* that bore,
Through the ſalt-waues, young *Phryxus* to the ſhore.
The barren Earth oft ceaſeth to ſupply,
And leaues to yield his wonted fragrancie.
Summer is bare: The *Dogge* whome heat did vex,
With moiſture oftner doth the world perplexe.
The furious Winds are fiercer growne; and more,
The thundring billowes rend the conquered ſhore:
As when our Ile, from *Belgia's* fore-land rent,
Did yield her ſelfe to that proud Element.
So when the Chariot of the golden Sun
By the firſt cradle of the world did run;
In wandring from its path, did often ſtray,
And ignorant did leaue th'vntracked way:
Or with its proper weight depreſt, did take
A doubtfull courſe, and different times did make
Confuſedly the ſame; when Heate did cloy
The *Thracian* ſhafts, and Cold the Dogge annoy.
Strange ſignes are theſe, yet more then theſe, doth rage
Feare in our Harts that nothing can aſſwage;
Miſ-giuing minds foretell our ills, and ſhow
Th'vnſure condition of the world below,
Whoſe Loue is ſourſe of all theſe feares. Then kill
And ſacrifice the Cauſe of all this ill;

THE PREFACE.

This offring ſhall thee expiate, and giue
By death deſeru'd, deſerued power to liue.
O would our Soules vpon themſelues reflect,
And ſearch from whence Content they might expect;
Which mindfull of their birth, do ſcorne to flye
At other marke then faire Eternity!
Then ſhould wee ſee, how like the Towring Fyre
They would to Heau'n their home, their *Spheare*, aſpire
Which only is their Center. Heere below
Hope ſailes with Feare, and Ioyes with Sorrowes flow;
No true content is had. A tottring ſand
That fleeting yields, and leaues not where to ſtand
Is our ſhort life. Our pleaſures, like the gold
The *Alchymiſt* produceth, to behold
Beauteous inough, but by the powerfull flame
Straight turn'd to ſmoke, or matter whence it came.
Our Ioyes are dy'de with Oaker, euery ſhowre
Defaceth their falſe Luſtre. *Honours*, *Power*,
Are only vapours, which the growing day
Or hoater Sun diſſolues, and driues away.
Beauty's vnperfect, like that plenteous fry
Halfe fleſh, halfe mud, that on *Niles* bancks doth lye.
Riches a crazed Ship, vnſure defence
In need to thoſe that there put confidence.
Our *Knowledge* skilfull Ignorance; and Art
The plague *Prometheus* did to man impart
By his ſtolne fire, that makes our ſoules to fry
With feauers of fond Curioſitie.
All vnder Heau'n is vaine: *Wealth*, *Dignitie*,
Knowledge, and *Beauty*, *Principalitie*,
Are diſtant from the *Spheare* where *Ioy* doth moue;
Reſt dwells below them, *Happineſſe* aboue.
Then giue a little time, and ſee how heere

These

THE PREFACE.

These *Heröes* ſcorning what the world holds deere,
Did make a way to *Immortality*,
And by Contempt attain'd *Felicity*.
Heere ſhall you ſee no ſumptuous Houſes fraught
With Banquets, or with Viands dearely bought;
No coſtly Beds ſhining with *Tyrian* dye,
No Iewell faing'd for gliſtering brauerye,
No roomes replete with Muſickes charming ſound,
No Followers with eyes fixt on the ground:
But Woods and naked Rocks, and thereupon
Horrour expreſſ't. Heere baſe Refection;
Small time to ſleep allotted; Bodyes clad
In baſeſt rayment; Men in penance glad,
Delighted in their paynes, whome Life did tyre,
Whoſe Hope was Heau'n, and Death their cheif Deſire.
But yet no cruell *Furies* do perplexe
Their quiet reſt; no pining Cares do vexe
Or trouble their Content; nor Enuy clad
In faire appearance, euer made them ſad.
True Reſt, great Ioyes in their ſmall Cells reſide,
And perfect ſmiles from ſpotleſſe hearts do glide;
Whoſe ſoules remembring whence they came, contayne
Themſelues and Heau'n, and ſtriue it to regayne.
Then looſe thy ſelfe with theſe, with theſe to winne
That Heritage, which thou haſt loſt by Sinne.

THE

THE TABLE

OF THE LIVES.

S. MALA-

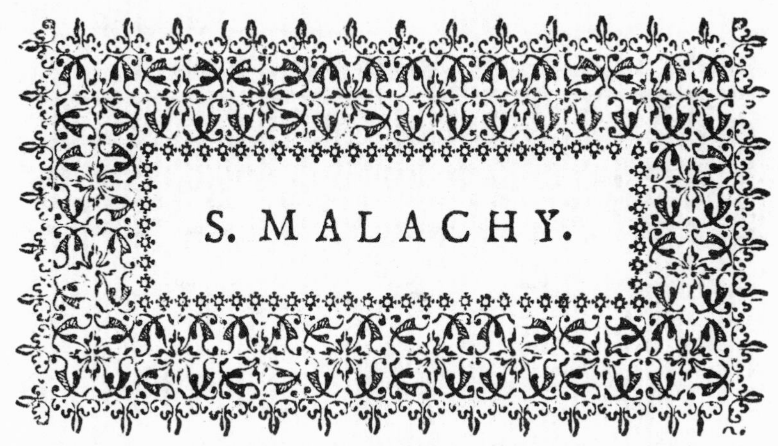

S. MALACHY.

THE ARGVMENT.

BOrne in the Land, ſurrounded with the mayne
Of the Vergiuian deepe, *S. MALACHY*
Appeares, and ſhewes vnpoliſht ſhells containe
Pearles often fraught with richeſt brauery.
We honour by our deeds, not Countries gaine,
And do our ſelues infect, vnſtaynd thereby,
And learne to note, how ere we riſe or fall,
We, and our *Soiles* are not reciprocall.
See how in tender yeares the world he leaues,
And from his childhood beares th'appointed croſſe:
Try'de with affliction, nothing Grace bereaues,
No paynes are hard, no worldly domage loſſe;
No falſe allurements mooue, no fraud deceyues
Him of his hopes, no Vanity doth toſſe
His conſtant ſoule, nor from his Hauen driue;
Where we, if like, ſhall like to him arriue.

THE LIFE OF S. MALACHY BISHOP OF IRELAND,

Written by *S. Bernard*.

Of his Birth, Minority, *and the first* Flower *of his Youth*. Chap. I.

SAINT *MALACHY*, borne in *Hybernia*, or as we call it, *Ireland*, in the Citty of *Ardmach*, was there through the particular fauour of the Diuine Clemency, bred and brought vp in such sort, as from the Natiue Barbarisme of the place, he drew no more then Fishes do from the brackish Seas. Whence it comes to be a thing most delightfull, that so vnciuill and rude a Nation, should seeme to yield vs a person of so gentle behauiour, & celestiall manners. He who deriues the hony from Stones, & fetches oyle from the hardest Rockes, hath moreouer wrought this wonder. True it is, the Parents of *S. Malachy* were both of noble Bloud, and of high Degree; and the Mother no lesse generous of Mynd then Lineage, was very solicitous to shew to the Child, as yet tender, the true way of Saluation,

Saluation, making a great deale more reckoning thereof, then of the ſwelling Literature of the world, and yet wanted not the Child a good towardnes for eyther of both profeſſions. In ſchoole he learned the Grāmer, at home the feare of God; & continually through his profit, did ſatisfy both Mother and Mayſter. Which thing ſhould not ſeeme to others to be any whit vntrue; he hauing through eſpeciall fauour from heauen, the lot to haue ſo good a Soule, which made him as well docible, as ſtrangely amiable and gracious.

From Mothers breaſt, inſteed of milke, he ſucked the waters of Wiſedome, and day by day, became more wiſe. More wiſe, ſhall we ſay, or more Holy? If I ſay, both the one and other, I ſhould not much repent me, becauſe I ſhould haue ſayd but truth. For manners he was graue, a child indeed yeares, but voyd of childiſh ſportfullnes: and howbeit, held in veneration and admiration of all, yet became he not thereby, as generally others do, haughty or inſolent, but rather quiet and ſubmiſſe with all meekenes. He was not impatient of gouernment; not ſtubborne to diſcipline; not dull for ſtudies; and finally not delighted with games, the proper and general affect of that age: ſo as in learning, which was competent for him, he out-ſtripe all his equalls of the ſame age: but in Goodnes of life and purchaſe of vertues, he excelled as many, as taught him; and that not only through the induſtry of his Mother, but euen alſo by the Vnction of the ſpirit; wherwith being interiourly ſolicited & puſhed on, he was neuer backward in diuine Exerciſes; as to retire himſelfe in ſolitude; to meditate the holy law of *Chriſt*; to make often prayer; to be temperate in dyet; to vanquiſh ſleep. And wheras from publique frequenting of Churches he was partly hindred through ſchoole, and partly kept backe through a certayne reſpectfull modeſty; yet forbare he not the leſſe, to lift vp his Mynd to the ſupernall Father, & to adore him euen likewiſe with exteriour geſtures, whereſoeuer in ſecret he could find occaſion thereunto: being at ſuch tymes very cautious and circumſpect to eſchew vayne glory, the moſt certaine poyſon of vertues.

There lyes not farre off from *Ardmach*, a village whither his Maiſter went often to walke, without other company, thē this beloued Diſciple. Now therfore on a tyme, while they were walking both together, *Malachy* obſeruing the Maiſter in a deep ſtudy with himſelf, making a ſtep (as he related afterwards) remayned ſomewhat behind, and on the ſuddayne lifting vp his innocent hands from the bow of his hart euer bent, sent forth enflamed Iaculatoryes to the Starres;& for not to be discouered, very slyly would he be putting himselfe agayne somewhat handsomely on the way: and with so pious a theft, would the blessed youth from tyme to tyme be deceiuing his Guide. It boots not heere to relate all the acts, which made his greener yeares very illustrious and admirable. My penne makes hast to much greater things. And yet neuerthelesse will I not seeme to let passe this one thing by the way, which in that tẽdernes of his, gaue matter, not only of a good, but of a soueraigne hope.

Being now arriued at last somwhat towards the end of the first arts, and thirsting after the grauer Sciences, being moued through the fame of a learned Doctour, he went his wayes with great diligence, though somewhat farre off, to be acquainted with him. But finding him at his entring into the howse very busy, scoring of the wall very impertinently with an awle, being disgusted with such a leuity, and immediately pulling backe his foote from thence, he had no list to reuisite him any more; so much (howbeit neuer so greedy of Learning he were) he preferred honesty before knowledge. In this sort then, he passed ouer his childish yeares, and yet in Youth reteyned he still, as it were, the same tenour of candour & purity; saue only that together with yeares, did Wisedome and grace, both with God and men alike increase in him: with this besides, that continually there beganne more high and sage reflections, and discourses to awake in his breast. For that the prudent youth beholding on the one side the malignity of the world, and on the other the quality of the Spirit which swayed within his mind; came more thẽ once to speake within himselfe in this sort.

My spirit is no whit secular; for what hath it to do therewith, since there is no more resemblance betweene them, then betweene night and day? Mine seemes, to proceed from God, nor am I ignorant of the gifts, which he hath vouchsafed me. From him, do I acknowledge the stole of innocency I enioy, with the flower of continency in me preserued hitherto. From him, that glory of myne so much securer, as it is more secret, consisting wholy in the testimony of the proper conscience. None of all which possessions can abide without much dãger vnder the Prince of this naughty world. Besides, I go carrying so great a treasure in an earthen vessell, and there is good reason to feare, least it come to take a knock, and be brokẽ, & the Oyle of gladnes within be vnhappily spilt. And how

is

is it possible not to take a knock among so many stones, & amidst so many rocks of this way, & life so full of turnings, windings, & rubs? And shall I seeme in a moment to be loosing of all these blessings of holy sweetenes, wherewith the Eternall Goodnes from the beginning hath preuented me? Rather I resolue to secure the same in the hand of him, who hath giuen it me, & my selfe likewise therewith; since also I am his, I will temporally loose my life for not to loose it eternally. And where may the same with my being, & all what I am, be in more safety, then in the right hand of the giuer? For who is more wary then he in keeping? who more potent in deffending, and more faythfull in restoring? He will keepe it safely; he wil restore it in his tyme. I shal not loose a iot of whatsoeuer I shall seeme to distribute in workes of piety. Perhaps moreouer, I may looke for a good returne. This magnificent Bancher, is wont to redouble with vsury, the things which he hath giuen of courtesy. Such were the thoughts of *S. Malachy*, and he really went about to execute the same, as knowing most cleerely, that good wils without good effects are of litle, or no profit.

How S. Malachy *submits himselfe to the discipline of* Imarius, *and is first made Deacon, and then Priest.* Chap. 2.

THERE was a holy man in *Ardmach, Imarius* by name, of a very austere life, and a most implacable chastiser of his proper flesh; he dwelt reclused in a Cell, neere the great Church, in performing there very hard penañce with continual prayer. To this man went *S. Malachy* to be instructed, and guided in a spirituall life, by him, though lyuing, yet voluntarily condemned to the graue. And though from a Child (as we said) he had God himselfe for Maister in the art of louing God, yet now more ancient, as a rude disciple, would he needs submit himselfe to the rule of a man. Heere now let those note well this point, who vndertake to teach the same which they haue not learned, and go gathering and multiplying Scholers without euer hauing been at schoole; blind guiders of the blind. And if *S. Malachyes* example suffice them not, yet let them marke what the *Apostle S. Paul* practised. For had not he, trow you receiued the Ghospell from Christ himselfe? And yet thought he it not amisse to cõmunicate the same with men, least his way & labors might prooue otherwise in vaine. Where *S. Paul* holds not himself secure, do I hold me lesse. And let him who vnderstands it otherwise, beware his security proue not presumption.

But returne we now to the fact of *S. Malachy*, whose fame being incontinently spread, all were astonished at such a nouelty; but yet all not discoursed alike thereof. Many through humane affect, were bitterly sory, that so delicate a youth, and of so good dispositiō should so of his owne choyce be obliged to so great sharpnes & austerity. Others attributing the same to ficklenes and youthfull heate disdaynefully blamed him, for putting himselfe vpō an enterprize, so farre beyond his forces. But they wrongfully layd the blame vpon him, while he could not be culpable of temerity, who so adhered to the counsayle of the Prophet, saying: *It is good for him, that shall carry the yoke, from his youth.* But such an act in *S. Malachy* seemed so strait a way, as had not been seene to be trod by others steps; nor vntill that tyme, had any Student of the same Academy euer entred in. So as he was faygne to be exercised a good while without a fellow of any ranke, sitting in silence and submission, all the while at the feete of *Imarius*, and refining his vnderstanding & will with entire Obedience, with perpetuall mortification, and with al those industries and arts, which easily conduct a soule, that is both feruent and meeke, to the top of Euangelicall perfection. It was not long neuertheles, that others being enflamed through his example, began to giue themselues to the selfe same Discipline they seemed to abhor so much the other day: In so much as where he was solitary at first, and the only sōne of his Father, very soone he came to be the eldest of many Brothers; but as he was more ancient in Cōuersation, so was he more sublime in Contēplation. Whence he seemed to the Archbishop *Celsus*, as likewise to *Imarius*, who by this tyme knew him well, to be worthy of Sacred *Deaconship*, & so they ordayned him.

From that tyme this new Leuit, seemed to buckle himselfe publiquely to all the workes of piety, but especially to those which are ordinarily held in most contempt with others. And with particular diligence would he attend to the Funerals & Exequies of the Poore deceased, whiles this Office to him seemed to be of no lesse humility, then humanity. And therin our *Toby* had the temptation of a wicked woman, or rather of the ancient Serpent, by her meanes, because a Sister of his, esteeming it a dishonour to her, that he should imploy himselfe in such affayres. What dost thou (would she say) thou foole as thou art? Let the dead go, and bury their dead. And with such sayings would she neuer cease to molest him euery day. But the foolish woman had her answere giuen her, very apt therunto: O wretch, you seeme to know well the Syllables of the sacred Sentence, but not a whit the sense therof. And so in this sort would he be cheerefully pursuing that Exercise, so gratefull to the eyes of the Diuine Goodnes. And for his perseuerance therein, his Superiours holding him moreouer to be worthy of *Priesthood*, without delay promoted him thereto, notwithstanding all the resistance which he could make. *S. Malachy* was found at that tyme, to be 25. yeares of age. In which two Ordinations, if the Decree of the *Canons* were not strictly obserued, which prescribes the 25. to the one, & the 30. yeare to the other, it may well be imputed, both to the zeale of the Ordaynant, and merits of the Ordayned. True it is, that as such anticipation of tyme in so eminent a subiect, is no way reprehensible; so for my part I would not seeme to counsaile the same to any other quality of persons. But yet the same was not inough to the iudicious Archbishop, who made him moreouer his Vicar in the preaching of the diuine Word, and in the Catechisme of that rude and sauage people. Nor was *S. Malachy* skant of his trauayle, but rather with feruour, accepted the same, as not willing to couer the talents he had, but to negotiate with them, according to the will of the *Highest*.

The labours and trauels of S. Malachy *in his functions, and how he goeth to* Malcus *Bishop of* Lesmor. Chap. 3.

BEhold how *S. Malachy* anon, with his mystical tooles, puts himselfe to delue vp stumps, to breake vp lands, to tread out pathwaies, to leuell banks, & with a Gyants hart to be at hād, now heere now there. He seemed to be a flame amidst the Forrests, & a hooke among naughty plants. In lieu of barbarous customes, he inserts Ecclesiasticall rites. All ranke superstitions (which were not few) all diabolicall charmes, & finally whatsoeuer heeretofore he iudged to be disordinate, indecent, or out of square, endured not long in his sight, but as fruite with the hayle, or as dust with winds. So before the face of this holy Reformer, abuses and vices were quite defeated or dispersed. But as on euery side he endeauoured to set down Lawes & Rules full of iustice and honesty, yet laboured he still with particular care to introduce the Apostolicall Constitutions, the approued

ued Councells, and aboue all the Traditions and Obseruances of the holy *Roman Church*. And hence it grew, that whereas at first, not so much as in the principall Cittyes of *Ireland*, were Diuine Offices celebrated with solemne harmony; now, not only in Cittyes, but in Townes and Villages also, were sung the Masses, and Canonicall howers, no lesse then in the rest of Christianity. Wherto it helped not a little, that *S. Malachy* from a youth had attended to his part in Musique. But that which more imports, he renewed the vse of the Sacraments, and in particular of *Confession, Confirmation*, and of *Matrimony*, things that eyther out of malice, or ignorance, had bene heeretofore as it were, wholy forgotten, and dismissed.

Amidst these labours and trauailes, and many others, which for breuity sake are let passe; we may belieue for certayne, this Seruant of *Christ*, had receiued great gusts and consolations from heauen: and yet neuerthelesse, being as he was of a most delicate Conscience, & thinking very lowly of himselfe, & for that to him it seemed he had neyther practice nor Learning sufficient for so high employments; those same delights came to be much watered, with a continuall feare which he had, least through his imprudence any opinions or customes might be introduced in some points discordant to the Custome of Catholique Institutes. So as, to get out of these anxietyes, for his better instruction, he was resolued, with the approbation of the *Prelats*, to transferre himselfe for a tyme to *Malcus* Bishop of *Lesmor*, being a famous Citty of *Momonia*, in the Southerne part of *Ireland*. Which *Malcus*, being now surcharged with yeares, as well for profoundnes of wisedome, as for singular sanctity of life, & likewise for the gift of Myracles which he had; was held in those Regions, as an Oracle of Truth, and a common refuge of the afflicted. *S. Malachy* being courteously receiued by this good old man, while he carefully ministers to him, and likewise with diligence goes on obseruing the things appertayning to diuine Seruice, & to the cure of Soules, through an vnlook't for accident, was a noble field laid open to him to exercise *Charity*.

How Cormacus *King of* Momonia *repayres to* Celsus; *and being put out of his Kingdome, is by friendly succours restored againe.* Chap. 4.

IRELAND in those tymes (as it likewise ought to be at this present) was deuided into certayne little kingdomes, and by conse-

consequence subiect to warres, seditions, and tumults. Now there being a great discord risen betweene *Cormacus* King of *Momonia*, & a wicked brother of his; the King being vanquished in battayle, and thurst out of his seate, made his recourse in persõ to the Bishop *Malcus*, to be succoured by him; not for recouering his scepter, but rather to saue his soule, as being timourous of him, who takes away the spirit of Princes, & as very much alienated from sheding of Christian bloud for temporall interests. At the newes of such a Ghest, did *Malcus* make preparation to receiue him with due honour: but he would not consent thereto, affirming his intention was to liue with him in a priuate and quiet manner; and laying aside all memory of royall pompes, to betake himselfe to the discipline, and fare of the other *Canonists*. *Malcus*, at such a resolution by how much more astonished, accepting the offer of a contrite hart, assigned to the King a little howse to lodge in, *S. Malachy* for his Maister, with bread and water for his sustenance. Nor did the *Prince* himselfe desire hence forth any cheere or delicates; remayning in a place of all other sweetenes most satisfied with the incorruptible gusts and celestial viãds ministred him by *S. Malachy*. Through which, notwithstanding remayning more mollifyed, he rightly bewayled his sinnes, and extinguished the incentiues of the flesh, with baths of the coldest water, with *David*, crying to our Lord: *Behold my basenes and my misery, & pardon me all my offences.* Nor were the *Soueraigne Iudges* eares found deafe to such a prayer; but rather heard he the supplication made, not only in the sense he vttered it, wholy spirituall and internall; but euen likewise (conformable to his infinite Goodnes) in the materiall and extrinsecall. And as he reserues not all sentences to the *Tribunall* there, he was pleased to succour likewise in this life, the depressed innocency of *Cormacus*, by exciting the spirit of a certayne King neere vnto *Momonia* into so great an indignation for the iniustice offered, as that cõming in post to the Cell of the poore Penitent, he laboured to encourage him to a generous returne, in setting the goodnes of the cause before him, the perfidiousnes of the Rebels, the fauourable right hand of the *Highest*; & this, for the more efficacy with feruent exhortations, mingled with large promises. With engines thus addressed, he sought to stirre vp & prouoke that afflicted *Prince*, but perceiuing the obiects of Soueraignity, and motiues of selfe-loue, were not of force inough to preuayle with him, he turned himselfe with dexterity, to those of Christian piety, and the publique weale, most liuely representing to him the miserable oppressiõ of his subiects, the insolencies and iniuryes of the intruding Tyrant, and the obligation which a lawfull and naturall Lord hath to deliuer, to his power, his vassals from so great afflictions and miseryes. In which point the friendly King dilated himselfe with greater vehemency then before, as hoping sure with such a battery at last to make the mynd of *Cormacus* to render vp its hold.

But finding him to be firme notwithstanding all this, in his determinatiõ, & more fixed then euer; at last, as to a sacred Anker, he made his repayre to *Malcus* the Bishop, and to *S. Malachy:* who both being voluntarily enclined therto, as to be the greater glory of God, without much difficulty was he won to their opinion. In such sort as *Cormacus* enforced through the authority and commaund of both the one and other, did finally accept the humanity & promptnes of his Neighbour, and with his ayde, and much more through his presence *Who can do all*, the impious and wicked Intruder was put to flight, and he not without the infinite ioy of the people, was installed agayne into his Royall throne; and from that tyme euer after did he loue and respect *S. Malachy*. Who after he had for some tyme, not without notable emprouement, enioyed the familiarity and discourses of *Malcus*, being by Letters and Messages recalled by *Celsus*, and *Imarius* (who could no longer endure his absence) he accordingly made his returne backe into his Countrey.

How S. Malachy *had a vision, and deliuers his sisters soule from Purgatory: with the noble resolution of his Vncle, in surrending vp an Abbay to* S. Malachy. Chap. 5.

IN the meane tyme his Sister was departed this life, of whome we made some mention aboue. Concerning her, it behooues vs not to passe ouer in silence a Vision, which the Man of God had. Because that although while she liued in flesh, he abhorred her behauiour, in such sort, as that after some yeares, he made a vow not to see her any more: yet now she being quit of body, he himselfe remayned discharged of the vow: and beganne to reuisit her in spirit, whome he had no will to see euer any more aliue. For so much as on a night, it seemed to him in sleepe, that he was aduertised by a Man in hast, that his Sister attended without, in the Churchyard in a browne habit, without hauing tasted any thing for these thirty dayes

dayes together. At which voyce, now *S. Malachy* being awaked, he presently vnderstood, what manner of famine tormented her: and exactly casting vp the tyme, he found it had been iust thirty dayes, since he had said Masse for her. And in regard the Seruant of *Christ* loued the soule, as much as he hated the imperfections of his Sister, without delay he returned to his suffrages so intermitted. Nor was it long ere the dead Woman appeared to him, vpon the threshall of the Church (but yet bard from entring in) and apparelled in black. But her Brother perseuering still in assisting her without euer omitting any morning, wherein some Sacrifice was not offered vp for her, he espyed her very soon in a grayish gowne, within the Church indeed, but not admitted as yet to the Aultar. In summe, he ceased not to celebrate for such intention, vntill finally she appeared to him, not only within the Church, but euen likewise neare to the Aultar in a white garment, amidst a most happy troupe of blessed Spirits, who in like manner hauing now finished the purgatiue paynes, were noted with the same candour. Whence cleerely appeares, how great is the valew and force of the *Sacred Masse*, to the cancelling of sinnes, to vanquish the aduerse powers, and to lead into Heauen, the Creatures taken out of the earth, and mire, or rather from the mouth of *Hell* it selfe. *S. Malachy* tooke exceeding contentment at so certayne a Deliuery of his Sister, and felt no lesse ioy in himselfe for the pious and magnanimous resolution of an Vncle of his. The which, to the end it may the better be vnderstoood, & pōdered, this it was.

We must vnderstand, that in a place of those parts, called *Benchor*, was anciently founded a Monastery, by a certayne holy Abbot, called *Congellus*, with so prosperous increase, as well of meanes, as of subiects, as that from thence, as from a fruitefull *Metropolis* were sent, as it were, infinite Colonies into diuers regions. And it is a constant rumour, that one child only of that Blessed *Congregation*, called *Siluanus*, had planted alone in diuers countryes, full a hundred Conuents. From thence came also *S. Columbanus* into *France*, and after into *Italy*, and among other Monasteryes erected that of *Luxonium*, so numerous, and frequent, as that the Quires succeeding by turnes, there was no intermission had from diuine Offices, perpetually night, or day. But that of *Benchor*, as the origin and fountayne of all, retayned the chiefe dignity, vntill such tyme, as through the fury of the outragious Free-booters, it was wholy deſtroyed, yet withall enriched with a great number of venerable *Reliques*: ſince, beſids ſo many other bodyes of Religious Men, who there repoſed in peace, there were by the ſame Free-booters, in one day only, martyred and ſlayne nyne hundred. With ſo cruell a deſtruction, that moſt noble Seminary though quite extinct, yet the inhabitants notwithſtanding, ceaſed not ſucceſſiuely, to create by a certayne forme, a Secular *Abbot*, who without any thought of Religion, attended only to the gathering vp of rents, and conuerting them ſacrilegiouſly to his proper vſes.

In this tyme now, *S. Malachy* had an Vncle (of whome we ſpake before) who had this rich Abbay in his hands: who eyther prickt with a Synderiſis, or ſting of conſcience, or moued with the Examples and Exhortations of his wiſe Nephew, determined while he had ſpace for holeſome pennance, not only to quit his hands of ſuch adminiſtration, but to renounce the world outright, and to apply that huge benefice, together with his perſon to diuine worſhip, and to the inſtitutes of *S. Malachy*; who notwithſtanding he were vnder the direction of *Imarius* had now begunne to haue many imitatours and followers. The man of God being glad of ſuch a Vocation, did voluntarily accept of the care of his Vncle, and the plot, for ſome reſtauration of the building. But as one tenacious of the pouerty of Chriſt, would by no meanes admit of the poſſeſſions, ſuffering the people to depute another to ſuch affayres. The which afterwards (as we ſhall ſee in its place) repayed the beneficence of the diuine man, with abominable ingratitude. The renuntiation being made in this ſort, and the poſſeſſion taken of the holy place, *S. Malachy* by commiſſion of *Imarius* went thither with ten brothers, and ſome Carpenters, and immediately put himſelfe to worke. Nor was it long, ere that, in approbation as it were of the enterprize, there happened vpon the fact, a notable wonder.

S. Malachy *workes a miracle, and is made Rectour of the forſayd Abbay: with one, or two miracles beſids.* Chap. 6.

ON a day *S. Malachy*, for the encouragement of others, was labouring with his proper hands, & with great diligence hewing of certayne tymber. Now while he ſtood with the axe ſuſpended in the ayre, as ready to giue the ſtroke; behold one of the workemen, improuidently putting himſelfe betweene the arme of *S.*

Ma-

Malachy, and the axe, receyued the whole blow vpon the very ridge of the backe, which should haue fallen plumpe vpon the designed subiect, whē presently, being depriued of his senses, he fell downe for dead. At the sight wherof euery one came running in with pittyfull cryes. The wound was searched, and the shirt was found to be slit from the collar to the reynes, but the flesh wholy entire, and not hurt, except, that only the vpper skinne was only touched so lightly, as the marke thereof could hardly be discerned; so as the labourer arose suddaynely very ioyfull and lusty, with so much the more gladnes of the standers by, as more probably it hence was cōcluded, that their trauayles and paynes, as we sayd, were gratefull and acceptable to the Diuine Goodnes. Whereupon with fresh vigour they set thēselues to worke agayne. So as in few dayes was the Oratory finished with polished timber, & firme couplings, a worke for those swaynes and people, very gracious. And this was the beginning of the miracles of *S. Malachy*; & from that tyme began they to attend afresh to diuine Offices with like piety, though not with equall number of persons.

There *S. Malachy* himselfe was *Rectour* a good while, through commaundent of *Imarius*. Who as he was of degree aboue others, so likewise in his deportments was he a liuing Rule, & bright glasse, and as a booke layd open to those Clerks, for as much as in all his proceedings, there were true precepts of Religious cōuersation to be read. And he not only, in cōmon obseruance, seemed to go alwaies before that little flocke, in sanctity & iustice in the sight of God; but would moreouer be doing particuler pennances, and other acts of Perfection, which no man was able to equall. Which things the common Aduersary, not being able to brooke, put into the hart of a familiar friend there about, lying sick, (whose name was *Malcus*) that *S. Malachy* cōming in to him, as he was wont to visit him, he should suddaynely with a knife giue him his death. The good Father, being aware therof, (the sick man not being able to keep it in silence) betaking himselfe to the armes of prayer did notwithstanding freely present himselfe before him, and with the Signe of the *Crosse*, on a sudden banished the malady frō his body, & the diabolicall thought from his mynd. This man was the naturall brother of *Christianus*, *Abbot* of *Mellifont*. He was conuerted to our Lord vpon so great a benefit, and with the habit tooke vpon him new behauiour: & at this day do both liue a great deale more vnited in spirit then bloud.

In the selfe same place he restored to health, a certayne Cleарke, named *Michael*, afflicted with a most grieuous dissentery, and despaired of Phisitiās, with the only sending him frō his table a litle of his portion. This *Michael* fell afterwards into another dangerous malady, and the seruant of Christ cured him anone, not only in his limmes, but in his mind also; & he in like manner for feare of worse, did enter into Religion, and is now (as I vnderstand) abiding in *Scotland*, Superiour of the Monastery, which *S. Malachy* foūded lately in those parts.

S. Malachy *is made Bishop of* Conerthen. *His labours there, and the fruit which he wrought in that Diocesse.* Chap. 7.

BY such actions as these, the fame and family of this great *Abbot* increased euery day; so as the Church of *Conerthen*, not farre frō *Benchor*, hauing beene now a long tyme vacant, those to whome belonged the Election of the Bishop, resolued vpon the person of *S. Malachy*; nor did any thing hinder the expedition, but the resistāce only of the Elect himselfe. Although afterwards, at last, he was cōmanded by *Celsus* and *Imarius* his lawfull Superiours, to yield & affoard his Consent, being as then of the age of about some 30. yeares. When after the solemne Consecration, being led into the Citty, he suddaynly applyed himselfe to exercise of his pastorall Office, with such ardour of spirit, as was requisite for so important a cure.

But scarce had he begunne the gouernement, when he saw himself doubtles to be there not destined for the rule of men, but, setting *Baptisme* asyde, very properly of beasts. In no place had he euer yet noted a people of so ill a breeding; of so detestable superstitions; of so stiffe a hart to Faith-wards; so vncapable to law; so vntoward to good institutes; nor finally of so foule and dishonest conuersatiō. They were Christians by name, in life Pagans. There was no vse of Tithes, or tendring the first fruites, nor of Confession, or demaunding penances; nor likewise who to demaund them of, so rare were Priests in those parts; and those that were to be had, so negligent & careles, as in Churches was no preaching, or diuine Office sung. In this Forrest now of sauadge beasts, what course should this Champion of *Christ* take? Of force must he eyther shamfully retire himselfe, or els combate with daunger. But he as a good Souldyer & good Pastour withall, determined to stand fast, and not to budge a foote,

foote, as ready to giue vp his life, for his flock, when neede should require the same.

And howbeit, it might wel be sayd, they were not sheepe, but so many wolues; yet stood the couragious Keeper amidst the wolues, seeking by all wayes and remedyes, from wolues to render thē as Sheepe. So as he ceased not feruently to admonish al in publike & with teares to reprehend euery one in priuate; heere to vse sweetnes, there to deale with sharpenes. And such like meanes would he continually be vsing, to draw them out of the snares of the deuil, wherewith they were so fast entangled. And if these his pious endeauours fayled, he would seeme to recurre to Prayer; and accompany his Deuotions with profoūd humility of hart, & propitiatory afflictions of body. How many nights passed he ouer without sleepe, and in making supplication for them? How often in person, went he in the Citty vp and downe a seeking of the fugitiues, and constrayning them with sweete violence to appeare in the Church? Nor was the faythfull Steward of *Christ* lesse anxious for the soules, which were scattered through the Countrey, hastning now heere, now there, with that holy troupe of Conuictours, neuer frō his side. He went, and dealt among those spightfull & thankelesse people, whole measures of corne, which some reaped in such aboundance, that at last they became fit to be layd vp in Gods barne. And let no man thinke, he vsed to ride in any of these iourneys: for lo, he walked continually a foote; shewing himselfe euen in this poynt, to be an Apostolicall Person. Nor is there a tongue able to expresse, what this Father, tender of such cruell and wicked Children, hath suffered in so frequent Pilgrimages, and Episcopall visits. The tribulations, affronts, and iniuryes, which he susteyned cannot fully be related. How often through their faults, was he like to perish for hūger, and thirst? How often afflicted with cold, and nakednes? & with a thousand other incommodityes? And yet still, with the Enemyes of peace, was he pacificall, and still importuned them in season & out of season, to amend their wicked liues. For curses, he afforded blessings: being strookē, he would ward himselfe with the buckler of Patience: being scorned and made a laughing stocke, he prayed more instantly to God for them: and perseuering after this manner so long in knocking at the gate of the *Diuine Mercy*, at last, it was set open to him, & through the power of the *Omnipotent*, the stones were mollifyed, barbarisme mitigated, and crabbed minds began to

mellow,

mellow, and by little and little to acquaynt themſelues with things appertayning to their ſaluatiō, & to admit of diſcipline & precepts. And in ſumme, through diuine Grace, they were ſnatched out, as it were, frō the clawes of the rauenous and greedy deuourer, in whoſe hands they had alwayes beene; out of whoſe diabolicall cuſtody being ſet free, they made ſo notable a change, as at this day to thoſe people, theſe words ſuite well, which God ſeemed to vtter by *Eſay* the *Prophet: The people which heeretofore were none of mine, are now become my people.*

The Citty of Conerthen *is deſtroyed, and* S. Malachy *with his, repayre to* Cormacus. *The Church of* Ardmach *fell into Seculars. With the Reſolution of* Celſus *therupon.* Chap. 8.

AFTER a certayne number of yeares now paſſed ouer, for better purging of ſinnes, ſucceeded an incurſion vpon them, by the barbarous Inhabitants of the *North,* when a great part of the Citty of *Conerthen* was deſtroied: in ſo much as *S. Malachy,* with his *Religious,* who were about an hundred and twenty, was conſtrayned to go his wayes out of that Citty. But yet his departure frō thence, proued not altogeather vnprofitable, becauſe that repairing himſelf into the kingdome of *Momonia* (whereof we haue ſpoken before) hee erected there a goodly Monaſtery, at the coſt of *Cormacus,* being very mindfull of the good Offices, and Charity affoarded him, in tyme of his baniſhment. So as beſides his cōming in perſō to meete and receaue him, and his conuerſing with him afterwards, & with the reſt of his Company, with much familiarity & loue, he concurred moreouer, as we ſaid, very royally to the Fabrick Whereby in ſhort tyme it was fully accompliſhed, and wonderfully increaſed in annuall rents, and moueables; and that which is yet more to be eſteemed, in ſubiects. Who, to the end, they might walke with the better will, by the ſtrait and difficult way, the Bleſſed Man ceaſed not, being a Biſhop, and a Maiſter as he was, as if but then he had newly become a Nouice, to be the firſt in obſeruing the Traditions and Rules.

He ſerued in his turne, now in the Kitchin, now in the Refectory. In the Antiphons, Leſſons, Ceremonyes, or labours of the Quire, he would haue no manner of priuiledge at all, performing alwayes his part, as one of the leaſt. Heere likewiſe he ſhewed himſelfe

selfe to be so ardent a louer of voluntary *Pouerty*, as in courting and seruing the same, among all the Riuals there was none could seeme to come any whit neare him. And howbeit for the maintenance of the place, he iudged it fit to admit of rēts in cōmon; he was yet notwithstanding very vigilant, least the publique, through human frailty, might degenerate into priuate. Amidst such cares as these, whilest in holy peace he aduaunceth by all meanes, the profit of his, & the glory of God, for his greater probation, there came an assault vpon him, no lesse slyly, then vnlooked for. Which truly the better to vnderstād, it shall be needfull for vs to fetch the narration a prety way off.

The Church of *Ardmach*, as it is the Mother of the other Churches of *Ireland*, so is it more illustrious and farre more reuerenced, then all. Besides that, heere was the residence of *S. Patrick*, and the sacred bones heere left of that first *Apostle*, & first *Father* of all those Nations. Whose fame & esteeme with great reason, is heere so famous, that euen his Successours, be what they will, do come to be feared and obeyed, not only of the inferiour, & the rest of the Clergy, but euen likewise of any Baron, Lord, or Peere of the Iland. But as all the affayres of mortal mē, seeme euer to incline to the worse, there had entred in now a good while since, a very execrable abuse; to retayne (forsooth) the Pastorall Chayre in a certayne family: In so much as from one Vsurper passing to another, it had there so endured now for fifteene continuall generations, and vnder a Diabolicall tytle of imaginary Prescription, they were so rooted in the wicked possession, as that when there were found to be no Clerks in the family, they would be substituting the marryed: and of the same condition, before *Celsus*, there had beene to the number of eight, men though learned for the most, yet as I sayd, without sacred Orders. And hence came the dissolution of the whole Christianity with the spirituall ruine and temporall likewise of all *Ireland*, in creating and changing heere & there Bishops, at euery capriccio of the wicked Metropolitan: yea a thing which was neuer heard of, in making in one Bishopricke only, for euery people, as it were, an infamous Bishop, with a hellish multiplication of most vnworthy administratours.

Now then to take away so pernicious a scandall, it pleased the Diuine Maiesty, the Miter should lastly light on the head of *Celsus*; Who though of the same stocke, yet notwithstanding he being

prickt

prickt with the feare of God, as soone as through a mortall infirmity he perceiued the end of his dayes to approach, he determined to put in execution the designe, which he had a pretty while before, that is, to cut off indeed, that infenall line of inheritance, by freely yielding vp the Archbishopricke into the hands of *S. Malachy*, whose reputation and credit he knew well to be very sufficient in this case, to purchase to himselfe the fauour of the Citty, and to oppose himselfe as a firme wall to the ambition and greedines of Tyrants.

To which effect, as it were by way of Testament, he declared his mynd to be, that the Sea being vacant, by all meanes the holy Bishop *Malachy* should be placed therein, since there was not to be found a person, more deseruing it then he. To which purpose he most earnestly desired that the *Primacy* might be (after his decease) transferred vpon him. For the better manifestation of his ardent desire, he not only declared this intent *viua voce*, to the standers by, but euen likewise did intimate and recommend the same by letters and precepts, on the behalfe of *S. Patricke* to such as were absent, and especially to personages of quality; and very particulerly to both the Kings of the vpper and lower *Momonia*. These through diuine inspiration were the thoughts of *Celsus*: and they had a glad successe, though not so easy, nor yet so speedy as he would haue wished.

S. Malachy *is elected Bishop.* Mauritius *holds still possession, whilst* S. Malachy *refusing the charge, is enforced by* Malcus, *and the Popes Legate to accept it.* Chap. 9.

THE occasion of the delay, was, for that *Celsus* departing this life, & the Electours being come to the Diet, the greater & better number of suffrages, without controuersy elected *S. Malachy*: and the rest of the voices were for a certaine Cousen of *Celsus*, called *Mauritius*. This man through his presence and power ouer-swaying quite all iustice and reason, was temerariously planted in the Archiepiscopall Throne, to the infinite griefe of all good men, and especially of *Malcus* the Bishop (euen now so extolled by vs) and of the Bishop *Gilbert*, Legate of the Apostolike Sea, for all the Kingdomes of *Ireland*. These two great Prelates, with many others of ech quality, made great instance, and offered whatsoeuer they were worth to *S. Malachy*, not to refuse to enter into *Ardmach*, and

and to take vpon him the spirituall gouernment thereof, according to the determination of *Celsus*. But the humble seruant of Christ, who esteemed euery climing to be his owne precipice; stood very stiffe in refusing the interprize, while he thoght he had a good pretext for the same, through the perill of seditions and tumults, that might happen to arise thereupon. With such delayes were now three yeares already passed, when the two zealous Bishops aboue mentioned, being not longer able to endure the adultery of the prime Church of *Ireland*, and the dishonour of *Christ*, assembling anew the Clergy & Princes, & with common consent made their recourse to *S. Malachy*, as prest to constrayne him with mayne force, in case he should seeme to perseuer in the negatiue.

But the Friend of quietnes still shewed himselfe to be more backward, alleadging the difficulties of the busines, the multitude, the power, the couetousnes of the Aduersaryes; that he had not conrage inough to stand in contention with the meanest fellow, and much lesse with so many, and such as those, and for the space of 200. yeares so rooted in the Sanctuary, whence how should he euer be able to roote them out, they being especially his Ancestours in possession? Nor was it worth the while, that for his occasion should follow manslaughters, and the earth by dyed with human bloud. And he finally obiected the cõiunction he had already made with another lawfull Spouse, from whome he saw no reason how he could disunite himselfe. With such like words and defences, the dexterous Souldiour went skirmishing in the continuall velitations and assaults of them that loued him so much. But his Friends notwithstanding all this, now afresh pressed him hard, and much more those that were of greater authority, to accept of the Archiepiscopall gouernment. Which he agayne denying, they threatned him with open Excommunication; for now they would not admit of any excuse. Whereupon he made them this finall Reply: You draw me violently to my ruyne (sayd the *holy Man*) and I will follow, whilst it seemes to me, I shall heerby gayne the glorious Crowne of Martyrdome. But if no persuasions will content you, let vs make a bargayne first, ere I enter into the field: That if it shall please God (according to your desire) to put some order in affayres, and to take out of impious hands the dominion vsurpatiously possest, there may be some other sufficient Rectour immediatly substituted into the dignity, that you now go about to put vpon me:

and that I be licenced to returne agayne to my present Spouse, and to my most beloued *Pouerty*.

This was the last and most resolute answere of *S. Malachy*. Whereby very cleerely may be seene a great purity conioyned with an equall Fortitude; since on the one side without simulation he fled honour; and for iustice sake on the other, he feared not death.

In summe, by no meanes for prayers or threats, would he seeme to yield his assent thereto, vntill such tyme as promise and firme word was giuen him, vpon the conditions propounded. Assoone as he was in security therof, he finally accommodated himselfe to assume the charge; & so much the rather, as besides the vnanimous, and perseuering instances of such like personages, it seemed to him he had yet some other manifest signes of the diuine will: whereof one is worthy of ponderation, and very considerable. There appeared to him (euen about the sicknes of *Celsus*, while he was then a farre off, and knew nothing thereof) a woman of a tall stature, and of a graue aspect, who being demaunded by him, who she was, made him answere, *she was the Wife of Celsus*, and without more ado, putting the staffe of gouernment into his hand, she suddaynely vanished. And within a few dayes after, while *Celsus* now drew neere to his death, he really sent him indeed in signe of Succession, a rod euen iust of the figure of the same Fantastique one. The memory whereof, and the correspondency of the tymes, was a matter of much moment in the mynd of *S. Malachy*, and iustly made him feare, least standing out longer, in such an occasion, he might seeme apparently to wrastle with God himselfe. He accepted then the charge; but yet without euer entring into the Citty, whiles the intruder liued; and the same he did, for not to giue on his part any manner of perturbation, by which otherwise they might hap to loose their liues, to whome he was rather come to affoard the same. So as for the space of two yeares, (for so long that ambitious man escaped) did *S. Malachy* attend to exercise the office, abroad through the Prouince.

Mauritius *being dead*, Nigrettus *succeeded. A Diet is called to install* S. Malachy: *The opposers are defeated, and stroken by the hand of God.* Chap. 10.

M*Auritius* being now dead, another of that dãnable race, called *Nigrettus*, or *Nigerrimus* rather, with the like impudency, steps anon to the sterne; while the malicious Predecessour, to adde sinne to sinne, had a prety while before, wrought notable practices, to haue him first for heyre in the world, and after his Companion and follower into Hell. The rumour and disdayne of this great audaciousnes being spread through all parts, a new Diet was called, to install at last the good *S. Malachy* into the degree, now for so many yeares, and that for so many reasons, due vnto him. But behold how the Sinagogue of the malicious Hel-hounds, opposeth against him. One of the Children of *Belial*, being a notable fauourer of *Nigrettus*, and very prompt and potent to euill, as he knew the place where the States were to assemble themselues, with a good number of Ruffians, layd himselfe in ambush in the next hill, with a full deliberation, when the Councell should be set, by treacheryes to come forth suddaynely, and to rush in vpon them without fayle, but aboue all to take away *S. Malachyes* life; and for the lesse dãger of reuenge likewise to kil one of the two Kings, who was there also to meete. And now stood matters in a readynes, the Conspiratours in wayte for effusion of bloud, and the Good men vpon the point of going to the shambles; when through the diuine Benignity, the innocent *S. Malachy* opportunely had intelligence of the cruell plot & without making a noise, or putting his people into a hurly-burly did no more but enter into the Church, and lifting vp his hands, craue succour of the Omnipotent, whose prayer was easily heard, & tooke effect accordingly.

For behold on a sudden the heauens to be couered, the ayre ouer darkened, flashes of lightning to breake forth, cracks of thunder, impetuous stormes, and hideous tempests to arise, the day of wrath and extreme iudgment to be represented to mortals. And to the end all men might discerne how forcible the prayer of *S. Malachy* was to disturbe, and to put the Elements thus in commotion, those were only punished with so sharpe menaces, & with so wonderful, dreadfull, and cruell a tempest, who more then the rest seemed to thirst to take away the life of the Holy Man. The head of this diuelish faction, with three others of the principall, being stroken with a thunderbolt miserably perished: & the day following were their bodyes seene to be blasted & disfigured, one vpon this, another vpon that bough of the trees, wheresoeuer through the violence of the thunder, ech one was furiously cast. Three others were foũd to be halfe dead on the ground. The rest of the baser crew, were dispersed into diuers parts very confusedly, and with exceeding great horrour, and they went about lyke men distracted. Whereas those of the part of *S. Malachy* so neere to the place amidst so perilous accidents, had no molestation with such prodigyes, nor hurt at all, nay not so much as a hayre of their heads were diminished; Which bred a farre greater admiration in the mynds of the people, wherby they euidently beheld that God himselfe tooke *S. Malachyes* part. The vnhappy *Nigrettus*, with his cõplices, through the fury of the people, was thurst out of the Citty, and with the greatest ioy that might be, the true Bishop and Primat of all *Ireland* introduced into his place, being at that tyme of some thirty eight yeares of age. But yet for all this neyther within or without, was he wholy free from persecutions and troubles, as shall presently appeare.

Nigrettus *his craft, as also the plot of his wicked* Complices: *& how all turned to a perfect Reconciliation.* Chap. 11.

THE Diet being now dissolued, and the aforesaid King, with the other defenders of the right and equity of *S. Malachyes* cause departed from *Ardmach*; that viperous race not able to brooke the priuation of the ancient dominion, began to exclayme bitterly, and complayne for being ouer borne and oppressed by the more potent; and with all endeauour and art, gaue themselues within the towne to renew seditions and tumults, against the Seruant of *Christ*: & the fugitiue *Nigrettus* without, was not wanting the while with fraud and subtilityes to stirre vp seditions abroad, and to put euery thing into garboyle, rebellions, and disorders.

In the Sacristy of *Ardmach*, among other things of best esteeme, are two famous Reliques very charily kept. Whereof one is a certaine *Text* of the Ghospells, which had been heeretofore belonging to the *Blessed S. Patrick*. The other a Staffe, all couered with gold, & beset with most rich Iewels, which they call *Iesus Staffe*, as holding

for

for certayne that our *Sauiour* himselfe had framed it, and vsed it with his owne hands. Now these two reliques, as I sayd, are by those people had in so great Veneration, as the Simple, in whose possessiō they see them, do hold them to be the true & lawfull Successours of *S. Patricke*. Which thing *Nigrettus* knowing very well, flying had priuily carryed them away with him; and with these tokens and pledges, did carry himselfe as the true Archbishop, and went about to withdraw the people, as much as he could, from their Obediēce to *S. Malachy*.

But a principall man of the same stock, seemed to play the fury aboue the rest; who not regarding eyther the promise made to the King, not to molest the most holy Priest of God, nor yet the hostages giuen for that end; with a crew of seruants and kinsfolkes did practize how to murder *S. Malachy*. And for as much as he could not publikely attempt the same without manifest danger, in respect of the Deuotion which the people bare to so great a Pastour, he determined together with the others, to rid him away by some treacherous meanes, in causing him to come improuidently to his house vnder the pretence of confirming a new amity with him. With this concept in his head, the roomes being furnished in good tyme with armed men, one day while the Archbishop was singing of Vespers in the great Church, he sent certayne men in hast, very humbly to intreate him (the Office being ended) to vouchsafe to come to him, as soone as he could, it being so needfull for them to establish the accord. Which thing seemed to be very extrauagant to the followers of *S. Malachy*; and being aware of the deceipt made answere, that more fit it were he should come himselfe to the Prelate; & that the Church was a more competent place for acts of that quality. The Messengers replyed, their Lord could not come with safety, nor durst he aduenture for the multitude, who but yesterday were ready to cut him in peeces.

While such manner of contentions passed betweene them, the diuine Man, who desired peace, and feared not death: Let me alone (saith he) Brothers for Gods sake: let me follow the example of my Maister. And shall I be a Christian, if I do not in some sort imitate Christ? Peraduenture this my submission will mollify the hart of our Aduersary, and in the meane tyme, with this Example I shal giue you some Edification. And if this sauage people should teare me in peeces, I will willingly yeild my life into their bloudy hāds,

to

to the end I might leaue you a patterne how you ſhould order the courſe of your life. Beſides, by this occaſion you ſhall truly ſee whether your Superiour haue learned of *Chriſt* to be affrayd of death for *Chriſt*, or no. And with this, ryſing vp on his feete, he beganne to walke on with an vndaunted geſture: howbeyt his freinds & Diſciples with teares trickling downe their cheeks, humbly beſought him not to be ſo willfull, as to hazard the ſheading of his bloud among thoſe bloud-ſuckers: becauſe a great multitude of the faithful were like to be left deſolate, who in all things wholy depended vpon him. But he confiding, and fixed in the Diuine protection (his eares being ſtopt to ſighes and laments) went boldly on, accompanyed which no more, then with three diſciples only, being prōpt and diſpoſed to lay downe their lyues with him.

In this manner he came to the Enemyes gate, he had no ſooner put in his feete, but he was ſeene to be encompaſſed round with a great Troupe of terrible Hackſters, he ſtanding the while, like an innocent Victime, expoſed to the ſtrokes of whoſoeuer had the will to ſacrifice the ſame. But (O force! O power of Chriſtian confidence!) while they were all expecting the ſigne to ſet vpon him, he with the only caſt of an Eye, with one ſerene looke only, did mitigate them in ſuch ſort, as there was none of the moſt forwardeſt or couragious, durſt ſo much as offer any manner of violence vnto his perſon, the diuine power did ſo bridle their fury. Nay, rather the Prince himſelfe, and Captayne of them, ſuddaynely changed his inhumane intention, and inſteed of tearing him to peeces, & deſtroying him wholy, aroſe to do him great Reuerence and honour, ſhewing an incredible deſire of a ſincere concord. At which wordes, *S. Malachy* exceedingly reioyced, and was no whit ſlacke in a matter ſought for by him, with ſo great daunger of his life. A ſolemne peace then was ratifyed between them with ſuch ſincerity as that he who before was ſo grieuous and dangerous an Aduerſary, was not only ſatisfyed now with the Election made, but ſhewed himſelfe afterwards alwayes louing, and much deuoted to *S. Malachy*. For which ſucceſſe the good conceiued an incredible ioy, in beholding him to eſcape ſo that day, who had no fault, & through his merits ſo many ſoules deliuered from the perill of eternal death. This action of his, made not only the name and reſpect of *S. Malachy* now to dilate it ſelfe more then euer; but euen likewiſe wrought a great dread in all people, who vnderſtood that two of his moſt

fierce

fierce and potent Persecutours, were with a sudden & diuine power, made prostrate, though in a very diuerse manner; the one, being terribly punished in body, the other benignly compunct, and changed in mind.

Nigretus *is constreyned to render vp the pledges to* S. Malachy *: the Iudgement of God is seuerely shewed vpon two bitter Raylers against* S. Malachy. Chap. 12.

SVCH difficult Encounters, and grieuous disturbances being now passed ouer, the holy Archbishop began very freely to ordeyne and dispose whatsoeuer might seeme in any wise to belong to his Ministery, but yet neuer without some eminent daunger of his life, while he found no tyme, or place secure from treacheryes. Wherupon by publique counsayle there was a Guard of select men appoynted for his person day and night, although he was resolued (as we haue said) euer to relye much more vpon diuine protection, then on human guards. And because the banished *Nigretus* was continually working of no small domage in stirring vp the rude people and causing of separations and discordes in the Church of God; it seemed conuenient to *S. Malachy* to vse his best endeauours against a disorder & scandall of so great importance. And therefore the good Archbishop applyed himselfe withall care and industry to wype away this great scandall; and did vse such effectuall meanes to stop vp the wayes to the minister of the Deuill, as the wretched Man was constreyned, in despight of himselfe, to yeild, and restore the stolne pledges, and for euer after to rest quiet, and subiect himselfe withall humility. And thus *S. Malachy*, though amidst so many difficultyes and Tribulations, notwithstanding with the fauour of God went prosperously on, procuring the saluation of many Soules, and proceeding successiuely day by day. Nor were the malefactours only, but euen likewise his detractours chastized by diuine Iustice. Wherof, among others, vpon a certayne peruerse fellow, was a notable demonstration shewed.

This man not content to thinke vnworthyly of the great Archbishop, and to maligne him agaynst all reason: but moreouer endeauoured to defame and wound him with bitter speaches, and shamefull calumnyes in publique meetings & more eminent places, helping himselfe therein with a certaine pernicious Eloquence,

 wher-

wherwith he was endued, and with the fauour of Princes, & great Ones, purchased through base flatteryes & scurrile iests. And now was he arriued to such enormous insolence, as that wheresouer he met with *S. Malachy*, & especially in the more publique assemblies, he would not spare to vse him discourteously both in words and gestures. But this manner of audaciousnes did cost the wretch full deare; for the instrument of rayling in him, was so putrifyed, and swoln vp, as that after he had for seauen continuall dayes done nothing but spit out wormes, which seemed to swarme from his diuelish tongue; being finally consumed quite, and pined away with abominable corruption issuing from thence, he gaue vp the Ghost, leauing his filthy Carkasse to be meate for wormes of the Earth.

The other was a Woman of that accursed generatiō, so enuious, & alwayes bearing such an implacable hatred towards Blessed *Malachy*, as she euer abhorred his very sight. Notwithstāding as she wēt to heare him preach to the people, the wretched and shameles creature did not forbeare to lift vp her voyce in that assembly, & call him Hypocrite, and a robber of other mens goods, adioyning besides, to so bitter iniuries, outragious taunts, vpon the Baldenes of the man of God: who being wise and meeke, gaue no answere himselfe of any kind; but the great God (who reserues reuenge & glory to himselfe) sufficiently made answere for him: for that the wicked and damnable wreth thereupon lost her wits, became furious and frantique, continually crying out, she was strangled by *S. Malachy*, nor ceased she from horrible screeches, til she likewise yielded vp her vitall Spirit. Insomuch, as hauing vsurped the ancient Nickname of *Elizæus*, through the iust iudgement of God, she found to her cost, another *Elizæus*.

In the meane tyme there happened a cruell Plague to rage in *Ardmach*: by which pestilence an infinite multitude of people consumed euery day away. Whereupon *S. Malachy* ordayned a solemne procession, and sent vp enflamed darts (both of iaculatory and vocall prayers) which pierced the skyes, and came to the Throne of his diuine Maiesty; who graunted his humble request, and very speedily caused it to cease.

And this thing bred a wonder in the people, who did obserue the sanctity of the great Archbishop, and euer after caused them to haue a farre more reuerent respect to his sacred person; and likewise it stopped the mouthes of the malignant, and in particular those of the

the ſeede of *Chanaan*, who being by this and other examples terrifyed, and conuinced by ſuch soueraygne wonders, ſayd likewiſe with the *Egyptians: Let vs fly from* S. Malachy, *becauſe the Lord ſeemes to fight for him.* But to late were they aware of their owne wretchednes: nor were they able to auert the heauenly Indignation, ſince within a litle while after, that vnfortunate race was quite annihilated and extinguiſhed, not without the terrour, and amazement of as many as knew the ſame.

S. Malachy *ſurrenders the Archbiſhopricke, and returnes to* Conerthen: *and ſoone after reſolues vpon a iourney to* Rome. Chap. 13.

BY theſe meanes the affayres of *Ardmach*, being now reduced to good termes, the Clergy reformed, the rumours quieted, & the Enemyes by this tyme taken away; *S. Malachy*, whoſe breaſt was inflamed with the loue of Humility, after he had now brought peace to others, determines to procure the ſame likewiſe for himſelfe. And calling a new Diet of Prieſts & Layks, obteyned in vertue of the former Pact (though not without their great ſorrow & griefe) to diſcharge himſelfe at laſt of that cure ſo burdenſome, and in his roome to ſubſtitute a perſon of rare and approued vertues, by name *Gelaſius*. Whome as ſoone as he had conſecrated, and ſeriouſly recommended to the principall of the kingdome, being loaden with victories and triumphes, he returnes agayne to his firſt charge of *Conerthen*, which by this time was reaſonably well recouered of the loſſe receiued from the barbarous people. And in this returne ſeemed *S. Malachy* to giue forth apparent ſignes now more cleere then euer of Chriſtian Modeſty; or to ſay better, of the greatnes of a ſingular courage.

The Dioceſſe of *Conerthen* of ancient tymes, had two Epiſcopal Seates; but afterwards through the couetouſnes, and ambition of a great *Incumbent*, they were confounded together, and reduced to one only. Which thing our *S. Malachy* diſlyking, for iuſt reſpects, deuided it anew, and renounced that of *Conerthen*, being the better prouided with Rents, and more noble of the two, for another, much inferiour to the former for wealth; It is called *Dune*, a place obſcure and little, which our Bleſſed Man chooſe rather to reteyne to himſelfe. And to that purpoſe he paſſed from *Conerthen* to *Dune*, accōpanyed with a few diſciples; and likewiſe immediately forſooke the eminent Title of *Archbishop* of *Ardmach*, to a poore title of Bishop of *Dune*. O pure hart! O eye of the Doue! Let all men be euen rauished at this Example of exceeding great *Humility*, which shined bright in the course of thy whole transitory life! Where are they now, who so earnestly contend about their lymits and bounds? Who meerely for a base cottage, or a plot of ground, do wage Law, and stirre vp such fearefull tragedyes? But let vs desist from entring into such manner of discourses, and rather proceede to declare the rest of the life of this great Saint. From Metropolitan and Primate of *Ireland*, being thus made Bishop of *Dune*, the first thing he endeauours, is to haue (as he was wont) a flourishing Colledge about him of Regular Clerks.

And behold now another tyme, how our new Souldyer of *Christ*, puts himself agayne into spiritual combats; he harnesseth himselfe with complete armour of *Mortification*, and perpetuall Meditation, although by this his desire, he seemed to obteyne the merit, rather then the effect; it being impossible for him to deny his endeauour, counsaile, and presence to such a number of persons, as eyther touched with good inspirations, or tempted with sundry temptations, repaired to him as to a safe refuge & true Oracle. Besides which, the obligation he had of trauayling through the Prouince, to sow the word of God, to visite the parishes, and to ordeyne all things as one of the *Apostles*, did employ him not a little. And commonly there was none would say vnto him; In whose authority do you this? so great was the opinion and credit he purchased; partly through the life he lead, partly also for the signes & Miracles which he wrought. And yet for all that, while it seemed to him, that he could not with security promote so high affayres, without the expresse commission of the holy *Apostolike Sea*; he determined to trauayle in person towards *Rome*, and that so much the rather, as he had many other occasions besids of no light importance, mouing him to this long and tedious pilgrimage: Whereof one the most vrgent was this which we shall now tell.

Within the costs of *Ireland*, are two Metropolitan seates, the one of *Adrmach*, whereof we haue spoken heertofore more ofren, illustrious, rich, and founded euen from the tyme of *S. Patricke*: the other (whose name is vnknowne vnto me) of a meaner quality, and but newly erected by *Celsus*, and subordinate to the first, and not confirmed hitherto by the *Vicar* of *Christ*. To both these Seas,

now

now, *S. Malachy* desired for their greater complement of honour & reputation to obtayne the vse of the sacred Pall: and to the second as more late, the consent also of Apostolicall approbation. And to this effect, he went about to prepare for his iourney. But as the same came to be knowne abroad, not only his domestiques, but al others likewise were infinitely sorry thereat: while it seemed to be a very hard matter for them, to remayne so long without him: and fearing withall, in so great and difficult a voyage by Sea and land, some sinister accident, might betyde him.

Their anxiety was increased the more, by reason of the death of *Christianus* Bishop and Brother of *S. Malachy*, which happened much about those dayes: a Prelate indeed, though second in glory, yet for zeale and sanctity, peraduenture not much inferiour to him. By reason of this fresh and grieuous a losse, came now the departure of the blessed Father, to be continually more difficult. And they all affirmed with one voyce, they would by no meanes consent, their only prop should depart from them; the country in the meane tyme abyding in so manifest danger of a totall ruine, if both such pillars should thence be taken away at one tyme. So as all from the highest to the lowest, with one and the selfe same spirit, ran hastily to him, and hauing in vayne mixed their reasons, coniurations, and protestations to moue him; did at last playnely giue him to vnderstand, that when they saw Loue would not preuayle with him, they would detayne him by force: When lo, the Seruant of God, with a seuere countenance, threatning them with chastisement from Heauen, endeauoured to pacify them: and yet was it not possisible for him to hinder them, but that for a finall conclusion, the matter should be remitted to a decision by Lots; and yet notwithstanding all that, so great was the pertinacity of them, as that after the first, & then the second being drawne in fauour of the Bishop; yet they with exclamations and plaints, would needs haue him come to a third Election: when still finding the same to be conformable to the afore passed, and for that they iudged it to be enacted by the supreme *Head*, and *Disposer* of all things, agaynst their wills they yield to his desire. But before they would let him go, they desired and humbly requested him to ordeyne one to supply the place & Episcopall Seate of his Brother deceased. To which he willingly condescended, and therefore calling into his presence some three of his Schollers, was much perplexed in mynd and vncertayne which of them were the most sufficient for such a high and eminent Ministery. And when he had taken a carefull and diligent suruey of them all: *Do thou Edanus* (sayth he, for so was one of thē called) *take vpon thee the charge*. But the poore Wretch excused himselfe, in the best manner he could, and powred forth a shower of brinish teares. *Feare not* (replyed he) *since thou hast been designed to me by our Lord himselfe, and I haue seene thee already with the ring of the mysticall Espousalls on thy finger. Whereupon* Edanus *assuming more confidence then before, very humbly obeyed.*

S. Malachy *in his way to Rome goes to* Yorke. *He visits* Claraualllis *by the way, and arriues at Rome.* Chap. 14.

SAINT *Malachy* hauing now consecrated *Edanus* Bishop, puts himselfe on his iourney, and with an easy and short cut passed ouer into *Scotland*. From thence being come to *York*, a Citty in England, a certaine *Priest, Sicarus* by name,, hauing the spirit of prophecy, beholding *S. Malachy* in the face, albeyt he neuer saw him befor, yet did he point at him with the fingar, to the stāders by, saying: *Behold him heere whome I told you of, that a holy Bishop should come out of Ireland, who sees into the thoughts of men.* Moreouer, the said *Sicarus*, discouered to *S. Malachy* many hidden things, which were with al punctuality found to be most true. And being demaunded by some of the Bishops companions, concerning the successe of that pilgrimage of theirs, among other things he answered, they were not al of thē like to returne backe with him into *Ireland* agayne. Wherupon they fell into some suspition of their dying by the way, but their prediction came to be verifyed indeed in another sense. For as much, as in the returne which *S. Malachy* made from *Rome*, as we shall set downe in its place, he left part of them in the Conuent of *Claraualllis*. And so much may suffice of the Prophet *Sicarus*.

In the same Citty of *York* came to the holy Bishop a Noble mā, whose name was *William*, being at that tyme Prior of the Canons of *Circham*, and now Monke, and Father of the Monkes, in our house of *Mailros*: who after he had very humbly recommended himselfe to his prayers, did him a noble act of courtesy; which was, that seeing the trayne of the Bishop to be somwhat great, & his prouisiō of horse but slender (for hauing with him besides Seruants & Clearks, some fiue Priests, he had no more then three horses for thē al) he he made him a friendly present of a horse of his: which because he was outward for the saddle, & of a naughty pace, *William* did ingenuously alleadge for himselfe how sory he was for the defects, and that he would haue more willingly giuen the same, if he had been much better. Whereto *S. Malachy* made answere: And I like him so much the more, as you seeme to depaynt him worse; and turning himselfe to his followers: Make ready (sayd he) this *Beast for me for he is like to proue well inough, and will hold out for a long voyage.* And so got vp, & though in the beginning he found him to be rude, & of a very hard trot; notwithstanding shortly through a meruaylous chaũge it appeared he now had a very dexterous Rider on his backe: and for confirmation of whatsoeuer he had prognosticated of him, for nine whole yeares togeather which *S. Malachy* suruiued, he alwayes serued his turne, becoming really a very excellent & prized horse; & for a later empromement, wheras before he had a coate of a darke gray, he beganne to wax white, in such sort, as within a short space there could hardly be seen a whiter beast.

These and other like Offices of friendship, found *S. Malachy*, in that pilgrimage: and I my selfe likewise had the hap to know such a Man, and to be fed, and enriched with his spirituall Discourses; and he mutually made shew likewise of some contentment taken in me a Sinner, and loued me deerely, euen to the end of his life. Moreouer he seemed not to thinke much, to lodge in our homely Cottages, giuing also to all the Monks a rare and singular Example of *Christian Perfection*, and wee receiuing alwayes from his followers some manner of edification. And so hauing taken the place & Inhabitants into those his bowels of Piety, giuing vs all his holy Benediction, he departed from vs, not without sorrow and great lamentation of the people. Hasting now forward in his iourney, our blessed Pilgrime arriues at the City of *S. Claude*, where he presently cured his Hosts child in the place where it lay in extremity. From thence by the shortest way he passed to *Rome*, where *Pope Innocent* the second at that tyme did gouerne the Ship of *S. Peter*; who graciously receiued him, and tooke much compassion vpon him for the grieuous paines he had sustey ned, and the hard trauayles he had takẽ in so tedious a iourney.

S. Malachy

S. Malachy *remaynes a while in Rome. He is made Apostolicall Legate: and returnes homeward by* Clarauallis. Chap. 15.

ALbeyt *S. Malachy* were nothing vnmyndfull of his principall busynes: yet before all other things, he began to demaund the fauour to leaue off the Episcopall Office, and to retire himself to liue and dy in our Monastery of *Clarauallis*. Which howbeyt denyed by the *Vicar* of *Christ*, because it seemed to him not iust, that a person so helpfull to the world, should so be shut vp in a corner therof, he had notwithstanding obteined from *Christ* himself, some part of what he desired; since it was afforded him by the *Diuine Goodnes*, if not to liue, at least to dye in *Clarauallis*, as shall be declared in its due place. *S. Malachy* remayned for a whole Moneth in the holy Citty, visiting with singular deuotion those places which were consecrated with the bloud of *Martyrs*. And in the meane tyme, the *Pope* informed himselfe by him, more fully and at large of the estate and custemes of the Churches in *Ireland*. At last vpon mature deliberation with his *Cardinals*, he declared our Blessed *S. Malachy* his *Vicegerent* and *Apostolicall Legat*, through all that *Iland*, in the place of the Bishop *Gilbert*, who being surcharged with yeares, most humbly craued to be discharged. After which did *S. Malachy* propose his demaunds, which were, for the confirmation of the new *Metropolis*; and for the *Pals* both of the one and other. And as for the *Confirmation*, he obteyned it without difficulty. But for the *Palls*, the *Pope* answered; *It was conuenient, the matter should be treated of more solemnely. Wherfore as soone as you shall be arriued at home, shall you assemble a generall Synod: & by common Decree, you shall procure for the said Palls that some worthy persons with speed may be sent hither, that the same may benignly be affoarded them.* So sayd *Innocent*, and then taking off the *Miter* from his head he put it on *S. Malachy*: and besides he pleased to giue him from his owne vestments of the *Masse*, a stole and maniple. And then with the louing kisse of peace, and *Apostolicall benediction*, very courteously licenced him to depart.

In his returne homeward, he reuisited *Clarauallis*, & reuiued vs a new with his most gratefull aspect, he being exceedingly grieued that he could not alwayes make his aboade with vs, and then with deepe sighes he spake to vs, as followeth. Seeing it is not the Diuine pleasure of Almighty God, that I shal heere remaine with you: yet

yet I beseech you at least, that insteed of my person you would take some of my Clerks vnto you: Who with you being made good disciples, may serue to supply vs afterwards with Maisters: adding moreouer, they shall serue vs for seed, and in their seed shall people be blessed: People (I say) who though by ancient Tradition haue had some kind of knowledge of Monasticall functions; yet hitherto haue neuer seen any Monks amongst them. Leauing then some foure of them behind, he departed from thence, who succeeding very wel in the probation, were admitted into the Order: and within a litle while afterwards were some others sent thither, and those likewise being admitted, and instructed with diligence, were together with the first, sent back into *Ireland*, vnder the care of the holy Brother *Christianus*, (being of the same family) with an addition of so many of ours of *Clareuallis*, as being al together, sufficed for a formall *Abbay*: which likewise in processe of tyme, conceiued, and brought forth some fiue daughters. From whence with multiplyed seed, the number of *Religious* euery day increased, according to the prediction and vow of *S. Malachy*.

S. Malachy *arriueth in* Scotland, *and there cureth King* Dauids *sonne. He passeth from thence into* Ireland, *and comes to the Monastery of* Benchor. Chap. 16.

THE venerable Ghest being departed from vs, & prosperously landing in *Scotland*; found there King *Dauid*, in a certayne castle of his, with his only Sonne, lying sicke of an incurable disease. Where being intreated to stay, and that he would be pleased to afford him health, he sprinckled him with water by him blessed, & looking him in the face, said to him: *Be of good cheere, my Sonne since you are not to dye at this present*. These were his words; & immediatly the effect followed: For the day after, the *Prince* recouered his health to the exceeding consolation of the King, and the infinite iubiley, and ioy of all the Court, and finally to the stupour and amazement of al that heard and knew the same. The rumour therof being spread there was nothing euery where but bonfyers, ringing of bells, and giuing of thankes, and voyces of prayse, as well for the vnexpected recouery of their Lord, as for the greatnes & nouelty of the Myracle it selfe. This *Dauid* the father, and *Henry* the sonne, being now valourous, and wise Souldiours, are yet lyuing to this day: and as at that tyme, they vsed much importunity to retayne *S. Malachy* their Ghest with them, to make much of him; so while he liued, they alwayes striued to honour him, and to shew themselues, not to be vnmyndfull, and very gratefull for such a benefit, and therefore offered to him many rich Presents.

But the wise Contemner of transitory Rewards, and worldly pompe, by any meanes, on the next Morning would needs depart from thence; and passing by the way of *Crugeldus*, restored speach to a certaine young Girle.

And in the Iland of *S. Michael*, he cured, in the presence of all the people, a woman so possessed with Deuils, as her friends were enforced to hold her very streightly bound with cords, & sometymes in chaynes of Iron.

From thence being come to the hauen of *Lapisperius*, while he expected commodity to passe ouer into *Ireland*, he was not ydle, but among other things gaue order, and himselfe likewise put hands to a certayne Oratory of grates or lattuce-worke, & encompassed it round with a fense, leauing in the midst a certayne space for the buryall of the dead; and blessed the same. Which was so efficacious, as that euen to this day, from diuers parts are brought thither many lãguishing persons, and ill affected, and from thence returne with strength, and wished comfort.

That same also was very notable, which happened there to a certayne insolent fellow: who being entred into that inuiolable Cemeter, with foule and impious intents to profane the same; he was seized vpon by an vgly and horrible Toade, which suddenly shewing it selfforth, with a swelling looke fell a spitting of venome vpon him. Whereat the poore wretch being sorely astonished and affrighted, threw himselfe ouer the sacred rayles, euen headlong the shortest way.

But to leaue these degressions, and returne to *S. Malachy*; after he had embarqued himselfe in the said Port, with a good gale, he very happily arriued at the Monastery of *Benchor*, to the end that his first Children, perhaps might likewise be the first, to gayne his Benediction. And who were able sufficiently to expresse the ioy they felt in the reuiew and receiuing of such a *Father*, returned safe and sound from parts so remote? Nor the said *Congregation* only, but euen all those people also thereabout, did shew forth such ioy for his returne, that euen from Cittyes, Castles, and Townes they ran thither

thither in great troupes, to do him Reuerence, & bid him welcome. And he himselfe, not to hold his new *Legation* in vayne, without delay endeauours to visit all those kingdomes, distributing on euery side very holsome gifts of Apostolicall Facultyes, in such sort, as no Sex, nor Age, nor Condition, or Professi on whatsoeuer remayned without feeling of some part of the Comfort.

He celebrated likewise some Nationall Councells, in the more conuenient Citties. Where, for the sound and Catholique Religion, were most profitable Canons and Decrees established: carrying in the meane while, his eyes continually fixed vpon the necessityes of euery one, and applying remedyes allwayes as need required; now with sweetnes, and now with seuerity. Nor was there heere to be found any one that would seeme to contradict his precepts, or proudly contemne his admonishments, but they were rather accepted of all, as holsome medicines, and as constitutions deriued from Heauen. And how could it be otherwise, while al was confirmed by so many workes aboue nature. In testimony wherof, besides those others we haue touched already, we wil in the Chapters following relate some others most to our purpose; since to recount & vnfold them all, were not possible: and I on the other side am more willing to dilate my self. in things conducing to *Imitation*, then such as may only excite *Admiration*.

A briefe Description of S. Malachyes *manner of life, as an introduction to the ensuing miracles, which he wrought.* Chap. 17.

IN my iudgment truly, the first, and most stupendious myracle that *S. Malachy* wrought, was *S. Malachy* himselfe. For why; setting apart the interiour man, whose beauty, worth, and sincerity sufficiently shined most brightly in his life and actions, what shall we say of the exteriour only; which with conformity of manners, to wit, most modest and decent, he would be alwayes shewing in such sort, as not the least thing could euer be discouered therin, that might any wayes seeme to offend the eyes of the beholders? Let vs come to the tongue: It is surely most certayne, that for a man not to trip in talking is a very great perfection. And yet what man, so curious let him be, was euer knowne, that could euer espye, or note in *S. Malachy*, I say not a word, but so much as an ill gesture? Who euer saw him to moue eyther hand or foote with vanity? Nay wherin gaue he not Edification to his Neighbours, in walking, in his habit, and semblance? He had so perpetuall a serenity in his cõtenance, as neyther with the grauity of Melancholy, or leuity of Laughing, was he euer seen to be distempered. All was discipline in him, all harmony, all Vertue. He was an Enemy to scoffs, but yet not austere, or froward. Remisse would he be sometymes, but dissolute neuer. Careles in nothing, though in many he knew wel how to dissemble, till tyme and place. Quiet oftentymes, but yet not once would seeme to be slouthfull.

From the day of his conuersion, vnto his last breath, he had neuer any thing proper, not seruants, nor farmes, nor messuages, nor finally any manner of rents, eyther Ecclesiasticall or secular. For his Episcopall table, he had no assignement made him at all: yea the good Prelate indeed, had not so much as a determinate dwelling to put his head in; as he who spent all his life, as it were, in visiting of Villages and Parishes; so seruing the Ghospell, and by the Ghospell therefore susteyning himselfe, according to the order and decree of our *Lord*. It is true, that he and his companions, because they would not be burdensome, or put any to expences, would mainteyne themselues oftentymes with the sweat of their browes, and labours of their proper hands. And when at such tymes he had need of some rest, he would vsually be taking it in pious places, dispersed by himselfe heere and there through *Ireland*: and if he chanced to abyde any where, he would allwayes so conforme himselfe to the customes and obseruances of the house, as neyther at Table, or elswhere, would he seeme to haue any thing in particular: nor euen at first sight could there any the least difference be discouered betweene him, and the rest of the Brothers.

What more can be sayd of him? Euen inough to conteyne many Volumes, his life was so admirable, & a mirrour to all Mortals. But my scope and intention is only, to demonstrate those thinges which in his life are most imitable, as I said aboue. To proceed then, although our blessed *S. Malachy*, were now an aged man, and *Legate* of the *highest Bishop*; yet did he neuer giue ouer his ancient vse to go on foote, to preach himselfe in person, still causing such others as he lead along with him to do the like; a forme very truly Euangelicall, and so much the more recommendable in *S. Malachy*, as it is found to be lesse in practice with others. Whereas he, who doth such things, may worthily be called the lawfull heyre, and Succes-

sour

four of the Apostles. What wonder is it then, if the diuine Man, did worke such admirable things, he being so admirable himselfe, though he wrought them not of himselfe, but God in him, since we read; *Tu es Deus qui facis mirabilia?*

By occasion of the loud acclamations of these his transcendent Vertues, & most notable working of Miracles; his fame beganne to spread it self throughout all the neighbouring places, nay euen ouer the whole Country; and there resorted dayly many to be cured by him of all kind of diseases; and among the rest a woman extremely vexed with the deuill, who dwelt in a Citty which is called *Cultafin*. Her parents thereupon procured *S. Malachy* to be sent for: Who comming into the house, presently fell vnto his prayers, and commaunds the vniust possessour in the name of the highest, to goforth of that body; he obeys, but instantly leapes into another Woman present. *S. Malachy* perceiuing this, spake thus to the accursed Enemy of Mākind: *I haue not so quit thee of her, as that thou shouldst seeme to assaile that other. Therefore I charge thee agayne in the name of the Highest, that thou let her go also.* The Fiend being constrained thereto, obeyes his behest, but yet returnes to his former habitation. When the Blessed Seruant of *Christ*, obseruing the deceypt of our Aduersary, expells him a new from thence, he then flyes agayne into the second. This bobb the peruerse spirit gaue to him for a pretty while, in chopping so alwayes, and flying from one into the other. At last *S. Malachy* being stirred vp with a holy zeale, and not without iust indignation, to see him so mocked by an vncleane Spirit, recollected himselfe a little, and resuming more intense forces from Heauen, withall violence quite banished him from both: leauing the cruell Serpent (so full of fraude and deceipt) enraged thereat, thinking perhaps by that policy to make the *Holy man* desist from further troubling himself. But peraduenture some will admire at this long delay heerein, and resistance of the Aduersary, attributing the same (it may be) to the power of the malignant Spirit. To such persons I answere, that it pleased the Diuine Dispensatour of all things, *Qui omnia bene & suauiter disponit*, to try the patience of his Seruant *S. Malachy*, and to the end that by such delay and changes, both the presence of the Enemy, and victory of *S. Malachy*, more cleerely might appeare. Which thing is yet more illustrated, and made to appeare to be true: therefore attend heere a while to that which elswhere this great Seruant of *Christ* seemed to worke, not in person, as before is declared, but in absence. Which yet surely had been a great deale more easy for him to haue done at hand, then so farre asunder.

A man is dispossessed of euill spirits, by the power of S. Malachy *in his absence. With diuers other miracles besides.* Chap. 18

IN the Northern parts of *Ireland*, in a certayne howse, where *S. Malachy* before had happened to lodge, lay one afflicted, and terribly tormented with Deuils. Who on a night, ouer heard some discourses they had among them; Wherin they sayd to ech other: Beware this wretch do not touch any of the straw there, wherin that Hippocrit had sometymes slept, least perhappes he escape out of our hands. Frō which words, the sick man did gather that those infernall Spirits meant it of *S. Malachy*; and then taking courage began to approach by creeping thereunto, as well as he could: but being weake in body, he could not get thither by crawling; yet was he very strong in fayth, for he desisted not to go forward, as he was able. Wherupon you might heare in the ayre certayne feareful cryes, and perplexed voyces, *Hold, hold him off, or we loose the prey.* But he trāsported with hope and desire, made so much the greater hast, to reach thereunto: & through diuine Mercy, being come to the blessed Litter of straw, fell a stretching himselfe thereon, and wallowing vp & downe therin: While the infernall furyes with howling & lamēts most bitterly exclamed: *Alas, alas, we haue bewrayed our selues: we haue deceiued our selues. For loe, he is euen now made sound.* And so he was indeed, being whole in a moment of all his lymnes, and freed of the diabolicall affrights and horrours, which he suffered.

In *Lesmor* likewise did *S. Malachy* deliuer a Lunatike person; & made him whole and perfect in all his senses. Moreouer, our great *Saint* did restore another person to his former wits, who dwelt in *Praginia*. And in the same Countrey, by causing a frantike woman to wash her selfe with a water which he blessed, she was presently released of her chaynes, and disease. Another woman in like sort being enraged, so as she would be a biting, & tearing her flesh with her teeth, was by him through Prayer, & a simple touch only restored to health. There was likewise a Man, who in phrensy could seeme to foretell certayne things to come, and so impetuous and terrible withall, as the greatest cords were hardly able to with hold

hold him. And yet this Man in a moment was freed also through the prayers of *S. Malachy*, & restored to his wits. I could name the place where this fel out; but because it happened in a place of so barbarous a name, that (as it happens often in many other words of that Nation) it may scarce seeme fit to be expressed with the voyce much lesse represented with the pen, I thinke it a thing very conuenient, to let it passe namelesse.

There was in the aforesayd Citty of *Lesmor*, a certayne young girle very dumbe, whome her Parents hauing humbly put in the presence of *S. Malachy*, as he passed along, the man of God made a stop, and touching her tongue with a little of his spittle, without more ado, in the sight of all, affoarded her the vse of speach. Another tyme going forth of the Church, with a great trayne after him, a woman was presented to him at the Porch, by a distressed Man her Husband, wholy depriued likewise of her pronunciation. Whē *S. Malachy* beheld this miserable woman, he signed her with the most holy Crosse, and commaunded her in the presence of all, to recite the prayer of our Lord: which she presently sayd very punctually. The multitude seeing this Myracle, gaue glory to the diuine Goodnes. In a certayne place called *Obentreb*, a rich man being mortally sick, had now for some twelue dayes continually remayned without once being able in any wise to vtter a word, and consequently was hindered from making his Confession. But *S. Malachy* comming to visit him, immediately he recouered his lost speach, & being armed with the *Sacraments*, with singular Confidence of eternall life, gaue vp the Ghost.

A certayne Baron being in *S. Malachyes* Inne, while he was treating there with him, about some affayres; as one full of faith, stole away but three rushes only from his poore little Couch, and with that pious theft, wrought wonderous things; which we haue not tyme to relate in this place. The Man of God being come to *Duenuania*, there came in to him a Gentleman of that Citty, as he sat at table, earnestly beseeching him on the behalfe of his wife, who was not without great feare & daunger of her Child-birth, being longer thē the ordinary terme required. The Bishop of *Mehome* likewise with others that were present at that sitting, did very earnestly recommend the case vnto him. When *S. Malachy* heard this, he answered: *I am not a little sorry for it, in reguard that she is a very good Matron.* And without more adoe, reaching to the Husband, a cup by him blessed

blessed, added : *Go your wayes, and giue her this drinke. and bid her not feare any thing.* So the Noble man did as he was commaunded, and the next night without any difficulty at all, the woman was safely deliuered. *S. Malachy* happening to abide in the Champion countryes, with the *Count* of *Vlidia*, behold a woman appeared before him, very great with Child, now at least for fifteen months and twenty dayes gone : and who finding no humane remedy, with piteous teares came seeking for succour from the Seruant of *Christ*. *Malachy* being moued with so new and vnexpected an accident, puts himselfe into Prayer, & sudenly there in the place the poore wretch without any trauaile at all, brought forth the creature into the world,

A rehearsall of other myracles of S. Malachy, *vpon sundry occasions.* Chap. 19.

ANother thing yet of no lesse wonder, though in a diuerse kind happened in the land of *Vlidia*. A certayne Souldiour of the Count of *Vlidia*, hauing no regard vnto Gods commaundements, and without hauing any feare of his heauy displeasure, kept the Concubine of his owne Brother. *Saint Malachy* hauing notice heereof, performed, like another *S. Iohn Baptist*, the very same office of charity in reprehending the wicked man. But that wretchlesse creature, representing *Herod*, not onely disobeyed him, but made him answere moreouer, with swearing, in the hearing of all, that *he would neuer abandon his Mistris*. *S. Malachy*, the true seruant of *Christ*, being fraught with the zeale of Iustice, answered; *God may then disseuer you, agaynst your will.* For which the incestuous wretch as caring but litle, in a most despightfull manner, went his wayes from him. He had scarce gone a mile from that place, and within lesse then a full houre, but God punished him for this his enormous crime; by being assayled by certayne men, and that so desperatly, as wounds were the beginning of their fray, and stabbes euen to the heart, were the period. In this bloudy onset, his Soule payed for the transgression of his disobedience. For one of the Ruffians sent him on a rufull message to Grand *Lucifer*. At this newes euery one remayned astonished, especially seeing the speedy execution of the sentence of *S. Malachy* : and other wicked men being heerby gently admonished, were truly conuerted. In the same coũtrey, Count *Dermitius*, through manifest disorders of Gluttony, & and other Sensualityes, had layne now sicke, and vnweildy a long

tyme

tyme. This man being visited by *S. Malachy*, & first sharpely rebuked for the scandall, and ill example he had giuen, and after blessed with holy water, was sudenly raysed, & beyond the expectation of him and his, very nimbly mounted on his horse. In the City of *Cassel*, came one to *S. Malachy*, with a sonne of his, being sick of the palsey crauing pitty at his hands. The holy Bishop thẽ lifting vp his mynd to our Lord, said to the Father of that child: *Goe thy wayes, for thy sõne shall recouer*. He went then, but returned the next Morning, with the child not yet cured. *S. Malachy* making his prayer for the Child somewhat longer then before, cheered him vp, and gaue strict order to the Father of the lame child, to dedicate him to the diuine Seruice, which he faithfully promised to do. But yet afterwards kept not his word. Wherupon the youth after some yeares relapsed agayne into the same palsey.

Another Man likewise brought his sonne to the holy Man, frõ parts farre distant. This child had withered feete, and was not able to moue awhit. *S. Malachy* demaunded how the same happened. I thinke (answered the Man) it was the worke of the Deuill, because my sonne, being, on a tyme, childishy disporting himselfe in a certayne meadow, that accursed Fiend (if I be not deceiued) made him to fall a sleepe, & then awaking, I know not how, he was foũd taken in this manner. And speaking thes words, he powred forth abundance of teares, and humbly prayed the Diuine Man, to giue his sonne some succour. Who being mollifyed therwith (according to his custome) cõmaunded the lame child, to giue himself to sleepe while he prayed; who did as much: and when *S. Malachy* had ended his prayer, the child immediately stood vpon his feete, very iocund and lusty. The holy man kept him afterwards with him, a prety while, and instructed him well in the Rudiments of the Christian Fayth, carrying him along with him, into diuers places with his other Domestiques.

A certaine poore Man, serued in a Mill of the Monastery of *Benchor*, maynteyning himselfe partly with that labour, partly also with dayly almes. This man had likewise been lame now for these twelue yeares, in such sort, as he was compelled to go with his hãds on the ground, and trayling his dead feete after him. Now *S. Malachy*, beholding him one day before his Cell, to be somewhat sadder then ordinary; with the bowels of Charity, demaunded of him, the *reason why he was so pensiue*? The disconsolate man answered: *You see, alas, how long now it is, that I miserable Caytiue haue suffered this same: and how the hand of God seemes verily to oppresse me, and for a greater increase therof, how I receiue dayly nothing but scornes and reproaches of such, as should rather compassionate my Case.* The benigne Father, being wholy moued with these words, with eyes and hands lifted vp towards the Mercy-Seate of *God*, made his prayer to that Soueraigne *Iudge*; & to the end they should be more efficacious, he retires himselfe into his Cel, where falling prostrate on the ground, he most hũbly beseeched the diuine Mercy, to restore that poore creature to his former strẽgth. His prayer was quickly heard. For the Man arising from the groũd, stood vp firme on his feete. This thing seemed to him a Dreame, for he did nothing but looke about him, to see whether it were true or no. And yet neuerthelesse making some proofe to moue his Legs, & to frame his Steps, he at last acknowledged the diuine Mercy to be shewed vpon him: and then nimbly returned home to the Mill, with much ioy, and with infinite rendring of thankes to *God*. Wherupon his Companions, and the others who knew right well who he was, remayned astonished, and amazed, as it were, at the sight of some phantasme; attributing the same to the Goodnes of God, and the Sanctity of their blessed *Bishop*.

In the same place, was a Man cured of the dropsy, through the only Intercession of *S. Malachy*. Who afterwards remayned in the seruice of the Monastery.

There was a certayne Gentlewoman of parentage very well descended, but yet farre more illustrious for her vertue, which made her most deere to the blessed *Pastour*. This woman, was grieuously afflicted with the bloudy flux; & this her disease was so vehement, as she, in processe of tyme, was brought to an extreme debility, & euen, through the aboundant issuing of bloud, was ready to giue and yeild vp her spotlesse Soule into the hands of her mercifull *Redeemer*. Her friends seeing her in this lamentable case, sent a messenger with all speede to *S. Malachy*, to entreate him to vouchsafe to come and visit her, and affoard her some Comfort in this her Extremity. When the holy *Bishop* heard this heauy Newes, he was strooke very sad, for the losse he saw would ensue of a Matron of that great worth and rare Example, as she was of. And sudenly determined to go his wayes thither: but afterwards fearing to arriue too late, called to him *Malcus*, a man of a singular integrity of Conscience, (of whome we made mention before) and a very dexte-

rous

rous young man. *Go your wayes* (said he) *in hast, to the sick woman, and carry her these three apples blessed by me; I hope in our Lord, that hauing once tasted of them, she shall not come to tast of Death, before she see me, though I be not otherwise able to come so speedily as I would.* The good *Malcus* obeyed with expedition: and with efficacious meanes exhorted the dying woman to tast of the Present, which was sent her by the Bishop *S. Malachy.* She being cōforted somewhat with the most gratefull name of her spirituall Father, beckens to her Mayd, (being not otherwise able to speake, or to moue her self) to put vp her pillow a litle. Wherupon, taking one of the apples, with a trembling hand she beganne to bite the same, and being newly reuiued with the only tast therof, brake forth into words and prayses of God. By & by her sleepe, which together with her tast had now for a good while been lost, returned to her agayne, and she reposing with great sweetnes, the bloud in the meane tyme came to make a stop. In so much as being now awake without more ado, she found her selfe to be altogeather whole although not without some mãner of weakenes, the which notwithstanding by the next day did likewise leaue her, at the vnexpected presence of *S. Malachy.*

A Continuation of the Miracles, which S. Malachy *wrought, vpon diuers other Occasions.* Chap. 20.

THere dwelt neere to *Benchor*, an Honourable Knight whose wife being arriued at the article or point of death, *S. Malachy* was speedily sent for to help her with fit accomodations, and with the *Extreme Vnction*. Who came thither, and hauing cheered her at first with his only aspect, prepares himself to apply the holy Oyle without delay: It seemed notwithstanding to al her friends very behoouefull (I know not vpon what occasion) and farre better, to differre the same till the next Morning. The good Father (very loath) yeilds thereunto, and making the signe of the Crosse vpon the sick woman, retyred himself into the other Chambers. He had not been there long, but behold you might easily haue heard, some pittyfull cryes, plaints, and noyses sounding through all the howse, that their *Mistris was dead.* The blessed man of God hearing this tumult, runs with his disciples, and approaching to the bed, certainely found she had giuen vp her last breath. Whereat he was full of sorrow & heauynes, laying the fault on himselfe, for that she had so departed

 with-

without that *Sacrament*; and then lifting vp his hands to heauen, with great affect: *Lord* (said he) *I cry thee mercy for I haue playd the foole, and been too negligent heerein. It is I, euen I, that haue sinned, with this prolongation, & not this poore wretch, who for her part had a very good wil therunto.* After he had thus exclaymed, he vowed to take no more Comfort or repose of any sort, till he had rendred to the dead, what he had wrongfully taken from her: and so standing with his face ouer the corps, endeauours to warme and foment those frozen limmes with bitter teares, and burning sighs, supplying to his power, the passed want: and turning towards his Company, from tyme to tyme, would be saying to them: *Watch, and pray,* So as they with Psalters and deuout prayers, he with deepe Sighes, passed away the whole night, without a winke of sleep; when as lo the Morning came, it pleased the *Diuine Clemency*, to listen vnto the vnspeakeable sighes of his most faythfull Seruant. What more? She opens her eyes, who was dead before: She sits vp right, and knowing *S. Malachy*, with a deuoute bow, saluted him. Whereat as many as beheld the sight, & heard so meruaylous things, were exceedingly amazed; and all the sadnes turned into ioy. Yet *S. Malachy*, (though there appeared no more danger for the present) very piously would needes annoynt the reuiued, as knowing well, how assuredly in that Mistery sinnes are remitted, and how likewise the body feeles a help. After he had finished this good act, he departed from thence. As for her, she (to the greater glory of God) suruiued for some tyme in good health: & hauing performed the Penance imposed her by *S. Malachy*, fell sicke afterwards agayne, & with the wonted succours of the holy *Church*, very happily dyed.

There was moreouer a Woman so afflicted with the spirit of anger and fury, as not only her kinsfolkes and neighbours seemed to shun her conuersation; but euen her owne children could hardly endure to inhabite with her. Wheresoeuer she was, there was nothing but scolding, rancour, and a hideous storme, bold, fyery, audacious, gibing, light of fingers, vntollerable, and fastidious to euery one. By reason whereof, her afflicted Children not finding other way of redresse, from so continuall and bitter grieuances, resolued to bring her (as dexterously they did) into the presence of *S. Malachy*, where breaking forth into teares and laments, they humbly demaund succour of the seruant of God. He taking compassion, as well on the danger of the Mother, as on the Childrens infelici-

infelicity, tooke her a little asyde, and demaunds of her with great affect, and gracious semblance: *Whether she had euer been confessed in her dayes*, and she answering, *No. Do you now then confesse* (sayd he to her.) Which the furious woman did, through diuine instinct: and he hauing enioyned her a conuenient pennance, & prayed awhile ouer her, commaunded her on the behalfe of *Christ* our *Lord*, that from thence forth, *she should be angry no more.* A thing incredible: there suddenly grew such a meeknes, and so great a patience in her, that euery one might know, there could be nothing therein, but meerly a change from Heauen. Which was so great a comfort to her children, as cannot be expressed. She is yet lyuing, and is sayd to be of so fayre a condition, & of so deep a Tranquillity, as where before she was wont to exasperate and offend euery one; she is now not troubled a whit withall the losses, iniuries, or tribulations that can befall her.

Now let euery one, esteeme of things as he please. If with the *Apostle* it may be lawfull for me, to abound in my sense, I dare say, that greater was the exploit of this amendement, then was the recalling of the Gentlewoman spoken aboue from death to life: because in the former was the exteriour Man raysed, in the later, only the interiour. But let vs go forward.

A secular man of good quality, came to condole with *S. Malachy* for the sterility of his soule; beseeching him to obteyne for him at the hands of God some plenty of teares. With that, the *holy Man* of God, with a cheerfull countenance approaching to him, in signe, as it were of friendship, layd his cheeke to his, and added withall, *That grace be giuen thee.* From that tyme forward, had the lay man so great aboundance of water in his eyes, as that sentence of the Scripture, seemed to be verifyed in him: *A Fountayne from the gardens: A spring of liuing waters.* This aboundance of teares the Man had to his dying day, which made his soule white, and pure from the staynes of Mortall sinne. And being so washed and cleansed from those spots of Capitall sinnes, his innocent Soule ascended on high to him, *Qui in altis habitat*, there to giue him laudes and prayses, and continually to sing the celestiall Song of *Alleluia*.

S. Malachy, *through his prayers multiplyed Fishes: With other Miracles of that kind.* Chap. 21.

SAINT *Malachy* in trauayling (as we haue sayd) to preach the word of God, did many Miracles, whereof this is one. The holy Bishop, endeauouring withall power to spread the Ghospell of *Christ Iesus*, throughout all the Kingdome of *Ireland*; fell by chance on a certayne Iland, in former tymes very famous for fishing, but afterwards, for the sinnes of the people, reduced to so great a sterility, as the poore Inhabitants were brought into very hard straytes for want thereof, and ready to be famished. It was reuealed, through the diuine *Clemency*, to a certain woman, that the intercessiõ of *S. Malachy* were the only remedy to help them to their former aboundance of fishes. This was the reason that the people flocked about him, as soone as he was landed, being a great deale more anxious and sollicitous for fish, then for preaching, or doctrine: so as they were neuer frõ his sides, cõiuring him, that laying aside, for the present, all other care whatsoeuer, he would vouchsafe to cast his eyes vpon their foresayd necessity. But the true seruant of *Christ*, answered them, that he was come thither, not to catch fishes, but soules: yet they notwithstanding, went still recommending themselues with so much more feruour, as at last it seemed good to *S. Malachy*, not to set light by the notable fayth which they shewed. Kneeling then downe on the same shore, he besought our *Lord* to affoard the grace to these men, though altogether vnworthy thereof. His praier no sooner came to the diuine throne, then a good quantity of fishes somwhat greater then vsuall ascẽded to the top of the waters, and euen to this day doth the plenty continue. What wonder is it then, that the prayer of the Iust, which penetrates heauen, should likewise diue into the Abysses, and call from thence such like, and so many squadrons of waterish creatures?

On a tyme *S. Malachy*, with three other Bishops, arriued at the towne of *Fochart*, where they all lodged, at the house of a certayne *Priest*; who finding himselfe, but ill prouided for such Ghests as they, sayd to *S. Malachy*: *How shall I do, trow you, that haue no manner of fish at all?* Seeke for some, answered he, of the *Fishermen*. O, replyed the Priest, *It is now two yeares since that there could none be found in the riuer, in so much as these poore men, through despaire haue been faigne to abandon the trade.* Then *S. Malachy* replyed. *Do you cause in the name of God, the nets to be cast.* Which was accordingly performed, and at the

the first draught there came vp some twelue Salmons at once, & as many at the second: so as all the company had meate inough to feed on, and to celebrate the Eternall Benignity. And to the end, that this thing, without all controuersy, might be attributed to the Merits of *S. Malachy*, after the feast was consumated, the former sterility did returne, and so continued for two yeares.

From these pleasant aduentures, and as it were of sport, let vs passe to a graue example of the diuine Seuerity, yet euer mixed with his wonted Mercy. There was in *Lesmor* a Clerk, of good example for the rest, but of Fayth not so orthodoxe. This man taking much complacence in his knowledge, and for the sharpnes of wit which he tooke himselfe to haue, durst impiously affirme, that in the *Eucharist*, howbeit the *Sacrament* were there, or *Sanctification*, to say rather; yet was there not therefore, the Thing of the Sacrament (as *Deuines* vse to say) that is, the reall Body, and Bloud of *Christ* our *Lord*. Vpon which so abominable errour of his, being often secretly admonished by *S. Malachy*, but euer in vaine; at last he was cited to appeare before a certaine Congregatiō of Ecclesiasticall persons, without the accesse of any secular person, that with the least shame that were possible, he might come to acknowledge his errour. Licence was there giuen him, freely to propound and argue: he endeauoured withall the forces he had to mainteine his falshood. But *S. Malachy* disputing against him, and with liuely reasons, and sound authorityes shewing how farre he was from the truth (and besides *S. Malachy*, the rest likewise confuted him) yet notwithstanding that arrogant man persisted still in his diabolicall opinion: he departed from thence indeed much confounded, but not amended, shamefully alleadging he was not conuinced through force of learning, but meerely ouerborne and oppressed with Episcopall power. *And thou* Malachy (he stucke not to say) *shouldst not haue dealt with me in this manner, in speaking thus against the truth, and (if thou wilt but confesse the matter as it is) euen in truth against your owne Conscience*. The holy Pastor being exceedingly contristated with so pertinacious an impudency as well for the losse of that erring soule, as for the loue of the Catholike Fayth, causeth the *Clerke* anew to make his appearance in a more solemne and numerous assembly: and heere the fallacyes & vanity of that contumacious wretch, being afresh layd open, and confuted, he publikely exhorted him to acknowledge the falshood, and depose his pertinacy. The same admonition did many other

Priests

Priests and the grauest *Prelats* affoard him. But being not able to remoue him an inch, at last they declare him a manifest *Heretique*, and by consequence deuided from Christian Society. And yet notwithstanding all this, that ignorant and proud Wretch, perseuering still in esteeming himselfe more wise and learned then all that were present, and further vpbrayding them for partiality, whereas he only freely but defended the Ghospell; *S. Malachy* at last being prouoked therewith, spake out with a lowd voyce: *Since thou wilt not willingly confesse the Truth, let God then make thee to confesse it by force.* And the Heeretike answering, *Amen*, the *Councell* was dismissed: & that excommunicated person, not being able to suffer so great dishonour and infamy, determined to runne into some forrain parts; & now with his fardell was in readynesse for the way, when behold him ouertaken on a suddayne with a grieuous infirmity; and feeling his strength to fayle him, he cast himselfe on the ground very weary and anxious.

In the meane tyme, there happened to passe by, a certayne vagabond distracted fellow: Who seeing him lye on the ground in that manner, demaunded of him; *what dost thou heere?* And the miserable Wretch answered, *he was not well*, and therefore not able to go backwards or forwards. *This malady* (sayd the mad man) *is nothing els but death it selfe; Get vp then, and go home agayne, and I will help thee.* Which words were not vttered by chaunce, but through Diuine disposition, that he might be cōstreyned to obey a mad fellow, that would not seeme to consent to so many learned and wise men. In summe, being guided by him, he was faygne to returne back into the Citty against his will, where hauing now better bethought himselfe, at last comes truly to repent his cryme, and with a great deale of contrition causeth the Bishop to be sent for to him, and as it were in a moment confesseth the fault, detests the opinion, receiues absolution, and giues vp the Ghost. In this manner that delict seemed to cost him no lesse then his life, and as many as had heard the imprecation, were astonished at the efficacy therof.

Two notable accidents, vpon certayne faythles Men, for breach of accord with S. Malachy *and an other Bishop, about certaine differences amongst them.* Chap. 21.

GReat, doubtles was the trauaile, which *S. Malachy* tooke, in the reduction of that man we mentioned aboue. But he suffered

no

no lesse paynes, nor shewed he lesse vertue, in according certayne people, now entered into a sharpe contention in matter of Confines. At what tyme *S. Malachy* resided in the Conuēt of *Benchor*, those people happened to be in a great difference; to compose which, on all sides they accorded to stand to the arbitrement of *S. Malachy* the true Seruant of *Christ Iesus*. But he was at that tyme very much troubled with many cares, which was the reason he gaue the charge to decide that cōtrouersy to another Bishop. But he also excused himselfe, saying, that *S. Malachy, and not he, was required for the effect*. And therfore he desired to be quitted of that toyle, for that they would contemne him, & he take paynes to no purpose. *Go your wayes* (sayth he) *and our Lord shall be with you*. And the other Bishop replyed: *I am content to vndertake the charge, but if they listen not to me, then know for certayne that I will send for you to determine this debate, which is rysen amongst them*. At which words, *S. Malachy* smiling: Do so then, answered he. Wherupon the Bishop condescended to vndertake the taske, and so departed.

Within a short tyme after, this Bishop caused the partyes to be assembled together. The cause was throughly debated on both sides: and for that tyme they were attoned, in such sort as they came to the signing of some articles of agreement betweene them, agreed vpon with full Consent on all sides: and theerupon they went home to their owne howses. But scarce were they gone on the way, when one of the Company being tempted by the accursed enemy of Mākind, raysed a sedition betweene them, hauing a fayre opportunity offered him. For the other was turning homwards carelesse on the way, supposing they were now out of all daunger, and therefore were naked, I meane, without any manner of defensiue or offensiue weapons about them. Wherupon that wicked Company wherof we first spake, began to say among themselues: *What do we stand vpon? We haue already the victory in our hands, and we may now worke our owne reuenge*. With this fatall resolution they furiously turning back, made hast to ouertake them on the suddayne, and vnawares. Which the *Bishop* perceiuing hyed him to the Captayne of that Rout, or assembly, and began to complayne for so great an iniustice, and for so open and vntolerable a treason; but his complaynt auayling little, he addes protestations, he alleadgeth the respect and authority of him that sent him thither, he menaceth the wrath of God, & in fine vsed all possible meanes to diuert him from so great a perfidiousnes.

ousnes. But the barbarous man, after he had let him awhile coniure & cry, at last turning himselfe to him with a proud countenãce: *Do you think* (answered he) *that for your sake we should let the malefactours get out of our Clawes, whome God as a prey, hath so deliuered to vs?* Then the poore Bishop remembring himselfe of the admonishment giuen at his departure, stretching his eyes and armes towards the Monastery began vehemently to weepe & exclayme: *O man of God, where are you now? Where are you? Did not I presage as much before? O Father? Wretch that I am, vnhappy I! Hither I came to do good, and not any hurt. And behold heere, through my occasion do those there loose their bodyes, and these their soules.*

In this manner the good *Prelate* went vp and downe afflicting himselfe, and calling vpon his *S. Malachy*. When on a suddaine amõg the wicked Persecutours, was heard a terribly voyce, (nor could it euer be knowne from whence it came) as if certayne other of their Neighbours with armed troupes, had made some incursiõ into their country, and put all to fire and sword, leading their wiues and children captiues without mercy. At which rumour, though vayne, their boldnes immediately being repressed, euery one betooke him to his heeles, leauing the rest to shift for themselues: and as it chaunceth in like tumults, the confusion was so great, as the hindmost not hauing once heard the said voyce, nor knowing wherefore, let thẽselues be led by the formost, vntill such tyme as comming into their countrey, and fynding there no such matter as they stood in feare of, remayned ashamed, and came to know, how in recompence of the malice and pride, which they had shewed to the messenger of *S. Malachy*, they had through diuine Iudgment, been giuen into the power of the Spirit of Lying. Wherat the Bishop reioyceing, he speedily returned back to carry the newes to *S. Malachy*. Who seeing things notwithstanding as yet very broken, and still fearing new disorders, determined to go thither in person, to establish betweene those sauage Nations, a sound and sincere concord indeed.

But yet neyther could he for the present seeme to bring his designe to passe, in regard the Conditions being freshly renewed, not without much adoe, & particular oathes hauing been takẽ of such, as the busines concerned, those who had been abused, being mindful of the iniury done them before, did impiously agree among themselues to cry quittance with the periurious and perfidious people: And so they went after them, as sure to ouertake them embroyled with domestique cares, wherby they might handle them as they list.

But

But it fell out, through diuine dispensation, that hauing easily passed ouer a certaine great Riuer, which lay in the way, they were yet stayed with a little brooke, not farre off, & in despight of thẽselues were constreined to make a stop. For now to them it seemed to be more then the wonted brooke, yea a very huge water, which on euery side denyed them passage; in so much as being al in admiratiõ, they said: *Whence comes this inundation? the weather is fayre, the mõtaines without snow, there hath fallen no rayne of late; and though it should chãce to haue rayned, yet which of vs can remember this little torrent, with any waters euer to haue been swolne in this sort, as to come thus to couer the land, and to ouer flow the champaines? The hand of God without doubt is heere. He hath cut off our way, for loue of this Saint, whose pacts we haue not obserued, and haue likewise violated his precepts.* So as these also without satisfying their greedy desires, full of shame, & dread, now turned their backs. The fame whereof was spread all about, and euery one blessed the Diuine *Maiesty*, that knowes so well to catch the crafty in their owne snares; to pull downe the crests of the proud; and to exalt such as humbly and faythfully serue him. Which is likewise made more manifest in the case we shall presently tell you.

Two other terrible examples of the iudgement of God, shewed vpon the contemners of S. Malachy; *yet mingled with mercy for his sake.* Chap. 23.

A Principall Gentleman of *Ireland*, falling out with one of those *Kings*, though he dealt about reconciliation, yet by no meanes would he seeme to trust him, vnlesse such a one as *S. Malachy* at least would seeme to interpose himselfe as surety between them. And certaynely not without cause, as the sequell will make apparent. For asmuch as that Gentleman assuring himselfe, not so much vpon the word of the King, as on the authority and promise of the mediatour, who was euen *S. Malachy* himselfe, while appearing in publique he walked without feare at all, behold vnawares is cast into prison by the King; who could not subdue the inueterated passion in him, nor Christianly forget that ancient hatred. The friends & kinsfolkes of the poore knight beholding him with their infinite sorrow in manifest perill of death, recurre to *S. Malachy*; vnder whose surety that other had put himselfe into the power of the King.

The Seruant of *Christ*, being stroken heerwith, and affronted withall at so iust a quarrell, what he intends to do in this case, we will declare. Hauing so sure a foundation, as the past promise of the King, he quickly reares vp a strong Bullwarke agaynst ensuing assaults, and endeauours withall power to suppresse this enormous treason; to effect which, he musters vp a braue army, to wit, a good company of his disciples, and with them presenting himselfe before the king, demaunds the prisoner at his hands: and being shamefully denyed, *You wrong* (saith he) *at once the diuine Maiesty, your selfe, & me, in violating the pact. And if you haue no care therof; yet haue I truly. This good man was perswaded by me; he founded himself vpon my word. If he chaũce to dye, I am he that haue betrayed him, and am by consequence guilty of his bloud: to what purpose would you seeme to make me a Traytour, and you disloyall? Then know for certayne, that neyther I, nor these of myne, are resolued to tast any food, vntill such tyme, as the innocent, be put into liberty, as he ought.* That sayd, he entred with them into the Temple, where all that day, with the next night, they perseuered together in Fasting and Prayer. But the King who dwelt hard by, fearing least their prayers, he being so neere, might seeme to haue too much force vpon him, with a foolish caution and aduise, tooke the resolution to absent himselfe from thence. But he no sooner was departed, but God, who reserues reuenge vnto himselfe, stroke him blind, and hauing lost wholy his sight, was glad to restore the prisoner; and to be as an other *Saul* to *Ananias*, so he to the holy Bishop, being led vnto him, where humbly crauing pardon, and mercy, through the benigne & feruent intercession of him, that could not be mindfull of iniuries, with a double miracle he had presently his sight. And in fine, the Gentleman being deliuered, an inuiolable friendship was accorded on. This surely was a great demonstration of the diuine Iudgement; but perhaps, this other, which (God assisting vs) we intend to declare, will by the wise arbitratours, be held no lesse.

We haue related aboue, that *S. Malachy* accepting the Abbay of *Benchor*, being content with the Church, and Seate, had voluntarily yielded the rents and demeanes to a certayne lay man. This mã paying as commonly is wont so great a benefit with great discourtesy and ingratitude, from the tyme he entred into the administration of those goods, beganne to vse many insolencies agaynst the holy *Abbot* and agaynst his *Religious*; annoying them in euery thing, persecuting them on euery side, and endeauouring alwayes to vilify,

lify, and denigrate their actions and deportments; but he escaped not free for so great iniustice. He had an only sonne, who through the example of the wicked Father being likewise bent to molest & offend the Man of God, within the terme of a yeare onely, made a miserable End. The matter succeeded in this sort.

It seemed good to *S. Malachy*, for the increase of diuine worship, to build an Oratory of stone worke, as he had seene done in other countryes, and the foundations now being layd, those barbarous people, fell a wondering thereat, as at a thing very vnusuall with them. But that malicious and proud yong man aboue the rest, of whome we spake, shewed not only with the others an admiration thereof, but such rancour withall, as he could not conteyne himselfe from murmuring heere and there agaynst the same: and after he had with diuers instigations and calumnies endeauoured to stirre vp those people agaynst the Seruant of *Christ*; at last comming with a shole of Townsmen, vpon the heate of the busines, and with a scornefull eye, beholding *S. Malachy*. *Hold* (sayth he) *O you Syr: what cappriccio is now come into your head, to bring such a nouelty into our house? We are in* Ireland, *not in* France: *What a leuity is this? What need is there of such a sumptuous and proud worke? Where haue you meanes to finish it, poore thing as you are? Who shall euer see it come to the roofe? It is surely the tricke of a mad man, to set hand to a worke so beyond his compasse. Hold, hold your hand; Desist from a vanity so great, or otherwise shall we make you giue ouer, nor will we suffer you to go forward by any meanes about such a building, impossible to be brought to perfection.* In which words, the hayr-brayne and rash man came to discouer his wicked intention, without once reflecting on his small forces. Forasmuch as his followers, in whome he confided so much, as soone as they came in sight of the venerable Bishop, being suddenly chaunged in hart, returned home to their houses; that impious, seditious and wretched Leader being quite aboandoned, as he deserued. To whome with Fortitude and Mercy withall, the man of God, answered: *Thou miserable wretch, this worke which thou heere seest begunne, and beholdest with an ill countenance, shall be finished without doubt, and many shall see it accomplished. But thou, because thou hast no will thereunto, shalt neuer see it: And looke you to it, least Death surprize you not in your sinne.* So *S. Malachy* sayd; & so fell it out: He dyed, and the worke was finished: but he saw it not, because, as we sayd, he dyed the very same yeare.

Now the Father of that wicked wretch, hauing known of thē *Saints* prediction, he hath kild (sayth he) my sonne, and was so incensed agaynst him for it, as in the presence of the Captayne and of the Chiefe of the Country there, he had no respect to him awhit, but called him Enuious, hollow-harted, and a meere Cosener; and lastly for a greater spight, termed him a Moncky. To which bitter contumelies, the follower of Christ answered not a word: But yet the great God would not seeme to hold his peace, throgh whose will, on that very day, that impious wretch, being seized on by an infernall spirit, and cast into the fire, was by his friends very hardly taken forth from thence, with his lymmes all burnt, with his wits crackt, with his face awry & foaming as the mouth, sending forth such horrible cryes, & framing such strange gestuures of the body, as put a terrour into euery one, and many togeather had much ado to hold him. Heerupon *Saint Malachy* was called to the spectacle, and with wonted clemency making his prayer for him, was heard, but not to the full; Because that in chastisement and memory of the offence committed agaynst the holy Father; he had after that, euen to this day, certayne grieuous fits, which at changes of the Mooue, doe most bitterly afflict him.

S. Malachy *lights on a treasure to build with, the modell was presented to him in a vision. Together with his gift of Prophesy.* Chap. 24.

REturne we now to the building: for which in truth, *S. Malachy* had no manner of meanes at all, eyther little or much; but yet felt in his hart, a certayne firme confidence in God. Whereof he was not a whit deceiued; since our Lord, perceiuing this Seruant of his not to go founding himselfe in treasures any wayes by him purchased, made him to light vpon one, within the scituation it selfe, neuer touched or knowne till that very hower. *S. Malachy* then seemed to find in the purse of God, what he could not haue found in his owne: and that worthily truly. For what was more reasonable, then for him to haue the coffer in common with God, who had nothing proper of his owne? While he in fine, that hath a liuely fayth, hath all the riches of the world. And what els is the world, but an inexhanstible Banck of the diuine Clemency? *The whole circuit of the world is myne* (sayth he) *and whatsoeuer is conteyned therin.* And hence it is that *S. Malachy* discouered those moneys, not disposing thē or laying them

them vp, but exposing them indeed ; ordeyning so large a donary of the Creatour, should wholy without sparing a whit be spent in the seruice of the Creatour: and so much the rather, as by a passed Reuelation, he knew that Edifice to be acceptable to his diuine Maiesty. Because that hauing first before he once set hand vnto it, conferred the intent with his Domestiques, and finding them somwhat dubious, by reason of the charges; he gaue himselfe to prayer, to find out by that meanes the will of God therupon.

When returning one day from a certayne Pilgrimage, which he made, being now somewhat neare to the place designed, he lifted vp his eyes, and behold, he seemed to discerne a very goodly Oratory of stone, and of excellent workmanship withall, & regarding the scite, the former, & cōposition therof, impressed the same in his fantasy with that tenacity, as the thing being cōmunicated with some few of his owne disciples of the more ancient sort of them, he gaue beginning to the building, & finished with such diligence the scite, the modell, and prorportion, with all the circumstances, by degrees, as the plot came iust to answere the fold; as if he also with *Moyses* had heard, *See you do all according to the plat-forme, which was shewed you in the mountayne.* He had afterwards a like vision to this of that other Oratory, which he built in a place called *Sabelline*, sauing that he saw the fashion not only of the Oratory there, but cuē of the whole Monastery likewise.

These said manifestations were of material and sensible things. But that which now we shall set downe, was of an edifice meerely spirituall. *S. Malachy* passing along by a certayne Citty, and a great multitude concurring thither to meete with him, by chaunce he discouered among the troupes, a yong man very curious to view him, who mounting on the top of a huge stone, was standing there a tiptoe, for that purpose to behold him, extēding forth his neck as much as he could: and *S. Malachy* being certifyed from heauen, how that person stood there with the spirit and vertue of *Zachæus*, yet the friēd of God held his peace for that tyme, making shew as if he had not heeded the same. But after at night in his Lodging, he told some of his how he had not seene him only, but also foreseen what should betyde him. The third day was not passed, when that deuout man appeared at his Inne, in the company of a Gentleman his Maister: who courteously proposing to *S. Malachy*, the good desires of the young man, besought his Paternity to accept him, among his chil-

dren.

dren, and followers. *S. Malachy* acknowledged him presently, and added: *He had no need to be recōmended by men, who already by God had bin so recommended to him.* And so taking him louingly by the hand consigned him to other *Fathers*, & *Brothers* of his, & liues (if I be not deceiued) at this day, a chiefe Lay-Brother in the Monastery of *Suria*, with an excellent fame of religion and sanctity.

The Blessed Bishop, likewise shewed a great gift of *Prophesy*, euen at the tyme of his saying *Masse* when being aware of a certayne crime which lay hid in the Deacon, for that tyme did no more but looke vpon him, and fetch a sigh, but after the sacred Mistery was ended, he examined the minister himselfe in secret, as touching his conscience: and he ingenuously confessed, that night he had felt an illusion. Wherupon the most chast *Priest* enioyning him a secret pēnance; this day, sayd he, thou oughtest not to appeare at the Aultar, but chastly and modestly rather to haue withdrawne thy selfe, and to haue carryed the respect due to the most holy Sacrament: to the end that being purged with such humiliation, thou mightst haue been found more worthy hereafter to so noble an office.

And so another tyme, while he was offering the *Host*, with accustomed reuerence & purity of hart. There was a glorious doue seen to enter in at the window of the Tēple, which illumining the whole Church, that was somwhat obscure before, after it had flown heere & there, came lastly to rest vpon the Crosse, before the face of the *Celebrant*. He that serued was astonished at the nouelty as well of the light, as of the Bird it selfe, (which is rarely seen in those coūtryes) & as halfe dead, fell groueling on the ground, so as he hardly came to himselfe all the tyme of the ministery. When *Masse* was ended *S. Malachy* did forbid him vnder mortall sinne, to discouer the thing as long as he liued. He being at *Ardmach*, in company with another Bishop his Collegue, they arose by night togeather with others, to visit deuoutly the Sepulchers of the holy Martyrs there, layd vp in the Cemeter of the blessed *Patrick*. And behold how one of those Aultars did seeme to burne into liuely flames. Whence *S. Malachy* ghessing the great merits of such as reposed there, ran in of a suden, and plunging himselfe into the midst of the flames, with opē armes imbraced the Aultar. Where what he did, or felt in the place there is no mā knowes. This is true, that the Man of God came forth of that fire more enflamed with celestiall Loue, then euer: as all his more dearest friends very easily perceiued.

S. Ma-

S. Malachy *remembring his purpose, calls a Synod about the Palls. And vndertakes a second voyage to* Rome. Chap. 25.

NOw at last, let vs heere make a stop to the signes and prodigyes from the diuine arme, shewed forth in fauour of *S. Malachy* by an entire catalogue therof. It sufficeth that noting the same with some diligence, which we haue already touched, the Iudicious wil assuredly acknowledge all the species, at least of the anciẽt myracles; as Prophesies, Reuelations, Chasticements of the wicked, Healths of body, Conuersions of mynds, Resurrection of the Dead. Besides which, through his so excellent vertues, he was magnifyed of our Lord likewise in the sight of Kings, and the greatest Men: he was full of merits, and after many and grieuous persecutions, surmounted at last, euen Enuy it selfe. From so honorable a Race, what might be expected heere, but a glorious yssue? Let vs now see then in what manner he went forth.

On a day *S. Malachy*, and the Brethren togeather were in a holy recreation, conferring amongst themselues of the last passage: and euery one being inuited by turnes, discouered where, & when it would like him best to depose his terrene carkas, while some insinuating one, and some another solemnity; some this, some that Cemeter or Churchyard; *S. Malachy* (when it came to his turne to answere) standing first a litle in suspense, for the place distinguished: That if he were to remayne in *Ireland*, it would be most gratefull to him, to be where he might arise in the company of the holy Apostle *S. Patricke*: & if in forraine parts, no where more willingly would he repose his bones, then in the church of *Clareuallis*. As for the tyme he chose the day of All-soules: to the end to be accompanyed then with greatest number of suffrages, that might be. Now if this were *S. Malachyes* desire, he had the fauour afforded; If an Oracle, it missed not a iot, as we shall see.

The feruent desire, which *S. Malachy* euer had to adorne the two Metropolitans with the sacred Palls, was not a whit extinguished, though for a tyme buryed in the ashes of obliuion. Which now he vnraked, and was wholy enflamed with a desire to put it in present execution. Which to performe effectually, after he had recommended himselfe to our Lord, he gathered a generall Synod in *Ireland*: and after the dispatch of other particulars, came to the foresayd point of the Palls. The proposition pleased all for the most; but with condition, that the enterprize should be committed to some other, besides him. Yet notwithstanding *S. Malachy* made great instance to go, in regard Pope *Innocent* was dead, & *Eugenius*, a Monke of *Clareuallis*, was mutually chosen for his Successour: yet had he no cause to feare a repulse, in renewing of his memorial; for he was a Man of that benignity and sanctimony, as the fame therof spread it selfe throughout the world: and likewise in respect, *Pope Eugenius* for publique affayres, was then resident in *France*, which was a short way, and lesse daungerous, then the first he vndertooke. The Prelates perceiuing the great desire he had to vndergoe that paynefull iourney, durst not much oppose themselues agaynst the will of the holy man, but consented to his desire: Which he vndertooke as soone as the Councell was dissolued.

Amongst a great number of his friends, which accompanyed him to the Sea syde, one was called by name *Catholicus*, who was sorely molested with an Epilepsy; in such sort as often tymes in a day he would fall on the ground, to the exceeding great brusing of his whole body, which to preuent he had alwayes one to attend vpon him. This miserable wretch turning himselfe to *S. Malachy*, with a lamentable voyce, and full of teares, sayd. *Ay me, Father, you go now your wayes, and know in how great, and how many afflictions you leaue me, and yet can you help it, if you please: and though I for my sinnes, haue, and do deserue all euill, yet alas, what fault haue these poore Brothers done, to whome for my sake is not permitted an houre of rest?* with this plaint the hart of the Blessed Bishop was as it were, now spilt asunder: When he deerly imbracing the sick man, made the signe of the Crosse on his breast, saying: *Rest secure yet, and be confident that you shall not fall into the like fit agayne, till my returne.* That malady the poore man had susteyned for six yeares togeather. But now at the only speach of *S. Malachy*, he was recouered in such sort, as he neuer fell more thereinto, being in a moment deliuered from so grieuous, & bitter a payne, and the assistants themselues from a long and yrksome a custody.

After which, as *S. Malachy* was taking ship, came two of his most inward friends to him, for to craue a notable boone at his hands; and he demanding what their request was: we will not tell you, sayd they, till you promise vs first to comfort vs: he promised so to do; then they replyed. We will (sayd they) that you faithfully

fully promiſe vs another thing, which is to make your returne to *Ireland* agayne, very ſafe and ſound: the very ſame did all the others beſeech him. Whereupon the ſeruant of *Christ*, retiring a litle, as he was wont, within himſelfe; and being ſorry firſt for hauing ſo engaged his word, not knowing how to diſcharge himſelfe, being willing on the one ſyde to come out of debt, and ſory on the other to leaue *Clareuallis*. But after the ſame, at laſt reſolued with himſelfe, to comply with that which preſſed him moſt, that is, not to fayle in his promiſe, remitting the reſt to the diuine pleaſure. Then though with an euill will he anſwered, yea: and his diſciples being comforted not a litle heerwith, he cauſed them to hoyſe vp ſayle. But in the midſt of the Sea, he was driuen backe agayne vpon the coſt of *Ireland*, by a ſudden contrary wind. Where he landed, and paſſed the night in a Church of his, acknowledging and thanking the diuine goodnes, for that without the preiudice of any, he had by that meanes acquit him from all wherein he was bound to his Monkes. And in the morning being afreſh embarqued, he landed very happily on the ſame day in the Kingdome of *Scotland*, & after two dayes more arriued at *Verdeſtagnus*, where leauing certayne ſubiects for a Ciſtercian Abbay which he had founded there, he purſued his iourney, and being honorably receiued by King *Dauid*, in the confines there, ſtaying in that place for ſome dayes, not without a great deale of fruite, he paſſed into *England*.

In Gisburne *in England* S. Malachy *cures a woman of a Canker. And after arriues at* Clareuallis, *where he fals mortally ſick.* Chap. 26.

SAINT *Malachy* at his entrance into the kingdome of England lodged in the Canonry of *Gisburne*: where he contracted a very ſtreight friendſhip with thoſe Prieſts there of ſingular fame. Moreouer in that place, a woman was preſented to him, very much deformed, and eaten with a horrible Canker: He bleſſed a little water, & therewith ſprinkled the ſoares ſo efficaciouſly, as the paines therof ſudenly ceaſing, the next day they could hardly be ſeene.

Departing from thence, he went to the Sea ſide, where he met with an vnlookt for impediment, cauſed through certayne differēces riſen at that tyme betweene the Apoſtolique Sea, and the King of England about iuriſdiction; which were then growne ſo hoat, as he through aboundāt iealouſy permitted no Prelate to go forth of the

Iland; and for the same respect, was the Bishop *Malachy* likewise reteyned for some tyme. Who on the one syde though he were sory to be delayed in that sort from his businesses: yet was he not aware on the other syde, that this very delay seemed to fauour his vowes, & designes. Because, if he had presently gon into *Fraunce*, he had been feigne, leauing *Clareuallis*, and passing the Alps, with diligence to haue measured the greater part of *Italy*; the Pope *Eugenius* being already gone forth of France, & approached to *Rome*. Where as now by this delay through a sea-passage, his iourney by diuine prouidence came to be disposed in that manner as he arriued at *Clareuallis*, euen at the point himselfe desired. Where being receiued by vs, as an Angell descended from Paradise; what a light seemed to shine vpon this our habitation, and what a solemne Feast was it for vs al? and I my selfe now trembling, and weake as I was, being reuiued with the newes, ran full of exultation and iubiley to his holy kisses and imbraces; and he reciprocally, shewed himselfe to vs, as he was wont, very pleasant and affable, and wonderfully gratefull to euery one.

Now by this tyme were some foure or fiue dayes of our common gladnes passed ouer, when behold on the Feast of the glorious *S. Luke* the Euangelist, after he had with extraordinary deuotion celebrated Masse in publique, he was taken with a feuer. Wherupon falling downe on his bed, he fell sick, and all our ioy was turned to sadnes; though somewhat moderated the while, in that the feuer as yet was not very violent nor rigid. So as recouering hope, you might haue seene, what running there was vp and downe in the howse, some to prouide medicins, some to apply fomẽtations, some to bring him meate, some to exhort and intreate him to eate, euery one striuing to serue such a Ghest, and accompting themselues most happy that could haue most accesse to that holy & blessed man Whẽ *S. Malachy* beholding thẽ with a benigne countenance: *All these paynes* (would he say) *are too much for you to take: but yet for your sakes I refuse them not, and willingly do what you cõmaund me*. He knew right well his latest hower approched: and to his companions, who would seeme to comfort him with saying there appeared in him no mortall signe, *It is conuenient* (would he answere) *by all meanes that* Malachy *this yeare depart this life. The day approches now, which I, as you very well know, haue alwayes wished to be the last of my short dayes. I know well in whome I trust: and now that I haue part of my intent, I am certaine, and secure in like fort that my desire shalbe graunted in the rest. He that brought me through his clemency to this place I desired so much; will not deny me the tyme nor terme: and for as much as concernes this weary body of myne, I will heere repose it: for the soule he shall prouide for it, who giues saluation to such as put their trust in him: Nor haue I any small confidence in the same day, wherin by the lyuing is purchased so great a help to the dead.*

And now approached full neere the day indeed, when he spake so freely of it: so as not to loose any tyme, he craued for the *Extreme vnction*. And while the Monks were about to descend into the *Church* to fetch the holy Oyle with procession thence vnto his chamber, he would not seeme to consent thereunto by any meanes: but would in person be led downe thither, where with the greatest veneration that might be, hauing taken the holy Oyle, as also the heauenly *Viatique*, he returned to his bed, and recommended himselfe to the prayers of the Brethren, as he likewise mutually recommended thē to our Lord. And it is a meruaylous thing, how from an vpper chāber that was somewhat high, wherin he was lodged, he came forth and descended on his feete, while he affirmed notwithstanding, that death had knocked at the doore. And yet, who would belieue it? He was not pale in the face, nor meagre, nor wrinckled in the brow, nor had his eyes sunck, nor his nose sharpe, nor his lips cōtracted, nor black his teeth, nor leane & slender his neck, nor crūpt in the shoulders, nor finally had he the flesh of the whole body any whit fallen away. Thus far hath my pen gon on its course; now it seemes, as it were, to runne a ground, and loath to passe to that which by all meanes is conuenient to be written, as immediately followes.

The blessed Death of the most venerable Bishop S. Malachy. *With a myracle which fell out after.* Chap. 27.

THe ioyfull Commemoration of *All-Saints*, arriued at last; whē we entred into the Quire, but with a dolefull musique, & yet was it necessity for vs to sing in mourning. *S. Malachy* though he could not sing, yet mourned not, but reioyced rather for his approach so neare to the triumph at hand. His defect of voyce he supplied with a iubiley of the mind. He honoured that Blessed Society, wherof he was very soone to make vp one: he payed to others that tribute, which within little after was likewise to be payed to him.

The sacred Offices being ended, as well as they could be, *S. Malachy* now approched, not to night, but euen to *Aurora*, as it were; nor was it *Aurora* indeed, since darknes being now banished, the day was come: so as the feuer renforcing it selfe, the vitall parts begã throgh all the lyms to put forth first a boyling, and then a cold sweat. To the end that euen that blessed soule it selfe likewised might seeme to passe through fire and water, into rest.

And now hope being quite lost on all sides, and ech one resuming his owne prognosticat, and acknowledging those of the sicke to be likewise true; we were called on his behalfe to the Cel where he lay, & he casting his eyes towards vs: *With a great desire* (sayd he) *haue I desired to make this present Pascha with your Charities: Thanks be to the supernal Piety, that I see not my self defrauded of my hope. If I be able I shall not be vnmindfull of you. Go to, I shall. I haue put my trust in God, and euery thing is possible to the belieuer. I haue loued God, I haue loued you: Loue is without terme.* Hereupon looking vp to heauẽ, he adds, *O Lord conserue these in thy name, and not these only, but all those who by meanes of thy word, and my ministery, haue beene dedicated to thy holy seruice.* After which imposing hands vpon all, one by one, he makes vs to go rest our selues: alledging the extremest article was not yet arriued. We went our wayes then, and about midnight, being newly awaked, we ran to him againe, who was now vpon departure. The chamber, and all the howse was filled; there hauing beene besides our owne family, many Abbots repayred hither from other places. And so with psalmes, hymnes, and spirituall Canticles accompanyed we our friend in his way homwards.

Thus *S. Malachy* Bishop of *Ireland*, & Legate of the Apostolique Sea, assumpted as it were from our hands by the Angels, in the yeare of our *Lord*. 1148. and of his age 54. in tha day and place by him chosen & prognosticated before, most peaceably slept in our Lord. And may be said to sleepe; Since we all hauing our eyes fixed vpon that venerable face of his, were none of vs aware of his last breath; there not appearing in the dead the least signe to distinguish him awhit from what he was liuing. And such was the freshnes of that whole angelicall countenance of his, as he might seeme to haue receiued rather an ornamẽt from death, then any iniury at all. And finally himselfe was not changed awhit, but he changed vs rather: Forsomuch as in a moment, our mourning was turned to Iubiley, playnt to song, and the domesticall discipline also, which was somwhat troubled before with ſo grieuous an accident, was now returned to its frame agayne.

The ſacred Body being taken out of the chamber, vpon Abbots ſhoulders, was carryed (according to his owne deſigne) into the Chappell of the moſt bleſſed *Virgin*. There were the Exequies performed with great celebrity; the Maſſe was ſolemnely ſung, nor was there any want of thoſe diligences, which appertayne to ſuch a worke of piety. Nor is it to be ſilenced the while, how a certaine child ſtanding in the meane time a pretty way off, with a dead arme of his, not without a grieuous impediment and deformity to him; I my ſelf being aware thereof, becked to him, to come to me, when taking the withered arme, I applyed it to the hand of the glorious Biſhop, and he publikely on a ſudden, retyred from thence with his arme, and hand made whole and ſound. That done, thoſe Organs of the holy Ghoſt, were depoſed in the appointed Sepulcher.

In this manner the good *S. Malachy*, hauing happily runne his cariere, went his wayes to the immortall crownes: leauing vs all no leſſe full of ſolid edification, then of laudable Enuy. It reſts now O *Sauiour*, and our *Ieſus*, that as we being put in truſt with this moſt noble treaſure of yours, ready to reſtore it whenſoeuer you ſhalbe pleaſed tn require the ſame: ſo your *Maieſty*, would vouchſafe not to take it from hence, without the ſpoyles of ſo many companions and friends; but as we haue had him, as a Gheſt, and Conuictour in this tranſitory life; ſo may we haue him as a Guide & Conductor into heauen, for to raigne there with thee, and him, world without end.

FINIS.

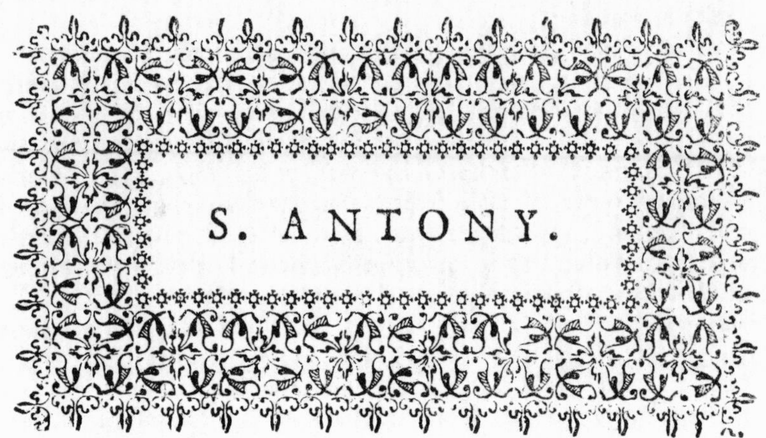

S. ANTONY.

THE ARGVMENT.

SPeake, O yee ſhores, neere which the Sunne doth riſe,
How bright from you his golden Chariot flyes,
Reflecting his ſtrong luſtre on your ſtreames,
And makes your gemmes vye purple with his beames:
Expreſſe you this, and we may parallell
The glorious light that iſſued from the Cell
Of this deare Saint; which made th' enamor'd sky,
To wonder at a State, ſo low, ſo high.

Behold his faſting, watching, dayly ſtrife
With helliſh Foes, his troubles during lyfe;
Yet like the Palme with greater burden preſt
Rayſ'd more aloft, by paynes obtayning reſt.
Contempt of riches did a treaſure gaine
Immortall, precious. He caſt downe, doth raygne
Aboue the Sphæres. And we from him may know
Heau'ns high way lyes not through the world below.

THE

THE LIFE OF

S. ANTONY ABBOT.

Taken out *S. Athanasius*, from *S. Hierome*, *Palladius*, and others.

The Genius and disposition of S. Antony: *With his Vocation, and Renuntiation of the World.* Chap. I.

SAINT ANTONY of Ægypt, that glorious Conquerour of himselfe, and triumpher of the Princes, and powers of darknes, was borne in the confines of *Heraclea*, in a place called of *Sozomenus* by the name of *Coma*, and by *Nychephorus Conia* (a variety sprung peraduenture from the errour of the Copyers: and so it is to be thought, since *Coma* in the Greeke tongue doth signify a Bourg, and therefore it is a common opinion of some, that eyther of both the Authours had so written. But howsoeuer it be, it appeares very well, that) *S. Anthony* from the first beginning was destined to high enterprizes; since Nature, Education, and grace haue concurred with so liberall a hand, to fauour and adorne him. He had an able, and liuely temperature of body; an aspect both graue and pleasant; a sacacious iudgement; a memory tenacious; a witt

 docible

docible, acute, and constant. Besides he was bred of Christian parents, very honourable, with singular care and custody, and with so much the greater facility, as the Child of his owne accord, being much aliened from childish sports, and profane studies, shewed him selfe most amorous of silence, and of Churches; attentiue to the word of God, content with simple fare, and without any delicacies. To such matters, and addresses as these, the holy Ghost added the forme, and the ornaments, which presently we shall see. For that indeed in the most dangerous passage of his age, which was of 18. or 20. being left an Orphã, with one Sister only, certaine things began to come into his mynd, which formerly he had heard, or read, of the Counsayles of Christ, of the conuersation of his disciples, and of the meruailous feruour of the primitiue Church, at such tyme as the faythfull, replenished with charity, selling their houses and liuings, and whatsoeuer els they possessed in the world, went voluntarily, bringing the price thereof, and laying the same at the feete of the *Apostles.* Considering withall, the inestimable rewards, wherewith for the same they were to be recompenced in *Heauen*.

These thoughts, went *S. Antony* reuoluing in his mind; when as it happened through diuine disposition, being entred into a Tẽple, according to custome, he heard in the very same instant, these words of the Ghospell recited; *Si vis perfectus esse, vade, & vende omnia quaecumque habes, & da pauperibus, & veni sequere me, & habebis thesaurum in caelo.* The words were not sung to a deafe man: they suddenly pierced with extraordinary feeling vnto the marrow & hart. Wherupon the Sacrifiec being ended, he returned home from thẽce without delay: and gaue liberally the rents of his Patrimony to his kindred, which were 300. acres of very fertill land, as *S. Athanasius* affirmes (to whose Greeke text I do particularly adhere, though others haue accompted it for some 300. trees of fruitfull Palmes) and this to auoyd all manner of contention. For the moueables he put them to sale, and taking from thence a summe of money, distributed the same to the poore; reseruing to himselfe, but a very small part for necessities occurring, and especially for his Sisters sake. But within litle after, being returned to the Church, and hearing that other aduise of the chiefe *Verity*; *Nolite cogitare de crastino*: with a generous resolution he made an end of selling the rest, and placing the child his Sister, in the company of some noble and deuout Virgins,

he

he distributed the rest that remayned, to the poore. Thence leauing his house, and parents, being replenished with singular confidence, he made his entry into the sharpe way of perfect Vertue.

At that tyme, there were not on foote so many Monasteryes in *Egipt*, as were afterwards to be seene: and in the Deserts which were more remote (none can remember) that euer any one inhabited, till that tyme: But, he that would with particular study, giue himselfe to diuine Seruice, and attend to the saluation of his soule, for the most, recollected himselfe into some little Lodging, neare to his country, and there would exercise and apply himselfe with sundry meanes to pacify the heauenly wrath, to amend his manners, & to prepare himselfe for death. The holy youth hauing got some notice of one of these Exercitants, being now of good yeares, and wel experienced, disposed himselfe to do as much. And likewise sequestring himselfe from the conuersation of seculars, began first to deale with him, and afterwards with others, frõ time to tyme, such as dayly he discouered to be addicted to that manner of life: and not for curiosity to know sundry inclinations of natures, or features of faces, but with diligence only to obserue the industryes, and vertuous qualityes of all, and in ech one to imitate whatsoeuer might seeme more admirable in him; and so like a wise Bee, for the framing of his misticall hony, in visiting them at tymes, and shewing himselfe officious, obsequious, and obedient to them, he went on with a great deale of iudgment; collecting abstinence from hence, thence affability, from one dexterity in conuersation, from another vigilancy in praying, from this heere patience and meekenes, from him there sharpe penance and mortification, and from all together a feare of God, and christian charity to his Neighbour. And it is truly a thing worthy of note, that he contending so with euery one to his power in so noble an enterprize, would be doing the same with such circumspection, and with so much sweetnes; as not only he was free from rancour and enuy, but likewise highly beloued and esteemed of euery one. And moreouer now hauing made the renunciation of his goods, and hauing nothing to susteyne himselfe, he would not liue with the sweat of other mens browes, but would giue some tyme to the labour of his hands, & of the price which he purchased with his trauells, reteyning onely to himselfe, so much as might suffice him for a little bread, he would diuide the rest with very great charity, among the poore.

S. Anthony *is twice tempted by the euill Spirits: but reiects them both.* Chap. 2.

TO so fayre a beginning, and so happy a progresse, the subtile & cruell Enemy of human kind, opposeth himselfe, vsing all art, and framing euery engin, to withdraw the new souldiour from his glorious purposes. First he beginnes on the one side, to reduce into his mynd, his parentall inheritance, the commodity and delights of his home; his nobility of bloud, with the hope of new purposes. On the other, the streight way of vertue, the frailty of flesh, the difficulty of pennances, especially in the spatiousnes of a long life, which with apparent reasons, he would seeme to make him promise to himselfe. He added moreouer, the due sollicitude of his kindred, & particularly of the virgin his Sister; who though recommended to others, yet if peraduenture any sad disastre should betide her, she might iustly in the sight of God & men, cōplaine of him. With these suggestions, gaue Sathan the first assaults to *S. Antony*: and perceiuing himselfe to be so valiantly repelled with words of the diuine scripture, through liuely fayth, and with the memory of the Pouerty, of the dolours, and Passion of *Christ*; he reenforced the battayle afresh, with a squadron of bestiall & carnall thoughts, enflaming in an instant, the naturall incentiues of youthfull age, and representing in his imagination day and night, sundry formes of beautifull and lasciuious women. This new warre, as it was continuall and perilous to *S. Antony*, so was it grieuous and troublesome to him beyond measure, and the Enemyes so much the more audacious and fierce, as their intelligence on earth was greater, and their enflamed darts seemed to penetrate more neere to the Fort of the soule.

Neuertheles, the stout and faythfull Guardian, opposed so many rampiers of vigils, fastings, considerations of infernal paynes and of the last iudgment; and aboue all obteyned with humble and feruent prayer so much succour from heauen, as euen likewise from these battayles, he seemed to carry away alwayes a happy & glorious victory. Whereupon the restles Aduersary did tēpt him with arrogancy, and vanity, hoping by that meanes to depriue him of the crowne. Within a little after, the Enuious & diabolicall wretch appeared to the blessed young man, in the shape of a horrid, & yong Blackamore, complayning with a human voyce, & prostrate at his feete,

feete, sayd to him: Many, and many, O *Antony*, haue I deceiued in my tyme, but as by other *Saints*, so likewise now by thee, and thy valour, am I put to confusion. Being demaunded, who he was: I am said he, the fried of Carnality. I am he that moues debates, & in sundry manners, do cause perplexities in youth; & therfore they do call me, the spirit of Fornication. How many, that haue beene disposed to liue in Chastity, haue I made them already to alter their purposes? How many, that haue begun to keepe the same, haue I reduced agayne to their obscenes and vncleanes, as before? I am he, through whose occasion, the *Prophet* so reprehends the lapsed, saying: *Spiritu fornicationis seducti estis:* & surely with reason too, since I, & no other but I, am he that deceiued them. And I finally, am he, who haue tempted thee often, yet hitherto could I neuer ensnare thee.

At these words, *S. Anthony* acknowledging, all good to come from heauen, sudenly gaue thanks to the diuine Goodnes, & thence taking new confidence, thus answered the Deuill. Thou then for ought I can see, art a very coward, and hast little in thee: and likewise the age, and hew thou hast taken vpon thee, are right signes of great weakenes and basenes in thee: and added, For this reason alone, (quoth he) I will not care for thee. And concluded with great iubiley of hart: *Dominus mihi adiutor, & ego despiciam inimicos meos.* Scarcely had he begun to sing this goodly verse, of the hundred & seauenteenth psalme, when the infamous seducer vanished quite, ful of rage, and confusion. And it was but iust, that the fierce encounters, and vererate stratagems of that immortall substance, which had once the impious boldnes, to rise vp against the *Highest*; should remayne thus scorned & reproached by a yong man, encombred with flesh, and encompassed with infirmity.

But yet for all this, *S. Antony* held not himselfe a whit secure, or out of danger: because he had well vnderstood ere now, how the wicked spirits, haue a thousand inuentions to hurt with. Heerupon taking alwais new courage, at the presence of God, he would neuer lay down the armes of iustice; nor yet discouered he only, from the strongest tower of holy fayth, with high contemplation, the country afarre off, but euen lay also in wayt with particular attention to be alwayes ready agaynst the domesticall enemies, not suffering in the Ports of the hart any thought to haue entrance, not throughly examined, and well known. He had all his parts subdued and restreyned with seuere lawes, and heasts. He would passe very often whole nights in prayer, and when through extreme necessity it behoued him to rest somewhat, he had no other bedd, then a peece of a mat, or the bare ground. Some two or three dayes togeather, would he be without eating or drinking a whit, and at last would refresh himselfe with nothing els, but bread, and a litle water, and salt.

And heere it is to be noted, that he slackt not his rigour after he had thus continued a while as if he had done inough; nor measured he the greatnes of his profit by continuance of tyme: But day by day, he would suppose he did but then beginne, remembring that saying of *Elias*: *The Lord liues, in whose sight I do stand to day*. In which saying, *S. Antony* would ponder on that word, *to day*: being well aduised, that the souldier of Christ, were to make no reckoning of the trauayles, and yeares now passed ouer; but as if euery day, he had but newly entred into the lists, so were he to be alwayes in a readines, to giue forth himselfe, as a glad spectacle to the diuine Maiesty, Men, and Angels. And now since mention is made of *Elias*, I will not spare to add, how the blessed *S. Antony* according to the light he had in raysing vp his thoughts, from tyme to tyme, was purposed at last, with singular study to expresse in himselfe, the lyfe and manners of that louer, not of Prophecy so much, as of retirednes, and solitude.

S. Antony *betakes himselfe into a Cell in the Desart; and is therefore maligned by the wicked Spirits.* Chap. 3.

NOt farre off from *S. Antonyes* Cottage, were many ancient ruines, not inhabited by any. In one of which causing himselfe to be shut vp, by a certayne friend of his, with order taken with him, to bring him bread within such a space; he heere would treate with none other, then himselfe, and God alone. For which the Prince of darknes, being now anew enflamed with rage, and fearing if he put not remedy to it in tyme, he should soone behold (to his irreparable losse) the desert likewise filled with Monasteries & Monkes: sending presently to the Cell of *S. Antony*, a great number of cruell Ministers, caused him (through diuine dispensation) to be so sharpely scourged & whipped, as he was left on the ground, deuoyd of speach or breath: and he himselfe likewise related afterwards, that the smart of those stroakes exceeded any torment, which were

were humanly supportable.

While then he lay along stretched forth in this manner; behold (through diuine prouidẽce) his coadiutour came now to him with his wonted prouision. Who opening the doore, and finding the poore *S. Antony* in so ill a plight; tooke him vp for dead on his shoulders, & with much cõpassion carryed him so to the Parish Church. Heere now, who were able to explicate the concourse of freinds, Parents, and Neighbours, who came suddenly to behold him, to bewayle him, and to prepare his obsequyes? Some lamented the thred of so heroicall actions should so beyond al opinion be cut off. Others very bitterly deplored the losse of such a Father and Maister, and perhaps there wanted not those (such is the nature of men) that for lack of consideration, would seeme to reprehend him of immoderate feruour, & foolish temerity. The Euening being passed with such discourses, while they stood about the Corps with many lights officiously, expecting the Exequyes; by little and little (as it happens) they fell a sleep. And now it was about midnight, when *S. Antony* being returned to himselfe, & opening his eyes, was aware, that all the Standers by were oppressed with a profound sleepe, excepting his familiar friend, who through his much sollicitude and charity, was continually in suspence, and vigilant. Which *S. Antony* perceiuing, coniured him so much, partly with signes, and partly with a low voyce, as in fine he obteyned, without any noyse to be conueighed back into his cell againe. Where being not able, throgh the many soares he had, eyther to kneele, or to stand on his feete, he was feyn first, as he lay, to make his prayer a prety while, & after that with a greater courage thẽ euer, began he with a lowd tone to defy the infernall squadrons, saying.

Behold me *Antony*, heere I am, I fly not your skirmishes, how fierce soeuer they be, nor shal euer any thing in the world be able to seuer me from *Christ*; and presently gaue himselfe to singing of Psalmes, saying: *Si consistant aduersum me castra, non timebit cor meum*; whẽ as the Authour of Pride conuerting himselfe to his cursed Crew, See you (saith he) this vntamed beast, how after so many punishments, and bitter woes, he dares yet to prouok vs thus? Take vp your armes afresh, and assayle him now more sharpely then euer; that he may once come to learne, whome he hath to deale with. *Lucifer* had yet now scarcely finished his commaunds, when the foundation being shaken with a horrible Earth-quake, and the foure sides of the poore

Cell

Cell layd open. There entred in a moment by those chincks a huge multidue of vncleane spirits, in sundry and dreadfull figures of Lyons, Buls, Leopards, Beares, Wolues, Aspes, Scorpions, and Serpents, beating the ayre, and bestirring themselues, ech one, according to its proper forme, and nature. The greedy Lion roared, ready to deuoure: The Bull lowed, threatning with his cruell hornes: The Dragon hissed, with the neck stretched forth, and a pestilent breath: The rauenous Wolfe fell a houling, with open mouth, and sharp teeth: and all the sauage beasts, in fine, with eyes enflamed, and open iawes, fell a brissling themselues, being ech of power, if not hindred from aboue, to teare *S. Antony* into a thousand peeces. But as they had no power vpon the lyfe of the *Saint*: so on the person, as farre as they had leaue, they striue now agayne, to worke him what domage and outrage they could.

At which very tyme the inuincible Champion, though otherwise groaning amidst all those terible blowes, yet fayling not a whit of his courage, reproachfully rebuked the malignant spirits, saying: If there were any force in you, some one of you alone, were inough (I trow) for so light a conflict, but because God hath taken away your forces from you, therefore you do go thus about to affright me with multitudes, and with strange figures of beasts, being surely an euident token of your misery. And mansfully inferred moreouer: If you haue any power in you; If God hath giuen you any authority ouer me, am I not now heere in your hands? Then do you swallow me vp, & glut your appetites vpon me: but if you haue no such lycence, why trouble you your selues in vayne? See you not, how the signe of the holy crosse, & the Fayth in God serues christians, as impregnable walls.

At these words, the wicked fiends, encompassed him round, & euen fretted, and gnashed their teeth at him: When the Seruant of God, in lifting vp his eyes, beheld incontinent, the roofe to open it selfe, and the ayre to appeare with a celestiall ray; wherupon the roome was illuminated at once, the Enemyes vanished, the payne ceased, and the building shaken and disioynted before, came suddaynely now to be vnited agayne, & reduced to the former estate. And from thence in a moment, *S. Antony* was informed of the presence of God, and sending forth a deepe sigh, to the vision-wards, exclaymed. Where wast thou, O good *Iesus*, where wast thou? Why wast thou not heere from the first beginning to remedy my wounds? In answere

answere whereof, was heard this voyce: *Antony*, I was heere in presēce with thee, but stood expecting thee. And since thou hast shewed thy selfe to be thus stoute, & daunted not awhit, I will alwayes succour thee, and shall make thy name famous through the world. With this Visitation *S. Antony* rose vp from the ground, with a great deale more vigour, then before he euer receyued. And was euen iust at that tyme, of the age of 35. yeares.

S. Antony *retires himselfe into more inhabitable places. He meetes with the illusions of the Diuells: and shuts himself vp.* Chap. 4.

SAint *Antony* being now by this tyme enflamed to greater enterprizes, determines to penetrate further into the more inhabitable places, and most remote from humane society: yet thought it not meete to conceale this determination of his, from his first and deerest Mayster, but rather communicating with him his whole designe, inuited him also to be partaker with him of so illustrious a cōquest. But he excusing himselfe, through his old age, with other difficultyes besides, *S. Antony* doth put himselfe alone on the way: And while he hauing confidence in God, goes forward, very suddenly he beheld a great siluer Bason on the ground. At which sight, making a stop, and glauncing his eyes, obseruing the apparition, did presently perceyue the subtility of him, that had forged the same, and began to discourse with himselfe. Whence might this siluer vessell seeme to come hither? The place is quite out of the way, heere are no steps of any passengers, and when peraduenture one should loose it, yet such is the greatnes thereof, as suddenly he must needs be aware thereof, or at least would he afterwards haue turned backe at leasure to seeke it out: so as this is thy trick, O Sathā, nor thinke thou thus to hinder my intention heerby. Go thy waies then with thy mettall with a mischiefe.

This sayd, the Plate immediately vanished like smoke, when *S. Antony* pursuing his iourney, but a little way off discouered a very great wedge of gold on the ground, and that not counterfayte and phantasticall, as the siluer was: yet could not be discerned, whether it were by diabolicall operation, or els (for the greater proofe of the Seruant of God) by some heauenly power, there put in that sort. But this is well known the gold was not imaginary, but true & perfect. At the quantity and brightnes wherof, while *S. Antony* wondered:

dered, to the end so betwitching an obiect, might not penetrate the mynd, starting away from it, as it were from fire; he passed on his way, with his eyes shut, & flying through the playnes, neuer made stop, till he had quite lost the sight of the place. When taking some breath, & renewing his holy purposes againe, he arriued at a Moũtayne, where was a Castle halfe ruined, and inhabited with serpẽts and hurtfull beasts, insteed of men. Which at the appearing of the *Saint*, as if they had been chased, went headlong away in al post; & he damming vp the gate, with stone & tymber, remayned within, with prouision of bread for six months: hauing left order with his friends, that twice a yeare (for which space and more some *Egiptians* knew, & especially the *Thebans*, how to bake breake, & make it last) should supply be made him, from tyme to tyme: with which sustenance, and with a little water only to be had in the same place, continued he his admirable sobriety, and singular abstinence.

There came many to visit him, while he himself notwithstãding being shut vp, saw them not, nor would suffer himselfe to be seen of any: and the bread I spake of, was let downe to him by certayne holes in the roofe. In the meane while, his friends, attending with great desire at the doore, and passing that way many tymes by day and night, might heare from tyme to tyme, a very great noise within the roome, with raylings and outcryes, which sayd to him: Get you hence, out of our house. What haue you heere to do, in this desert? You shall neuer be able to endure our persecutions. The friends of *S. Antony* now hearing such quarrels, and menaces, without, did verily belieue some ill disposed persons, and enemies of the *Saint*, had byn gotten in with a ladder, from the top: but afterwards, looking in very curiously through a chincke, they caused some to get vpon the roofe, and by diligent search they could finally discerne no such matter: It was presently knowne, that those horrible clamours, proceeded from none, but infernall spirits. Whereupon, the poore people, being now affrighted, began suddenly to call vpon *S. Antony* by name, & to craue his succour: Who regarding the good of these, more then the menaces of those, approching to the doore, exhorted thẽ with fayre speeches to retire from thence, and not to feare, since the Deuill is commonly wont (if you be fearefull) to increase your vaine and needles feares. Go home then on Gods name, and do you make the signe of the holy Crosse. Go your wayes, home, I say, in the name of the Highest, & leaue them

them heere in fine to be illude themselues.

With this conge, the visible friends giue backe, and departed thence, and he alone remayned behind to stand in contest with the inuisible Enemies: although from henceforth in all bickerings, he had not much to do with them, partly in regard, that they, through so many losses, became continually more weary & feeble: partly also, because he felt himselfe euery day more couragious and stoute, being very often comforted with diuine Visitations, and with often triumphes ouer his now vanquished Enemyes. In the meane time, new troupes of people, ceased not to resort from Cittyes and Villages to *S. Antonyes* Cell: Who making accompt to haue found him allready dead, beyond all hope, did heare him sing. *Exurgat Deus, & dissipentur inimici eius, & fugiant qui oderunt eum, à facie eius: sicut deficit fumus deficiant, sicut fluit cera à facie eius, sic pereant peccatores a facie Dei.* And likewise: *Omnes gentes circumdederunt me, & in nomine Domini, quia vltus sum in eos.* With such and other like darts, the valourous Champion, transfixed so the rebels of *Christ*, as in all the encounters, they had euer the worst.

S. Antony *remaynes reclused. His fame spreads through all parts: whereby many come to renounce the world.* Chap. 5.

IN this manner of inclosure, the seruant of God, remayned for 20. yeares continually, without once seeing to yssue forth, or euer being seen of any person. Whereupon, the fame of *S. Antony* was so spread, and was in so great eredit, of more then humane vertue; as day by day, there assembled about him a greater concourse of diuers Nations, and conditions of persons, then euer. Some came with desire to be instructed, and trayned vp by him: & others to be deliuered from the Deuill, and from sundry infirmities. Others in fine desired, to behold such an Hermit as he, with their proper eyes, and so rare and liuely example of perfection, and to speake in a word, such an *Angell* on earth. Who, by how much more through humility retyred, so much greater thirst was excited in men of his conuersation. And in briefe, the matter went so farre, as they being able no longer to endure the expectation, pulling away the obstacles by violency, and breaking vpon him with boldnes and reuerence alike; they intreated him so much, as he was able to resist no longer, but forthwith he came out of a Sanctuary, where he had

had beene, as it were, annoynted with the diuine hands, consecrated and promoted for the gouernement of soules. And it may well be conceyued the while, what a plenitude of grace, he receiued from Heauen; since loe, the very same redounding likewise to the body, after so many yeares of pennance, so great fastings, and such meditations, combats, and vigils, appeared to be of so good a cõplexion, as if in all that tyme, he had attended to his health, and had entertayned himselfe in pleasant pastimes.

With this was matched such a manner of composition, modesty, and grauity, as well beseemed a foster-child of the supreme wisedome, and Citizen of the supernall country. In such wise, as to haue met him, after so long a retirement in so great a multitude of men, applying themselues to him, and euen profuse in his prayses & renowne, yet should you not haue seene any signe of perturbation in him, or of vayne contentmẽt, but was alwayes found with Reason in the Sterne most firme, constant, and equall. He had so cheerefull & serene a coũtenance, as all men that looked vpon him, were comforted therwith. But what shall we say of the other Gifts of the holy Ghost? The dispossest of euill Spirits may suffice to winne beliefe: the infirme also whome he hath restored: And the many besides aflicted and disconsolate, through diuers occasions, which with sweet & efficacious words he hath recomforted. How many emnityes, and how many strifes hath he reduced to peace and concord? He would exhort all with great vehemency of spirit, nor yet lesse with the weight of reason, and examples, by no meanes to preferre any wordly thing, before the loue of our *Lord Iesus*. And he would also discourse of the future goods, and of the excessiue charity of God towards miserable mortals: since for their Redemption and Saluation he would not seeme to pardon his owne most welbeloued Sonne, but rather in satisfaction of our debts, deliuer him ouer to so cruell and bitter a death. With which discourses and admonishments, *S. Antony* went mouing the people in such sort, as many conceauing a like desire of the Eternity, and contempt of the world; determined themselues likewise to be sequestred from the vulgar, & to giue themselues to a solitary life.

From hence so many Monasteryes tooke their beginnings, wherewith in a very short tyme, were all those craggy mountaynes and champians of *Egipt* filled. And he, so long as he liued, had the superintendency and sollicitous care ouer them all: receauing with singular

singular affect of charity, such as for diuers occurences of good gouernement, would be making their repayre vnto him: and he himselfe also would no lesse be visiting them in person, when tyme required, without sparing any labour, or respect of manifest perils, hauing alwayes the heauenly custody with him, which miraculously defended him from all disasters.

As it happened once among other tymes, in his visit of the coũtry of *Arsinoe*; whither trauayling with some of his, and being to wade ouer a branch of the riuer of *Nilus*, full of Crocadills, & most cruell Enemyes & Deuoures of men, hauing made his praier a litle, entred into the water, and passed quite through it, both going and comming, without any manner of hurt at all of himselfe or his Cõpanions. Being now returned to his Cell, he gaue himselfe to his wonted labours and exercises, as before: and aboue all to his pastorall care, by inducing alwaies the Monks to greater perfection, with words and deeds, full of holsome incitements, and holy doctrine. Nor was it hard for him to assemble an Auditory, so great was the hunger which euery one had of his words, and so singular the grace of his discourse, vouchsafed him by our *Lord*. But especially, one day, there being met together a very great concourse of people, to heare him, the venerable *Abbot* with accustomed modesty, & candour of mynd, in the Egyptian tongue, began to deliuer himselfe, as it followeth in the next chapter.

The Exhortation of S. Antony *to the Monkes, and people of the Desart.* Chap. 6.

ALthough the diuine Scriptures (my Children, and most beloued Brethren) are sufficient of themselnes for the instruction, and erudition of men: Yet is it a thing notwithstanding very reasonable, and iust, that euen Men no lesse knowing themselues, with mutuall incitements, excite one another to the execution of that, which they haue well vnderstood; and with pertaking ech one with the rest, the inspirations and lights he obteynes of God, they may all come to be euery day more wise, and expert in his holy seruice. Wherfore you, my children, whensoeuer you shall haue any good conceipt, to propose vnto others, & to me your Father; omit it not, and I also as more auncient in yeares, and most ready for the glory of God, will participate with you, in as much of that kind, as

I haue hitherto any wayes, eyther by document of others, or of my owne experience, been able to comprehend.

The first then, and principall aduertisement for all, is this, that ech one of vs, endeauour two things. The one, not to diminish awhit of our labour or industry, reputing our selues, to haue done inough. The other, not to loose courage, while the affayre seemes too prolix and tedious to vs; but rather, we are to make accompt, that euery day is the first beginning, and to be alwayes a conseruing and increasing our holy purposes. Because, that as the whole age of a man, is very short, in comparison of what succeeds: so is al the created tyme, as nothing, being paraleled with Eternity. And truly in this life, things are ordinarily bought at a iust price, & in human traffiques is accompt made of so much, for iust so much: but in our case it is not so: while the Eternall Crowne seemes to stand vs indeed, but in a very little.

We read in the *Psalmes*: *Dies annorum nostrorum in ipsis, septuaginta anni: Si autem in potentatibus, octoginta, & amplius eorum labor & dolor.* Whence put the case, we do spend the same whole space of eighty, or a hundred yeares, in the diuine seruice, thinke you the reward therof to be equal? The trauaile exceeds not an age, the guerdon endures foreuer; the toyles are on earth, the recompence in heauen; the body comes to be rotten and consumed, but recouers a glorious, and vncorruptible one. So as my Children, let vs not go foulding our armes; Let vs not thinke it to be ouer long; or that we haue done already any great matter, since according to the *Apostle*: *The Tribulations of the present life, haue not any proportion with the glory, which is to be manifest in vs.* Nor, casting our Eyes to the world, belieue, that we haue forsaken any great matter. For as much as the whole roundnes of the Earth, is but a point, in respect of the vniuersall fabrique of the world: and yet supposing we were Lords of as much as the Sun warmes, and should haue quite renounced such a Monarchy, for the Loue of Christ; yet for all that would it be nothing at all, if we regard but the Realme of the Heauens, which is proposed to vs. And who is he, that would not willingly seeme to cast away a dramme of yron, to haue for the same a hundred of gold? Euen so a Man, that should abandon for God, all these earthly Signoryes, should afford very little, and receiue a hundred for one.

Now, if all the Earth at once, may not seeme to contest with the worth of Paradise; it is cleere, that for one to depriue himselfe

of

of farmes, or houses, or summes of money, he should not yet seeme to take eyther any vayne glory, or foolish sadnes for the same: especially considering, that though we despoyle not our selues of these things for the loue of Christ, yet of force are we very soone to forgo them, when we come to dye; and to leaue them very often, to such, as we thinke least of, as *Ecclesiastes* well notes. Why then do we not make a vertue of necessity? Wherefore exchange we not, a transitory patrimony, for an incorruptible inheritance? And if it be folly, to be tenacious of that which we possesse, much lesse being once disentangled from the same, should we be turning our thought agayne vpon such a purchase? but alwayes aspire to the gaining of such things, as follow vs after the departure of the Soule from the body: such as are the merits of Prudence, Temperance, Iustice, Wisedome, Fortitude, Humanity, Liberality, Fayth in *Christ*, Meekenes, Hospitality, and other such like merchandise: whereof if we make vs prouision in tyme, being once recalled from this banishment, we shall find them to haue gone before vs, as Harbingers, to prepare vs a Mansion, in the Citty of the Blessed.

These things, being well considered, should surely shake off, from the mynd all negligence, and weake pusillanimity: but when they suffice not, at least we ought to be moued, with the strictnes of obligation we haue to God. He truly is our lawfull *Lord*, and we his naturall vassayles and slaues. Now then, as a slaue dares neuer to mutter thus much, and say, I haue laboured yesterday inough, too day therefore I will do nothing: No, but day by day (as the Gospell sayth) still shew forth the selfe-same promptnes, which he did before, presuming not at all vpon his passed toyles, nor thinke thereby to be idle, eyther now, nor heerafter; to the end, he might conserue himselfe in grace, with his Mayster, and not to be thrust out of his seruice: so likewise should we, euery day be encouraging ech other to Religious Discipline, assuring our selues, that if we cease from working one day only, we shall not obtayne remission, in vertue of any former seruices done, but shall be punished rather for this dayes demerits. For so sayd the Prophet *Ezechiel*; *That after death, euery one shall be iudged, according to the state, he shall then be found in.* And *Iudas* also for his ill carrage (if I might so say) of one night onely, did loose the fruite of all his yeares forpassed.

So as, attend we, my children, to the true Obseruation of our Rules, and not suffer our selues to be vanquished with tediousnes, as knowing

knowing, that according to the *Apostle*, *Our Lord is not backward a-whit to cooperate with him that hath a good will, and endeauours to help himselfe*. It shall likewse auayle vs not a little, to chase away Slouth, to carry alwayes in the memory, that saying of the *Apostle* himselfe, *Quotidie morior*. And if we likewise would be alwayes thinking with our selues, that this present day were to be our last, & awaking in the morning, we would but suppose not to arriue to the Euening; and agayne being layd downe at night, not promise to our selues to liue till morning: If we would regard, how vncertayne the end is, and how the diuine Prouidence, seemes to measure, and number our steps, & how it hath continually the Eyes vpon vs; we should certainely not sinne, nor sufferre our selues to be carryed away with vnbrideled desires, nor should we be angry with our Neighbour, nor giue our selues to lay vp treasure in earth: but we should hũbly yeild to others, in all, & throughout, & should abhore all sensuall pleasures, as a lewd and transitory thing, remayning alwayes with our wits about vs, & with the Eyes turned towards the Tribunall, where we are all to be iudged. And after this manner shall the feare of euerlasting torments, be of more power to extinguish, then the delicatenes of the flesh to enflame the desires of the Old man. And with such a Stay shall the Soule sustayne it selfe, though enclining already to a miserable precipice.

S. Antony *proceeds yet in his Exhortation: And giues them other aduises besides.* Chap. 7.

NOw therefore, beginning a new, as if to day we but entred into the way of Perfection; let vs enforce our selues, to arriue to the End; and let no man turne his face to looke back, as did the wife of Lot, especially our *Lord* hauing said so expressely, *That whosoeuer hauing once set his hand to the plough, should turne his face to heed what remaynes behind, were not apt for the heauenly kingdome*. And this turning back, is nothing els, then for a man to repent himselfe of his good beginning, & to returne yet agayne to wordly thoughts & actions. But some peraduenture may be affrighted with the name of vertue? Go to then, yet let it not seeme strange or impossible, since neyther is it farre from vs, or extrinsecall to vs, but rather within vs: and the matter is easy to him, that truly disposeth himselfe to seeke it out. Let the *Grecians*, and other profane Louers of themselues, go their wayes

wayes to seeke it out, in forren Prouinces: let them plough the seas, crosse mountaynes, runne ouer the playnes, & countries: For vs, there is no need to make any voyages for it, by sea or land, since that, as the Prime Verity affirmes, *The Kingdome of Heauen is with in vs.* In so much as to obteyne the same (supposing the diuine Grace, as inclined to all) on our parts there requires no more, thē a meere efficacious will. For so much as looke when the superiour part of the Soule, should be reduced to its naturall state, it would come to haue in it selfe a solid and formall vertue indeed: since the naturall state seemes to be nothing els but the great rectitude, & much goodnes, wherein it was framed by the soueraygne *Creatour*.

And hence it was, that the captayne *Iesus Naue* sayd to the Hebrew people: *Direct your hart to the Lord of Israel:* And *S. Iohn Baptist*, *Do you rectify your wayes*. Because it is proper to the nature of a Soule, to haue no wrinesse or crookednes in it. But whē it goes bending to this or that side, then looseth it the naturall rectitude, & that bending so, is worthily termed malice. From whence may appeare, that the enterprise is not so bad, as it seemes. For that if we, with the helpe of our *Lord*, but conserue our selues, such as we were framed by him; we may come without more a do, to possesse Vertue: but if through election, we adhere to the euill, we do voluntarily become wicked. If then the matter be not to be sought for else-where, but only consists in our selues, let vs beware of vncleane cogitations; and since from God we haue receyued our soule, as in *deposito*, let vs so deale that in his time, he may acknowledge his own workemanship in vs, and find the soule to be such, as himselfe had formed at first.

Let vs fight manfully, that we be not tirannized by wrath, nor yet ouersswayd with concupiscence: While it is written, *The anger of a man, workes not the iustice of God*: and concupiscence after its conception, doth bring forth sinne: and sinne being put in effect begets death. Let vs then be circumspect, in the gouernement of our selues, and stand we alwayes vpon our ward: and as the sacred Scripture aduiseth vs, let vs guard our hart withal the warynes that may be; because, though our enemyes on the one side, be infeebled, and deiected, notwithstanding on the other, are they very sagacious, great dissemblers, and most subtle withall; and as the holy *Apostle* well notes: *Non est nobis colluctatio aduersus carnem, & sanguinem, sed aduersus principatus, potestates, aduersus mundi rectores tenebrarum harum, contra spiritualia nequitiæ, in cælestibus.* Great is their number, in this lower region of the ayre, nor are they in truth farre off from vs: They are likewise very different from ech other, in nature, and species; of which differences surely might a long discourse be had, but being a matter so litle necessary to our present purpose, & worthy of a more sublime vnderstanding, then mine is; It shall suffice me for this tyme, to touch that only which more imports vs; to wit, the fraudes, and stratagemes, which those maligne substances do worke, to the offence, and domage of our soules.

The blessed *S. Antony*, being come to this passage, made a pause for a while: and then began more at large, to discouer diuers arts and subtilities of *Sathan*, for that tyme as yet very new, and vnknown; at this day notwithstanding by the obseruation of so many ages, God be thanked, now very common, and vulgar. And then began he afresh, to declare a certayne remedy agaynst them, which was a vigilant, and continuall memory of God, conioyned with spirituall gladnes, with the firme confidence of the fatherly Prouidence, and with the care which our *Lord*, taketh of his *Seruāts*. In which state so long as the Christian stands, and the Religious also, he hath no need to feare any thing. Since as the Diuels, withall their fury, and rage, when he stands in his owne defence, cannot endomage him, with force; so are they not wont to assault him, with open warre, but with ambushes, and snares: wherein yet lying in wayte, if they note the Citty of the soule, to be neglected, ill prouided, and vnquiet; then rushing in on a sudden, they will enkindle seditions, multiply breaches and put all in confusion and disorder. And this in summe sayd the blessed *Antony*, for asmuch as concernes temptations, and inuisible traynes.

But for apparitions, and visions, to be able well, and securely to distinguish them; he counsayled the Monkes, in such a case, not to be dismayed awhit, nor to shew any signe of feare at all: but be the Spectacle what it will, couragiously to speake vnto it, and demand, *who art thou, and from whence comst thou*? For that if it be good it will suddaynely cleare thee in that point, through diuine power, and will replenish thee together with true gladnes: If naught, it shall loose its forces in a moment, in beholding the mynd so stout, and constant; since to demaund in that manner, is a manifest signe of assurednes, & tranquillity. In this manner we may see *Iesus Naue* to be cleered by the Angell of light; and others not to be deceyued with

with that of darknes.

The Exhortation ended; a certayne Probleme is handled among the Fathers of the Desert: wherein euery one passeth his verdict. Chap. 8.

VVHile the holy *Abbot* spake in this sort, it canont be expressed, what comfort and consolation the Auditory felt; so as the tepid, were enflamed with the loue of vertue, the pusillanimous seemed to pretend now great hope. And some on the contrary, being full of vayne persuasion before, came now to be humble, and to thinke more modestly of themselnes; and finally all remayned astonished at the discretion of spirits, wherewith our Lord had seemed to endue *S. Antony*. Of which so precious a gift, since we are now fallen vpon it; we cannot so slightly passe ouer in silence that so famous a discourse, that to this purpose *Iohn Cassian* declares, with the Morall therupon; which was, that some of those ancient Fathers, on a tyme, being come to the blessed *S. Antony*, in *Thebais*, to conferre with him, about spirituall matters; the conference it selfe grew so hoat betweene them as it lasted from the beginning of the night, to the next day morning.

The Probleme was this. What vertue, or what obseruance, might seeme more efficacions, and more secure, to preserue a Monke alwayes assured from diabolicall snares, and deceipts, and to leade him by the stricter way, and with greater fredome to the top of Perfection? Concerning which doubt, ech one, according to his capacity, produced what he thought best. Some there were, who placed al in fastings, and vigils, affirming for proofe therof, that the soule, being extenuated therby, and made pure of hart, & body, comes more easily to be vnited with God. Others extolled entire pouerty, and the totall contempt of worldly things; in reguard the mynd, being naked, & quite stript of all those things, without doubt, being now light, and discharged of all, may sudenly mount to the heauenly delights. By some others, was giuen the palme to the loue of solitude, and the deserts for being the true, and only way to become familiar with God, and to be alwayes vnited with his infinite Goodnes. Nor were they wanting, who preferred the works of mercy, and fraternall charity, before all other Exercises whatsoeuer: alleadging that especially to these is the kingdome of heauen promised in the Ghospell. Thus euery one, hauing now vnfolded his mind, and more spaciously enlarged himselfe, in proofe of his proper assertion; the greater part of the night, as we said, being spent already, did the blessed *S. Antony*, beganne to speake in the manner following.

It cannot be denyed, my Reuerend Fathers, but that the same propositions by you made, are of singular auayle, for him that hath the loue of God in him, & hath a longing desire to come vnto him. Neuerthelesse to place a principall foundation theron, innumerable proofes and seuerall euents, occuring to diuers persons, wil not afford me to do it. For as much as I haue seen heeretofore some men being giuen to wonderous abstinence from meate, and sleepe, incredibly retired from all human society, so addicted to Pouerty, as they would not reserue a penny to themselues, or a loafe of bread for the tyme to come, being wholy employed with exceeding deuotion, and with singular feruour in hospitality, and in the comfort and succour of Neighbours; to fall at last into such errours & illusions, as their issue proued nothing answerable to their generous beginnings, and magnanimous enterprizes. So as we may clerely discerne, which way is the better, to arriue to God by. If with diligence we seeke, and search into the occasion of the ruine, and perdition of those vnhappy ones, who most certayne it is, had been gathering together, a long tyme a notable treasure of good, and holy workes; what then was it, that made them not perseuere vnto Death? Surely the only lacke of *Discretion*, they hauing not sufficiently learned of their Maysters, the rules and conditions of this Vertue, which shunning eyther extremes, continually maintaynes vs vpon the high way, and lets vs be carryed away with the right hand of spirituall consolations, to superfluous & vnmeasurable feruours; nor yet with the left of temptations and aridities, vnder colour of care of the body, to fall into slouth, and sensuality.

This *Discretion* is that, which by the Lord and Sauiour of mãkind, is called the Eye, and Lampe of our body. Which eye being simple, the whole body shall be replenished with light: but when the Eye is too blame and naught, all the body shall be as full of darkenes: the reason is, for that to this faculty of the soule it belonges, to weigh, ballance, and discerne all the thoughts, and operations of man. Whence being corrupted, that is, not founded in true knowledge, or some errour, it comes to obscure the whole body, in blinding the vnderstanding and folding it vp in the night of vices,

and

and of disordinate passions: and immediately our *Sauiour* himselfe adds the cause thereof; *For that if the light which is in thee, be darkenes, how great then shall the darknes it selfe be?* And in truth, who sees not, that when the iudgement, through ignorance, remayning in the darke, goes doubtfull and wauering; but needs must the thoughts and actions, depending thereon, come thence to be entrapped in a greater and thicker myst of sinnes? Of which truth, he doth giue vs sufficient testimony, who by the eternall Maiesty, being chosen the first King of *Israel*, for not hauing this eye of discretion sound, but all members ill affected with darknes, deserued to loose the Kingdome; while he thought to be more seruiceable to God, in sacrificing to him, then obeying of *Samuel*; incurring thereby the diuine offence in the selfe same thing, wherein he made full rekoning to gayne his fauour.

The defect of this knowledge, after that glorious triumph, perswaded *Achab*, that mercy and clemency were better then seuerity, and the execution of that rigorous and cruell command, as it seemed to him. Through which cōsidering, being mollifyed, whilst he would needs seeme to be contemning with an act of piety, the bloudy victory, as he thought, through indiscreet compassion, being himselfe likewise obscured in his whole person, was without remission condemned to death. This is that *Discretion*, which is not only called by the *Apostle*, a *Lampe*, but a *Sunne* also, where he saith; *Let not the sunne seeme to set vpon your anger.* This in like manner is called the Gouernment of our life, according to that saying: *Such as haue no gouernment with them, do fall like leaues.* This is worthily tearmed *Counsayle*, without the which to do any thing, is by the holy Scripture, so precisely forbidden vs, as neyther are we to take otherwise the spirituall wine it selfe, which is, that Gladnes that cheeres vp the hart of man, while *Salomon* saith; *Do you euery thing with Counsaile; and with Counsaile likewyse do you drinke your wyne.* And elsewhere; *Who workes without Counsayle, is like to a Citty, which is dismantled quite, and destroyed:* as shewing with this similitude, how pernicious to the soule, is the lack of such a vertue. In this, knowledge, in this the vnderstanding, and iudgment consists, according to that aduertisement, which saith; with wisedome is the house built, & with vnderstāding repayred; with iudgment is the Cellar replenished withall the best and most precious things. This I say, is that solid foode, that can not be taken, but of strong, & perfect men. Whence the *Apostle* sayth: *To the perfect belonges a solid foode, who through long experience, let the senses be well exercised in the discretion of good and ill.* What more? It is so profitable, and necessary, as it comes to be numbred among the other diuine attributes, according to the sentence of the sainte S. Paul: *Quick and liuely is the word of God, and very efficacious, and more penetrant farre, then the sharpest knife, arriuing to the diuision of the soule & spirit, yea euen to the ioynts & marrow, & is a discerner of the thoughts and intentions of the hart.* Out of which authorityes, it is manifestly shewed, that without the grace of *Discretion,* it is impossible, eyther perfectly to purchase, or long to conserue any vertue whatsoeuer.

This then in matter of Perfection, was the iudgment, this the Doctrine of *S. Antony.* The which, being first by that sacred Session of Fathers, without reluctatiõ approued, & after, with good reason, by *Cassian,* as we said, inserted into his Collations, hath also seemed good to vs, for the publique vtility, to transferre into our present discourse.

The multitude of Monks increaseth. The Angelicall life of S. Antony: *And of the persecution raysed by* Maximilian *against the Church.* Chap. 9.

IN the meane season, the number of Monks did meruaylously increase, and throughout all those hills, could nothing els be seene but Cells and Monasteryes, like to Pauillions applyed to a sacred warfare, full of Psalmes, Conferences, Lessons, Prayers, Fasts, and vigils, accompanyed partly with a iubiley of hart, through expectation of the future goods; partly also with the industry, and labour of the hands, to purchase almes for the poore. Who shall expresse then, the chast dilection, and streight concord amongst thẽ? In such sort, as casting the eyes vpon those countryes, a Man verily seemed to behold, a Region as wholy dedicated to the worship & Iustice of God. Heere raigned not, eyther open, or hidden factions, not practices or designes of transitory, or terrene things, but only a multitude well ordered of men, all applyed to the study of the more eminent vertues. So as one beholding them, & the Orders withall, might truly breake forth, into that exclamation of *Numbers, the 23. chapter. Quam bona domus tuæ Iacob, tabernacula tua Israel, tamquam nemora obumbrantia, tamquam Paradisus super flumina, tamquam tabernacula, quæ fixa sunt à Domino, tamquam cedri Libani circa aquas.*

But yet in so vniuersall a feruour, did the Lampe of *S. Antony* alwayes seeme farre to excede, both in heate and splendour, the other

other lights: who neuer ceasing his angelicall customes, did alwaies to his power keepe silence, and augment his pennances: aspiring day and night to the happy mansions of Heauen. Whereupon, as likewise the imitation of the more glorious *Saints*, he had so fixed his mynd, that whensoeuer it was needfull for him to eate or sleep, or in any other manner to serue the body, he beheld the noblenes of the Soule, so miserably abased with so vile an exercise. And thus through compulsion, he would take his refection, now alone, & now with others, not omitting through occasion thereof, to remẽber his disciples, how much it behoued them very seriously to attend to the soule, and to seeke after the profit thereof, in spending as litle tyme, as might be in the care of the body, that the spirit be not pulled downwards by sensuall delights, but the flesh to be reduced rather into the seruitude, and power of the spirit; and this sayd he, was the sense of those wordes of the Ghospell. *Nolite soliciti esse animæ vestræ quid manducetis, neque corpori, quid induamini: hæc enim omnia gentes inquirunt: Scit enim Pater vester, quod his omnibus indigetis: Quærite autem regnum Dei, & hæc omnia adijcientur vobis.*

At the same tyme, while *S. Antony* was instructing, and guiding his Monkes in this manner; was raised in *Egypt*, that cruell persecution of *Maximinian*, agaynst the Church of God. At the newes whereof, the holy *Abbot*, being desirous to shed his bloud for *Christ*, went his way in hast to *Alexandria*, accompanyed with many, saying: let vs be present by all meanes at the glorious combats of the Champions of *Christ*: for that God will eyther make vs worthy of that glorious Fellowship with them, or at least, if our Vocation extend not so high, their fayth and fortitude will affoard vs a noble spectacle, and of much edification. In the meane tyme, he puts himselfe in publique to help and encourage them. First in the mines, and in prisons, and afterwards much more, when they brought them to the vniust Tribunall. And heere is the manifest Prouidence of God to be noted, that as he had destined him to the gouernment, and example of Religious, (and in truth many, being inuited only with the example, aspect, and manners of the man of God, renounced the world) so he neuer suffered the Tyrant to lay hands vpon him.

True it is, that hauing once vnderstood, he was in the Citty, and succoured the Christians, he made an Edict, that no Monke should approch to the prisons, and that all should depart from *Alexandria*

xandria. But yet the valourous *Confessour*, was not terrifyed with this, but rather on the day appointed for the wicked Execution, and at the publique Act of *Matrtyrdome*, while the other Monkes, were a hiding themselues, he alone, accompanyed the combatants to the scaffold, exhorting them alwayes to perseuere inuincible, and couragious. From hence, to the end to be more easily seene, or rather to draw the eyes of the Prefect himselfe vpon him, being clothed with a garment, which was very conspicuous; he gets vp on a place of aduantage, somewhat neere vnto the scaffold, and there stood confidēt to the very end of al; with a holy Emulation for the Crownes, which the faithfull of *Christ*, seemed to purchase by their deaths: declaring thereby the promptnes and fortitude, which in such occurrences, they are to haue, who are truly *Christians.* In so much, as the Prefect descending from the Tribunall, & with all his Guard, passing by *S. Antony*, remayned astonished at the grauity and fortitude of the *Saint.* Who since he saw himselfe, not without griefe, to be thus deceiued of the hope, returned afresh to the prisons, and caues to serue, and comfort the Confessours of Christ, as he was wont; vntill such tyme, as the blessed Bishop *Peter* being martyred, the rage of the Persecutours, came finally to cease.

Vpon occasion wherof, *S. Antony* retiring to his Monastery, there gaue himselfe to participate as well as he could, of the Palmes of the Martyrs, with bitter austerityes, abstinence, and voluntary punishments: not wearing any other within, but Cilices, and skins without; and neuer washing his body, nor so much as his feet, but when he chaunced on the way to wade ouer any water. And it is held most certayne, that vntill his buryall, he was neuer seene to be stript, or naked.

S. Antony *dispossesseth one of the Deuill: and heares a voyce from heauen which directs him what to do.* Chap. 10.

NOw *S. Antony*, being thus recollected, with purpose not to be seene of any, for a tyme; a certayne Captayne called *Martinianus*, with a daughter of his, very shrewdly tormented by the deuill, and with a great troupe of people, approached to the Cel, & there stood knocking, and beseeching *S. Antony* with a lowd voyce, to come forth in publique, and to pray to God for the Mayden. To which cryes, hauing now stopped his eares for a pretty while, he came

came at last of meere compassion, to a litle chinck of the wall, and said, *Hola, Who do you call for? I am yet mortall: If you belieue in that Lord whome I serue, go your wayes, and pray to him, and according to your faith, shall the grace be done you.* The Captayne shewed not himselfe to be any thing backe-ward to such aduises, but immediately conuerting himselfe from Paganisme, began to inuoke the name of *Christ*; and on a suddayne, the daughter of that Captayne was found to be safe and sound. After this, many other aswell Lunatique, as infirme persons, who could not come to haue any audience of the *Saint*, lay prostrate at the doore, and there recommended themselues, so long to his intercessions, as they came thence wholy cured.

At which meruayles, and at the concourse of new troupes of people, was *S. Antony* sore molested: fearing in his mynd, some motion of *Pride*, or at least, the world might come to frame too high a conceipt of him. Making then, mature deliberation herupon, he determined to leaue that Cell, and to conueigh himselfe secretly into the vpper *Thebais*, in some part, where he might not be known of any liuing body.

To this effect, being departed, with some loaues of bread, to the shore of *Nilus*, while he was sitting there, expecting commodity of passage, he heard a voyce from Heauen, which with a cleare tone pronounced these words: *Antony, whither art thou going? and wherfore?* And he not being troubled thereat, as being already acquainted with such things, made answere: *These people will not let my rest, whereupon I am resolued to passe into the vpper Thebais, as well to eschew the sayd disturbances, as principally also for not to be requested in things, which exceed my power.* The voyce adds: *Although thou goest thy wayes hence to Thebais, and endeauourest to hide thy selfe* (as thy designe is) *among the sheapeards Cottages there: Yet know, thou shalt thence but purchase to thy selfe a double trauayle: Whereas if thou wilt find true rest indeed, thou must go into the hart of the Desert.* And S. Antony replying: *who shall shew mee the way thither to some place, to the purpose, since I my selfe was never there?* when presently was shewed him a squadron, or to say rather a company of *Saracens*, who comming to *Egypt* for traffique sake, were now in their returne into *Arabia*, and were bound to trauaile just that way.

Then *S. Anthony* approching to them, intreated them fayrely they would be pleased to take him along for a pretty way with thẽ, and so they did, as if they had had commandment from *God*: and at the end of three dayes, and three nights, they arriued at a very high mountayne, at the foote whereof, went gliding a fresh, and christall water, and not farre from thence certayne trees were to be seene of sauage, and wild palmes. At the discouery of such a sight *S. Antony* did exceedingly reioyce, and sayd within himselfe, that same was surely the seate appointed for him. So as taking his leaue, with a thousand thankes, of the *Saracens* (who gaue him moreouer some of their bread) he remayned there alone in the Mountayne, & tooke it as his deere habitation, susteyning himselfe with water, and the Dates thereby, and with the new supply, which the *Saracen* passengers, from tyme to tyme, admiring so great a vertue, did afterwards affoard him: Vntill such tyme, as the Monkes at last, being come to the knowledge of the place, tooke vpon them, the care to prouide for him; howbeit the holy man, perceyuing by this occasion, they were like to be troubled much, and forced to take a great deale of paynes for his sake, was resolued to spare that labour: & causing some plough-irons to be brought vnto him, with a litle seed corne, he beganne to till and sow a plot of ground, so as euery yeare, he reaped sufficient to liue on: being much comforted the while, that he was heerby no whit offensiue or troublesome to any person of the world, being a thing, to his power, which he had euer auoyded. But seeing afterwards, for all this, that Ghests forbore not to resort thither, he sowed there moreouer, some hearbes, for to be able to giue some manner of entertaynement, to passengers, wearyed with so long and difficult a iourney. And forasmuch as diuers sauage beasts, being inuited by the water there, came thither to drinke, and did withall some hurt to his corne; he catching one of them, sayd very mildly to it, & the rest: Why do you wrong mee so, that offend not you? Go your wayes, and come you hither no more, for our *Lords* sake. A very admirable thing; they being terrifyed, as it were, with such a commandement, durst neuer more seeme to returne thither.

S. Antony *is much troubled with the assaults of the Diuell: He heares of* S. Paul *the great Hermit, and goes to seeke him out.* Chap. 11.

AMidst such labours of body & mynd, the seruant of God being now growne old, yet continued his wonted discipline, and neuer left to afflict himselfe. Wherupon the Monks being moued to

pitty,

pitty, did bring him Oliues, with oyle, and pulse, for these were delicacyes amongst thē. But in that place so remote, it cannot be told what combats the blessed *S. Antony* continually susteyned from Sathan. Such as went thither, for their deuotion, were afterwards wont to relate, they had heard besides, great tumults, and noyses there, with many cryes and clamours, and clashing of armes, and seene the mountaine all couered ouer with sparkles of fire, and the *Saint* vpon his knees, making his praier, against the fury of the outragious Enemyes. And surely it was an admirable thing, that a solitary man, in so great a vastnes of regions, should haue no feare, neyther of infernall spirits, nor of dragons, nor wild beasts: but truly, according to the *Psalmist*, confiding in our *Lord*, like to Mount Sion, had alwayes his mind very peaceable, and quiet: so as the deuills had occasion to feare him, and the beasts laying their poyson and cruelty aside, became very meeke and tractable to him.

But yet *Lucifer* ceased not to tempt him agayne, and to seeke alwayes to worke his annoyance, gnashing and grinding his teeth at him. And one night, among the rest, while *S. Antony* was busy in prayer, he had leaue to set against him as many hurtfull beasts, as were to be found in those desert cliffs; who as forced to come forth of their dennes, were set on to encompasse the Seruant of *Christ*, making a proffer (as others heeretofore) to swallow and deuour him quite: but he vnderstanding the subtility of the Aduersary, told them, That if they had power from heauen, they might deuoure him, but if otherwise they came as sent by the deuill, without delay they should go their wayes, for he was the seruant of *Christ*. With which protestations, the brutish troupes, being affrighted & scourged, did suddainly fly away.

From thence within few dayes, while he was making baskets, as he was wont, to bestow on them that dealt very charitably with him; he perceiued one of the wickers of his worke to be drawne to the doore-wards, and raysing vp himselfe, sees a monster, from the head to the hips, which appeared like a man, & frō the hips downewards, was like an Asse. And yet was *S. Antony* not astonished awhit at so new, and straunge a spectacle; but rather making the signe of the Crosse on himselfe, defyed it boldly, as he was wont: whereupon the beast being scared, togeather with the spirits that guided it, so impetuously ranne from thence, as falling downe headlong, it dyed, representing in that fal the vnhappy aduenture of such as would go about to driue away *S. Antony* from the Desert.

Now after so many toyles of body and mynd, the Seruant of God was become Ninety yeares of age; & could no more without manifest daunger, endure austerites as before. Wherupon, with a pious violence, the Monkes enforced him to accept of two of them, to beare him company, and to haue care of him. The one called *Amathas*, and the other *Macarius*. About which tyme, the glorious doctour *S. Ierom* declares, how *S. Antony* bethinking himselfe, that hitherto neuer had any *Monke* gone further into the desart then he, it was reuealed to him, on the night following, that he was deceiued, since there was another yet, more ancient and perfect then he that likewise inhabited therein, and that by all meanes, he should go to seek him. *S. Antony* was nothing slack to obey. For scarce had the *Aurora* put forth, when without any other companion, then a little staffe, he puts himselfe into the voyage: and now was it about high Noone, and the parching rayes of the sunne beganne to scorch the head of the holy Old man, and yet neuerthelesse, would he not seeme to desist from going forwards, saying within himselfe: I haue a firme confidence in God, that he will shew me him he hath promised me to see. And standing to muse thereupon, behold a Hippo-centaur appeares before him, to wit, halfe a man, and halfe a horse. At which sight, arming himselfe with the holsome signe, on his forhead: *Hola*, said he, *where abouts I pray you, inhabits a certayne man of God?* To which demaund, the beast, with a confused voyce, made offer to answere, and withall stretching forth the right hand, seemed to point him the way, and flying vanished, nor could it euer be knowne, whether the same were a feigned apparition, or some reall thing.

With such direction, did *S. Antony* follow on his way, deeply considering with himselfe on that strange figure, which he beheld a little before. He had not passed farre, thus musing with himselfe, but there appeared to him, in a craggy valley, a man of a little stature, with a hawked nose, and horned countenance, who with a gratefull aspect, approaching to him, did offer him Dates, in signe of peace. Whereat *S. Antony* stood still, and laying hand on his wonted armes, doubted not to aske him, *who he was*, and he answered so plainely as *S. Antony* was much astonished thereat. I am likewise mortall, said he, as you are, and one of the Inhabitants of the wildernes, adored by the blind Gentility, vnder the name of *Fauns*, *Satyrs*

tyrs, and *Incubi*. I come to thee now, as an Embassadour of my Companions, beseeching thee in the name of all, to make intercessiō for vs likewise, to the common God, for we haue now vnderstood he is come, for the saluation of the world. At which words, the holy *Abbot* beganne to sheed teares for ioy, in beholding how the glory of *Christ* was dilated, and the power of Sathan annihilated, and smiting the ground with his staffe, addes: Wo be to thee *Alexandria* who giues the honour due to God, vnto Monsters & Portents: Wo be to thee meretricious Citty, where haue all the superstitions of the world, built their neast now, wilt thou say? The beasts doe seeme to confesse *Christ*, and yet do you neuertheles, stand adoring of Idols.

S. Antony had not yet ended these wordes, when the Satyr as betaking himselfe to his wings in a moment, was quite vanished away. And to the end, that not any may hold it for a fabulous thing, it is to be vnderstood, that a like Monster to this, was brought a-liue to *Alexandria*, where after it had been wel seene, and reuiewed, by all the people, it came to dye. Whereupon being opened, and powdred with salt, it was lastly conueighed to *Antioch*, to satisfy the eyes also, of that Citty there, and of the *Emperour* himselfe.

S. Antony *trauayling on his way, espies a wolfe comming forth of a* Caue; *where entring in, he finds* S. Paul *the* Theban *retired.* Chap. 12.

TO returne to *S. Antony*, the good old man went on his way, and not discouering ought els, then the tract of beasts, and infinite wasts of sand withall, there remayned now no other sustenance to him, then a firme confidence of the Protection of *Christ*. By this tyme, two dayes were spent, and the night following, the seruāt of God did consume in prayer; when in the dawning of the day, he discouers a farre off, a thirsty she-wolfe, which panting and seeking for water, approched to the foote of the Hill. The wary trauayler looke after her, and as soone as she was departed from the denne, he likewise comming thither, began to looke in, though in vayne, because so great was the darknes there, as he could not discerne any thing. It was truly a horrible and dreadfull thing to behold, but *Charity* banished feare; he taking courage to himselfe, and going very softly and tenderly in, as he could, at last amidst those obscurities going forwards not farre off, there appeared a light wherewith being inuited, while greedily he makes hast thereunto, he stumbles on a stone ,and with the noyse thereof, gaue occasion to him, that was within, on a sudden to shut & make fast the door vpon himselfe.

The caue lay open on the one side thereof, but well shadowed the while with a plan-tree, very great and full of leaues, and in the same playne arose a most cleere spring, from whence a litle brooke streaming along for a litle space, went creeping vnder the ground. The same place in tymes past, had beene the receptacle of those wicked Forgers, who in the tyme of *Cleopatra*, and *Mark-Antony*, in that place, had been coyning of false money; as do well testify the many anuils, & hammers there scattered vp & downe in those cauernes. And lastly for auoyding the persecution of *Decius*, & *Valerianus*, and to leade a holy lyfe, was the blessed *Paul* the *Theban* there shrowded from his youth, and had there perseuered with incredible constancy to the age of 113. yeares. Now *S. Antony* perceiuing himselfe to be shut forth, in this mãner, with exceeding great griefe lying prostrate at the doore, remayned there vntil the sixt houre, & vpwards, continually intreating to be admitted, & saying: You know well inough, who I am, and whence I come, and though vnworthy (I confesse) of your sight, yet without such a grace, I will not depart hence. Whereas you that affoard harbour to beasts, why banish you a Man? who according to the Ghospell, hauing sought and found already, doth now knock to be let in. Which if I attayne not, I shal dye heere in the very Entry, and when that happens you shall be constrayned to bury mee. Which will be to troublesome to you.

The *Pilgrime* hauing thus continued a prety while, in this mãner of intreaty, at last *S. Paul* smiling within himselfe, made answere: This same is a prety custome indeed, to beseech in brauing thus, to charge so, and calumniate with teares? And is it so straunge to you, that I receiue you not, if you seeme to come hither to leaue your life? In this manner of iesting, did *S. Paul* open the doore, & the straungers, howbeyt new, and as yet vnacquanted, very louingly embracing ech other, did salute notwithstanding one another by name, giuing infinite thankes to the diuine Goodnes. And after the holy kisse of peace, being both set downe, *S. Paul* began to speake in this manner: You see heere, *Antony*, him, whome you haue sought for thus, with so much trauayle, rude, worne, frayle, & decrepit,

decrepit, & one in briefe, who within a very litle shall become dust. But in the meane while, for Charity sake, tell me, what is done in the world? Who rules? Go they about to reedify the cittyes agayne, already destroyed? And is the Deuill yet worshipped there, as he hath euer (almost generally) beene heeretofore?

Now while they sate thus sweetely discoursing together in lifting vp their eyes, they behold a Crow pearching on the bough of a tree thereby, which descending downe with a moderate flight, let fall betweene them, a whole loafe of bread, and so went its wayes. Wherupon said *S. Paul*: Go to, our Lord hath sent vs our dynner heere, truly pious, truly mercifull. It is now full sixty yeares, that I haue hitherto receiued my halfe loafe euery day: Whereas now at your comming hither, he hath redoubled the allowance to his Seruants. After which, the Benediction giuen, they both sate down, by the side of a cristall fountaine: but yet before they fell to their meate, there was no litle ado betweene them which of the two, should breake the bread, in streyning courtesy the one with the other, with religious modesty, and with diuers reasons, in the point of preheminency before ech other. *S. Paul* did principally ground himselfe in the Lawes of hospitality, wherto *S. Antony* opposeth the maiority of yeares. The strife seemed to last a good while, and the day in the meane tyme passing away, at last, the duell ceased, vpon agreement made to take hold of the loafe between them, and to pull it, so as to ech might remayne his share in his hand; and so it iust fell out, and without more dispute, hauing taken the bread, and finally stooping, sipt a litle water, with thankes-giuing, they passed that night in Psalmes and Vigils.

S. Paul *discouers to* S. Antony *his death approching. He dyes in* S. Antonies *absence, and is afterwards buryed by him.* Chap. 13.

THe morning being come, *S. Paul* begins to speake to his Ghest in this sort: It is now a good while, my Brother, since I haue knowne that you haue dwelt in these parts, and your presence hath beene promised me heeretofore by our common Lord. But now in fine that I am arriued to my last passage, there remaynes me nought els, but to go my waies vnto *Christ*, as I haue alwaies desired. Know then, you haue been sent hither by God to performe my Exequyes, & to couer my lymmes with Earth. *S. Antony* hearing this, beganne to weepe, and beseech him, not to leaue him behind, but to admit him for companion on the way. When *S. Paul* replyed: You are not to reguard your owne cõtent, but the profit of others. He might seeme to fauour you indeed, hauing layd down the burthen of your flesh, to cause you to fly into Heauen; but he should not therby answere the expectation of the Brothers, that should remayne behind depriued of your guidance, and example. Wherefore I pray, be it not troublesome to you, for Charityes sake, to returne your wayes home, to fetch hither the Cloke, which was once giuen you by *Athanasius* the Bishop, to fold vp my carkas in, and so to commit it to the Earth. Which request the Blessed *Paul* made, not that he cared much to be putrifyed, eyther naked, or clothed, especially not hauing for so long tyme, vsed to couer himselfe with other, then with the leaues of Palmes, being wouen together with his owne hands; but he did it, that he might not grieue him, by expiring in his sight.

S. Antony remayned amazed at the thing, which he heard, & particularly for the Cloke, and with veneration, acknowledging our *Lord* in the person of *S. Paul*, without reply, kissing the eyes and hands of the *Saint*, went his wayes in hast to his Hermitage: and at his approach, his two disciples demaunding of him, with great anxiety, where he had been so long, he answered: Wo be to me Synner, and false Monke: I haue seen *Elias*, I haue seen *Iohn Baptist* in the desart, or to say better, I haue seen *Paul* in Paradise. Then holding his peace, in knocking his breast, he tooke the Cloke of *Athanasius* out of the Cell; when as his Companions importuned him yet to vouchsafe to speake more cleare, but he differing the same to its time without more delay, or affording any nourishment to his body so lõg fasting & wel nigh spent; went suddainly forth, with his mynd wholy fixed on his sweet Host, fearing (as it fell out) least in his absence, he might giue vp the ghost. And now by this tyme, he had gone in great hast, as it were, half the way, when as lifting vp his eyes aloft, he sees among the happy troupes of elect spirits, the blessed soule of *S. Paul*, very glorious & radiant, to ascend vp to heauen. And suddenly casting himselfe on the ground, beganne to sprinckle his head with sand, and to weepe and lament, saying: Why leaue you me O *Paul*? Why go you away so before I had taken my leaue of you? So lately knowne; alas so soone parted!

S. Antony himselfe recounted afterwards, that he had passed the rest of the way, with the swiftnes of a Bird: and so it was knowne

in

in the proofe, since entring into the Caue, he found the holy corps yet kneeling, and the necke vpright, and hands lifted vp; insomuch as notwithstanding the triumph, which he had seen before, he was almost of the mind that he was yet aliue: but then not perceyuing any breath, or signe of life, he endeauoured with bitter playnts to kisse him; and folding him vp in the sayd garment of *S. Athanasius*, he brought him forth with Hymnes, and Psalmes. But then not hauing any instrument to digg his graue with, and with great anxiety thinking, & bethinking himself what to do: Behold two Lyons, with their hayre layd open to the wind, to come running at that tyme. Whence he at first being somewhat affrayd, and then taking courage in God, attended their comming, as so many Doues; and they being arriued to the corps, did humbly cast themselues at the feete thereof, with fanning in their manner, and bitterly roaring in signe of the sorrow they felt: and presently began with their feete to plough vp the sands, vntill such tyme, as there remayned sufficient roome for a man. Which being done, and as it were for their hire, receiuing the benediction of *S. Antony*, they quietly went their wayes: and he putting his shoulders to the sacred burthen, did bury it in the trench.

After this, surueying the Heritage of the dead, for not to go thence, altogether empty handed, he tooke hold of the Cassocke of Palmes; and being returned home agayne as long as he liued afterwards in the solemnities of *Easter* and *Pentecost*, he would alwaies reuest himselfe therewith. After these workes of charity were ended he was intreated by a great number of Monkes, now comming in hast to him, where he was, to visit anew, & to recomfort the Cōuents. He went then along with them, and while they were on the way, there fell out another notable meruaile. That way was al very craggy and barren, & the heates excessiue, so as it was not long ere prouision of water fayled them, and the Monkes not knowing what to do, letting their Camell go loose, being scortched, and afflicted, lay downe; When the holy old man, not a litle contristate at so great a perill of theirs, sequestred himselfe a litle, and kneeling on the ground, & lifting his hands to the starres, began to beseech God, with so much fayth and feruour, as suddenly in the self same place of prayer, sprung forth the desired liquour. Whence all were reuiued, and others being satisfyed, as they anxiously sought for the Camell, did suddenly find him by the cord of the headstall, through a new miracle, entangled in a rocke. Loading him then, to their great contentment, they came very safe, and sound to their Cells agayne.

S. Antony *is very wellcome to all at his returne: and giues holsome Documents to ech one, vpon good occasions.* Chap. 14.

NOw it would be long, and superfluous heere, to explicate the ioy, which the Disciples shewed at the comming of their most sweest Father and Mayster, and he likewise reioyced as much to see them all, to be so feruent, with his presence and renewed in spirit. He had besides no small consolation, to find his *Sister* so perseuering in the diuine seruice, being come to be Superiour of a most Noble, and numerous Conuent of Virgins. Now the arriuall of the *Saint* being knowne throughout all those Parts, a great multitude of persons of all qualityes resorted thither, to salute him, and to visit him as they were wont, and especially of the Religious: to whome he for entertaynement sake, insteed of presents, and gifts, would be giuing of precious aduertisements and aduises, saying: They should alwayes hold firme their fayth, and dilection to God, and the Neighbour: They should guard themselues from vncleane thoughts, and delights: They should not not suffer themselues to be deceyued with Gluttony: and should fly Vayne glory: continue their prayers: lay vp the documents of the holy Scripture in their breast: be allwayes reuoluing the actions, and manners of *Saints*, in mynd; endeauouring to reforme themselues, through the imitation of them.

And principally, he aduised them not to cease to meditate on those words of the *Apostle S. Paul*: *Sol non occidat super iracundiam vestrã*, and added thereunto, nor yet vpon any other sinne whatsoeuer: it being a thing very fit and necessary, that neyther the Sunne accuse vs of our diurnall malice, nor the Moone of nocturnall sinnes. For which end (said he) shall the preceps of the *Prophet* himself, help you much: *Iudge your selues, and examine your selues well.* Let ech one, euery day, take accompt from his proper soule of his actions, words, and thoughts. And hauing erred, let him amend; hauing done wel, not exalt himselfe, but seeke to perseuere, and not become negligent: and let him beware, *he iudge no man, nor iustify himselfe,* (as *S. Paul* said another tyme) *vntill such tyme as our Lord comes, who shal discouer the hidden*

hidden things; in regard, that we in our actions, many tymes do deceaue our selues. But our *Lord* beholds euery thing very cleerely: and therefore we should seeme to haue the same reguard to others as to our selues, and to compassionate one another. It shall be also very profitable for vs to suruey with our Memory, the motions of our soule, and the workes which we dayly performe, and set them downe in writing, as if we were to giue accompt therof to others. Whence it shall come to passe, that for shame to be manifested to the world, we shall keepe our selues from falling into things which are worthy of reprehension. And with such a discipline refrayning the appetites, and subduing the flesh, we shall be able, very easily to conserue our selues in the grace of our Lord.

These, and such like instructions, he fayled not to giue to his Monks, vpon good occasions. And for as much as among the secular multitude, there was continually a great number of lame, & diseased people; he prayed afresh for them, but obteyned not equally for all: our Lord dispencing his graces, according to his good pleasure. And *S. Antony*, euen as when he was heard seemed not to vaunt himselfe; so when he suffered repulses, murmured he not, but alwayes gaue thankes to our *Lord*; & exhorted the afflicted to haue Patience, and to be satisfyed, that their cure depended not on him, nor on men, but on God only, who affoardes health, when he wil, and to whome he lists. Wherupon, the languishing receiuing the words of the Old man, as from the mouth of God, learned to attēd, and suffer, and the cured came to acknowledge themselues bound not so much to *S. Antony* therefore, as purely to God. But what shall we say, besides al this, of the efficacy, which the Prayers of *S. Antony* had euen in persons, and places farre remote?

He being in the Monastery, and on this side of the mountayne, the Count *Hercolaus* came humbly to beseech him to vouchsafe to intercede for the health of *Policratia* virgin of the Citty of *Laodicea*, a great seruant of God, who through much abstinence, and maccratiōs of the body, did feele most bitter dolours of the hips & stomack and was quite fallen away and come to nothing: which the holy Father did with a very good will, and the Count noted the while in a little scrole the very day of the prayer. And being afterwards returned to *Laodicea*, and finding the virgin to be now on foote, & free from all manner of paynes, to satisfy himselfe more fully, whether it were to be attributed to the prayer of the *Saints*, or no; he demaunded of her, on what day she began to feele her selfe well; and hauing heard it, he presently tooke out the scrole, & with the great astonishment of all, they found the *Saints* prayers, and recouery to haue happened on the selfe same day.

In like manner, a certaine Courtier, called *Frontone*, that being tormented with a raging infirmity would haue eaten his tongue, & pluckt out his eyes, had recourse to *S. Antony*. Who without any more ado, sayd to him: Go thy wayes, and thou shalt be healed. But *Frōtone* standing yet still for all that, and not departing thence for some dayes, the seruant of God replyed to him: Thou canst not be cured heere; Go thy wayes then into *Egipt*, & thou shalt see wonders. And so it fell out, for scarcely was he arriued in those confines there, but his vehement sicknesse quite forsooke him.

Many others likewise, whome it were too long to recount in this place, were by meanes of the *Saint*, deliuered from sundry, & daungerous maladyes. Though the miracle of *Frontone* it seemes, apperteynes not so much to the gift of *Curing*, as that of *Prophecy*. Which in *S. Antony* how eminent it was, though by diuers things aforesaid, may seeme in some manner to be comprehended: yet shall the same more clearely appeare, by that which we shall presently declare.

S. Antony *relieues a Monke in distresse: and sees the soule of* Ammon, *in a vision, to ascend to Heauen.* Chap. 15.

TWO *Monkes* on a tyme, being trauayling in the desert, came to fayle of water; in so much as the one of them dyed thereof, and the other seemed to lye in extremes. This, being reuealed to *S. Antony*, he commaunded the two which were in his company, to go their wayes, and runne presently with a vessell of water to the said place, being distant frō the Monastery, a dayes iourney at least, and tels them wherfore. And they diligently performing the same, found the one, as I said, departed, whome they buryed, & brought succour to the other in good tyme, and being so escaped they conducted him to the *Saint*. Now for what cause, the same was not shewed him before, and why God would conserue the one, and not the other, seemes not to concerne me so curiously to seeke into. It sufficeth, that in so great a distance of place, was manifested to *S. Antony* what passed.

Another day, he sitting on a hill, in company of others, sees one

one ascending in the ayre, and many meeting of him, with very great ioy. Whereat *S. Antony*, remayning in admiration, and exceedingly desirous to know who it was; it was reuealed to him, to be the soule of *Ammon* a Monke, who dwelling in the Desart of *Nitria*, about some 13. dayes iourney from the residence of *S. Antony*, was wont notwithstanding to come sometymes to visit him. He was a person of rare vertue, and many miracles are likewise reported of him: and this one among others, that being once to passe ouer the riuer *Licus*, which at that tyme, was very much ouerflowne, he prayed *Theodore* his companion for his sake, to follow some distance from him, to the end by wading together, they might not be seene to ech other naked. So did the other, and yet for all that was *Ammon* afterwards abashed at his owne skinne. And while he stood vpon such points, and bethought him thereof, I know not how, without touching the water, he sees himselfe on the other shore, in the twinckling of an eye: where likewise the other, being afterwards arriued, and seeing *Ammon* to be all clothed, and without any signe of wet vpon him, demanded the manner how he passed ouer, and seeing he refused to participate the same with him, he tooke hold of his feete, and wrong him, and coniured him so much, as in fine he vnfolded the quality of his passage to him, with this pact notwithstanding, that he should not discouer it to any, till his death.

Now the Monkes, as I sayd, seeing *S. Antony* with eyes so attentiue and suspended, very deerely intreated him, not to conceale from them, what he saw: when as he answered, that *Ammon* was departed from these miseries, and was was gone triumphant to Heauen. Whereupon the disciples noted the day, and after a month some Brothers coming from *Nitria*, making a diligent comparison of tymes, they found, that *Ammon*, on that very very day, had passed to a better life.

Another tyme, *S. Antony* sayling with some Monkes and other Seculars, began to smell a very loathsome sauour, and all affirming it to be the smell of salt fish, and of dryed figs, he replyed, he felt another sent. And while he was thus affirming, there was heard a horrible cry to come from a yong man possessed of the deuill, who lay hid vnder the vpper decke of the ship. Then *S. Antony* rebuked the Deuill, and on the behalfe of *Christ* constreynes him to depart, as he did, leauing the young man sound, and the others astonished not so much at the miracle, as at the purity of a soule, so quicke of sent, as to sauour the neerenes of the vncleane spirit. Besides, he was wont also to perceyue before hand, the comming of such, as came to see him, and the occasion wherefore: and many tymes, would foretell the one, and other, some three or foure dayes, and somtymes a month before they arriued at him. But that which happened to *Eulogius* of *Alexandria*, was a matter of particular edification, and caution to all.

The life of Eulogius *briefely set downe, and especially a notable act of Charity of his, concluded happily through* S. Antonyes *aduise.* Chap. 16.

THis *Eulogius*, was a man, (as *Palladius* declares) of a good disposition, and hauing distributed already the greater part of his substance for the loue of God, yet neuerthelesse had not the hart, eyther to lead a solitary life, or to liue vnder obedience. Whereupon finding by chaunce a miserable wretch, to lye in the streetes, forsaken of all, maymed, without his hands and feete, depriued of the vse of all his lymmes, except his tongue: he made choyce, for his Mortification, and for the Exercise of christian vertue, to take care of that poore wretch, to keep him at home, and to serue him til death: and to the end the worke might become more meritorious, being all in feruour, he made a votiue promise thereof to our *Lord*. Hauing taken him then to him, he attended to the gouernement of him, to prouide him of victuals, and cloathing, bathes, medicines, & phisitians; in fine to serue him, as he had been some good Benefactour, or Patron of his.

In which ministery hauing now perseuered, at least for fifteene yeares, with equall sollicitude of his, and gratitude of the other, at last the Cripple was assayled with so strange and diabolicall temptation, as he now beganne, not to suffer himselfe to be gouerned any longer, making very earnest instance to be exposed forth anew in publique; alleadging that he was now glutted with *Eulogius* his entertaynement, and could endure no longer so retyred a life, nor so much abstinence. *Eulogius* wonders at such a manner of mutation in him, and though he had no small occasion of iust indignation against him; notwithstanding ouercoming himselfe, he wêt about to cherish the Wretch, more now then euer, in giuing him dainty meates, and procuring him some good and pleasant conuersation;

tion, but all in vayne: The more he laboured therein, the more did the other perseuer, requiting the good *Father* with nothing els, but complaynts, grumbling, & iniuryes. At last, the deuill had brought him into that rage, and desperation, as he was euen vpon the point as it were, to kill himselfe.

Now the matter hauing passed thus a prety while, the trouble on the one side was intollerable to *Eulogius*, and he was now euen ready to acquit himselfe therof: on the other it seemed to him a great folly to loose through impatience, the trauayles and toyles of so lōg a tyme. Moreouer he was stung with the offering, which he had made to our *Lord God*. Amidst these perplexityes and agitations of mynd, he resolues for a last dispatch to cōmunicate the whole with some neighbour Monks: Of whome he was counsayled, that since the great *S. Antony* was aliue, he should be contented to repayre to that *Oracle*, and seeke fit remedy at his hands. Wherupon *Eulogius* did thinke it best so to do, in regard he had heard much commendatiōs of the great Sanctity of that Holy man, and was glad to haue this opportunity to see him. To which end, *Eulogius* had prepared, though with great difficulty, a barke to put the Criple into, but not without much ado he got the miserable Wretch to be conueyed thereinto, with him: and so both of them went by water to the Monastery of the *Saint*, where being once arriued, *Eulogius* gladly attended his comming from the Hermitage, to visit the Brothers, and Ghests, as he was wont. Nor was it long; for on the night following the seruant of God, came into the publique view, intermitting for a tyme his diuine contemplations, and attending now to the good of his Brethren; & causing all the strangers to be assembled, according to custome, he suddaynely calls for *Eulogius*, very often by name, not known to him before: Who thinking there had been some other *Eulogius* present, held his peace for that tyme: But afterwards hearing himselfe to be called vpon a new, being halfe astonished, made answere; *Behold I am heere*.

S. Antony requires the cause of his voyage, and *Eulogius* replyes: There is no need, Father, that I should tell it to you: He that hath so manifested my name vnto you, may as well likewise discouer my necessity. I know it very well, replyed the *Saint*; but yet for edification of the standers by, I would haue it declared from your own mouth. *Eulogius* obeyed: when he had ended the narration, the holy *Abbot* stood vp, and with bended browes, looking him in the face:

Thou

Thou art ready to abandon (sayth he) this poore man, and lefst thy selfe to be vanquished with perturbation and tediousnes: Know then, if thou leauest him so, that God will receiue him by the meanes of another, that is better then thee. With which words, *Eulogius* being much terrifyed, durst open his mouth no more. When *S. Antony* turning himselfe to the infirme man, with a seuere countenance, and with a terrible voyce, beyond all expectation, sayd to him: Thou peruerse and abhominable Wretch, vnworthy both of Heauen, and earth: Thou neuer leauest fretting, & quarrelling, to the offence of God: knowest thou not, that he who serues thee is *Christ*? How darst thou then so to mutter agaynst the diuine *Maiesty*? Is it not cleere, that *Eulogius*, only for the Loue of *Christ*, hath vndertaken to haue care of thee, & to do thee good? This sayd, he attended to giue audience to the others, and after some space of tyme, returning to those two againe, with more benignity of speach, aduised them, saying: Beware my Children, you part not from ech other: but laying aside all rancour, & bitternes returne you home againe, where you haue liued together, for so long tyme, because our *Lord* will soone be calling for you: and know, that so cruell a temptation, hath not befallen you for ought els, then for being now so neere your End, and the reward of your labours: and take heed, you do not otherwise, for that if the Angell find you not so, you are in great daunger of loosing your Crownes.

This manner of reprehension, with both, had the weight it ought to haue, and they departing without delay, by accord, went to their former habitation, and there passed not 24. dayes, but *Eulogius* dyed: & after three dayes more the Leaper followed him, very well disposed in the inward man, & exceeding contrite. This successe was attentiuely obserued, not without a great deale of glory to our Lord, and much profit to soules.

S. Antony *enioyeth sundry visions. And fortels diuers things of the* Arrian *Heretiques.* Chap. 17.

TO this kind of visions, and Reuelations, may others be added, no lesse to the purpose of exciting the feare of God, and very worthy to be alwayes conserued in memory. Wherof one was, that *S. Antony* being one day in prayer, about the hower of Noone, before meate, he felt himselfe sudenly to be rauished in spirit, and it

seemed

ſeemed to him that he was carryed to Heauen, by ſome fauourable ſpirit. But in aſcending ſome others of a proud and fierce aſpect, oppoſed themſelues againſt him, who being repulſed by the Guard of *S. Antony*, beganne to quarrell, and alleadge the power they had frō aboue, to examine whoſoeuer paſſed. With this denunciation, they preuayled to performe their office, but the wicked ſpirits being willing to demaund an accompt of *S. Antony* from the day of his Natiuity, it was not permitted them to do ſo, but only from the tyme he became a Religious perſon, in regard that all the tranſgreſſions behind, were now cancelled, and remitted by the diuine piety.

Then did the infernall Miniſters dilate themſelues againſt the ſeruant of *Christ*, in diuers accuſations and calumnyes, but not being able to proue any, ſo aſhamed, and confounded, in ſpight of themſelues they were feigne to let him paſſe. And at that very inſtant agayne, did *S. Antony* returne to himſelfe, ſo ſtrooke and aſtoniſhed withall, as that forgetting his refection, he remayned all the reſt of the day, and all the night, a ſighing, and conſidering, with how many Enemyes vnhappy Man hath to deale withall. It came into his mind beſides, how the *Apostle* not without good reaſon ſeemes to call the deuils, the *Princes and Rulers of this ayre:* exhorting the faythfull, to betake them to the armour of God, that they may be able to reſiſt him in that dreadfull day, and the ſpightful accuſer may not haue wherewith to conuince them at that houre.

Another tyme, after he had a while talked of the immortality of the Soule, with ſome that came to viſit him; the next night, he heard himſelfe called from aboue, with theſe words: *Antony stand vp go forth, and behold.* Being gone out, he ſees a foule and horrible Mōſter, who with the head ſeemed to reach to the clouds; and ſome others beſides, with wings, which endeauoured to fly, but he ſtretching forth his vnmeaſurable hands, ſtrooke ſome of them downe to the Earth; others he could not hinder from mounting on high: and as for the one he fretted with rage, and gnaſhed his teeth; ſo he reioyced for the other, and made great triumph: When ſuddenly a voyce ſayd to *S. Antony: Marke well what thou ſeest:* & ſo cōming a new light vpon him, he perceyued it to be the paſſage of ſoules, and that great Giant to be the diuell, who had power & authority vpon his Subiects only; but was wholy impotent againſt thoſe, who in life had not been obedient to him.

Another day, he ſeemed to behold infinite ſnares, gins, and

pit-falls, to be spread on the face of the Earth, saying with a lowd sigh: *And who shall be able to come off safe, amidst so many nets, and traps?* he heard this answere: *Humility only*. With these and other such like illustrations of the vnderstanding, came *S. Antony* continually to be more enflamed to the study of Perfection, and to vanquish himselfe: and as vpon such accidents, he was euer wont to stand musing, and be extraordinarily recollected; so the Disciples would be easily aware, that some such like extasies or abstractions, or other had happened to him: & they would be comming about him, with so many prayers and coniurations, as he could not conceale them, especially considering the fruite they might gather from them.

Another tyme, after these, he approaching now towards the end of his life, and sitting in contemplation, he was rapt in like mãner, & turning himselfe to the standers by, beganne to fetch a deep sigh, and trembling all ouer, kneeles on the ground, and so remayning a good while in prayer, he arose agayne, all bathed in teares. Wherupon the disciples being affrayd, enforced him to manifest to thẽ, that which happened to him. Then the *Saint*, with many sobs, and with words interrupted, answered: O children, how much better were it to dye outright, then to behold the things to fall out, which haue now been declared to me. When they yet vrging him agayne, he addes, but with deepe sighs: The wrath of God hangs ouer the holy *Church*. For lo, it is to be giuen vp into the power of bestiall persons. I haue seen the table of our *Lord* encompassed roũd with lasciuious and vnbrideled mules, that with many kicks of the heeles, oppresse the Priests, and turne euery thing vpside downe. At which sight, I sighing amayne, and desirous to know the mistery, this voyce seemed to land in myne eares: *My Aultar shall be profaned, and full of abhominations*. But yet together with this euill newes, I haue likewise learned, how the storme shall soone passe ouer, and fayre weather agayne shall returne to the *Catholiques*. Both which Prophesyes, were shortly fulfilled. First in the sacrilegious boldnes and insolency of the *Arrians*: and then with the demonstration of the diuine iustice, and with the punishments which in part, at least they payd for all.

These Ministers of the deuill, had sacked the Temple of *Christ*, and within sacred cloysters had violated the Virgins and Matrons there, made hauock of the pious people, and stayned the Yards, & Chappels with innocent bloud, brought in the rabble, and the vilest artisans artizans, the worshippers of Idols, to contaminate the vessels, to trample the Baptisteryes, and Sacraments; and in summe, committed such things, as without horrour and shame cãnot be related. But so impious, and licentious prosperity of theirs, lasted not long. For lo, the rauenous wolues now fallen into hatred with al Natiõs, for such impietyes; and chased away with the fury of the selfe same people, whome they had stirred vp, fled out of the Cittyes, & basely went lurking agayne in their wonted holes. Wherupon the true & ancient Religion, came agayne to dilate it selfe; and the faythfull saw to their great content and consolation, the predictions of *S. Antony* to be verifyed. Whereof since we haue now treated sufficiently already; we will conclude this matter, with a notable case, which happened in the tyme of *Nestorius* the Gouernour of *Alexandria*, to a certaine man called *Balatius*, a Captayne in *Egypt*.

The Iudgement of God shewed vpon Balatius *the Heretique: and how* S. Antony *opposeth himselfe against the* Arrians. Chap. 18.

THis *Balatius* was a great fauourer of the *Arrians*, & consequently a most cruell Persecutour of Catholiques, and particularly of the Religious: in so much, as he made the Monkes to be publiquely whipt starke naked: nor was ashamed likewyse to scourge the sacred Virgins, and the Seruants of *Christ*. Where with *S. Antony*, being moued, resolued to write to him a briefe Letter, of the tenour following. I see the wrath of Heauen to come vpon thee: Do thou cease then to deale with the Christians in this manner, that it may not come and ouertake thee. The *Heretique* laughed and scoffed at these menaces of his, and casting the letter to the ground, & spitting vpon it, he bad the bearers thereof (after he had vilely intreated them) to returne to *S. Antony*, with this message: Since you seeme to take such thought for the Monkes, it will be now tyme for mee to call you to accompt also. But there passed not ouer a full day, when the diuine vengeance appeared vpon that vnhappy Wretch. Forasmuch, as he and *Nestorius* going to a place called *Cherius*, but a dayes iourney distant from the Citty, vpon two horses, that of *Balatius* being the gentlest in his stable, the sayd horses began to play together, when as that, wheron *Nestorius* sate (being they stiller and quieter of the two) giuing suddenly a gripe to *Balatius*, pulled him downe, and leaping vpon him, most cruelly brake his hippe, whence being carryed to *Alexandria*, he dyed within three dayes, while all remayned astonished to see, how suddenly *S. Antonyes* menaces were executed vpon him.

In whose soule, besides so noble a gift of *Prophesy*, was seene also a rich ornament of *Wisedome*; not sprung from the curiosity of vnderstanding, but from purity of affect: not founded in meere speculation or discourses, but in a sensible knowledge, and diuine Loue: not refined with the chayres, and scholasticall disputes, or written Bookes, but with liuely fayth, deuoute aspirations vpon the meruaylous volume of this great fabrique: Insomuch as the immensity, and most swift, and ordinate motions of the heauenly sphears, the generation & corruption of sublunary things, the discording concord of simple bodyes, the formes and differences of the mixt, the variety of inuentions, arts, customes, and accidents of men: but aboue all the sweet disposition, and infallible gouernement of the Eternall Prouidence, were to him, as well a glasse of verity, as an incentiue of Charity. And that which is more to be celebrated with these so great gifts, and treasures of profound knowledg; he was so farre from being puffed vp with them; or once to thinke but vainely of himselfe, as how much more knowledge he got, so much the more he increased in true Modesty and Humility. And especially he carryed a very singular respect, with an interiour and exteriour reuerence to the Interpreters & Depositarians of the diuine Scripture, such as are the Clarks, and Prelates of the holy Church, and as willingly demaunded, & learned of them all, as if he had been the most rude and ignorant of the world: albeit on the other side, when need was, he would not sticke to giue a good account of himself, and of the fayth he imbraced to any person of what quality soeuer.

The *Arians* had spread throughout all *Alexandria*, with subtile lying, that *S. Antony* was of their opinion: which the Seruāt of God hearing, admiring so great impudency in them, by the iudgement of the Catholike Bishops, and of the Brothers withall, he descended from the hill, and being in the citty, in the presence of al the people, beganne to detest that peruerse Sect, calling it a pestilent heresy, & the Messenger of *Antichrist*; teaching, and aduertising all how the Sonne of God is no created thing, nor made of nothing, but is the selfe same substance, and wisedome of the eternall Father. Whence were it a great impiety to say, there was once a tyme, when he was not

not: for as much as he, the word of the Father, was eternal with him. Wherupon he concluded: Wherfore, haue you no communication with those wicked followers of *Arius*, since the light hath nothing to do with darkenes; and you that obserue the due Worship of God with reason do call your selues, and are truly *Christians*. But they in tearming the Sonne, and the Word of God the *Father*, a creature, are nothing different from Gentils; nay rather do you hold it most certaine, that the creatures themselues, are al incensed against such wicked persons, that dare to number and put among things created, the *Creatour*, and *Lord* of the *Vniuerse*, in whome, & through whome hath beene made, and hath being, whatsoeuer is therin.

From such like aduertisements and protestations of the *Saint* the hearers tooke a great deale of pleasure, in seeing that pestiferous opinion so anathematized by such a Man: and all the inhabitants of the Citty, as well the Laicks, as Ecclesiasticall, as well Gentils as Christians, did striue to be the first in the Temple, to see the Man of God, (for so was he called of all) and there likewise, in the sight of them all, would he worke many Miracles, partly in expelling deuils, partly in curing: in so much as the very *Pagans* themselues, made instance to be touching at least of the garment of *S. Antony*. Finally, in that short space of tyme, there were made more *Christiãs*, then were in a whole yeare before: and he himself, besides the truth of the doctrin he deliuered, & the vertue of the miracles he wroght, and the Prudence which in his dayly actions he shewed, was of so attractiue, and gracious a countenance, as howbeit of stature he were not different from others; neuerthelesse the strangers that arriued thither, hauing neuer seen him before, could easely distinguish him from the multitude, and point him out with the fingar to be such a one. To this serenity of countenance, were answerable his behauiours, so iudicious, and complete, as if he had alwayes liued not in Caues, or in the Forrests, but in populous lands, and in conuersation with the Nobles.

S. Antony *sends away two Philosophers well satisfyed, who came to proue, and tempt him; Besides others, that came to iest at him.* Chap. 19.

THERE came on a tyme, as *S. Antony* was on this syde of the Mountayne, two Pagan Philosophers to him, to try him awhile, and to proue what was in him: and he knowing a farre off, what manner of men they were, went forth to meete them, & said to them by meanes of a good Interpreter: Wherfore haue you, being sage, and Philosophers as you are, taken such paynes, so to come to the house of a foole? When they answering, he was no foole, but prudent, and wise; *S. Anthony* replyed, and pressed them with this dilemma: If you would seeme to visit me, your labour were superfluous: If you take me to be sensible, and wise, then do yee become Christians as I am, since conuenient it were, we should seeke to imitate the better: and, if I were to repayre to you, I would surely endeauour to follow your steps; so do you, that haue procured to see and know mee thus, not refuse to do that which I doe. With such like words as these, with some miracles, which they had seene him but lately worke, these curious men, being amazed thereat, departed thence, not without some amendement in themselues.

Others came afterwards of purpose to iest at him, as an Idiot, to whome he sayd: What thinke you? Which was the first, eyther wit or learning? Whereto the Philosophers answering, that without doubt, Wit was the first; and that by it, learning was found out. *S. Antony* did reply: if it be so, then he that hath his wits sound, hath no need of learning. With this cōclusion, as well the Doctors themselues, as the standers by, with reason were astonished. After whome came in others in like manner to demand of *S. Antony*, acc̄opt of the Christian Religion. These men also were very learned, & versed not only in Poets fables, but no lesse in the imaginations of *Plato*, and *Pithagoras*. Now then, they beginning to sophisticate with him, and gibe at the Gospell, the blessed *S. Antony*, stood awhile as it were in a study, and thence with great compassion of their blindnes, discoursed in manner following.

What is more honourable, thinke you Philosophers, eyther to confesse the Crosse, or to adore, as Gods, such as are announced for adulterous, and full of wicked carnality? The thing, which Christians professe, at least, is the signe of Fortitude, and contempt of death: your glories are nothing els, but passions of intemperance, lasciuiousnes, and vnbridled desires: which is better to say, the Eternall *Word*, without leauing his Diuinity, for the benefit of the world, hath taken human flesh, to make vs partakers of the diuine [illegible]ture: or insteed of the great God, to worship (as you do) the bru[illegible]sts, and dead men? And with what face then, dare you to scoffe

ſcoffe at Chriſtians for affirming *Christ*, the Sonne of God, for the Redemption of mortalls, without leauing what he was before, to become what he was not, and to be ſo abaſed, as the humility derogates not a whit from Maieſty; while you others, ſo vnworthily intreate a ſubſtance ſo fayre, and noble, as are reaſonable ſoules? Forasmuch, as on the one ſide, you would haue them to be ſtreames, braunches, and ſemblances of a ſupreme Intelligence, engendred of the higheſt God: & on the other, you do ſeeme to precipitate them from the top of Heauen, euen downe to Earth beneath: Whereas indeed a leſſe euill it were for you, to ſhut them vp only in human bodyes, but you cloth them, or to ſay better, put on them, the ſhapes of Aſſes, Dogs, Wolues, and Serpents, and that which is worſe, with ſhifting and thruſting them now into one body, now into another, you do make them perpetual erratiques & vagabonds. With which villany notwithſtãding you perceiue not a whit, being ſo blind, how much you do iniure withall that ſoueraygne mynd whence they are deriued, and whome they ſeeme to reſemble, ſince looke what the image is, the ſame by all likelyhood, muſt the architype be, & yet that which is worſe by this meanes do you come alſo to diminiſh the dignity of *God* himſelf, the father and origine of that moſt excellent Intelligence.

But come we to the miſtery of the Croſſe, which you ſo much vpbraid. Now tell me then, which of the two were fitter to be choſen, to ſuffer without default the ſnares of the wicked, and for defence of Honeſty & Truth, to expoſe ones ſelfe to all bitternes of puniſhments: or els to giue credit to fables, and adore the errours of *Oſiris*, & *Iſis*, and the deceipts of *Tiphon*, & the flight of *Saturn*, & the deuouring of children, and murdering of Parents, for ſuch are your opinions, and your articles. Beſides this, you that flout ſo, at the reproach of death, why ſeeme you not to admire the glory of the *Reſurrection*? And yet thoſe that preach the one, proclayme the other: and how remember you the croſſe, & paſſe ouer in ſilence, ſo many dead men rayſed, blind reſtored, palſey men cured, leapers cleanſed, the walking vpon waters, & other infinite miracles? Al which ſeeme to ſhew very cleerely, that *Chriſt* was not purely Man, but true God and *Man* together. And ſurely it cannot be denyed, but you proceed very vniuſtly with vs, and deale not with our ſcriptures as you ought; foraſmuch, as if you regarded them, with an equall eye, you ſhould find, without doubt, how all the actions of *Chriſt*, do manifest and discouer him to be *God*.

And now produce you awhile your tryumphs against vs? Though indeed frõ irrationall substances, what els can you bring forth, but crueltyes and bestialityes? And if forsooth (as I vnderstand you would seeme to answere) that such things, are but allegorically meant by you, and that they haue a good interpretation with thẽ, while in *Proserpina* is vnderstood the earth: in *Iuno*, the ayre: in *Diana*, the Moone; In *Neptune*, the Sea; and so of the other: yet for all that, you can not deny your selues to be seruants and worshippers of the creature, to the open disparagement and grieuous dishonour of the *Creatour* himselfe. Whereas, if the beauty of the visible things, were it that moued you so much, such a motion were inough indeed to make you to admire them, and no more; but you insteed thereof, fall a deifying them, and the honour which is due to the Artificer, do you giue to the masonry it self, the same of the Architect to the house, and that of the Captayne to the Souldiour. What thẽ do you answere to all those things? Do but tell vs, I pray, that we also may learne, if things so worthy of laughter, may seeme to be cõteyned in the Crosse.

S. Antony *proceeds in his discourse: and what followed therupon.* Chap. 20.

THE *Philosophers* now being brought into streights, & forced to shift heere and there, *S. Antony* smiling, proceeded forward. The truth of the things, which I haue told you, is euen to be seen with the very eyes; and yet neuerthelesse, whereas you, as Professours of Logick, ground your selues vpon sillogismes, and without such instruments, allow not Religion: tell me first, The knowledge of God, is it more exactly purchased by dialecticall demonstrations, or by operations of *Fayth*, occasioned through workes, or demonstration founded in words? And they answering, that *Faith* proceeding from workes, without doubt, was the more ancient of the two, and brought the greater certainety with it. You haue answered well, said *S. Antony*, because indeed Fayth consists in a certayne interiour disposition of the *Mynd*; whereas Logique seemes to leane meerly vpon the artificiousnes of those, which put the words and the propositions together; in such wise, as when one, by the meanes of Fayth, hath the vertue to worke, he hath no need of the art of argumentation at all; since the very same which Faith teacheth

teacheth vs, do you ſeeke to proue by reaſons and diſcourſes, and many tymes are you not able ſo much, as to expreſſe with wordes, that which we penetrate with the vnderſtanding: and no meruayle, beauſe the Chriſtian law, is not founded in ſpecious & pompous reaſons, but in that power and Vertue, which by *Christ*, is ſubminiſtred to vs, from the Eternall God.

And that this is true, behold vs heere, who neuer hauing learned any letters, do belieue in God, acknowledging in his facture, the Prouidence, he hath of the Vniuerſe. And this our habit of mynd, how operatiue, and efficacious it is, you may gather at leaſt from hence: That whereas, the fooliſh Inuentions, Sects, Phantaſyes, and Idols of you *Grecians*, in effect do vaniſh, and come to nothing: the Chriſtian Verity extendes it ſelfe on all ſides, & you with all your Sophiſtryes, conuert not the *Christians* to *Gentiliſme*: but we, not propoſing, nor teaching any other then the *Fayth* in Chriſt, go daily defacing your vnhappy ſuperſtitions, and diabolicall ceremonyes, in making *Christ* manifeſt to all, to be truly *God*, and the *Sonne* of *God*: and you withall your ſmooth, and elegant ſpeech, are not able to hinder the progreſſe of the Chriſtian doctrine: wheras we only with the name of the *Croſſe*, do ſuddaynly chaſe away thoſe very deuils thēſelues, which you dread, & adore for Gods. And where, but the ſigne of the Croſſe is made, can no art Magique auayle, nor haue Sorceryes there any force at all. And if not, then tell me, I pray, where now are your Oracles? Where your Egiptian Enchaunters? When ceaſed, and vaniſhed trow you theſe infernall arts, but ſince the coming of the croſſe of Chriſt?

And do you now then thinke the *Croſſe*, to be worthy of ſcorne; & not rather the things, by it conuinced, annihilated, & deſtroyed? And that ſo much the more, as your rites were neuer yet perſecuted of any, but haue beene alwayes for the moſt part receiued, and honoured of the world: Whereas the Chriſtian Fayth with al the perſecutions & tribulations, which it hath hitherto ſuffered frō Kings and Princes, continually flouriſheth and multiplyes, now more thē euer. And when was there euer in the world, more light, & greater knowledge of God? When euer attended they ſo much to Sobriety, Continency, and Virginity? When was death ſo much euer contēned, as ſince the holy *Croſſe* hath beene knowne, and adored? & he that belieues it not, may behold ſo many ſquadrons of Martyrs, and ſuch a number of Virgins, who for the loue of *Christ*, haue conſerued their bodyes immaculate, and vntouched. And howbeyt the things already said, are most sufficient for the cleering of our Fayth: neuerthelesse since you yet stand requiring of demonstrations, behold the persons possessed with ill spirits (and by good hap some were present at that tyme,) and causing them to come forth in the midst, he said, as followes. Eyther do you with your sillogismes, or with any other art you haue of Enchauntments, or inuocations of your Idols, deliuer this people; Or else if you cannot, leaue of to entercounter with vs, & acknowledge the Omnipotency of our *Sauiour*.

Heereupon *S. Antony* inuoking the name of *Christ*, he made two or three signes of the crosse vpon the possessed, who from the cryes they gaue, and from prancks they played, and from the torments, and violences they suffered, being suddaynely returned to full and perfect health, became now very still, and gaue infinite thanks to our *Lord God*. Whereat the *Philosophers*, with reason, remayning astonished, *S. Antony* spake to them in this sort. Why do you so wonder heereat? These are no workes of ours, but of *Christ*, by the meanes of such as belieue in him. Do you then belieue in him likewise, and become Christians, and you shall see, that ours are no bablings awhit, but meerely the effects of a liuely Faith, which if you had, you should not neede, to go begging of arguments. These were the words of *S. Antony*, and they likewise admiring the same, wẽt their wayes, shewing him great Reuerence, and confessing withall how much they had beene helped by him.

How the fame of S. Antony *increased: And especiallly what credit he had with Princes.* Chap. 21.

BY these and such like things, may euery one easily imagine, how much daily the fame and renowne of *S. Antony*, went dilating it selfe: insomuch as at last not only persons afflicted with infirmityes, and euill Spirits, or such as were desirous to be guided in the way of our Lord; came to the mountayne to visit him, and to request help and counsayle at his hands: But euen likewise the very Magistrates, and Iudges of *Alexandria* themselues. Who for to haue more easy accesse vnto him, sent to entreate the same at his hands, by meanes of prisoners, and guilty persons, who were subiect to criminall sentences, as knowing well such cases and necessityes, ſtyes, would not be deſpiſed of the ſeruant of Chriſt. Nor were they deceiued, ſince being vanquiſhed by their prayers and teares, he went forth of his Hermitage, and came to exhort the Gouernour in paſſing ſentence vpon them, by any meanes to preferre the feare of God before any paſſion, or human reſpect: remembring them withall of that ſaying in the Ghoſpell, *What meaſure you affoard to others, shal be likewiſe giuen to you.* And with ſuch manner of aduiſes as theſe, obteyned he, very many diſpatches of ſuites, and releaſes of Innocents.

For other perſonages, he forbare not with admirable modeſty to remember them likewiſe of the vanity of the world, and the felicity of a ſolitary life: nor the ſame without fruite, for that many hauing left great riches, and honours, as well of warre, as of peace, haue conuerted themſelues to a religious life. And in ſumme, in the perſon of *S. Antony, Chriſt* had affoarded a famous Phiſitian to all *Egypt*. What hart oppreſſed with ſadnes which parted not cheerfull and content from him? What dolorous ſoule, for the death of their deereſt friends, depoſed not on a ſudden their heauynes and murmuring? What wrathfull perſon, was not preſently reduced to concord? What beggar or Wretch, with his wordes and examples, that came not to make litle reckoning of money, and willingly to ſuffer the neceſſityes of life? What tepid Monke, reſumed not againe new feruour? What young man, with the ſight and diſcourſes of *S. Antony*, was not ſuddenly enamoured with chaſtity? What conſcience afflicted and tempted of the Enemy, or moleſted with irkſome thoughts, that was not immediately quietted. Becauſe indeed among the vertues of this holy man (as we haue ſaid aboue) one was ſo acute a diſcretion of ſpirits, as in the twinckling of an eye, he would know their inclinations and motions; and would not only ſuffe himſelfe to be deceyued, but likewiſe giue opportune and excellent remedy to others, according to the neceſſityes of euery one. Beſides, how many Virgins, already deſtined to matrimony, that with the only beholding of *S. Antony* a far off, haue been conſecrated to *Chriſt*? And finally, as many as repayred to him, haue come their wayes from him much encouraged agaynſt the Diuell, inſtructed againſt euill cogitations, comforted in tribulations, and full of vertuous, and holy purpoſes.

True it is, that ſuch manner of conuerſation with men, was very cautiouſly diſpenſed by him, nor did he ſo giue himſelfe to the care of others, as to be any whit vnmindfull of himſelfe, but rather assoone, as could be, in imtation of *Christ*, leauing the multitude, he would retire himself to prayer and solitude. Nor was the sweetnes of friends, or power of Princes, able to withdraw him from such manner of obseruance. To which purpose, we are not to passe ouer in silence, how a certayne Captayne, after he had visited him, being willing to entertayne him further in discourse, he gently excused himselfe, with that similitude of Fishes (so renowned afterwards, and brought into a Prouerbe) that euen as those, remaining on the land, giue ouer and dye, so Monkes abiding too much with Seculars, do loose the feruour of the spirit; with which comparison, the Captayne was well satisfyed, though much grieued the while to be seuered from him. But what great matter may it seeme, that *S. Antonyes* friendship, should so be desired of Rulers or Prefects of some Prouinces only, since we see it sought for no lesse of very Monarkes themselues, and of the Emperours of the world?

It is a knowne thing, how *Constantinus Augustus*, and the Princes his sonnes, *Constans* and *Constantius*, sent him letters, as to a Father, intreating him to vouchsafe to send them greeting, and good counsayle: but he was so alienate from worldly fauours, and so abhorred he euery least apparence of vanity, as he was vpon the point, not to accept the Epistles sent, saying to the Monkes, to whome it seemed to be some great honour to be so courteously greeted by the *Cæsars*: Why meruayle you that a King should write to a man? Nay wonder rather, the immortall God, should write so his law to mortals, yea euen speake to them face to face by meanes of his only begotten Sonne. The magnanimous *Abbot* then (as we haue sayd) within a litle had refused to receiue the letters, at least he was resolued not to answere them at all, if through the prayers of his Monkes, and scruple which would arise of litle Edification, he had not been enforced in a manner to write backe, as he did: first with praysing those *Lords*, for the fayth they professed, & then exhorting thē to make no great reckoning of their present greatnes but to haue alwayes the future Iudgement in mynd, & to acknowledge *Christ* only, for the true, and eternall King; he concluded lastly in persuading them to be courteous and benigne, and to haue speciall care of the poore, and of Iustice. Which aduises, were receyued of the Emperour and Princes with great ioy and consolation.

This

This was the credit and reputation, whereto the Seruant of Chist, euen in his tyme, was arriued, surmounting the Enuy, and detraction of the world; and the same not so much, through fame of great learning, or of extraordinary Eloquence, or of Bookes put forth to light, or of any of those arts, which are in price with the world, as through a sanctity of manners only, and by the grace of God, who is delighted to exalt the humble, to manifest such as are willing to hide themselues, and withall to giue the world to vnderstand, how the diuine precepts and counsayles, are not impossible to those, that will disentangle themselus, and walke couragiously in the way of vertues. But be this sufficiently sayd for the present of the glorious acts, and rare parts of *S. Antony*, rather as intimated to the faythfull only, then any wyse explicated as they deserue. And now remaines it for vs to touch somewhat of his *Death*, that to him was a sweet, and blessed Birth-day.

S. Antony *being now come to the end of his dayes, presageth his death. With his happy departure out of this life.* Chap. 22.

THe holy Old man, was now arriued to the age of one hundred and fiue yeares old, with a great ability of body. He wāted not a tooth, though his gumms indeed were somwhat fallē: He had his sight very excellent good; hauing his eyes yet sound, and quite without blemish: his feete, and armes he had still very actiue, and that which is more to be merueyled at, was this; that notwithstanding he was so giuen, from his childhood, to Fastings, Vigils, Solitudes, Cloysters, with other of the sharpest penances that are, without shifting (as we sayd aboue) his garments, or euer bathing himself; he had yet, so fresh, and fayre a skynne, as if he had beene alwayes trayned vp in feasts, and banquets, stoues, and baths, and other addresses of human delicacyes. In this state, had he an interiour feeling in himselfe, of the speedy approach of his last dayes. Wherupon going forth againe from the inmost part of the wildernes to reuisite and comfort the Conuents abroad, and causing the Brothers to be assembled together as to a Congregation, he cleerly spake to them in this sort.

This is the last visit, and surely is it much, that in this present life, we haue enioyed one another so long. But now it is tyme at last, that I goe my wayes. For I haue liued in the world my part already. The disciples in hearing this, beganne to weep, and to giue very deare imbraces, and holy kisses of peace to their Mayster. Who being now very glad to go forth of this exile, and to passe into his Countrey, in the meane while he went about, to put them in mynd, that they would not suffer the trauayles of Religion to seeme tedious to them, but dayly seeme to expect death: that they endeauour to keep, the soule from vncleane thoughts: that they purpose to imitate the manners of *Saints*, and wholy fly the cōmerce of Schismatiques, and Heretiques, not suffering themselues to bend this way, or that way; through feare of Magistrates, or Princes, whose forces are but little, and not durable.

With these, and other such like aduises, making an Epilogue as it were of the rest, he tooke leaue of his children, who vsing all violence to reteine him there, that they might be receiuing his last spirit, they could not procure the fauour, as well for many respects which he cōcealed, as principally, to auoyd a certayne abuse, which the *Egiptians* had, to conserue with some art or other, the bodyes of persons of quality, vpon certaine beds, in performing their wonted Exequies indeed, & enwrappiug them after their manner in sheetes, but yet auoyding to put them vnder the ground, as a thing wholy vnworthy of them. Now was this abuse alwayes very much displeasing to *S. Antony*, and he had been reprehending the people for it at sundry tymes, and intreated the Bishops, often to remedy the same: alleadging that euen from the auncient *Prophets* themselues, were seen to bee sepulchers extant, yea that the body of *Christ* our *Lord* himselfe, had beene put into a Monument, and was couered with a great stone, who arose the third day. With which examples, howbeyt already, he had reduced many persons, to bury their dead; yet neuerthelesse, knowing the custome, and inclination of that people, he would not trust the multitude with his spoyles, but retiring himselfe into his Cell, from whence had he departed, within few months after fell sicke: and calling his two disciples to him, who had now some fifteene yeares been present with him, he spake to them in manner following.

I am now (my deerest) vpon walking the way of my Fathers, and I feele my selfe to be called of our Lord. As for you, be you wary and vigilant, and take heed, you loose not the labours of so long a tyme: but as if you had but now begunne, do you enforce your selues to mayntеyne your wonted feruour and study. Then know you the

the snares, and rages of the inuisible Enemies, and know you likewise, how through diuine Iudgment, they haue lost their forces. Do you not feare them then, but alwayes aspire to *Christ*, and fixing a liuely fayth in him, expect euery moment to be cited before him, & so attend to your selues, still remembring the rules, and documents, you haue had from me; especially to fly as fyre, the conuersation of *Arrians*, and *Meletians*, and whosoeuer shall haue seuered themselues from the Fayth, and communion of the Catholique Church, since you know, how I no lesse haue alwayes abhorred them. But rather seeke to vnite your selues with *Christ*, and with his *Saints*; that after death, they may acknowledge you as Friends, and be receyuing you into the Eternall tabernacles. Be this your opinion then, and this your discourse.

And if you haue any care of me also, as of a *Father*, doe not suffer my Corps, by any meanes, to be carryed to *Egypt*, with the hazard of being put vp in some house, according to the peruerse custome of the Country there; but hide me rather in the earth, in a place, where no person of the world, may know besids your selues, because if it be cōsumed for the present, it shall yet be restored agayne very glorious in the Resurrection. You shall distribute my Garments in such sort, as that *Athanasius* the Bishop may haue one of my *Melots* (which were only poore sheep skins sowed together) and the *Mantle* whereupon I was wont to lye. To the Bishop *Serapion*, you shall giue the other *Melot*: and you, in memory of mee shall keep the *Cilice*: and with this my Sonnes, remayne in peace, for *Antony* passeth, and shall be no more abiding with you.

These were his last words, and then with a cheerefull countenance, shewing the *Angels* and *Saints* to reioyce, who came to meete him, he gaue vp the Ghost. And the disciples, though sad for loosing such a Father on earth, neuerthelesse being recomforted, for hauing purchased such an Intercessour in Heauen, did bury him, according as he had ordyned. And to the Bishops, they gaue the garments, as welcome, and as much esteemed of them, as those who had gotten a very rich inheritance. And the great *Athanasius*, recounts of himselfe, how he wore the same afterwards, very willingly: whereby it seemed to him, that he carryed about him, a perfect Memorial of the wholesome aduises, and documents of *S. Antony*. Such a course, and end, made the great Seruant of *Christ*: whose life (as we insinuated aboue) *Athanasius* himselfe first wrote, in the Greeke tongue; who

though

though he were of another vocation, notwithstanding in fayth & will was he most vnited with him. The blessed *Euagrius* translated the same into latin, who liued very neere those tymes, and was the disciple of both the *Macarius*, enriching the same with some things receiued, as it is probable, of such as had much familiarity & conuersation with the Man of God. Moreouer, as many as haue framed the Ecclesiasticall History, and other most graue *Authours* besides, haue likewise touched his acts, and made very pious, and honourable mētion of him: God vndoubtedly so disposing the same, not so much in recompence of the labours of *S. Antony* (who enioying eternall felicity in heauen, should seeme to care very little to be renowned in earth) as for the profit of all man kind. To the end, so perfect, and noble deeds, words, and manners, might not seeme to be shut vp within the termes of one people, or of one age only; but should dilate themselues into all parts, and serue for instruction, glasse, & incitement to all Nations, and to all posterity.

FINIS.

S. PACHO-

S. PACHOMIVS.

THE ARGVMENT.

I BORNE of miſbelieuing Parents, gaind
Not by my ſelfe but Heau'n, the ſauing light,
Quickned the grace which I had entertaind,
And left the world, that I more ſafe might fight
Againſt my foes: I victory obtaind,
Finding this way to countermand their ſpite:
And ſlighting what the world doth moſt commend
More eaſily I did my ſelfe defend.
What ere he be that ſtriues to haue a ſhare
Within the manſion of Eternity,
Let him in this beſtow his greateſt care
To ſhun th'indearements of Mortality.
Soules haue no parts, harts vndeuided are,
Heau'n and the world haue no affinity,
Like as of Senſe, on ſeuerall obiects bent,
The ſtrength is weakned, and is leſſe intent.

THE LIFE OF S. PACHOMIVS ABBOT.

Written by Simeon Metaphrastes.

Of the Birth of S. Pachomius, *and his miraculous Conuersion to the Christian Fayth.* Chap. I.

N the same age (some few yeares after) the blessed *Pachomius* did flourish, a great Father likewise and an excellent Mayster of Monkes: whose vertue, and Religion, no doubt was so much the more memorable, as the helpe of Education, which he had was lesse, being borne of Gẽtiles both Father and Mother, & brought vp in *Thebais*, without any knowledge of our *Sauiour Christ*, vntill such tyme, as he arriued vnto military age. Some notable signes did forerun his Vocation. One was, that when they gaue him to drinke any wine, or other liquour, which had been offered to the Idols, with a certaine hidden auersion of the stomacke, he would suddenly be vomiting it forth. And another signe also was there yet of more

more wonder: for that, he being once conducted to a Sacrifice, which was to be performed, by a riuers side, hard by, there could be nothing done; for that at his presence, the Priest could neyther finish his ceremonies, nor would the Diuels seeme to enter into the Statues, to giue forth answeres, from thence, as they were wont: so as their wicked Minister, hauing finally vnderstood the occasion thereof, with furious brawling, began to controule the Parents of *Pachomius*, as hauing brought thither, an enemy of the immortall Gods: and commaunded them, suddenly to thrust him forth, as fearing least some heauenly wrath, or vengeance might light on their Sonne.

Amidst so impious superstitions of his house, & the rudiments of Egiptian learning and doctrine, *S. Bachomius* being arriued to the twentith yeare of his life, was enrolled as a Souldiour in a new leuy of men, which in the name of *Constantius*, was then made in diuers parts, against the Tyrant *Maxentius.* And with this occasion, being conducted by water with others, to a certayne Citty, neare vnto *Thebes*, he fell into great necessity, together with the whole army, through the smal prouision that was made of victuals for thẽ. Which being vnderstood, by those of the Country there, who by good hap, were of the faythfull people of *Christ*, and very friendly to the Neighbour, they suddenly prouided for the afflicted Souldiours, what was needfull for them; and that with so great sollicitude and charity, as *S. Pachomius* was astonished thereat: & demaunding what nation they were of, that was so hospitable, and benigne; answere was made him they were Christians. When demaunding againe, of what manner of life & institute they were, he vnderstood, that they did belieue in *Iesus Christ*, the only Sonne of God, and did well to all sorts of persons, with firme confidence, to haue some large remuneration for it, at the hands of the same God.

S. Pachomius, had scarcely heard these words, but that full, as well of interiour consolation, as of an vnusuall light, retyring himselfe from the company, and being somwhat in a deepe study with himselfe, he lifted vp his hands to the starres, saying: *Lord God*, who framedst the Heauen and earth, if thou shalt vouchsafe to regard my basenes, and my trauayles, and giue me the knowledge of thy Diuinity; I promise to serue thee, and obey thy precepts while I breath. With this prayer, and promise, the loue of vertue so increased in him, as he began, from that tyme forwards through the diuine Grace to resist all sensuality, and valiantly to suffer Tribulations; helping himselfe with the memory of his first purposes, vntill such tyme, as the *Emperour*, hauing gotten a glorious victory vpon the Tyrant, he was cashiered with others: and not seeing opportunity there to become a Christian, he immediately went his wayes to *Chemosium*, a Towne of the higher *Thebais*, where remayned some notable and venerable Seruants of God. Of whome, being instructed in the holy Fayth, he was baptized: and the very same night, that he receiued this wholsome Sacrament, he sees in his Sleepe his right hand to be filled with dew, which falling from heauen, did incorporate it selfe in forme of hony, and withall heard a voyce, which said: *Open the eyes of thy vnderstanding Pachomius, and know, that this is a signe of the grace, which is affoarded thee by Christ.* This vision was not in vayne or vnprofitable a whit, but rather *Pachomius* felt himselfe so compunct therewith, and enflamed with diuine Loue, as he determined, without delay, to renounce the world, & to consecrate himselfe to a monasticall life. And hauing heard of a famous Hermit, called *Palemon*, that dwelt in those desarts, he wēt his wayes to him, to submit himselfe to his discipline.

S. Pachomius *craues of* Palemon *to be receiued into his discipline, and is admitted: with the manner of their liues togeather.* Chap. 2.

THis *Palemon* for yeares was very graue, seuere of countenance, & so rigid and mortifyed in his cōuersation, as by many he was iudged to be inimitable. So soone as he heard then, one knocking at his cell, opening the doore, he sayd to *Pachomius*. *Who art thou? and what seekes thou?* To whome the good young man answering: *God sends me to you to be admitted into your estate of life.* The old man replyed. This is no worke for you, nor so easy as you thinke; for some three or foure others, haue come hither likewise that haue not been so well able to stand to it afterwards. Then *Pachomius*: All men are not made of the same mould. Do you receiue me, and in tyme (I trow) you shall be cleered in that point. I haue told you already (replyed the Hermit) that you cannot brooke the labour. Go your wayes then first to do pennance in some other place: and if you shall then thinke your selfe able to endure it, do you come to me, & then perhaps I shall accept of you. Because indeed my manner of liuing (for to tell it you) is very sharpe, and difficult. I susteyne my selfe

selfe (God be thanked) with no other thing, then bread and salt. Neither wine nor oyle euer enters into my mouth. Halfe of the night, or there abouts, do I spend, part in praier, part in reading, and ruminating the diuine Scripture.

These and the like words, though deliuered with a harsh voice, and a horride brow, were not sufficient to terrify the constant *Pachomius*, but rather, as a litle water spurted on a great fyre, enkindled such a flame in his breast, as with much reuerence, he most cheerfully affirmed, that he felt in his mynd, a firme beliefe, that the diuine Goodnes, by meanes of the intercession of the same *Palemon* (whose life was a mirrour to all Mortalls) would make him a disciple not vnworthy of so noble a Mayster. From such perseuerance, vnited with like piety, the *Anchoret*, now easily gathered, that *Pachomius* had an extraordinary feeling, and a manifest vocation of God. Whereupon, hauing now some confidence of a happy successe, without more ado, he admits him into his Cell, and giues him his habit. And from thence, they began to liue together, spending the greater part of the tyme in deuotions, and the rest, in twisting of Camels hayre, and making of sacks, and that not to pick out money for their owne profit, but to relieue the poore with, as the *Apostle* counsayles.

At night then, in tyme of prayer, and Psalmes, if *Palemon* perceiued the disciple to be somewhat pressed with sleep, taking him forth of his Cell, with a basket in hand, he would employ himselfe with him, in carrying of heapes of sand, to and fro, vntill such tyme, as the superfluous vapours of the body being dispersed by this meanes, he might come to be prompt, & nimble againe, and haue the spirit now throughly awaked; and would besides be admonishing him, saying: be you sober and attentiue *O Pachomius*, that you be not ouercaught by the Tempter, and all our labours proue not to be in vayne. But the feruent *Nouice*, gaue not much occasion vnto spurs and incitements, and the holy *Father* exulted in himselfe, and glorifyed the Diuine Clemency, to see him become euery day, more obedient then other, to see him more addicted to mortification, and abstinence, he not sparing in the meane while to go alwayes before him, with a liuely, and continuall example.

So as once vpon Easter day, *Pachomius* to solemnize that Feast, hauing dressed him a litle Oyle, seasoned with salt, when *Palemon* saw him to reach it to him, suddaynely striking his forhead, & cafling forth a deepe sigh, with teares he sayd: My Lord was put on the Crosse, he was loaden with iniuryes, cuffs, and buffets, in his greatest thirst he was made to drinke both Vinegar and Gaule, and shall I be pampered heere, and be soothing my palate which oyled meates? Nor with all the instance, and intreatyes, that *Pachomius* could vse by any meanes, he would seeme to breake his Fast, vntill such tyme, as that seasoned Oyle being taken away, and some other brought him which was pure, and simple (in blessing it first, with the signe of the Crosse, and rendering most humble thankes to the high *Creatour* for it) he finally fell to. In such like acts *Pachomius* continually beheld himselfe, as in a glasse: and as from the excellency of the Mayster, he was hourely encouraged more to follow the good; so from others defects, became he alwayes more cautious to beware the euill.

The iudgement of God shewed vpon a Monke. S. Pachomius *founds a Monastery, and* Palemon *dyes.* Chap. 3.

AN audacious *Monke* but ill founded in the knowledge of himselfe, and human frailty, came on a tyme to see *Palemon* and *Pachomius*, while they had made by chaunce a very good fyre: & after he had sate downe with them a pretty while, entertayning themselues with spirituall discourses, arising on a sudden, sayd to *Palemon*: if you, and your disciple haue true Fayth, shew me heere some Euangelicall experience thereof, and make your prayer, heere barefoote, vpon these burning coales. *Palemon* reprehending him for it, and aduising him, not to suffer himselfe to be deceyued so by the enemy; he puffed vp with greater pride, and presumption, went voluntarily vpon the Coales, and the Diuine Maiesty, permitting it so, the Diuell had power to preserue him without hurt at all. Whereupon that miserable Wretch, with malapert insolency, vpbrayding *Palemon* and *Pachomius*, with saying: where was their fayth? went his wayes very proud, from thence. But it was not long, ere he payd very soundly for it.

For first, being deluded by the ancient Aduersary with lascitiuous shapes, and therupon very grieuously strooke and afflicted, he repayred agayne, after some dayes to *Palemon*, with sighes confessing his errour, saying: Know that I am vndon, for not hauing obeyed you, and now I do pray you, to succour me, with your prayers, for that

that I stand in great daunger, to be slayne of the infernall Enemy. The wretch was yet a speaking, and *Palemon* and *Pachomius* a weeping for compassion; when lo, on a sudden, the deuill assaults him, takes him out of the Cell, and like a sauage beast, chasing him a good while through the Crags, and Mountaynes, finally in the Citty, which is called *Pus*, tooke away his wits, so as he cast himselfe headlong into a fornace of a bath, where suddaynely he dyed.

S. Pachomius being admonished with these so horrible, & strāge accidents, from thence learned to feare the Iudgment of God, and to re-enforce the guard vpon his hart, by resisting the appetites, bridling anger, and the other passions, and endeauouring to found himselfe, by all meanes, in true humility. Besides, when he read or recited any things of the sacred scripture, he posted not in hast, as many are wont, but tasting, and ruminating the sentences, & precepts, one by one, he sought to deriue profit from them, and to serue the Highest with fit attention. Being often sent barfoote, to make wood, in a certayne forrest, very full of sharpe thornes, while he felt his flesh to be torne, and wounded, he would be suffering all the dolours thereof with alacrity, in remembring the Nayles, which pierced the sacred feete and hands of our *Lord* and *Sauiour Christ Iesus*, & continually treating with God in those solitary places would he pray for himselfe, and for all human kind, that he might be preserued from the snares of the common Aduersary. In summe, with these manner of Exercises, was he arriued to such a point of perfection, as the Maister himselfe remayned much comforted, and astonished thereat.

It happened to him afterwards, on a tyme, by a certayne occasion, to arriue at the Iland, and Towne of *Tabenna*; where, being in a long, and profound Prayer, he heard a voyce to say to him: *Pachomius, stay heere, and set vp a Monastery in this place, because many shall come vnto thee with desire to be saued whome thou shalt guide, according to the instruction, which I shall giue thee.* And with this, an *Angell* appeared, and gaue him a Table, wherein the same Institute was conteyned, which for many ages afterwards, the Monks of *Tabenna* obserued. Then *Pachomius*, with the discretion of spirits which he had purchased, very cleerely perceiued, that as well the vision, as the Rule was a heauenly thing: and receiuing the same with great Reuerēce, he went to his Mayster, and communicated the whole with him; beseeching him to be pleased, to put to his helping hand, in the exe-

cution

cution of what, had beene ordeyned him, by the Angell. And though *Palemon* otherwise, would very vnwillingly haue left his auncient Cell, notwithstanding to comfort so good and vertuous a disciple, he was perswaded to go thither, and they both set vp there a poore habitation, in forme of a Monastery. But it was not long, ere *Palemon*, being now spent, partly with old age, and partly with maceration of the body, arriued to the end of his dayes; and *Pachomius*, as in life he had alwayes obeyed, and serued him, with exquisite diligence; so after death, with extraordinary feeling, buryed him, with his owne hands, with a great deale of Lamentation, but not without Canticles and Hymnes.

A Brother of S. Pachomius *ioynes himselfe with him in his manner of lyfe; and what followed.* Chap. 4.

AFter this, a naturall Brother of *S. Pachomius*, becomming a Christian, and called by the name of *Iohn*, being likewise touched with a laudable desire of a perfect life, came to seeke him, and to inhabite with him. They remayned full fifteene yeares together continually exercising themselues, in acts of religion, & pennance. At the end wherof, while now it seemed to *Pachomiubs*, it would not be long, ere that came to effect, which had been promised him of the multiplication of Monkes, he began anew, to enlarge the dwelling, to be able to receiue them all. This fact of his, was displeasing to *Iohn*, and as he, who was the elder in yeares, and perhappes, knew not, or not fully belieued, what was signifyed to *Pachomius* from Heauen, esteemed such a building, to be against Pouerty, and therfore reprehended his Brother, somewhat bitterly for it, saying, he should cease from committing such follyes, so to seeke to enlarge himselfe, more then needed. To which words, though he answered nothing, yet did he inwardly thinke vpon thē; and after hauing some remorse at such a thought, retyring himselfe at night in the new building, he puts himselfe into bitter Laments, and turning himselfe to God, with great dolour cryed out in this manner.

Alas, that the prudence of the world, should be yet continually raigning in me! I am still a carnall man, and after so many yeares of Religious warfarre, doe I yet suffer my selfe to be vanquished by wrath, vnder a colourable pretext of good. Mercy Lord, least I vtterly

terly perish, because that if thou establish me not, in thy patience, and that the Enemy come to find somewhat of his in me, I shall be subiect to him, since it is written: That if any one but sayle in one, he is made guilty of all. I belieue thy benignity is exceeding great, help me *Lord*, & I shall walke in the way of thy Elect; aduauncing my self alwaies forward, & forgetting quite what remaines behind. Euen as they likewise through thy grace, haue done, to their euerlasting prayse, and crowne, but to the great affliction, and vtter confusion of the aduersary: otherwise, how shall I be able to instruct those, whome thou saydst, thou wouldst giue me in charge, if first I shall not subdue the passions, which by meanes of the flesh, make warre against the spirit, and if I shall not haue learned to obserue thy Law inuiolable? But I hope Lord, through the help of thy high and mighty hand, I shall do that, which may like thee best, and thou pardon all my defects.

In such accusations of himselfe as these, ioyned with bitter playnts, with burning prayers, and with solid purposes, spent he all that night, & at the apearing of the day he found on the ground, a certaine durt which was there caused through the continuall teares, that streamed from his eyes; as also with the excessiue sweat, which tricked downe from all his body. Nor let any one seeme to attribute this, to an exaggeration of words: for that besides the humour, which contrition wrong from him, and affliction of mynd; it was then likewise the season of Summer, and the place of its nature was exceeding hoat: nor was the seruant of God, then making his prayer in a carelesse kind of composition of body, but eyther on his knees, or prostrate, or bolt vpright, with the armes erected & distended in forme of a Crosse, without letting them once to fall, or leaning himselfe to any thing, vntill the tyme he had purposed to himselfe; and this, as well to suffer something with *Christ*, and for *Christ*, as by that meanes to keep his mynd more vigilant, and attentiue.

With this sacrifice of an humble and penitent hart, he obteyned so much fauour from heauen, as for the tyme to come, he perseuered with his Brother, in meruaylous Peace, and Patience: and assoone as he passed into a better life, he interred him, with all due piety, & with the wonted Exequyes. Frō hence, remayning quite alone, as he had but then entred into the Wildernes, he gaue himselfe with a fresh vigour to his accustomed spirituall exercises, not

R for

forbearing the while, like another *Noe*, to be building the Arke for those, that were to be saued therin, according to the Angelicall prediction, which howbeit slow in coming to passe, yet was he certayne, it would not fayle.

S. Pachomius *is tempted by Deuils in sundry sorts. He sees a vision; & many repayre vnto him, to be admitted into his Institute.* Chap. 5.

IN the meane tyme *S. Pachomius* was very grieuously molested by Hellish Monsters, being all enflamed with Enuy against him, & desirous to put any obstacle soeuer to so great a good; so as putting in practize whatsoeuer was permitted them, with diuers apparitions and strange phantasmes, they sought to affright the seruant of God. Among other on a time, being about to kneele to his Prayers, the earth on a sudden fell a gaping before him, in forme of a deepe Cesterne, to swallow him vp. At other times, returning from the more remote deserts, where sometymes through desire of greater solitude, he was accustomed to retire himselfe; vpon the sudden, the same peruerse spirits were before him, marching as it were in order of battaile, and saying with a loud voyce: Giue place to the Man of God. They endeauoured likewise to shatter the new building in such sort, as it seemed they would haue turned it topsy-turuy from the very foundations. Besides, sitting on a day at some handy worke, after he had made his prayer, there seemed a Cock to be represented to him of an vnmeasurable greatnes, which redoubling very fierce, and horrible crowings, aduentured from tyme to tyme to fly in his face, and with the clawes, and spurs most cruelly scratched him.

These, and other affrights and iniuryes *S. Pachomius*, being full of a high confidence in God, very easely repelled, now with the signe of the most holy crosse, now with some verse of the sacred Psalter. Wherupon the malignant spirits, perceiuing the way of feare, succeeded not with them; turned themselues by agreement to tempt him, with laughter, in shewing themselues very busy & earnest to remoue certayne leaues of a tree therby, tying them with great ropes, and exhorting one another to pull hard, with voyces and vnited forces, much after the manner, as Carpenters are wont to do, when they lift some huge piece of tymber. But this trick of theirs, was not any whit sufficient to moue the grauity, and constancy,

ſtancy of the Chriſtian Philoſopher; but rather ſighing, inſteed of laughter, and ſetting his mynd on the Crucifix, he attended to proſecute the exerciſe in hand, in ſuch wiſe, as the powers of darknes, being thus ſcorned by a mortall man, and put to confuſion, went their wayes.

But yet for all this, they ceaſed not afterwards, to renew the battaile agayne, by taking the habit and forme of beautifull women and endeauouring to ſit downe at the Table with the Man of God in tyme of refection, and to be impudently putting their hands into that poore fare, which he had before him; when ſeeing themſelues to be howerly vanquiſhed and deſpiſed, chaunging their figures by diuine diſpenſation to the greater crowne of the *Saint*, they afflicted him more then once with ſundry paynes & cruel torments. Wherin as he, through the help of *Christ*, remayned alwayes victorious; ſo according to the ſaying of the Scripture, it often happened, that he walked, and that without hurt, vpon venemous beaſts; and which is more, being to paſſe the Riuer of *Nilus*, when need was, the Crocodils themſelues, inſteed of a bark, would ſecurely be wafting him ouer.

With ſuch proofes, and ſo glorious victoryes, *S. Pachomius* now being arriued to the higheſt degree of hope and charity, the Angell appeared to him anew, and ſayd to him: *God is pleaſed*, O *Pachomius, with thy ſeruice, and would haue thee reconcile the Gentils vnto him*. When not many dayes after, ſome perſons, deſirous to ſaue their Soules, and glutted with the world, beganne to repayre vnto him from diuers places, who benignly receiued them all, but yet gaue thẽ not the Monaſticall habit, till firſt he had proued euery one with a long and exact probation.

The manner he held in the inſtructing of all together, and ech one in particuler, conſiſted, in keeping them free, and farre off from all traffique, and tranſitory cares; and to vnite them, firſt from the world, then from the hauing of things proper, and laſtly from thẽſelues. And foraſmuch as to exhort others to the Croſſe, examples do moue a great deale more, then words; he was the firſt in obſeruing of Silence, in Edification, Leſſons, Faſts, Vigils, and other labours, and auſterityes of the Monaſtery, to prepare the Table, to cultiuate the garden, to anſwere at the gate, to be ſeruing of the Sick both night and day, and hence with louing aduices, and remembrances withall, would he afterwards very eaſely conduct others, to liue according to the obligation of such a vocation. It was not long ere the good odour, & fame of this new Institute was spread euery where, in such sort as the multitude of Monks, came soone to ariue to the number of a hundred.

S. Pachomius *highly regardeth the Clergy; and visits the great* Athanasius. Chap. 6.

AMōg these Monkes, was not yet seene to be any *Priest*: wherupon when they were to communicate, some Priest was called for, of the neighbour Villages, so rare was Priesthood in those dayes, and held in the esteeme it ought to be. And as for *S. Pachomius* he suffered not any of his disciples to aspire to such a dignity, or any other honours, or degres at all, affirming that from like desire, doe grow emulations, strifes, and contentions; and added, that as a least sparckle of fyre, falling in a barne, if not speedily oppressed, will vnluckily consume the whole yeares haruest: so *Ambition*, or the thought of a Clerkship, with what pretext soeuer it enter once into Cloysters, and be not suddenly extinguished, will come to put all the Religion in tumult, or ruine rather and vtter destruction. Notwithstanding afterwards, if any one being a Priest already, should offer himselfe to follow the Rule, *Pachomius* would not refuse to accept him, and with such quality of persons, so carryed himselfe, as how much more respectfull, he shewed himselfe towards them for the sacred Orders sake which they had taken; so much more humble & meeke would they become through the Vertue, and example they saw in him.

Besides that, he was full of Piety to all, especially towards the aged and infirme persons. To young men likewise, he would vse discretion, dexterity, and longanimity to saue their Soules, wherof he was meruaylously zealous, & sollicitous. And because not far from his Conuent, was a certayne Village without a Pastour, and consequently depriued of the word of God, and the holy Communion, he dealt very charitably about the same with *Aprion* Bishop of *Tentiri*, in whose Diocesse the sayd place was; and with his consent, set vpon the building of a Church, where afterwards a Parish was appointed. And he in the meane time, not fayled to go thither with some companions, to instruct thē in the Christian doctrine, performing that exercise with such deuotiō, & with so much grace,

&

& composition of body and mynd, as to the Seculars it seemed they heard, and saw an Angell, and no mortall man, nor were the faythfull only confirmed, by this meanes, but many Infidels likewise conuerted to the Fayth. And as *S. Pachomius* receyued those who belieued in the Ghospell with extraordinary ioy; so for the losse of the obstinate and incredulous persons, he would feele extreme dolour, and for the same be shedding of continuall teares.

At that very tyme, the great *Athanasius* had taken possession of the Bishoprique of *Alexandria*; & being gone in progresse, as a good Pastour, in person to visit the Churches of *Egipt*, & especially of the vpper *Thebais*, and *Siena*, by that occasion he was likewise to passe by *Tabenna*, when *S. Pachomius* knowing some part of the trauailes, and persecutions which the holy Bishop had suffered for the *Catholique* fayth, went forth to meete him, in company of all his *Monkes* with iubiley and festiuity of Psalmes, of Hymnes, and Canticles. True it is, that hauing vnderstood before hand, how meanes was made by the Bishop of *Tentiri* to *Athanasius*, for his promotion to a higher state, for not to be seene nor knowne by him, he hid himselfe of purpose, in the throng. Whether he spake with him afterwards, or no, is not found written any where. But as this Chanpion of *Christ*, was a great friend, and much deuoted to the Catholique Prelates; so could he not suffer so much as the name of *Arrius* and *Meletius*, and the other Heretiques and Scismatiques to be mentioned of any by name: and for their writings he could not endure them by any meanes to be had or read of his Monkes. He was likewise very cautious in forbidding them to murmur at all, especially against the Clerks and Prelates of the church, and if by chance they had fallen into such a default, he would suddenly oppose himselfe against them, in citing some verses & sentences out of the holy Scripture to that purpose, together with the example of *Mary* the sister of *Moyses*, so seuerely punished by God, for hauing murmured against her Brother. And finally by how much more sweete and plyable he was to all, in that which lawfully he might; so much more rigid, and inflexible he shewed himselfe, where it stood not with the least point of the honour of God, or the *Neighbour*.

S. Pachomius *is visited by his Sister, who afterwards retires her selfe into a Monastery.* Chap. 7.

SAint *Pachomius* kept himselfe wholy from the conuersation & familiarity of his Parents, except when he had good hope to help them in Spirit. And thersore lastly being visited by a Sister of his, he sent her answere by the porter in thes words. Behold thou hast heard I am yet aliue: Go thy wayes then, and take it not ill, that I let thee not see me. I will promise thee, that if thou wilt happily imitate this manner of life of myne, to obteyne together with me pardon & Mercy of our Lord, some fit dwelling or other shal be assigned thee, in a conuenient place to liue in peace and silence, and by that occasion peraduenture, it may happen the diuine Goodnes will call some other women likewise to do pennance with thee, since in fine there is no other consolation on earth, then for one to do well, & to serue God.

With this answere, the good woman was so compunct, as she brake forth into plaints, and without more ado, determined to obey the counsayle of her Brother; who according to promise, caused certayne Lodgings to be built for her, not farre from the Monastery, very apt for the end pretended: wherin she exercising her selfe, according to the directions and orders of *S. Pachomius*, it was not long ere there came many other women likewise to her for the same purpose, who increasing continually in number, she was elected to be the *Mother* & *Abbesse* of them. Whence he attended with more sollicitude then euer to instruct them well, and to conduct them safely to a good Port.

A certayne venerable and discreet Father, called *Peter*, had the superintendency ouer that Conuent, by commission of *S. Pachomius*, who at his tymes would visit, and exhort them to Perfection; and if it happened now and then to any Monke, hauing some kinswomen there to haue occasion to go to any such, he was accompanied thither, by some ancient, and graue person, or other, of approued vertue: nor could he speake with such a one, but in the presence of the *Mother*, and some of the principall of the Monastery. To giue, or take any thing with them, or els to eate, or drinke in that place, vnder any pretext whatsoeuer, was wholy prohibited. When any of the Sisters came to dye, the others very decently composing the corps,

corps, would depose it with Psalmes in a determinate place, neere vnto the conuent, Whence after the Monkes wold conuey the same in manner of procession, and bury it with deuout prayers & accustomed Canticles in the hill neer at hand. Through the fame of these things, a certayne yong youth (among others) of some fourteene yeares old, by name *Theodore*, a Christian of noble Bloud, being moued, gaue himselfe likewise to the discipline of *S. Pachomius*, by the occasion which I shall presently tell you.

The history of Theodore, *and how he and his Mother entred into the discipline of* S. Pachomius.

THeodore once on a festiuall day, beholding the riches, the delights, and the ornaments of his owne house, felt himselfe suddenly to be interiourly moued by the diuine grace, & began to discourse with himselfe in this manner, saying: What shall all these eases, contentments, and momentary pleasures auayle me (Wretch as I am) if I come to be depriued of the Eternall? Forasmuch as none for the present can attend to these, and in the future enioy the others: and fetching suddenly a great sigh, retyred himselfe into a more secret place of the house, where prostrate in teares, he sayd: *O Lord*, who seest the secrets of harts, thou knowest, I prefer not any thing of this life before thy loue: vouchsafe then to illumine me, so as I may be able to vnderstand thy will; and that perfectly executing the same, I may glorify, and prayse thee foreuer.

After this, refusing the commodityes and the cherishments of his Mother, he began to giue himselfe seriously to abstinence, and fastings, with other mortifications and asperityes, wherin hauing exercised himself for some two yeares together, he recollected himselfe in the company of some Seruants of God. One of which, (the vespers being ended) discoursing according to the custome amõgst them of spirituall things, he entred in, to speake of the *Tabernacle*, and of the *Sancta Sanctorum*, of the ancient Law; interpreting the exteriour Tabernacle (as that which was of the manner of manufacture) to signify the first people of the Iewes; but that of the *Sancta Sanctorum*, should figure the vocation of the Gentils, as hauing a more sumptuous and mysticall entry with it; whence in the place of Sacrifices of beasts, and insteed of the Thurible, of the Table, of the Arke, of the Candlesticke, of the Propitiatory, and of all those o-

thers

ther ancient symbols, for our saluation, hath succeeded the diuine word it selfe: who assuming our human flesh, hath taken vs from the paynes of our sinnes, through the holy light of the Ghospell, and with the satisfaction of his infinite merits.

This said, he confessed he had heard this interpretation from the great *Pachomius* himselfe, who had lately gathered togeather a good number of Monks in the Iland of *Tabenna*, and gouerned them with merueilous discipline; and I hope (added he) that the mentiō of this Man of God, now made by me, may impetrate for vs some indulgence of our sinnes. The good Monke had scarce finished his discourse, when *Theodore* was enflamed with the relation made, with an exceeding desire of knowing *S. Pachomius* by sight, and to giue himselfe wholy to be gouerned by him. In so much, as a vertuous and good Old man, called *Pecusius*, being come thither from *Tabenna*, for to visit that Congregation there, was by *Theodor* intreated at his returne, with great affectiō, he would be pleased to conduct him with him to the blessed *Pachomius*, as he did with a very good will, and being arriued at the holy place, the youth, not being able to conteyne himselfe from teares of Ioy, was receiued by him with a great deale of charity, and numbred with the others; where in a short tyme, he profited so much in all manner of vertues, as *S. Pachomius* himselfe, did wonder at it.

There was afterwards an occasion presented to make the constancy and feruour of this *Novice* more renowned. In reguard the Mother, being now become a widow, and not brooking the absence of her sonne; came to *Tabenna* in person, bringing letters frō the Bishops with expresse order to haue him restored her agayne. Heere now, she being receiued by the Nuns, as a guest, she speedily sent the letters to *S. Pachomius*, vrging the execution therof. When the seruant of *Christ*, hauing called *Theodore* to him, said to him in this sort: I vnderstand thy Mother is come to see thee, behold the Letters of the Bishops, which she hath brought me, for that end. Go thy wayes then, and comfort her, especially for the Prelates sakes who haue recommended it to me. *Theodore* answered. Do you giue me security then, *Reuerend Father*, that this little edification, which I shall giue vnto others, with such an enterview, be not imputed to me, at the day of Iudgment? Forasmuch as if in the tymes before grace, the children of *Leui*, did quite forsake their Parents, howbeyt most deere vnto them, for to serue the *Lord God* wholy: how much rather should I, that haue receyued so great mercy and light from the same *Lord God*, keep my selfe from preferring in any wise the affection to flesh, before the loue, and seruice of his diuine *Maiesty?* seeing our *Sauiour* hath sayd openly to vs: *He that loues his Father, or Mother more then me, is not worthy of me.* Then *S. Pachomius* declared himselfe better vnto him, with saying: If it seeme not expedient to thee my *Sonne*, I will not vrge thee to it, but rather confesse the other to be of more perfection; because indeed the Monke is to fly al worldly commerce, and be louing, with an ordinate affection, & without passion, all those who through fayth, are members of *Christ*. And if any would seeme to oppose, that he may not desist from wishing well to his owne bloud, let him note that saying of the Scripture, *That euery one becomes the slaue of him, that vanquisheth him.*

By this manner of speach, the good Youth, being now confirmed more, and more, would by no meanes, shew himselfe to his Mother. And it pleased our Lord, through this austerity of his, that she remained so astonished and moued to deuotion as she determined likewise herselfe to leaue the world, and with the approbation of *S. Pachomius*, was receiued into the number of the Seruants of *Christ*. Whence may be gathered, that things being done to the greater glory of God, howbeit in the beginning sometymes, they may seeme perilous and bitter: yet neuerthelesse through diuine disposition, do they produce many tymes most sweet fruites.

The Griefe which S. Pachomius *tooke for the lapsed: Togeather with this Discretion, and Patience in all occasions.* Chap. 9.

FRom these, and other such like successes, looke how much consolation *S. Pachomius* tooke in our Lord; so much griefe and sorrow felt he for the ill proceeding of some, who tyred with labour, & to much giuen to carnall prudence, would neuer throughly renounce themselues, nor be despoyled of the old man. The holy Man would seeke to help such by all meanes possible, but in vayne. Because they, partly not knowing how to deny their proper will; partly affrighted with the difficulty of vertue, and with the examples of the pennances and Mortifications which they saw in others; finally being vanquished by the spirit of pusillanimity, and vayne feare, did suffer themselues to be caryed from the port, into the dāgerous tempests of the world: Yet this departure of theirs was not altogether vnprofitable to others, since the field of our *Lord* heerupon, being purged from weeds and cockle, became continually more pleasant and fruitfull. And besides, from thence might be gathered, how that euen as the austerity of the Monasticall life doth not hurt Seculars, if they wil but help themselues with it, in some part; so neyther the aduice, good carriage, nor the Prayers of others do benefit Monkes, if they resolue not to shake of quite, very manfully all manner of Slouth and Cowardise.

But to conserue, and to promote Men of good disposition, one of the principall industryes of this great Louer of the Crosse, was, not to permit, that in the treating of his person, should be vsed particularityes with him, of any sort whatsoeuer, as we shall see by the ensuing acts. He being gone on a tyme, in company of some Monks to reaping in an Iland called *Threa* (where euery one had built him a houell to retyre himselfe to, in due tymes) the good Father, whether it were, through age, or with ouermuch worke, fell sick of a feuer, and *Theodore,* in his cold fit, being ready to couer him with a Shepheards mantle wouen with hayre, *S. Pachomius* would by no meanes suffer it, but willed him to take it away sudenly, and to couer him only with a Mat, as the custome was to do with others; which done, *Theodore* brings him a handful of dates. exhorting him to refresh himselfe with them: Whereat the good *Father,* with teares in his eyes, replyed.

Why, *Theodore*, because we haue power ouer the labours of our Brethren, and to vs the care belonges to prouide and distribute the portions among them; should we therefore at our pleasure, and without any regard be treating of our selues in this sort, or be taking of any thing superfluous, or out of tyme, and comon custome? And where should our holy *Feare* be then, if we should do so? For tell me, *Brother*, haue you runne through al the houels, & certifyed your selfe, that there is no other sick body, more necessitous then I? deceiue not your self so, *Theodore,* iniquity is abominable in the sight of God, not only in great, but euen also in smaller matters. If others then, with diuine help, can patiently suffer afflictions, and discommodityes; why should not I seeme to suffer the same? And with this answere, he sent the *Disciple* away exceedingly edifyed and instructed. *S. Pachomius* likewise had obteyned of our *Lord*, together with the discretion of spirits, that same likewise of the Infirmityes, so as he could very well distinguish, which proceeded from natural causes,

causes, and which from the operation of the Enemy; who many tymes, for to hinder the diuine seruice, is wont to alter the humours of human bodyes, and to cause indispositions in them. Wherupon *S. Pachomius* being assayled on a tyme in the Monastery with a most grieuous feuer; it seemed to him very requisit, to cause him thereby increase his abstinence (since by this meanes for fiue continuall dayes, he remayned without eating and drinking) but yet slackt not awhit to rise in the meane tyme vnto Prayer. Wherwith, being cured, he went with the rest into the Refectory, giuing thankes to the Eternall Goodnes.

But yet with all this rigour, which he vsed with him selfe, let no man thinke, he was hard or mercyles towatds others, but rather (as hath been sayd aboue) was he wonderfull tender, and compassionate to all, and afforded all possible succours to relieue their necessityes. Besides that, as farre as reason of gouernement would permit, setting all arrogancy a part, he would be shewing himselfe equall, or rather inferiour to all. In so much, as being weauing on a tyme, and controuled by a child with saying, *Father*, you worke not right, for lo, our maister weaues not in that manner; he arose vp sudenly from his seate, and whereas another would eyther haue seemed, as if he had not heard him, or haue chastised his little modesty: The holy Old Man with a cheerefull countenance, approching to the Maister, and quietly taking instruction from him, went sudenly to execute the same, with singular humility, and with the great edification of as many as were present. With these and such like things not only particular and profane men, being now inuited at last, but euen whole congregations likewise of other Monks, came to ioyne, and submit themselues to *S. Pachomius*, to whome with equall charity, he afforded Rules, and Superiours.

The History of Ionas *the Monke in the desart there. And* S. Pachomius *his solution of a doubt.* Chap. 10.

IN one of those Monasteryes, called *Muchosa*, there was a Religious man whose name was *Ionas* a man of so great perfection & fame as we cannot choose but step a little from our purpose, to say something of him. This Religious person had continued in the diuine Seruice, and in the cloyster, some 85. yeares, with very good example: and it is a memorable thing, that he hauing alone had alwayes care of the garden, and therin had planted diuers trees, yet he neuer had tasted to his death, so much as one fruite of them, being notwithstanding very francke therof to the Brothers, and to the Ghests, and to all the Neighbours about, who at their pleasure were satisfied with them. His clothing as well for sommer, as winter, was of three sheepe skins, sowed together, saue only, to go to the holy Communion, he would put ouer a coate, somewhat more decent, but being then risen from the sacred table, he would presently despoyle himselfe therof; and so had he conserued it neate and cleane, for all that space of 85. yeares.

He was so great a friend of Labour, as he knew not, as it were what Rest was, nor yet the Infirmary. He neuer eate any boyled thing: he liued vpon hearbs chopt in vinegar: He neuer lay stretcht forth in length, but laboured by day in the garden, & at the setting of the Sunne, taking his refection, he would retire himselfe into his cell, and sitting on a stoole in the midst of the roome, attend to the knitting of bull-rushes, and to make ropes, vntill the ringing to Office; shutting his eyes sometymes, scarcely as much as necessity required. And this his worke he performed, not by the light of a Lampe, or of fire, but through much practice and dexterity, wholy by darke, for to be able in the meane tyme, the better to attend to the Meditation of holy Scripture, wherof he had cõmitted a good part to memory.

We let passe besids, many other meruaylous things of this holy Man, for breuityes sake, but yet we may not seeme to passe ouer in silence, the manner of his last act. Because he was foũd by the Mõks starke dead to sit in his Cell, with rushes in his hands (according to his wont) & with his feete and armes stretcht forth, & stiffe withal in such sort, as they would not seeme to change that composition of his, nor to pull off his furrd coate frõ his back, but were feigne so to fold him, as in a trusse; and in that manner were they glad to carry him to be buryed.

But now let vs returne agayne to *S. Pachomius*, who neuer ceased with words and deeds to enflame and guide his disciples to Perfection: exhorting them sometymes, and sometyme agayne resoluing their doubts, with a great deale of wisedome, and no lesse charity. He was demanded once (among other things) by one of his Monks; What was the cause, that while a man, is in peace before temptation, he discourseth so well of Temperance, Humility, and other

other Vertues; and when the time of execution comes afterwards to put that in practise which was in discourse, we find our selues so frayle and feeble to performe the same? As for example, in the tyme of Anger, to shew acts of Patience; in bitternes and rancour, to be forgetfull of iniuries receyued; when we are paysed of others, to be wary of vayneglory; in these (I say) and other the like occurrences? Then the *Saint*: The reason is (answered he) for that, we know not how to prepare our selues, nor to meditate as we ought, for to keepe the spirit prompt and vigilant in the tyme of battayle. Whence it behoues vs euery day, and euery houre, with a fresh resolution to renew our good purposes, and to power into the contẽplatiue part of the Soule, the oyle of holy feare, which may serue as well to re-enforce it to do good, as to illumine the same to discerne, and distinguish the Obiects, which are represented to it by the wily and subtile Aduersary. In such wise, as standing cõtinually vpon its guard, it suffer not it selfe to be easily moued to disdayne, nor rancour, nor to other disordinate passions: and besides that, raysing it selfe aloft, and thinking of inuisible, and eternall things, it may come to assume great courage, and consequently to contemne all diabolicall suggestions, and finally to walke (as the Scripture sayth) *vpon Serpents, and Scorpious, and aboue all the powers of the Enemy.*

With such aduertisements, and counsayles went *S. Pachomius* opportunely encouraging, and instructing his Subiects. And howbeit in amending their defects, he would more willingly be vsing of sweet remedyes and lenitiues, as more conformable to his proper genius, and to Christian clemency; notwithstanding, when it was expedient for him, he knew well also, how to apply more bitter and biting medicines: as by reading this ensuing discourse the iudicious Reader may easily perceiue.

The life of Siluanus *the Monke. And what a blessed end he made, through the help of* S. Pachomius. Chap. 11.

SAINT *Pachomius* had in his Conuent, a certayne Monke called *Siluanus*. This man in the world had been a Comediant, and of a lyfe (as commonly such persons are) very wild and dissolute. Whereupon, at his entrance into Religion, *S. Pachomius* had particulerly exhorted him to stand vpon his guard, and to mainteyne himselfe sober, and vigilant, that he might not be carryed away with sensuality, and the diuell, to vices, and leuityes past. And so had he promised to do: then he tooke the habit, and indeed so walked he, as long as the feruour of deuotion lasted; but afterwards, through wearines of combating, and subtraction of grace (as it happens, for one to be tepid without being, as it were, aware of it) so began he by litle and litle to grow looser in his conuersation, and to returne to his secular iests, and scoffs, as before. *S. Pachomius* gaue him many wholesome admonitions, which being not inough, he likewise added sundry seuere chastisements: and at last, where he seemed to him to be incorrigible, some twenty yeares after he had receyued him, he ordeyned in the presence of all the Monkes, that he should be stript of his habit, and thrust out of the Congregation.

Whereat *Siluanus* being wholy confounded and contrite, did cast himselfe at the feete of the *Saint*, with saying: Pardon me, *Father*, yet for this tyme, for I hope in our *Sauiour*, that he will graunt me true Penance, and to your Paternity much consolation in my actions. To whome *S. Pachomius* answered: Thou knowest, how I haue borne with thee all this while, how many chasticemēts haue I both against my wil and custome inflicted vpon thee? since then neyther with fayre meanes, nor yet with foule, thou wilt amend thy selfe, how can I, or how should I permit so contagious and infected a mēber, should go wasting thus, and consuming the whole body of Religion? To this so bitter an answere, *Siluanus* replyed, with new humiliations and promises. And yet *S. Pachomius* stood firme in his purpose, till being conuinced with the perseuerant submission of the other, he required pledges, which might giue security of his chaunge of manners. When immediatly a venerable man, by name *Petronius*, being moued out of Charity, tooke the Obligation vpon him; and full of diuine confidence, gaue his word, that *Siluanus* should be renewed in spirit, and should giue himselfe seriously to the exercise of vertue. With this intercession was *S. Pachomius* content to prolong his tearme. Nor was the grace affoarded in vayne, or the promise any way temerariously made, since from that tyme, *Siluanus* began to wage a sharpe warre with himselfe, and to go forward in such sort, as in a short tyme, he became a mirrour of perfection to all the Cōuent, hauing got (among other things) so great a gift of teares, as they streamed from his eyes, like a perpetual riuer: so as, neyther in the presence of strangers, nor at the Table, could he possibly conteyne himselfe from them: While that saying of the Psalme agreed with him; *Cinerem tamquam panem manducabam, & potum*

[illegible]

meum cum fletu miscebam.

He was instanced by some, that if he could not absteyne altogeather, yet by all meanes at least, he would forbeare in the presence of the Ghests. When he affirmed, he had endeauoured the same many tymes, but not by any meanes could he refrayne; they answered, that a deuout soule may well abide allwayes with internall compunction, without breaking into open demonstration therof; and in summe, they brought him to represse them in tyme of refection, because many being confounded, & moued with such a spectacle, refrayned from taking their necessary nourishment: whē *Siluanus* not being angry with any other then himselfe only, with great feeling, brake forth into those words; Would you haue me to stint my teares (I pray) in seeing so many *Saints*, with whome I am not worthy to be numbred, to attend vpō me, most vile wretch with so much diligence, hauing been accustomed heeretofore to gayne my liuing on the Stage? Whereas rather, I deserue not to kisse the very place, where they set their feet. I weepe indeed, as fearing euery houre, least the earth should swallow me vp, as once it happened to the profane *Dathan* and *Abiron*: since I hauing had from Heauen, both light and grace, more then inough, should haue vsed them so ill, & haue reaped so litle fruit. Then am I not through shame to forbeare from discoueting my selfe to be a sinner, since for such indeed do I acknowledge my selfe to be. Whereas truly if I should lay downe my life in doing pennance for the same, yet were it nothing in comparison of my demerits.

With such like answeres, *Siluanus* stopt the mouths of such, as dealt with him about this matter: nor was it contrition of words only, as often it happens, but his sayings and workes accorded in such manner, as *S. Pachomius* himselfe being full of meruayle thereat, for true humility preferred him before all in the Monastery; and within eight yeares afterward, was certifyed, how be was nothing deceiued, when he beheld that Soule going forth of the body, to fly vnto Heauen, with a great troupe of glorious Angells in company with it. This then was the fruite, which sprung from the seasonable rigour of *S. Pachomius*: and no lesse worthy of memory likewise, was another act of seuerity of his, which we will put down in the Chapter following.

How

How a Monke was penanced by S. Pachomius *for Vayne glory, and another for Disobedience.* Chap. 12.

IT happened on a tyme, while *S. Pachomius* was sitting in company with other graue Fathers, that a Brother who had made that day two mats, with double the labour he was obliged to do by the Rule, being ouercome with vayne glory would by no meanes cōteyne himselfe, but needs must he set them forth to view, at his cell, right ouer agaynst the place, where *S. Pachomius* was, as thinking verily to haue been much praysed aud esteemed of him for his diligence therein: whereof the wise *Pastour* being aware, fetching a deep sigh, said to the standers by: behold I pray, this Brother heere, who hath been labouring all this while from the Morning hitherto, to dedicate afterwards all his sweats to the Diuell, without leauing any merit or fruite thereof for his owne soule, since he hath had for end, the satisfaction of men, rather then the pleasure of God.

Heerupon, causing him to come before him, he gaue him a sound reprehension for it; and to the end, he might learne to rectify the intention, in whatsoeuer he should worke heerafter, enioyned him in pennance, that while the Brothers were in prayer, he holding both those mats in his hands, should cry vnto them, with a lowd voyce: I beseech you Brothers, to pray for this miserable soule of myne, which hath preferred two small mats before the Kingdome of Heauen. And in the same manner, caused him to stand in the Refectory, till the Table was ended: and for addition shut him vp in his Cell, for fiue moneths space, with order that no man should visit him the while, & that he should eate nothing, but bread and salt. Such accompt was made in those dayes of purity of hart, and to fly those sinnes, which in our age, peraduenture, are accompted very veniall and light. And if yet this chastisement, perhaps, shal seeme to any to be too disproportionate to the fault, let him know, that to the Man of God, there wanted no sufficient motiues for the same.

The holy *Abbot*, made great accompt also of sincere Obedience, which especially consists in simply executing what is cōmāded, without curiously examining the designes of the Superiours, nor putting into controuersy the quality of the thing commaunded. Now, he hauing committed to some Officers, that while he went

on

on a certayne Pilgrimage they should haue some respect to the tender age of certayne Nouices, who were not able to performe so much abstinence, as the other: It happened, the same Officers, perceyuing the Community had not eaten the herbes, and Oliues, which were boyled, had giuen ouer to prouide any more of them, contenting themselues with distributing of dry bread onely, to all the Refectory. *S. Pachomius* returned, and all the Monkes, being gone forth to meete with him, and to receyue him; one of the innocents, began to say with a lowd voyce. Verily *Father*, since the tyme, that you went from hence, to this day, hath there beene no herbes boyled for vs. To whome the *Saint* answered, with a cheerfull countenance. Trouble not your selfe (my Sonne) for I will prouide for you. Entring then into the kitchin, and the Cooke being busy in knitting of rushes, he sayd to him, in this manner: Tell me Brother, how long since is it, that you boyled any herbes? It is now some two Monthes ago (answered he;) and being demaunded the reason, he alleadgeth, that scarce any of them had eate thereof, when they were before him, but only the youths: whereupon, he had a scruple to bestow so in vayne, both the labour, and the cost: And to the end, this same might not be imputed as Slouth vnto him, he had employed himself in the meane time with his fellowes, to worke the Mats. And how many haue you made of them, demaunded *S. Pachomius*? Some 500. answered he. Now bring them hither then to me (sayd the Father.) Which being brought, he caused them suddaynely to be all cast into the fire: giuing cleerly to vnderstand by that act of his, and with the words he spake to that purpose, that as it is the proper office and prayse of the Superiour, to moderate and discerne: so from the subiect, is not required so much prudence, and circumspection, as a prompt execution, and perfect Obedience. To this example, the same also was not much vnlike, which followes in the next Chapter.

How two Stewards of S. Pachomius, *were checked by him, for doing against Obedience.* Chap. 13.

THere hapned so great a dearth of corne, as scarcely was any to be found, throughout all the Land of *Egipt*. Which *S. Pachomius* wel knowing, sent one of the Brothers, to make his prouision therof as much as an hundred peeces of gold, of a certaine coyne, was able to procure him, being taken out of cōmon stock, of the Labours of the Monastery. The Procuratour or Steward went his wayes therwith, into diuers forren parts, without finding the desired cōmerce, till lastly arriuing at the citty of *Hermothen*, it pleased our *Lord*, that he should meete by chaunce with an honest Gentleman, who had the whole corne of the countrey in his custody. This man, being required of the Monke, so much corne, as might amount to the said summe, answered: Truly Father, I haue not any of myne owne, but if I had, I would take it from my childrens mouthes, to spare it for you, whose vertue, and holy life, hath now a good while since, beene notifyed to me. But harke you *Father*, I haue yet now the publique grayne vnder my charge, which hitherto the Magistrates haue not seemed to require at my hands, nor do I thinke, they will demaund it, till the new be gotten in. If you suppose by that tyme, you can restore it me agayne, do you take therof, as much as you please. When the Monke told him, how he durst not vndertake to returne it so soone; but if it seemed to him, that he might well dispose thereof, as he had said, he would willingly take a quātity to the valew of the price aforesaid of a hundred peeces.

I shall not only afford you so much (replyed the Commissary) but euen likewise as much more, if it please you to accept the same. Do me but only the fauour the while to pray for me. Whereto the buyer made answere, that for the present, he had no more money to bestow. When the other very courteously affirmed, that it imported nothing, but he might take the grayne with a good will, and yeild him the price therof at his commodity, so liberall an offer seemed now to the Monk, not fit to be refused. Wherefore he suddainely freightes a great bark therwith of some thirteen Tun, so great indeed, as one half thereof, was not to be found else where in all those countryes therabout, & with great ioy went his wayes therwith to the Monastery, as thinking he had done some great peece of seruice to the whole company, and especially to *S. Pachomius*. But he was very much deceiued in his accompt.

Because the *Saint* had no sooner vnderstood of the arriuall of the barke, so laden, & knowne the manner how it came to be so freighted, but he sent a man to the wharfe in post, with expresse order, they should not vnlade any whit therof, saying: Let the Steward assuredly know, that not a gayne of that corne of his, shall seeme to enter into our howse; nor shall his person appeare before me, vntill

he

he haue satisfyed the errour committed, in so gouerning himselfe to be led with auarice, in taking the same vpon Credit, and abusing withall the goodnes of him, that sold him the corne. Now therefore since he hath so exceeded the precepts giuen, let him go suddainely to all these neighbour-places, and sell the same according to the price set him downe by the seller; and hauing carryed him the summe, let him buy according to the price, so much, and no more as he may haue with the money which he receiued of vs, for that effect. Which being executed, and no more then fiue measures & a half, conueyed to the house, the Monke was depriued of his Steward-ship, and restrayned in the Monastery. Nor had the Procuratour yet much better successe. Who was appointed to sell some of the labours of the Monkes, at a stinted rate how much he was to take for them. He went then to the inhabitants with those merchandize, and finding them to amount to thrice so much, as he was prescribed to take, it seemed to him a folly to put them away for lesse, and so returned he his wayes home, with his purse fuller, then was pretended. Which being vnderstood, *S. Pachomius* made him immediatly to returne into the Market, and to restore to the buyers, all that, which exceeded the rate set downe. Whereupon, he likewise being depriued of his office, was shut vp, and had a good pennance enioyned him. With thes demonstrations the *Saint*, it seemes, besides the purity which he required in Obedience, would likewise manifest, how far off they are to be from all manner of couetousnes, who seeme to manage the temporals affayres in Religion. But as this man of good, was an Enemy of tepidity, and of pusillanimity; so on the other side, approued he not immoderate feruours, which ordinarily succeed but ill, and such was the euent we shall presently tell you.

An Example of the indiscreet zeale of a Monke of S. Pachomius; *and the happy Life he led afterwards.* Chap. 14.

A Person there was of a good disposition, rather then of any great reach, who after he had attended a while to a spirituall life, of himselfe, came at last of his owne accord (as others did) to submit himselfe, to *S. Pachomius*; nor was it long ere being prickt forward with excessiue feruour, and youthfull heat, he began very earnestly to instance the said holy *Father* to obteyne him from heauen, some commodity, & occasion to spend his bloud, for the Catholike fayth. The world, at that tyme, was all in peace, and the Church of God enioyed an vnwonted tranquility, through the deuotion, & by the vertue of the most Christiã Emperour *Constantine*. In so much as the importunity of the Monke, besides his being too bold in a certaine manner, came likewise to be vnreasonable, and foolish withall. *S. Pachomius* then answered him, that forbearing for the present to thinke of Martyrdome, he might do well to conuert his thoughts, to the taming of his Passions, & to combat with himselfe, alleadging that in a sort he was depriued of the glory of *Martyrs*, who perseuered to the end, in Cloysters, without reprehension.

But that other, not satisfyed heerewith: and renewing oft the same request, *S. Pachomius* at last said to him. Since you wil not cease to prouoke me so, I will pray for this thy intention, and I hope I shal be heard. But thou on the other side, beware that cõming afterwards to the Triall, insteed of confessing our *Lord Christ*, thou cõmest not to renounce him quite. Because in truth, thou dost but delude thy selfe, so to tempt thy God, and thus to seeke, those perils, which our *Maister* and *Sauiour* himselfe, hath taught vs to shun. So sayd the expert Captayne: But neyther authority nor reasons, were of power to bridle the confidence, or to say better, the presumption of the Monke.

From hence, within two yeares after, it chaunced to *S. Pachomius*, to send certayne Brothers to a place, not far from thence, to prouide some marish rushes for mats and cottages, and a litle after he sent the audacious Wretch thither also: & presaging, as it were, the encounter he was to meete withall on the way, vpon his departure aduised him to stand vpon his guard; and in manner of an Enigma, added those words of *S. Paul: Ecce nunc tempus acceptabile, ecce nunc dies salutis: nullam in aliquo demus offensionem, vt non vituperetur ministerium nostrum.* These marishes where the Monkes were working, were scituate at the feete of certayne mountaynes, inhabited by sauage & barbarous people, and continually drowned in Paganisme: some of which, at that tyme being descended into the playne, to fetch water, found in those deserts, the poore Trauayler alone; when causing him to a light on a sudden, they bind his hands, and lead him together with his Asse into the Mountaine: at whose approch, the other Gentils, who as then were ready to offer their sacrifice, and had killed many beasts for that purpose, began with great laugh-

laughters to scorne him, saying: *Come thy wayes hither, O Monke, and adore our Gods*: and leading him before their Aultar, they forced him to do, as they did. At the first, he refused to do it, and shewed them some resistance thereunto; but when the Pagans being angry, layd hands on their weapons, and that he saw the ponyard at his bosom, and the swords which glittered round about him, being now forgetfull, in an instant of al the stout purposes made, the poore wretch yielded, and being terrifyed, stuck not to tast of the wyne & flesh dedicated to Diuels, being a thing which (as for the essentiall of Idolatry) was as much, as if he had offered incense with them.

Heereupon, being licenced to depart by that wicked people while on the way, he had leysure inough, to enter into himselt, looking back into the fowle enormous and impious cryme committed, the vnhappy wretch beganne to fill the ayre with laments & sighes, and to lay on most furiously on his cheekes with his fist, & to curse his temerity, which had brought him into those tearmes. With this disaster, & with vncertayne, and wandering paces, being now come home in this piteous plight, and beholding the sayd *Pachomius* to meet him on the way, who had the reuelation of the whole euent, falling downe prostrate on the Earth, and weeping amayne, he cryed out alowd: I haue sinned before God, and you, holy *Father*, with following my owne will, and not obeying your counsayles. Then replyed *S. Pachomius*: Get vp, poore Wretch, thou hast indeed depriued thy selfe of the chiefest good. Assuredly, the crowne was already prepared for thee. Thou wast euen ready to enter into the Catalogue of the glorious Martyrs of *Christ*, and thou willingly hast made thy selfe vnworthy of that blessed fellowship. Our *Lord* was prepared with his Angels, to haue enuironed thy head with an immortal Diademe, and thou hast renounced the Diuine Maiesty for a moment of life. And while thou fearedst the first death (which by no meanes shalt thou euer be able to auoyd) art thou fallen into the second, which shall neuer haue end. Where are the words now which thou vtteredst once? Where the enflamed desire of suffering? Where those so many, and so great promises made?

To this, the Wretch could not answere a word, nor open his mouth, any otherwise, then to detest his crime, and to confesse himselfe, wholy vnworthy of pardon; yea now was his affliction, passed so farre, as he held himselfe altogether vncapable of pennance: whereof *S. Pachomius* being suddaynely aware, least he might cast himselfe headlong into the gulfe of dispayre added: thou for thy part, hast not fayled to become the enemy of thy *Creatour* & *Lord*; yet neuertheles, so great is that diuine goodnes of his, as it is able to drowne in the Abysses all our sinnes whatsoeuer, so that on our part, we dispose our selues with true sorrow, and due contrition to be partakers of his mercies: wherefore be thou not dismaied, for yet is there left thee some hope of saluation, since the tree, though pruned, yet springs agayne. Go thy wayes then into thy Cell, & stay there recluded in watching, and making thy prayer, & bewayling bitterly thy great offence. For a whole day thou shalt eate nothing, after that, shalt thou feed of nought els but bread, salt, and water: & not to eate of other mens labours, thou shalt make thy two matts a day; & if thou shalt perseuer in this manner during life, I trust in the merits of *Christ*, thou shalt not be excluded from the diuine Clemency.

From these words, it cannot be explicated, what comfort this poore soule felt. He shuts vp himselfe then sudely, & redoubling the labours, fasts, and macerations of the body, gaue himselfe to satisfy what he ought, with all the power he was able. It is true indeed, that for his spirituall help, it was permitted him by the holy *Abbot*, to go forth sometymes to comfort him with *Theodore*, & with some other Old men of the perfectest. And thus hauing perseuered for the space of ten yeares, being surprized at last by a most grieuous infirmity, he chaunged the temporall miseryes for the Eternall felicity, as *S. Pachomius* was afterward certifyed from Heauen. With whome God was wont to communicate things very far off, and hidden, and by his meanes to worke other wonderfull effects: as by the following Examples, we shall see in some part.

A Woman cured of the bloudy Flux, with other Miracles wrought by S. Pachomius. Chap. 15.

THere was in *Tentiri*, a woman that suffered an incurable flux of bloud: She hauing heard the renowne of *S. Pachomius* his sanctity, and not hauing the audacity to deale with such a *Father*, she instantly prayed the Bishop *Dionysius*, that vnder the pretext of some other busines of importance, he would procure him to come into the

the Citty. Hauing called him then, & after prayer, being set downe in the Church with him, while there they were discoursing with ech other of diuine things, the woman by little and litle stealing behind them, touched his hood, with so much fayth, as she suddenly recouered, and feeling her selfe to be wholy deliuered, did prostrate her selfe on the ground, giuing thankes to the diuine Mercy. *S. Pachomius* was aware of the practice had with him by the Bishop, & giuing his benediction to the woman without more ado, returned back agayne to his Conuent.

There hath beene already mention made of a certaine *Monke*, of great fame, whose name was *Ionas*, being the Gardiner of the Monastery of *Muchosa*. Now *S. Pachomius* being gone to visit the same Monastery, at his entry thither, espyed some young Nouices, that secretly had climbed vp a fig-tree, which was very high, for to gather of the fruit, & to eate them without any leaue. When the *Saint* approching nearer, perceiuing a deuil sitting on the top of the tree; the expert Phisitian of soules, knew it presently to be the vncleane spirit of Gluttony, the familiar enemy, & impostour of that greener age; & calling for *Ionas* without delay, appointed him to cut downe that tree, since it stood not well within the cloysters, and did afford but matter of temptation to those, who were not yet so well rooted in vertue. *Ionas* was sad thereat, and answered; *Noe, for Gods sake Father, since euery yeare it brings vs forth no little fruite.*

Then *S. Pachomius* not to seeme to disgust the good Old man (whose goodnes otherwise he well knew) held his peace. But the day after, behold, how the Tree was withered; so as there was neyther fruite, nor leafe, which was not dead thereupon: a thing so much more admirable, as the fig-tree of its nature, is more humid, and more repugnant to aridity. Wherupon, *Ionas* comprehending the vertue, and heauenly grace of the *Saint*, was very sory, for not hauing obeyed him with all dexterity. On a day, as he was making an exhortation to his Monks, according to custome, he was suddainely eleuated in spirit, and being awhile in that manner, he afterwards whispered in the eares of the vicar. Go your wayes into that next cell, and see what such a Monke is doing, since insteed of attending to the word of God, he lyes sleeping the while, exposed to the snares of the Enemy, who seekes nothing else, but to draw him into perdition, and the world. The vicar went thither, and found him very drowzy indeed. And a little after, notwithstanding they aduises

ses of the blessed *Pachomius*, though his negligence, the miserable Wretch, forsooke the Religion.

Another, being now brought into the extremity of sicknesse in the Monastery of *Chenebоscus*, and desiring before he closed his eyes to comfort himselfe with the sight of *S. Pachomius*, and to haue his holy Benediction; he sent to him, to beseech him that he would be pleased to come vnto him. At the newes whereof, the amorous *Father*, very suddenly puts himselfe on the way thither, with some companions: and while with diligence they went walking together, some two or three myles before their arriuall to the sayd place, *S. Pachomius* stopping on a sudden, stood looking vp into the Heauens, and beheld the soule of the Brother, enuironed with Angels, with a sweet harmony to mount vp into Paradise. In the meane while, the companions, not hearing the Musique, nor seeing the triumphe, sayd to the *Father*, who had his eyes still fixed on the Stars: Why stayes your Paternity thus? let vs make hast to find the Brother aliue. Whereto he answered: Nay rather let vs hast to arriue, whither he is now conducted, that is, to eternall beatitude. Whereupon they vnderstood, he had a Vision of the Saluation of the Soule, to represent it to them as well as he could. And diligent inquisition being afterwards made, it was found, the sayd sickman expired, euen iust at that houre, wherein *S. Pachomius* stood still in that manner.

S. Pachomius *procures through prayer, the gift of tongues. He falleth sick, & appoints his Successour, and so dieth.* Chap. 16.

SAint *Pachomius* on a tyme, visiting (as he was wont) his subiects to see how they carryed themselues, and to demaund particular accompt of profit, and conscience of euery one, found himselfe to be much perplexed with a certaine straung Monke, of great reputation: who being come from the parts of *Rome*, by how much he was more skillfull in the Latin and Greeke tongues, so much more raw and ignorant was he in the Egyptian tongue. In such as *S. Pachomius*, not hauing other language, then his owne, it was impossible for him to declare himselfe to him, or to vnderstand him well. To which was added another impediment, that the Roman Monke, being desirous to discouer to the holy Pastour, his ancient miseries, and to confesse his sinnes committed, would not admit of other

other meanes, nor communicate his secrets to a third person. Wherupon *S. Pachomius* with great sorrow, seeing himselfe to be excluded from the meanes of being able to help that soule, causing the Interpreter to go his wayes, and hauing beckned to the Roman to expect a while; he retired himselfe into a place apart, and there stretching forth his hands to Heauen, made this deuout prayer.

Almighty Lord, if I through defect of language, be not able to help such men, as come vnto me from countryes so remote, to what purpose were it so send them hither? And if yet thou wouldst haue me to be an instrument of the saluation of others; Graunt, *Lord*, (to whome nothing is impossible) that I be not ignorant of that, which they would say vnto me. Hauing thus perseuered in this prayer, for full three howers continually together, with extraordinary feruour; he espyed a sheete of paper, in a hand written in forme of an Epistle, to fall from heauen. Which as soone as he read (a wonderfull thing) he suddenly felt within himselfe the gift of all Tongues: for which, giuing thankes to the diuine Goodnes, he returned very cheerefull to the stranger, and began to talke to him in the Greeke and Latin tongues, with so much propriety and variey of words, as to the other, it seemed the Abbot in eloquence outstript all the learned men of the world. Hauing heard his confession then, and with holsome aduices enioyned him due penance, he proceeded to deale with the rest.

These, and the like demonstrations, which the diuine Maiesty gaue, from tyme to tyme, in fauour of *S. Pachomius*, especially ioyned (as hath beene said) with a perpetual tenour of a most holy life, it cannot easely be explicated, how much reputation and reuerēce they won him, not with Religious only, but euen Seculars also. Through which meanes, this great Gardiner of *Christ*, after he had sent to the table of his *Lord*, many fruites very seasonable and ripe, himselfe also being called to the rewards of so great labours, fell sick; when perceiuing the deposition of his Tabernacle to draw neare, causing the Monks to be assembled together, & brought before him, with a louing and gratefull countenance, he said to them, in this sort: I, Brothers, now at last, am entring into the passage, which al the children of *Eue* are to make, and do feele, how our *Lord* now cals me to him. Do you then, reteyning in memory, the fatherly aduices, which I haue giuen you, endeauour to stand continually on the guard of your soules. Eschew all things, that may any wayes

V coole

coole fraternall charity in you, and bring in factions or discords amongst you. Attending to the marke, which our *Sauiour* gaue vs to know his disciples withall, which truly is no other, then a mutuall loue, & sincere coniunction of mynds. Wherfore, I do exhort you, aboue all things, to abhor the commerce, & dealing, not only with *Meletius*, and *Arrius*, but euen likewise with any other, who shall but step an inch from the Apostolicall Traditions, and from the holy vniuersall Church. And since I am to depart, as I haue said, endeauour you to choose in my place, a person, that may be a spirituall help vnto you, and conduct you at last, to the end you haue all proposed. To which enterprize I do see none more sufficient, them our most beloued *Petronius*.

This said, the brothers sent sudenly to the Monastery of *Chenebofcus*, to call for him. And *S. Pachomius* in the meane tyme, composing his body, and recommending himselfe to our Lord with due preparations, very happily expired, betweene the armes, and sighes of his deere *Congregation*, on the 14. day of the month of May. As for the yeare, and other circumstances of tymes and places, there is no memory to be found. The sacred corps, with much veneration and solemne offices, was committed to the Sepulcher, & the blessed spirit, with singular feasting, receiued into the heauenly countrey, leauing on earth an exact modell of perfect exercitation to al those, who being aware of the false flatteryes of the flesh, of the vayne hopes of the world, and of the pernicious subtilityes of the deuill; aspire to the durable goods, & to the blessed vision of the most holy *Trinity*. To which be all glory & benediction, and yeilding of thāks for euer and euer. Amen.

FINIS.

S. MAR-

S. MARTIN.

THE ARGVMENT.

IN warfare bred, I chose a nobler foe
By nature, then the worlds vast realme doth yield,
My selfe; I first then him did ouerthrow:
Subdu'de, I gaind the glory of the field.
Conquerd, and Conqueror in one fight, I show
Our owne depression is our strongest shield,
 To check his fierce assaults, and soules to free
 From Sathans rage, and hellish slauery.
Dead to the world, like *Nigers* streames I rose,
That in the earth his buried floud enwombes,
And hauing made a naturall bridge, he goes
Farre vnder ground, but vp farre greater comes;
Whẽ the dead world to quicken Heau'n me chose,
And in a Bishops Chaire, to shew his doomes:
 Who cloathd himselfe for man, in flesh of Man,
 He cloathes receiues from me, his * *Ionathan*.

* Expoliauit se Ionathã tunica qua erat indutus, & dedit eam Dauid. 1 Reg. c. 18.

THE LIFE OF S. MARTIN BISHOP OF TOVVERS.

Taken out *Seuerus Sulpicius*, and others.

S. Martin *being the Sonne of a Gentill, becomes a Christian, and is enrolled a Souldiour of the Emperour.* Chap. I.

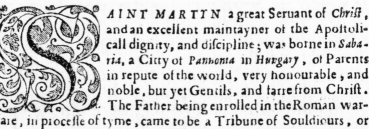

SAINT MARTYN a great Seruant of *Christ*, and an excellent maintayner of the Apostolicall dignity, and discipline; was borne in *Sabaria*, a Citty of *Pannonia* in *Hungary*, of Parents in repute of the world, very honourable, and noble, but yet Gentils, and farre from Christ. The Father being enrolled in the Roman warfare, in processe of tyme, came to be a Tribune of Souldiours, or as we say, a Coronell of a Regiment, by whome *S. Martin*, being lead into *Italy*, yet a child, was trayned vp in *Pauia*, in feates of armes; howbeit, though naturall instinct, he was enclined a great deale more to the acts of peace, or rather to Christian Religion. In so much, as being yet but ten yeares old, agaynst the will of his friends, he went secretly to the Church, and with instance demanded

manded to be made a Catechumen. Within two yeares after, he desired likewise to retire himselfe into the desert: & he had done it in effect, if his tender age had not been an impediment to him. To wch disturbance of his holy designes, was further added a new leuy, which then was made of military men, with expresse order, that all the sonnes of old Souldiers, should be put into the roule, and conducted to the war. Whereupon *S. Martin*, being now some fifteene yeares old, being discouered by his owne Father, was against his will, enforced to repayre to the Ensignes of *Constantius* the *Emperour*. He would haue no other in his company, then a slaue only, whome yet he would be seruing rather, then be serued by him, to wit, in often pulling off his shoes, and brushing his clothes, & furnishing the table with what was needfull.

With this disposition of mind, being come to the field, some three yeares before his baptisme, he allwayes preserued himselfe wonderous pure, and vntouched of those vices and debauchements, in which Souldiours are for the most part wont to be inuolued. First for his person, he would seeme to content himselfe with fare so moderate and simple, as from that tyme he seemed to be rather a Monke, then a Souldiour: besids he would seeme to content himselfe with those kind of meates, which others vtterly refused to eate off: moreouer he would shew himself very benigne and courteous, to his Camerades, and to all others, bearing with their defects, and supplying the necessity of euery one, with extraordinary charity, patience, and humility. He would comfort the afflicted with loue and dexterity, and be very helpfull to the sicke: and without thinking of the morrow, he would feed most liberally the hungry, but with particular tendernes cloth the naked; in which worke of piety, was a certayne act of his very memorable, which we shall tell you in the next Chapter.

The singular Charity of S. Martyn *to a poore man. And how he leaues the warres, and betakes him to another Course.* Chap. 2.

THe Roman Army, at this tyme, was lodged in *France*, in exceeding cold places, and in the hart of a winter much more cruell, then vsed to be in that place; in so much as many men, euen dyed frozen in the streetes. Now it happened, in the Gate of *Amiens*, that a poore man, quaking with his naked body exposed to the sharpenes

penes of the ayre, very pittifully craued some succour of the souldiours, that passed then along, in the company of S. *Martyn*; and the wretch being not heeded by any of them, *M. Martyn* apprehended straight, how that merit by the diuine prouidence, was reserued for him. But what could he do, in such a case? He had not a penny of mony about him, hauing now already spent all, in other Almes: And in fyne, had nothing els but his armes, and a short cloake on his back. What resolution tooke then the Man of God? Taking out his sword, of a sudden, he diuided the same into halfes, and giues the one part therof to the wretch, and the other keepes to himselfe to couer him the best he could. At the sight of such a strang habit, & remnant of cloath, as some of the more youthfull of them, could hardly conteyne themselues from laughing, so others more stayed then they, were worthily touched therwith, as knowing how wel they might haue cloathed him, without despoyling of themselues.

Now in truth, how much God was pleased with this charity of *S. Martyn*, he seemed to demonstrate the night following, appearing before him, with that piece of garment, on his owne person, and bidding him to looke and marke well, whether it were not the Garment he had giuen to the poore man, the day before. Wherupon with a sweet countenance turning himself to a multitude of Angels which attended him, he added with a lowd voyce: *Martyn, being but yet a Catechumen, hath clothed me with this mantle.* Words surely well worthy of the bowels of Christ, and agreeable to those other, which he sayd, conuersing with men, and which he will repeate agayne, at the Iudgement day: *Quamdiu vni de minimis meis fecistis, mihi fecistis.*

From this so noble a vision *S. Martyn* tooke not a whit of vayne glory, but acknowledging and magnifying in all, and through all the heauenly grace; he tooke rather a motiue thence of greater humility and diligence, in the diuine seruice. So as without more delay, he hyed him to Baptisme, being then about eighteen yeares of age, and withall to giue himselfe more freely to a perfect life, he was euen ready to bid adieu to the military state, but being constreyned through the importunity of his Tribune (who hauing finished his office, promised to follow him,) he differed yet the execution of his holy purpose, for the space of two yeares: in all which tyme, remayning in person in the field, he had his thoughts in the Cell, and Quire, so as well he may be sayd a Souldiour, by name, rather then

then exercise.

In the meane tyme, a huge Army of *Almans*, being entred into *France*, which did nothing but wast the Roman Empire, *Iulianus Cesar*, being sent by *Constantius*, to that seruice, made the leuy of his men, in the territory of the *Vangion*, which at this day is called *Spire*, or as others would haue it, to be that of *Wormes*, where before his cõming to encounter with the Enemy, he would needs haue giuen a largesse to the Souldiours. They began then, according to custome to be called one by one, before the Maister of the Campe. Whereupon *S. Martyn*, esteming this, to be a good occasion for him to take his leaue, when it came to his turne, with Christian liberty, said to *Cesar*. Hitherto, haue I beene at your pay, now then do but graunt me leaue to become a souldiour of Christ: as for my part of the donation, be it giuen to others, since it is not lawfull for me any more to embrew my selfe in bloud.

At these words, the Tyrant being angry, lookt sowrely vpon him, and said, that *Martin* had craued licence, not so much for deuotion sake, as for feare of the battaile, which was to be on the day following: Then the seruant of God, so much more bold and vndaunted, as the feare was greater they obiected to him: Behold answered he, O *Cæsar*, whether my refusing mony, do seeme rather to spring of feare, then piety. To morrow, am I ready, on the point of ioyning battayle, to present my selfe, before the first ranckes, without Target, or Helmet, or other armes, but only with the signe of the holy Crosse, and with this confidence alone, to thrust my selfe into the thickest squadrons of those barbarous people. With this so couragious an answere, *Iulian* being incensed much the more, caused him suddenly to be put in prison, to come to the proofe, and to expose him vnarmed, to the face of the enemy.

This thing gaue much matter of talke to the whole Army, and with diuers affects of mynd, they were all expecting the yssue; when betymes in the morning, behold, beyond all expectation, the Embassadour of that fierce Nation, came in with Heralds, and Interpreters, not only to craue peace, but also to submit themselues humbly to the obedience of *Cæsar*. This matter was held of all, to proceed from Heauen, and such as were priuy to the sanctity of *S. Martin*, in particular, attributed without doubt, so suddayne a mutation, and so greet a Victory so easily gotten to nothing els, then to his merits; because there wanted not meanes, to the diuine

power,

power, to saue him amidst a thousand swords & launces, and to discomfite, and put to flight, as many as should attempt to offend him: notwithstanding it seemed to be more conformable to the sweet disposition of the eternall prouidence, and more agreable to the peacefull nature, and manners of *S. Martin*, to free him rather by the way of such an accord, then by the meanes of death, and slaughter.

S. Martyn *repayres* to S. Hilary *Bishop. And departing homewards meetes with a Diuell, whome he stoutly foyles; and what followed.* Chap. 3.

DVring the common ioy aboue mentioned, *S. Martyn* being deliuered, and the warre now wholy concluded, repayred to *S. Hilary* Bishop of *Poytiers*, a person in those tymes of rare and eminent Goodnes. Heere did he giue forth such demonstrations of himselfe, as *S. Hilary* to retayne such a labourer in that vineyard, attempted often to make him Deacon, but *S. Martyn* alwayes resisting, and still affirming; & crying out, that he was not worthy of that degree, the discreet Pastour was aduised, there was no other way to constreyne this man therto, then to giue him some kind of office, which in a certayne manner might rather be held a disparagement to him, then any dignity at all: nor was he herein deceiued awhit, since offering him vp the charge of an Exorcist, which was held to be the meanest and lowest of all, *S. Martin* at last, not to seeme to haue it in scorne or disdayne, was persuaded to accept thereof.

Not long after, being admonished by God, in sleepe, to go his wayes to reuisite his countrey, and help his friends, who as yet were not out of their Paganisme, he demaunded leaue for this end, of the holy Bishop, to go thither: Who graunted it, indeed, though with a very ill will; intreating & coniuring him, not without teares, to returne backe againe, as soone as he could. And so likewise *S. Martyn* (as it is said) departed with no great good will himselfe, foreseeing the difficultyes of the enterprize, and protesting to his Brothers, that therein he was like to suffer great trauayles and aduersityes, as it fell out afterwards in effect. For that first, in his passage ouer the Alpes, he fell into the hands of the Bandits, one of which lifting vp his axe now ouer his head, was stayed by the arme of another lesse cruell then he, who notwithstanding binding his hands behind him, gaue him to the custody and spoyle of of another who for that end, leading him to a place more remote began to demaund of him, who he was? and *S. Martin* answered, he was a Christian. Art thou not affrayd, replyed the Thiefe? And he with an incredible constancy affirmed, that he was neuer lesse afrayd in his life, since he knew very well, the diuine Mercy, to be then most present, with such as trusted therin, when they found themselues in the greatest perils of all: but I am sory for thee (quoth he) that makest thy selfe wholy vncapable, & vnworthy therof, by the life thou leadest. And with this ouerture very dextrously falling into the Ghospell, with holsome and efficacious words, so moued that soule, as he was conuerted to *Christ*, and with a full deliberatiõ of changing his manners, did secretly put the Pilgrime in his way, beseeching his Charity to vouchsafe to recõmend him to our Lord: which he did, and not without fruite, forasmuch as this very Thiefe afterwards came to be a Religious man, who euen told vs this particular himselfe.

S. Martyn then pursuing his voyage, hauing passed *Milan*, was met by the Deuill, in forme of a man, who would needs know, whither he went: and being told by *S. Martyn*, that he was going whither God had called him, the Enemy replyed: Go whither thou wilt, or whatsoeuer thou takest in hand, Know, that the Deuil wil be alwayes contrary to thee. Then *S. Martyn* answered with the *Prophet*: *Dominus mihi adiutor, non timebo quid faciat mihi homo*. At which words, the Impostour immediately vanished: and *S. Martyn* after some dayes, being arriued in his Country, attended the first thing he did, with all endeauour to procure the saluation of his Parents, but not with like successe; since the Mother came to be a Christian while the Father could not be stirred from the impious worship of the Idols. Yet there wanted not in his place many others, who through the example, and with the exhortation of *S. Martyn*, were brought into the right way of eternall life.

Besides this, there was another occasion for him, to employ wel the talents which he had receiued, and to shew forth the zeale he had of the holy Fayth. Because the Arrian Heresy, at that tyme, with particular successe hauing extended it selfe into the parts of *Sclauonia*, and all those confines there, *S. Martyn* with all his might opposed himselfe to the Rebels of Christ, with so much more toyles and difficulty, as the fauour and succour was lesse, which he had from the Catholique Priests. Whence, taking the whole shock, and

X enuy

enuy on himselfe, being iniured and rackt with diuerse torments, and (among other things) hauing beene publiquely scourged, he was constrayned at last to turne back agayne into *France*.

S. Martin *is banished from* Millan, *and after escaping poyson, meetes with* S. Hilary *agayne*. Chap. 4.

Saint *Martin* hauing now vnderstood, on the the way as he went to *Françe*, that things were there turned vp-side downe, and that euen *S. Hilary* himselfe was by Heretiques, sent into banishment; he determined till better tymes, to entertayne himselfe in *Milan*, and there to set vp a litle Monastery: but neyther was he suffered so to do, by *Auxentius* the Head of the *Arrians*, who after many outrages, and persecutions, finally expelled him the Citty.

Whereupon *S. Martin*, being thus molested on euery side, falling into the company of a certayne Priest, a great seruant of God, determined for that tyme to hide themselues. To this end, they retired into a litle desert Iland, in the *Tyrrhen* sea, called by the name of *Gallinara*. Heer while the Man of God, liued in great abstinence of rootes and herbes, it chaunced vnawares, that he eate some *Hellebore*, which is a medicinable herbe: yet such notwithstanding, as that if the quantity be not moderate, and the simple well prepared, and corrected, through the great purgatiue it hath with it, it comes to be poysonous, and pestiferous, as *de facto* it had beene to *S. Martyn*, if being brought to extreames therewith he had not made his recourse to prayer, and with this remedy had not suddenly expelled all dolour and daunger.

After this, it was not long ere he knew, how *S. Hilary* hauing foũd grace with the *Emperour Constantius*, returned into *France*. At which newes being exceeding ioyfull, he trauayled towards *Rome*, to meete with him there, and to accompany him to his Church. But *S. Hilary* being now past by already, he met him neerer, and with great iubiley, being receyued by him, erected, out of the Citty of *Poytiers*, a poore Monastery for him, and as many as followed him. Among these, there was a certaine Catechumen, who falling sick of a violent feuer, while *S. Martin* was farre off (for three dayes only) about certaine affayres of the diuine seruice, beyond all expectation, departed this lyfe, and that which was worse, without Baptisme. The Conuent was sensible of this case: and *S. Martin* at his returne, finding

finding now the Exequies prepared, very sorowful and sad thereat approched his body. Heere now conceiuing in his pure mind new feruour of spirit, he makes them all go forth of the chamber; and the doores being shut stretches himselfe, like another *Elizaus*, vpon the cold bones of the deare Brother, and so hauing made a feruent prayer, and very soone perceiuing already, through diuine vertue, how the vitall spirits were vpon returne, standing something vpright agayne, with his eyes fixed on the face of the dead man, he stood couragiously expecting the effect of his prayers, and of the diuine clemency. There were not yet two houres of tyme past, when he saw the dead to moue his lymmes, by litle and litle, and panting to open the eyes, and to recouer the vse of his senses. Then *S. Martin* giuing thankes to our *Lord*, cryed out so lowd, as they who expected without, being moued with the noise therof, came rushing in, and all perceiued, to their infinite astonishment, the corps to respire, and take vigour agayne, which euen now they were ready to carry to buriall.

After so great a benefit had, the *Cathecumen* delayed not awhit to receiue the holy Baptisme, whereunto he suruiued many yeares after, and was wont sincerly to recount of himselfe, how being departed from the body, he was presented before a Tribunall, and by sentence confined to darkesome place, among the baser sort; but how at the same instant, two Angels relating to the Iudge, how it was he for whome *S. Martyn* had besought, to them was then Cōmission giuen, to restore him to life agayne, and to make a present of him to the seruant of God. This was the first wonder *S. Martyn* shewed forth in those parts; whence it followed, that being now held for holy, he begā afterwards to be esteemed also as a man very powerfull with God, and a person truly Apostolicall. Not long after this, passing through the fields of one *Lupicinus* an honourable & rich man, there met him a troupe of people, all full of laments, and teares, telling him, how one of the seruants of *Lupicinus*, had hanged himselfe, & so miserably had ended his dayes. *S. Martin* heerewith being moued to compassion, without delay intred into the chāber, where the vnhappy Wretch was deposed, and so from thence also dismissing the people, distending himselfe in like manner on the corps, made he his prayer: which was no lesse efficacious then the other, since that his hart now cold, already resuming the naturall heate, begān by litle and little to yield to the arteryes, & their pulse agayne, and motion to the nerues: so as the dead, with stretcht-forth armes, taking *S. Martin* by the right hand, arose on his feete, and accompanyed him to the gate of the house, in the presence of all that multitude; who replenished both with wonder and ioy, ceased not to glorify in *S. Martin*, the immense goodnes, and omnipotency of the Creatour.

S. Martyn *not without great contradiction of many, is chosen Bishop of* Towers. Chap. 5.

AT the very same tyme, the *Church* of *Towers*, being vacant, *S. Martyn*, by the vniuersall consent of the people there, was destined to that dignity. But he not being so easily to be taken forth from his Monastery; a certayne Citizen, being called *Ruritius*, his wife faygning to be grieuously sick, cast himselfe at the feete of the *Saint*, and coniured him so much, as he made him to come forth, to blesse her. With that pretext, a number of persons being couertly set in opportune places, *S. Martyn* was taken by them, and with a good guard brought into the Citty, where was already assẽbled togeather, a great concourse of people of all sorts, being met, according to the vse of those tymes, to passe their suffrages, for the election of a new Prelate: nor was there any person, great or litle that desired not to see *S. Martyn* installed in that seate, esteeming the country happy, vnder the care of such a Pastour.

Some Bishops only of the Neighbour-diocesses being called to the consecration, and some other principall persons stood earnestly against it; alleadging him to be a Person meane, of no Presence, with ill clothes, worse put on, and in summe, vnworthy to be nũbred among Bishops. With such oppositions, did these men seeke to alienate the people from the deuotion and fauour of *S. Martin*. But the matter fell out quite contrary with them, because the same obiections, as they were held of the people (who had the sounder iudgment) for the prayse and reputation of the Seruant of Christ; so on the other side, they came with litle edification to discouer the enuy and malignity of the Prelats. Whence they began also, by litle and little, to relent, one only excepted, more blind and obstinate then the rest, who cõtinued in resistance, till such time, as by diuine prouidence, a notable Iudgement was shewed vpon him, as we shall now declare.

This

This Prelate, in the *Church* of *Towers*, had the tytle of *Defender*, & by reason of that dignity was knowen of all. Now he being one day with the people in the Church, at the hower of diuine office; it happened, that the *Lectourer*, being not able to presse through the great thrung of people which was there, to approach the Quire, one of the Standers by in the meane while, laying hold of the Psalter, began to read the first verse, as it lay before him, being iust that same of the 8. psalme, which saith, *Ex ore infantium & lactentium perfecisti laudē, propter inimicos tuos, vt destruas inimicum, & defensorē*, the last word in that Text being so translated, insteed of *vltorem*. At which word so pronounced was lifted immediately a cry of the people vnto Heauen, to the extreme confusion & shame of the aduersary: and *S. Martin* without more resistance of any besides himselfe, was elected, or rather forcibly constrayned to the Bishopricke. In which administration, it may not easily be explicated, how fully, or rather superaboundantly, he gaue correspondency, to the full expectation, which was had of him: forasmuch as being disposed to that degree, with the exquisite addresses of a most chast mynd, in the sacred Vnction besids, he receyued so great aboundance of new graces, and gifts of Heauen, as continually outstripping himselfe, he reteyned both the vertue of a priuate person, & further added to his singular prayse, all the good qualtyes of a publique man.

S. Martin *retires himselfe out of the Towne, with his Monkes: and their manner of liuing there.* Chap. 6.

S*Aint Martin*, in the treating of his owne person would change nothing of his wonted manner; his fare, and apparell, was still the same as before, for habitation only he betooke himselfe into a litle Cell, hard by the Cathedrall Church: but euen likewise from thence, through too much importunity of frequent Visits, he suddenly retyred himselfe out of the Citty, into a marueylous commodious place, to distribute his tymes vnto *Martha* and *Mary*, since it was about two miles distant from the Towne. On the one side, it was girt in with a high inaccessable rock, on the other enuironed with the riuer *Loyre*: in so much, as there could be no entrance therinto, but by a narrow path. Within that enclosure *S. Martin* had built him a litle Cell of boards, & a part of his Monkes, who were some eighty in number, had done the like; and some agayne with in-

instruments had digged them in the rocky hill, certayne receptacles, but narrow, and more fit to meditate vpon *Death*, then to conserue life withall.

Heere no man held any thing proper to himselfe, all thinges were in common. To buy or sel, was not there permitted. To no manner of art, applyed they themselues, but to writing, and to this only, were the yonger deputed. Those of the more auncient sort, attended as it were, to nothing els, then to things diuine. Very rarely went any out of his Cell, but when they all assembled togeather in the Oratory to pacify God: besides, they did eate all togeather in the Euening. Wine was not affoarded to any, except to the sicke. The greater part would be wearing of cilices: clothes which had any finesse or softenesse in them were abhorred of ech one as a manifest scandall. A thing so much more admirable, as many of them were Noble of bloud, and dainetily bred. But for the loue of *Christ*, and the *Crosse* they did all very voluntarily, submit themselues to such a pennance. Of which number afterwards were many of them seen to be *Bishops*; while Citties striued to be gouerned in spirit by the Children of such a discipline. Nor could it be otherwise, but needs must succeed very excellent men vnder *S. Martin*, because not only with aduises and words, went he alwayes before them; but euen with workes and liuely incitements also of all perfection, and especially sincere humility, togeather with an ardent loue of the *Neighbour*.

Sulpitius Seuerus declared (who liued in those tymes, & knowing the *Saint* domestically as he did, very diligently wrote his life) how that going sometimes to visit him from countryes somewhat remote, he could neuer hinder him from washing his feet, and being to sit downe at table, from reaching him water, as well for his hands, as for those of his fellowes. The same man adds, how after he had fed the bodyes of his ghests with moderate victuals he would be afterwards affoarding them a most sweet food of spirituall discourses for their soules, exhorting them with like modesty and efficacy to nothing more then to fly the sensualityes of the present life, and to leaue the perilous trash of the world, to be able the more nimbly and free, to follow *Iesus*.

And to this purpose, he would set before them the fresh example of *S. Paulinus* Bishop of *Nola*, who after he had distributed very ample meanes for the loue of God, and help of the poore, did finally ly with an example of Christian piety, neuer heard of before, sell himselfe into a most cruell bondage, for the ransome of his subiects, who were held in *Affricke* slaues to the *Saracens*. With such manner of comparisons as this, and moreouer with precepts taken out of the sacred Writ, went *S. Martin* exciting in spirit, as many as came before him. Nor was it any great matter for him, that he should haue so much to giue to others, who so continually treasured vp for himself, remayning euen amidst exteriour actiõs alwayes with the hart so vnited with God, as neyther in words nor deeds, he would euer go forth of his presence. And as Smithes, without other matter to worke on, through vse, & for their pleasure only, will sometymes be laying on the anuile: so *S. Martyn*, not only in the tymes deputed to the Sacrifice, and diuine worship, but likewise at all houres besides, would eyther read or write, or be dealing with men: and through the great habit he had gotten, he would be continually recollected in the interiour man, conuersing sweetly with the heauenly Spouse, and with the giuer of all Graces.

He would neuer loose tyme in the day, and whole nights he would often passe ouer in labours, and watchings. To the body he gaue that refection, and that repose, which extreme necessity required, lying on the bare ground, couered only with a sharp cilice. He tooke heed with all caution from iudging the intentions of others, interpreting what he could ech thing to the better part, and alwayes very highly esteeming the reputation & fame of the neighbour: the iniuryes, detractions, & the enuyes of Persecutours, which in the whole course of his life were not wanting to him, he would recompence with weeping bitterly for their offences, and also (as occasion serued) with affording them benefits, & seruing them; not excluding any, what lay in him, from his holy freindship. He was neuer seen to laugh vainely, or to be contristate at any thing, conseruing alwayes the same tranquility of hart, and serenity of countenance, amidst al the varietyes of human accidents, eyther prosperous and cheerefull, or how straung, and aduerse soeuer they were: Wherof, those few actions, which we shall tell you anon, shall giue forth, a very euident testimony, though in ech one of these precious examples, do shine withall (as often it happens) many other vertues besides.

S. Mar-

S. Martyn *is much honoured by a miracle from God, for a charitable act of his.* Chap. 7.

S*Aint Martin* going one morning to the cathedrall Church, to celebrate in the winter tyme, was on the way demaunded an almes of a poore ragged wretch, that was ready to dy for cold. Now he, who in compassion, was still the same, calling his Archdeacon before him, commaunded him sudenly to be clothed; from thence, he pursued his way, and hauing adored our Lord, entred into the Sacristy to vest himself. There were in those dayes, certaine roomes adioyning to the Church, somewhat sequestred from the vulgar, which were called Oratoryes: In one of these (while the Chanons els where, were passing the tyme in Conuersation) *S. Martyn* according to yse, was alone in his *Pontificalibus*, sitting on a playne and simple seate, (for he would neuer vse any better), for that in the Church, he would neuer be seen, but on his knees, or standing vpright. Now while he was expecting there, amidst his holy meditations, at the houre of the Sacrifice, the very same Beggar, was seene agayne to appeare before him, who as it seemed (as necessity makes one ingenious) could tel how to cōtriue it so, as the Clerkes vnwitting therof, finding the Bishop retyred, presses in to him, & with a lamentable voyce, complaynes for that he was not prouided by the Archdeacon. Then *S. Martyn* without more ado, causing him to step aside, tooke off his owne Cassocke, not without some trouble, from vnder his vestments, and gaue it to the Wretch; who as for solliciting his sute had entred in without noyse, so now obteyning what he would, he went quietly away. A litle after, the Archdeacon enters to aduertise the Bishop, that now it was tyme for him to come forth, for the people were al expecting his cōming, when he answered: It were fit the while the poore (meaning himselfe) should first be clothed, or otherwise, he could not appeare in publique: but the Archdeacon (for that *S. Martyn* was outwardly clothed with the vestment, & could not penetrate the Enigma,) after many excuses finally added, how the poore man could not be foūd. Bring hither (said *S. Martyn*) the Garment prepared, for there shall not want one to put it on. With these words, the vnperfect man came to be troubled in himself, & being constreyned through necessity, went his wayes suddenly to a shop at hand, where hastily

ſtily hauing bought a poore coate, for ſome halfe a Crowne, being courſe, ſcant, and illfauourdly made, caſts it downe with a diſdainfull geſture, at the feete of *S. Martyn*, ſaying: behold the garment, but for the beggar now where is he? When the Venerable Biſhop, without looſing a whit his holy peace, cauſing the others to ſtand forth ſomewhat without the portall, procuring to be ſecret as much as he could, did reueſt himſelf with it; howbeit at laſt through the diuers circumſtances of the matter, the thing could not be concealed.

And beſides that, it pleaſed the diuine goodnes, to illuſtrate ſuch a fact, with an euident ſigne, becauſe the admirable *Prieſt*, going forth in that habit, while acording to the vſe, he bleſſeth the Aultar; behold a ball of fire to ſhine from his head, in mãner of a comet, which blazing towards Heauen, ſent vp a fyery ſtreame. True it is, that howbeit the ſame fell out on a ſolemne day, and in a great cõcourſe of people, yet did not any other ſee it, then one of the Virgins, , one Prieſt, and three Monkes only: as for the other, why they had not the fauour to behold it, appertaynes not to vs, to examine heere: it ſuffiſeth, that the teſtimonies, as well for number, as quality, are ſufficient to take away all doubt.

S. Martin *trauailing alone, was hardly vſed by Souldiours, not knowing who he was.* Chap. 8.

THE diuine Man, going in a viſit of his Dioceſſe (which he performed with ſingular care , and edification of all) his Companions by ſome accident or other remayned behind, while he going on his wayes, met with a Caroch of Souldiours trauayling vpon buſines; but the horſes ſtarting at the ſight of *S. Martyn*, in a caſſocke of hayry cloth , and a darke mantle which hung downe on one ſide, and affrighted therewith, were troubled in ſuch ſort, as the harneſſe being on a ſudden entangled together, could not eaſily be freed. Heerupon the cruell Souldiours being enraged alighted, and with ſtripes, and cudgells ſet vpon *S. Martin*: Who as he was very amorous of the Croſſe, as holding euery occaſion very deere, to be ill intreated, without once opening his mouth, ſtood to the blowes, vntill ſuch tyme, as being torne and halfe dead, he fell to the ground, when thoſe ſpightfull fellowes, hauing now atchieued ſo goodly an exploit, returned agayne to their Caroch.

This done, the companions of the *Saint*, being now arriued, and ſeeing him in that manner, to lye full of wounds, all in bloud, being ſad and heauy thereat lifted him vp, and layd him on an Aſſe, and with all the haſt that might be, got away out of that curſed place. But now, thoſe impious fellowes (though they had the aduantage to diſentangle the harneſſe, & to ſet them in order agayne) yet had they not the power to go forwards one foote further, but rather through diuine iuſtice, the horſes ſtood ſtill, immoueable like ſtatues, in the ſelfe ſame place, nor with cryes, threats, and cruell ſtrookes, could they be made to go on a ſtep. Finally, after they had ſpent in vayne, their whips, and Cudgells, which they had out of the next wood, theſe wicked fellowes began now to reflect, how this accident could not be human, but by diuine iuſtice; & hauing remorſe of conſcience, for the grieuous outrage they had cōmitted on the poore paſſenger right now, they went to enquire of ſome, that paſſed that way, who he was that went before in ſuch a habit, and with ſuch marks; and hauing vnderſtood to be *S. Martin* (whoſe name was a great deale more famous then his perſon) they acknowledged the Sacriledge committed, and the vengeance of God vpon them, and fearing yet worſe, they all ſtriued to follow the Seruants of God; and hauing ouertaken him, with deep ſighes and lamentable voyces, caſting themſelues proſtrate on the ground before him, ſprinckling their heads with duſt, and knocking their breaſts, they humbly beſought pardon of him, and licence to be gone.

The *Saint*, by diuine reuelation, had foreſeene the ſucceſſe already, and alſo acquainted his companions with it. Whence ſuch pennance was not awhit new to them, nor did he vpbrayd any of them, for the iniury done him: but receyued them all, with a benigne countenance; and with feruent prayers, hauing obteyned their diſpatch, he ſent them away confounded, and aſtoniſhed at ſo great a Clemency.

A notable Example of a diſſolute Monke, conuerted by S. Martyn *to a better life.* Chap. 9.

VVE may not ſeeme to conceale heere the Patience, and Meekenes, which *S. Martyn* ſhewed to a Prieſt of his Church, by name *Britius*. This man, being trayned vp in a Religious life, with the Obſeruance of Pouerty, and Modeſty, as he was aſſumpted

assumpted to the Clergy and Benefices, so suffered he himselfe to be drawne away, with the concupiscence of the Eyes, as without regard, eyther of his Life past, or present Degree, or the speach of people, he began to giue himselfe wholy to pleasures; to maintayne horses, and to buy very costly Slaues. These things now pierced the very hart of the holy *Pastour*, who after he had prayed to our *Lord* for him, stuck not with much sweetnes, and grauity, both of words and countenance, to set before him the enormous scandall that followed of so great a mutation of manners in him, intreating him withall to be thinke himselfe of the ancient purposes, and to consider, how the state of the Clergy, did not acquit him at all of the perfection of a Monke, but that rather the name did seeme to oblige him; to haue in horrour and contempt all the delights and pleasures of the world, since thereby was vnderstood, he had left to others their transitory things, and with the *Prophet* had chosen, for portion and inheritance, God only.

With such aduises, *S. Martyn* went about, to awake that vnhappy mã from this deadly sleepe: but as he was giuen ouer already in prey to sense, & found himselfe to be but little disposed to admonishments, for the present he held his peace; but feeling himselfe afterwards to be gauled with the truth, and with this occasion also more enflamed by the Diuell, he was so incensed therewith as that on the very next day turning the medicine into poyson, with great fury, he came to the Monastery, where the Man of God was sitting neare vnto his litle Cell. Heere *Britius*, full of anger, or full of phrensy rather, with sparkling eyes, and trembling lips, & changing often colour, vents forth his rage conceyued agaynst *S. Martyn* in presence of many, loading him with infinite contumelies and iniuries, and hardly also abstayning from laying violent hands vpon him. Nor yet was the sacrilegious temerity of this man, any thing new, or sudden, to the Seruant of *Christ*, hauing first before his arriuall, seen on the top of the hanging cliffe, two wicked Spirits, who triumphing, and ioyfull, calling *Britius* by name, with voyce, and gestures, stood egging him on, to reuenge the affront, and to handle the *Bishop* in that sort, as he might not dare heerafter to molest him any more.

Whence *S. Martin*, composing himselfe to all manner of *Patience*, endeauoured, with admirable dexterity and sweetnes, to mitigate the Wretch, the whilest he, letting wholy the reynes loose to his

Tongue, ceased not to abuse him with extreme insolency, and bitternes. And now hauing suffered his tongue to range at liberty on euery side, with the same fury he entred in, he went forth agayne: when by the prayers, no doubt of *S. Martin,* the darknes expelled, he began to be aware of his grieuous offence, and was so compunct for the same, as that suddenly turning his steps backe agayne, with blushing and shame, prostrating himselfe at the feete of the holy Man, besought him benignely to remit his fault. Nor was it any thing hard to obtayne this grace of him, who was sory, not for his owne abasement, but rather for the precipice of the other, yea, and to help him more, playnely expressed to him, how he had seene the two infernall furyes, that set him on.

In summe, with all affection he receiued him into his friendship agayne. Wherein he was found so constant, that howbeit, he had afterwards many, and grieuous complaints of him, yet notwithstanding, he could neuer be brought to depriue him, of his Priesthood, least vnder the shadow of publique chastisement, the priuate offence might seeme in some mãner to be punished by him. And to persons of quality, who seemed to wonder much at him, & not to like very well so much indulgence of his, *S. Martyn* would answere, among other things: *Iudas* was tollerated by *Christ*, and shall not I beare with a *Britius*? In this manner, went he still perseuering in these most intense acts of *Charity*. But who would say euer, that so obstinate, and vnbridled a man as *Britius* was, should come afterwards, to be so gracious in the eyes of God, as to become a *Bishop*, and a *Saint*?

And yet so fell it out, thankes be to the diuine Goodnes for it, & to the intercessions of *S. Martin*: who on a tyme, holding his eyes fixed on Heauen for a pretty while, and being therefore of *Britius* taxed of madnes: Know (sayd he to him) Sonne, that I haue obteyned of our Lord, that thou mayst come to be Bishop after me. Though thou must vnderstand, that in the Bisshopricque it selfe, thou shalt want no aduersities. Then *Britius* sayd: Lo you now, did not I affirme the truth, how this man was meerely out of his wits? But howsoeuer, in tyme he vnderstood, he was deceyued. Because that *S. Martin*, being once departed this life, it pleased the diuine prouidence, that *Britius*, though vayne and proud before, yet notwithstanding being held in high esteeme for *Chastity*, was without opposition, elected by the people, and Clergy, to the supreme

supreme gouernement of soules. In which office, acknowledging, and amending the errours of his youth, he most notably demeaned himselfe. And to the end, the Prophecy of his Predecessour, might be verifyed, with his great glory, he suffered, from the impious, and slaunderers, most grieuous persecutions.

How a certayne Virgin refused to be visited by S. Martyn: *and how patiently he tooke it.* Chap. 10..

TO returne now from whence we were digressed; a like fortitude to this, shewed *S. Martin* of an equall courage, and serene mind in another case, though light in esteeme perhaps, yet very difficult in practise: there was in the Diocesse of *Towers*, a Virgin, among others, of excellent fame, and vertuous behauiour; who now for these many yeares, of her owne accord, had made her abode in a certayne farme of hers, very streightly reclused, and onely attending to God, did fly the conuersation, & sight of men. *S. Martin* now, being inuited with such an odour (who otherwise was exceeding precise from spending any tyme with women) yet chancing to passe by those parts, determined to honour with his presence so rare a vertue, being a fauour so much more notable, as known to be more vnusuall with him: but the matter succeeded not accordingly, because the *Spouse* of *Christ*, would not giue way to remit a whit of her rigour, so much, as at the request of such a Prelate to be visited at all. So as *S. Martin*, with many of his company, being now arriued where she was, not doubting awhit of being admitted to her presence, hauing sent in a messenger to her, and that in vayne, so repulsed he departed thence.

Now what would an ordinary Priest haue done in this case? If not happily, taken it at least in ill part, and perhaps haue iudged the Virgin to be taynted with heresy, and worthy of excommunication? But the diuine man, was so farre from being offended therat, as reioycing at such a repulse receyued; began with magnificall words, to extoll the constancy and chastity of her, who had so retyred herselfe from him. Nor with words only shewed he forth, the high opinion he had framed of her, but with facts also: forasmuch as she afterward, in the Euening hauing sent him certayne presents of refection, and refreshment, *S. Martin*, who in his whole visit, till that tyme, had neuer accepted of any thing which was offered him, yet of what the Virgin sent him, he refused it not; alledging, it was not fitting for a Priest, to refuse the benediction of her, who deserued to be preferred before many Priests.

With such like words, and workes, from tyme to tyme, gaue *S. Martin* euident signes of a full victory gotten ouer his passions, & of the peacefull possession he maintayned in himselfe. But in regard, some will say perhaps, how these manner of prayses, are cōmon also with priuate persons; let vs come, to the proper parts of a true Prelate, and Apostolicall Guardian. Among which, it seemes that the zeale of the holy, and orthodoxe fayth, and of the sincere worship of God, doth hold the first place. For whose conseruation, *S. Martyn* was alwayes wonderfully sollicitous, and vigilant, keeping himselfe, and all all his flocke, from euery least contagion of Heretiques, or of others seuered from the Roman Sea. Heerwith did burne in his breast, an inextinguishable thirst to illustrate, and propagate the Christian verity, on euery side, and particularly in the neighbour parts; where it seemed to him an intollerable thing, that any relique of Paganisme, should yet be extant. He endeauoured then maynly to extinguish the same; and Almighty God most commonly for his part, with a powerfull hand, and stupendious workes, concurred thereunto.

S. Martin *restores a Womans sonne from Death to life: with other notable thinges.* Chap. 11.

Saint *Martin* on a tyme going, by occasion of the diuine seruice, to the Citty of *Chartres*, chanced to passe through a Village all of Gentils, who at the fame of the *Saint*, going forth of the Towne, put themselues in the high way to behold him; and at the same rumour, concurred so great a multitude of the neighbour countries, as all that playne was seene to be couered with an infinite people. At the sight of which sheep, for that the most were led astray, the holy *Bishop* sighing, and eleuated in spirit, beginnes to preach to them the word of *God*, and to inuite them to eternall saluation, and that with such a feeling, and with such a voyce, & action, as doubtles seemed to them somewhat more then humane.

Now while he thus discoursed, it pleased our *Lord*, that a Woman, whose only Sonne was dead at that tyme, comming before him, with hands lifted vp, presented him to the blessed *S. Martin*, saying:

ſaying: we vnderſtand, that thou art the friend of God, reſtore me my Sonne, which is the only Child I haue. To the prayers of the dolorous Mother, were added the ſighes, and interceſſions of the ſtanders by. So as *S. Martyn* perceyuing, how for the conuerſion of that people, ſome miracle were fit, lifting vp his eyes and mind to Heauen, and conceiuing thence an vndoubted certaynty of the diuine ayde, he tooke the body in his armes, and in the preſence of all, put himſelfe on his knees: and after a little ſpace the party aroſe vp, and ſo reſtored the child reuiued to the Mother, aſtoniſhed, and almoſt beſides herſelfe for ioy: whereupon a cry was lifted vp to the ſtarres, and all theſe people confeſſing *Chriſt* for true *God*, began in troupes with great vehemency to runne after *S. Martin*, moſt inſtantly intreating him to make them Chriſtians. And he full of iubiley, lifting vp his hands ouer them, made them Cathecumens all at once, giuing order beſids, that they might be inſtructed; affirming it, not vnfit to make Cathecumens, in the open fields, ſince in fields in like manner haue Martyrs beene conſecrated.

With this manner of purchaſe, our *S. Martin* reioyced much more then with the increaſe of rents, or tytles: and not onely from manners, and minds of perſons, but euen from their memory alſo, and eyes, endeauoured he to take away all apparence of profane, & Gentill worſhip: nor were the difficulties of the enterpriſe, nor magnificence of Antiquityes, able to diuert him from it. In the Caſtle of *Ambatia*, was a Tower of polliſhed ſtones, heertofore dedicated to a falſe God; which from the ſolid, and ſpacious foundations, ariſing more and more, came at the top, to finiſh in forme of a Pine-aple, a worke both of art, and coſt alike, and not only curious to behold, but alſo very firme and durable.

Now the holy Biſhop, hauing appointed *Marcellus* a Prieſt there dwelling, by all meanes to deſtroy ſuch an abhomination, & after ſome tyme finding the ſame, as yet on foote, reprehended his ſlacknes. But *Marcellus*, excuſing himſelfe with the difficulty therof, for that the making was ſuch, as hardly would an Army be able to demoliſh it, much leſſe a ſmall number of Clerks, or feeble Monks which liued with him; *S. Martin*, without more reply, hauing recourſe to his wonted tacklings, ſpent all that night and morning in prayer: When behold on a ſuden a vehement tempeſt of winds, lightning, and thunder, impetuouſly ſmiting the building, fetcht it vp by the ground, and layd it flat on the Earth:

In another place, stood a pillar of an vnmeasurable greatnes, on the top whereof, was an Idoll. And S. *Martyn*, being not able to endure so great an offence of the true God, determined by all meanes to leuell it with the ground, but not finding commodity, eyther of Masons, or instruments to affect it, he craued likewise the diuine succour, with so much ardour, and such efficacy withall, as the prayer being ended, the effect very sudenly followed: because that in the sight of all the standers by, there appeared from Heauen another Pillar no lesse then that, which descended with such a force vpon it, as reduced it into dust, together with the Idol.

How S. Martyn *by the signe of the Crosse, escaped Death: And how the people were conuerted thereupon, to the Faythof Christ.* Chap. 12.

SAINT *Martin*, in a certaine Bourge of the Infidels, hauing destroyed their Temple, would needs presently vpon it, cōmaund a tall Pine-tree there, that was consecrated to the Deuill, to be felled to the ground. But the Country-people, who through the diuine will had beene quiet at the one, very tumultuously afterwards opposed themselues to the other. *S. Martin* endeauoured to pacify that blind people what he could, & to make them capable of the Truth; shewing by diuers reasons, how one sole God was the Maker of euery thing, and that to him was due from the rationall creature, all honour, oblation, and Sacrifice, and not to the Angels thurst out of Paradise, deceiptfull, and proud, whome hitherto they had miserably serued; and went prouing withall, how in that Trunke, could be no matter worthy of veneration at all. Now while he was preaching in this sort with great charity, one of those Pagans, more impudent and more saucy then the rest, lifting vp his voyce, sayd to him: If thou hast such a confidence in this thy God, we our selues will cut downe this tree for thee, and do thou but set thy shoulders thereunto, and be propping it vp; and if thy Lord stand for thee, as thou sayest, thou shalt not suffer a whit. The magnanimous Bishop accepted the Condition, and all that barbarous company accorded likewise, exchanging very willingly the losse of such a plant, with the death of one, that was so great a Persecutour of the Idols.

That Pine, of its nature, was bending in such sort, as it cleerly appeared, in cutting it downe, wherabout of necessity it must light. On that very side, did *S. Martin* suffer himselfe to be placed, with his legs

legs tyed, by those rude rustiques, where he stood as a statue. And the people presently vpon this, diuided themselues, very glad and ioyfull the while at so new a spectable, and some with axes, in hast began to cut downe the Pine-tree. The man of God, from thence had made his Monks to sequester thẽselues, who laboured in vayne to hinder such a proofe, and being pale, and full of sadnes, with tẽder eyes ech momẽt stood expecting the losse of their deere Maister, and the tree now ready to totter with redoubled stroakes, seemed to threaten the fal. And yet stood *S. Martin* very firme and vndaunted; when finally the ruine, with a terrible noyse, directly bended towards him, & now was euẽ ready to oppresse him, when he without being troubled awhit, lifting vp his arme, opposed thereto the signe of the Crosse, and nothing els besides. A thing truly very admirable, that euen at the holsome signe so made, was sudenly that great trunck, as it were beate back with a violent Engine, & went with such a fury to the contrary side, as it almost had crushed the very Infidels thẽselues, who were hewing it downe.

What effect now this so sudden euent might cause in their minds may more easely be imagined, then written. The Monkes beholding now beyond all hope, *S. Martin* to be safe, and sound, with consolation and iubiley giuing thankes to our Lord for it, wept out right, and the rude people being conuinced with so great a miracle, holding vp their hands and voyces to Heauen, did finally yield, and acknowledge the errour of their life past, and were willingly conuerted to *Christ*; insomuch as where before, there were no faythfull, as it were, to be seen thereabouts, within a litle tyme, by meanes of the vertue, and diligence, and the exemplar manner of the holy *Bishop*, there remayned not a place, that was not very full of Christians, of Churches, and Monasteryes: Because the seruant of God was wont, as soone as he had demolished any house of the Idols, to erect in the same scituation, some deuout Oratory, or Religious Conuent, or other.

S. Martin *stayes the flames of fire from doing any harme. With other wonders which he wrought.* Chap. 13.

VVE may not seeme to let passe in silence, a thing, which if it had not happened in publique, might perhaps haue seemed incredibie to some. *S. Martin*, hauing in those countries therabout, set fire to a very noble, & most ancient Temple of the Idols, it happened, that a wind arising, did carry the flame to a house hard by, not without manifest danger of dilating it selfe further, and of stirring vp, with the sense of their priuat losses, the tender minds of that Community. *S. Martyn* then being aware of the danger, with the wonted courage of a liuely fayth, mounted vp speedily to the roofe, & puts himself against the flames; and it is certaine, that at the only appearing of the Man of God, the flames, as timerous to offend him, in a moment seemed to fetch about, & to be retorted, and gathered within themselues, & in the sight of all, in striuing against the violence of the wind, to retire in such sort, as the priuate buildings remayned very safe; and *S. Martyn* with his only presence, effected that which al the people, with their instruments, & water, could not so easily haue brought to passe.

In the Leapers Bourge (as they called it) likewise, hauing attempted to ruin a temple, very famous, no lesse for the great riches therof, then for the much superstition vsed about it; he was repelled by the Gentils, not without much outrage, and iniuryes don him. Wherupon, retiring himselfe into some place thereby, he remayned in fasting for three whole dayes togeather, and praying in sackloth and ashes: and at last appeared two champions vnto him of the heauenly warfare, being armed with speares & shields, saying how they came, as sent from our Lord to succour him, against that multitude of swaynes. That therfore, he might returne bouldly to the enterprize agayne, and not feare any impediment whatsoeuer. So *St Martin* did, and in the presence of all those Pagans, who through diuine power, stood the while immoueable, he ruined the profane bulke from the very foundations, destroyed the Aultars, & reduced the images vnto dust. Whence succeeded another great benefit, that the Gentils, perceiuing themselues so bound and stupifyed, without being able to rise against the Bishop, knew the effect to be caused by a supreme power, and they all, as it were, came to belieue in *Christ*, exclayming with one voyce, and confessing, that the only *God* of *S. Martin*, was to be adored, and that, for the Idols, they were to make no reckoning of them, since in such a necessity of theirs, they were not able to helpe themselues.

Two other stupendious things, are recounted in this matter: one was, that in the country of *Burgundy*, there being a great number of country swaynes risen agaynst *S. Martin*, in defence of a Tēple,

ple, one of them drawing out his ſword, ſet vpon him; when the holy man, ſuddenly laying his cloake aſide, offered him his naked necke, nor was that impious fellow any whit ſlack, to haue giuen the ſtroake: but lifting vp his arme, in the preſence of all, fell flat backwards himſelfe, and cryed for peace, and pardon. The other was, that from a like diſdayne, another wicked fellow, being minded to kill him, the very ſword fell out of his hand, in ſuch wiſe, as it was neuer ſeene more. True it is, that he rarely came into ſuch termes, becauſe for the moſt part, *S. Martyn* with meekenes, and with preaching, would be tempring and perſuading the people, in ſuch ſort, as themſelues vnderſtanding the truth once, would condemne their owne madnes, & deſtroying the Idols with their proper hands, be conuerted to *Chriſt*. To which effect of conuerſion of ſoules, *S. Martyn* was wont very induſtriouſly to make vſe of the great gift he had, in curing the ſicke, and deliuering poſſeſſed perſons of euill ſpirits; as among others, he did heere with a perſon of great quality, by name *Tetradius*.

This man, being moued to compaſſion, for a deere ſeruant of his, very cruelly oppreſſed and tormented by the infernall enemy, with great inſtance intreated *S. Martyn* to vouchſafe ſo much as to cure him. The holy man then, willed him to be brought before him: but the maligne ſpirit would not endure, to be led from home reſiſting the ſame very obſtinately, euer with biting, and ſcratching. Whereupon *Tetradius*, repayring to the holy *Bishop*, puts himſelf on his knees to beſeech him, he would be pleaſed to come to the lodging himſelfe. And with this occaſion, *S. Martyn* began very dexterouſly to help this ſoule, with ſhewing himſelfe ſomewhat backward therein; and with ſaying, that it was not lawfull for him to enter into the houſe of a Gentile, and profane man;& could tell how to diſcourſe ſo well, as *Tetradius* promiſed him to become a Chriſtian, if he could ſee but his ſeruant deliuered once of his paine, and malady. Vpon this pact, *S. Martin* was content to go thither, and ſo holding his hand ouer him, on a ſudden expelled the Diuell. Nor did *Tetradius* fayle of his word, being made a Cathecumen out of hand, and a litle after baptized, and while he liued thenceforth, did alwayes beare very great reuerence, and loue to *S. Martin*.

The gifts, and naturall talents of S. Martin: *with a certayne miracle that he wrought.* Chap. 14.

THus did this great *Captaine* by all meanes continually wage warre against the Prince of this world, and went dispossessing him apace from his ancient tiranny. Nor let any esteeme this zeale of his, to be awhit deuoyd of prudence, or discretion: forasmuch as *S. Martin* being assisted with diuine grace, and profound humility, could very well distinguish of inspirations, good or euill, as of the Angels themselues, of light or darknes, (which in diuers figures, and with sundry intentions, would visit him often.) Moreouer howbeyt, through many impediments, he was not able to attend to the schooles; yet with a viuacity of wit, and with sobriety and vigilancy, together with such reading, as his businesses would permit, and much more through an excellent purity of hart, and by keeping the mind euer fixed in God; he arriued to so high a degree of true science, & of a solid, and masculine eloquence, that he was able to expound very difficult places of diuine Scripture, with incredible cleerenes. And in answering to cases of conscience, could alwayes touch the very point of matters; as also in discourses, as well publique, as priuate, teach and moue the Auditours, with so much more fruite, as he sought euer more, the only glory of God, and abhorred his owne.

But aboue all, he would giue a very singular accompt of the Christian fayth, and was sufficient to refute with very pregnant reasons, whomesoeuer should seeme to haue the impious boldnes to assayle the same. He was wont also, to gather very profitable, and spirituall conceipts, from things which dayly would occurre vnto him. As once when he saw a sheep newly shorne, he pleasantly sayd to the standers by: This sheep heere, hath already fulfilled the precept of the Ghospell, because of two coates, he hath parted with one, to such as had need; and so should you likewise doe. Beholding one, that was keeping of swine, very cold, and but halfe couered with a poore, and curtayle coate of skinnes, he sayd: Behold *Adam*, chased out of Paradise; but let vs, leauing the old *Adam*, cloth our selues with the new.

There was a great and goodly meadow, where in one part the oxen fed; another fouly rooted vp by swyne; the third as yet vn-

vn touched, and diapred with pleasant colours, gaue wonderfull delight to human eyes. Now *S. Martyn*, turning to his cōpanions, said: That peece which you see so fed on, may seeme to demonstrate the state of *Matrimony*, because that howbeit, it haue not wholy lost the honour of its greenesse, yet is it depriued of the grace, and ornament of the flowers therof: that other so grubd, and turned vp, as you see by those vncleane beasts, resembles the filthy vice of *Fornication*: but the remaynder, which hath not hitherto, suffered any manner of iniury, represents the glory of *Virginity*, since being clothed with very frequent and fresh hearbs, rich of fruites, & distinguished with pleasant flowers, in manner of fine pearls, emeralds, and rubyes, shynes aboue all the beauty of art, and workmanship of hand. O blessed semblance, and right worthy of God, forasmuch, as there is nothing in the world, that may seeme to compare with the gift of holy *Virginity*!

In the visit of his diocesse, arriuing once at a certayne riuer, in company of many other seruants of God; he saw a great shole of Foule, very busy a fishing, and greedily attending to gorge themselues. Then sayd he to such, as were about him: these rauenous birds, resemble much the infernall enemyes, that lye alwayes in wayte, to catch the vnwary soules, to take them on a sudden, and to deuour them vp, without end of satiating themselues. To these words, he added, a notable miracle, which was, to commaund the foule, with the powerfull vertue of words, to leaue the waters, wherin they were floating, & to go their wayes to the vplands, & desert places. At which voyce, being suddenly assembled togeather, leauing the waters, they flew to the woods and mountaynes; while the multitude of Spectatours with reason remayned astonished to behold, that *S. Martin* should haue likewise power to commaund the birds.

In this manner then, ech creature serued the purifyed eyes of the *Saint*, as a liuely glasse of truth, and without labour, or rather with delight, gathering, as I said, the best documents from euery thing, he came alwayes to maynteyne his hart, and of those he dealt with, in chast thoughts, procuring withall possible industryes, that rationall soules, should dispose themselues, to afford a cleane and gratefull lodging to the diuine Goodnes. To which effect, likewise he sought to keep his subiects exercised in prayer, to be prompt in pardoning iniuryes & offences, and lastly to exchange the delights of the Sense, with the pleasures of the Spirit.

S. Martyn *through fasts, and prayers to Almighty God, appeaseth the wrath of* Valentinian *the Emperour.* Chap. 15.

THe charity of *S. Martyn* was not conteyned within those more high and Noble workes of Mercy alone, but extended it selfe very tenderly also to the Corporall workes, and exteriour necessityes, in curing of the sicke, in visiting, and defending of the Orphans and widowes, succouring the afflicted, and oppressed with vniust power, or by any other human accident, shewing no lesse promptnes in vndertaking such like enterprizes, then greatnes of courage, in susteyning them, and setting them forwards by al meanes possible. To which purpose, we may not conceale, how he being gone vpon such occasions, to the Court of *Valentinian* the *Emperour*, a man very proud, and haughty by nature, and besides by his *Arrian* Wife, much prouoked against the Catholiques; he had heere a large field likewise, to shew his constancy in. In regard, that the *Emperour*, hauing heard before hand of the comming of the Man of God, and of the affayres he was to treat of, suddenly gaue order, he should not be admitted into the Pallace. So as *S. Martin*, after he had once, or twice, endeuoured in vayne to get audience, not loosing a whit of his courage the while, nor yet troubled for the repulses had, with his wonted fayth, and fortitude, layd hold of his ancient remedyes. He puts on a course Cilice, sprinckles himselfe with ashes, takes leaue of all sorts of meate, & drinke. From thence entring into sighes, and prayers, he perseuered so long, till on the seauenth day, an Angell from Heauen appeared to him, & bad him boldly go to the Pallace, for the gates, though of purpose shut against him, should now stand open to him, & the pride of the mercylesse Prince, should fall by one meanes, or other.

With this confidence, *S. Martyn* going thither, found his entry so easy, as without any impedimẽt, he came to the roome, where *Valentinian* himselfe was, who seeing him a farre off, was exceeding angry therewith at the first, and with frowning lookes, cryed out vpon his Guards for admitting him in; and thereupon stood immoueable, without saying any more, or giuing any manner of entertaynement to the blessed Bishop: When behold on a sudden, the Royall Throne was enuironed with flames, which approaching to that part of his body, wherewith he sate, enforced him against

his

his will to stand on his feete; and was affrighted therat in such sort as being humbled, with many imbraces, and courtesyes, he now receiued him, whome a little before he could not endure to see: & immediately, without expecting supplications from him did fauour him with whatsoeuer he desired. After which, he would inuite him very often to familiar discours, yea, and to banquets also: & lastly at his parting, offered him diuers rich presents. But the faythfull friend of Pouerty, with much edification of all the Court, without accepting of any one, repayred to his cure, and diocesse, as soone as might be. In this manner, the Seruant of *Christ*, with patience, and with prayer ouercoming all obstacles, guided his busynesses to a fayre port: & as he suffered not himselfe, to be deiected awhit with indignityes, and affronts; so kept he himselfe amidst fauours, and prosperityes, perpetually immutuable.

How S. Martin *was honoured, and esteemed by the Emperour* Maximus, *to the great honour of the Clergy.* Chap 16.

IF euer any Prelate were welcome and made much of, by great Princes, this holy man had as much respect of them as any: for in the number of his most rare gifts, shined no lesse Apostolicall Maiesty, then Religious modesty. Whereof *Maximus* the *Emperour* among others, hath giuen vs a very good testimony: who within a while after the Death of *Valentinian*, being assumpted by the souldiours to the Empire, though on the one side, he were very tenacious, and committed many extorsions; yet on the other, shewed he himselfe, to be desirous of eternall saluation, and a man of timerous conscience, being much furthered therein by the Empresse his wife, a woman of great vertue, and no lesse ready to fauour, for her part, the Catholike Prelates, then that *Arrian* was sollicitous, to hinder them.

By these two personages now, it cannot be expressed, how *S. Martyn* was reuerenced, and esteemed. So as going at those times likewise to the Court, by occasion of deliuering of certayne prisoners, releasing of *Bandits*, and recouering from the Treasury some goods confiscated, and of other such workes of paternall charity; *Maximus* did receiue him with singular veneration, and after he had dispatched with him the aforesayd businesses, he would call him aside, and very willingly heare him discourse, of the vncertaynty of pre-

present things, of the Eternity of the future world, of the glory of the Blessed, and of the vnspeakable greatnesse of God. At which discourses, the deuout *Queene* was alwayes present, being his deere consort no lesse in Religion, then in the Empire, sitting humbly on the ground, still hanging in suspence, with all recollection, and silence, on the words, and gestures of the man of God; wherewith now being warmed, she was soone enflamed with so great a feruour, as acknowledging with a liuely, and most chast fayth in the person of her Ghest, the same of *Christ*, she determined to represent in her selfe both the *Sisters* of *Lazarus*: and as in sitting at the feete of the *Saint*, and hearing of the diuine word, she had imitated *Mary*; so in seruing, and feeding him she would not be awhit inferiour to *Martha*.

With this purpose, she intreated him, very earnestly to daigne to receiue a sober refection particularly from her: which *S. Martin* precisely denying her, as he, who abhorred all vanity, and such like familiarity with women, yet she very firme in her deliberation had recourse to her husband, and with him togeather, began afresh to importune the *Bishop*; in so much, as partly not to contristate such Princes, and partly not to preiudice the cause of the poore, which then he handled, at last suffered himselfe to be ouercome. Whereupon the good *Empresse*, without other wayters as all, hauing set him at the table, began to put before him the meate which she had dressed and seasoned with her owne hands, and likewise presented him his drinke, and in summe, during the dinner, like an humble handmayd, stood attending with her eyes modestly fixed on the Table, & with her whole person attentiue and prompt to the seruice. And finally, the cloth being reuerently taken away, and the remainder, with the crums, with diligence voyded, she tooke them with her, most triumphant, and glad, with infinite thanks to God, as one laden with many exceeding rich spoyles.

Surely, not without a great confusion, and shame to some women of our tymes, who not bearing respect, eyther to the Decrees of *Councells*, or euen to the dreadfull *Mistery* of the *Aultar*, are wont themselues no lesse impious, then impudently, to be serued by the Priests of the Highest, insteed of Wayters, and Pages. Though indeed the Clerks themselues for their parts, are not wholy without fault, since they for the vile interests of ambition, or gayne, permit that degree to be trampled on by men, which euen the Angels thẽselues

ſelues do reuerence. From which adulation and baſenes of theyrs, how far off *S. Martyn* euer was, and with what decorum, eſpecially in publique, he conſerued the Epiſcopall dignity, may be eaſily gathered by that which we ſhall ſet downe in the next Chapter.

How S. Martyn *was feaſted by the Emperour: & how he bare himſelfe therin.* Chap. 17.

THe aforeſaid *Maximus* had very oftentymes inuited *S. Martin* to dyne with him, but alwayes in vayne; yet notwithſtanding he ſo perſeuered with intreatyes, as finally he yeilded thereunto, with no leſſe gladnes of the *Emperour*, then if he had conquered a kingdome. There were thither inuited withall, as to a great feaſt, three principall Lords of the Court, the Conſull *Euodius*, and two *Counts*, the one the Brother, the other the vncle to the *Emperour*: between theſe two, was placed the *Prieſt*, who was *S. Martins* companion. The holy Biſhops Chayr, was put beſides *Maximus* himſelfe. The Feaſt was now by this tyme, prety forwards, when according to cuſtome, there was a Cup of wine preſented to the *Emperour*, who commaunded it ſudenly to be commended to *S. Martyn*, expecting with a kind of ambition, to receiue it afterwards from his hand. But the great *Prelat*, hauing taſted therof, drank to his *Prieſt*, giuing to vnderſtand therby, in that aſſembly was none more worthy then he to pledge him; eſteeming he had done ill, if eyther the *Emperour* himſelfe, or his chiefeſt Fauourits, or neereſt to him, had beene preferred by him before that poore Seruant of God.

They receiued all much edification heerat: & being ſlighted in that caſe, tooke it ſo much the better, as the moſt of the other Biſhops in Court were ſubiect to baſe flattery, and with much indignity ſought the grace and fauour of the Officers, and Miniſters of *Ceſar*. True it is, that this liberty, and confidence of *S. Martin*, had not been ſo conuenient and fit for all, not hauing equal ſplendour of life, nor ſuch diuinity of miracles, as he. Wherof, though we haue mentioned ſome already, notwithſtanding of an infinite number of others yet remayning, we ſhall not ſpare to ſet downe ſome few, which without preiudice to the Reader, and in ſome manner without iniury of the *Saint* himſelfe, may not well be let paſſed.

How S. Martin *miraculously escaped burning.* Chap. 18.

SAINT *Martyn* being gone, in the midst of winter, to visit a place of his diocesse, a lodging was prepared him by his Clerks, in the precincts of the Church, and to ayre the chamber there was a great fire made vnderneath, and insteed of a bed, was strewed a good quantity of dry litter and straw; whereon *S. Martin* at night reposing, and setling himselfe to sleepe, and being accustomed (as we haue said) to lye on the hard ground, could not away with such softnes, and as it were displeased therewith, immediately putting the straw aside, returned to his ordinary manner of lodging: but as the flore was broken, and full of clefts, it happened, that the force of the fire piercing through them, by little, and little, it came to enkindle the straw, and furiously to burne. Whereupon, *S. Martyn* awaking, and seeing himselfe sudenly in so great a danger, without hauing tyme, or to say better, aduertence to call vpon the diuine ayde, with a naturall motion which he had, got vp on his feete, & ran in hast to open the doore, but it pleased God he found it so barred, as that while he laboured and toyled himselfe, to put back the bolt, the fire approaching had now taken hold of his Cassock.

Then finally *S. Martin* returning to himselfe, and perceiuing that his remedy consisted not in flying away, but in crauing ayde from heauen, taking hold of the sheild of fayth, and prayer; casts himselfe on his knees in the midst of the flames, which euen heere likewise sudenly, as it were affrighted thereat, withdrew themselues, while he stood immoueable still pursuing his prayers. In the meane tyme, the Monks, who were companions to the *Saint*, remayning in the next Chamber, being awaked with the noyse, and terrifyed at the chance, by force, and not without some delay & difficulty, brake open the doore, and thinking by that tyme to haue found the blessed Father consumed and dead, they saw him, beyond all hope, amidst the flames both aliue, and entire; and comming boldly vnto him, tooke out his body from thence. The blessed man confessed afterwards, not without sighs, his owne fault. For that he hauing among other his spirituall employments, an ancient custome, in awaking alwayes, before any other thing, to lift vp his mind to God, and to sanctify with the perfume of prayer, the Aultar of his hart, and so to shut vp the Temple of his soule, that no

vn-

vncleane, or hurtfull beast of euill thoughts, might seeme to put their foote therinto; yet howsoeuer at that tyme, eyther out of humane feare, or subtility of the enemy, being quite, as it were, besides himselfe, and wholy vnmindfull of his good custome, he had first made his recourse to visible remedyes, then to the inuisible: affirming for certayne, that he was in extreme danger of burning, being alone, while he laboured, with a troubled mind to open the bolt. But that after he had betaken himselfe to the armes of the holy Crosse, and prayer, the flames were on a sudden (as he sayd) so contracted within themselues, as they left him vntouched, through diuine power.

How Euantius *was cured of a grieuous sicknes by* S. Martin: *and what other notable things he wrought besides.* Chap. 19.

ABout this tyme, a certayne honourable person, and a man of much piety, by name *Euantius*, fell mortally sicke, and being now as it were despaired of by the Phisitians, with a great deale of fayth called for *S. Martyn*, who without all delay, went his waies thither. An admirable thing: he was not yet gone halfe way, when the sicke man felt the benefit thereof, and hauing suddenly receiued health, came in person to meete with him, and to entertayne him as a Ghest. And *S. Martin* being willing to depart the next day, with humble intreatyes and much importunity, he was enforced at last to remayne a while with him. In that interim, a Page of the house, was stung with a venemous Serpent, so pestiferous indeed, as he was now euen ready to giue vp the last breath. When lo, the same *Euantius*, taking him on his shoulders, with great confidence, carryed him to the feete of the *Saint*. And now was the euill already spread through all his lymmes; when you might haue seene the skinne to swell in euery veyne, and the vitall parts to stretch like a bladder, till *S. Martyn* which his blessed hand feeling them heere & there, at last with his finger touched the wound it selfe. At the point whereof, might cleerely be seen, the poyson retyring it selfe, to runne to the fingars end, and thence by the narrow mouth of the wound, with long spinning to gush forth mingled with bloud, like the milke which sprinkles from the teats, being hardly wrung. Wherewith the youth arose vp sound, and the standers by remayned astonished, confessing vnder Heauen, nothing to be any awhit comparable to *S. Martin*. Nor was the worke lesse famous, that followes after.

There was in the City of *Chartres*, a young girle of twelue yeare old, so dumbe, as till that time, she could neuer frame a word. Now *S. Martin* being in the company of other two Bishops, *Valentinian* and *Vitricius* by name, the sayd little girle, was presented to him by her sad Father, that by his meanes, her tongue might be loosed: when as *S. Martin*, with much modesty began to put of that office to those two Prelates; alledging, that to their fayth, and vertue, nothing would be impossible. But they on the other side, vniting their intreatyes with the Suppliant, began to vrge him much to vouchsafe to comfort him. Whereupon *S. Martin*, without more delay, shewing no lesse piety, in the prompt execution, then humility in the first refusall, gaue order, that the multitude of people, should stand off, and he remayning only, with the Bishops, and with the Father of the child, according to his custome puts himselfe into prayer: then blessing a litle oyle, with the preface of the Exorcisme, and taking hold of the tongue of the dumbe Creature with his fingar, he dropped a litle of that holy liquour vpon it, not without present effect. Because the Girle, being demaunded what was her Fathers name, suddenly answered thereunto very readily. Whereat, the sayd Father, lifting vp his voyce with ioy, & teares at once, very deerly imbraced the knees of the Man of God, affirming this to be the first word, that he had euer heard his daughter speake; who afterwards, with the vniuersall wonder of all, reteyned still the vse of her speach. And this truly was vpon one alone, but that which now we shall tell you, concerned many together.

For there being entred into the family of a principall man, by name *Licontius*, a kind of disease, so grieuous and contagious withall, as that throughout the whole howse, there was nothing to be seen, heere and there, but the sick to lye, vp and downe, without hope or strength: *Licontius* for a last refuge, craued succour of *S. Martyn*, by letters; to whome the blessed man answered, it would be a very difficult thing to do, forseeing in spirit, that the scourge of God, was ouer that howse: and yet notwithstanding for compassion, he disposed himself to pacify by all meanes the heauēly wrath, and retiring himselfe, he continued in fasting, and cilices for seauē whole nights and dayes together, with so feruent prayer, as finally he obteined what he would. Wherupon *Licontius*, being exceedingly ly comforted, went flying in hast, with a thousand thanks, to bring the good newes to *S. Martyn.* And offered him moreouer, a hundred pounds of siluer: Which the holy Bishop, neyther refused, nor altogether accepted, but with a meane betweene both, & not suffering the same to enter into the gates of his Monastery, applied it sudainly to the ransome of Captiues; When it being suggested to him by the Mōks, to retayne some part therof, for the necessityes of the house, which at that tyme, was in some distresse, he answered, that the ordinary assignement of his Church, was sufficient for that purpose.

This cure wrought *S. Martin*, and many others of sundry infirmityes, as well in presence, as in absence. But what wonder is it, that he should haue power vpon humane bodyes, who had so much power ouer spirits? This is certaine, the possessed being brought to the Cathedrall Church to be deliuered by him, assoone as he put but his foote forth of his Cell, to come to the Citty, they would begin to schreech with horrid gestures, and houlings, full of dreadfulnes to behold: insomuch as the Clerks, with this signe only, were wont to vnderstand before hand of the Bishops comming thither. And he besides, not as other *Exorcists* are wont, who through force of threats, and cryes, vse to cast out Deuils; but being sprinckled with ashes, with wearing sharpe cilices, with prostrating himselfe on the groūd and with the armes of holy prayer withall, would mayster them. Nor yet let any thinke the while, that among so many graces from Heauen, that *S. Martin* was wholy without the Gift of Prophecy also. Forasmuch as diuers accidents being farre remote in tyme, & place, were manifested to him, partly immediately from God, partly also through the ministery (as hath beene sayd) of the Angels. Of which, and of many other meruayles besides (for breuity sake vntouched by vs) whosoeuer would seeme to haue a more distinct notice, let him read *Sulpitius Seuerus* in his *Dialogues*: howbeyt, he also, not to be tedious, confesseth, that of purpose, he had concealed a great part of them. But now, it is tyme, in fine, for vs to come to the last act of this representation, certainely no lesse notable, or lesse perfect, then the others; but so much more worthy of applause, as it more assures vs of the reward.

The Death of S. Martin, *with the Lamentation made by all, & the great strife for his Body.* Chap. 20.

THE blessed Man, was now arriued to the 81. yeare, or as others will haue it, to the 87. of his age, when through diuine reuelation, he himselfe knew, that his end approached, and cleerely foretold it to his disciples. But yet for all that, continued he his wonted deuotions and abstinences, and diligently attended to his pastorall office. And because, in those dayes, there fell out a scandalous discord, among the Clerks of a certayne place, which is called *Candacum*, he determined in person to go thither, to quiet them; esteeming he could not more happily end his life, then by leauing all his Churches in good peace and concord. Being gone then thither, and with diuine grace, hauing setled matters, he was now ready to turne backe to his Monastery agayne, when he began to feele in himselfe, some notable defect of forces: and therefore gathering his disciples togeather, he told them how his Tabernacle was now ready to be dissolued, whence of necessity he must needs leaue them.

When lo, amidst very dolefull sighes and teares, there was raysed this common voyce amongst them, saying: And why do you leaue vs so, holy Father? To whome do you recommend vs so disconsolate, and afflicted? The rauenous wolues will assayle your flocke, and the Shepheard being lost, who is he that can defend vs? We know very well, you desire to go to *Christ*, but your rewards are safe inough, and guerdons which differred awhile, are not lessened awhit: then take you pitty on vs rather, who remayne in such manifest danger. The Seruant of *Christ*, being mollifyed at these words, could not conteyne himselfe from weeping, but with great affect, turning himselfe to Heauen, sayd: *O Lord*, if I yet be necessary to this people, I fly no labour, thy most holy will be done. Wherein, being as it were put in ballance, he shewed, he knew not, which of the two was deerest to him, eyther to remaine on earth for *Christ*, or to leaue the earth for *Christ*. Wherein he gaue example to the faythfull, how in such prayers, they are not to encline with desire, eyther to the one, or other side; but a with reall, and simple indifferency, to remit themselues in all, and through all, to the diuine arbitrement.

The

The good *Bishop*, for some dayes now, was tormented with a cruell feuer, and yet neuerthelesse continued he night and day in meditation and vigils, susteyning with the vehemency of his spirit, the weakenes of his body, lying so, in that his soft and delicate bed of ashes, and hayrecloth; when being with much instance intreated by his Monkes, to suffer at least some vile sackloth to lye vnder him: It is not fit, sayd he, O children, that a Christian should seeme to dye otherwise, then vpon ashes: and if I giue you not example thereof, the fault is mine. This sayd, he turned with his face vpwards, to cast vp his eyes and hands to the starres. In which position now immoueable, lying as drawing to his end, he was very earnestly intreated by the Priests (who in great number were come to visit him) to turne himselfe at least on one side, to take some rest, but he replyed: Let me alone *Brothers*, and suffer me rather to looke to heauen-wards, then to the earth, and to put my soule into into the right way, being euen now ready to passe to the *Creatour*.

After this, seing the Deuil to appeare before him: What dost thou heere (sayd he) thou bloudy beast? Thou shalt find nothing in me. O Thiefe! *Arahams* bosome lyes open, and ready for me. And with these words, he yeilded vp his spirit, vpon Saturday about midnight, in the tyme of *Honorius*, and *Arcadius* Emperours, in the yeare of our Lord 397. or as others will haue it 402. hauing his face so resplendant, and all those members and flesh of his, so ill intreated before, and mortifyed, now so white, fresh, and sweete to behold, as they seemed already to be transformed into the state of glory. At the very same tyme, were heard most sweet harmonyes aboue, of Angelicall Quires; and this not only in those parts, but euen likewise in the Citty of *Colen*, where the blessed *Seuerinus* Bishop, together with his *Archdeacon*, was partaker of so gratefull accents also: and the same Bishop, had reuelation besides, how in that sound, so continued in his eares, the seuere ministers of the eternall Iustice, were, at his passage, though in vayne, withholding and examining *S. Martyn*. Whence euery one may consider with what rigour, sinners are there handled, since so without respect, the very Iust are so strictly dealt with.

The newes being spread abroad of his descease, who were able to expresse the mourning of all, and the solemnity of the Exequyes there made? When not only of *Towers*, and all the Countrey thereabous, but euen from sundry other neighbour Cittyes likewise all

all the Inhabitants came forth to honour the body, while the contrary affects at once then combated in their soules, both of ioy & sadnes: notwithstanding the number of those was much greater, who moued with the losse of such a Father, Pastour, and Maister, and of their only refuge, went sighing and lamenting bitterly amidst the hymnes & canticles. But especially the assembly of two thousand Monkes, all trayned vp by the *Saint*; and partly a chast and deuout Quire of Virgins, all eleuated in spirit, & diuine praises, gaue forth a pious, and noble spectacle to behold.

With such a trayne then, a great deale more glorious, then the triumphes of Emperours, and of *Cæsars*, were the sacred spoyles deposed, in a certaine place of that Countrey, vntill it was throughly determined, where it should be placed, in a proper and stable Sepulcher. Now there being in those dayes, a great controuersy risen thereabouts, betweene the inhabitants of *Towers*, and those of *Poytiers*; in the one of which places, *S. Martin* had led a good while a priuate life, and in the other had gouerned the Church to his dying day: And they being not able, in so great diuersity of minds, by humane wayes, to come vnto accord therin; and both the one and other people cōtending with ech other about the same, in strict vigil and custody of the sacred treasure: It pleased our Lord, that those of *Poytiers*, about midnight should remayne all oppressed, with so profound a sleepe, as that their aduersaries being aware therof, had the space to let downe the body quietly by a window, into a Barke there ready in the riuer. Whereupon looke with how much ioy & triumph for so great a purchase, they went conducting it home: so the others, became as sorowfull & perplexed for the losse, the next day morning.

There was afterwards, by the *Bishops*, successours to *S. Martyn*, built to his honour in *Towers*, a sumptuous & magnificent Church, where with great veneration was kept, that noble instrument of diuine wisedome, vntill this vnhappy age, in which the Sunne hath not seen a worse deed, then the impious scattering of those blessed Reliques in the riuer of *Lucra*, by the hands of sacrilegious Heretiques. But howbeyt, through diuine permission, they had the force, to disperse the bones, and ashes of the *Saint*: Yet were they not able, nor euer shall be, to extinguish the memory of his manifold miracles, nor the good odour of his excellent Vertues.

FINIS.

S. FVL-

THE ARGVMENT.

NAture and Art, behold conioyn'd in one,
A *Genius*, void of affectation,
Most affable; Victorious grace to fight
Agaynst rebellious sense, and appetite:
The world orecome by slighting it, a Crowne
Of glory got, and by contempt Renowne.
See how, although a thousand crosses band
Agaynst the good, in spite of all they stand
Firme in their godly purpose; mou'd no more
Then rocks by waters, forced on the shore.
Happy Selfe-will, when Will it selfe subdues,
And for a guide, and sternes-man Heauen doth vse.

THE LIFE OF S. FVLGENTIVS BISHOP OF RVSPA.

Written by a Disciple of his.

The Parentage, Birth, and Education of S. Fulgentius: *& his Vocation to Religion.* Chap. I.

AT such tyme as *Hunnericus* King of the *Vandalls* tooke *Carthage*, *Gordianus* Senatour of that Citty, with all the others of the same Order, being spoyled of his goods, and driuen into Italy, dyed there, leauing Sonnes behind him; wherof two of them, with hope of recouering their Fathers estate, returning into *Affrick*, found their house to be giuen away already to an *Arrian* Priest, so as they had no commodity to recouer the same, and to inhabit in *Carthage*, though they had the fauour to enter into some part of their substance, with which they got themselues into the Citty of *Leste*; where one of them, by name *Claudius*, hauing taken to wife, a pious & honourable Woman called *Mariana*, by her had the blessed *Fulgentius*, whose life we take in hand to write.

This

This woman hauing in her first yeares lost her husband, tooke no small care to set her sonne to schoole. And forasmuch as in those tymes, was made great accompt of the Greeke tongue, she suffered him not to attend to the Latin, vntill such tyme, as he had the workes of *Homer* by hart, and was also well versed in the Poet *Menander*: and as the youth was of a noble wit, and of a happy memory, he so profited in that study, as in the Greeke pronunciation and accents, he seemed, as it were, a naturall Grecian. After this, he gaue himselfe to the Latin, wherein likewise he made a happy progresse: but as it chanceth in like cases, very suddenly he was forced to leaue them both, while the gouernement of the whole family fel vpon him; but yet so, as in that manage of his estate he would neuer subtract himselfe frō the obedience of his Mother. Who in her widdow-hood, tooke meruailous consolation from the good deportements of her prudent sonne; perceyuing how dexterous he was, in entertayning friends, reasonable in opposing enemies, how meeke towards seruants and seuere withal, how diligent in the care of his patrimony, and discreet in purchasing the grace of Princes, whereby he came very soone to such reputation, as he was made a chiefe Magistrate of the Common wealth.

Now while in this Office, he endeauours to proceed with all sweetnes, and to gather the Imposts without exaction, or the offēce of any; it was not long, ere the weight of secular businesses appeared very grieuous, and the vanity of pompe & vayne felicity, came to be tedious to him. Wherwith he began to giue himselfe to prayer more then ordinary, to the vse of deuout bookes, and to conuerse with Religious: through whose conuersation he was well aduised that as transitory pleasures and delights, are not there among them, so are neither the disgusts, nor molestations of the world: he perceiued them secure, and free from calumnyes, and with holy loue to be most conioyned within themselues: he considered many yong men amongst them, who with a glorious victory ouer their appetits, cōserued perfect, and perpetuall chastity. With whose examples being moued, he did finally breake forth with himself, into these words.

Alas! we wretches of the world to what end is all this toyling, without hope of eternall goods! What shall the world be euer able to afford vs! If we like Ioy (though indeed better it were to mourne with safety, then to laugh with danger) how much more iocond are these men that haue the conscience setled & quiet in God! Who haue nothing to do with these Sergeants, or Prouost-Marshals! no feare, but of sinne: who attend to nothing but to obserue the diuine Precepts; nor are anxious a whit to loose their possessiõs, in gayning their lyuing with their proper hands, day by day. Let vs imitate so vertuous a people: Let vs likewise vndertake so commendable a a manner of life; and let not the light be in vayne which God hath giuen vs: Change we, our former customes, and alter we our employments, so farre forth, as whereas hitherto we haue contended with our friends about points of Nobility, we may now striue no lesse in pouerty with the seruants of God. If heeretofore, we applyed our selues to sollicite debtours, we may now attend to conuert Synners. Our Lord Christ, is wont to frame holy Doctours, euen of the profanest exactors. Frõ Custome-house it selfe was *S. Mathew* called to the Apostle ship: Which is not yet spoken to make comparison betweene him and vs, but only that if he hauing left the ministery of the Tole-howse, haue receiued the office of preaching, why may it not be lawful for me, laying downe my Procuratour-ship, to take penance in hand? Our refuge is God: whence I am not to feare at the age I am of, since he himselfe, who affoarded the gift of continence to so many yong men that liue in the Monastery, may likewise afford it me a Synner. With such thoughts as these reuolued in mind, at last he resolued to leaue wholy the delights of the world, and to giue himselfe to a Monasticall life.

S. Fulgentius *presents himselfe to Bishop* Faustus, *to be his Disciple. With the difficultyes he had with his Mother* Mariana. Chap. 2.

TRue it is, that not to passe with hazard from one extreme to another, *S. Fulgentius* began first to fast secretly, then to shunne by little and little, his ancient acquaintance, and now more then euer to attend to his deuotions. To which effect, being retyred into the country, through diuine grace, he went so farre, as that being yet a Layman, he seemed to be a perfect Monke. His familiars in the meane tyme, were astonished thereat; nor wanted there some, according to custome, who attributed such abstinence, & retirement of the yong man, vnto basenes of mynd, or to some other sinister accident. But he being enflamed euery day more & more, in the loue of perfection, while it seemed to him he had made sufficient proofe of himselfe, being touched with a discourse of *S. Augustin*, vpon the

36. Psalme, he determined to put off no longer the change of his habit, to discouer his vocation, and to quit himselfe wholy of the danger of those secular commerces, with further hope besides, to be able to helpe others with his example: and not without reason. For what man how meane a condition soeuer he were of, would once be ashamed, or affrayd to become a Monke, in beholding such a one as *S. Fulgentius* was, with so notable a contempt of all sensuality, and all greatnes, so to walke by the way of abstinence, and humility? And thus hauing great familiarity with the Bishop *Faustus*, who for the Catholique Fayth, being put forth of his Church, by the wicked King, had built him a monastery in those confines, and there liued very holyly with others; where it pleased *Fulgentius*, to linck himselfe with him, and vnder his obedience to dedicate himselfe to the diuine worship.

But he well vnderstanding the Parentage of the yong man, & how deliciously he had beene bred, began to suspect some manner of fiction in the matter, and said to him: Wherfore, my Sonne, do you iest so with the Seruants of God? For art thou likely to be a Monke, and to relinquish so on a sudden all thy delicacyes, and exchange thy banquets into grosse fare, and those sumptuous suits of apparell, into course and abiect clothing? Thou hadst first need to be a lesse dainety Lay-man, and so perhaps we shall belieue thou wilt, and mayst forsake the world. But the yong man, heerewith being more enflamed, taking, and reuerently kissing the hand of *Faustus*, with his eyes fixed on the Earth, replyed: He is well able, O Father, to giue me power, who hath affoarded me the will; do you but only giue me leaue to follow you: Open me the doore, admit me as one of your disciples, and God shall, I trust, find wayes inough to deliuer me from my iniquityes. The blessed old man hearing this, had a scruple to resist the diuine inspiration, and without more adoe, consented to the yong man, saying: Remayne thē with vs, my Sonne, as thou wilt thy selfe. Let vs try for some dayes, if deeds, will accord with words, or no: God graunt my feare may proue to be in vayne, and thy desire stable. And thus *S. Fulgentius*, being receiued into probation, the matter was sudenly diuulged, to the ioy of the good, & confusion of the wicked: nor was there wāting some of his deerest companions, that being prickt therewithal, euen spurned likewise at the world, and no lesse then he, became religious.

But the forlorne *Mariana*, as soone, as she had vnderstood what had passed, as if she had presently lost her Sonne, wholy anxious, and troubled, being full of teares and laments, flew immediately to the Conuent: Where being halfe besides her selfe, with a loade of Outrages, she began to exclayme agaynst *Faustus*, to render the Sonne agayne to his Mother, the Maister to his Seruants; and how it was no office of a good Priest, so to ruine the howse of a poore widow. Such words as these, notwithstanding were not of force inough to sting the prudent old mã; but rather with a fayre & serene countenance, compassionating the motherly affects, he so sought to appease her, as he suffered her not yet to see her sonne. Then *Mariana*, as knowing well, how much otherwise that sweet Child of hers esteemed and reuerenced her, and how great loue he bare her, thought it expedient to plant her selfe at the gate of the Monastery, and there to fix her selfe, as she did, lamenting outright, and with great exclamations exaggerating much her sad misfortune, in calling againe and agayne vpon her deer *Fulgentius* by name.

This first temptation, gaue a great shake to the good yong man, while the sighes and groanes of his so deere & louing Mother euen pierced him to the hart; but yet neuerthelesse, lifting vp his mind vnto heauen, with a pious cruelty enforced himselfe not to heare them; vntill such tyme, as being assisted by diuine grace, he remayned triumphant ouer flesh and bloud. Wherupon the blessed *Faustus*, not without cause framing a great conceipt of such a vocation, turning himselfe to the Monks, & with a cheerfulnes withall said to them: This yong man heere, shall well be able to suffer any paynes of religion whatsoeuer, since for Christ he hath beene able so to neglect the dolour of a Mother. Who going and comming to and fro more then once, after in vayne she had giuen many molestations to the Bishop, and layd many snares before her Sonne, being now quite tyred withall, she finally gaue ouer.

S. Fulgentius *makes a donation of all to his Mother: And was afterwards terribly persecuted by an* Arrian *Priest*. Chap. 3.

IN the meane while, *S. Fulgentius* giuing himselfe to the maceration of the body, among other voluntary afflictions, & austerityes, did wholy absteyne, not only from wine, but euen from oyle also, being the common cates of those places. Whereupon in short tyme,

tyme he became to be spent, in such sort, as the withered skinne was cleft on all sides, and by litle & litle all filled ouer with a scab. Whence truly, whereas some thought he should be faigne to coole & languish in diuine seruice, he endeauoured notwithstāding to go alwayes forward, and to attend to the health of his soule, remitting that same of the body, to the prouidence of the Creatour; & was not a whit deceiued of his trust the while, since without other help, his health was very soone restored him agayne to the great consolatiō of all. And now the tyme of renunciation being come, he thought it expedient to make a free donation of all his goods vnto his Mother, as well to solace there with the sad desolation of the afflicted widdow, and likewise to bridle a certaine obstinate and stiff-neckt yonger Brother of his, making accompt, that the feare at least of loosing his goods, would force him so to be very tractable, and obedient to his Mother.

After this, there arising a new persecution agaynst the Catholique Bishops, *Faustus* was enforced to fly away, and to hide himselfe heer and there, to the great domage & preiudice of his Monks. Whereupon *Fulgentius*, with his leaue retyred himselfe into another Monastery thereby, where a great friend of his, by name *Felix* was Superiour, who knowing the worth and sanctity of *Fulgentius*, receiued him not only with great content, but further vsed all industry, to substitute him in the gouernement: which being not able to gayne of *Fulgentius*, after a long contention and strife betweene them about the matter of subiection, he obtayned at last, he would accept of part of the rule and gouernement: and so was the care deuided betweene them both, in such sort, as *Fulgentius* presided, and had the care of the spirituall matters, and *Felix* of the temporall affayres. In which offices they both demeaning themselues with great concord, and much edification, there happened a sudden incursion of the Moores: whereupon, the holy Family was constrayned with theyr Pastours to forsake that country, & to seeke them a securer mansion in parts more remote.

Now then, after a long voyage, and sundry aduentures had, being arriued at last, at the fruitfull territory of *Sicca*, they were inuited, as well through the quality of the soyle, as the gentlenes of the inhabitants to remayne there, as they did, attending ech one to his office, and especially *Fulgentius*, to reduce the Heretiques vnto the true fayth, and to help those soules both with wordes and examples

examples in all vertues. There preached at that tyme in the villagē of *Babardilla*, an Arrian priest, very rich in substance, in behauiour barbarous, and a most cruell persecutour of the Catholiques. This man, vnderstanding of the life, and goodly workes of *S. Fulgentius*, and suspecting he was come, vnder the false habit of a Monke to alienate men from Arianisme, laying some wayt and ambushes in diuers places, caused him, and his Collegue *Felix*, to be taken and brought before him, and with fierce eyes, and a wry countenance sayd to them: Wherefore are you come hither from your house to peruert the Christians? And without otherwise attending an answere, commaunded them to be cruelly beaten.

When the good *Felix*, being moued with compassion, for *S. Fulgentius*: Be not (sayd he) so cruell against this my Brother, and companion heere, being so tender of complexion, as he is like to dye in your hands; but do you wreake your selues rather on me alone, for all the fault is in me only. With which words, the Minister of the Deuill being astonished, made *Fulgentius* awhile to stand aside, and more seuerely appoynted *Felix* to be smitten then before; who amidst the blowes of the hangmen, tempered his sorrow somwhat with the ioy he had to behold *Fulgentius* exempted. But this contentment of his, lasted not long: forasmuch as that wicked *Arrian*, being pushed thereunto of his natiue fiercenes, after he had so ill intreated the one, began to handle the other worse; nor sufficed the example of so rare a charity, nor the noble and venerable aspect of *S. Fulgentius*, to moue his obdurate hart to compassion.

But *S. Fulgentius* rather amidst the smart of the blowes, (which to him was as it were intolerable,) hauing with humble voyce, demaunded so much fauour, as to speake some three or foure words, he gaue him truce and respit the while, as thinking him enclined to confesse the Arrian opinions, and to renounce the ancient religion: but noting him to enter into a formall discourse, about giuing accompt of their life and pilgrimage had; being fraught with rage, he caused him to be more, cruelly intreated then euer; & lastly shauing & stripping them both, bad them be gon: and they reioycing within themselues, for hauing suffered for Christ, so dispoyled of their rayments, but inuested with glory, returned home to their Cells agayne.

The fame, and rumour of this accident, *S. Fulgentius* himselfe being a personage so illustrious as he was, dilated it selfe to the Generall

nerall discontent of all, euen to the Citty of *Carthage*. So farre forth as the Bishop of the Arrians himselfe, resented it much, & was ready to make demonstration therof, if the offended had made but any complaint therof, at all. Whereunto many exhorting *S. Fulgentius*, he suffered not himselfe to be induced; neyther withal their persuasions nor yet with the grieuousnes of the iniury receiued to seeke reuẽge, saying, that besides that such things are to be remitted to God, it would be also a scandall to see a religious Catholique man, to recurre to the tribunall of an Arrian. Howbeit, to mitigate the fury & persecutiõ of that peruerse sect, he determined to go into some place where it ruled not. Wherfore withall his Monks, he passed to his former dwelling, as choosing rather, to haue the Moores his Neighbours, then the Heretiques.

S. Fulgentius *leaues* Carthage, *and goes to* Alexandria, *where he met with* Eulalius *Bishop: and returnes back againe by* Rome. Chap. 4.

NOt farre from the Citty of *Loda*, began *S. Fulgentius* and *Felix* to found them a new Monestery: Where while they attended to their accustomed offices of piety, *S. Fulgentius* lighted on a booke of the Liues and spirituall Conferences of the Monks, and Hermits of Egipt. Through this reading and meditation, he became so enflamed to the greater study of al perfect vertue, as without more ado he resolued to go his wayes secretly into those parts, as wel to lay off the name, and charge of Abbot; as also to tye himselfe to a more rigorous and streight Rule. Which mutation of place, was in those dayes tolerated, in certaine Religious, as then not hauing made any expresse vow of any particular congregation.

So as *S. Fulgentius*, vnder the pretext of dispatch of some affayres in *Carthage*, being arriued to the wals of that Citty, with only one companion, by name *Redemptus*, insteed of entring into the Towne tooke shipping for *Alexandria*, without other viatique with him, thẽ a firme confidence in God, through whose disposition being caryed by the winds to *Siracusa* of *Sicily*, he there met with the holy Bishop *Eulalius*, a person of great sanctity, and much affected to Religious persons, as hauing moreouer a proper Monastery of his owne where he would recollect himselfe sometymes from his other Ecclesiasticall occupations. *S. Fulgentius* with other Pilgrims being courteously receiued by this good Prelate, while at table they dis-

 coursed

coursed of spirit and learning, it could not be, but the wise & prudent Bishop, must needs be aware of his doctrine and sufficiency. After dynner then calling him aside, he sayd to him: Thou madest mention at table of certayne Institutes, and Collations of the Fathers, I pray thee now, bring me the Booke if thou hast it: which *S. Fulgentius* did without delay, and withall at the earnest instance of the *Bishop*, declared the whole argument therof, in a few and very apt words.

The *Bishop* admiring the yong mans wit and erudition, and solacing himselfe, with hauing such a Ghest in his howse, began familiarly to request of him an accompt of his trauayle. And *S. Fulgentius*, to couer with humility his designe, said he went to seeke his Parents, whome he vnderstood to liue in the parts of *Egipt*; & he said but truth in saying so, since he held allthẽ for his parents, that might further him in spirit. The Bishop perceyued the answere was ambiguous, & easily gathered by discourse from the other cõpanion, who was a man of much simplicity, what passed in effect: When the blessed *Fulgentius*, now finding himselfe besides expectation, to be be discouered, confessed of himselfe, how the matter stood with him; to wit, that he had left his home, with the mynd to enter into the inmost solitude of *Thebais*, to be able there, being altogeather vnknowne, and dead to the world, to lead his life more perfectly, with hauing euery day new examples of vertue and pennance from so great a number of the seruants of God. Thou doest well answered *Eulalius*, to desire continually a greater perfection: but know on the other side, it is impossible for any to please God, without the true fayth. The land wherto thou tendest, is separated now long since from the Sea Apostolique. Al those Monkes, whose rigour and abstinence is growne so renowned, will beware of communicating with thee. And then what shall it auayle thee, with fastings to afflict the flesh, while the soule shall want its nourishment? Wherefore returne my Son, whence thou camest, least while thou desirest a more holy conuersation, thou sufferest shipwracke of a sound Religion. I likewise, for my part in my youth, before vnworthy as I am I was assumpted to this degree, haue had the selfe same thought, which now thou hast, but the respect which I now told thee of, did quit me of it.

The blessed *Fulgentius*, yielded to the counsayles of the holy *Bishop*: yet neuerthelesse, for the more perspicuity in that point, iudged

ged it expedient, to seeke also thereupon the iudgment of the *Bishop Ruffinianus*; who being fled out of *Affricke* for the persecution of the *Vandals*, as hath been sayd, hid himselfe vnder a monasticall life, in a certayne litle Iland neer vnto *Sicily*. From whome hauing likewise receiued the same answere without seeking any further, he determined by all meanes to returne backe agayne; yet so as he fayled not by the way, to repayre, of meere deuotion, to the Citty of *Rome*. Where after he had humbly visited those holy places; it chanced besides, beyond expectation, that he was present there, at a spectacle of the greatest pompe & magnificence of that Court; there ariuing at the same tyme, *Theodoricke* King of the *Gothes*, where in a place called the Golden Palme, he made a speach to the whole Nobility, distinguished according to the degrees, and the honour of ech one: and where likewise were heard the acclamations and applauses, which the people vniuersally gaue.

Through which sight notwithstanding *S. Fulgentius* being nothing caught with those transitory things, but lifting rather vp the mind and affect to the celestiall glory, sayd to his Friends: How beautyfull trow you, must the heauenly Hierusalem needs be, since *Rome* so glitters heere beneath? And if heere in this world, so great a pompe and splendour be affoarded to the friends of vanity; what glory trow you, and triumph, is due in the other to such as contemplate the truth? And after he had spoken many things to this purpose, with the profit and consolation of the hearers; taking his iourney againe, with diligence, he passed into *Sardinia*, and from thence into *Affrick*, where he was receiued with extreme ioy, not only of the Monks, but euen of the lay men also, & strangers there; among which, a wealthy gentleman, noting with how much perill and incommodity, the seruants of God there inhabited in those confines, being moued of piety, offered them a good and secure scituation in the Prouince of *Bizacco*. Which proffer *Fulgentius* accepting, with great thanks, heere founded a new howse, with a notable increase of Monks, and extraordinary helpe of soules in those countryes.

S. Fulgentius *to shun the title of Abbot, hides himselfe in vayne: & shunning afterwards a Bishopricke, is made Bishop of* Ruspa. Chap. 5.

NOtwithstanding the great pleasure and contentment, which *S. Fulgentius* tooke on the one side, for the great fruit of soules which was made, yet on the other he felt exceeding sorrow, in perceiuing himselfe by such occupations much hindred from his vnion with God, and sweet contemplation of inuisible things. Besides the which, the tytle of *Abbot* and charge of commaunding others, was of small contentment to him, while he called to mynd that Christ our Lord himselfe, had sayd, that he came to serue, and not to be serued, and to performe not his proper will, but that of the eternall Father. With such kind of thoughts as these, being newly pushed on to abase, and hide himselfe by all meanes; after a long consideration, at last he tooke the resolution, which we will shew you now.

There washes the banckes of *Vinci*, and *Bennese*, an arme of the Sea, full of shelfs and rockes. In the one of which, being so dry as day by day, they were fayne to procure fresh water to be brought them with litle boates, was found to be a Conuent of Monks, who vnder the care of two Reuerend Prelats there, perseuered in extreme pennance, and pouerty. To this Monastery now the blessed *Fulgentius* being retired, he began to relish agayne the desired fruits of a priuate life, and of holy humility, mortifying through obedience all proper will, in taming continually the flesh with fastings, prayers, and vigils, and diuing at pleasure into the profound mysteryes of the Eternity: and yet interupting withall, at tymes, his mentall exercises, in copying forth, with his owne hand, some good booke or other, which he could do very excellently well; or els in weauing, for sundry vses, the leaues of Palmes, wherin likewise he had beene very dexterous heertofore; so as it seemed to him he was now in that state he wished for so much: but yet was it not affoarded him, to remayne therein, as long as he would.

Because that *Felix* his Collegue, and the other his Monkes, hauing notice thereof, first of all, vsed all the meanes possible they could themselues, to haue him agayne: but while their prayers and persuasions, were not of force thereunto, they finally interposed the authority of the Venerable *Faustus* the Bishop, by whome

S. Fulgen-

S. Fulgentius was constrayned at last, to returne backe agayne; and to the end, he might be engaged to remayne there with a new obligation, he was forthwith ordayned both Priest and Abbot: with which chaynes being now tyed, he began to set his hart at rest, and to attend with all study and care, to that which God had commended vnto him: whereupon in short tyme was spread so good an odour, as the Abbot *S. Fulgentius*, in all that territory was held to be a common Father and Pastour of all, with a vniuersall desire to choose him, and no other for Bishop, when tyme should serue: of which conceipt *S. Fulgentius* was aware, but in regard that as then, by Edict of King *Trasamond* the ordinations of Bishops were prohibited, he was acquit of all doubt thereof, esteeming it in vayne to fly the dignities, which could neyther be giuen, or taken.

But after that, the holy Colledge of Bishops yet remayning, through zeale of the diuine glory, and the common good, with publike Decree had freely defined, that notwithstanding the Kings prohibition, ordination of Bishops should be made in euery Diocesse, and heerupon that holy decree was begun to be executed on all sides: & the people, the while striuing to appeare no lesse pious and diligent then others, heere it was, that the blessed *Fulgentius*, went about to preuent their designes, and to hide himselfe in such wise, as there was no possible meanes to find him out. So as the inhabitants were fayne to resolue to expect till such time, as he might appeare in sight; but fearing in the meane while, some new inhibition should proceed from Court, they were enforced agaynst their wills to make one of their Clerks, a Bishop: and so in a very short space, were almost all the Churches furnished with Pastours, and that with so great dislike of the King, as he tooke order to banish the Bishops, and caused the Archbishop *S. Victor* himselfe to be cast into prison at *Carthage*, to the great lamentation, and disturbance of the Catholique part.

The which as soone as *S. Fulgentius* vnderstood, as thinking himselfe to be now out of all daunger of any such honour, he stayd not a whit from returning agayne to the custody of his litle flocke. But it pleased the diuine prouidence, that the humble Seruant of God should be deceyued of this purpose. Forasmuch indeed, as among those people which as yet now were destitute of a Bishop, was that of *Ruspa*, a famous Citty and very full of rich and noble inhabitants. Which delay of theirs, had sprung from the ambition of a certayne Deacon there, one *Felix* by name, who the more audaciously he pretended to the Chayre, was the more maynely resisted by good men: and though himselfe, through fauour of his kindred and friends, had a faction sufficient to hinder others from the dignity, yet not inough it seemed to procure it to himselfe.

Among those discords, and ciuill broyls, it was sudainely vnderstood, that *S. Fulgentius*, who could neuer be discouered before, at the tyme of the creation past, did now appeare at last. In the meane while, the Arch-Bishop, happening to passe by *Ruspa*, in his conduction to *Carthage*, the Gentleman of the Citty, with some Catholique Bishops there, had accesse vnto him, and easely obteyned full licence, to create *S. Fulgentius* the Pastour of *Ruspa*. Heereupon many Cittizens with great hast presented themselues to the Seruant of God, who remayned in his Cell infirme of his eyes, & so taking him vp as it were, on their shoulders, with mayne force they led him into their countrey, and then consecrating him with due ceremonyes, placed him in the Pontifical seate. But in conducting him thither, there happened a notable thing which followes.

A Deacon layes an ambush to assayle S. Fulgentius, *but missed of his purpose. He is confined afterwards with other Prelats into the Iland of* Sardinia. Chap. 6.

THE foresaid Deacon, hauing taken vp the way with a strong guard, to hinder the passage of *S. Fulgentius*, his company the while through the secret instinct of heauen, tooke another way; & so was the aduersary illuded, and the new Bishop, with common iubiley, & with solemne preparation, hauing publiquely said Masse communicated the faythfull with his owne hands; and then after to vanquish euill, according to Christian perfection, endeauoured to honour his enemy *Felix*, in making him Priest: the which dignity in those dayes, was esteemed according to the merit and greatnes of the degree. But howbeit *S. Fulgentius*, so benignly remitted the offence; yet so passed not the malice without due punishment: since *Felix* dyed within a yeare, and the publique Procuratour of *Ruspa*, who had beene his principall Fautour, being so potent as he was, came sudenly to loose his riches, and to fall into great streights, and necessityes. Whence the others, were brought to dread the diuine iudgments, and for euer after to haue the blessed *Fulgentius* in greater veneration.

Whose

Whoſe vocation, as it had beene wholy ſincere and celeſtiall, ſo it affoarded a large feild to the holy man, to manifeſt himſelfe to be alike inuincible in proſperity, and aduerſity: which he was to the full, while in ſuch a mutation of eſtate, with ſo moderate a decorum of his perſonage, he alwayes reteyned, not only the ſame meekenes and affability, but euen likewiſe the monaſticall habit, & clothing as before: nor ſo much as in his diet he made any alteration at all, ſaue only for age he was conſtrayned to vſe the ſeaſoning of oyle, and when he fell ſick, to mingle his water with a little wine, ſo as qualifying only the rawnes therof, he felt no whit of the ſent, or fauour of that precious liquour. In the night, riſing alwayes before others, he endeauoured to reſtore vnto ſtudy and prayer, thoſe howers, which the occupations of the day, for the publique neceſſity, had wreſted from him. He was neuer ſeen to inhabit in any place, without the company of his Monks. But rather the firſt fauour, which he demaunded of the Cittizens of *Ruſpa*, was, the commodity of building there, a conuenient Monaſtery for his rule. In which many ſtriuing to haue the merit therof, it pleaſed him to make vſe of the charity of one *Poſthumianus*, a moſt principall Gentleman of vertue, and of bloud, from whome hauing a fayre ſcituation affoarded him ſomewhat neere to the Church, with a pleaſant groue of Pynes, which ſerued likewiſe very fit for the fabrique, he conuayed the Abbot *Felix* thither with almoſt all his congregation, leauing only ſome few Monkes in the other, vnder the care of one *Vitalis*; yet in ſuch ſort he did it, as both the Conuents did liue with the ſame diſcipline, and communicated together, not as gheſts and ſtrangers, but as Brothers and members of the ſame body. And the bleſſed *S. Fulgentius*, howbeyt moſt ſeriouſly buſyed in his Dioceſſe, fayled not the while to haue ſtill a paternall care & prouidence of the one and other.

In the meane while the King of the *Vandals*, hauing already confined the Catholique Biſhops to *Sardinia*, ordayned likewiſe that *S. Fulgentius* ſhould be carryed thither. Which ſucceeded to the great comfort of thoſe innocent Prelates, ſince they reaped not only a notable help from the learning, and conuerſation of the holy man, but likewiſe in the publique acts of that ſacred Colledge, and in the particular occurences of their Churches, they did greatly auayle thēſelues, of the ſuccour and charity of *S. Fulgentius*, as being very eloquent in tongue and pen: ſo as all the letters they had to ſend, for

matters

matters of importance, were dictated by him, and if any were fit to be reprehended, or admonished, or els to be reconciled vnto the Church, the charge therof, was most commonly recommended to him.

And for asmuch, as according to custome, S. *Fulgentius* had departed from *Affricke* exceeding poore, and without prouision, and accompanyed only with a few Monks, he perswaded two of the number of those Bishops, to wit, *Illustris* and *Felix*, with their domestiques to lead with him, in the Citty of *Calari*, a religious and common life: so as they being assembled togeather, and sweetely lincked with the band of charity, both the Clerks and the Monks, had the same table, and the selfe same prayers, lessons, and spiritual exhortations. Whereby not only, those of the Conuent, but euen also, the others of the Citty were greatly assisted. There was no person distressed and afflicted, who in that holy place, found not refuge, none desirous of the word of God, who there might not freely heare the same; to the doubts of Scripture, and Cases of conscience, continually answere and resolution was giuen; Peace and concord put betweene playntifes, and enemyes; Almes dealt to the needy & necessitous. And particularly besides, S. *Fulgentius* would be euer ayding them, not only by absoluing them of their sinnes, but also following the Counsayles of Christ, in not reguarding therin, the litle or much substance they had to leaue, but the affect they shewed of a voluntary and full renunciation.

King Trasamond *seeks to entrappe* S. Fulgentius *with curious questions: and the* Arrian *Ministers do exasperate him agaynst him.* Chap. 7.

AT the same tyme, King *Trasamond* had found out another more subtile way to subuert the faythfull in *Affricke*, in pretending openly that he sought nothing els, but truth in all things, and sometymes proposing sundry demaunds and questions to simple Catholikes: and howbeyt, now and then neuerthelesse, there wãted not men sufficient inough, to cõuince their heresies; yet would the King seeme to make but light accompt of them, still vaunting himselfe to haue had the vpper hand in the disputes, and controuersies of fayth. Wherin, while he labored now with this man, now with that, he was put in mind of the blessed *Fulgentius*, as of a person of rare learning, and very able to solue all the knots and difficultyes,

cultyes occurring in such matters. So as sending a Messenger with diligence for him, he was conducted to *Carthage*: where in a poore lodging, the first thing he attended to (and not without fruite) was to confirme the Catholikes, and to informe the Heretiques of their blindnes, in prouing with liuely and pregnant reasons, that one only substance in persons distinct, was truly to be adored in the most holy *Trinity*. There being afterwards a writing presented vnto him, on the behalfe of the King, full of fallacyes, & cunning quircks and demands; he, inserting therewithall the words of the scripture it selfe, answered from point to point, with so much acumen, perspicuity, and breuity, as the King himself, though obstinate in his perfidiousnes, remayned astonished at the doctrine: and the people of *Carthage*, diuulging the said answere, continued more and more, well affected to the Catholique faith.

After this, the King not contented with the former demaunds, proposed yet some others a new, but without giuing leaue, or scope to *S. Fulgentius*, to answere with commodity, that he might not quote his words, as formerly he did, and giue the world to vnderstand the impertinency of them; but constreyned him rather, hauing read the paper, to help himselfe, what he might, with his memory, and to answere out of hand without more adoe. The which condition, seeming, as in truth it was, full of iniustice, the holy man for awhile, differred to make his reply: but the King imperiously pressing him to it, and attributing the caution to diffidence, least the Arrian Ministers might likewise seeme to do the same, & diuulge with their accustomed vanity, they had stopped his mouth; *Fulgentius* disposeth himselfe to answere vnto it the best he could, reducing to his mynd, what was but once permitted him to read, & in three little admirable Treatises of the *Incarnation of our Lord* (for the question of the King, was of that subiect) he apparantly shewed, how the same Sonne of God, equall in all, and throughout, to the eternall Father, in clothing himselfe with our mortality, tooke truly and really a reasonable soule.

With which wisedome and subtility of his, King *Trasamond* being much astonished, durst question him no more; howbeyt a false Bishop of his, called *Pinta*, rather through intemperance of tongue, then sufficiency of learning, would needes be replying, I know not what thereunto, giuing heerewith occasion to *S. Fulgentius*, to frame another worke therupon, to conuince anew the temerity, &

ignorance of the enemyes of *Christ*. There was likewise moued to him, a certayne controuersy, about the holy Ghost, by a Priest called *Abrazilla*, which further gaue a fit occasion to *S. Fulgentius*, to let it appeare, with many and cleare demonstrations, how the *Holy Ghost*, with the *Father*, & the *Sonne*, ought simply to be confessed one God. Which things, by how much they brought more honour and esteeme to the seruant of God, so much the more, the Ministers of the Deuill, conspired in one, to aduise the King, not to let the matter proceed any further, protesting withall the harbouring of such an aduersary in *Carthage*, would be the ruine of the Arrian religion, and that if he remedyed not the same in tyme, he would come shortly to haue so many Followers, as that with al the forces of the kingdome, they could hardly be resisted.

The King being terrifyed with these, and such like suggestiōs, though in a manner against his will, commaunded, without more delay, that *S. Fulgentius* should returne to his former confines, and for auoyding of all popular tumult, he should be embarqued in the night. Whereto he obediently yielded for his part; but the diuine Goodnes, being not willing, with such a departure, the faythfull should seeme to be depriued of the sight & comfort of such a Father; deteyned the ship so long, with contrary winds, in the Hauen, as well nigh all the Citty had space to salute him, and to receiue *the most holy Sacrament* at his hands: When behold a faire gale of wind now comming about, and a certaine religious man, one *Ginliatus* by name, among others bewayling his departure, the holy *Bishop* being moued to compassion vpon him, and full of a propheticall spirit, sayd cleerely to him: *Trouble not your selfe my Son, for soone shall this whole persecution cease, and we shall returne to you agayne: but I pray thee, keepe this secret, for I could not choose but discouer it to thee, being moued so with tendernes, and Charity towards thee.* And this *S. Fulgentius* added, for the great care he had to conceale his gifts, and to eschew all human glory, contenting himselfe the while with the testimony of a good conscience, and with the inward grace affoarded him; so as likely he did not, nor euer would worke Myracles: and if now, & then perhaps he did any, he would still rather attribute the same, to the fayth of another, then his owne vertue.

But for the most part, whensoeuer he was sought vnto, to pray to our Lord for the sick, and afflicted; he would frame his prayers, with these words, or the like: Thou knowest, O Lord, what is fit for the health

health of our soules, while thou succourest our corporal necessities, in such sort, as they hinder not the spirituall profit. He was wont to say, that the Gift of miracles serued not to make a man more iust, but to cause him rather to be renowned in the world: A thing truly, which auayles, but litle to eternall beatitude, where vertuous and hood men, howbeit obscure and vnknowne, are not hindred awhit from getting into Heauen. Though if we speake of supernaturall effects, those workes, which others performe in curing of bōdyes, seeme vnto me not to be so admirable, as those, which he wrought, in curing of Soules, in conuerting with his fayre exhortations, and good example, so many Heretiques to the Church, and so man sinners vnto pennance.

S. Fulgentius *builds him a new Conuent in* Calari. *The persecution ceaseth. Prelates are recalled from banishment.* Chap. 8.

VVIth these, and other the like exercises, which accompanyed *S. Fulgentius* still in ech tyme and place, being now brought backe to the Iland of *Sardinia*; he was agayne no small cōsolation, to the afflicted *Bishops.* And hauing led with him from *Affricke*, a good number of Monkes, with the leaue of *Brumasius* Bishop of *Calari*, he built him there a new Conuent without the Citty neare to the Church of *S. Saturninus*, attending with all care and sollicitude to conseue religious discipline most pure; hauing principally an eye, that none of the Monkes (who were about some 50. in number) should seeme to haue any thing proper. And for to take away all occasion thereof, he would himselfe distribute with great discretion, the necessary things appertayning to them, according to the forces and infirmity of ech one. True it is, that such, as enioyed any particular thing at his hands, he would require to be notable in humility: protesting vnto them, that in Congregations, whosoeuer receiues of the publique substance, more then others, becoms a debtour to each one of them, to whome the goods do belong; and how he cannot satisfy the debt, as iustice requires, without shewing himselfe very obedient, lowly, meeke, and tractable to all. By these waies, the *Saint* would seeme to remedy the scandals from such inequalityes.

And as he was exceeding sollicitous in preuenting the suites, requests, & importunityes of the Monkes, in giuing them before hād what reason or necessity required: so towards the importunate, & not resigned, he would shew himselfe to be very seuere, in denying them sometimes, euen that which they had otherwise deserued; affirming, that they should otherwise incurre the displeasure of the Highest, if they should desire things superfluous; and that it playnely denoted a weake spirit, and of litle vertue. Forasmuch as such as they, through a former renunciation now seeing themselues to be shut of all manner of trafficque, and gayne of the world, with such kind of demaunds, do seeme to supply the vse of trading. He addded moreouer, that such only are worthy of the name of religious, who mortifying quite their proper wills, are ready to will, and not to wil that only, which is insinuated to them by the Superiour. Nor made he any reckoning of those handy workes, not well conioyned with interiour acts: as wishing, that the spirit of deuotion, should be the season of ech operation. Besids, he would shew himselfe to be sweet and affable to all, without any arrogancy or imperiousnes awhit (though in his tyme, he knew also to vse due grauity;) and the subiect how simple and ignorant he were, had full freedome to make any request vnto him, and that as often as he would; & the good Father would likewise heare him with all patience, or without shewing himselfe weary, with reasons & examples, vntill such tyme as the party himselfe had freely confessed, he was throughly satisfyed and contented.

In this tyme of banishment, he wrote to those of *Carthage*, an Epistle of high Counsails, and Aduertisements, discouering among other things, with great cleerenes, the deceipts, & flatteryes wherwith miserable soules are conducted to Hell. And at the instance of one *Monimus*, a religious person, he cōposed two bookes *Of the remission of sinnes*, and instructed him besides, in the matter of *Predestination*, and of the differences of *Grace*. Moreouer, he sent often letters of edification into diuers places of *Sardinia*, and *Affrick*, & likewise to *Rome*, especially to the principall Senatours there, vnto Ladyes, & Widowes of good name. To *Proba*, the Virgin of Christ, he wrote two little bookes of *Fasting*, and *Prayer*. Furthermore with seauen bookes, he partly interpreted the doctrine of *Faustus*, a Frēch Bishop in the best sense, and partly also openly confuted some opinions of the same man, inclining to the Arrian sect. Which worke of his, well appeares, how gratefull it was vnto God, since scarcely had he finished the same, but the whole persecution ceased, by the death of of King *Trasamond*, and the succession of *Hilderick*, a person of meruailous goodnes, by whome the Catholike Religion was sudenly restored, and the Bishops recalled from banishment, according to the prophesy of the blessed *S. Fulgentius.*

That glorious troupe then of *Confessours* returned back agayne to *Affrick*, to the great consolation of the people there, being desolate and disconsolate so long, and was met with, and receiued, euen at the very sea side, by an infinite multitude of people, most especially for the loue of *S. Fulgentius*; at whose appearing in sight, were infinite cryes and shouts lifted vp to heauen, while euery one made hast to behold and salute him, and to receiue his benediction, and euen to touch at least, but the hemne of his garments. And so great was the concourse and presse of people, in conducting him with the others, to the Church of *S. Agileus*, that some Deuotes of his were fayne to make a ring, or circle about him, for to passe without perill.

S. Fulgentius *at his arriuall puts himselfe into a Monastery agayne: and after reconciles himselfe to Bishop* Quod-vult-deus. *And so makes a blessed End.* Chap. 19.

THere happened likewise another notable thing in the same procession, which was, that the heauens being darkened on a suddayne, and a great shower of rayne powring downe, there was yet not a Man to be seen, that left the company, to retire himselfe to some shelter: but many rather, as in imitation of *Christ* our *Lord* in *Hierusalem*, in taking off their proper cloakes, made very readyly a Pent-house therof, for to shelter the Blessed *Fulgentius*. Who were able to explicate the welcomes, with the honours, and festiuityes, which were made him, first in the Citty of *Carthage*, and after in all the countryes, and lands where he happened to passe through in returning to his Diocesse? With all which things notwithstanding, that noble Follower of Christ, was not only not proud awhit, but eueͯ as soone as he arriued at his Church, put himself anew into his Monastery, very freely deposing all superiority of the Conuent; in so much as the publique gouerment of the Church, depending wholy on him, yet in the domesticall and dayly discipline, he would humbly depend on the *Abbot Felix*.

In the rule of the Clergy moreouer, he had a singular care, to prohibite all wanton and costly apparell, and to prouide, that for secular busynesses, none should be absent from home, or exempt frõ the Quire; for which cause he would haue all to inhabite close to the Church, and for the tyme they had to spare, they should spend partly in cultiuating some litle garden, with their hands, partly in exercising themselues in singing of psalmes, and pronouncing the words very wel. He ordeyned besides, that all the Clerks, and all the widdowes, and likewise all the other Laymen, who had no iust impediment, should fast on the Wednesdayes & frydayes throughout the yeare, and that all should be present euery day at the diuine Offices. He would chastize the vnquiet, as need required, now with priuate and publike reprehensions, now with pennances, & scourges, to the end, that with the penalty of one, all the other might take example. Through which proceeding, and perpetuall innocency of his manners, he was now in such veneration, as not only his subiects, but euen very strangers also that were well disposed, would remit their contentions and strifes, though neuer so spleenfull and inueterated, to the arbitrement and decision of the *Saint*: and among others, the people of *Massimiana* who by no meanes would accept the Bishop that was ordayned them, were finally with the authority and admonishments of *S. Fulgentius*, well pacifyed with him, putting an end to that so contumacious, and scãdalous a contention between them.

Notwithstanding all this, the *Saint* wanted not his contradictours, and emulous, as is wont to happen; whome he striued to ouercome which patience, and submission. Among others, a certaine Bishop by name *Quod-vult-deus* seemed to take it very grieuously, to haue *S. Fulgentius* preferred before him, in the Councell of *Vinci*. Whereof the Seruant of God being aware, expected the occasion of the *Suffetan* Councel: And at the commencing therof, sought and obteyned with an excellent example, there to haue the lower place of the aforesayd Bishop; endeauouring with such an act of humility to reconcile vnto him, and to gayne that soule, though without any fault of his so disgusted and alienated from him. Now heere what will they say, who are euery foote striuing for precedence? Let them learne heere of the blessed *Fulgentius*, to execute the precepts of *Christ*, and to seeke alwayes the lowest place.

In Sermons moreouer (wherof he made, and wrote many) he was wont to haue reguard not to the applause a whit, but rather to the motion and compunction of the people. Wheerin he had so great

great a grace, as that (among other tymes) preaching once two dayes together one after the other, at the dedication of the Church of *Burni*, euen *Boniface* himselfe *Bishop* of *Carthage* being there present, could by no meanes hold from weeping out-right, in giuing God thanks, for that of his infinite mercy, there were alwayes found very excellent Doctours in the Catholique Church. After his returne frō banishment, besides the Sermons and Bookes already written, he wrote anew ten others, against the lyes and falshods of *Fabianus*; & three of *Predestination*, and *Grace*. Amidst such manner of exercises as these, *S. Fulgentius* approaching to the end of his life, as presaging what was shortly to follow, with a few Brothers for a yeare before retyred himselfe a fresh, to do pennance, and bewayle himselfe, in a little rock of the Iland of *Cercinna*, vntill such tyme, as through the prayers and lamentations of such, as he had left behind him, he was constreyned to returne to his Diocesse againe, and to resume the gouerment.

But long it was not, ere he fell into a grieuous infirmity, which for 70. dayes afflicted him sorely, with most bitter paynes; wherein looking vp to heauen, he was wont to vtter no other words, then these: *Lord, do thou giue me now patience, and afterwards indulgence.* Finally feeling the houre of his passage to approach, and calling all the Clerks and Monks vnto him, he humbly besought pardon of them, if perhaps he had disgusted any, praying withall our Lord God, to prouide them a good Pastour. After this he disposed of the monyes, which as yet were left him, as a most faythfull Steward, as he had alwayes beene of the Ecclesiasticall rents: and recounting by name, all the widowes, Orphans, Pilgrims, & other of the poore, as well of the Lay, as Clerks, one by one, he ordayned what he had to be giuen by poul, without leauing so much as a farthing vnbequeathed.

Heereupon, turning himselfe to prayer, and tenderly blessing as many as entred vnto him, he remayned in his senses and iudgment vnto the last breath, which he rendered vp to our Lord, towards the Euening, in the yeare of our Lord 461. on the first day of Ianuary, in the 65. yeare of his age, which was the 25. of his Bishoprike. In the meane space, while the prouince of *Bizacena*, was sacked, and harrowed with fires and assaults of Moores, the country and Citty of *Ruspa* (through the merits doubtles of the holy *Pastour*) had alwayes enioyed a secure and quiet peace. His body was watched

ched all the night, with psalmes, and spirituall Canticles. Then the morning being come, with an infinite concourse of people, he was carryed, and layd by the hands of Priests, in the Church which is called *Secunda:* Where himselfe had deuoutly placed the venerable Reliques of the Apostles; and where for the reuerence of the place, till that tyme, no man had beene buryed.

FINIS.

S. THEO-

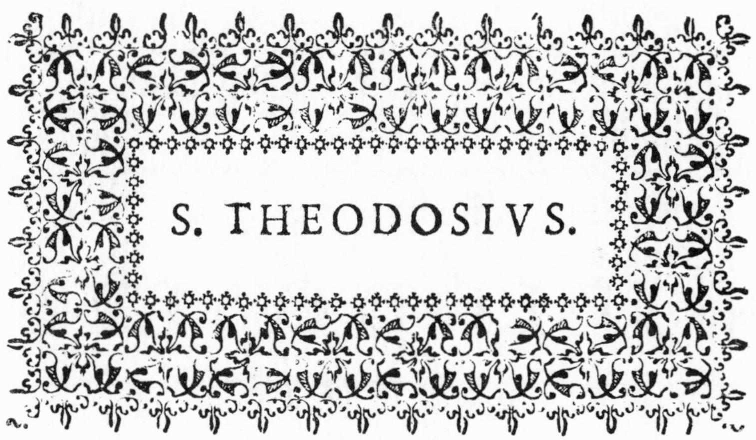

THE ARGVMENT.

DEare Saint: The ancient Ages did esteeme
Thy Country-men * as Pigmyes; so they seeme
Compard to others: yet thy Towring mynd
Did ouerlooke the world, which thou didst find
A painted Harlot, whose discoloured face
Did maske in faygned beauty, borrowed grace.
Her thou discouering with a piercing eye,
Such base indearments quickly didst descrye,
And taughtst to others: thousãds didst thou free
When her impostures blazond were by thee.
Both friend and foe one action doth auerre,
Thee to the world no friend, no foe to her.
Might tyme, but like the billowes of the maine
Reduce it selfe into its spring agayne;
Or Eagle-like could once it selfe renew,
That we its ancient offspring might reuiew;
We should confesse, past Ages hardly saw
One from the world, the world more to withdraw.

* The Cappadocians vvere esteemed Pigmyes, as the Chaldean Paraphrase Ezech. 27. interpreteth the Hebrevv vvord.

THE LIFE OF
S. THEODOSIVS
ABBOT.

The Parents, Country, and Education of S. Theodosius: *His Vocation, and how he met with* Stelites. *With his arriuall afterwards at* Hierusalem. Chap. I.

THE great Father and Maister of Monks *S. Theodosius*, was one of the number of those, who not receiuing from their Natiue Countrey, eyther splendour or renowne, haue yet through their proper actions, and eminent vertues, enobled the same. The blessed Man, was borne in *Magariassus* of *Cappadocia*, a place obscure, and vnknown before, but after by so happy a plant, deseruedly famous and illustrious. His Parents were *Procesius* & *Eulogia*, both Christians, & according to the quality of the land there, very honourable, & wealthy. By these, the *Child* being nurtured with great care, both in the feare of God, and in some knowledge of good literature; assoone as he arriued to yeares of discretion, (as he was among other his gifts, of a prompt and ready wit, and of a cleare voyce, and distinct pronunciation) he was set to recite the diuine scriptures to the people assembled in the Temple, on determinate dayes. In which exercise, while

while many examples, & precepts of sanctity, were presented vnto him; and while he notes in the old Testament, the exact obedience of *Abraham*, in going forth of his Country, and sacrifizing his only begotten sonne; and in the sacred Ghospell considers the rewards proposed to such as leaue their Parēts, or goods for the loue of God; this doctrine anon sunck very deepe into the hart of the prudent youth: so as now generously contemning the delights of that age, & reiecting with a sterne brow, the subtile flatteryes of the Sense, he determined to walke by the narrow, and vnbeaten way, vnto the glorious confines of the true Beatitude.

To which effect, knowing what need there was of the celestiall grace, to obtayne it more easily, and in greater aboundance; the first thing he did, was, that recommending himselfe to God, he applyed his thoughts, vnto the pilgrimage of *Palestine*, to see & adore the Land, so dyed with the bloud, and printed with the steps of our Sauiour; and through the liuely memory of his cruell torments, to gather from thence aboundant fruite of spirit, and perseuerance. Such in summe, was the Vocation of *S. Thedosius*, while the *Councell* of *Calcedon* was then assembling. And forasmuch, as at that time, the fame of *Simeon Stelites* the Greater, was very illustrious, who neare vnto *Antioch*, standing day and night on the top of a pillar, wholy exposed to the iniury of the elements, to the great admiration of the world, performed very sharpe pennance; it seemed good to the deuout Pilgrime to go that way, to take thereby the benediction and spirituall precepts of so worthy, and admirable a personage. Trauayling then towards the same Countrey, he no sooner approched to that strange habitation, but that before he opened his mouth, he heard himselfe with a lowd voyce to be called vpon, and saluted by the holy old man, by his proper name; who hauing notice from Heauen of the quality and intention of this new Trauaylour, thus began to cry out at the first sight of him: *Thou art wellcome, thou man of God, O Theodosius.* At which very sound, the fresh Disciple of the eternall Wisedome, being stocke with astonishmēt, as it were, and prostrating himselfe on the ground, most humbly saluted him agayne, and then recollecting himselfe from the feare he was in, and with a set ladder getting vp the Pillar; he was not only most deerely imbraced by *Simeon* but also fully certifyed of all his future euents and aduentures, of the numerous rationall flocke, which in processe of tyme, he was to assemble togeather, and to feed, and of the great multitude of soules, which he through diuine help, was in time to take forth of the iawes of the infernall wolfe; & as much also in summe, as in the whole course of his present life, through diuine disposition, were like to betyde him.

To this prophesy were adioyned counsayles, and exhortations, full of wisedome and truth; wherewith *S. Theodosius* being much comforted, very cheerfully proceeded in his way, and safely arriued at *Hierusalem*, while the Blessed *Iuuenall* did gouerne that *Metropolis*. Heere hauing visited with great cōsolation those most holy places, he began to thinke with himselfe, what manner of life, he might choose to discharge himselfe of all terrene affects, and to be vnited more easily with the eternall goodnes. A consultation by how much more necessary, so much the more dubious and perplexed it was vnto him, as appeares in the Chapter following.

The conflict S. Theodosius *had in himselfe about his vocation; with his resolution thereupon. And how fearing Prelacy, he flyes into a Caue.* Chap. 2.

THeodosius heereupon, on the one side, felt himselfe to be carryed with a vehement desire vnto solitude; while to him it seemed that therein, without al impediment, he might giue himselfe wholy to Prayer; and on the other, he was not ignorant, how dangerous it was, with a mind not fully purged, to depriue ones selfe of all human direction, and succour: since that in the desart, the disordinate passions, like fire raked vp in the ashes, or as wild beasts in the woods, do lurke, & awayt occasion, to wreake their natiue cruelty: Whereas amidst human Society, they being discouered through dayly encounters, and thrust out of their dens; are more easely destroyed; insomuch, as the Soule victorious of it selfe, and dissolued from the bands of corrupt nature, mounts vp very lightly vnto high thoughts, and to the free contemplation of celestiall things. These, and other such like reasons, on the one and other side, this new Philosopher puts into the ballance, and hauing poysed them maturely, in the diuine sight, at last takes himselfe to the securer side, with resolution to become, not a Doctour before a Scholler, & not enter on the stage, before he had learned the art of fencing. So as being aduertized, that in *Dauids* Tower (a place so called in those parts) was an old souldiour of Christ liuing, by name *Longinus*, growing

ing into friendship with him, he easily obteyned to be admitted into his howse, to be guided and instructed by him, in all, and thoughout. Whereunto he disposed himselfe, with so great submission of the vnderstanding, and with so much feruour of the will, as that through meanes of the dayly exercise of vertues, and diligent instruction of the Maister, with the noble strife of his fellow-pupils, he became very sudenly perfect in the rules of profitably taming the flesh, of knowing and readily discerning of spirits, of restrayning with a hard hand the motions of pride; and finally to walke in the presence of God, with perpetuall recollection of the bodily senses, and of the powers of the soule.

S. Theodosius in this wise, hauing made, in monasticall profession, so notable a conquest of himselfe, as in the iudgement of all, he might well be a Guide, and Maister to others; notwithstanding seemed to himselfe only, to be still, but as it were, in the beginning. He had perseuered yet more yeares in the same schoole, if an impediment had not happened, which heere we shall speake of. A certaine pious, and honourable Matron, by name *Iulia*, hauing at her cost built a magnificent Temple, to the honour of the *Queene* of *Angels*, not farre off from the habitatiõ of *Longinus*, obtayned with great instance of him, that he would appoint *Theodosius* by name, to the custody of that sacred place, while things were preparing about the full exercise of Religion, with the choyce of Quiristers, & Clerks, & of all things els belonging to the splendour of diuine seruice therin. *Theodosius* was but vnwillingly drawne from his deere conuersation, and going thereupon to the said Church, remayned there vntill such tyme, as he thought he might well stay there without perill; but in processe of tyme, being aware how busines went, about preferring him to the formall Rectorship of that Colledge, he stayed not till the matter might be concluded, when he could not be able to make resistance; but in imitation of the *Sauiour* of the World, who in the like occasion, preuented before hand the inclinatiõ of the people, he fled away secretly vnto the top of a moũtayne, and got himselfe into a great caue, where by ancient Tradition, it is held the three *Magi* had lodged, when as they, hauing adored the King of Heauen, and illuded that King of the Earth, they returned from *Iudea*, into their country by stealth.

Heere now, *S. Theodosius* being quite rid of all disturbance, began that manner of life, which a good while since he had designed;

 where

where Prayer, and Psalmes, with order and deuotion seemed to hold their turns; the vigils often endured throughout the whole night, and the eyes were become a perpetuall fountaine of teares; to the habit, which was a grosse, and course Cassocke, his food suited very well, as being the rootes of hearbes, windfall acorns, the fruite of palmes, some pulse; or when these fayled, the shells of dates soaked in water. In this manner, the seruant of God, spent his dayes, with so much the more consolation, as he was further remoued from al testimony of men, that might put him into vayne glory and consequently diminish a good part of the merit. With this warinesse, concealed he himselfe to his power. But the diuine clemecy enclining alwayes to the vniuersall good, could not brooke so great a light, should be shut vp, & enclosed so in that horrid rock. Wherof assoone as some ray had appeared in those countryes thereabout, there wanted not Louers of the chiefest good, & contemners of the world to shew themselues; who to be guided securely to the end proposed, with all affection, craued to be admitted, and to enioy the instruction of *S. Theodosius*. To whome, though he to maintayne himselfe in his secret intention, would willingly haue giuen a constant repulse; yet remembring himselfe, of the prophesy of *Simeon Stelites*, & weighing the great seruice, which is done to the highest wisedome, in cooperating with it, to the saluation of soules; after he had excused himselfe, to those suiters some while, at last he permitted himselfe to be vanquished, & won, to accept them for his disciplíne, with reteyning alwayes in himselfe the interiour humility, as before, and a vigilant care of himselfe.

Two notable signes of the Prouidence of God, towards his Seruants in their greater necessities, through the prayers and merits of Saint Theodosius. Chap. 4.

IT followed hence, that *S. Theodosius*, shewing himselfe such a liuely mirrour of all laudable actions, increased day by day the cōceipt was had of the sanctity of the Superiour, being a thing of inestimable moment for the quietnes, cheerfullnes, and incitement of the subiects. And *God* cherished this opinion of others with meruaylous signes now and then. Among which was one, that the Feast of *Easter* being come, & the Monkes hauing a desire to keep that day sacred, and also very festiuall, with some recreation of the body

body and spirit; there was in that Hermitage, no oyle or bread, or any manner of food, to be had, for the purpose of such a Solemnity. Whereupon being sad and disconsolate, they stood, as it were, reflecting thereon and exaggerating their great misfortune. *Theodosius* heerwith, notes their countenances to be changed, and vnderstanding the occasion of their sadnes, commaunds on the Saturday ouer night, that an Aultar should be set vp, and some forme of a Refectory be put in order for the next day. Which thing, seeming very absurd to those, who knew the want there was of all manner of victual: Do you make ready notwithstanding, sayd *Theodosius*, what I bid to be done, and for the rest, take you no care: He that nourished so many thousands of *Israelites* in the desart, and after satisfyed fiue thousand persons, with fiue loaues of bread, will surely likewise haue compassion of vs, being now no lesse prouident, nor a whit lesse potent, then he was.

The venerable Father, had scarce made an end to speake, when behold, two Mules appeared, well loaden with all those nourishments, which were fit for the present solemnity, and monasticall professiō. Whereat they yeilding endles thankes to the diuine mercy and acknowledging the truth of the promisses, and efficacy of the prayers of the *Saint*, the sacrifice being finished the next morning, and the prouision disposed in order, they all very cheerefully refreshed themselues, in eyther kinds. And after some tyme, that poore family, falling into streights agayne, and euen ready to murmur thereat, not so firme and assured of the former succour, as deiected and oppressed with the present necessity; *S. Theodosius* encouraged them the while, with saying among other things: Who euer trusted in our Lord, and hath beene abandoned by him? Who hath euer faythfully depended on him, & hath not beene comforted? Let *Ieremy* the *Prophet* answere for me: he hath replenished ech soule, that was a hungry. Let *Iob*, and *Dauid* answere likewise: He prepares food for the crowes, and their yong ones. So as hence we may learne at last, how much the diuine Prouidence, excells any human industry, which euen of set purpose many tymes, lets things be brought to extremes, that the remedy may proue more gratefull, and be held more worthy of acknowledgement. And we plainely see the while, euen in this life also, how largely he requited all those things, which for his sake, we haue left in the world.

In this manner, went *S. Theodosius*, comforting those faynt minds

minds; when it pleased God, that a rich distributer of almes, riding along those craggy mountaines, to relieue certayne others in necessity, as soone as he approached to the side of *S. Theodosius* his Caue, perceiued on a sudden, his beast first of all to stand still, and then after to bend very violently that way; whereat the rider merueyling much, who as yet had no notice of the retirement of *S. Theodosius*, after he had a good while beene spurring and kicking the beast onwards in vayne, at last resolues to let the reynes go loose, and to see whither the secret instinct would seeme to lead him: and the beast therupō went directly to the vnknown caue, where the good man perceiuing with his owne eyes, the distresses of those religious there, did blesse the diuine Maiesty for the occasion affoarded him, to merit so, and redoubling the almes he intended to haue giuen vnto others, he left those soules, though feeble otherwise, & vnexpert Nouices, so prouided and contented withall, as they had a iust occasion, to rely euer after on the heauenly protection, & neuer more to make any doubt thereof.

The number of S. Theodosius *his disciples increaseth. He builds a more ample Conuent, according to the miraculous direction of God.* Chap. 4.

IN the meane tyme, with the fame of *S. Theodosius* increased the number of his Disciples, and Conuictours; insomuch as now the first habitation not sufficing, with all the cottages adioyning therunto, it was needfull for him, to apply himselfe to a formall building, that were capable of an extraordinary multitude; nor was it any difficult matter for him, to take such an enterprize in hand, while the wealthy and deuout persons of all those countryes therabout, so readily concurred thereunto. He stood yet a good while in suspence, about the election of the seate therof: in which consultation, hauing more then once considered many places, both neere and further off, he finally resolued to be certifyed of the best, and more gratefull to God, in the manner following.

He tooke then a Thurible in his hand, full of coles, and putting incense thereon, but without any fire, went his wayes through all the desart, deuoutly singing of prayers, very apt for the purpose, as these: O God, who by the meanes of many, and stupendious proofes, perswadedst *Moyses*, to take the gouernment of the *Israelits* in hand, and with them likewise, with affects aboue nature, procuredst

curedst him credit, who changedst the rod into a serpent, the sound into a leprous hand, and in a moment restoredst the same from leprous, as cleane and sound as euer; who conuertedst water into bloud, and the bloud agayne into water. Thou who with shewing the fleece, madst *Gedeon* secure of the victory. Thou who hast framed all things, and still conseruest the same. Thou who declaredst to *Ezechias*, with Sunne-dyall reuerst, the addition of his yeares. Thou who at the prayer of *Elias*, for the conuersion of Idolatours, didst send downe fire from Heauen, which in a moment, consumed both the victime, the moist wood, and the water thereabout, togeather with the stones of the Aultar themselues. Thou I say say, O Lord, who art now the same thou wast then; heare me also, thy poore Seruant, and vouchsafe to intimate to me, where it pleaseth thee, I should now erect a Temple to thy diuine Maiesty, and a dwelling for my children. And I shall vnderstand that plot, to like thee best, where thou shalt cause these coles to enkindle of themselues.

With these inuocations, went he circling about all those mountaynes, nor euer left, till he arriued at *Cutilla*, and the bankes of the lake *Assaltite*. But seeing the coales in the Thurible to be yet cold, and dead, laying the default on his demerits, he returned against his will; when not farre from the Caue, he suddenly sees a smoke to rise vp from the coles, through diuine power, as it were, enkindled of themselues. Wherewith, being fully satisfyed of the diuine will, while the large contributions of the faythfull fayled him not; first of all, he began to erect a Church, with diuers Chappells, & Quires, distinguished in such sort, as without hindering one another, the sacred Offices, might there be sung at the same tyme, in sundry languages, by seuerall nations. Whence it was afterwards, a thing of great consolation to heare Psalmes, and Hymmes sunge at once with order, and sweetnes, by *Palestines*, *Bessians*, *Greeks*, and *Armenians*.

The house of God being finished, he passed to that of Men, with such distinction, and so much scope and amplenes, as that the first Cloyster was for the vse of the Monkes, with all the Offices requisite, and with a partition, which is called in the Greeke tongue, Γηροκομεῖον, for the commodity of such, as being toyled out with labours, and worne with yeares, were not able, to wield themselues, or keep them to the obseruance of the order. Next to the same, the Ghestory, or roomes for secular strangers; yet deuided into two parts, the one for persons of quality, the other for the meaner sort. Then followed the Hospitall of the poore, and sicke of euery sort, and in the last the lodgings of persons possessed with spirits. Because that among other workes of mercy, *S. Theodosius* gaue himself, with particular diligence most benignly to receiue a number of Hermits, who without first purging their soule with due remedies, through false apparence of good, and proud presumption of their owne knowledge, hiding themselues, some in this & some in that caue, were thereby, through the iust iudgement of God, most miserably abused and oppressed by the Diuell. To these, besids corporall sustenance, he would also giue wholesome aduises, and seeke to take away the false opinions from their mynds: and a good part of the tyme, which they had free from torments, he would cause them to spend in prayers, and psalmes. He would enter moreouer by day & night into the sickmens chambers; and with particulrar tendernes, comfort the lame, the wounded, and leaprous, feeding them with his owne hands, washing the stincking and noysome vlcers now of this, and then of that man, and lastly with frequent kisses, and amourous armes, be deerly imbracing them.

The great Hospitality of S. Theodosius *in the tyme of a Dearth, and how God concurred therwithall: with his great zeale for the* Catholike Church. Chap. 5.

AT the fame of so great charity of *S. Theodosius*, were a great nūber of persons of all qualityes, assembled together at the said place, to all which, with much patience, and with very good order, was both diet, and lodging affoarded: and it would fall out now, and then, especially at some principall Feasts of the *Mother* of God, that at diuers houres of the day, they were fayne to furnish a hundred tables. And there happening afterwards an vniuersal dearth almost through all the prouinces of the East, there came such a multitude to that noble Monastery, as that the Officers, fearing some disorder, resolued to keep them out of the Cloysters, and with exact measure to deale them victuals by weight. The which, as soone as *S. Theodosius* once vnderstood; confiding now more then euer in the diuine Goodnes, causing the gates to be set open, in the sight of all most cheerefully admitted the presse of people; and in vertue of his firme

firme fayth, and enflamed prayers, the prouision increased of it selfe in the Cellars and Pantryes, in such sort, as that all being satisfied at table, there was plenty inough yet left for such as wayted.

Among which occupations of theirs, by how much fuller of distractions, they are of themselues, so much the more vigilantly watched the good *Pastour* for the spirituall conseruation, and the interiour piety of his Monks, endeauouring by all meanes, that at certaine houres, they might be recollected in necessary meditation of vertues, and of the fruitefull acknowledgment of their owne defects; and to the end, the ordinary meanes vnto purity of hart, might not turne into ceremonyes, and their frequent victoryes occasion security, (to which perils, religious are commonly exposed) besides his owne example, as we sayd, with workes, he would likewise excite the Family frõ tyme to tyme, with enflamed words, as thus: I beseech you, would he say, my brothers, by that Lord who hath giuen himselfe for our sinnes, let vs once apply our selues in earnest, and truly indeed, to the care of our soules. Let vs bitterly bewayle our dayes vnprofitably spent, and endeauour not to loose those same which remayne. Let vs not suffer our selues to be slouthfull in sensuality; nor the occasions of this present day escape out of our hands, through the foolish hopes of the morrow, least death surprizing vs voyd of merits with the foolish virgins, we come to be excluded from the blessed nuptials, whence we shall afterwards bewayle, when it will be too late to repent. Behold now is the acceptable tyme, behold the day of saluation. This is the course of labours, that same shall be the ioy of rewards. This the sowing of teares, and that the fruite of consolation. For the present, God is very fauourable to such as conuert themselues to him: then shall he be a terrible Iudge, and a strict examiner of ech worke, word, & thought of ours. We now do enioy his *Longanimity*, then shall we experience his *Iustice*, when we come to arise agayne, some to eternall felicity, and others to the qualityes, and demeanours of ech one. How long then shal it be, ere were fully obey the counsayls of Christ, who with so especiall a vocation inuites vs to the heauenly kingdome? Shall we not awake from the sleepe of slouthfulnes? Shall we not rayse our selues from baser thoughts, to Euangelicall perfection? And yet, forsooth, we professe to aspire to the cou͂try of the blessed, and on the other side, we forslow the meanes that leades vs to it. And surely this is a great vanity of ours, that flying the

the labours of the warfare, we should promise to our selues the crownes of the victory.

With such like reasons, *S. Theodosius* awaked his subiects, and confirmed them, as need required, not only with ancient and moderne examples, but also with diuers authorityes of the sacred writ, explayning the difficult places thereof, with such clarity, and impressing them strongly with such an energy withal, as the Auditors remayned therewith much illumined in the vnderstanding, & enflamed in the will. He was moreouer exceedingly versed in the ancient Traditions, and in the Orthodox, and sincere doctrine of the *Fathers*, and especially of the Great *Basil*, whose writings, & principally those of monastical constitutions, he held in great veneration. Nor was this great zeale of his, restrained awhit within the bounds of that house, or among the inhabitants of that Prouince only; but nobly dilated it selfe vnto the common benefit of the Catholique Church, and to the conseruation of the right fayth, against the subtilityes, and lewd machinations of perfidious people, ambitious, & friends of nouelty, as appeares in the chapter following.

The ancient Heresies arising, are maynly resisted by S. Theodosius; *and for that cause he is banished by the Emperour: who dying shortly after, the Church flourished agayne.* Chap. 6.

THere arose agayne in those dayes, through the secret iudgemēt of God, reuiued by diuers Sectaries, worthily called *Acephali*, the pestiferous opinions of *Nestorius, Eutiches, Dioscorus*, and *Seuerus*, already condemned by foure Generall Councels, the *Nicen*, *Ephesin*, *Cōstantinople*, & *Calcedon*; and among the other multitude, was the *Emperour Anastasius* very miserably seduced by them, insomuch as he laboured to amplify his Sect, by all meanes possible. But the principall assault he vsed, was to gayne the holyer Prelates to him, or to take them away, by disquietting, and assayling now this, now that, by himselfe and his Ministers; now with prayers, and then with perswasions, now with monyes and titles, and then with menaces, depressions, and banishments.

In this manner, hauing tempted, and preuayled with diuers, he finally resolued to set vpon *S. Theodosius*, as seeming to himselfe, that he should make a great conquest, if he could but reduce an *Abbot* of so great a fame, and reputation vnto his part. To this intent, by by men for the purpose, he sent him letters, full of feygned friendship, peruerse counsayles, and deep malice, and for the greater efficacy, vnder the shew of piety, adioyned therunto a rich present, of thirty pounds of gold, for the holy man to bestow at his pleasure in workes of mercy. With this deuise the *Emperour* thought to batter the fortresse of *S. Theodosius*; but he found himself to be much deceyued of his presumption. For the *Seruant* of *Christ* indeed, accepted the gift, and faytufully shared it amongst the poore; but for the particular of Religion, most freely answered the *Emperour*, and his Messengers, that he would please not to enter into such practise with him, since he was fully resolued to loose not one life only, but a hundred liues, rather then once to mooue an inch from the doctrine of the vniuersall *Church*, and from the articles, and *Decrees* of the *Sacred Councells*.

To this effect was the answere of the glorious *Abbot*: which made such impression in the *Emperour* at first, as he being touched therewith, and acknowledging the errour, returned him fresh letters agayne, protesting those motions and troubles, wherein the Christians were then embroyled, were not caused, or occasioned by him, but through the pride, and vnquiet nature of some Priests, from whome particularly he should rather haue expected all care, to maintayne the people of God in peace, and concord. Wherefore now the more earnestly, he exhorted the *Blessed Father*, to continue still in his good purposes, and to renforce, togeather with the other Monks, the vsuall prayers for the quiet of the common wealth. Such demonstrations as these, for that time *Anastasius* shewed being of a better mynd; but (as he was of a nature exceeding vnconstant and mutable) it was not long ere that suffering himselfe to be turned agayne, and deceyued through perfidious Counsailours, he entred into rage more then euer. And besides the placing in diuers Coūtryes of false ministers of the Ghospell; he sent withall, a great company of Souldiours, to hinder by force the Preachings, Consults, and assemblies of the maintayners, and fauourers of the truth. Which commaund was immediately put into execution.

But *S. Theodosius* for all this, ceased not to prosecute his generous actions: but rather with redoubled feruour hauing made choyce of exemplar, learned, and zealous labourers; began with them, to visit and make his progresse through the villages, castles, and Cittyes thereabout, and to preuent with fit antidotes, and holsome medecins, the hellish poyson of heresy; in catechizing the ignorant, reclayming the strayed, encouraging the wauering, confirming the stable: and in summe, not forslowing any meanes, which appertayned to the help of soules, and to the glory of *Christ*, wherby at last he came to promote things so farre, as that notwithstanding the frownes of the souldiours, and subtilityes of the aduersary, mounting the pulpit, with a most extraordinary concourse of people, he publiquely declared, all those to be excommunicated, who departed from the authority, and constitutions of the foresayd foure Generall Councels. Which as soone as *Anastasius* the *Emperour* heard of, forgetting quite the veneration he had shewed before to the persõ of *S. Theodosius*, and together without conscience, hauing wholy lost all shame, without respect disgracefully expulsed him the monastery, and condemned him, with opprobrious and iniurious words, to perpetuall banishment. Which notwithstanding, through diuine Goodnes, continued not long. For that the *Emperour*, within a few months, being with a heauenly mace sommoned before that Tribunall which cannot erre, had for his Successour the famous *Iustin*; through whose valour and prudence the clouds of calumnyes were quite dispersed, the furious winds of persecutions ceased, and a fayre tranquility returned to the *Church* of *Christ* againe.

S. Theodosius *being returned agayne to his Charge, cured a woman of a Canker. And works other myracles besides.* Chap. 7.

NOW *S. Theodosius*, with the ioy and Iubiley of al the faythful, being remitted agayne into his former charge, betooke himselfe with fresh courage to his wonted exercises; the which how acceptable and gratefull they were to the diuine Maiesty, besides the aforesaid signes, may likewise appeare by the merueilous things that follow. The *Exaltation* of the holy Crosse, was kept festiuall there, in a certayne Temple built by *Constantine* for that purpose, in those countryes. And to this Solemnity went *S. Theodosius*, with many of his Monks. Wherof a certaine woman hauing got some notice, that had beene cruelly tormented a long while with a horrible canker in one of her breasts, and who had proued diuers medicins in vayne; resolued at last vpon diuine remedyes, and remembring her selfe of the generous resolution of that famous *Hemoroissa*, with like fayth & greatnes of courage, she entered into the Church

while

while the Office was celebrated. And being shewed the Man of God (whome she knew not by face) with stealing paces, & without noyse, approached behind him, and dexterously applying the agreiued part, to the hood of the *Saint*, most certayne it is, at the first touch of the sacred cloth, all payne on a sudden abãdoned the breast and left no scarre of the vlcer.

This sudden, and so perfect a cure, to the great glory of God, was proclamed through the *East*. Besides which, that other which succeeded in his returne from *Bethleem*, gaue great matter of acknowledging, and praysing the diuine power in the person of *S. Theodosius*; when as he being lodged in the Conuent of the *Abbot Martian*, caused through this benediction, from one sole grayne of corne, in a few houres, so great a quãtity to be multiplied, as that the granary being not able to hold the same, in the sight of all men, the corne brake forth at the doore.

Elswhere agayne, a child being fallen into a deep well, through the same intercession, being held past all human succour, in the presence of many, to the inestimable ioy of the afflicted and dolourous Mother, came forth agayne, very safe and sound. Through the fame of these, and other such like meruaylous things, a certaine *Count* of the *East*, whose name was *Cericus*, being to passe with his army, agaynst the *Persians*, first visiting the holy Citty of *Hierusalem*, repayred also to the Monastery of *S. Thedosius*, by whome being exhorted, with liuely reasons, not to place his hopes of the Victory, in the multitude, or force of his souldiours, but in the ayde of him, who as well can worke wonders with a few, as with infinite nũbers, he became so enflamed with the admonitions, & mãners of the blessed Man; as that to enter into battaile, he esteemed he could not make vse of armour of better proofe, then of the Cilice that *S. Theosius* was wont to weare on his naked skin. Wherewith, being armed, together with the benediction of the sayd Father, going his wayes, with his army, towards the enemy, he came very suddenly to handy blowes, and that with so much the greater confidence, as he had besides the foresayd coate of male, the person of *S. Theodosius* also euer in his eyes; who in the heate of the battayle, with pointing, and signes of the hand, went shewing him still, what part to enforce, what aduantages to take, where the ensignes should be aduanced, and where couragiously he should spur his horse. By which apparition, the deuout Champion, being greatly encouraged

ged on euery side where he seemed but to cast his eyes, as that putting the Pagans to flight, and terrour; it was not long, ere he returned backe full of ioy and glory, to giue *S. Theodosius* a distinct accompt of all that dayes worke, with immortall thankes.

Many other apparitions, are recompted of this diuine Man, as heertofore of *S. Nicolas*. By meanes wherof, heere one at sea very happily escapes out of cruell tempests; and heere another in the land from sauage beasts; and some from this perill, and some from that. There are likewise told diuers predictions of his, whence it appeares, how eminent he was in the spirit of *Prophesy*. But setting apart such like graces, being common with men, sometymes of no good life, my pen more willingly conuerts it selfe, to the intermitted discourse of his religious Vertue.

The Humility, and Patience of the Man of God, especially in his extremity of sicknes. And how sweetly he gaue vp the Ghost. Chap. 8.

AMong the vertues of this Venerable man, the sollicitude he had of manteyning continuall peace, and true concord between his Subiects, not deserued the least place. And this care of his, so boyled in his breast, as that when any of them, by some accident had broken any friendship betweene them, if by no other meanes, he could not peece, and reunite them agayne, he would not stick to cast himselfe downe at their feete, and to pray and coniure ech part so long, as that being mollifyed with tendernes, and confounded with shame, deposing all rancour, they became reconciled to ech other. From whence, may likewise be gathered, how great was the humility of the holy man, most worthy of admiratiō, were it only for this, that by such acts he lost no reputation, but rather how much greater contempt he shewed of himselfe, he was so much the more esteemed, and reuerenced by othes.

With this submission of his, was the vertue of *Patience* seene to march hand in hand with him, being a safe buckler, and secure bulwark of the souldiours of *Christ*, against the hoat and furious assaults of the ancient aduersary. Of which kind of armes, how dexterously the Man of God would be helping himselfe, he notably shewed in his extreme age. Because, that being oppressed, through a most grieuous infirmity, which made him more then a yeare to keep his bed, with most sharpe dolours; yet for all that, he fayled not of

his

his inward peace, nor yet forslew his accustomed prayer, and familiarity with God. And they affirmed who assisted him day & night, that in the greatest extremity of all, and fury of his fits, he did nothing, or sayd any word vnworthy of Christian magnanimity, or of his former behauiour.

But euen rather the said assistants auerre: That a certaine venerable old man, being come to visit him, and through compassion, bidding him pray to God, to deliuer him of so great affliction, and he should easily be heard; with no pleasing countenance, contrary to custome, he answered thus: Of charity, *Father*, speake not to me any more in this manner, for as often as such thoughts haue come into my mind, I euer held them, as suggestions of the enemy, & with all endeauour haue expelled them from me, discoursing in this manner with my selfe; that to abate the pride that may arise in me from the credit, which God hath plesed to giue me on earth, these agonyes, and humiliations are to very good purpose. And what share, trow you, are we like to haue in the consolations of the Eternity, if in this short space, or rather moment of tyme, we suffer not some manner of affliction? In truth, Father, we needs must resolue to suffer at this present, if we would not worthily be vpbrayded with these words herafter, *Recepisti bona tua in vita tua*. Thus *S. Theodosius* spake: and the Monke admiring, and touched withal, went his wayes.

In the meane tyme, the Man of God, feeling himselfe to decay more and more, & calling at last his sad disciples to his Cell, with his owne and their great feeling, he exhorted them to perseuere in their vocation, and stoutly to resist all temptations; and aboue all, to maynteyne faythfull and prompt Obedience, to whome soeuer with lawful election should come to succed him in the gouerment. Moreouer, very humbly calling for three of the Bishops of those countryes, and communicating with them, some things of importance for the publique seruice; in the presence of them, and of all the Monkes in teares, he alone being ioyfull, and glad, hauing with diligence procured already all things necessary for such a presage, did lift vp his eyes and hands to heauen, and then decently resting them on his breast, without any difficulty, yeilded vp his spirit, being now of 105. yeares old.

And it pleased our Lord, that a man possessed of an ill spirit, who till that tyme could neuer be deliuered from so great a calamity; now finally casting himselfe downe, with many teares, and bitter sighes, on the couch of the *Saint*, at the first touch of the venerable Reliques (but yet more tormented then euer) in the presence of as many as were there, was freed, and secure from that horrid tyranny.

The blessed Pope *Hormisda*, had the care of the Vniuersall Church at that tyme (though others according to *S. Cyrill*, would haue him to haue arriued to the tymes of *Pope Agapitus*, that is, to the yeare 536.) and in particular of *Hierusalem*, in the tyme of the Patriarch *Peter*; who at the first aduertisement of the departure of *S. Theodosius*, came in hast to the Monastery, while an infinite number of people, of all parts, came likewise in to obtayne some shred of the Garment, or Capuch of the blessed man, or at least to come neare him, and contemplate more freely on those chast lymmes of his, which had beene such efficacious instruments of the high *Creatour*. Whereupon to satisfy the pious desire of the multitude, the sacred corps of force remayned vnburyed, vntill such tyme, as the throng being somewhat ceased, he was, by his deerest, & most deuoted friends, with teares and sighes, deposed in the bosome of the cōmon Mother, from thence to arise agayne, at the sound of the last trumpet, with the other Elect, most glorious, and resplendant for all Eternity.

FINIS.

S. BENET

S. BENET ABBOT.

THE ARGVMENT.

LOoke how the Rosy Daughter of the morne,
The Starre that glads ech mortall with its light,
Leauing at first old *Titans* bed forlorne,
About the Spheres doth cast her Crimsom light;
Roses and Lillyes hurling through the skye,
Quenching the starres with rayes from thence that fly.
So glorious was thy morning, so bright rayes
Thy tender yeares did lighten, and foretold
The heauenly Sunshine of thy riper dayes,
Dispelling darkenesse, and inflaming cold
And senselesse hearts with fire of holy loue,
And drawing all to seeke the ioyes aboue.
Thou taughtst the way, remouing obstacles,
That as they rise depresse our mounting soules:
Thy doctrine thou confirmdst with miracles,
And heau'n by thee both Death and Hell controules.
If Starre, or Angell bring Heau'ns influence,
Thou art that *Starre*, thou that *Intelligence*.

THE LIFE OF S. BENET ABBOT.

Taken out of the Dialogues of *S. Gregory*.

The Infancy, and more tender yeares of S. Benet; *with his inclination to piety and religion: And how* Romanus *a Monke assisted him therein.* Chap. I.

SAINT *Benet*, Founder of the most noble Congregation of *Mount Casin*; gaue with his birth, no litle glory to *Nursia*, though otherwise, a notable and famous Citty, in the Confines of *Marca*, and *Vmbria*. It was in the yeare of our Lord 482. when *Gelasius* the first, gouerned the *Catholique Church*, and *Anastasius* the *Empire*. The Father of *S. Benet* was called *Proprius*, the Mother *Abundantia*, of the family of *Riguardati*, at that tyme, not only Honourable, but potent and Illustrious. The *Child* of a rare towardnes, in wit farre outstripping his yeares, in shewing himselfe to be aliened from all manner of pleasures and sports, was sent to *Rome*, to study, vnder the tutelage of one, that had a good care of him. Heere now being entred into profane schooles, he was soone aware of the perils, that

that hung ouer him, through vayne sciences, ill companyes, and the snares and intrications of the world. So as, fearing some precipice, he made hast to pluck out his foote betymes; with firme deliberation to repayre vnto the desart, and with all endeauour to attend to the diuine worship, and to the saluation of his Soule.

With this deliberation, the *Saint* and *Elect* of *God* first retyred himselfe from the concourse of *Rome*, into the castle of *Offida*, without other company, then only of his *Nurse*, that deerely loued him, from whome (as yet) he could not conueniently quit himselfe. Nor was it long, erre the *Diuine Goodnes* with euident signes, began to shew forth how gratefully he accepted the religious purposes of *S. Benet*. For that a Scry wherwith they winnow corne, being broken by chance in two peeces, which the *Nurse* had borrowed of her neighbours, and she poore woman most pittifully lamenting for it, the pious youth could by no meanes endure to see her so distressed. Whereupon putting himselfe into prayer, with the two peeces thereof by his side, as soone as he had ended the same, he found thẽ suddenly vnited, and the Vessell as whole, and sound, as if it had neuer beene broken or hurt at all. The miracle was great, & could not be concealed, whence all the inhabitants there-about, came running in to behold the same, blessing our Lord, and magnifying the *Child*, with the words that had been spoken heertofore of the holy *Precursour* of *Christ*: and further for memory of the fact, they did hang vp the sayd Scry publikely, at the entrance of the *Church*, where it remayed, till such tyme, as the *Country* was sackt by the *Lombards*.

These fauours & acclamations were a great spur vnto *S. Benet*, to fly away thence, and to hide himselfe, as soone as he could. So that abandoning his *Nurse*, and as many as knew him; he secretly got him to the Mountaynes of *Sublacum*, about some 40. miles distant from *Rome*; a territory but obscure in those dayes, though illustrious afterwards, through the abode and long conuersation of *S. Benet*. And it pleased God, that before his arriuall thither, he should hap to meete which a certayne Monke, by name *Romanus*, who courteously examining him of his life, and vnderstanding his heauenly Vocation, gaue him besids good counsayls, the habit moreouer of an Hermit, with promise withall to keep it secret, and to be assisting vnto him, in what he might. With such direction, the new *Champion* of *Christ* being come to *Sublacum*, puts himselfe into a most ſtrayt caue, and therein remayned ſhut vp, for three yeares continually together, without the knowledge of any perſon, in the world, except *Romanus*; who liuing not farre off, in a monaſtery vnder the Obedience of *S. Theodoſius Abbot*, fayled not to ſteale ſome part of his leaſure, and reſerue alſo ſome pittance of the food allowed him, to viſit from tyme to tyme, and to ſuſteyne his deere diſciple. And foraſmuch as from the Conuent to the caue, no path way was to be found, there hanging a very high cliff iuſt ouer the ſame; *Romanus* was wont to tye to a long cord, that little bread he could get, with a bell vnto it, by ſound wherof *S. Benet* might conueniently vnderſtand, when his refection was brought him.

Our Lord appeares to a Prieſt, and ſends him with victuals to S. Benet. *He is aſſayled with a cruell temptation, which he ſtrangely puts away. And afterwards eſcapes poyſoning.* Chap. 2.

NOw the auncient *Aduerſary*, not brooking well the charity of *Romanus*, and the life of *S. Benet*; in letting downe the cord abouesayd, threw downe a ſtone vpon the bell, & burſt it to peeces, which notwithſtanding *Romanus* fayled not to ſupply, and ſtill to perſeuer in that worke of mercy, vntill ſuch tyme, as our *Lord*, being willing to giue him reſt of ſuch labours, and to others the example of ſo high and ſublime vertue, appeared in viſion to a certayne Prieſt of thoſe countryes, who to feaſt himſelfe on the day of *Paſcha*, had made ready a good dynner to that end, and ſayd to him; *Thou ſtandſt heere preparing thee banquets, when loe, my Seruant the while, lyes ſtaruing yonder for hunger.* At which admoniſhment the good *Prieſt* ariſing ſudenly, on the ſame day of *Easter*, with his victuals, puts himſelfe on the way, and after he had fetcht ſome compaſſe about thoſe mountaynes and valleyes, a prety while, he found *S. Benet* at laſt, in the Caue. When ſaluting him fayrely, and making ſome prayer together with him: Let vs now, ſayd he, afford ſome little nouriſhment to the body, & reioyce in our *Lord*, for this is the Feaſt of the *Paſcha*. It is truly a Paſch to me, anſwered *S. Benet* (who in ſo great a ſolitude, vntill this tyme, haue not knowne the courſe of the yeare) and you haue afforded me a Feaſt ſufficient already with your preſence. Nay truly, not ſo (replyed the *Prieſt*) to day is celebrated the *Reſurrection of our Lord*, nor is it any wayes fit for you to faſt on this day, and that eſpecially ſo much the rather, as I am am sent hither of purpose, to communicate in charity with you on this day.

Then without more strife or contention they both blessing our *Lord*, fell to eating, and after a sweete, and spirituall discourse had betweene them, the *Priest* went his wayes. And now, as it were, at the same tyme, some shepheards also lighted on the said place: Who beholding amidst those brakes, the holy yōg man to be clothed with skyns, at first they tooke him for a beast that might lurke there, but after approching neere vnto him, and illumined with his admirable aduises, & christian doctrine; they knew anone themselues, who till that tyme, had beene but as brute beasts. Wherupon being touched with true Contrition, they gaue themselues from thenceforth to a more reasonable life. From whence, the fame of *S. Benet* began to spread it selfe, & the poore Caue to be frequented of many; who bringing him corporall food, returned from thence, well refreshed with spirituall nourishment.

On those dayes, he being once all alone, was assayled by the Deuill, in forme of a blacke Bird, being called a Moore-hen, which for a good space, did neuer giue ouer from flying in his face, with such importunity, and so neare withall, as he might easely haue taken her in his hand, if he had listed. But he chose rather to defend himselfe, with the signe of the holy crosse. Wherupon the bird flew away, leauing notwithstanding a cruell temptation with an intolerable passion, enkindled in the members of the yong man. In such wise, as the souldiour of Christ, stood now vpon staggering, & deliberating, as it were, to returne back into the world agayne; when being sudenly fortifyed with diuine Grace, he reentred into himself agayne, and beholding a bush of sharpe thornes, and stinging nettles at hand, with a generous force pulling off his clothes, on a sudden casts he himselfe therinto, & so long rouled his naked body theron, as that being full of wounds, and bloud all ouer, with the external heate he extinguished the internall, and through such a noble act remayned so victorious ouer the rebellions flesh, as that from thence forth (as himselfe reported to his Disciples) he neuer felt any more trouble therof.

After this, it pleased God, that diuers persons of sundry places should repayre to *S. Benet*, desirous not only of saluation, but euen likewise of perfection. And it was but iust, that he now possessing so peacefully the kingdome of his proper mynd, should be applyed

to

to the care & gouerment of others. For that we see also in the written Law, how the *Leuits*, in the seruour of their youth, were tyed to labour, & to serue in the Temple; nor before they were full 50. yeares old (at which tyme, it is supposed their passions, are in quiet, and the heart at rest) were they made the Guardians, and Sacristans of the holy Vessels, which are interpreted the reasonable soules. But among others, who approched to *S. Benet* the seruant of God for his help, were some religious of a neighbour Monastery thereby, who in those dayes being destitute of an *Abbot*, besought him to take the charge vpon him.

These men, were accustomed to a large, and more liberall life, and litle disposed to conforme themselues with the manners of *S. Benet*. And he being aware thereof, for a while made a strong resistance to their request. But being constrayned through the prayers and coniurations of the whole Family, he accepted the gouerment at last; and first with example, and after with words, endeauoured he to take away the abuses, and then to bring in a forme of liuing, worthy of the profession they made. But soone it appeared, how the good inspirations and desires they had, had taken but litle roote in their soules; because that shortly they were all aggrieued with the Rule, and reformation made; and the diabolicall instigations had gotten such power in some, as that not being able to endure in their sight, such a liuely and continuall example of extreme abstinence, & perfect manners, they determined to take him away, out of hand, with poyson. But the diuine iustice, suffered not their wicked designe to take affect: because that at the tyme of the refection, while one of them, was presenting the holy Father with a cup of poysoned wine, it pleased God, with the signe of the Crosse which *S. Benet*, according to custome, vsed to make thereupon, the glasse, as with the blow of a stone, fell suddenly into peeces, and the wine from the brothers hand, dropt downe to the ground. Whence the Man of God, knew presently, that drinke without doubt to be the potion of Death which could not endure the signe of life. And thereupon with a mind composed, and a face serene. turning himselfe to the Monkes; God forgiue you (sayd he) what a plot was this amongst you? Did I not tell you at first, my manners would neuer seeme to agree with yours? Then rest you in peace, and seeke you out some other, that may gouerne you better, And heerwith, leauing them quite confounded and astonished

he

he retired to his desired Caue agayne, and there attended seriously to himselfe.

How two principall Senatours of Rome *offer vp, and dedicate their children to* S. Benet: *and how a Monke was led away by a Deuill, which* S. Benet *discouers, and remedies.* Chap. 3.

TRue it is, that *S. Benet* was not suffered to enioy that estate any tyme, because that the odour of such a sanctity, continually spreading it selfe more and more; there repayred to him a new cõcurse of people, much touched with the *holy Ghost,* and cloyed with the world. With which multitude after a sufficient instruction had, he founded in those countryes, about a dozen Monasteryes, appointing Lawes, offices, and an Abbot to ech. So as diuers personages, and Senatours of *Rome,* began now to hold it a great felicity to haue any Children at such a tyme, to send to *S. Benet,* and to dedicate thẽ vnder the care of such a Father, to the seruice of the *diuine Maiesty*. Among which, were two principall, *Eutitius* and *Tertullus*. Wherof one offered *Maurus,* a yong man of so rare a wit and of such a spirit withall, as in short tyme, he became an assistant of the *Maister* himselfe. The other greatly addicted to the same discipline, with much veneration, offered in person his eldest sonne *Placidus* to him yet a Child, & then after made likewise, a free donation of a great masse of riches, farmes, manners, and Castles to the *Saint,* with cittyes both maritime, and in land, wherof the Catalogue would be heere too long: surely to the great confusion of our tymes, in which as the entring into Religion is ordinarily held desperatiõ, shame & madnes; so the taking away of subiects reputation and goods frõ them, is reputed, and that euen of those who call themselues *Christians,* to be good prudence, valour, and Iustice.

But to returne to *S. Benet*, vnto whome as well in the beginning, as in the progresse of his administration, there happened many notable things. The vigilant *Pastour,* with the greatest sollicitude that might be, was wont to apply his subiects to the study of prayer, as knowing well, how necessary the succour of Heauen must needs be, for the cutting off of disordinate affects, and repressing of passions withall, which euen from the mould whereof we are framed, do continually spring, For which cause, besids the particular deuotions of ech one, at certayne houres, he would assemble them all togeather, in a certayue place deputed for holy exercises. Now it happened, that in one of those assemblies, while diuine office being ended the Monks were meditating, & conuersing with God; one of them, being vanquished with tediousnes, went forth of the Quire, and partly went idly vp and downe heere and there, and partly busyed himselfe in some temporall matter of litle moment. Which being known to his *Abbot Pompeanus*, after he had admonished him thereof diuers tymes, but all in vayne, he brought him at last to *S. Benet* himselfe, who with a good reprehension sent him backe againe.

But yet this auayled not much, because after two dayes, the Monke returned to his old custome: and *Pompeanus* anew had recourse to the *Saint*, who being moued with compassiõ for the sheep nigh lost, determined immediately to go in person himselfe to apply by all possible meanes, some present remedy thereunto. Taking then *Maurus*, for his companion, and *Pompeanus* withall, he went his wayes thither: and setting himselfe to espy, in a fit place, what happened in tyme of prayer, he saw how a litle blacke boy, tooke the Monke by the hemme of his Cassocke, and went leading him forth of the Oratory. Then the vigilant *Prelate* sayd secrely to *Maurus* and *Pompeanus*. *Do you not see there who it is, that leades him thus away?* and they answering, no: *Let vs pray then*, sayd he, *that you may be likewise made partakers of the spectacle.* And so they did all for two daies togeather, at the end whereof, *Maurus* did deserue to see the reuelation, while the other found not the grace. Which done, yet *S. Benet* expected another day, and suddenly after prayer agayne, finding the Monke to be yet gadding as before, he gaue him a blow, which had so much efficacy with it, as that the diuell, as if himselfe had been lashed, had not the hart to returne any more to the same agayne. This acccident surely, was very memorable, but yet this other which followes, is no lesse glorious then it, though in a different kind.

S. Benet *causeth a spring to arise out on the top of a mountayne: With other accidents besides.* Chap. 4.

AMong the Monasteryes, whereof we haue made some mention aboue, three were seated on a high and craggy rocke, and so dry withall, as the Monkes were enforced, through those cliffs & steepy places, to fetch their water from the Lake, which as then the

riuer

riuer of *Teneron* caused, and that not only with extraordinary trauayle and paynes, but euen also with the manifest danger, & continuall feare of precipices. Whereupon the Monkes certifyed *S. Benet* of the greatnes of the difficulty they felt, and besought him hūbly, that he would be pleased to place them somewhere els. The benigne *Father*, was touched with tendernes at the request, and giuing them good hope, dismissed them anone, bidding them to returne to him on the next day. In the meane while, the night being come, without taking any other then the innocent *Placidus* with him, he went secretly to the top of those cliffs, where he made his prayer, and in the very same place, putting downe three stones, as a signe, with like secrecy as before, he returned home to his Cell againe. When day was come, behold the Monkes returne; to whome *S. Benet*, without more ado: Go your wayes, sayd he, towards such a place, & where you shall find three stones layd one vpon another, there dig, for God is able to produce water on the tops of mountaines to ease you of the paines of so tedious a iourney. And they going with great confidēce to the sayd place, found it already to wax moyst, & to spring vp water, increasing at last in so great abōdance, as vnto this present day, without diminishing a whit, it stil runs from that top, to the foote of the hill. With this remedy the *Saint* refreshed and eased his disciples of their trauayle and thirst: & with this other that followes gaue peace to a timorous, and anxious soule.

A certayne poore man in those dayes, was conuerted to the fayth, a Goth by nation, who putting himselfe into the hands of *S. Benet*, by whome being exercised in his tyme, as well in spirit as in bodyly labour, he was appointed after prayer, to fell downe a peece of wood, vpon the banck of the Lake there, to make a garden plot of. Now it happened, while the prompt Neophit attended with all his forces, to cut downe the bushes and bryers, that the head of his axe, flying off suddenly from the helue, fell into the deepe water, without hope of euer recouering it agayne. Whereupon, being afflicted for the losse, which it seemed to him, he had caused to the Conuent, he went trembling to accuse himselfe vnto *Maurus*, and to do penance for the same, in case he had committed any fault therin. *Maurus* was much edified at so tender a conscience; nor was he slack the while to acquaint the common Parent, & Maister therwith. Thē *S. Benet* being moued to compassion, went his wayes to the Lake, and taking the helue of the hatchet out of the *Gothes* hand, threw it into the water, and the head of the hatchet of it selfe immediately floating, tooke hold of the helue agayne, and came to the land: at which sight, the Goth being astonished, and quite as it were, besids himselfe, *S. Benet* puts the hatchet into his hand, saying: My sonne, Goe to worke agayne, and trouble not your selfe any further in the matter. There followes yet another act, no lesse admirable then this, and perhaps from the tyme of *S. Peter* the *Apostle* hitherto, not heard of before.

Placidus on a tyme, being gone to the said Lake for water, while he stoopes with his vessell, fell vnfortunately thereinto, and being snatcht by the streame, in a moment was caryed away, the distance for space of a bowes shot from the land. This in spirit *S. Benet* did behold, being shut vp in his Cell, and calling *Maurus* very suddenly vnto him: *Go thy wayes*, said he, *in all hast, for the Child is drowned.* The good subiect, was accustomed to hold the Superiours becks as Oracles. Wherfore, without other reply, he demaunds only his benediction of him: and hauing taken the same, ranne violently to the danger, and that with so much speed, as that going on the waters dry foote, he tooke *Placidus* by the hayre of his head, not being aware the while of the nature of the way he went on, vntill such tyme, as he had pulled him safe to the land. When returning into himselfe, and reflecting on what was past, his hayre stood an end, and giuing thankes to the highest God, led *Placidus* to the presence of *S. Benet*. Heere arose a noble contention of profound humility betweene the Mayster and disciple; while *S. Benet* ascribes the greatnes of such a miracle vnto the fayth and promptnes of *Maurus*, and *Maurus* attributes all to the merits and intercession of *S. Benet*. The youth himselfe, in part decides the controuersy, affirming, that in arising aloft, it seemed to him, that he saw the habit of *Father Abbot* ouer him; whereby, he tooke it that he was deliuered by him. But howsoeuer it passed, it is euident, the obedience of *Maurus* was worthy of eternall memory.

Florentius *a Priest, seekes to poyson* S. Benet, *but is preuented. He practiseth also to corrupt his Disciples; and is lastly punished by the hand of God.* Chap. 5.

IN the meane tyme, the Followers and Deuotes of *S. Benet*, do continually multiply and increase, esteeming themselues amidst the

the snares of this pilgrimage, very happy and secure, vnder the guiding of such a Leader. But as Enuy alwayes spurnes at vertue; a certaine *Priest* of that countrey, called *Florentius*, being of the number of those who couet the fruites of human prayses, and fly the purchase of solid vertues, could by no meanes endure so much reputation, & so prosperous successes of *S. Benet*. This vnfortunate wretch being stirred vp and excited through blind passion, began first, with euill words to detract from the merits, and actions of *S. Benet*, and then to hinder by all meanes possible, the concourse of people that went vnto him. After which perceiuing how he trauailed in vayne, and that, by how much he endeauoured to vilify, and depresse him, he was the more exalted by God, and reuerenced of men; he suffered himselfe at last to be led into the same very deuilish plot, whereinto those former traytours of the *Saint* had beene caryed. True it is that whereas they hid the fraud vnder a cup of wine, this vnder a loafe of bread. But as that was not able to deceiue the eyes of the Man of God, so was this also reuealed vnto him. Because *Florentius* vnder the shew of charity hauing sent him in almes, a Loafe of bread cōtempered with deadly poyson, the holy man stuck not to receiue it with thanks giuing. But being soone certifyed, through diuine power, of the wicked deceipt, at the houre of refection, he threw it downe to a Crow, which at that tyme was wont to come to him to take her meate at his hands, & said to her: On behalfe of our *Lord Iesus Christ*, take you heere this loafe of bread, & cary it to some place where it may not be touched of any person lyuing. At which words the Crow spreading her wings, and opening the mouth, began to houre, with croaking, and shewing a will and feare alike to touch that pestilent food: but the Man of God vrging her to obey, with confidence tooke it vp with her clawes, and flew away with it, and then after some three houre space, returned agayne to her wonted meate.

At such ill demeanours as these, *S. Benet* was exceedingly sory, not so much for his owne sake, as for compassion of his aduersary. But *Florentius* the while, being full of gaul and obstinate in malice since he could not murder the body of the Maister, endeuoured to destroy the disciples soules. And among other things, he had the impudence to contriue in the very garden of the Monastery, and in the sight of the Monkes themselues, a lasciuious daunce of naked womē. At which spectacle, the *Abbot*, with reason fearing some notable disorder, determined to giue wholy place to the fury of the Enemy, and to abandon the Country and mansion there built vp by himselfe, with so great expences. Setting then the affayres of the Conuents in order, and exhorting the Monks to perseuere in the study of perfection, with some of his companions, he puts himselfe on his iourney, and through diuine instinct, or rather through a cleare voyce which came to him from heauen, he trauayled towards a Castle, about some two dayes iourney from thence, by name *Caßin*, with ful purpose to announce the true light of the Ghospel vnto the Country people that inhabited there, which miserably lay yet blind in the darknes of Gentilisme, and the shadow of death.

Hardly was the seruant of God, departed from *Sublacum*, when as vengeance from heauen, appeared vpon *Florentius*: because his howse, being otherwise safe and sound, the roofe only of the roome where he then remayned, falling downe on a sudden, with a remedyles ruine, burst all the bones of his body, and for his soule, that went to the tribunall of the eternall iustice. The accident was suddenly diuulged, and one of the Monks, ran immediately in hast after the holy *Abbot*, to carry him the newes, as he thought, very glad and welcome to him: but *S. Benet*, insteed of reioycing thereat sent forth sighes vnto heauen for that soule, & with seuere words gaue a sharpe rebuke to the Monke, who therein had shewed in himselfe not so Christian a mynd, as he ought. From thence, proceeding on his way, he arriued at last at the foresaid Castle, scituated on the side of a steepy and high hill, in the top wherof, was a Temple seene amid the thickest of the woods, being dedicated to *Apollo*. Where *S. Benet* wanted not matter to worke on, or what to encounter.

But before he would enter into battayle, he would seeme to prepare himselfe for that purpose, with especiall care, by retyring him into some remote place: and there for fourty dayes continually together, remaynes he in prayer, fastings, and vigils. After which with the odour of so good a life, and with the efficacy of his preaching, being the fittest batteryes to Fayth; he sets himselfe, through diuine fauour, couragiously to destroy paganisme, and so brake the Idol, demolisheth the Aultar, hewes downe the woodes; & where before was the Oracle of the false God, he erects an Oratory to *S. Martin*, and in place of an Aultar builds a Chapell vnto *S. Iohn Baptist*, through whose intercession, obteyning alwayes new graces, & offering vp most pure and acceptable sacrifices to the *Creatour*, he neuer

uer left labouring to acquit, and discharge poore mortalls from the cruell seruitude of the Deuill.

The Diuell appeares to S. Benet; *He throwes downe a wall new built vp, and kills one of the Monkes in the ruines thereof, who is restored to lyfe agayne: with other illusions of the Diuell.* Chap. 6.

THe ancient Tyrant, no longer able to endure to foresayd enterprises of *S. Benet*, besides the diuers difficultyes and impediments which in vayne he stirred against the messenger of Christ; began also to appeare vnto him, not through in imagination, or dreame, but with open vision, and with dreadfull figures, casting forth, by the mouth and eyes, infernall smoake, and flames of sulphure, and with a raging voyce, howling, and lamenting in such manner, as that the disciples, though they were not permitted to behold him, yet playnely might heare him to say, among other things; *Benedicte, Benedicte:* and while the Man of God, vouchsafed not to answere him, outragiously he added: *Maledicte*, and not *Benedicte, what hast thou to do with me? Wherefore dost thou persecute me thus?* And heerewith, fell a vomiting of most horrible blaspemies, and menaces; whereof, though the *Saint* seemed to make but light accompt, yet the standers by euen the while feared grieuously.

That which increased his fury, was a certayne building begun by the Monkes for their habitation, which in processe of tyme, from meane beginnings, amounted after to the magnificence we see at this present. Whereupon being incensed more and more with anger, he appeared one day to *S Benet*, in his Cell, while the Monkes were a labouring, and freting sayd openly to him, that he was then going to worke what mischiefe he could, both to the labourers, & to the worke in hand. Whereat the holy Father, sends suddenly to aduertise his disciples thereof, and to admonish them, to retire thēselues without delay: but the messenger arriued not so soone, but that the diuell had already throwne downe to ground, a very high wall, which they had built, and thereby crushed to peeces a Monke vnderneath the ruines: in so much, as to shew him to *S. Benet*, it was needfull to gather the peeces, and to put them vp in a sacke together: When the man of God, causing them to be layd forth, where he was wont to make his prayer, and dismissing the Monkes, shut himselfe in the Cell, & prayed with such feruour

vnto

vnto God, as euen at that houre he restored the yong man all whole and sound agayne, and as able as the rest, to continue and go forward with the worke interrupted.

Nor did the malignant spirit only in weighty matters, thus vent his choler; but euen sometymes also in things, that were halfe ridiculous in themselues: as was that of a stone, of no great bignes, which being to be placed in the wall, he sets himselfe vpon it, insomuch, as they did but labour in vayne, to place it aright, being not able to stirre it awhit, vntill such tyme, as the Man of God, in person, had giuen his benediction thereon. Whereat the deuill, as he is wont, goes his wayes, and the stone was suddenly lifted, & lightned, as it had beene of wax only. After which, it seemed good vnto all, to dig somwhat deep, & they found out an Idoll of brasse, which after some houres casting by chãce into the kitchin, it seemed to send forth fire on all sides, as it would doubtlesse haue burned vp the roome. This sight, put the Conuent into a hurly-burly, all striuing to runne in with their buckets of water, and calling for help. At which noyse of theirs, the admirable *Abbot* arriuing, with one only cast of the eye, was presently aware of the illusion; and then bowing the head prayes awhile, and bids the Monkes, to make the signe of the Crosse vpon their eyes: which done, the flames immediatly vanished, and so euery one vnderstood it to haue been only a fantasticall flame, and not true fire.

Through these persecutions, and troubles, *Lucifer* did in fine effect no more, then to affoard new occasions to *S. Benet*, to illustrate the name of *Christ*, and to purchase to himselfe credit continually more and more, as well with the faythfull, as Gentills; and that so much the more, as to this so rare a grace of miracles, was added an extraordinary Gift of *Prophesy*, as by the following examples, may cleerely be gathered.

A secular man, but exceeding pious withall, was wont euery yeare, to go from home, a good way off, to the Monastery; as wel to take the benediction of the holy Father, as also to visit a Brother of his, whome there he had in religion. And to the end the voyage might be the more meritorious, he would make it on foote, and remayne fasting, vntill his arriuall vnto the presence of *S. Benet*. Now it hapened on a tyme, that another trauayler kept him cõpany on the way, who had brought along with him, good prouision of victuals; and after they had gone thus a pretty way togeather, while

while it grew somwhat late, the trauayler inuited him very friendly to eate a bit with him, and to refresh themselues, as well as they might. God forbid, Brother, said he, since my custome is, for to arriue fasting vnto *Father Abbot*. With this answere as then, the inuiter was quiet, but yet after a space agayne, he vrged him afresh, that now it was ful tyme of dynner. But the Man being resolued to keep abstinence, still denyed him againe a second tyme; so as the other was feigne to comply with him.

But not long after, behold a goodly meadow, with a limpid spring, presents it selfe to them, which opportunely inuited them to recreate themselues; when he that caryed the victuals, sayd: O what water! O what a pasture is this! O what a place to repose in awhile, and to take some repast, rest, and breath of our trauaile! The sunne by this tyme was growne very forward on its way, the mẽbers weary, the sound of the Byrds very sweete to the Eares, the flowers and hearbs as seeming to flatter the eyes; besides which many fayre pretences fayled not the sensuality, to excuse withall. What more? The deuout pilgrim at last was ouercome. But then at the euening, being come into the presence of the Man of God, & crauing his benediction, as he was wont, the *Saint* stucke not very dexterously to vpbrayd him, with what had passed with him on the way, saying. How goes the matter brother? The wicked enemy who spake to thee so, by the meanes of that Trauayler there on the way, neyther at the first, nor second tyme could moue thee away whit, till at last, at the third he brought thee to his bent. The poore man hearing this, and acknowledging his great vnconstancy, casts himselfe at his feete, full of teares, and confusion. A fayre reuelation surely: but yet is this that followes, no lesse prety, and admirable, then it.

The Gift of Prophecy, which S. Benet *discouers by occasion of* Totila, *endeauouring to abuse him by a tricke. And how he discouers, and chastizeth his Monkes, through the same Gift.* Chap. 7.

TOtila the King of the *Gotes*, hauing heard of the wonders of *S. Benet*, and measuring others manners by his owne perfidious mynd; determined with a subtile inuention to informe himselfe better of the truth thereof. Trauayling therefore to *Mount Casin*, he stayd a little way off, & sent to certify the worthy *Abbot*, that he was now come to visit him : and being answered, he might come when he pleased, he caused a Fauourite of his, by name *Rigone,* to be decked vp with his Princely robes, and commaunded him to be accompanyed by his whole Court, and attended by three principall Barons, vnto the presence of *S. Benet*, as if it had beene the person of *Totila* himselfe ; and gaue good order besides, that no inckling of the fiction, might come to the conuent. *Rigone* trauayling with such Maiesty, and so great a pompe, was hardly arriued at the Cell, but the *Saint*, began a farre off to call vnto him, with a lowd voyce: Lay away, my sonne, put off those things thou wearest so, for they are none of thyne. At which words, the Barbarian, as strucken with thunder, fell suddenly downe to the ground, and feared worse, for his great presumption, in abusing and mocking so great a Man. At which terrour likewise, all fell humbly prostrate before him, & not daring to approach neerer, returned to the King, with pale countenances, and with faltering speech, related vnto him how sodainely the deceipt was discouered by the Man of God.

Then *Totila* himselfe, went thither in person, with so much submission, and reuerence withall, as that being come in the sight of *S. Benet*, who was sitting a farre off, he casts himselfe presently on the ground ; and howbeyt the Man of God, some twice, or thrice, said to him, *Get vp I pray*; yet durst he not do it, vntill such tyme as *S. Benet*, with his owne hands, went and lifted him vp. And after this, in few words in priuate, he reprehended him shrewdly of his euill manners, and acquainted him besides, with what was like to succeed with him, saying: Thou dost much mischiefe, & many euils thou hast hitherto wrought, but now refrayne frō thy iniquityes at last, & know thou shalt enter heereafter into *Rome*, thou shalt crosse the Seas, nine yeares thou shalt raigne, and dye on the tenth. With these newes, *Totila* being exceedingly terrifyed, most humbly crauing the intercession of the Seruant of *Christ*, departed thence : and from that tyme afterwards, began to be lesse cruell and fierce. Not long after the same, he entred into *Rome*: from thence he sayled into *Sicily*, and being arriued vnto the tenth yeare of his raigne, through diuine Iustice, came to loose both life and kingdome at once.

The foresayd reuelations of the *Saint*, and other the like, which for breuity sake we let passe, haue happened with strangers only : While these others haue succeeded, partly for amendement, & part for the consolation of his Monkes.

Two

Two whereof, being once gone forth, about some worke of *Charity*, the businesse held them so long, as the poore Monkes were persuaded to eate in the house of a certayne deuout woman. Wherupon returning late to the Monastery, and crauing the wonted benediction of the *Venerable Father*; he suddaynely demaunded, where they had dyned, and they answering confidently, in no place; he replyed, why tell you me a lye in this manner? For you did enter into the house of such a woman; and did you not eate of such and such meates? And haue not ech of you drunke so often? They being conuinced with these circumstances, and with ech particular thereof, being full of confusion withall, cast themselues at his feet confessing the fault, and demaunding pardon at his hands. And the good *Father* shewed mercy to them, as knowing they would run no more into the like default.

There was not farre from the Monastery, a village inhabited by many, conuerted by *S. Benet*, among whome; were found some Women, consecrated to the diuine worship; and the sollicitous *Pastour*, being carefull to conserue that flocke, was wont often to send some one of his disciples thither, to make some spirituall exhortations to them. One of which, hauing ended his discourse with them, was persuaded through the intreaty of those deuout Women, to accept a small present of lynnen cloth, at their hands, and so he puts it vp in his bosome; but the Gift cost him full deare, because returning to the Monastery, he had of *S. Benet* a most bitter reprehension for it: for among other things, it was demaunded of him, how crept that iniquity into his breast? when as he halfe besides himselfe, had quite forgot his fault, nor could well tell, wherfore he was so accused; when lo, the holy *Abbot* replyes: Belike then, I was present with thee, when thou receiuedst so that lynnen cloth of the Seruants of God, and didst put it in thy bosome? With this, at last the Monke came to acknowledge his fault, and with a great deale of contrition, taking it forth of his Cassocke, threw it away to the ground.

S. Benet *discouers a temptation of Pride in the hart of one of his Monks: with a briefe Relation of the life of* S. Scholastica *his Sister*. Chap. 8.

ON a tyme, in the euening, the man of God taking some litle repast, a certayne Monke stood holding him a candle, who in the world had beene the Sonne of a certaine *Protectour*, which in those dayes was an Office of great dignity. Now while he wayted in that manner vpon him, he was halfe vanquished with a grieuous temptation of *Pride*, saying within himselfe: Who is this heere, that sitting at the Table, I should not only not sit besides him, but stand holding him the candle, and serue him as a Page? He had hardly giuen place in his soule to these suggestions, but that the *Saint*, with great vehemency of spirit, began to rouse him vp, saying; Make the signe of the Crosse on thy hart, Brother: what is that thou thinkst on? Make the signe of the Crosse I say: and sudenly calling in others, he made them to take the candle out of his hand, and willed him to sit downe at the table himselfe. He being afterwards demaunded of the Monks apart, what was that which he was thinking of at that tyme, he ingenuously confessed, the assault of pride which he then had, and the formall words, he was then framing in himselfe. They all wondered the while, and were much astonished thereat. Nor can it easily be expressed, what a spurre to perfection were these kind of discoueryes, and fatherly admonitions of his, vnto them. And thus *S. Benet* of purpose, vsed some acerbity with them, as knowing that medicines for the most, are the more holsome, as they haue more bitternes in them: whereupon the disciples of necessity must needs stand the more on their guard, & become more vigilant vpon their defects, in beholding the maysters eyes still so vpon them, and alwayes intentiue, not onely to what they did, but euen likewise to what they thought.

But as the diuine *Prelate*, with such oracles as these, vsed to cause a great feare and sollicitude in his subiects: so with others in its turn he would deale as sweetly, and giue as much security and comfort. At such tyme then as Mount *Cassin*, and all the arable Land thereabout was oppressed with a great and extraordinary dearth, that sacred Conuent also, what with the nourishments of those of the howse, as with the almes which were distributed to strangers, was brought to such straits, as there remayned no more, then fiue loaues of bread in the Monastery, & the Granary quite empty. Wherupon the Monkes, but litle acquainted with such manner of extremityes, were now so sad and constristate with it, as they could not choose but in words, & countenance, bewray their pusillanimity. The man of God then being aware therof, very modestly reprehẽded such diffidence in them; & after that afforded them great hopes

not

notwithstāding, affirming that though they had but small prouision for that day, yet should they haue the next day following a great aboundance. Nor stayed he in his promises, since on the very next day were found at the Gate 100. bushells of meale in sacks, without knowing euer by what way or meanes Almighty God had sent them thither: whereby, the Seruant of *Christ*, besides the help and consolation they felt therein, had likewise occasion to dilate their harts, and to trust in the diuine Goodnesse, and in their greater scarcity not to doubt of reliefe any more.

The newes also of the happy passage of *S. Scholastica* out of this lyfe, gaue them extraordinary contentment. This same was the natural Sister of *S. Benet*, & wholy dedicated to the diuine seruice from a child. Who being of riper age was wont euery yeare to visit her Brother, and to receiue spirituall instructions from him, who in cōpany of some disciples of his, would go forth to meete with her somtymes, at a certayne Grange of the Conuent. Now in their last visit, there happened a thing of great astonishment; which was this, that they hauing passed ouer a whole day togeather in sweet and deuout discourses, and then after, in the euening, hauing giuen some refection to their body, *S. Benet* being about to take his leaue of her to returne to his Cell agayne; the holy Virgin, being then more taken with his sweet conceypts, and discourses then euer; began to intreate him, with the greatest instance that might be, he would please to stay with her, and there passe away that night in such discourses, and particularly in treating of the future life, and of the glory of Paradise. At which request, *S. Benet* being angry, as it were, seuerely answered: What say you Sister? And know you not, that by no meanes, it is lawfull for me to lye out of the Monastery? And thereupon being ready to arise, and go his wayes, *Scholastica* obtayning yet some delay, and grasping her hands vpon the table, put her head thereon, & powring forth a floud of teares, made secretly her prayer to God. A strange thing! the Heauens before being so cleere, as no cloud appeared in the skies, on the sudden, in the lifting vp of her head, there followed such thunder, & hideous noyse thereupon in the ayre, & such a floud of rayne withall, as it was impossible for *S. Benet*, and his companions, to put forth of doores that night.

Then the venerable *Abbot*, perceiuing himselfe to be thus layd vp as it were, being ful of sorrow for it: God forgiue thee Sister (said he) what hast thou done? When she answered; I intreated you, Syr, and you would not heare me, and I prayed to my God, and he hath vouchsafed to heare me: now then go forth if you can, and leauing me, returne to your Cell. In the meane while, the storme so increased, as the holy old man was enforced to remayne there, against his will, for to satisfy the desire of the thirsty virgin to heare the word of God. The morning being come, she vrged no more, but taking her leaue of *S. Benet*, he returned to the Conuent, & after three dayes, remayning in a closet of his chamber, and lifting vp his eyes, beholds the blessed spirit of his said Sister, to go forth of her body, in forme of a doue, & thence to fly vnto heauen. For which, he first gaue due thankes to God, with psalmes, and hymnes, and thẽ likewise acquainted the Monks therwith, to their extreme ioy, & so sent them without delay to fetch the sacred corps, & to carry it into the Church, where he caused it to be layd in the Sepulcher, which already he had prepared for himselfe, to the end that as their mynds had beene alwayes vnited in life; so their spoyles after death might not seeme to be seuered and disioyned. This same was surely a notable vision, and full both of iubily and wonder. But yet was that other, more straunge and admirable, which he had in the Monastery of the Abbot *Seruandus*, not farre from Mount *Caßin*.

A Notable vision of S. Benet, *together with* Seruandus *Abbot: with diuers other admirable things.* Chap. 9.

SEruandus was a person of a great spirit, and very learned withal, and as he often visited *S. Benet*, to conferre with him about matters of the diuine seruice; so *S. Benet* mutually, from tyme to tyme, would repayre to him: & one day among others, after they had talked a prety while together of God, thirsting after the heauenly coũtrey, whither as yet they could not arriue; the houre of rest being come, *S. Benet* retires himselfe vnto the vpper Chambers in a tower where he then lodged, and *Seruandus* rested in another beneath; & right ouer against the said tower the Monkes lodged in a great howse. Now *S. Benet* arising by night, according to his manner, some while before the others to contemplate, and treate with God, standing at the window, and looking vp to Heauen-wards, espyes a sudden light to illuminate the ayre, with so great a splendour, as it farre surpassed the brightnes of the day it selfe. In which specula-

tion

tion of his, happened an incredible thing, if the *Saint* himselfe had not reported the same, which was this: That the whole world was represented to his sight, as gathered together through, diuine power, vnder a beame, as it were of the Sunne. And while he fixeth his eyes in the purest light; he sees also, by an inexplicable way, the soule of the blessed *Germanus* Bishop of *Capua*, to be conueyed to Heauen, by the Angels, in a Globe of fire.

Then *S. Benet*, that he might haue some companion of so glorious, and admirable a spectacle, with a voyce, as lowd as he could called the Abbot *Seruandus* to him, some twice or thrice: who being awaked, and troubled with the noyse, made extraordinary hast to get vp to him; but yet came but to a peece only of that great light. Howsoeuer, he was much astonished thereat, & so much the more when he vnderstood, what first his holy Ghest had seen. And howbeyt, the matter was such, as there could be no doubt made of any false imagination therein, yet for the greater euidence, it seemed not amisse to send that night, a graue and pious Monke, by name *Theodosius*, vnto the Citty of *Capua* it selfe, to vnderstand what was become of the holy Bishop. And in effect it was found, that he was dead indeed; and informing himselfe more punctually of the matter he was certifyed, his passage was iust at that houre, or rather in that very moment, wherein the man of God, had seene him to ascend to eternall glory.

The blessed *Gregory* the Great, relates other visions, and prophesyes of him; which to declare at length, would seeme a superfluous thing, and farre from our purpose: and much longer would it be, to vnfold one by one, all the other merueylous works, which in diuers subiects are recounted of him. While once he lamented & foretold a long tyme before, the destruction of Mount *Cassin*, which followed through the incursion of the *Lombards*, and agayne of the ruine of *Rome*, not by the hand of the armed *Barbarians*, but through Earthquakes, winds, thunders, & horrible tempests from Heauen; he appeared to some Monks in sleepe, who were sent to *Terracina*, to set vp a Conuent there, and gaue them the whole modell, and order of the building. He threatned excommunication to two Religious women of a naughty and slaunderous tongue, if they amended not the same, and after the menace giuen, without more adoe the effect followed, since dying in that vice, and buryed in the Church, they were seene to go forth, as often as Masse was celebra-

ted

ted there: nor euer found any rest vntill such tyme, as the Man of God, with his owne hand, had giuen an host to the Priest to offer for them.

A certayne yong Monke, going forth of the Monastery, without leaue, to see his Father and Mother, was suddenly at his arriuall thither fallen dead in the house; and there was no meanes to keep the body in the Sepulcher, vntill such tyme, as *S. Benet*, had caused a consecrated host, to be put on his breast; when the earth being so pacifyed, as it were, with the same, reteyned him still. With another Monke being fickle and vnconstant, and who with great importunity had obtayned leaue to go forth of Religion, he so wrought with his prayers, as that going forth of the Monastery, he was assayled by a dragon with open mouth; with which terrour he calling for help, had the grace to returne into his Cell agayne, where gathering his wits togeather, he persisted allwayes after very sound in his Vocation.

A child being couered all ouer with leprosy, insomuch as the hayre fell off his head, and his skinne all swolne and puffed vp, being brought into the presence of the *Saint*, was suddenly cured. Through prayer he got likewise a good summe of money for a man that was shrewedly vexed by his Creditour; and that inough, not only to satisfy and defray the debt, but euen also to liue, and mantayne himselfe withall afterward.

In the tyme of the dearth aforesayd, he ordayned that a litle oyle which remayned in the Dispense, should bee giuen to *Agapitus*, a subdeacon, who had demaunded some of him: and knowing the Dispensier had not executed his order, he comaunded the vessell which was of glasse, should be throwne out of the window, which was done; and howbeyt the place beneath was all very rugged, and full of the sharpest stones, yet remayned the vessell as entire, as it had fallen vpon soft feathers. When causing it to be presently giuen to *Agapitus*, he puts himselfe with the Monks into prayer ouer another vessell which was empty, & couered; and it was not long ere it was full of oyle, insomuch as it heaued vp the couer withal, & ran ouer on the ground. Heerewith the *Saint* made an end of his prayer, and the flowing liquor ceased. Whereby the disobedience, & infidelity of that Monke, became iustly reprehended.

Another old Monke, in whome the deuill was entred, and whome he cruelly tormented; a secular man being poysoned by his enemy

enemy; a Country swayn, being miserably beaten, and tyed with cords by a Souldiour of *Totila*, were all quite deliuered. The first, with a light stroke; the second with a simple touch; the third only with a glaunce of *S. Benets* eye.

Another country man, with much fayth, and a great deale of teares, laying his dead child at the gates of the Monastery, had him agayne restored by the *Saint* aliue and lusty. The like effects aboue nature wrought, through diuine power, by meanes of *S. Benet*, are worthily celebrated by Writers. But I for my part, do make a farre greater reckoning of the burning zeale, which he had of the glory of God, and of the eternall saluation of Men, then of all these: in reguard that the vertue of miracles, and other such like gifts of Heauen, are seene also sometymes to be found in the reprobate; while Charity is it that makes vs gratefull, and acceptacle to the diuine Maiesty.

S. Benet *hauing founded many Conuents, and giuen a Rule to his Monks, knowing the tyme of his death before hand, made a most blessed End.* Chap. 10.

Saint Benet, as we haue said aboue, was no sooner taken out of the caue, through diuine prouidence (where for three yeares continually together, so exposed to the iniuryes of the ayre, incommodityes of the body, and temptations of the enemy, he had exercised a very sharp and strict penance) but that with all his power he attended to the reducing of mortals, according to the capacity of ech one, partly to the precepts, and partly to the counsayles of Christ. Nor being content with the founding of many howses of Monks well ordered in the same Country, he went in person, with a few souldiours of his, to assayle the Idolatry of Mount *Cassin*, and to chase away the deuill from those old lodgings & ancient holds of his. Nor there only by himselfe, and others, did he fortify & establish whatsoeuer he had gayned to God: but likewise sent very choyce Captaynes into diuers and remote prouinces, to promote & conserue the Catholique Faith. Moreouer, though he left good orders & rules of life to the Conuents there which from tyme to tyme he had founded: yet neuerthelesse he wrote afterwards of purpose rules full of wisedome and equity for the whole vniuersal Religiō, which being published to the world, were, and are continually of singular auayle.

Among these Heroicall enterprizes, *S. Benet* by this tyme approaching to the end of his trauayles, had knowledge a little before of the day of his death, and openly auerred as much, partly by word of mouth to his disciples present, and partly by letters to others absent: and moreouer added, he should haue from heauen some manifest signe therof ere it came. Nor was this last prophesy of his awhit in vayne, since what he told infallibly fell out. As yet, there appeared no other infirmity in him then meerely of old age, when six dayes before his passage, he caused his sepulcher to be opened, and prepared. And from that tyme, being taken with a burning feauer, which went alwayes increasing more & more; on the sixt day he made himselfe to be caryed into the Oratory, where fortifying himselfe with the holsome viatique of the *Body* and *Bloud* of our Lord, & with the help of his deere disciples, putting himselfe on his feete, & lifting vp his eyes and hands to heauen, amidst very amorous and sweet words of holy prayers and diuine colloquyes, he gaue vp the ghost: and two Monks in diuers places, on the selfe same day, had a like reuelation therof.

For they saw a way in the ayre, adorned with rich tapestryes, and shining all with innumerable lamps, extending it selfe from *S. Benets* Cell, by a strait path, to the East-wards: vpon which a certaine person presenting himselfe in a venerable habit very glorious, enquired of them, what way was that they saw there, and they answering they knew not, he told them, how this was the way by which *Benet the beloued of God, ascended vp to heauen*. So as according to his promise, as well the absent, as present had knowledge of his passage. He was buryed in the Oratory of *S. Iohn Baptist*, neer to his Sister *S. Scholastica*: and as well heere, as at the Caue of *Sublacum*, fell out afterwards, and still do happen, according to the disposition of the faythfull, many very great, and manifest miracles. Though to me truly, this only one seemes to be the notablest of all, to see that illustrious Cōgregation to haue held out so long, afterwards in holy discipline, and in that ancient feruour of spirit it beganne with, & to haue brought forth such, and so great lights of sanctity, & knowledge, as it may worthily be called a fruitfull Seminary of perfect Monks, eminent Doctours, and irreprehensible Prelats, & Pastours of soules.

FINIS.

S. STE-

S. STEPHEN KING.

THE ARGVMENT.

THe goods of Fortune like our garments are,
That heat do giue, but first from vs it take.
Riches do good to those that can them spare
For their soules health: our mynd alone doth make
Them good or bad; from thence they haue their Fate,
And thence are happy or infortunate.
This Saint adorn'd with Royalty, enricht
With all the ornaments great Princes haue,
Glittering in pompe that hearts and eyes bewitcht,
What was most deare vnto his Sauiour gaue:
And last himselfe a free-will-offering brings,
So doing homage to the King of Kings.
Looke how the weary Hart desires to tast,
The chrystall brooke, or siluer streaming fount:
So seem'd his rauisht soule to thee to hast,
O dearest Sauiour, that dost farre surmount
All pleasures, treasures which we heer possesse,
The summe and scope of all our happinesse.

THE LIFE OF S. STEPHEN THE first King of *Hungary*.

Ghiesa *Prince of* Hungary, *endeauouring the conuersion of that Country, sees a comfortable vision to that purpose; and entertaynes* S. Adalbert *comming thither to that end.* Chap. I.

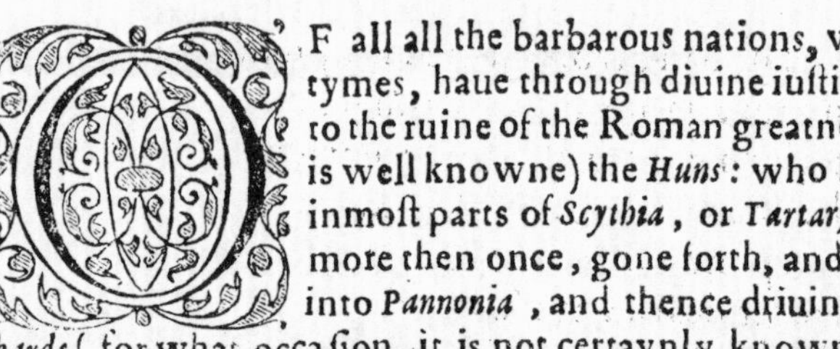

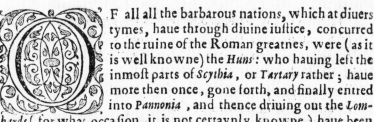

OF all all the barbarous nations, which at diuers tymes, haue through diuine iustice, concurred to the ruine of the Roman greatnes, were (as it is well knowne) the *Huns*: who hauing left the inmost parts of *Scythia*, or *Tartary* rather; haue more then once, gone forth, and finally entred into *Pannonia*, and thence driuing out the *Lombards* (for what occasion, it is not certaynly knowne) haue been called by the new name of *Hungars*. From which tyme, with a natiue fiercenes and rapacity, they haue not ceased, to molest the Church of God; being giuen wholy to the impure worship of Idols, and rather guiding themselues, with vnbridled wills, then with lawes or decrees, vnder the heads which sucessiuely they made choyce of. Of these heads, *Gheisa* was the fourth, who though cruel and seuere by nature; yet neuerthelesse, eyther by instinct of reason, or through the noyse which ran euery where of Christian Religion

ligion, becomming more temperate, & desirous to haue a distincter knowledge of the same Religion; procured of purpose to make peace with all the neighbour Prouinces about him, and with publique Proclamation, gaue not onely secure passage to as many Christians, as would enter into *Hungary*, but ordeyned further that they might all euery where be cheerfully receyued, and benignely intreated: & particularly extending humanity towards the Clerks. and Religious, he began to admit them into his sight without difficulty, & with attention to listen to what they seemed to propose. In so much as what with the example of their life, and the efficacy of the diuine word, and the power of the heauenly rayes, and the excellent disposition of *Gheisa* himselfe; came the holesome seed of the ghospell, by litle and litle to take roote, and to bud in his breast. And in short tyme, the matter went so farre, as that he, not only with a good part of his familiars, tooke the water of holy Baptisme, but likewise made a full purpose, to bring as many as were vnder his gouernment, to the same fayth.

To which effect, according to the instructions of the seruants of God, he designed missions of preachers, building of Churches, foundations of Parishes and Bishopprickes: when on a night, there appeared to him sleep, a yong man of more then human beauty who sayd to him: God saue thee, O elect of Christ; Leaue of these plots of thine, for they are not to be perfected by thee, who hast thy hands too much embrued in bloud; but thou shalt haue a Son, who through the diuine will, shall put the things in execution which now thou proiectst in mynd; and he shall be a King, and be of the number of those, whome God hath predestinated, first to a temporall crowne, and then likewise to an eternall. In the meane while, shall come to thee a personage, with spirituall embassies. See thou receiue him honourably, and haue him in much veneration, and giue thou full credit, and perfect obedience to his aduises, and exhortations.

Gheisa, being astonished at this vision, and considering the same with himselfe, made his Domestiques acquainted therewith, and being humbly prostrate, with infinite thankes, and abondance of teares, recommended himselfe and his states, togeather with the sonne he was to haue, to the care and protection of him, that neuer sleeps, nor shuts his eyes. After which, remayning in much suspense of mynd, about the aforesayd Embassadour; behold the newes, that *S. Adalbert*, Bishop as then of *Prage* (which came afterwards to be the *Metropolis* of *Bohemia*) was coming to him, to procure the conuersion, & saluation of soules. This newes was of great consolation to those *Neophites*; when without delay, the *Prince*, with all the Court, went to meete with the Man of God, and receyuing him with al honour, shewed himselfe most prompt and ready to an entire and filiall obedience.

This *Prelate*, was of great fame, & of the illustrious bloud of *Bohemia*, & of science no lesse then zeale, & as one who hauing twice in person, visited the Mother of all Churches, and humbly adored the *Bishop* of Rome, had among other emprouements from thence suckt forth the pure milke of Apostolicall doctrine, and further obteyned a most ample leaue, in case his *Bohemians* should obstinately resist the Ghospell, to passe into any country of the Infidels, to announce the kingdome of Heauen. It cannot be then explicated, while he saw through the goodnes of God, so great a gate set open to him, vnto the *Hungars*, with how much feruour, and with what industry, he suddenly applyed himselfe to all the ordinary meanes, requisite to the eternall saluation of his Neighbours; the secular Power for its part, concurring likewise to the same, as hath beene sayd; the which euery one sees, of what moment it is, for the happy progresse of the Ecclesiasticall.

S. Stephen *appeares in sleepe to* Saroltha *the Princesse, deliuered afterwards of a Sonne, by name* Stephen; *to whome his Father in his life tyme surrenders his Kingdome.* Chap. 2.

IN those dayes, *Saroltha* the wife of Geisa, being now some what neere to her childbirth, for the greater confirmation of the heauenly promises; there appeared to her in sleepe, euen he, who had the glory to be the first that shed his bloud for *Iesus Christ*, in the habit of a Leuit, & called to her with a sweet countenance, saying: Be of good cheere, *Saroltha*, and know for certaine, thou shalt haue a Sonne, who shall bring into thy howse, the title and crowne of a King, and as soone as he is borne, see thou impose my name vpon him at the sacred Font. At these words, full of wonder and consolation, the *Woman* demaunds of the *Saint*, who he was, and how he was called? whereto hauing answered, that he was *S. Stephen* the *Protomartyr*, without any more, he vanished away. This happened about the yeare of our *Lord* 969. in the *City* of *Strigonium*, where within a few dayes after, the child was very happily borne: & being baptized, with due rites in the lauer of water, by the hands of *S. Adalbert*, according to the precept of the vision & Crowne that attẽded him, had the glorious name of *Stephen* imposed on him.

There liued as then, in those parts, an Italian Knight, thurst out of his Coũtrey by Ciuil warres, by name *Theodatus San-seuerinus*, who by nobility of bloud, and much more, through his valour, & dexterity, was risen to a high degree, both of reputation, & fauour with *Geisa*. This was a wise, & discreet *Baron*, and the Princes Godfather at his entrance into the Christian warfare, and then after, his Mayster and Tutour in behauiour: and therefore after the Italian manner, with a childish simplicity holding him to be his Father, he would salute him by the name of *Tara*; & *Theodatus* in memory of so pleasant a word, founded a towne & Monastery of Religious men hard by *Danubius*, which being afterwards increased by the great *Matthias Coruinus*, with stately buildings, gardens, lakes, & fishpõds, euen to this present day, is called still by the name of *Tara*.

And as the pious child, was very diligently brought vp by *San-seuerinus* in princely manners; so in the elements of the Christiã faith and in those vertues, which are most gratefull to the eyes of God, he was instructed, with great care by *S. Adalbert*, in such sort, as that hardly was he weaned frõ the beast, but he brought forth the name of *Iesus* before that of bread; and in his childhood, together with the Grãmar, he became very expert in the Catechisme; and being now entred into his adolescency, with his acts, gaue not only a noble example of Christian piety, but euen also in publique meetings, he would euer speake with merueilous efficacy, of the deformity of vice, of the beauty of vertue, of the feare of God, of humility, of charity, and of all iustice: seeking by all meanes possible, to mollify the natiue fiercenes of the *Hungars*, and to reduce them, through diuine assistance, vnto a feeling of humanity, and to the vse of right reason. And was so enflamed with the loue of equity, and amendment of the people, that as occasions happened, he would not stick to accuse, and sometymes also to reprehend, in conuenient manner his very Father himselfe, yea and to supply now and then at his request, with the singular approbation of al, the principall cares, in giuing audience, dispatching of publique and priuate businesses, in admitting of the Embassadours of Princes, & giuing them answers,

with

with all satisfaction, that might be.

So that *Geisa*, being now weary with trauailes, and worne out with yeares, acknowledging, with his infinit contentment, very able & sufficient qualityes in the yong man, for an ample gouernemēt, wished nothing more, then to discharge himself of the weight and to lay the burden on his shoulders, and forthwith to behold him with his eyes, inuested in the throne, which he well deserued. And to that end hauing called a generall diet, he had no great difficulty, to perswade the States, to dispose themselues to honour his sonne before hand, by substituting him in his place, being now already spent, and wholy vnable, admitting him to be their lawfull Prince and Lord, and affording him all prompt subiection, and assured oath of fidelity. At so earnest exhortations, and iust request of *Geisa*, the mind of the multitude, remayned so enflamed, as that without delay, in the eyes of the old man (which euen for ioy were powring forth teares) *Stephen* was with great applause, proclaymed not *Duke*, or *Vayuod*, but lawfull *King*, & on the shoulders of the great men, lifted vp to the highest throne, and thence conueighed, with the same applause, to the Souldiours tents.

Heere had he likewise, the title of *King* afforded him, with the greatest veneration, and consent of all, that possible might be. For which benefit, *Geisa* shewing himself to be no whit vngratful, with ample donaryes, with taking away the old aggreeuances, with scattering of mony to the people, and words of much courtesy, continually obliged to him, & his sonne more & more the harts of men, and (that which more imports) was not behind to acknowledge the diuine goodnes, with solemne sacrifice, & extraordinary yielding of thankes. Through which, in the space of a few dayes being oppressed with age, & with a great Catarh, he dyed in the yeare of our *Lord* 997. and the new King, as he had alwayes borne due reuerence in life to so worthy & well deseruing a Father, so ceased he not to performe the same, after his death, with deuout prayers, and most sumptuous exequyes.

King

King Stephen *makes peace with his Neighbours, and seeks to pacify all at home, but is resisted by one* Cupa *a Rebell, whome he labours to suppresse.* Chap. 3.

IN the meane tyme, *Saint Stephen* applying himselfe with more liberty, and exacter diligence to the gouerment, the first thing he sought for, was to haue the glory of God for his finall end, in all his actions, esteeming him euer to be no lesse a Censour and seuere Iudge, then a benigne Father, and bountifull rewarder. And that by so much the more, as he vnderstood of what importance, the Example of a Prince was, as well to the good direction, as the ill gouerment, and totall ruyne of his people. And not to be at the same tyme distracted with internall and external cares and molestations, and with the thoughts both of peace & warre at once, he earnestly laboured in the reestablishing of friendship, and the Capitulations already concluded by his Father with his neighbours, as well by Embassies, as letters, cutting off by this meanes likewise all hope of forraine succours to any male-content with the present State, or who should otherwise be any wayes desirous of nouelty. And forasmuch, as he well vnderstood, how the nerues, and sinewes of empire and rule do principally consist in iustice, as well towards God as to mortalls, he trusting but litle in his owne knowledge, would ordinarily recurre partly to the documẽts of diuine scriptures, wherin day and night, he made himselfe very conuersant, and partly to the counsayle of prudent and learned men, & such as feared God, but especially of *S. Adalbert*; who now perceiuing, through diuine clemency, and the valour of *S. Stephen*, how well matters had proceeded in *Hungary*, determined to passe ouer into other countryes more remote, and which seemed to stand in more need of the light.

Taking then his leaue of the *King*, though giuen with a very ill will; he went his wayes with two choyce companions, and no more, towards *Prussia*, where till that tyme had arriued no knowledge of the Ghospell. Heere while he trauayles, to deliuer the *Pagans* from the seruitude of the diuell, & from their ancient warlique exercises, fierce customes of Barriers, Tourneaments, and the like, vnto the knowledge of the true God, and loue of Christian meekenes; being taken by that wicked nation, and tyed to a stake on the top of a high and steepy hill, & so transfixed with seauen launces,

ces, was added to the merit of his preaching, the palme of a glorious martyrdome. In this interim, *S. Stephen* ceased not also, to hew downe the woods, and to cultiuate the deserts of that Gentility; being resolued, eyther to reduce all his subiects, vnto the knowledge of the Creatour, or in the enterprize, to part with his Kingdome, and life at once.

And for that a good part of that people being brought to be Christians, rather to please the Prince, and for terren ends and designes of theirs, then through any deliberate consent, & stable will; and many others, by no meanes would seeme to admit of such māner of doctrine, *S. Stephen* was enforced against his will, to vse now & then, somewhat bitter, and biting remedyes, wherby he came to exasperate some Nobles in such sort, as that shaking off the yoke of subiection, partly despising the simplicity, and partly hating the seuerity of the Euangelicall discipline, they rose vp in armes agaynst him, and in the lower *Hungary* began to wast, rob, and destroy the deuout places, and persons there, and such as were found to be most obedient to the name of *Christ*, and of *S. Stephen*.

The *Baron of Singia*, by name *Cupa*, was the head and Captayne of the Seditious; a man of exceeding power, and greatly followed of many, who a good while since, hauing by indirect waies, aspired to the Kingdome, now taking occasion from these nodeltyes, went raysing vp the people in such sort, as that what with large promises, what with subtile calumnyes agaynst the persons of *S. Stephen*, and *Gheisa* the Father, and with horrible blasphemies agaynst the Religion brought in of new, as enemy to the Gods, and of their auncient ceremonies and institutes, as also of the glory of the *Hungarian* name, so alwayes mayntayned and augmented, not by the way of bookes, or of slouthfull ease, but with hardy enterprises, and expeditions of armes, being not content with harrying the Champenys, boroughs, and villages, with in a few dayes he lifts vp his horns, to the assaulting euen of the walled townes, nor doubts he a whit to the greater despite, and contempt of the holy *King*, to besiege the towne of *Vesprinio* it selfe, being a Citty very especially beloued, and fauoured of him. Who at the first tydings of the rebellion, hauing tryed with all possible meanes, to temper the mynd of *Cupas*, to winne the people, and to quiet the tumults, at last after many, and earnest intreatyes, gathering a full and competent army, vnder the ensignes of *S. Martin*, the glory of the

the *Hungars*, and of *S. George* that renowned Martyr, and marching along towards his Enemy, he entrenches himselfe in *Cupa* his sight, along the riuer of *Gara*.

Saint Stephen *makes* Vencellinus *his Lieutenant Generall*, *and giues battell to* Cupa, *who is slayne. And the Rebells being defeated*, *the King ordaynes Bishopprickes, Parishes, and Monasteryes.* Chap. 4.

SAint Stephen, among other personages of quality, had three noble *Alman Lords* with him, very zealous Christians, and exceeding expert in feates of Armes, who from the first newes of the pious inclination of *Ghiesa*, had voluntarily put themselues into his seruice, to help and promote the holy Ghospell, to their vtmost power. One of these, by name *Vencellinus*, was by *S. Stephen* declared Lieutenant Generall of his forces; & between the other two *Hunte* and *Pasna*, was the Cauallery, or horse deuided; while the charge of the Fantery, or foote, were distributed to excellent Collonells and Captaynes: and as soone as the Souldiours had taken a little breath, and repose, *S. Stephen* was not slacke, with great courage, and good order, to offer battayle to the perfidious Enemy. Nor was *Cupa* himselfe a whit behind to go forth to meete him, with great vehemency, and with equall hope of victory. The encounter endured many houres, not without a great slaughter betweene them, & still with vncertayne and doubtfull euent: the King himselfe went heer and there very manfully vp and downe the troups, encouraging the doubtfull, inciting the valiant, hartening the cowards, and very readily sending still succour where greater necessity appeared; and aboue all, neuer ceased he to inuoke the diuine assistance, in a cause so iust: and his prayers were not cast into the winds, because, that *Vencellinus*, who had the right wing in charge, perceiuing himselfe to be secretly renforced, as it were, with new breath; after he had fought a good while, with his eye vpon the disloyall *Cupa*, finally knew him, and went suddenly to meete him, & while they both were buckling together, hand to hand, the *King* perceyuing the encounter, with a good number of choyce horse made hast to succour him; whē approching neerer, he sees *Vencellinus* hauing now vnhorsed his enemy, to be cutting of his head with his owne hands; the which to the great ioy of the Christians, was put on the point of a speare, and being carryed heer and there, did giue great terrour to the Rebels, for without more adoe, they fell into route, and direct flight: while our men pursued them with hoat executions, and with the same violence entring into the enemies trenches, neuer gaue ouer from cutting in peeces, as many as they fonnd therein, vntill *S. Stephen*, who grieued at the effusion of so much bloud, caused the retrayt to be sounded.

The Captiues as guilty of high treason, escaped not without cōuenient punishmēt: one quarter of *Cupas* body, in terrour of the rest, was affixed on the gate of *Vesprinio*; another of *Strigonium*; the third at *Gauerino*; and the fourth, at *Alba Iulia*, the principall Citty of *Transiluania*. And if *S. Stephē* in chastizing had vsed iustice, he shewed it no lesse, in largely rewarding his Captaynes, and souldiours, according to the dignity and deportement of ech one: but his principall study was, amidst such prosperous euents, to shun vayne-glory, and to shew forth that piety and gratitude, which he owed to the Authour of all good, and the Court of Heauen. And to that end, deuout processions being made, with solemne masses, he began from the very foundations a magnificent Temple to *S. Martyn* his Protectour, in a scite, which is called the holy *Hill*; where is sayd, the great Seruant of God, was wont to remayne in contemplation, for the litle tyme he abode in that Country: and besides the applying of the third part of the spoyles to the fabricque, he assigned for all the Priests that should inhabite there, the whole Tithes of corne, wine, & of cattell; and moreouer of the children themselues of the inhabitants of the Citty and territory of *Simigia*. And the rest of the goods which he might well haue put into the Fiscall, he deputed part to the maintenance of the poore, & part to the increase of the diuine worship. And being inflamed with new feruour of charity, he neuer left crauing of the Highest, at all houres, & somtymes in sackcloth & ashes, the grace to see before his death, all *Hungary* conuerted vnto the fayth, as forseing for certayne, that being so, it should come to be (as it fell out afterwards) a perpetuall, and strong bulwarke for the *Church* of *Christ*, agaynst the violence of the *Barbarians*.

Many difficultyes seemed to crosse this pious desire of his, but none greater, then the want of sufficient Cathechists, & Preachers; while the number of them who had come to those parts, in the tyme of *Geisa*, through diuers accidents, was much diminished. Whereupon in imitation of his Father, with ample patents, and very liberall offers, he sent to al the religious Orders of Christendom, to inuite the good, and learned vnto him: Insomuch, as many Monkes, and Priests repayred thither, partly moued at so honest a request, and partly also of their proper will. Among which, was one *Astricus* a Benedictin Abbot, called *Anastasius* by another name, with some disciples of his, who in the lower *Hungary*, receyued some wounds for *Christ*. From *Polony*, resorted two famous Hermits, *Andrew* and *Benet*; whereof the one was famous for miracles, the other honoured with sacred martyrdome. By meanes of these, & others, who came to that worke; the *King* attended to instruct the Gentils in the principles, and manners truly Christian; alluring them with sweetnes of words and workes, and likewise when need required, constrayning thẽ by mayne force, to forsake the impious worship of the Idols. Nor euer ceased he from the worke vntill such tyme, as he had purged all those lands of their profane rites, and abhominable filth of the Diuells. And to the end, that all might proceed with due forme, and that the fruit of these labours, might be durable, he takes in hand, with mature consideration, & with the counsayle of the wise, to ordayne in fit places, with sufficient rents, Parochiall, and Collegiate Churches, & diuers Conuents of Monkes; and diuided the Kingdome it selfe into ten Bishoprickes, declaring the Citty of *Strigonium* the Mother of them all, & choosing Prelates of honourable fame for ech one, and such as were apt, with the word to feed the flocke, and to lead them with good workes.

King Stephen *sends to* Rome *an Embassadour, to submit himselfe, and his Kingdome to the Sea Apostolique: & marryes with Gisla, of the house of* Bauary. Chap. 5.

THe rumour and applause of these so heroicall actions of *S. Stephen*, immediately ran through all *Europe*; and there was none who vnderstood the noble proceedings, and spirituall conquests of the new *King*, that deemed him not worthy of eternall prayse, and royall Maiesty. Yet he alone could not satisfy himselfe, nor euer repute that Hierarchy Canonicall, or the Title acceptable to God vnles the free assent, and full confirmation of the Pope were added thereunto, who in those dayes was *Benedictus* VIII. Some foure yeares then, after the death of *Geisa*, the Rebels for the most being suppressed, the publique affayres put in good order, and the faith dilated now as farre as *Danubius*, he sent Embassadour to the Citty of *Rome*, with a goodly and decent pompe the aforesaid *Anastasius*, by him named already *Bishop* of *Colotz*: who after kissing of the feet, and tender of obedience, and a full relation of what had happened in *Hungary* in these latter yeares, was humbly to beseech his *Holynes* for three things. First, that he would daigne to blesse, and admit that new Christianity into the mysticall body of the faythfull. The second, to ratify, with his supreme power, what *S. Stephen* had already disposed, about the Bishopriques, & Metropolis. The third, to approue, and declare valid the name of *King*, wherewith he had beene voluntarily honoured by his subiects; to the end, that the iudgment of the *vicar* of *Christ* concurring thereunto, he might, with so much the greater authority, seeme to promote the diuine seruice, whereto only had all his industryes, thoughts, and designes their whole scope.

The *Pope* at so noble an Embassage, and ioyfull tydings, felt extraordinary consolation in himselfe, nor euer ceased frō praysing God for the happy increase of the Catholique Church, especially there hauing beene that yeare likewise, *Polony* vnited thereto, vnder the *Duke Mischa*, and thither come from thence in like manner an Embassage, to acknowledge the chiefe Sea, and to yeild due obedience to his *Holynes*: wherefore very freely with the generall consent of the sacred Colledge, it pleased his *Holynesse* to giue full satisfactiō to the petitions of *S. Stephen*, & to accept the *Hungars* into the flock of *Christ*. And for royall Ensignes (being a thing that seemed most iust to all) he made him a gift of a Crowne of gold, of great price, and of excellent workmanship: and moreouer sent him a Crosse, to be caryed before him in publique, in signe of the Apostleship, and adorning the presents, with these very words: I am, said he, an Apostolique man, but he may worthily be called the Apostle of God, since through his meanes, *Christ* hath gayned so great a multitude: and therefore, do we remit also to this good *King*, the care of reducing those Churches to better forme, with Parishes and Diocesses.

In this manner, *Anastasius* with a happy expedition, hauing now obtayned what he would, returned agayne very glad into *Hungary*. In whose approch to *Strigonium*, he was met by *S. Stephen* forth of the territory there, with a great multitude of the Clergy, & Nobility. Then were the Apostolicall Briefs read, and the Crowne and Crosse presented; which things *S. Stephen* receiued, not only with

with extreme ioy, but also with much veneration, kneeling himselfe, among other things, in publique, at ech mention which was made of the holy *Father*, to excite with his example, his subiects to a great esteeme and reuerence due to the Roman Sea. Then being anoynted, consecrated, and crowned, with solemne ceremonyes & triumphes, by the *Arch-Bishop*, he attended with more seriousnes thẽ euer, to take away the impediments quite from the course of the Ghospell, maynteyning the external peace with a good neighbourhood, and louing offices, and the internall, with Edicts, & Lawes full of iustice, and equity.

And forasmuch, as to conserue the state, and life of the *Prince*, and to restrayne the pride and animosity of the more stubborne subiects, it is of no light regard besides the good intelligence, of neighbour-Potentats, to haue likewise some number of Children; he determined, with the iudgement, of his more trusty and wise Counsaylours, not to differre his mariage any longer, especially there offering it self, the most noble cõdition of *Gisla*, of the illustrious bloud *Bauary*, and Sister of *Henry* the second, being he that comming into *Italy*, and crowned by the *Pope*, to his immortal prayse, had chased away the *Saracens*, and their fauourits from *Capua*; and those neighbour countryes. The *Spouse* then, was decently conducted to the *Husband*: and as that Sacrament was celebrated with all the circumstances, and respects due vnto Christian Princes; so is it no wõder, the match succeeded to be one of the most blessed, which for many yeares haue flourished since in the world. Into that royall house neuer entered any vayne pompes, no importune iealousyes, no false suspitions, nor bitter contentions; while the happy couple stri-ued not between themselues but in charity vnfaigned, & in the continuall study of the diuine glory. For which end, hauing obteyned (as we haue said) confirmation from *Rome*, of the *Strigonian Metropolis*, and of the Seas subordinat thereunto, to eschew all occasion of strifes, he cleerly determined and lymited the confines of ech; & the same did he also, to diuerse Abbacyes, founded by him.

Saint Stephen *and his Queene build many Monasteryes. His piety shewed to all; and the marueilous eleuation of his in prayer.* Chap. 6.

IT cannot easily be expressed what sollicitude, and magnificẽce *Saint Stephen* alwayes shewed in sacred buildings. He built a marueilous

ueilous goodly Temple in *Alba-regalis*, to the most Blessed *Virgin* (to whome he was singularly deuoted, and so would he likewise haue all those vnder him, and to keep the vigils of all her Feasts, and especially of the *Assumption*) prouiding it with most ample priuiledges, of large rents, and sumptuous furnitures, of vessels both of siluer, and gold, beset with iewels, and so finely wrought, as the metall though of exceeding price, was the least part of the valew therof. In the ancient *Buda*, called *Sicambria* of old, he erected a most noble Temple to the glorious Apostles *S. Peter* & *S. Paul*, hauing for that end, with great rewards, caused certaine Architects to come from *Greece*, and as many artificers, as he could procure to come thither. And to the end, the *Hungars* might conuerse more freely in *Rome*, and continue alwayes firme in deuotion to the chief *Bishop*; he dedicated that gallant Temple of *Mont Celius* there, to *S. Stephen* the *Protomartyr*, without sparing any cost, which for the figure is commonly called the *Rotundo*, and there richly founded withal a Colledge of twelue Priests: and built in the *Vatican*, & sufficiently prouided an Inne, for a welcome receptacle of those of his nation, who should go to visit the *Princes* of the *Apostles*. And extending his liberality also into *Thracia*, and *Soria*, he erected in *Constantinople*, a holy place very statly and goodly to behold; and a conuent of Religious in *Hierusalem*, that ech day at the holy Sepulcher, sacrifices might be offered for the publique good.

These, and other very pious places, are recounted to be built by that holy *King*. And the *Queene Gisla* also, besides the participation she had with his merits, in applauding her husband in all things, & concurring therto as much as she might, would needs build likewise at her proper assignements, and adorn at all points, the *Church* of *Vesprinio*, and there maynteyne at her owne costs, a good number of Priests to say diuine seruice. And if such were the greatnes of mind of these two happy *Princes*, and continuall profusion of expẽces, in materiall wals, and other dumbe works; euery one may easily ghesse, how much their benignity was, and how great their tendernes to men, created for the heauenly country, and oppressed and afflicted in this banishment of theirs, through various necessityes & miseryes. It is reported of *S. Stephen*, that there neuer came any pilgrime to him, whome he lodged not, and after dismissed with a viatique. He had an extraordinary care of the sicke, he would send them, besides dayly relief, now and then some louing present or other, and immediately cured some of those, whome he but commaunded to arise in the name of God. By night, with a pleasing, and cheerfull countenance, he would put himselfe, to wash the feet of most abiect people, and then at last bestow mony vpon them. He would further in the night go alone vnknowne, to visit the Hospitalls of the poore with his full purse.

And it happened on a tyme, that some of them, eyther through greedines of the present obiect, or for some other vniust occasion, meeting with the pious benefactour, most furious and vngratefull as they were, fell a pulling of his beard; with which fact of theirs notwithstanding he was nothing moued, but passing from thence, to the Church of the *Mother* of *God*, gaue her thankes, with all his hart, for that through her intercession, our *Lord* had vouchsafed him, in some manner, to make him partaker of the most vnworthy outrages, villanyes, and iniuries done vnto him. And from thenceforth, more earnestly pursued he to giue large almes, to all sorts of miserable, and calamitous people as well in publique, as in secret, with his owne hands, and by meanes of his familiars, and especially of the blessed *Gunther* of *Bohemia*, an *Hermit*.

And as often, as this *Gunther* the man of God, did come from his Country, to visit him; *King Stephen* would put all the prouisiõs & store of the pallace into his hands; when the *Hermit* distributing what he found, vnto widdowes, Orphans, strangers, and beggars, would soone leaue the Royall Pallace voyd and destitute of all things. Whereat *Saint Stephen* would take very great contentment; feeling himselfe by such acts of charity, towards his neighbour continually enflamed, more and more in the loue of *Christ*, and to the sweet contemplation of inuisible things. And now and then was so highly rauished withall; as that praying once, on a tyme, in his Pauillion, in the open fields, he was playnely seene with the pauillion it selfe, quite raysed a pretty way from the earth.

The Bessians of Bulgary *do forrage* Hungary, *but are defeated by* S. Stephen: *and* Conrade *the Emperour with great forces being ready to giue him battell, is miraculosly preuented.* Chap. 7.

KIng *Stephen* had likewise through the great familiarity, which he had with God, some reuelations of no small importance: as then when the *Bessians* (being a people of *Bulgaria*, with whome afterwards they confounded their proper name) and Pagans at that tyme accustomed to rapine, and most bitter enemyes of the *Hungars*, were euen ready to forrage and destroy *Transiluania*; whereof S. *Stephen* in the night being aduertised from Heauen, dispatched immediatly with all care and diligence, a Post vnto *Alba-Iulia*, who arriued so early thither, as that all the country people of those parts, had space sufficient, to retire themselues, with their most precious commodityes, into walled townes: and there remayned exposed to fire and sword, and pillage of the Enemies, the houses only with the beasts, aud such like Cattell. With which notwithstanding that rauenons people went not long away so triumphant and proud: Because S. *Stephen*, being prouoked with new iniuries, made incursions into their Confines, with a flourishing army, and comming to encounter with *Cea*, the head of the *Beßians*, slew him, and taking his baggage, made a most rich booty of him, and without cōuerting it to priuate vses, applyed it to pious workes, and to the ornament of Churches.

Heerupon the fame of S. *Stephen* now continually increasing, and spreading it selfe through the world; it fell out, that whereas at first, for the instruction and conuersion of *Hungary* there had come thither from diuers parts, very learned and pious men; now for to learne good lawes and laudable customes, began thither to resort many rude and ignorant people, with desire of instruction, & light. As among others some sixty of the principall *Beßians* themselues, though not without great perill and danger, through default of the garrisons appointed there by *S. Stephen* in those frontiers, who at the appearing of such a troupe (which besides the rich furnitures of their personages, brought with them a good number of carriages) eyther allured by the greatnes of the booty, or moued of hatred, or iealousy towards them, without more ado, set vpon them, & not satisfyed with the vniust spoiles they tooke, some they killed, & others they left halfe dead, & wounded. The *King* receiuing the complaint of so haynous a fact, caused without tumult and delay the malefactors to be brought into his presence; & after a shrewd reprehensiō giuen, setting vp gibbets in all the principall passages of the Kingdome, he made them publikely to be hanged vp by two and two. Through which seuerity, besides the punishing of the insolence and presumption past, he so wrought, that while he liued afterwards there was no more any violence offered to any stranger. To this zeale of Iustice,

Iustice, and care of strangers, may be attributed a great part of the continuall protection, which the diuine Maiesty had of him, in his greatest daungers: whereof besides the euents declared aboue, the aduentures which now we shall speake of, doe giue ample testimony.

His Cousen *Henry* being dead, *Conrardus Suenus* entred into the Empire. Agaynst this man, while for diuers respects he differred his going to *Rome*, the Dukes & Communaltyes of *Italy* making a conspicacy, to set themselues at liberty, fell flatly into rebellion; and the better to stand agaynst the power of *Cæsar*, besides the cōbining of themselues togeather, they further demaunded ayde of strangers, and especially of King *Stephen*, and the *Sclauonian* nations which extend themselues from the vtmost bancks of the Adriatique Sea, through *Dalmatia*, *Bohemia*, *Seruia*, *Bulgaria* and *Polonia*, euen to the Artique pole, by the meanes of commerce of a common language amongst them. With all which preparation notwithstanding, *Italy* was not of power sufficient to resist the forces of *Conrad*; who at the fame of such comotions, descended with a dreadfull army vnto *Millan*, and so strayghtly besieged that Citty, as all the rest being terrifyed therwith, laying aside all stubbornes of hart admitted him, with all humble homage and obsequiousnes that might be. Whence applying himselfe to find out the origen and trace of the whole cōspiracy; he found that among other stayes and vpholders, it was fouded particularly on the succours promised by the *Hungars*, as wel for the naturall auersion they had from the name of the *Dutch*, as for the especiall deuotion they bare, from the tyme they receyued the *Holy fayth*, to the Italian name, & to the Bishop of *Rome*.

Conrad, being exasperated with these informations, and moued to a bitter desire of reuenge, was no sooner returned into *Germany* agayne, but he tooke vp armes anew to reuenge himselfe of his aduersaryes, and after he had wasted *Bohemia*, and the neighbour countryes, and seuerely chastized *Boleslaus* the new *Duke* of *Polony*, and chased away his Sonne *Mestou* thence, he sets forth a great Army agaynst *Hungary*: at which newes *S. Stephen*, though a great deale inferiour in forces, endeauours notwithstanding to gather vp an army, and to prepare for his defence, confiding yet aboue all things in the diuine succours. Of which his confidence at this tyme neyther, was he awhit deceyued. Because the *High-dutch* very fiercely entring into those parts, and being now encamped in a place commo-

commodious, *S. Stephen* was not slacke to meete them with his squadrons, and now were matters disposed on both sides, for a cruell and bloudy battell; when besids all opinion, appeares in the field, an Imperial Herald, who running through all the tents of the Captaynes and souldiours, gaue expresse order, to take vp the pauillions, and bagage, and to returne agayne into *Almany*. There could not happen to *Conrad*, a thing more strange, and new at that tyme, who examining his officers with great diligence, and not finding he had giuen any such commaundement at all; was satisfied at last, how that Herald could be no other, then an Angell sent from Heauen, in fauour of S. *Stephen*; and being touched with religion, not only for the present renewed a firme peace with the *Hungars*, but holily resolued withall, perpetually to beware of molesting such any more, whome he manifestly saw to be so safe, and secure vnder the diuine protection.

Gynla *the vncle of* S. Stephen *rayseth a rebellion, and is ouerthrowne: & after that receiueth Baptisme. With another notable conspiracy against him discouered, and punishad.* Chap. 8.

THe good *King*, being thus deliuered from so great a dãger, had soone after, a new occasion, to acknowledge the eyes of the diuine clemency to be cast vpon him. Among the remaynder of the rebellious and contumations people, against the yoke of *Christ*, & obedience of the *Prince*; was an vncle of his, by name *Gynla*, who had the mountaynes of *Transiluania* in his gouerment. This man, after he had often sought to recall to the anciẽt profane rites, not only the people but euen his Nephew himselfe; takes vpon him through diabolicall instinct, to endomage with inrodes and incursions the *Lower Transiluania*, & the *Cityes* of *Hungary* it selfe. While *S. Stephen*, on the other side, hauing tryed all wayes to quiet *Gynla*, and to put him in the way of saluation; being finally enforced to recurre to armes, had so much furtherance from him that can do all things, as that passing into his *Vncles* gouerment, in a few monthes, he subdued him quite, and conuerting the neighbour people to the Fayth, led *Gynla* with him prisoner into *Hungary*, with his wife, and children: and lastly also hauing induced them to Baptisme, he set them at liberty and treated them alwayes very honourably. To this persecution, there succeeded afterwards another, so much more daungerous, as it was

was more secret.

Foure of the principall Palatynes of his Kingdome, with many familiars of the Court, being but ill founded in human and diuine fayth, and not able to endure the present tranquility & peace, and throwly resolued ere Christian religion tooke deeper roote, to reduce *Hungary* agayne to the ancient fiercenes; determined first of al to take away *S. Stephens* life, and thence afterwards to put all into hurly-burly, and to stirre vp heere and there, reuolutions and tumults: With this purpose, one of the conspiratours, being the most temerarious of the rest, hiding his Scimetre vnder his coate, and entring one Euening into the Pallace, in the shutting of the night, before that candles were lighted (it being then sommer tyme) went priuily insinuating himselfe into the Kings lodging; where while he goes feeling the wals vp and downe into the darke, with dubious hands; behold his Fauchon vnawars fals from him: at the noyse whereof the *King* crying out, the Palatyne being wholy terrifyed and confounded, found no better euasion then to present himselfe vnto his presence, & humbly to craue pardon at his hands; nor was the same denyed by the *King*: who making neuerthelesse most diligent inquisition of the cōplices, for publique example, would haue them by no meanes to be left without due punishments.

The Sanctity, and vertues of B. Emericus, *sonne to* S. Stephen: *his especial gift of discerning the merits of others. And how* Maurus *a Monke was especially honoured by the said King.* Chap. 9.

SAint *Stephen*, in the meane tyme, had many Children, & among them, one *Emericus*, who being adorned with more then human vertues, was by posterity afterwards, with the authority of the Pope Beatifyed. It cannot easily be explicated, what consolation tooke, not only the Parents from the bud, but euen likewise all those, who being neere him had any knowledge of him. For first, being preuented from heauen, with plenty of benedictions, and alwayes afterwards brought vp with exact tendance of Nurses, Tutours, and very excellent choyce Maisters, and principally assisted by the liuely examples, and holsome documents and admonishments of the Father, (who not content with his present aduices to help him, did write himselfe also a Booke of that matter) he came in short tyme to worke those fruits which from so rare a towardnes, & diligent edu-

 cation,

cation, the world might well expect.

And among other notable things, recounted of him, this was one, that euen from his tender age, through his great moderation of dyet, restrayning himselfe, with much watching; he would rise at midnight, to recite deuoutly the diuine the office, and pausing betweene psalme and psalme, examine the distractions suffered therin, and with hart contrite, craue pardon of God for them; and would endeauour besides with heauenly grace, to reduce his actuall intention to a most perfect habit. *S. Stephen* sometymes beholds the same through a certaine chincke of the wall, and keeps it secret, reioycing in himselfe, at so new and pleasing a spectacle. Now the holy *King* was wont (according to his commissions and facultyes, receiued from *Rome*,) to obserue the customes, and behauiours of Ecclesiasticall persons, and to go in person to visit the Churches and Conuents of his Kingdome: and among others, going once to *S. Martyns* hill, where (as hath beene said) many Monks of the *Order* of *S. Benet* did liue very orderly & regularly togeather; it pleased him once, to cary his beloued *Emericus* thither with him, & at his coming neere to the place, perceiuing the venerable family to come in processiõ towards him, he sudenly sent his Sonne before to meete them, & entertayne them the while, who being receiued with great honour by the Seruants of God, began in the sight of his Father, to kisse him one by one, but yet not all alike, since that knowing by diuine reuelation the merits of ech one, to some he gaue two kisses, to others three or foure, and fiue to many, saue only to *Maurus* he gaue seauen. Whereat the *King* merueyling much, and thinking it likely not to happẽ by chance, would needs be satisfyed therof; when Masse was ended he familiarly demaunded of *Emericus*, what was the reason, that to one, and the selfe same habit of Religous, with the same manner of salutation of kissing, he had obserued so great diuersity in the number: whereto the *Youth* very promptly answered, that in such distribution he had had regard to the purity and continency of ech one, & that with the number of seauen so perfect, it pleased him to honour him so, who from a child to that tyme, had kept his virginity entire.

The Father remayned with this answere, much more in suspense, then before: and to be the better certifyed therof, taking his leaue from thence for the present, returned thither agayne, a little after vnknowne, with two only familiars, and no more: and dexterously

terously comming by night into the Quire, in time of the Mattins, the office being ended, he noted how the greatest part of those Regulars, immediately retyred themselues, to repose in their Cells, & how such only as *Emericus* had fauoured most, remayning behind, went to hide themselues in certayne corners, to continue their feruent prayer. Then *S. Stephen* approching first to one, and then to another a part, discouering who he was, very courteously saluted them all; who at the sight of his Royall Maiesty interrupting both prayer and silence not fayled to salute agayne with all reuerence: but so did not *Maurus*, being wholy rauished the while with celestiall things; for being saluted by the *King*, with most sweet words, he opened not his Mouth, and being sharply rebuked by him for it conttnued still mute. Whereupon the day following the *King* for better proofe of the inward qualityes of *Maurus*, causing the bell to sound to a Chapter, in the presence of all, with seuere countenance, at last charged him with many things that by no meanes became a religious person: but the disciple of Christ, confiding in the testimony of a good conscience, and in the iudgement of him that sees all, keeping alwayes a good composition, and modesty with him, answered not a word. Whereupon the *King* apprehended the sanctity of this man, was with reason so singularly honoured by his sonne *Emericus*, & laying all dissimulation aside, he discouered most cleerly to the Monkes, the intent wherefore he came thither, and the experience he would needs make of *Maurus*. Nor did he extoll him only for the present, with extraordinary prayse, but further elected him a litle after, to the Bishopricke of *Cinq-Eglises*, and obtayned the full confirmation therof from his *Holynes*.

A singular act of Chastity in Emericus, *preseruing his virginall purity in the state of Matrimony.* Chap. 9.

IN this meane while, *Emericus* went dayly increasing, both in yeares and vertues, & felt a generous desire to burne in his breast of doing some notable seruice to the diuine Maiesty. With this deuotion, entering on a tyme, with one page only, into the *Church* of *S. George*; he puts himselfe on his knees to meditate, and to find out with himselfe, what Present to offer, that might be most grateful & acceptable to the eyes of his *Creatour*: and behold on a sudden, the whole place to be replenished with an immense light, and a voyce heard

heard which said: *Virginity* is a fayre and beautifull thing; this is that which I seeke entirely of thee, as well in mind, as body; This then, do thou offer to God, and see thou perseuere therein with full purpose. These words arriuing in the eares of the Page withall, did so penetrate the mind of *Emericus*, and so wrought with him, as that being enflamed with the desire of obeying, and distrustfull withall of his owne forces, he prayed in this manner.

My *Lord God*, to whose eyes euery thing is open, and naked, & who, as thou knowest, through thy iust iudgment how to take away the life from great men, and are very dreadful to the Kings of the earth; so to their frailty, who presume not of themselues canst tell how to afford opportune succour; Graunt I beseech thee, thy most holy will, may completely be performed in me, and with the dew of thy mercy, extinguish in my hart al noxious concupiscéces: Fortify the weaknes of thy poore Seruant through thy benignity, that he may neuer swearue from the right way: Guard him from al the allurements of sensuality, and cause that he neuer commit any thing, whence he may seeme to fall from thy grace.

The Colloquy ended, *Emericus* felt himselfe to be fully replenished with extraordinary consolation, & wonderfully encouraged withall, yet to eschew vain-glory, would neuer reueal the fauour to any, but commaunded his seruant vnder grieuous paynes, as long as he liued, to keepe it secret. When cooperating afterwards, with the diuine mercy, he neuer left at tymes to macerate the flesh, with prayer fastings, and vigils: and that with reason too, because God, (who is not pleased with vertues not come to the Chisel, and proued by the Hammer) disposed, that by meanes of his Father, he should be tépted to marry with a yong Lady of rare qualityes, and of Princely bloud, though by Authours vnnamed. To which importunity, after *Emericus* had resisted a prety while at last, not to contristate his Parents, he yields, secure the while, that the diuine Goodnes for the obseruance of his promise, would not fayle him of some succour or other, as indeed after he found it so.

For that as soone, as he had with solemne ceremonyes, publiquely accepted the Spouse, in priuat being assisted from heauen, as well with reasons, as with prayers, he easily induced her, to cōserue with him, vnder the cloake of Matrimony, the flower of virginity, preferring it (wisely) before all respect of yssue, and all the greatnesses, & Signoryes of the world. Wherof in progresse of tyme,

S. Stephen was aware; but yet setting the greater glory of God before his eyes, by all meanes he absteyned frõ withdrawing *Emericus* frõ his holy purpose. Amidst so great variety of human accidents, & among so many prosperityes of glorious victories and ioyfull successes, had S. *Stephen* no want notwithstanding of his probation & scourges. For of so numerous an of-spring, which he had, while one dyed after another, in their childhood, there was only *Emericus* left him, with whose safety alone, to him it seemed were counterpoysed all other losses whatsoeuer; when he also, in the flower of his age, was snatched away, so accomplished with merits, to be an aduocat in Heauen, for those nations, which in earth by lawful inheritance belonged to him.

S. Stephen neuerthelesse at so grieuous a blow felt incredible sorow; especially so redoubled a little after, by the death of his wife, not finding the while, any one of his stock, to whome securely he might leaue the gouerment: and the whole kingdome standing in daunger to returne to their old vomit, and customes as before, whẽ through want of a good successour, the good exercises began, should be quite giuen ouer. *Emericus* his exequies were celebrated in *Alba-Regalis*, some 30. dayes after his happy passage, with so euident miracles, and so full persuasion of his eternall felicity, as in a moment all the cloudes of sadnes and mourning were vanished quite, when his wife, now Widdow, gaue faythfull testimony of her husbands virginity, and the Page to confirme the same, discouered what had happened in *S. Georges* Church.

How S. Stephen *dyes, and is buryed with pompe in the Church of our Lady which himselfe had built, where he workes many miracles. With the translation of his holy Body afterwards.* Chap. 10.

Saint *Stephen* perseuering still in his wonted yielding of due thankes vnto God, and conforming himselfe with the diuine will in all things, came shortly after to fall into a grieuous palsey, wherewith being held more then 30. months in his bed, he was finally seized with a strong feauer, which brought him to the end of human miseryes. And now at last, peceyuing himselfe to decay, causing the Prelats and Barons which were in Court, to be called vnto him, he delt with them about a future Election, hauing alwayes an eye on the diuine seruice, & increase of his holy fayth, &

exhorted them with fatherly affect, to esteeme it aboue all things, and for the same to be ready to spend their bloud, when occasion should require. Moreouer, he recommended to them the obseruance of the diuine precepts, & of the Popes ordinations, the maintenance of Iustice, concord, and of peace, not only among themselues, but likewise with strangers: In summe, to shew themselues Christians to euery one, and faythfull no lesse in hart, and deeds, then profession, and title.

In this manner in substance, *S. Stephen* spake to the principall of the Kingdome, with the great resentement, and sorrow of as many as heard him; when lifting vp his eyes and hands to heauen, not without teares, but with voyce interrupted, he spake in this manner; O glorious Queene of Heauen, O noble restorer of the world, into thy hands do I recommend, togeather with my soule, the Churches, the Clergy, the Primates, and the people of *Hungary*. Heerupon, hauing receyued, in the presence of all, after the Sacrament of *Pennance*, the celestiall *Viatique*, & *Extreme vnction*, he quietly rendred his spirit, vpon the very Feast of the *Assumption*, as he had alwayes desired, a happy day, and with reason euer celebrated by him from a child with singular ioy, being then the yeare of our Lord, one thousand thirty & eyght, or thirty foure, as some will haue it, being the 69. of his *Stephens* life, and 41. of his Crowne.

His body, with magnificall pompe, and most frequent concourse of all the States, was carryed likewise to *Alba regalis*, there to be deposed in the Temple of the most *blessed Virgin*, by him built, as we haue said aboue: but being not yet consecrated, it seemed good to the Bishops, that ceremony should first precede the funeralls, which being ended, he was there placed with psalmes and canticles, and other solemnityes, in a vault of white marble; where a long tyme the diuine Goodnes continually glorifyed his seruant, giuing health to the lame and diseased; and consolation, and succour to the miserable & afflicted. There were heard also in the same place, oftentymes by night, angelicall songs, with a most fragrant odour diffused on euery side. The precious members lay there in a Sepulcher, some 45. yeares: at which tyme *Ladislaus* the 7. raygning, there came order from *Rome*, that diligent search, and enquiry should be made of all the reliques of such, as from the beginning had been the instruments of God, in the preaching of the Word, & conuersion of *Hungary*; and for the renewing of the memory of such labours,

labours, and so great merits, that a very Honourable, and Noble translation, should be made of their bodyes.

In vertue of this Order, by the vniuersall Dyet, was a Fast intimated of three dayes, with prayers and almes; after which *Ladislaus*, with much veneration, being accompanied by the Court & people, came first to the Monument of *S. Stephen*: but with all the engins, and strength that might be, was it not possible to be opened and discouered; vntill such tyme, as by the aduise of a Virgin, whose name was *Carite* (who being immured besides the Church of our *Sauiour*, was held in great opinion of sanctity) he was resolued to deliuer *Salomon* his brother, imprisoned by him for grieuous strifes and disgusts betweene them. Heerupon now the Fast being redoubled, that immoueable stone, was so easily remoued as it had been of wooll, or straw. The Coffin then of lead being taken from thence, and carryed in procession, and the Vespers sung, it was reuerently deposed vpon a most glorious Aultar, in the midst of the Church; and all that day, and the night following, there continued very euident miracles.

In the morning, which was the 20. of August, the Masse being celebrated, and prayer ended; the *King*, with the principall of the Clergy, and Nobility, approching to the coffin, keeping the multitude off, for feare of some theft, with deuotion they opened the same, and now the flesh being dissolued, the bones appeared to lye within a certayne liquour, like balme, which euen sauoured of an odour of Paradise, being much consumed with tyme. *Ladislaus* beheld it attentiuely, and with great curiosity seeking for the ring of *S. Stephen*, caused for that purpose, the said oyle to be laded forth by hands of the worthyest Prelats, into siluer vessells: but by how much the coffin was emptyed by others, it was agayne filled vp of it selfe, and all their diligence succeeded in vayne: being then amazed thereat, they powred it in agayne, and yet the quantity increased not a whit eyther more or lesse. When the bones withall, being put thereinto, they were thence translated, into a most sumptuous, and rich Chapell.

An Angell appeares to Mercurius *a Monke, and deliuers him a hand with the Ring of* S. Stephen. *With a Miracle happening at the shrine of* Emericus. Chap. 11.

OF the number of those, to whome, in the ministery of the Priests, was denyed accesse to the sacred reliques, was a Mōke whose name was *Mercury*, deputed to the seruice and custody of that Church. This man, taking it very heauily to hart, that he could not be suffered at pleasure, to behold and kisse that great treasure, retired himselfe a part; and there in the dead tyme of the night, sat mourning and lamenting, when besides all hope, there appeared to him a yong man, of a heauenly countenance, who reaching him a peece of fine holland, enfolded and wrapped vp together: Take heere (said he) O *Mercury*, the same which thou hast so much desired, & when thou hast kept it *in deposito* for a day, do thou carry it to the *King*. After these words, the Angell vanished away: and *Mercury* ful of vnspeakable sweetnes, vnfolding the cloth, found there the hād and Ring, so much sought for of the *King*, and when it seemed to him, to be now high tyme, he went and made a present thereof to the King *Ladislaus*, who receiued it most ioyfully, & in a sumptuous Reliquary, caused it to be layed apart in another Oratory. And it was but iust, that so beneficious a right hand, with particular care, without all iniury should be kept and reuerenced, in a place by it selfe, which so often had beene so profusedly stretched forth, to the benigne succour, and liberall reliefe of the poore.

This particular, from a heape of relations, we haue thought good to select forth, about the life, customes, and greatnesses of *S. Stephen*, the first *King* of *Hungary*. With which, since we haue accidētally likewise fallen vpon those of the blessed *Emericus*; it may not happily be amisse, to conclude the whole narration, with an admirable effect, wherof they both, though not equally, might seeme to participate.

In the tyme of the same *King Ladislaus* before mentioned by vs, a certaine High-dutchmā, one *Conrad* by name, a man of a most wicked life, and plunged in all manner of debauchnes, being at last compunct, and contrite for all; went his wayes to *Rome*, and there making a generall Confession of his whole life, had for his penāce, to weare on his bare flesh, a breast plate of steele, tyed on with fiue chaynes

chaynes of iron, with a sheet of paper written therein, wherein his more enormous crymes were conteyned, signed with the seale of his *Holynes*, and in this habit to go visit the holy places of Christendome, vntill such tyme, as through diuine power the bands should be vndone, & the writing be wholy cancelled. This man obeyed with great promptnes, and after he had beene at *Hierusalem*, and other famous Monuments of *Saints*, he came at last vnto *Alba-regalis*, & there putting himself in prayer, at the shrine of the holy *King Stephē*, he determined not to arise from thence, vntill he had perfectly obteyned the grace. And now he had perseuered from one, to nine a clock at night, when sleepe through wearynes oppressed him, and immediately the *glorious King* appeared vnto him, saying: Get vp friend; and go thy wayes to the Chapell hard by, of my sonne *Emericus*, who through especiall priuiledge of incorrupt virginity, shall obtayne thee vndoubtedly pardon of thy so great crymes, he being one of the number of those, who haue neuer defiled their garments, but accompany the *Lambe* wheresoeuer he goes, and who stand singing before the Throne of God, that new song.

Which said he vanisheth; & the *Penitent* without delay, passing to the Monument of *Blessed Emericus*, had no sooner begun to frame new prayers, but that in a moment, his hard knots fell loose of thēselues, & the seale broke open, & discouered the paper to be blank. At the noyse of the cheynes falling off, the Keepers of the Church, & others, at that tyme entring to do their deuotions, came running to him, and some of them vnderstanding particularly by relation, and the rest with their owne eyes what had happened, neuer ceased to magnify God, the giuer of all good, and merueilous in his *Saints*. To whome be all honour, power, and benediction for all eternity. *Amen.*

S. EDVVARD KING.

THE ARGVMENT.

AN Orphan left, and in minority,
Heau'en was my Guardian; this did mee protect:
To this I did assigne my custody;
My raging foes heerby suppress't and checkt
Yielding to it, did grant me liberty
To serue my deare Aduancer, and reflect
    On this false world, which promising content
    Doth only yield vs matter to repent.
As those that in the Eternall Essence see
What ere falls out, what euer was before:
Veyl'd vnder bread, Deare Lord, I view'd in thee
The machinations of the Prince * that bore * The Dane.
A Rauen bath'd in Martiall Gules, to bee
Dissolu'd: I stretcht mine Empire past the shore
    That *Albion* bounds: my force did *Ireland* tame
    That thought my standards fatall where they came.
Treasures so much I slighted, that I view'd,
Vnmoued thereat, my treasures borne away.
The stately Fane at * *Thorney* rays'd, hath shewd * Now VVestminster
My end, Heau'ns glory: Still it doth display
A mynd with true Magnificence endu'de.
Heerby I gaind what neuer shall decay:
    And with a Ring espous'd me to the skie,
    Where my Raygne done, I raygne Eternally.

THE LIFE OF S. EDVVARD KING OF ENGLAND.

Written by *Alred* Abbot of *Ridall*, of the Order of *Cisterce*.

S. Edward *is chosen King in his Mothers wombe.* Ethelrede *the Father dying,* Edmund *succeeds.* Canutus *rages.* Emma *flies with her two yonger Sonnes into* Normandy: *with the great towardlines of* S Edward.

IT pleased God, the Blessed *Edward*, through especiall prerogatiue, should be chosen *King* before his appearing to the world: for that at the instance of his *Father Ethelred* King of *England*, a Parliament being called, as well for other publique affayres, as to declare, & sweare to a new Prince, howbeit already there were two sones of his of strong constitution, *Edmond*, and *Alfred*: yet the Nobility & Clergy, being but little satisfyed with eyther of them, with a wonderous inclination, concurred to yeild homage vnto an vncertaine yssue,

yſſue, as yet encloſed in the Mothers wombe, which being born a little after, was called by the name of *Edward*. True it is, that *Ethelred* dying in thoſe dayes, and moſt cruell tempeſts threatning the *Iland* on euery ſide, with conſent of the *Barons*, not to leaue things altogether without a head; the ſaid *Edmond*, tooke the rule vpon him. Nor was it long, but that a terrible inundation of the Barbarous *Danes*, came ruſhing into *England*, vnder the *Tyrant Canutus*. Who beginning to put all things to fire and ſword, the *Queene Mother*, whoſe name was *Emma*, a *Norman* by natiõ, was conuayed for greater ſecurity, with her yonger ſonnes, into her *Fathers* Country.

Heere the child *Edward*, began betymes to giue forth very euident ſignes of the mature piety he was like to atteyne in tyme. In reguard, that hauing in ſcorne all childiſh ſports, he attended ſtill, among other tokens of a Chriſtian mind, to viſit now this, now that holy *Conuent*, and to linck ſtreight amityes with the moſt famous Seruants of God. In the meane tyme, in *England* the fury of the *Enemy* grew day by day more cruell, then other: nor was now to be ſeen at laſt, or heard any other then ſlaughters, rapins, bitter plaints, and terrible outcrys. The *Temples* burned, the ſacred habitations ruined, the Guardians, and Paſtours of ſoules, for feare of the worſt puniſhments, hid themſelues in the moſt craggy, and deſert places.

Among which, was *Britwald Biſhop* of *Wincheſter*, a man of great prayer, and of a notable ſpirit Who praying one day, with many teares, for the health of the *Kingdome*, and powring forth his afflicted hart with ſighs and laments before the diuine preſence, after much wearynes of mind, and body, fell finally aſleepe. Where behold the *Prince* of the *Apoſtles* appeared to him, from an eminent place, with *S. Edward* before him, a youth very gracious in countenance, and adorned with a ſcepter, diadem, and royall mantle, who after he had with ſolemne vnction, conſecrated him with his owne hands, gaue him many good documents withall, full of verity and life; and in particular exhorted him, to keepe virginity, reuealing to him beſiſides, for how many yeares he ſhould hold the dominion.

Now *Britwald* being ſorely aſtoniſhed at ſuch a viſion, as ſoone as he returned agayne to himſelfe, tooke hart, & beſeeched *S. Peter* to vouchſafe to manifeſt to him ſome things of the eſtate of that miſerable Coũtry, & of the end of the troubles, which afflicted the ſame. To which demaund, the *Apoſtle* anſwered, with a ſeren countenãce.

King-

Kingdomes, *O Bishop*, are of God, he is the *Lord*, and *Maister* of all; he at his pleasure alters, and changes gouernments, & for the sinnes of nations, doth oftẽ exalt the Hypocrit. The *diuine Maiesty*, is grieuously offended with thy people, and therfore they are fallẽ into the hands of their most capitall aduersaryes: but yet neuerthelesse God shall not be vnmindfull of his wonted mercy, nor stretch forth his iust vengeance, for euer vpon them: because many yeares shall not passe after thy death, but the present calamityes shall cease, and the wished redemption shal come to this people since his eternal goodnes, hath already destined a man, according to his hart, and wholy at his deuotion; who being placed through my help in the royall Throne, with the infinite consolation of the subiects, shall abate the forces, and bridle the *Danish* fury; and who after he hath many wayes raysed, and aduanced the *Church*, being deere to God, very acceptable to his friends, and dreadfull to his enemyes, shall termine his glorious life, with a most holy end.

From this so benigne an answere, together with the sight of him there promised, the *Bishop* tooke new courage, and stuck not to enquire of the Oracle it selfe, of the posterity, and successours of *Edward*. To which demaund, with obscure and dubious words, the *Apostle* replyed no more, but that, *God was Lord, and after this, he would prouide another, according to his good pleasure.*

Edmund *with his Children are put to the sword.* Alfred *is made away.* S. Edward *prayes, and makes a vow to God and* S. Peter; *and* Canutus *with his children dying, is recalled into* England *agayne.* Chap. 2.

THe English troubles, continuing still, with ciuill discord among themselues, being ioyned at last with externe warres, came to be so mischeiuous and pernicious, as that despising all law of fayth, all vicinity of bloud, all obligation of friendship, al things were full of fraud, factions, and iealousies. And euen malice proceeded so farre, as that the *Nobles* themselues, forgetting their oath shamefully renouncing their lawfull Kings, and putting *Edmond* to the sword, with his children at Nurse, they continually prepared tragedyes. *Canutus* with a wicked marriage, possessing the *Widdow* the *Wife* of *Edmond*, left nothing vntryed, to confirme himselfe, in the vnlawfull vsurpation of the Kingdome. Wherein he had so fast a hold, that *Alfred* for the quieting of tumults in some manner, too boldly passing ouer from *Normandy* into his *Country*, was with extreme cruelty, made away, as well by the *Danes*, as *English*, and at the same tyme, the desolate *Queene Emma* dyed in her *Fathers* house.

Then *Edward*, being depriued of all human succour on earth, and fearing euery houre, his last ruine from others, amidst many troubles, and anguishes, prostrating himselfe most humbly before the diuine presence, prayed in this sort. Behold, *Lord*, how I haue now, no more help in me, and my neerest friends are farre of from me: my friends, and neigbours, are all become my aduersaryes; I haue neyther Father, nor Mother in the world; my Brothers and Nephewes, are betrayd and slayne; the widdow my kinswoman, is become our aduersaryes wife. So as I am left without all stay, & they seeke moreouer, to take away my lyfe. But I (*O Lord*) poore wretch, am left to thee, and thou shalt succour the orphan, as heeretofore in a meruailous manner, thou hast done to *King Edwin*, enuironed on euery side. Thou, that madest *S. Oswald*, the ornament of *England*, of an exile, to be *King*, and by meanes of the signe of the Crosse, didst subiect to him, all those that hated him; If thou shalt be with me, and through thy protection, remit me into my *Fathers* kingdomes, thou shalt be alwayes my God, and the blessed *Apostle Peter*, shall be my especiall Protectour, whose most holy reliques, I do promise to visit in the Citty of *Rome*, with his direction.

With this Vow, *S. Edward* felt himselfe exceedingly reuiued, and replenished with no vayne hopes. For that *Canutus* in few daies dyed, and his children also, of tender age, not long suruiued. By occasion whereof, the *English*, as awakened out of a dead sleepe, very suddenly tooke vp armes, and shaking of the yoke of intruding tyranny, recalled the desired *Edward* into the land agayne, and receyuing him with all the honour possible, with one accord, they placed him in the royall throne. At the comming of *S. Edward*, all good arts, and Christian vertues did returne from banishment. The vacant Seas were soone replenished, Churches, and Monasteryes repayred, and the diuine seruice, in short tyme brought to its auncient splendour agayne. Hence through welcome peace, ensued the tillage of the wast and desert champaynes, and the Iudges and Magistrats being kept in their duty, more through example of the *King*, then feare of punishments, attended to administer vpright iustice, to all sorts of persons. The iubily, and content of the present

ſent felicity, was much augmented by the freſh memory of the miſeryes paſt; inſomuch as not only the reaſonable creatures with prayſes and thankes-giuing, but euen the land it ſelfe, with extraordinary fruitfulnes, the ayre with fayre and ſerene weather, the ſea with ſtill and quiet waues, and ſmiling countenance, ſeemed to acknowledge him, and the Cittyes daily to multiply in laudable cuſtomes, riches, and multitude of inhabitants.

Two notable examples in S. Edward *of contempt of Riches. With his vow of chaſtity, maintayned in the ſtate of Matrimony.* Chap. 3.

IT was not long, ere the fame of ſo great proſperity, extended to the Prouinces beyond the Seas. And from all the *Potentates*, the *Dane* excepted (for they left not their pride) came very honourable Embaſſages, from tyme to tyme, to congratulate, to make leagues of freindſhip, and to eſtabliſh ſome good correſpondence with *S. Edward*. And he the while, not puffed vp with pride, nor diſſolute with vayne triumphs, hauing alwayes the *diuine Maieſty*, before his eyes, with an euen tenour of life, carryed himſelfe very meeke to his domeſtiques, reuerent to Prieſts, gracious to the people, compaſſionate to the afflicted, and aboue all things, a great Almoner, & a ſtrange neglecter of money; inſomuch, as once, among the reſt lying on his bed, & his priuate Treaſurer, *Hugoline* by name, hauing vnawares, left open a cheſt of mony in that chamber, a groome of the place, being inuited through the commodity of the purchaſe and the ſeeming ſleepe of the *Prince*, approaching boldly, tooke away from thence a good quantity therof, & put it vp in his pocket; and being glad of ſo happy a ſucceſſe, returned againe a ſecond tyme and ſo a third; When as the *King*, who had feigned till then, perceiuing *Hugoline* to be comming, brake ſilence, and with friendly voyce, ſaid to the wretch: Get thee gone, for the Treaſurer comes; who if he chaunce to catch thee once, will not leaue thee a farthing of all thou haſt. At this voyce, the fellow fled aſſoone, and ſcarcely had got his feete forth of one doore, but *Hugoline* entred by the other, and finding ſo great a ſumme of treaſure to be wanting, he was euen ready at firſt to faynt for griefe, then entring into a rage with himſelfe began to rent the ayre with cryes and ſighes: When *S. Edward*, ariſing from his bed, & ſtill diſſembling the matter, quietly demaunded the occaſion of ſo great a heauynes, and hauing heard it:

Hold thy peace man (said he) perhaps he who hath taken it away had more need thereof, then we: Much good may it do him, the rest I hope will serue for vs. With such quietnes, he passed ouer that act. Whence may be gathered, how well subdued he had his passions, & how farre he was, from all rapine of others goods, that was so prōpt to yeild his owne.

To which purpose likewise, we may not let this passe; there hauing beene in his *Fathers* tyme, a most grieuous taxation, layd on the people, in respect of an army to be leuyed against the *Danes*, and yet the same exaction still continuing (as it happens) though the warre were ended; *S. Edward* as a good Father, and Pastour of his people, with princely liberality, discharged them thereof, for euer: whereto, besides the greatnes of his mynd, he was likewise moued by seeing playnely, vpon a heape of the same money, an vgly Deuill to sit, and sport himselfe. In such like acts as these of religion, equity and bounty, with the edification of all the world would *S. Edward* spend the tyme afforded him for the purchase of the Eternity. And yet among these same honourable thoughts, he forgot not a whit, the virginall title, so seriously recommeded to him by *S. Peter* the Apostle: which thing indeed, proued to be so much more violently assaulted by his green yeares, hoat complexion, easy accesse vnto delights, as through the subtilityes of the enemy, and store of seruants, most prompt to him at euery becke. Which assaults notwithstanding, though grieuous and fastidious, yet most commonly being open and manifest, *S. Edward* did manfully resist, through diuine grace, and went continually away with glorious triumphes. The battayles which perpetually day and night he suffered, from the Communalty, and states of the land, were cloaked with honesty, and coloured with the publique good, and consequently more treacherous, and terrible to him; who shewing infinite care of the vniuersall peace, and security, which greatly depended on the future succession of the *King*, neuer left vrging opportunely, and importunely, in tyme and out of season, with reasons, and examples, with prayers and coniurations, and those mingled now and then with some manner of threats, that he, forsooth, hauing pitty on his country, and of the daungers, that hung ouer it through his single life, would be pleased to differ no longer to prouide for progeny, to wit, some fruitfull and honourable mate.

Such were the requests, and supplications of the people, and

Barons. Among which, with apparence of right intention, and holy zeale the *Earle Godwin* shewed himselfe most earnest, being a person, very potent, politique, and ambitious, and who by the opinion of all, had a hand with the tyrant *Canutus*, in the impious murder of *Alfred*; and now with thoughts, wholy pointing to his priuate greatnes, plotted to mary his daughter *Edith* with *Edward*, and that to the notable increase of his estate, to see her Queen. This *Lady*, was not any thing like to the *Father*, as one that feared *God*, being a friend of abstinence, very prompt to read and worke, farre from pratling, & all feminin disports; in summe, a rose sprung from thornes, ordained by God for a faithfull Companion of *S. Edward* in all vertues. This *yong Virgin*, by publique decree, was commended and tendred to the good *Edward*, with the common importunityes and prayers perseuering still; so much more liuely, as the necessities of the Kingdome, and qualityes of the *Spouse*, made a repulse to the more inexcusable. All this now, the *King* knew very wel, but on the one side being resolued, not to manifest, or breake his solid purpose of virginall chastity; & on the other, very hardly able to resist any longer, the petitions and most earnest importunities of his subiects; being put into such streights, and fallen into an agony, he could find no better remedy, then euen the same by him so often tryed, of voluntary pennances, and feruent prayers. So as after many fastings, and other corporall afflictions, which doubtles do serue very much, to render the *diuine Maiesty* propitious to a man, being prostrate on the earth, full of humble affect, and firme fayth, he spake to his *Creatour* & *Lord*, in this manner following: *O good Iesu*, by thee the *three Childrē* haue been deliuered from the *Chaldean flames* of old. Through thee *Ioseph* leauing his cloake behind, had saued this honour: and the constant *Susanna* got the victory of the lewd old Men: and the holy *Iudith* through thy help could not be tempted by *Holofernes*. Behold mee heere, thy seruant, and as I haue beene heertofore, fauoured and beloued of thee, in diuers accidents: So succour mee now also, *O Lord*, in this necessity, and graunt, that in some manner, of imitation of *Mary* thy *Mother*, and *Ioseph* her faythfull Guardian, such espousalls may be had betweene *Edith*, and *Mee*, that my Chastity may suffer no wrong, or empeschement whatsoeuer. So *Edward* prayed, and moreouer added thereunto the efficacious intercession of the *Queene* of *Angells* herselfe: by whose intercession and meanes, so great desire of purity, was infused into

 the

the *Spouses* mind, as that being brought with solemne pompe and royall preparations to her *husband*, she was by him, without the mediation of any other testimony at all, in the diuine sight, very easily brought to a perpetuall purpose of entire *Virginity*; in such sort as being both vnited with the holy band, contenting themselues with the *Sacrament* of *Matrimony*, they alwayes kept themselues pure and far from any worke of wedlocke.

S. Edward *being myndfull of his vow of Pilgrimage, consults with the Peeres of his Kingdome thereof: But after debate resolues, & is dispensed therewith by the Pope.* Chap. 4.

THis difficulty, now by diuine help, being so passed ouer, there remayned yet another, of some moment; which was the fulfilling of his vow (as we haue sayd) heertofore, in his greater troubles, to visit personally in *Rome*, the Memory of the *Apostles*. The pious *King*, kept faythfull record still of this so great an obligation, and the care he had of performing the same, did now continually burne in his breast. Whereupon, as soone as matters seemed to affoard opportunity, he immediately began to make prouision of magnificent and sumptuous gifts, for to offer vp at the holy *Aultars* of *Rome*; & besides went putting of things in order for the voyage. To this effect, calling the chiefe of the Kingdome into counsayle, he discouered this thought of his vnto them; and reducing to all their memoryes, the vnhappy state, and extreame calamityes of their country, which had brought him to recommend himselfe to the diuine *Clemency*, and to make a vow of pilgrimage to *Rome*, to obteyne more easily the Protection of the *Prince* of the *Apostles*, he demonstrated with many reasons, how abominable, and impious it was, to forget ones duty, and to become vngratefull to him, who had deliuered the whole nation from the hand of most cruell enemyes: wherefore, euery one sincerely should propound, what best occurred to him, about the accommodating of things, in such sort as through his absence, might neyther the traffique by sea, nor cõmerce by land, nor Townes, Castles, or Cityes, nor finally the priuate, or publique affayres come to suffer any hurt: and lastly bids them be of good cheere, affirming, he was most secure that the *Great God*, would both assiste him, in so long a iourney, and conserue his subiects in the peace and abundance, which of his benignity

nignity he had graunted to them of late.

To this sense did *S. Edward* speake, and scarcely had he finished, but all those *Counsellors*, and heads of the Prouinces, began to complayne with a lowd voyce at such a resolution, as not being fit the land should so be abandoned of its guide, and the subiects exposed to the slaughters, and outrages of the Enemyes, who were ready at al occasions, that should be offered them, to returne againe into the Iland in armes: His vow was laudable, but yet coũterpoysed with too grieuous and manifest perils. In this sort contended they a good while, and after many answeres, & replyes to and fro, he finally tooke resolution, to remit all to his *Holynes*, being at that tyme *Pope Leo*, the *Ninth* of that name; who being fully informed by expresse men, and letters at large, wrote back to the *King*, in this forme.

Leo Bishop, the *Seruant* of the *Seruants* of God, to his deerely beloued Sonne *Edward*, *King* of the *English*, Health, and Apostolical benediction. Knowing thy good desires, worthy of prayse, and most acceptable to God, we do yeild due thanks for the same, to him through whose meanes Kings and Princes do rule and gouerne, & execute iustice: but forasmuch, as God in euery place, is neere to those that call vpon his name, in truth and equity, and the *holy Apostles* are vnited with their head, with one, and the selfe same spirit; and that he equally attends to pious prayers: And that besides being euident, the *Kingdome* of *England* would come to be in great daungers, if thou shouldst leaue the same, that with the bridle of thy power restreynest the seditious motions of the people: We by the authority committed to vs from God, & his holy *Apostles*, do absolue thee from the band of that vow, for which thou fearest to offend the *diuine Maiesty*; and likewise, in vertue of that power, which was graunted to vs, by our Lord, in the person of the blessed *Peter*, when he said: *Quæcumq; solueris super terram, erunt soluta & in cælis*, we do first absolue thee, as well from this band, as from all other negligences and defaults whatsoeuer, incurred in thy whole life: then, in vertue of holy *Obedience*, and by title of penance, we do commaund thee, thou distribute the money, assigned to this Pilgrimage to the poore; and to erect besides, a Monastery of *Religious*, vnto the honour of the *Prince* of the *Apostles*: yet leauing still to thy discretion, eyther to reare it from the first foundations, or to repayre or augmẽt some other in ill plight, and ruined already through iniury of tymes or other accidents: & furthermore, that thou endow the same, with

tents

rents sufficient, to maynteine a good number of the Seruants of *God*, to the end, that while they there attend to prayse the *diuine Maiesty*, the glory may redound to the *Saints*, and pardon and indulgence to thee. Besides, we do will and declare, whatsoeuer so conferred & applyed, eyther by thee, or any others, to be firme and stable, and to be alwayes the habitation of the Monks, and not to be subiect to any secular person whosoeuer, except the *King*. Moreouer we confirme, with most ample authority, what priuiledges may seeme good to thee, to be graunted, so as truly they may be to the honour of God. And for conclusion, we do curse him with eternal maledictiō, whosoeuer shall once seeme to haue the boldnes to violate, or break the same.

This Briefe of the Pope, though otherwise true and authenticall inough, was notwithstanding by the diuine will, confirmed with an admirable euent, as followeth.

S. Peter *appeares to an Hermit, and bids him in his name to aduise* S. Edward, *not to doubt of the Popes Briefe. The ioy of the King heereat: and what followed therupon.* Chap. 5.

THere liued in those countryes a *holy Hermit*, who hauing beene now, for many yeares voluntarily shut vp, in a deepe Caue, with desire of *Contemplation*, came at last, to receiue the crowne of Iustice. To this man, on a night *S. Peter* appeared, and said to him: K. *Edward*, through anxiety which he feeles, for a certaine vow that he made, in the banishment from his Country, & for the care, which he hath for the quiet of the Kingdome, and necessityes of his Subiects, hath taken resolution, to seeke the pleasure of the *Pope* of *Rome*: Let him know then, that of myne authority, he is dispensed of the same obligation, with condition to found a Monastery to my honour and therefore he shall make no doubt of the *Apostolicall Brief*, but shall endeuour to dispose himselfe without delay, to performe what he commaunds him to do for that end. Because the whole order proceeds from me, being his ancient *Protectour*, and perpetuall Aduocate. And to the end, he may see the better to resolue vpō the execution therof; let him know, that in the west side of *London*, are yet to be seen the ruines of a most noble Temple, and Conuent of the Monkes of *S. Benet*, which heertofore hath beene fauoured with my presence, illustrated with miracles, and consecrated moreouer with my proper hands. This place is called *Thorney*; which for the sins ſinnes of the Inhabitants there, now for many yeares, being giuen ouer into the hands of barbarous people, of very opulent, and famous, is now become moſt poore and deſpicable. This would I haue the *King* take in hand to renew, adorne, and endow with ſacred pictures, ſtately buildings, and rich poſſeſſions, that well may they ſay thereof: Heere truly is the howſe of God, and the Gate of heauen. Heere will I ſet vp a ladder, by which the *Angels* may aſcend, to cary vp the ſupplications of Mortals; and I will not fayle according to the diſpoſitiõ of ech one, to open him the gates of heauen. But do thou, for the preſent, put downe in writing, what heere thou haſt heard, and vnderſtood of me, and without delay ſend the ſcroule to the *King*, that ſo he may reſt both the more ſecure of the diſpenſation, and more prompt to obedience, and ſtable in my deuotion. Which ſayd, the *Apoſtle* vaniſhed, and the *Hermits* relation, came into the hands of the *King*, euen iuſt at the howre, when the *Apoſtolique* Brief was deliuered and read.

Of which concurrence ſo together, it cannot eaſily be expreſſed, how glad *S. Edward* was thereat, and how greatly aſtoniſhed were all the ſtanders by. From hence, he did wholy apply himſelf to the execution of the precept: and the firſt thing he did, was to diſtribute to the poore, that whole ſumme of mony, which was prepared for the voyage of *Rome*; and then after, hauing taken very diligent information of the place of *Thorney*, he came to vnderſtand, how in the tyme of *Ethelbert*, who reigned in the Country of *Kent*, and was conuerted to the Fayth, by meanes of the bleſſed *Auguſtin*, being ſent into thoſe parts by *Gregory* the great to preach the Ghoſpell, his *Nephew Sebert* who ruled the Eaſterne part of *England*, at that tyme, was likewiſe baptized by the ſame *Seruant* of *Chriſt*, & in ſigne of his true piety, built a *Church* in honour of *S. Paul*, within the walls of his principall Citty by name *London*, & gaue good rents to *Mellitus*, for that purpoſe, newly created *Biſhop*. Then after, without the walls, to the Weſt-ward, he built, and richly endowed another, with a ſumptuous Monaſtery, in honour of the *Prince* of the *Apoſtles*.

Now being to make the *Dedication* of the *Temple*, the night before, the ſame *Apoſtle S. Peter*, appeared to a Fiſherman of the Riuer of *Thames* which paſſeth along that *Monaſtery*, vpon the banks thereof on the other ſide, in the habit of a *Pilgrime*, who promiſing the Fiſherman a good reward, made him to waft him ouer, and paſſing out of the barke, in ſight of the Fiſherman, went directly into the *Church*, and behold on a ſudden, a ſplendour ſo bright and glorious, as baniſhing all darknes, made of an obſcure night, a goodly day. There was then preſent with the *Apoſtle*, a multitude of the *Bleßed*, who by turns went in and out, and melody was heard from Heauen, while odours of vnſpeakeable ſweetnes, were ſpread vp and downe.

The *Conſecration* being finiſhed, the *Great Fisher* of *Men* returned agayne to the *Fisher* of *Fish*, and finding him amazed & aſtoniſhed at that vnquoth diuine light, entring agayne into his boate with him, ſayd to him: Haſt thou not ſomething to eate? and he replying. The hire you promiſed, ſo contented me at firſt, and then thoſe heauenly rayes, did ſo quite bereaue mee of my ſenſes, as I had no thought at all of taking any fiſh. Go to then, ſayd *S. Peter*, caſt thy net into the water. And ſo he did without reſiſtance, when in a moment, he tooke a huge multitude of fiſhes, and all of one ſort, ſaue one of an vnmeaſurable Greatnes; which being drawne to the ſhore, the *Apoſtle* ſayd: Thou ſhalt make a preſent to the *Bishop Mellitus* of this heere, which exceeds ſo much the other in worth, & bignes. The reſt, do thou keep to thy ſelfe, for thy hyre: & know that as long as thou liueſt, thou ſhalt alſo haue ſtore of them, & likewiſe thy Succeſſours for a long time after; ſo that you all take heed, not to fiſh vpon *Sundayes*. I am *Peter* that ſpeakes ſo vnto thee, and who in company of other *Cittizens* of *Heauen*, haue dedicated this *Church*, as Titular to me, and with this ceremony haue been pleaſed to ſupply the Epiſcopall rite therein. Do thou tell then *Mellitus*, what thou haſt ſeen and heard, and for his more ſecurity heereof do thou ſhew him, the ſignes which are left in the walls. Whence he ſhall not need to reiterate the ſame any more, but there only to celebrate a *Solemne Maſſe*, and preaching to the people, giue them plainly to vnderſtand, that I ſhall often viſit that place, and there be fauourable to the vowes and praiers of the faithfull, to open them the gates of Heauen, and to euery one heere beneath, who ſhall lead a ſober, pious, and iuſt life.

At the end of theſe words, the *Saint* was ſeene no more. When the morning being come, and the *Bishop* now in going in proceſſion to dedicate the *Church*; the Fiſherman went to meete him, with that great fiſh, and declared to him faythfully, what was recommended to him. *Mellitus* ſtood wonderfully in ſuſpence heerat, and opening

opening the Church, finds the flore to be all markt with the Greek, and Latin Alphabet, and the walls in twelue seuerall places to be anoynted with holy oyle, and as many ends of wax tapers, set vpon twelue Crosses, and all these things, as fresh as they seemed to haue been but now finished. At which sight, the good *Bishop*, with all the multitude, beginnes to blesse, and thanke the *diuine Goodnes*, without end. Nor fayled the prophecy of its effect likewise, in the promise made to the Fisherman, forasmuch as he, and all his posterity had euer after a lucky fishing; & in signe of gratitude for it, they were volūtarily wont to giue the Monastery the tithes therof: till at last, one of them, who would needs craftily haue subtracted the wonted tribute, came to be depriued of the benefit, vntill such tyme, as being humbly confessed, and penitent for it, he had made restitution thereof, and promised not to fall any more, into that fault.

S. Edward *sends to Pope* Nicolas *to confirme the Grants of his Predessour, which was accorded. He cures a Cripple, and the Kings euill; with diuers other Cures besides.*

S*Aint Edward* hauing had certayne notice, of such a tradition by diuers wayes, without more ado, was enflamed to the restauration, and reedification of the ancient *Thorney*: and for the obteining to that end, the confirmation of the priuiledges and spirituall graces already affoarded by the *Sea Apostolique*, he sent againe certaine men of purpose to *Rome*, with an Epistle, to the new *Pope*, in this tenour.

To *Nicolas*, chiefe *Father* of the vniuersall *Church*. I *Edward* throgh the grace of God, *King* of the *English*, do present all due subiection, and obedience: Let vs glorify God, who hath care of his elect, and who in place of a good Predecessour, hath substituted in his place, a very excellēt Successor. Wherupon we do thinke it meete, to come to your *Holynes*, as to a solid rocke, to refine and examine ech action of ours, how good soeuer it may otherwise seeme to be, that betweene vs, in our *Lord*, may still be receyued a due acknowledgement and sweet accord togeather; by meanes whereof, it may not be grieuous vnto you, to renew and amplify, at our instance, the grāunts and fauours, which your sayd Predecessour heertofore hath affoarded vnto vs; especially in dispensing with the vow, by me formerly made, of my comming to *Rome*, being changed not without the full remission of my sinnes, into the building of a Monastery of Religious, vnto the honour of *God*, and the blessed *Peter* his *Apostle*: as I also, for my part, will not fayle to confirme, & augment, the good customes of annuall contributions, which are made to the sayd *S. Peter*, in these my Prouinces: of which Collections, with other appendices, I do send your *Holines* a present, to vouchsafe to pray for me, and for the peace and tranquillity of my Kingdome, and to ordayne that continuall and solemne memory be had of all this *Nation*, before the *Aultar*, where the sacred *Bodyes* of the two most glorious *Princes* of the Earth be kept.

The *Pope*, very easily assented to his suites, so iust; he confirmed the dispensation, ratifyed the priuiledges, exempted those Monks from the iurisdiction of the Ordinary, and recommended to the *King*, not only the protection of the said place, but euen likewise the defence, and good direction of the *Churches* of the *Iland*. So that all things were done in name of the *Roman Bishop*, & with the assebly and counsayle of the *Abbots*, & *Bishops*. In this manner, an end was put to the busynes of the Pilgrimage: & the most deuout *King*, went so perseuering in holy workes, as it pleased the diuine Goodnes, to make him continually more great, and more illustrious then euer, not onely with fame, and worldly honours, but euen also, with the gift of *Curing*, and *Prophecy*, and of other not ordinary miracles.

He being once at his pallace, hard by the *Church* of *S. Peter*, there came thither a certaine *Irish man*, of a miserable forme, or figure; for that besides he was full of vlcers, and that the nerues and sinewes of his knees, were so shrunck vp, and so attracted together, as they had euen retorted his legs to his very backe, his shancks and shins stuck close to his reynes; whence he was forced, with certaine Pattins, in his hands, to go creeping on all foure, with trayling his lyms after him. This man hauing thus a good while been a burden to himselfe, to his owne exceeding payne, and trouble, and not finding any human remedy, recurred deuoutly to the diuine: and after he had recommended himselfe, many tymes, with great feruour, to the *Prince* of the *Apostles*; going lastly forth of the *Church*, & approaching neere to *Hugoline*, whome we mentioned aboue, being the Kings seruant and fauourit, he spake vnto him thus.

And will you not once looke vpon me? and haue you no compassion on me? and do not any so great miseryes moue you awhit? What wouldst thou haue me do to thee (said the other;) when the

Irish man replyed: It is now six times, that I haue gone, in this manner, as you see me heere, to visit the *Aultar* of the *Apostles*, in the *City* of *Rome*, to obteyne health, which yet at last *S. Peter* hath not denyed, but only seemed to differ awhile, and put me off, as willing to haue for company in the worke, his client *K. Edward*, for so hath he commaunded me to seeke him out, and to pray him to beare me on his sacred shoulders, into this *Church* at hand, with promise that if the *King* may once be brought thereunto, I shal recouer perfectly my lymmes.

Hugoline stood awhile in doubt, as at a thing that seemed so absurd at first: yet notwithstanding did the message to his *Lord*, who immediately gaue thankes to God for the same, and without delay, causing the *Cripple* to come before him, tooke him cheerfully on his back, and began to carry him to the place designed. Thus hung so poore & noysome a Wretch on the shoulders of so great a Monarke, who with botchy hands, and loathsome armes, clung fast to that royall breast, and neck. At this sight, some Courtiers fell a laughing; others with a scornefull and disdaynefull eye, lookt on the *Irish* mā, as a Dissembler and Hypocrite; others finally, who would seeme wise, began to tax the simplicity, and folly of the *Prince*: but he vnder this straung burden, had not gone many steps, when sudenly the nerues of the *Cripple*, began to stretch forth themselues, the bones to be setled agayne in their places, the dead flesh to wax warme, and the legs and feete, now vnloosed from the loynes, to returne agayne to their naturall place. Whereby a great quantity of corrupt humours, gushing out from diuers parts, did very fowly defile the embrodered Robes, wherwith the King was cloathed. Then could not the multitude cōteyne themselues from crying out alowd, *Hold, hold, for that the Irishman is made sound, the King need not to proceed any further so to weary himselfe, and to moyle and soyle his robes, in that manner*: While he on the contrary keeping the heauenly precept still fixed in his mind, shutting his eares to the Sirens songs, passed yet further, and entring into the Temple, reposed that sacrifice before the *Aultar*; and the *Wretch* moreouer hauing a good summe of mony for his Viatique, returned full of ioy, and iubiley to *Rome*, to giue due thanks to *God*, and his *Saints*.

A certaine woman, had kernells growing vnder her throat, or as we call it, the malady of the *Kings Euill*, which continually swelling with putrifyed bloud, besides the possessing of the whole, with a deformed aspect, gaue also forth an intolerable stench afarre off; this miserable wretch, after she had tryed many wayes, to be rid of this euill, was finally aduertized in sleepe, that her Health remained in the Kings hands, who if he would but once vouchsafe to touch, and wash the affected place, she should be cured without any more ado. The sick party, being encouraged with such an Oracle comes to the Pallace, declares the dreame, implores cõpassion. And the King, without any loathing of the fowle corruption, beginnes with his owne fingars, to stroake the tumours; then hauing washed them with water, he made the signe of the *Crosse* vpon them; Whẽ behold in a moment, the skynne being broken, came forth togeather with goare bloud, a great multitude of wormes, the kernels were asswaged, and the anguish went quite away. This is certayne likewise of some blind people, who hauing their Eyes spurted with the water, wherein the King had washed his hands, they recouered their sight in the presence of many. But leauing the meruayles of this sort; let vs come to some of the extraordinary reuelations which he had, as follow.

S. Edward *beholds, in vision, the King of* Denmarke *drowned, in comming to inuade* England. *With diuine iustice shewed vpon Earle* Godwyn, *for his periury.* Chap. 7.

The hatred of the inhabitants of *Denmarke* (as we haue said) against the *English* continued still. And so much the more increased their rage, as more happy, and glorious were the successes of this good King. In summe, the Enuy augmented so much, as that after long consults, they determined to vse all endeauours to recouer the possession agayne, whence they were so shamefully thrust out. In the meane tyme, *S. Edward* being at *Masse*, on the day of *Pentecost*, while the *Body* of *Christ* was eleuated, shewed a smiling countenãce, with the eyes attentiue, and fixed more then ordinary. The same, was much noted by the standers by, & the *Sacrifice* being ended, his most familiars were so bold in confidence, as to craue the occasion of such a nouelty: and he with his natiue candour, and humanity confessed what passed, saying thus.

The Danes had agreed with their King, to returne to their ancient exploits of armes, and to come and disturbe with hostility, that peace & quietnes, which the diuine Goodnes hath vouchsafed

safed to affoard vs: and for that they placed the foundation of the whole enterprise in their owne valour, not regarding the Highest to be the only Maister, and Distributer of victoryes; his diuine Maiesty hath been pleased, to let them see their vnmeasurable confidence. Now had they their army in readynes, and being iouiall, and proud of a prosperous gale, were at the point of hoysing sayle; when the King in leauing his long Boate, to board the Admirall, slipping with his foote betweene both the decks, fell downe into the sea, & was drowned without remedy, deliuering his followers at once from a new sinne, and vs from a new daunger. And this happened iust this very morning; and I hope in our Lord my God, and his most sweet Mother their impious designes shall take no effect in my tyme: & this is that which our Sauiour Christ hath cleerely shewed my this day. Great ioy and iubiley was this newes to the hearers; especially when sending some of purpose, to be fully enformed thereof, they found and reported the fact, the day and houre, to be iust the same, which was told by the King.

The Seruant of Christ, on a tyme sitting at table, and the *Earle Godwyn* his Father-in-law by him, it happened, that two Sonnes of the sayd *Earle*, yet children, the one *Harold* by name, and *Tosto* the other, in playing together, in the presence of the King, grew hot (as it happens) into a kind of quarell, & with bitter rancour, their sport was turned to a Duell. *Harold* being somewhat the more robustious and bold, sets vpon his Brother, and with both hands pulling him by the hayre of his head, ouerthrew him to the ground, & would haue stifled him doubtles, had he not beene suddenly taken forth of his hands. Then *S. Edward*, turning himself to *Godwyn* asked him if he did see nothing in the scuffling of these two boyes, but a simple fray? And he affirming, he did not. But to me, replyed the *King* in this childish brable of theirs, farre greater things then it, are represented. For that, as soone as both shall arriue to mans estate, they shall be taken with blind Enuy, and wicked Ambition: as first with traynes, and hidden frauds, they shall seeme to sport, and be in iest, with one another; but the stronger at last shall preuayle, & chase away the other: and then againe attempting to rebell, he shall againe be suppressed by him; and after he hath put him to death, it shall not be long ere himselfe do likewise come to ruine. Which to haue fallen out effectually, *England* it selfe saw afterwards, and truly may testify the same.

And

And since now we are fallen to speake of *Earle Godwin*: it is sayd of him, that he another tyme being at table with the King, one of the Squires stũbling with his foote vpon a rub, was ready to fall on his nose, had not the other foot which stood fast vpheld him the while. At which sight, the standers by reflecting, how one foot had helped his fellow; the *Earle* iested, Euen so it is (said he) when a Brother helps a Brother, and one succours the other, in his greatest need. Whereupon, replyed the King: And so might my Brother likewise haue done for me, had *Godwin* beene so pleased. At these words the *Traitour* was afrayd, and with a sad cheere sayd withall: I see *Syr*, I see very well you suspect me likewise for the death of your Brother, and giue credit to those that falsely terme me a Traytour. But God be the Iudge heerof, who knowes all secrets, and so may this morsell in my hand heer, do me good, as I was far from working any plot eyther agaynst thee, or thy Brother.

K. *Edward* accepted the condition, and gaue benediction to the meate, which as soone, as it came to the midst of the *Earles* throat, stucke there so fast, as he was neuer able, withall that he could do, eyther to swallow it downe, or to put it vp agayne, so as the passages of respiration, being stopt, his very eyes started forth in fearfull manner. Whereupon, as many as were present, were astonished and cleerly acknowledged the heauenly reuenge; when the King sayd to them: *Take away this dogg*, as they did. This wicked man, among many things, committed agaynst the diuine, and humane lawes, was growne at last to be so bold, and abused so much the goodnes of the King, as that to sway and rule alone, through diuers calumnies, he had banished by litle and litle, all the friends & kinsfolks that came from *Normandy* with the King. Nor was *Edward* vnaware thereof; but politiquely proceeding, not to put things into *burly-burly*, referred, and reserued all to the *Highest*, as knowing certaynely, he would make some demonstration therof in its time, which he foretold more then once, not only to others, but euen to *Godwin* himselfe.

One *Easter day*, the King sitting likewise at table (where euen amidst the royall Feasts and great assemblies of people, no lesse then when alone, he was wont to take many occasions to enter into God) he recollected himself more strictly then ordinary, & musing vpon the celestiall goods, with an eleuated mynd, acknowledged

the

the vnworthines and basenes of all worldly things: & while he remained thus in this consideratiō, his face was seen to be more seren then vsually, and his lips to moue with a modest smile, and then anone to become wholy sad and pensiue: the same was noted by by such as were present, and the Table being taken away, Duke *Harold*, with a Bishop, and an Abbot accompanying him to his chāber, were so bold, as to demaund, what had happened to him: When *S. Edward* answered.

The more a man shall seeme to subtract himselfe from transitory, and externall things, shall the true and essentiall make the more impression in him. Behold how I amidst the precious wines, and cates most delicate, and amidst the lustre of vessels of gold, & siluer, lifting the eyes of my mynd, to my Lord God, haue first felt my selfe to be replenished with spirituall consolation, and then in vnspeakable manner, haue been with the mynd, raysed to the sight of very sad disaduentures, which for these seauen yeares next, with a sudden mutation, shall hang ouer the head of mortalls. Because God, shall not fayle to visit the iniquityes of the Christian people. He shall deliuer them into the hands, and power of the Infidels, the subiects shall rebell agaynst their Lords: and Kings shall lay traps for Kings, Princes for Princes: and in euery Country, the cruell sword, shall reuenge the iniuries done to the Redeemer. Which things, and others like to these, fell out afterwards, euen iust in the manner, as the King had presaged. And this may suffice vs for his Prophecyes.

S. Edward *being at Masse beholds our blessed Sauiour on the Aultar. And being deuoted to* S. Iohn *Euangelist giues a ring to a Pilgrime for his sake, and dyes soone after.* Chap. 8.

KING *Edward*, was wōderfully deuout to all the Ecclesiasticall Sacraments, and particularly to the most holy *Eucharist*: and in this point had, from the diuine Goodnes, among others, one notable fauour. For being at Masse one day in the Monastery of *S. Peter*, before the Aultar of the indiuiduall Trinity, with one *Leofricus* an Earle (of whome it is said, that he liued very holily in the company of his wife *Gothgina*, and founded many religious Conuents) the Sauiour of the world appeared to him on the Aultar it self, & stretching forth his right hand, gaue him his heauēly benedidiction, with the signe of the Crosse, while the King in bowing with his head, was adoring the diuine presence. The sayd Earle *Leofricus* was likewise made partaker of the same apparition, who not knowing what passed in the Kings mynd, was approching to aduertise him thereof; whereof *S. Edward* being aware: Stand still *Leofrick*, said he, stand still: what thou seest, I see also: and then Masse being ended, he added: I cōiure thee, *O Earle*, for the Maiesty of him, we haue both seene too day, that while we are in this life, thou speake not a word of this vision, to the end, that eyther throgh popular applause, we may not fall into pride, or through so rare a nouelty, occasion may be giuen of murmuring to those, who belieue no more, then what they can touch or feele with the fingar.

Among these things, *S. Edward*, being now well stept in yeares, and loaden with merits, was certified, that now at last his reward approched, and his certificate was in this manner. He held (next *S. Peter*) *S. Iohn* Euangelist the beloued Disciple of *Iesus*, in greatest veneration: insomuch, as he neuer denyed any honest petition, that euer was made to him, in the name of *S. Iohn* Euangelist. When among other times it happened one day his priuy Almenour being absent, that a certayne Pilgrime, with the sayd inuocation, most importunely craued an almes of him, and he not hauing any thing at hand, pulling off a precious ring from his fingar, very graciously gaue it him. It fell out afterwards, that two English men, went in pilgrimage to the holy *Sepulcher*, & hauing crossed the Seas and now strayed vnawares, out of their way, in that errour they were ouertaken by the darke night, wherein very sad and afflicted, they could find neyther Guide, nor Counsayle, till beyond all hope appeared a venerable old man, who conducting them into the City of *Ierusalem*, benignely receyued them as ghests into his house, and after a dainety supper, brings them to their lodgings, with great charity. The morning being come, they both hauing giuen thankes, & ready to take their iourney, the good Host sayd to them.

Know Brethren, you are like to haue a good voyage, and shall returne safe, and sound againe into your Country: God shal be propitious to you, & I for your Kings sake, in all this time, will regard you still. I am *Iohn* the Apostle, that loues your King very tenderly for the excellency of his chastity. You shall carry him backe this ring

ring, which he gaue me some dayes since, when I appeared to him in forme of a Pilgrime: and acquaint him that the day of his deposition approches, and six months shall not passe ouer his head, ere I put him into the company *who follow the Lambe, wheresoeuer he goes.* Which said, the Apostle vanished, & they happily arriuing at home gaue faythfull accompt to the King, of what they had heard, and seene. Nor was the prediction vayne, because *S. Edward*, very soone after fell into his last sicknes: wherein purposing to edify by all manner of wayes, as many as conuersed with him, now feeling himselfe to decay apace, ordayned his death, should be presently published, though all the kingdome, that his soule, being loosed from prison might haue the suffrages of the faythfull, assoone as might be, and with this, he passed to his most desired Lord, on the 5. of Ianuary 1066. hauing held the scepter 23. yeares, 6. months, and 27. dayes.

He was bewayled, and buryed with that feeling and concurse of the people, as became such a Ruler and Gouernour. Two translations haue been made of that vessell of the holy Ghost: the one some 36. yeares after his happy passage, which vntil the other, was the space of 60. yeares. In both discoueryes, not only those sacred members, but euen also his Princely robe, and habit appeared very whole, and vncorrupted. The first Translation was made, to afford him a more honourable funerall. The other followed, at the tyme of his Canonization, vnder Pope *Alexander* the III. When deposing the venerable Reliques, there succeeded so many miracles anew, as would be too long a matter & far from our purpose, to make narratiõ of them. Whence we may, with reason hope through the merits, and intercessions of this great Seruant of God, that as so many particuler persons, haue obtayned the graces which they craued; euen so that most noble Kingdome, all scandals being taken away, and Heresies destroyed, may one day be reduced, to the vnion of the faythfull, and to the lap of the holy Catholique Church.

S. ANSELME.

THE ARGVMENT.

SEe in the West *Arabia's* wonder bred,
With gorgeous lustre fayre embellished;
Rich in all colours which our eyes behold,
Vying agaynst the Sunne his natiue Gold,
The Phœnix of his age. His Parents left
And of all help and succour quite bereft,
Heau'n vndertooke his charge. He needs not feare
The want of friends, whose friends, whose Hopes are (there.
Deuided from the world can *England* be,
The worlds chiefe Grace hauing espous'd in thee?
Or seeme discourag'd now, or hartlesse growne,
When such a Saint is denized her owne?
No, she may hope, that though some clouds may hide
A while the light, it will at length be spi'de:
And that th'offended Sunne will glister more,
And spread his rayes far brighter then before:
When you, Deare Saints, shall put an helping hand,
That you agayne may on our Altars stand.

THE LIFE OF S. ANSELME ARCHBISHOP OF CANTERBVRY.

Written by *Edinerus* a Monke of *Canterbury*, vvho liued in his tyme.

What the condition of S. Anselms *Parents was. The presage of his future life. His good inclinations, and first vocation to Religion.* Chap. I.

WE being to vnfold the Life and manners of *S. Anselme* Archbishop of *Canterbury*, a most noble City of England; will first touch some things of his Parents. His Father then was one *Gondolfus*, who being borne in *Lombardy* of *Italy*, and comming to liue in the Citty of *Augusta Prætoria*, now called *Aust*, in the confines of *Piemont*, tooke to wife a gentlewoman, whose name was *Ermenberga*. These two consorts, for riches & nobility were equall, but in manners and disposition far vnlike. Because the husband, being giuen to his pleasures, was held to be no good husband for his family

mily. While the wife on the contrary, being serious in the gouernment of the house, and a wise dispenceresse of his goods, gaue alwayes forth, a most excellent odour of her life vnto her last, leauing *Gondolfus* aliue; who seeing himselfe vnloosed from the bands of Matrimony, being now growne of great yeares, became a Monke, and dyed in his Monastery.

Of this couple *S. Anselme* was borne, of whome, as through a certayne presage of his future sanctity, it is reported, in his tender yeares, hauing heard his Mother say, that aboue in Heauen, was but one God only, who ruled and maynteyned the whole Vniuerse, he thought with a childish imagination, that the Heauens were shored vp, and susteyned by the mountaynes, & that from the tops of them, one might reach to the royall pallace of that great Monarke: and as he often had this though, it happened one night, that he seemed, to mount vp by one of those tops to the forsayd pallace, and beholds at the foote therof, certaine seruants of the King reaping of corne with much slouth and negligence: Whereat being scandalized, he determined to accuse them to the Lord himself. Whereupon, ascending to the top, and being admitted to the Pallace, he found the King, with the onely attendance of one Squire and no more, hauing sent away the rest of his family to reape, it being then haruest tyme. The child then entring into the hall, & being called by the King, approches neere him, and sits him downe at his feete. After which, being pleasantly demanded by him, who he was, and from whence, and wherefore he came: he answered to all without difficulty. And immediately heerupon he caused a loafe of most pure bread to be giuen him, which *S. Anselme* eating in the King his sight, felt meruaylous comfort. Being afterwards awakened in the morning, and reducing this vision to memory, the innocent child held it to be a certayne truth, & no fantastical thing; & verily belieued, he had been in Paradise indeed, and had tasted of the bread of our Lord, and so publikely affirmed to his companiõs.

He went after increasing in yeares, and vertue so, as for his good behauiour, he was beloued of all. Being sent to Schoole, as he was of an excellent wit, in a very short tyme, he profited exceedingly in learning: & for his choosing of a state of life, he was not yet entred into the 15. yeare of his age, when he began to thinke in what manner he might best obserue the diuine precepts, & saue his soule: and after a long discourse thereupon with himselfe, he came

at

at last to resolue, there was nothing more apt for the purpose, then to become a Monke, & to consecrate himselfe foreuer to the diuine Seruice. With this determination, he went his wayes to a certayne Abbot, intreating him to admit him into Religion. But that Prelate for feare of *Gondolfus*, durst not receyue him. And yet was not the good youth awhit coole therwith in his purpose: but rather besought God, he might fall into some grieuous malady, to the end the Abbot by meanes thereof, being moued to pitty, might admit him at last.

The prayers of *S. Anselme*, were more efficacious with God thē with men. Being suddenly sicke then of a dangerous infirmity, he besought the Abbot anew, he would daigne to accomplish his desires, and not suffer him to dye in the world. But he fearing yet the offence aforesayd, was still very stiff in the negatiue: and that not without the diuine Will, since the chast youth was destined to the help of other nations, and for other enterprises of greater glory of Christ, as we shall see anon. He recouered then his perfect health, & for that tyme withall renewed the good purposes; but afterwards what with the heate and feruour of youth, and the riches and commodityes of home, suffering himselfe to be carryed away with pleasures, and company keeping; he came wholy, as it were to loose, not only his Vocation, and spirit he had, but euen also the study of letters, wherein he had been so diligent before. One thing only for awhile, deteyned him somewhat, from complying too much with his senses therein, the respect of his deere Mother, whome he loued and reuerenced much. But after she was passed from this lyfe, being then meerly without any tye at all to hold him too, that frayle barke was carryed away into the waues and streames of the world.

S. Anselme *being tyred with the bitter vsage of his Father, goes into* Normandy *to* S. Lanfranke, *and becomes his Scholler.* Chap. 2.

IN his manner went *S. Anselme*, with the greater part of mortalls into manifest perdition; when the heauenly Father beholding him with the eyes of clemency, to vnty him from the world, permitted his Father to be so fraught with hatred, and auersion from him, as that equally the good and bad, or rather more the good actions of *S. Anselme*, then the bad, displeased him: nor was there any meanes left to pacify him, with all the humility and satisfaction the

yong

yongman could yield vnto him. Insomuch, as seing euery day, the old man to be more bitter to him, and intollerable then other; for feare of some great inconuenience, he determined to leaue his Country, Parents, and friends, as well to deliuer himselfe of so great tribulations and troubles, as to apply himselfe anew, more seriously to learning. Putting himself then in order, and laying his fardell on an Asse, he went towards *Burgundy*, with onely a certaine Clerke his familiar friend in his company: and passing ouer *Montsenese*, being not much accustomed to the labours of the body, he felt himselfe, so weary of the way, and of climbing vp the hill, and so afflicted withall, as not hauing other sustenance, he began to eate the very snow, insteed of food. Whereat the Clerke being moued to compassion, did presently looke into his sachell to see if there were somwhat there to eate: when besides all expectatiõ, he found therein a white and sauoury loafe of bread, which not in a dreame now as before, but really in effect gaue to *S. Anselme* lyfe, so as he arriued in few dayes to the place designed, very safe and sound, where partly in *Burgundy* it selfe, and partly also in *France*, for about the space of three yeares, he attended to his studyes.

There liued in those dayes in the Monastery of *Benedictins* at *Bec*, in the country of *Normandy*, one *Lanfranke* an Italian by nation, of the Citty of *Pauia*, a man so famous for knowledg & goodnes, as many youths from diuers parts of the world, repayred to him that were desirous of sound and perfect doctrine. Now *S. Anselme* being moued with the noyse and rumour of such a one; became so enflamed with desire of knowing *Lanfranke* by sight, and to conuerse with him, as he doubted not a whit, to go himself in hast into that prouince. And was in truth nothing deceyued of his expectation, finding in that Father, so rare gifts of wisedome, as he tooke it for no small happynes to haue him for Mayster, and to be admitted into particular familiarity with him.

With this occasion the feruent louer of liberall arts, without sparing eyther day or night employed himselfe with singular industry, to enrich his breast with sundry knowledges of high & extraordinary things, in giuing eare to the doctour, in turning of books, in gathering notes, in framing Epitomes, in rehearsing of thinges heard, and expounding others. In which occupations, while he suffers much paynes and many incommodityes (as it happens) now of cold, and now of heate, now of hunger, and then of sleep; it came

came agayne into his mind, that if he were a Monke, as heertofore he had desire to be, he should not suffer more troubles and paynes, nor do more pennance then now he did, while in a religious state besides, he should not loose the merit of so great labours; whereas in the life he then led, it was more vncertayne what fruite at last, he were like to gather thence. Wherefore in ruminating this, new purposes began to awake in his mynd of seruing God, and wholy renouncing secular designes.

Truly, it is well knowne that, that fier was as yet very feeble, and the flames ascended but impure, and full of smoake: whereupon, consulting with himselfe of the Monastery, he was to retyre vnto, he sayd within himselfe: If I enter into that of *Cluny*, it is somewhat too strayte, and I shall not be able to endure it: If in that of *Bec*, I shall not there be esteemed awhit, since the eminency of *Lanfranke* will doubtles obscure my name, and qualityes: Insomuch, as not onely I shall be able to help but few, but shall come also in a certayne manner to loose the tyme and paynes, I haue taken in studyes. It were conuenient therefore, I should seeke a place, where I might both help others, and giue forth some worthy demonstration of my selfe.. In these considerations, *S. Anselme* was remayning for some dayes: but then afterwards making his reflexion thereupon, through diuine grace he was soone aware how they spang from an euill spirit, and from a hart but ill mortifyed, & too much affected to the world. So, as reprehending himselfe for it: And doth this forsooth (sayth he) seeme Monachisme vnto thee, so to wish to be preferred before others, and to be more honoured & reputed then others? No truly: go to then, lay downe thy pride and become a Monke in a Conuent, where, as reason would, for the loue of God, thou beest the last, and the vilest, and most despised of all. And where may this be trow you, but surely in the Conuent of *Bec*? Since there is one to be found, who for his high wisedome and reputation purchased, is so sufficient for all, as there shall be no need of me at all. Heere then shall be my rest, heere my repose, heere God alone shall be my scope, heere his loue shall be my thought, heere the blessed and continuall memory of him, shallbe my happy entertaynement, and pleasant satiety.

Gondolfus *Father of* S. Anſelme *dyes, and leaues him his heyre. He conſults with* S. Lanfranke, *and the Archbishop of* Roan *what courſe of life to take, and afterward is made Prior of* Bec *in* Normandy. Chap. 3.

AMidſt theſe deliberations *S. Anſelme* was aduertiſed, that by the laſt will and teſtament of *Gondolfus* his Father, he was become the heyre and Succeſſour of all his ſubſtance. This newes puts his wits on the racke, not ſo, as to put himſelfe from the will of ſeruing his diuine Maieſty, but only made him to doubt, whether it were not, to the greater glory of God, to remayne in the world, & in the workes of Charity himſelfe to diſpence his goods to the poore. It would ſometymes likewiſe come to his mynd, that to be vnknowne, and to giue himſelfe wholy to contemplation, it were expedient to hide himſelfe, and to liue in the deſart. In this perplexity, it ſeemed good to him, not to make any firme reſolution therin, without the ſound and mature counſayle of ſome vnderſtanding and faythfull perſon, remembring the Scripture which ſayth: *Omnia fac cum conſilio, & poſt factum non pœnitebis*. Wherefore he went to *S. Lanfranke* and ſimply declared vnto him what paſſed in his mynd, he craued to be ſetled and eſtabliſhed by him, in what were beſt to be done to the greater ſeruice of God. *S. Lanfrancke* was not willing to be iudge in the matter, nor himſelfe to paſſe the ſentence alone, but exhorted *S. Anſelme*, to remit the whole, vnto the Venerable *Maurilius*, Archbiſhop of *Roan*, vnder whoſe obedience, at that tyme, the *Benedictines* of thoſe countryes gouerned.

S. Anſelme replyed not a word heerunto, and being guided by *Lanfrancke* they both went their wayes immediately towards the Archbiſhop: And ſo great was the deuotion and credit, which the good youth gaue to his Mayſter, as that paſſing through a great wood, betwixt *Bec* and the ſayd Citty of *Roan*, if *Lanfrancke* would but haue ſayd the word, that he would doubtles haue obeyed him therein. Being come to the Prelate *Maurilius*, they both togeather propoſed the occaſion of their iourney vnto him, & the difficulty which *S. Anſelme* felt, in chooſing a ſtate of life. Whereto without delay, the *Archbishop* anſwered, that ſurely the Monaſticall Profeſſion was the better, and moſt ſecure of all. To this anſwere, gaue *S. Anſelme* very humbly his conſent, and layng all care aſide, hauing diſpẽced his patrimony, as beſt ſeemed vnto him; he became Monke in in the same Monastery where *S. Lanfrank* was Prior; whose Abbot was called *Herlwin*, a person of good yeares, and of much esteeme, as well for his rare vertues, as also for hauing built and founded that Monastery at his owne cost, & charges.

S. Anselme being entred into this Academy of Christian Philosophy, and heauenly exercises, on the 27. yeare of his age, endeauours with great iudgment and attention to imitate (as we also read of *S. Antony*) all the qualityes, which he discouered to be more noble and perfect in euery one; through obseruation whereof, and with diuine assistance, walking apace from vertue to vertue, he became within the terme of three yeares, a most cleere mirrour of Religion. So as *S. Lanfranke* being assumpted to the gouernment of *Cadom*, *S. Anselme* was immediately substituted to him in the Priory of *Bec*: which dignity hindred him not awhit, from his wonted meditations, but rather continually recollecting himselfe, so much the more, he raysed himselfe to the vnderstanding of most high mysteries, and solued such Theologicall questions, as till that tyme had neuer beene treated before: wherein he was not so much assisted with intense speculation, as with purity of hart, and right intention which he had to expound the purity of diuine scripture, to the common benefit of all, and to defend the verityes of the Catholike fayth agaynst the malignant.

But among other knots that straytned him most, and held him in suspence, one was, In what manner the Prophets had seene at once both things past, and to come, as they had been present with them; and in what manner, with so much firmnes and resolution, they haue been able to preach and write them. In which passage while one night he was plunged before the houre of Mattins: behold from his bed with his eyes towards the dormitory, and temple he cleerely sees through the wals themselues, the Sacristans and the other Officers, about the Aultar and Quire, to prepare the bookes, to light the candles, and lastly one of them to take the rope, and to ring the bell, and at the pulse, all the Monkes to rise from their beds, to go to the Office. At which reuelation, merueyling not a litle, he came to comprehend, how easy a thing it was to God, to shew the Prophets in spirit the things most remote and distant from them, since to him it was affoarded so to behold them with the eyes of the body, there being so much distance of place, and so many impediments and obstacles betweene. In this manner came *S.*

Anselme to be cleered of the doubt, which tormented him so much.

But that which more imports, there was affoarded him from heauen, a discretion of spirits, so iudicious and subtile withall, as he easily diued, and penetrated into the customes and inclinations of ech sort of persons; and arriued sometymes so far, as to know the most hidden secrets of harts, and to discouer moreouer with extraordinary light, the very origens, and seeds, and proceedings of all vertues and vices; and finally to demonstrate with most cleere precepts and examples, in what manner to purchase the one, and eschew the other. To this so great liberality of God, corresponded he with all due thankefullnes and promptnes to serue him, & with the exact custody of himselfe from all that, which might any waies make him vnworthy and vncapable of so high fauours. In fasting he had now got such an habit, that how long so euer he differred his repasts, he neyther felt hunger in expecting, nor tooke any delight in the meate he eate: And yet did he feed as other men do, as knowing he could not otherwise susteyne himselfe, but did it sparingly, and so without sensuality, as he not only abhorred al daintyes and delicacyes, and gusts of the palate, but seemed (as we sayd) as if in him, the sense of tasting had quite been lost and extinct.

As for sleep, his holy occupations, and continuall labours gaue him but a very small tyme, answering and assisting euery one, that made their recourse to him for counsayle and direction. In which things the diuine man would be spending, not only the houres of the day, but euen those of the night also: and by night besides, he would attend, partly to amend, and correct bookes, which were dangerously marred, and corrupted; partly in meditating the life of his Redeemer, and contemplating the eternall Beatitude, through desire whereof, he would shed whole fluds of teares, as likewise he would do for his own defects, and through compassion of the sins of his neighbour, togeather with the miseryes of this lyfe, and the eternall losse of soules; insomuch as many nights he would often passe ouer without any sleep at all: and if perhaps he but chanced to shut his eyes, it would be but euen a litle before the houre of mattins, when how affectuous he would be in prayers, & vnited with the diuine goodnes, the prayers which he made at the instance of his friends and deuotes, set downe in writing, declare sufficiently.

S. Anselme *was enuyed much for his promotion to the the Priory, especially by one* Osborne *a Monke, who was afterwards reconciled to him; and dying, appeares* S. Anselme, *and reuealed his estate vnto him.* Chap. 4.

AMong all the vertues, and praysses, which are recounted of the holy man, to me none seeme more worthy of consolation, & imitation then the dexterity, & charity which he vsed in the gouernment and instruction of his subiects. To which purpose, we are to vnderstãd thus much, that assoone as he ascended to the Priorship, he wanted no few enuyers and persecutours; to whome it seemed an intollerable thing, and very vnworthy, to be subiected so, to the obedience of one, that might well be called a Nouice. Agaynst the peruersnes, & malice of these, *S. Anselme* opposed himselfe with all offices of benignity, that might be, and particularly vnto one, very yong of yeares, by name *Osborne*. This man being endowed with a rare wit, and of great hability, imploying his talents ill, and abhorring the interiour discipline & seruice; had cõceiued an auersion & hateful rancour against the holy Pastor, & stuck not to exercise the same, both openly & closely when occasion serued. Which malignity of his, though *S. Anselme* for himselfe, not much regarded: yet was he sory so noble a Subiect, of whome otherwise so much fruite might well be expected, should, through diabolicall operation, be so lewdly seduced, and as it were, vtterly lost.

Now then to reduce him into the righ way, first he sought by all meanes possible, to gayne his good will, and to win him to be confident. For which end he began to make exceeding much of him, to dissemble with his errours, to graunt him whatsoeuer was possible, without the manifest domage of the Order, and finally to omit nothing that might any wayes seeme to tame, and relent that so fierce and vnbridled wit of his. The youth tooke complacence at such deportements of *S. Anselme* towards him, and by little and litle being mollifyed and vanquished with so much humanity; began to be affected to him, and to take his fatherly aduises in good part, and euen voluntarily to compose himselfe to all modesty and grauity. Which the wise Rectour perceyuing, he proceeded to fauour him more then euer, to preuent his necessityes, not to suffer him to want any thing; and withall to prayse that emprouement and fruite which he noted in him, and sweetly to exhort, & pray him withal, continually to passe from good to better. From hence he went vntying him by litle and litle, from his accustomed leuityes, and very dexterously reuoked agayne those former indulgences which heertofore he affoarded him, and by all meanes endeauoured to reduce him to reason and religious maturity.

When as afterwards he saw himselfe to be fully possessed of him, continually restreyning him more and more, he fayled not to cut of quite that childishnes, which seemed as yet to remayne in him: and if he had noted him to relapse at any tyme into errours, he would chastize him, not only with words, but with pennances also. Which new seuerity, was supported by *Osborne* with admirable patience, being now assured and most secure of the fatherly bowels of *S. Anselme*, and of the amorous affect whence it seemed to proceed. In summe, with holsome and fit remedyes, that youth, who seemed so incorrigible before, came now to be amended and reformed in such manner, as looke what disquietnes and scandall he had giuen before, he now gaue as great example, and edification to all: When as thus cured in his soule, through diuine disposition he fell grieuously sicke.

Then did the good Pastour, shew no lesse diligence, in helping the exteriour man, then before he had vsed towards the interiour: so as he serued him in person, in supplying him his meate & drinke with his owne hands, & with extreme sollicitude, prouiding him of all things necessary, to rid that subiect of his infirmity, of whom now a good while since, he had promised to himselfe, great matters for the diuine seruice, and the good of Religion. But this pious industry of the Seruant of Christ, had not the desired end; since it pleased the diuine Maiesty, to cut of the threed of *Osborns* mortal life. Whereat *S. Anselme* grieuing with most tender affect (as much as Christian vertue suffered) in the houre of his passage, deerly intreated him, that if it were possible, after his death, he would giue him some tydings of him. The dying man did promise as much, and so expired.

The body, according to the vse being socked, clothed, & then layd forth on a beer, was carryed into the Church; while the Monkes sate singing of the wonted psalmes about the same. *S. Anselme* in the meane tyme to make his prayer more attentiue and feruent, retyred himselfe into a place somewhat a part from the others: heer while with teares, and sighs he begs of our Lord, the saluation of

that

that soule, being oppressed with sorrow & heauynes and his eyes now shut, he fell into a slumber: and in that repose, beholds in spirit certayne venerable persons, dressed vp in white garments, to be entred in the chamber of the deceased, and there to sit downe to iudge him. But not knowing, what sentence they had passed vpon him, & expecting with great anxiety to vnderstand the successe of that iudgmēt; behold *Osborn* appeares on a sudden, in face not vnlike to one that returns to himselfe againe, after a traunce, or fit of fainting. Whereat *S. Anselme* sayd presently to him: What is the matter sonne? How it is with thee now? The other answered: The ancient Serpent hath risen vp thrice agaynst mee, and thrice hath it fallen vpon his owne head, & the Bear-heards of God haue deliuered mee: after which words *S. Anselme* opened his eyes, and *Osborn* vanished.

This answere the dead man gaue, and *S. Anselme* himselfe, afterwards interpreted the same in this manner: That thrice the ancient Serpent arose agaynst *Osborne*; because first, he accused him of sinnes committed after Baptisme, before he had been offered vp by his Parents into the Monastery: secondly for those, which he had committed after his entry into the Monastery, and before the making of his vowes: in the third place, for those whereinto he had incurred after his vowes, euen to his death. But thrice agayne, was the accuser defeated; because the errours of the world, had been cācelled in vertue of the Fayth, and oblation of his Parents, when they presented him deuoutly to the diuine seruice: those of the Nouiciate, were remitted him in the new consecration of himselfe by meanes of his vowes. The faults which he had committed after the vowes, were pardoned him somwhat neere to his passage, by meanes of confession and pennance: So as the diuell, finding all his quarrels frustrate, being wholy confounded, was quite defeated, since all the instigations and subtilityes he had vsed to make that soule to fall into sinne, had redounded to his owne more grieuous torment, and greater damnation.

As for the Bear-heards of God, they are (said he) good Angels: for that, as they tame the beares, so do these restrayne the malignant spirits, from the cruelty and impetuosity, wherewith they vse to rush on, to the destruction of soules. After all these things, to shew himselfe a true friend, and father of his *Osborne*, no lesse after his death then before, he sayd euery day a Masse for him, though the whole

yeare

yeare following. And if sometymes, he were hindred from celebrating at all, he would seeke for some other, to supply the same, promising to do as much for that Priest, when he was requested. Besides which, he did send letters into diuers parts to procure suffrages and sacrifices for the same intention, and thereby obtayned a great number of them. Whence it followed, that not onely the deceased party felt (as is verily belieued) eyther opportune refreshment, or accidentall ioy: but euen also the liuing tooke excellent example of so burning and continuall charity of *S. Anselme*; yea euen his very enemyes tempered themselues, who before could not looke on him with a good eye; & at last ouercom & touched with the perpetuall tenour of such goodnes, tooke so great an affection to the holy man, as from murmurers and emulous, they became followers and proclaymers of his rare vertues. Although indeed to bring things to those termes, a certaine strange accident of no small moment, happened to one of those enemies of the blessed Pastour, that immediately followes.

A certayne ancient Monke, and great Enemy of S. Anselme, *at his death, was tormented with a dreadfull vision, which* S. Anselme *driueth away with the signe of the Crosse. And how he gaue himselfe to the trayning vp of Youth.* Chap. 5.

THere was one very ancient in Religion, who with implacable disdayne neuer ceased to bite and molest the good Father, and by no meanes could neuer endure him much lesse reuerence & acknowledge him in the place of Christ. Now then, through the iust iudgment of God it happened this miserable wretch fell sicke to death; and one night while all the Monkes were in bed, he began to giue forth very dreadfull cryes, & to seeke as it were, to shun the sight of some horrible figures; became very pale of visage, and full of trembling and great anxiety, and would withall be turning his head on this side, and that side, to hide himselfe. At these noyses, his neyghbours being now awakened, came suddenly in hast to aske what he ayled. You behold mee (sayd he) afflicted and distressed thus within the pawes of two most rauenous wolues, which are now euen ready to strangle me, and demaund you of mee, what I ayle? One of them that was present hearing this, by name *Ricolfus*, who was the Secretary of Conuent, without delay went running to *S. Anselme,* who at that tyme was correcting of a booke, and presently informed what passed with the sicke man.

At which newes, the venerable Prior being touched with his accustomed clemency, bad *Ricolfus* returne backe to the sickman: and he in the meane tyme recollecting himselfe a litle, ouertooke him in the Infirmary, and lifting vp his hand, made the signe of the Crosse vpon him, saying: *In nomine Patris, & Filij & Spiritus Sancti.* With which signe, the Wretch was suddenly quiet, and being somwhat cheerfull in face, with most inward affect of the hart, began to giue thankes to the diuine Goodnes: and added withall, that soueraygne signe he had seene to come forth of his mouth, as a fiery lance, which being brandished agaynst those wolues, had so terrified them, as made them suddenly to fly away.

Then *S. Anselme,* sweetly approching to him, dealt with him seriously of matters concerning the saluation of his soule, & brought him to a great compunction, and true confession of all his offences committed agaynst God: and after he had giuen him the absolution, told him playnely, he should render vp his spirit, about nine of the clocke: and so indeed it fell out, to the great astonishment of all. From hence forward, *S. Anselme* with a great deale more ease, began to administer the office: in which, as one that sought to promote to perfection all those, whome he had vnder his charge; so with particular application, he laboured especially in the help of youth, and alledged this reason for it: That euen as wax, when it is too hard, or too soft, takes not very well the impression vpon it, but if it be well tempered between the hard and soft, it most faythfully receyues the print of the Seale; so iust, do we see it to happen in the age of a man.

Take you one who from his infancy to his old age, hath been alwayes bred vp in the vanityes of the world, and begin to deale with him then of spirituall conceipts, of contemplation, of celestiall things, and of such other like discourses, and you shall find him to be not able to conceyue hardly, much lesse to put your aduices in practice, and due execution. Nor is it any wonder, since the wax is hardned, nor hath he spent his yeares in such practises, & hath alwayes had other obiects, and other designes. On the contrary side, take me a child, both tender of yeares, and of conscience, and who cannot as yet discerne the euill from the good, the very same shall happen with this, as with the other, the wax is too soft, and liquid for it, it admits no characters, or images. Betwixt these two then, the youth stands in the midst, as temperatly composed of stiff and tender. Do thou endeauour, to instruct such a one, and thou shalt imprint in his mind, what thou wilt. Which thing I noting (sayd *S. Anselme*) do employ my selfe with the more assiduity and sollicitude, in trayning vp of youth, and do labour from their soules to extirpate all the rootes of vices, and to plant the vertues in place of them: that being purged in this manner and well tempered, they may come to represent more to the lyfe, the true image of a perfect man. And these were the principall motiues of *S. Anselme*, for the education of youth.

S. Anselme *sueth to the Archbishop of* Roan, *to be discharged of his Office, but is denyed. Togeather with a Vision of* Ricoltus *concerning him.* Chap. 6.

IN the meane tyme, occupations and affaires continually increasing, and sorely oppressing the Man of God; he held himselfe to be so much disquieted and distracted therewith from interiour exercises of the mynd (which happened not so to him at the beginning) as he went for counsaile anew to the aforesayd Archbishop of *Roan*: before whome, he vnfolded the occasion of his comming, and bitterly bewayling his peace and tranquillity lost thereby, besought him, that he might be disburdned with all expedition of the charge. Whereto the Archbishop, being a person of much iudgement and sanctity withall, thus answered: Do not, my deerest sonne, make instance to forgo the charge, nor do thou seeke to subtract thy selfe from helping others, to attend to thy selfe only: for I tell thee, in good sooth, that I haue heard heertofore of many, and seen some also, who hauing vnder the coulour of their proper quietnes, abandoned the pastorall cure, & by that occasion being fallen into tepidity, haue likely gone from euill to worse. Which to the end the same may not fall vpon thee likewise (which God forbid) I commaund thee in vertue of holy Obedience, to reteine to thee still the Prelacy which thou hast, nor to suffer thy selfe to be induced any wayes to depose the same, vnlesse the Abbot do enioyne thee to it. And if thou shalt be called heerafter to any greater charge, that thou do not refuse by any meanes to accept therof: Because I know very well, thou art not like to stay any long tyme, in that wherein thou art, but shalt shortly be aduanced to a higher degree.

To these words sayd S. *Anselme*: Then woe to me poore miserable wretch: I am ready to faynt with the present burden, and yet when another more weighty shall be layd vpon me, I may not refuse the same! These sighes of S. *Anselme*, moued not the wise Archbishop a whit, but rather with the same seuerity, he rehearsed to him agayne the same precept, which he had giuen him. In this wise the Seruant of Christ, perceyuing himselfe to be quite excluded from that which he wished, fayled not at last to conforme his own to the diuine will: and returning home, with new feruour & new purposes gaue wholy himselfe to cherish & increase the more solide vertues in his Monkes. To which effect, knowing very well of what importance was the vnion and communication togeather of the subiects, with the Superiour; he pursued with all the meanes, that well he might, to procure to himselfe the loue of ech one, and that particularly with shewing of true compassion and tendernes to the sick, and indisposed; so as he stucke not to enter often into the Infirmary himselfe, and there not only with sweet countenance and gracious words to comfort the afflicted; but euen also (as we sayd of *Osborne*) to serue them, and prepare them their dyet & food with his owne hands, and with diligence to find out the state of ech one, and that which most would be gust-full, and pleasing to them.

Through which dealing of his, the bitternes and detractions not only ceased, if there were any yet left, but there followed a thing, which may truly be called, the very health of religion; to wit, a confidence, and a certaine coniunction of the members with the head, and that so strayt, and so great withall, as there was not any, who not suddenly to manifest his secrets, and ech passion, & thought which he had in his breast to the good Priour, as a child would do to his sweetest Mother. With which security, and sweet familiarity would S. *Anselme* be curing of the inward wounds, and remedying the temptations of his Monkes, and that with so much more ease, as their consciences were made more manifest and palpable to him. So as by this meanes, S. *Anselme* came continually to be held in greater grace and reuerence with all men.

And this good conceypt of theirs, increased so much the more, through a certayne meruayle, which newly happened to the aboue named *Ricolfus*. This man, while he went one night through the

the Cloyster, obseruing the houre of rising of the Monkes to Mattins, in passing by good hap before the Chapter-doore, peeped in with his eyes, and beheld *S. Anselme* in prayer, enuironed round as with a flaming circle of fire. *Ricolfus* was astonished at the sight, & after he had a litle thought with himselfe what it should be, he resolued to hye him to the Fathers celll, when seeing no body there, he returned to the Chapter agayne, and found there the Priour as before, but without the sayd flame, yet most assured the while, of that which at first he beheld so cleerly.

S. Anselme *in a case of necessity miraculously procures a fish from the Riuer neere by: And with the spirit of Prophesy foretels an accident to come. Togeather with the Bookes which he wrote.*

ON a certayne day, *S. Anselme* being sent vnto, by a principall Lord of *Normandy*, to come and deale with him about certaine affayres, he refused not to go; and hauing discoursed with him, till the Euening, he was not inuited at all by the Prince, to lodge there that night, though the Monastery of *Bec*, were farre from thence. Which the Man of God perceyuing, without speaking a word therof to any, tooke his leaue, and departed thence, not knowing where to lodge. In the meane time, meeting with one of the Monkes, of his owne Order, he asked him, Whither he went, and were they might harbour and retire themselues that night? The other answered: Father, we haue a house indeed, not far frõ hence, but there is no refection to be had for you, and your company, saue only bread and cheese.

Then sayd *S. Anselme*, with a cheerfull countenance: Doubt you not good brother; go thy wayes then before, and cast a net into the riuer there, and thou shalt presently find fish inough for vs all. So did the Monke without any doubt a whit, and calling in hast, a fisherman to him, bad him to throw in his net. Now was it indeed neyther tyme, nor place for such a draught, and therefore the fisherman laughed at such a bidden thing, and tooke himselfe to be mockt at by the Monke. But at last, being thereunto cõstrayned, as it were though his prayers and persuasions, he resolued to obey; and behold agaynst all hope, came forth of the water a Trout of an vncouth bignes, with another litle fish also: So as that fish was more then inough for *S Anselme*, and his company.

That

That other accident differed not much from this which happened to him in another house of a deere friend of his, called *Walter Tirel*, who being sory for want of fish, and with words of courtesy excusing himselfe, for not hauing prouision worthy of such a ghest; *S. Anselme* smiled, and replyed: There is now a Sturgeon brought in vnto you, and do you complayne for want of delicacies? As yet *Walter* verily belieued he had but iested with him, and would by no meanes giue any credit to it, when behold, two of his men came & entred into the house with a Sturgeō, the greatest they had seene a long tyme, being found (as they sayd) by the Stepheards vpon the bankes of the riuer of *Alteia*. Whence, though in a base and materiall subiect, yet may it well be gathered, that *S. Anselme*, amongst other gifts of heauen, had likewise the spirit of Prophesy.

About the same tyme, he composed three very subtile Treatises: one of the *Truth*, another of *Freewill*, the third of the Fall of the *Deuill*. By which treatises, may well appeare, wherein he had truly fixed his mind, though by such considerations and labours, he neuer subtracted himselfe from the care & consolation of his Monkes. He wrote also another booke, which he entituled; *The Grammarian*, wherein he introduceth a Scholer to dispute with him; he also in that booke goes soluing of many Logicall difficulties. He annexed thereto a litle Tract, which he called, by the Greeke terme, *Monologion*; for that speaking with himselfe alone, without medling with quoting of the holy Scripture, with meere reasons he proues *There is a God*, and that by no meanes it can be otherwise.

After this, it came into his mynd, whether with one short argument only, that same might not be solidly proued, which is so belieued and preached of God, to wit, that he is Eternall, Incommutable, Omnipotent, Incomprehensible, whole in euery place, iust, pious, mercifull, true, or rather Truth it selfe, Goodnes, Iustice, and some other attributes, and how all these things are one thing in him. This same proposition now did affoard him so much to do, as partly it tooke away his meate, and sleep; and partly also (for which he felt the greater griefe) held him exceedingly in suspence, and greatly distracted him in his Psalmody, and in the other diuine Offices: and by how much more violence he vsed thereunto, so much the more was he troubled with the foresayd question; vntill such tyme as waking one night, it pleased the diuine Mercy, to illumine his vnderstanding, and to giue him the knowledge of what he desired, with so much clarity, as he felt therewith a great iubiley of hart, and a wonderfull sweetnes and consolation of mynd. And supposing he might help others therewith (as he was far from all enuy, or basenes of mynd) he went suddenly about to put the thing in tables of wax (according to the vse of those tymes) and then gaue them in keeping, with great charge, to one of the Monkes.

Some dayes being now passed ouer, he demaunded the same of the party himselfe, and suddenly they were sought for in the self same place where they had been layd, but could not be found. Wherupon good diligēce was vsed to learne out if any of the house had taken them away, but yet could neuer come to haue the least inckling of thē. *S. Anselme* went about then againe to make others of the same matter, and with especiall recommendation gaue them in charge to another of his Monkes. He hides them in the secretest part of his owne bed: and the next day, beyond all suspition, finds them all to pieces on the ground, and the wax, with the characters, scattered heere & there. He gathers them vp as they were, & brings them to *S. Anselme*, who endeauours the best he could to set the pieces togeather and fits them at last with much ado, so as they might be read, and so kept them close vnited togeather. And to the end the same might happen no more, he causes them to be transcribed in parchment: and from thence, he drew afterwards a Volume, though litle in bulke, yet great and very admirable in conceipts & speculations, and called it *Proslogion*, wherein he discoursed eyther with God, or with himselfe. Which litle Worke, being written against, by a learned man, *S. Anselme* seemed to reioyce therat, and to yield thankes to the Censour, but made notwithstanding his Apology for it, and sent it backe to the sayd friend, beseeching him, or any other whosoeuer, that should once go about to taxe the aforsayd doctrine, not to publish the reprehension without likewise annexing the defence.

A most pious, and Excellent Epistle of S. Anselme, *to a certaine Launce-Knight, who was newly entred into the Monastery of* Cluny. Chap. 8.

VV Ith all these occupations, as well of gouernment, as also of more grauer studies, the Seruant of God neglected not to write also sundry letters of edification: Of one of which, we will

will heere insert a chapter, about the subiect of mutation of place, to the end yt may appeare, how much the same was impugned by this holy man, when it is not done through Obedience, or for some important occasion. He wrote then among other things, some aduises to a certaine Launce-knight, who was newly entred into the Conuent of *Cluny*, of the tenour following.

Thou art now entred, my dearest, into the lists and warfare of Christ, in which yt behoues thee, not only to resist the open battayles of the Enemy, but to beware likewise of the subtile traynes, which lye hid vnder the shew of a goood spirit. Because many tymes, when the wicked aduersary cannot come to ouerthrow a Nouice, with obiects of manifest sinne, he seekes to ruine and murder him with the poyson of false, but probable and apparent reasons: and so being not able to induce him to the harted of Religion, and the Institute which he hath made choyce of, at least he endeauours to make the conuersation, and dwelling tedious to him where he abides for the present: and though in some manner, he permit to reteyne yet the Monasticall life; notwithstanding he ceaseth not by a thousand wayes, to make the simple and foolish to imagine, that he knew not what he did, when he tooke the habit in such a place, or vnder such Superiours; or els in such a community, and this to the end, that making the wretch by these meanes, vngratefull for the benefit of his Vocation, through the iust iudgment of God, he may not only not go forward, but euen also haue much ado to hold his vocation, and to conserue himselfe in his good purposes. Because the mynd being once distracted into melancholy thoughts, eyther of changing the residence, or if this cannot be, at least of reprehending and blaming the foresayd causes of his determination, he hath no power to recollect himselfe, nor to aspire to that terme of vertue, whereto he ought to extend himselfe with all his forces. The cause is, for that the foundation being once vngratefull to him, he knowes not how to erect any frame of building thereon. Whence it followers, that euen as a yong tree, being often transplanted, or disquieted and shaken with many encounters, can not take any deep roote, nor commodiously suck in the moysture and nourishment of the earth, to giue forth the desired fruit in tyme: so the vnhappy Monke, if he seeme to remoue himself, now heer now there of his owne meere appetite, and not though any disposition of Superiours, or els euen remayning still where he is, per-

mits

mits himselfe to fall into tediousnes and disgust; he can neuer come to be well grounded in diuine loue, & consequently being dry and languishing in euery action of religion, he shall finally remaine very poore and despoyled of the fruites of good workes: & he seeing himselfe withall, to proceed from euill to worse (yt so he note the same) shall lay allwayes the fault thereof on others, and by this meanes abhorre euery day, more and more, euen those with whom he liueth and conuerseth.

For which cause, whosoeuer will bee a good Religious man indeed, yt behoues him, that looke into what Monastery he hath been first admitted, and dedicated to the diuine Seruice (if in that place be no manifest daunger to offend the diuine goodnes) with all study and attention he endeauour to establish himselfe there, and there to found himselfe in true Charity, and to beware by any meanes from iudging the manners of the place, whether they be publique or priuate, profitable or vnprofitable, so that openly they stand not against the precepts of God. But rather, reioycing for hauing found where to abide in the seruice of Christ, that he put away from himselfe all manner of suggestion, to remoue else whither; but with the greatest quiet that may bee, he seeke to attend vnto pious and deuout exercises. And yt peraduenture, yt may seeme to him, that he hath reguard to greater matters, & of more euident profit, then such as are practized in that Couuent there; let him thinke, that perhaps he is deceaued, in preferring things that are equall, before all others; or els in presuming, or promising too much of himselfe: and yf he cannot be brought to leaue of that opinion, at least let him belieue, he hath not deserued what he desires.

And if further he note he were deceaued; let him giue many thankes to the diuine clemency, in defending & setting himself free from such an errour, and for that he hath not suffered him, without gayne, or perhaps rather with losse, in prouing another habitation, and some other manner of gouernement, to fall into the blame of leuity, or lack of wit; or els, by imbracing of things too hard, in a very short tyme to become wearied, and fall into the former state, if not a worse. But if he truely desireth a thing more perfect indeed, and more conformable to him, let him make accompt, that for his sinnes, he hath not deserued the same; and let him patiently, suffer the diuine iudgment therein, which neuer denyes any one any thing, vniustly. And in summe, let him shun the offences of the

the diuine Maiesty, through murmur or muttering, but take in good part, and endure all with a sweet and holy peace, least perseuering otherwise, he come to exasperat the iust Iudge, and so remaine excluded from that which as yet he hath not receiued, and loose perhapps, what he holds already, or els to possesse it without any profit at all. But howsoeuer he do feele vpon himselfe, eyther the mercy or iudgment of God, in any case let him cheerefully giue him thanks, and in all, and through all, acknowledge that infinite benignity of his. And since he hath the grace to retire himselfe, into the Port (whatsoeuer) from the perilous stormes and tempests of the world, let him now auoyd to open in the Port it selfe any entry to the impetuous winds of impatience, and mutability; that the Soule abiding in the Lee, or harbour of constancy and meekenes, may remayne firme and intentiue ioyntly, and wholy to the sollicitude of feare, and the gust of diuine Loue; the one of which through caution conserues the hart, the other with sweetnes, euen perfects the Mynd.

I am not ignorant, how this matter would require more commodity of writing, or of discourse by word of mouth, to giue you to vnderstand with what subtiltyes in this matter of temptation, the ancient Serpent is wont to make the ignorant Monke to fall into his snares: & on the contrary, with what reasons and aduises, the wise Religious may dissolue and defeate his malicious perswasions. But for that I haue exceeded the breuity already, which an Epistle requires, and that whatsoeuer I haue sayd, or can otherwise say, consistes wholy to conserue this repose, and tranquillity of the Soule; it shall suffice me for this tyme, to haue proposed for your good what succinctly I haue don already. Nor would I haue you for this to imagin, that I hold you for vnquiet or malcontent: but forasmuch, as *Don Orsion* obliged me to giue you some aduertisements, I know not how to affoard you a better and more holsome one, then for a man to stand on his guard, in this kind of temptation, which I know is secretly wont to enter into some Nouices, and quite to ouerthrow them. So as (my friend, and most beloued Brother) behold how your deerest freind doth counsaye, admonish, and pray you, with the whole bowells of his hart, that with all the forces of your mind, you attend to the foresaid quiet of the hart, without which, it is impossible to discerne the snare of the treacherous Enemy, nor yet to penetrate with the eyes of the vnderstanding, the most strait and narrow way of vertue. To which tranquility, may no Religious, euer arriue without constancy and meeknes, which meekenes is the inseparable companion of patience: nor lesse shall he euer attayne thereto, yf he resolue not, to obserue and reuerence all the orders, and institutes of his Monastery not repugning to the diuine Law, though he see not the foundation of them, nor the reason why they were introduced, and prescribed. Farewell, and the blessed God direct & guide you in all your actions with perseuerance; so as, in the habit of iustice, you may one day appeare in his sight, and fully be satisfyed, when he shall manifest his glory.

A pretty Dialogue, betweene S. Anselme, *and another Abbot, concerning the trayning vp of youth.* Chap. 9.

THe like instructiõs gaue the diuine man in writing according to the occurrẽces that happened. Nor were those same lesse replenished with heauenly wisedome, which in diuers occasions, as we haue touched aboue, he deliuered by word of mouth: Whereof likewise for fuller satisfaction of the Reader, we will not spare to set downe some one example. It was the cõmon custome in those tymes, for Noblemen, as it were throughout all Christendome, to put their children of tender age into the Cõuents of Monkes, partly to consecrate them perpetually vnto Religion; and partly also to take them forth agayne, being piously trayned vp, for the benefit of the common wealth. Now it chanced that a certayne Abbot, in great opinion of Sanctity, discoursing with *S. Anselme*, of Monasticall gouernement, among other things, came to speake of these youths, to which purpose, he vsed these words: Tell me I pray, good Father, what we shall do with them, they are so peruerse and incorrigible; we neuer cease day and night from beating them, and yet still they grow worse and worse. Whereat *S. Anselme*, making a shew of some wonder, answered. You neuer leaue beating them: and when heerafter they come to be elder, what proue they then to be? Euen dolts, sayd the other, and very beasts. Then *S. Anselme*: O how well then, do you bestow the paynes to make beasts of men. And what can we do withall, replyed the Abbot? We seeke by all meanes to constreyn them to their profit, & it boots nothing. Do you forme them, or one, replyed *S. Anselme*?

Do but tell me a little Father Abbot: If you set but a plant in your garden, and bind it vp presently on euery side, so as it can not extend the branches any way: if you go after a yeare to take away the binder from it, how shall you find it? Certaynely with the boughes crooked, intricate, and inuolued. And who then should be in fault thereof, but your selfe, who so immoderatly restrayned the same? Iust so succeeds it with your pupils. They are planted by the oblation of their friends in the Garden of the holy Church to grow vp, and to giue forth good fruits to God. But you, with terrours, menaces, and stripes, do euen so strayten them, as that the poore wretches haue not a iot of liberty. So as being indiscreetly wrung and opprest, they produce and cherish in themselues, but ill discourses, which in manner of wreathed thornes, so grow & setle in them, as there is after no remedy to be found, or prop to sustaine and hold them vp, & to make them grow out straight agayne. And for that, they find no sparke of loue or pitty in you, nor any tendernes or sweetnes towards them, they cannot frame any good cōceipt of you, but do rather verily persuade themselues, that all your doings spring from hatred and malignity in you. And hence very miserably proceeds it, that the more they grow in body, so much the more increase they in auersion and iealousies, being alwayes inclined and ready to fall into all sorts of vices; and as in none they find any signes of true charity, so can they not reguard any one, but with an eye a skew, and quite awry.

But for the loue of God, I would feigne haue you tell me, what is the cause you are so strange & harsh vnto them? For are they not I pray, men, and of the same nature that you are? And would you, if you were in their place, thinke it well to be dealt with, in this wise? but be it, as you say, that you haue no other intentiō with you in such your rigours, but only to make them good. Did you euer in your life, behold a Gold smyth to frame with blowes and beatings only, any goodly figure of some masse of gold or siluer? I belieue not. What then? For to shape it with his instruments, now beates he it, and presseth it gently, and then with a discreet relieue, raysses he it vp, and frames it as he list. So, if you will seeme to introduce any good forme of manners into youth, it behooues you to geather with the depressions of pennance to vse some indulgences and helps withall of a fatherly tendernes and loue. To this point, the Abbot. What indulgences, (sayd he) what helps? We continu-

 ally

ally labour to constreyne them to vertue. And *S. Anselme*: It is well: and so euen bread, and other solid food, are good and holsome to such as are able to disgest the same. But do you try awhile to giue it to a sucking child, and you shall see it rather to be choaked, then fed therewith. Wherefore I need not tell it you, it is so cleere. But this I do affirme, that as sickly and strong bodies, haue their difference and proportionable food: so the weake and more feeble soules, require a food which is agreable to them, in measure and quality. The strong and able are fed, and delighted with the solid and substantiall food, that is, with Patience in tribulations, with breaking of the appetite, with exhibiting the left cheeke to him that strikes them on the right, praying for ones enemyes, with louing their persecutours, and with other the like. But that Soule, which is feeble as yet, in the diuine seruice, had need of tender milke, that is, to be intreated with sweetnes, with mercy, with a cheerefull countenance, with patience full of charity, & with such like carriages. If you would but accommodate your selfe in this manner with your feeble, and able ones, with the grace of God, what in you lyes, you would gayne all. With these words, the Abbot, being finally conuinced and touched withall, began to sigh, and said: We surely, Father, haue erred all this while from the right way, and to vs hath the Sunne of discretion, as yet not risen. Heervpon being prostrate on the ground, he confessed he had hitherto done ill; and with crauing pardon for what was passed, promised to amend heerafter.

Another Dialogue betweene S. Anselme, *and a certayne Procuratour of a Monastery*. Chap. 10.

VPon a tyme, there came to the holy man, a Procuratour of the same *Order*, who bewayled (as it happens now and then) his hard misfortune; for that being touched heertofore by heauenly inspiration, he had left the world to serue God, and now through obedience, was constrayned agayne to leaue God, to attend vnto the world. For as much, as the care of conseruing of rents, of following suites, of reuiewing of accompts, and of other such like secular affayres, did leaue him no tyme at all to recollect the powers & facultyes of his Soule, for contemplation of celestiall things; but put him rather in continuall danger of offending the diuine Maie-

sty.

ty, in diuers manners. To which complaint, *S. Anselme* answered, with the comparison following: The whole lyfe of man, may be well likened to a water Mill, seated on a swift riuer. Let there be then many millers belonging to this mill, some so negligẽt, as to let the meale fall into the water; others, to retayne part, and part agayne to let passe away; and some also, that gather vp all, and lay it vp, according as it is fit. Of this number, it is manifest, that he who hath reserued nothing, shall find but litle, he that hath held & saued all, shall be able to maynteyne himselfe more plentifully.

This Mill, as we sayd, may well be vnderstood this present life: the Meale represents the actions of men. Because, that euen as when the Mill workes, it goes allwayes round, and is euer continually wheeling about in it selfe; so likewise, human actions for the most, returne vnto their stations. As for example: Men plough, men sow, men reape, men grind, they make bread, they eate. Behold the Mill hath fetched a compasse. What then, doth it now stand still? No truly, because it returnes agayne to the foresaid tilling, sowing, reaping, grinding, making of bread, and nourishing withall. These things are exercised euery yeare: and like a Mill fetch agayne the same compasse, and turne about Let vs now take one, that doth all his workes for terren ends, and who in them hath no regard but to transitory things: this man, truly grinds and works indeed; but all the meale, which should be the fruite of his labours, through the course of secular desires, comes to be drowned, and caried quite away. This man, at the end of his life, when he shall turne back from the Mill to his howse, and that he would fayne feed on something, shall find nothing to eate, because the vehement streame hath caryed away the meale: Whence, wo to the wretch, for he is like to fast eternally.

Behold another, who looseth not the whole meale altogeather; because now he giues some almes, now hee goes deuoutly to visit Churches, and the sicke, and now he buries the dead, and so doth some other such like workes. But yet when this very person forbeares in nothing to giue himselfe to all sensuality, to be auẽged of iniuries receiued, to take complacence in human prayses, and that he cannot rid himselfe quite of impure and disordinate affects, the wretch looseth, ere he is aware, the greater part of the meale. And what shall become of him then in the other life, but euen to receiue rewards, according as he hath behaued himselfe?

Let vs now passe to the third quality of men; and let vs imagine it to be within religious. Suppose, when a Monke who hath made the Vow of Obedience, and what in him lyes, desires not to go forth of the Cloyster for any temporall busynes whatsoeuer, Such a one then, is enioyned by his Superiour to go abroad, to haue care of some possession of the Conuent; the good man excuseth himselfe, and prayes he may not be forced therevnto. And yet the Abbot still perseuers, and vrges his going thither. So as the subiect, being not able to resist, doth what he is commaunded. Behold he comes to the Mill, and needs must he grinde. There arise complaints heere and there, with murmurs and contentions. Heere now the prudent Monke is to looke well to his meale, and to receiue it warily into his sack, and not to let it fall into the Current: and how this? Let him do nothing out of vanity: Let him not be drawne to any manner of iniustice, for any gayne whatsoeuer. Let him execute Obedience in such manner, as he stifly defend with good reason all the Ecclesiasticall goods; but withall not seeke to increase them by vnlawfull wayes. If he walke in this manner, though he be sometymes enforced not to heare Masse, to breake silence, and other such like obseruances; Yet the vertue of holy Obedience, consummates all these defects, and with his sack both whole & sound, he conserues all his meale, whence after he shall haue plenty inough to feed on for all eternity: because such a one walkes not according to his Selfe-Will, but answearable to that of his Superiours, by meanes whereof, as the Apostle sayth, he comes to escape damnation.

Being now come to this passage, the Procuratour demaunded anew: & what then should we thinke of that Religious man, who offers himselfe voluntarily to such businesses, or rather practiseth them, with complements and flatteries? Wherto *S. Anselme* said, such question was not to the purpose of Religious men. To which the other replying, that he allwayes vnderstood it with condition, to wit, that the Monke so desirous of such occupations, should not after execute any thing without leaue of his Prelate; When *S. Anselme* answered: This leaue hath deceiued many such: because that in the matter, which we now treate of, there are two things wholy opposite, Obedience and Disobediēce: between these two contraryes, this leaue stands in the midst. He then, without being constreyned by Obedience to go forth of the Monastery, will yet neuertheles

uertheles goe forth, and by this meanes subtract himselfe from the rigour of the rule; though he do it with the full consent of the Superiour, & so seeme to iustify the act, by the licence obteyned; he remaines yet lyable to the sinne of disordinate and vnlawfull will and desire. Because that after one hath once left the world in person, he ought not to returne to it agayne, with desire: but yet while he would not performe it without the permission of his Superiour, the Obedience whereto he tyed himselfe, shall seeme indeed to excuse the exteriour fact; but that Will, which he had of his owne, shall cost him deare, if he do not penance in tyme for the same. Which some not reguarding, do suffer themselues, as I said, oftentymes to be deceiued through their appetite, vnder the shew of this leaue, or licence.

S. Anselme *had a vision in sleepe: His fame increased euery where: And through the importunity of the Abbot, was forced to take the whole Charge of the Monastery vpon him.* Chap. 11.

IN this manner, went *S. Anselme,* as well with wordes, as with the pen, & that which more imports, with works, inciting all to the contempt of the world, and to the seruice of the eternall God. When through his many labours, being seized with a most grieuous infirmity, in excesse of mind, he came to haue a Vision, that inflamed him much more to the desire of the eternall beatitude. For that, there seemed a very swift and swelling torrent to be represented to him, whereinto descended all the ordure and filth of the World; Which troubled, stincking, and filthy waters, with a violent force went promiscuously carying away all things with them, which they met with on the way, with all sorts of persons, both men and women, rich and poore. *S. Anselme* being astonished at so foule a spectacle, demaunded of one the company, Of what those miserable wretches liued, and whence they quenched their thirst? And being told they mainteyned themselues with that same water, wherewith they were more precipitously caried away. And how so, answered he? Is there any amongst them, that is not ashamed to swallow vp such filth? Whereto the other answered. Do not you seeme, Sir, to wonder heerat? This same, which you se heere, is the Torrent of the world, wherein sensuall men are so enwrapped, & caryed away: and by and by sayd: Wouldst thou feigne beheld,

what

what is a true Monke indeed? Yea mary would I, answered *S. Anselme*. When he replyed. Then looke round about thee, and see the walls of a Cloyster, being all lyned ouer with the finest siluer, and the grasse in the midst thereof, all of Siluer indeed, but soft and delicate, and most pleasant to behold. Which hath likewise another condition withall, that if one resteth thereon, it will gently seeme to yeild vnder him, and then rising agayne, be rising in like manner. This place so delightfull to see to, seemed to please *S. Anselme* beyond measure: When deliberating with himselfe, to choose the same for his owne habitation, the Guide began to aske him agayne, saying: Hola. Would you see now, what is true Patience? And *S. Anselme*, shewing forth as well with wordes, as gestures, a most ardent desire thereof, the Vision vanished on a suden, and he returned to himselfe agayne. By such apparitions he was filled with new light, and with a new feruour of spirit.

In this meane tyme, the name of *S. Anselme*, ran not only through out all Normandy, but euen likewise through the Countryes of France and Flaunders, yea and passing ouer the Sea, extended it selfe throughout all England, so as from diuers parts many noble and learned men, and Souldiours also had recourse to the diuine man, and dedicated themselues to the seruice of God vnder the custody of so great a Pastour: though he with great prudence tooke heed of perswading them, more to this, then to that Conuent, contenting himselfe with drawing them onely in generall to a Religious state, least they entring in without any proper deliberation of theirs to some Monastery, and then finding themselues afterwards, molested with molestations, temptations, and trauayles, might chance to murmur, and attribute their impatience and scandall to his persuasions. Whereupon the Conuent of *Bec*, came shortly to be amplifyed, both in number of subiects, and in plenty of possessions.

And the Abbot *Herlwin*, being lastly arriued to extreme old age, and now become decrepit withall, discharged himselfe of all things (touching the gouernement) & layd thẽ on the shoulders of *S. Anselme*; expressely ordayning that he should be well prouided of horses, & of all other accoutrements for iourneys, whensoeuer his busines required the same, and all should be kept as proper for his person. But he being affrighted with the name of propriety, when he returned from his iourneyes, would giue vp the same in common agayne; nor would he euer endure, that for his owne commodity, the others should seeme to suffer in any thing. And that no meruaile, since euen in the world it selfe, he was euer so amiable and courteous to all; as that when he saw his friends to want any thing, he would willingly supply them of his owne, according to his ability. For euen at that tyme also, the very light of reason, had dictated to him, that all the riches of the world, were created by the Eternall Father, for the common vtility of men, and that in the law of nature, they belonged no more to one man then another. And much more, after he was offered vp to God in Religion, as a perpetuall Holocaust, stood he allwayes firme and constant in voluntary pouerty. Nor wanted he occasions inough to exercise the same; in reguard, that besides the aforesaid priuiledges and particularities, which in vaine the Abbot *Herlwin* had enforced vpon him; there were brought now and then, no small summes of gold and siluer to spend, or keepe to himselfe for his owne commodity and pleasure, which yet the good religious man, would neuer yield to accept of, if they were not presented to the Abbot himselfe, for the benefit and vse of the whole community. And if the Benefactour himselfe, as it would happen now and then, replyed, that he had as then no intention to bestow it on the Abbot, or Conuent; he would answere, that he had no need of such things, and that, in that nature, he would receiue nothing at all of any person liuing. With these proceedings of his, he did allwayes yield forth a most sweet odour of himselfe. Whẽce he came to be inuited vnto diuers Abbyes, to make them spirituall exhortations, and to resolue their doubts, and to afford them his counsayle, as well in publique, as in priuate affayres: Which the man of Christ would do, with exceeding edification, and good of Soules.

Abbot Herlwin being dead, Saint Anselme *is chosen in his place. He is giuen much to Hospitality: And goes into* England *to visit* S. Lanfranke, and *King* William.

IN the meane tyme, *Herlwin* dyed, and *S. Anselme* with the common consent of all the Conuent, was elected for Successour. But he knowing the danger of such manner of dignityes, for many daies opposed himselfe with excuses & reasons as efficacious as he could, agaynst the sayd election. After which, perceyuing that he was not able to remoue the setled determination of the Monkes, lamenting and sending forth sighes, he cast himselfe at their feete, beseeching and coniuring them, through the bowels of the diuine mercy, to leaue of such a thought, and not to burden him with such wayght. But they on the contrary, being prostrate before *S. Anselme*, besought him to haue pitty on the Conuent, and to beware, that with such resistance he seemed not more to regard his proper commodity, the the publike weale and vtility. This perseuerance of the Monkes, togeather with the memory of that which was expressely commaunded him, by the Archbishop of *Roan*, ouercame him at last: otherwise, there had been no meanes possible, to haue brought him to accept of the Prelacy.

Being then consecrated, without altering awhit the manner of his customes, and liuing; he now proceeded to promote with all diligence his subiects to the end of their vocation, and with great vigilancy prouided, that the least wrong in the world might not be offered to any one, by the Officers and Procuratours, in the causes of the Monastery. Moreouer in receiuing, and lodging of Ghests (to which worke of charity, the family of *S. Benet* hath euer applied it selfe with particular industry, and prayse) *S. Anselme* was among others most wondefull liberall, & where ability fayled, he supplyed the defect with a great promptnes of the will, and withall serenity and cheeerfulnes of the countenance: and likewise, sometymes in case of necessity he would be taking from the refectory it selfe, the meate which was prepared for the Monkes, to set before strangers; though ordinarily, as he was a most prudent exactour of obseruance, so was he very accurate in procuring, that the Conuent should suffer no want: howbeit oftentymes, things arriued to those termes, as there would seeme to be no prouision left for the day following. In which cases, the Dispensiers, the Cellarians, and other the Ministers of the Monastery running with all anxiety vnto the holy Abbot, he would answere them with a graue & serene countenance, that if they would but haue confidence in the diuine Goodnes, he would not suffer them to want any necessaryes, nor were they deceiued awhit of his promise.

Because, euen in that very instant, or shortly after, you might haue seen to come from England (where many of the possessions of their Conuent lay) some ship well freighted with all manner of pro-

prouision; or els some extraordinary almes to arriue from some deuout person; or otherwise some wealthy man to come, and enter into Religion amongst them, wherby in time what manner of wãt soeuer, or disorder in this kind, might be easily remedyed. And forasmuch, as the forsayd possessions in *England*, for the better manage of good gouernment, required somtymes the visits and presence of the Abbot himselfe; *S. Anselme* was fayne now and then to go thither, being thereunto moued moreouer with desire to go and visit his deere, and most venerable Father and Mayster *S. Lanfranke*, who for his most excellent vertues, from the Abbot of *Cadom*, was assumpted to the Archbishoprike of *Canterbury*. Comming then to *England*, he was receiued with much ioy and honour, not only in the sayd Citty of *Canterbury*, but in all other places wheresoeuer he passed. And he alwayes according to custome, shewed himselfe most sweet and affable to all, accommodating himselfe to the genius and fashions of euery one; so much, as he would many tymes say, that he who in euery thing, wherein God may not seeme to be offended, endeauours to consent to the will of another, comes to merit exceedingly with the diuine Goodnes: that as he accordes with others in the present life, so with him in the future, may God and all created things, seeme likewise to accord. But he that dispising the neighbours contentment, will attend but his owne gust only; shal deserue often, with the iust Iudge, that euen as in this world, he would not seeme to conforme himselfe to the will of any; so in the other, shall no man accommodate himselfe to his. Since euen it is sayd by our Sauiour himselfe, that euery one, shall receyue according to the measure he hath proportioned to others.

The blessed *S. Anselme* now being moued with such like reasons, as we haue sayd, did shun by all meanes to be troublesome & grieuous to any: howbeyt, now and then, he was constrayned therefore to remit somwhat of the monasticall seuerity & discipline that he vsed otherwise, reputing it to redound to the greater glory and seruice of God, to condescend rather a litle now and then, with holy equity, to such Soules as he was to help, then by standing too much vpon rigour, to estrange, and alienate them from his speach and conuersation. Whence it followed, through the great affection, that all seemed to beare him, they came at last with a very good will to receiue very holesome and spirituall aduertisements from him: Which in truth haue neuer yet beene put in print, nor alwayes giuen in the same manner, but proportionable to the qualityes and estate of the hearers.

To the Monkes, aboue all things he would giue to vnderstand they should not seeme to neglect the least faults and trangressions of the Institute. And was wont to confirme the same, with a similitude of a Viuary, or Fish-trough, because that euen as when the holes, or chinks are not kept well stopt within them, the water by and litle goes running forth, & the fish doth euen perish the while: So in religious houses, when there is no heed taken of lighter faults, by litle and litle, is spirit togeather with obseruance lost.

He taught the Clearkes, how they were to maintayne the profession which euen by name they made, of hauing God only for inheritance, portion & lot, and aduised them to stand allwayes vpon their guard, least through negligence or tepidity, insteed of possessing God, they come to inherite the Deuill. To the maryed in like sort, he would giue aduertisements, very full of prudence and sanctity.

And in this doctrine of his, the diuine man proceeded not after the manner of the Maisters, and deep Deuines of the world, who beleiue they cannot seeme to maintayne their degree and dignity if they do not still propose very high and sublime conceipts, and not so easy to be apprehended of the vulgar: But *S. Anselme*, quite contrary to such, by reducing the highest points to the capacity of the meaner vnderstandings, and vnfolding the obscure and intricate passages, and declaring them by images and materiall examples (being a thing very proper to true and absolute Wisedome indeed) and confirming them moreouer with potent and manifest reasons; would seeme efficatiously to engrosse them in the breast and heart, so as euery one heard him with great cheerefullnes, and recurred to him in their doubts, with the greatest confidence that might be. Nor was there in England a personage at that tyme of importãce, that held it not a great misfortune to haue had no occasion to heare, honour, and serue such a man. Yea euen King *William* himselfe, who had, conquered that Nation by force of armes, and was commonly held to be fierce and cruell, shewed himselfe to *S. Anselme* so human and benigne, as they were all astonished at him.

K. Wil-

K. William *the Conquerour being dead, his Sonne* William Rufus *succedes. And* Lanfrancke *the Arch-Bishop deceasing*, S. Anselme *is chosen in his place.* Chap. 13.

FRom this tyme forwards, *S. Anselme* was much conuersant in *England*, and according to the occurrences that happened, he made frequent iourneys thither. And among other tymes that he went into those parts, one was, after the death of the said King *William*, to whom his Sonne succeeded of the same name, being a person very ill enclined, and who from a King became a Tyrant: and among other iniquityes of his, against all Iustice, he doubted not to pollute his impions hands, with the oppression of the Clergy and Religious, & with the vsurpation of the goods of the Church. Whereupon it seemed good to the Earle of *Chester*, and to other principall Lords of the kingdome, to giue him a Christian admonishment by the meanes of one of so great authority, as *S. Anselme* was; and with that occasion to comfort themselues with his presence and discourses, whom they wished to be the Phisitian, and Gouernour of their soules.

S Anselme then, being so earnestly inuited and intreated by this Man, and many others, with the greatest instance that might be; passed ouer agayne vnto *Canterbury*, where a litle before was deceased *S. Lanfrank* the Arch-Bishop, and where the Clergy and people, were in great care and desire, to supply the vacancy of that Seate, with the election of some worthy and sufficient Prelate. So as now at the appearing of *S. Anselme*, began to arise a generall whisper in the whole Citty, that a new Arch-Bishop was come already, and how they ought not to thinke of any other then of him. Which the humble Seruant of Christ perceiuing, immediately departed from thence, nor could he be induced by the prayers or intreaties of any, so much as to celebrate there on the Feast thẽ approching of the *Natiuity of the most blessed Virgin*. From hence, according to the necessity of the Churches, and the request of the Peeres, he refused not to go to the Court, where met with much reuerence by all the *Barons*, & the King himselfe likewise, with cheerfull countenance, came to receiue him, euen to the gate of the Pallace; and after most deere kisses, and louing imbraces, taking him by the right hand, he conducted him into a roome thereby. Where sitting

 downe,

downe, and some words of courtesy passing betweene them, *S. Anselme* shewed his desire to haue priuate audience with him: so as the standers by, went immediatly forth, when he without touching a whit the matters appertayning to his Monastery, for which it was thought, he had principally come to Court, with Christian liberty, began to discouer to the King, the sinister fame, that went of him; nor stuck he, to specify vnto him many particulars, that he might the more easily come to amend them.

The discourse being ended, he went his wayes, to seeke out the *Earle* of *Chester*, & was enforced to remayne there for some dayes. In the meane while, the King fell grieuously sicke, & fearing death was put in mynd by his followers, assoone as possible, to prouide for the principall Church of the Kingdome, being then without a Pastour, which was that of the aforesaid *Canterbury*. And now this counsayle seeming good to the King, he nominated the Abbot *Anselm*, and no other, for the same administration. The which declaration, was with admirable applause, receyued of all. The Abbot only, at the newes thereof, was strooke euen dead, as it were; but then gathering his forces to him agayne, he endeauours by all meanes possible to resist, but not being able to preuayle, agaynst the deliberate consent of the King, and of the whole Clergy, and people, he was snatched vp, and carryed into the Cathedrall Church, and placed in the Throne with much solemnity. From thence, he was straight conducted to *Winchester*, and lodged in the suburbs of the Citty there: where while he remaynes in the company of *Gondolfus* Bishop of *Rochester*, and of a certayne principall Monke, by name *Baldwin*: behold one night was a great fire enkindled in the neighbour-houses, which with fury went consuming whatsoeuer it met with in the way. It now approched to the house very neere vnto *S. Anselmes* Inne; when some familiar friends of the Hostesse or Mistres of the house, seeing so litle remedy agaynst the fire, began to carry away from thence the houshold-stuffe, into some safer place. But the woman, being full of fayth, forbad the same; very confidently affirming, there was no such cause of feare, while she had the Archbishop *S. Anselme* in her house. At which so generous words of hers, *Baldwin* being moued, intreated the holy Father, not to deny his succour to the deuout Matron: but he, with accustomed modesty & humility, answered: what should I helpe her? & wherein I pray? Go you but forth then, the other replyed, and make the signe of the holy

holy Crosse agaynst the fire: and who knowes, whether the diuine Clemency may not happily extinguish it by that meanes? When *S. Anselme* replyed agayne. What say you, by my meanes? You know not what you say. And yet neuertheles, for feare of the imminent danger, he went forth with the others; and in the sight of those furious flames, was constrayned by the Bishop of *Rochester*, and *Baldwin*, to oppose the holsome signe of the Crosse there to. A strange thing, he had no sooner lifted vp his hand, but (as likewise it is read of *S. Martin*) that flaming and impetuous floud of fire, retiring into it selfe, made a stop in its course: and the flames being extinguished on a sudden, left the buildings halfe burnt, so farre as it had gone.

S. Anselme *endeauours to put off the charge imposed vpon him, but in vayne. He after falls in disgrace with the King and is banished the Court. With a miracle that happened.* Chap. 14.

AFter all these things, *S. Anselme* did seeke very dexterously to put off from his shoulders, that new burthen of the Archbishoprique: and to that end had differred till then, the acceptation thereof, and his full consent thereunto. But so great were the motiues, and coniurations made of persons of ech quality; togeather with the scruple of *Obedience* thereunto added, which was imposed vpon him heertofore by the Archbishop of *Roan*, as that in fine a cõsent was violently extorted from him. And so was the blessed Man, with great ioy and solemnity, consecrated by all the Bishops of *England*, in the *Metropolis* of *Canterbury*. This consecration of his, was celebrated vpon the 4. of December, on the feast of the glorious *S. Barbara*: when loe, the *Natiuity of our Sauiour* comming shortly after, *S. Anselme* went his wayes to the King, to giue him the accustomed salutation of the good Newyeare: of whome he was first well intreated; but afterwards, partly out of malice, and the meere instability of the Kings owne disposition, and partly by the worke and instigation of wicked Courtiers and flatterers, the state of matters was quite changed: and the Kings mynd began with a sudden mutation to shew it selfe much aliened from the Archbishop: while to the foresayd occasions, was likewise added another of no small moment, which was, that *K. William* hoping for some great present from him at his first entrance, found himselfe to be quite deceiued of his expectation; since *S. Anselme*, was not willing at all to aggrieue his subiects with any exactions & loanes, to satisfy the disordinate appetites of the King.

So that perceyuing him now to be angry with him, he departed from Court, and retyred himselfe to a certayne Village of his called *Bregge*, to finish, and dedicate there a Church for that parish, which by the death of *S. Lanfranke* his Predecessour was yet imperfect. In which ceremony, succeeded a notable accident: which was, that a certayne Clerke, but ill disposed, comming from *London*, vnder shew of assisting at the sacred office, had thrust himsele into that troupe: where casting his eye on the vessell of holy Oyle, but ill lookt to as it seemed; he began to lay his sacrilegious hãds thereon, and so with silence went secretly his wayes, towards his home agayne. He was now gone a pretty way, as he thought, when cõtrary to his opinion, he found himselfe still in the same assembly, & in the selfe same place from whence he had fled; whereat wondering not a litle, he puts himselfe on the way againe: & behold within a while, finds himselfe still in the Church of *Bregge*: and so went turning his backe to it agayne and agayne, vntill such tyme as the people being aware of those erring and wandering steps of his, cast their eyes on the Clerke; and at the same instant were the Deacons aduised, that the vessell of Chrisme was not to be found, for which there arising a great cry, vpon good aduise, and discreet coniecture, the foresayd Clerke was immediately apprehended, and the vessell being found about him vnder his cloake, with menaces and rating, he was brought to *S. Anselme*, who being moued with compassion towards the wretch, with cheerfull countenance reprehended him Fatherly for it, and ordayned, he should be let go forthwith without punishment; and immediately the Man went directly home to his house.

This Dedication being finished, *S. Anselme* was very suddenly recalled agayne to the Court, of purpose, to giue his benediction to the King before he crossed the seas. He went then presently thither: and for that, the wind in those dayes was very contrary vnto him, he thought it his duty in the meane tyme, with all care and diligence, to admonish *K. William* agayne, of the great disorders & many abuses introduced into the kingdome, and to exhort him to relieue the afflicted Churches, and to help to reforme the same. He did it then in the best manner he could: but the King, being now troubled

troubled already, and wholy vncapable of good counſayle, not only ſlighted the man of God, with the Fatherly correction he gaue him: but euen alſo, with great diſdayne and contempt did baniſh him his preſence. Whereupon, ſome wicked and inſolent men preſent, tooke new courage, and boldnes agayne to offer wrongs and iniuries to Eccleſiaſticall perſons and their goods, bearing but litle reſpect to the dignity and merits of *S. Anſelme* himſelfe: who being much more ſeen and expert in the knowledge of ſpirits, then in the manage of temporall affayres, partly ſuffered himſelfe to be deceyued, not being able to perſuade himſelfe, that any one for tră-ſitory things, would willingly looſe the eternall; and partly alſo, was enforced to yield, hauing (as we ſayd) the King for aduerſary, and his grieuous enemy.

So as now being wholy anxious, he neuer ceaſed to bemoane himſelfe for the quiet and peace of a religious ſtate; nor found he any comfort, but when he could now & then, retire himſelfe from company, into Cloyſters. Nor would he neither within the Biſhoprique, nor yet without, euer liue without the company & aſſiſtance of ſome vertuous and approued Monkes, to his exceeding guſt, and to the great edification of as many as knew him. Beſides which, he fayled not to ſteale ſome tyme for meere contemplation, and to remedy the troubles of the Catholique Church, by meanes of his moſt learned writings. Among which, is that worke of his, moſt worthily renowned, which he wrote in the midſt of ſo great afflictions vpon the ſubiect of the *Incarnation of the Eternall Word:* wherewith, the errour of the Greeks, remayned diſcouered and conuinced, being ſo audacious, as to deny the Proceſſion of the holy Ghoſt from the ſecond perſon of the Bleſſed Trinity.

Nor only thus in his Cell, and ſtudies, but euen likewiſe at table, when they had giuen ouer reading, as a moſt excellent Deuine, he would ſolue very intricate knots, & expoũd difficult paſſages of the ſacred Scripture. He likewiſe feared ſo much euery offence, how light ſoeuer; as he often affirmed, with ſincerity, that if he had on the one ſide, the horrour of ſinne before his eyes, and the paynes of Hell on the other, with the neceſſity of being drenched or engulfed in this, or that; he would doubtles make choyce, rather of the infernall paynes, then of the offence of God; and ſooner accept of Hell, as pure and innocent, then the heauenly manſion being polluted with ſinne.

What occasions S. Anselme *would vsually take of spiritual Conceyts. How* K. William *returnes from beyond Seas : and* S. Anselme *goes to* Rome. Chap. 15.

THe Seruant of Christ, was wont with the gift which he had of knowledge, to gather spirituall & fruitfull conceipts from the things which daily occurred : as once certaine Seruants of his, had a course at a Hare, who after she had diuers wayes, very nimbly tryed to escape from them, by secret instinct, came at last to squat euen vnder *S. Anselmes* horse, who suddenly thereupon made a stop, so as the dogs, not daring to set vpon her, stood aloofe, baying at her, expecting her starting agayne. At which sight, the company laughing, and making much sport, *S. Anselme* fell a weeping: You laugh my Maysters (sayd he) but this poore little beast heere laughs not at all, or finds any sport. Her enemies encompasse her round about, and she with the agonies of death, recurres to vs for succour. The same indeed succeeds very often to the reasonable soule of man, which no sooner yssues from the body, but the hunters (malignant spirits) pursuing her as long as she liueth in flesh, by the diuers turnings, & crooked pathes of vices and iniquityes, euen to the article of death, do then cruelly stand ready to snatch her away, and to cast her headlong to eternall perdition, laughing & making great sport thereat; whiles the poore wretch lyes depriued and despoyled of all helps. And after these words, *S. Anselme* spurd on his horse, and commaunded them not to molest the poore creature; when by & by hauing escaped the dãger, she skippes againe into the meadowes & woodes from whence she had fled.

Another day, the holy Father seeing a boy in the stretes, holding in his hand, a certaine little Bird, fast tyed by the feete with a long thrid, taking much pleasure to let the thrid go and come now and then, and in the midst of its flight to pull it backe on a sudden agayne, and let it fall often to the ground. Whereat *S. Anselme* tooke compassion on the poore creature, and much desired to see the bird at liberty; when behold on a sudden the thrid brake, and the bird flew away, and the boy cryed. *S. Anselme* reioyced the while, & calling to his companions: haue you (sayd he) taken heed to the sport of the litle Boy heere? Whereto the others answering yea, he then replyed: And now such manner of sport for all the world, the ancient aduersary makes euery day with many sinners; he holds them so ſo entangled in his ſnares, and playing at his pleaſure, precipitates them now into this, and then into that vice. As for example, ſome be giuen to auarice, or els carnallity, or to ſome other ſuch like miſeries: To theſe will it happen now and then, that being touched with pennance and compunction, they make reflexion vpon the euill life which formerly they haue lead, for which they are moued to teares, & for that time make good purpoſes to amend themſelues. And now it ſeemes verily to them, they are looſe already, & at full liberty: but yet with the thrid, or lyne of euill cuſtome, in the very looſe and iumpe, as it were of their flying away, they are ſuddenly pulled backe agayne by the Deuill, and made to fall as before into the ſame ſinnes. And this thing happens very often, nor do they euer come to get forth of ſo abominable a ſeruitude, till with ſome great violence of theirs, & with the efficacious help of diuine grace, the ſame lyne comes once to be broken aſunder. With ſuch holy documents as theſe, the holy man, dayly excited himſelfe, and others, to the cuſtody of the hart, and purchaſe of vertues.

But to returne from whence we haue digreſſed. *King William*, after he had vnworthily baniſhed from his preſence the venerable man, ſo that *S. Anſelme*, ſeeing now all things to paſſe continually from ill to worſe, without hope of any preſent remedy, through the occaſion of obteyning his Epiſcopall Pall, reſolued to go to *Rome*, & to recurre vnto the Pope for help and counſaile, who in thoſe daies was *Vrban* the ſecond; for this end he went to demaund licence of the King, and after many repulſes, affronts, and iniuries receyued at his hands; did finally obteine it, with condition neuer to put foote into *England* more. Heerupon, with great feeling and teares, taking his leaue, firſt of the Monkes, and then of the Clergy, and people, he went to *Douer*, and there embarqued himſelfe for *France*: but in the midſt of his courſe, behold a contrary wind aroſe, in ſuch ſort as the mariners began to proteſt, that vnles he would needs be drowned, of neceſſity they muſt be fayne to turne backe agayne from whence they came. This newes, did much afflict the good Archbiſhop, enforcing him to ſay with ſighs: Since then, it pleaſeth the Almighty God of his iuſt iudgments to ſend me againe backe to my paſſed miſeries, rather then to let me go whither I had intended to arriue, let his diuine Maieſty do with me what he thinkes beſt, & gouerne and diſpoſe of euery thing, according to his good pleaſure. With theſe words growing téder, his eyes were all bathed in teares; when

 through

through diuine Clemency, the wind suddenly began to come about so as with a prosperous gale the ship arriued in *France* at a place called *Whitsand*: where they landing, was discouered another wonder, to wit, a leake in the barke of two foote broad, which through the merits of the holy man, amidst so great a tempest, and storme, had receaued no water.

As soone as it was known in Court, that *S. Anselme* was now on the other side, King *William* with impious boldnes, caused his possessions and goods to be seized vpon in his name: he cut of all the Acts & decrees by him made in the same Diocesse, & with strãge iniuries & wrongs stuck not to molest, and euen sucke out of the Church, for himselfe and his hungry flatterers, as much bloud, as he could. In the meane tyme, the Seruant of Christ being arriued at *Lyons*, there rested himselfe a while, & from thence passed safe to *Rome*, being euery where receyued of al, with much honour & reuerence; and especially of the Pope himselfe, causing chambers to be prouided him in his owne Pallace; and admitting him to audience, and kissing of the feet tooke him vp, and deerely imbraced him; & in the presence of all the Prelates, spake so much good of him, as the humble man being confounded thereat, had not the hart to lift vp his eyes from the ground, much lesse to endure such mãner of discourse. Wherefore with good opportunity he declared the state of the English Churches, and particularly that of *Canterbury*; when the Pope with gracious words promised, to take the businesse to hart, & prouide for the same in due tyme.

S. Anselme *being at* Capua, *miraculously causes water to spring vp in a stony soyle. And goeth with the Pope vnto the Councell of* Bari, *and thence to another.* Chap. 16.

IN the meane tyme, by reason it was then Summer, it seemed good to the Pope, that *S. Anselme*, being a person of so tender cõplexion as he was, should retire himselfe from that ayre, into a village of the *Benedictin* Monks, called *Schiana*, not far from *Capua*. This village, was seated on the top of a high and pleasant hill, but defectiue of water: insomuch, as they could get none at all, but at one Well only, which was there by, on the ridge of that hill, & this also but at certaine houres of the day, it remaining afterwards dry, in so much as the Guardian of the place with the inhabitants thereabout did suffer very much. Now the said Guardian cõceiued a great hope that

that though the sanctity of S. *Anselme* some remedy would be easily obtained from Heauē for so great a difficulty. And therupon he determined to dig a well in his owne house, howbeit the place being craggy and stony of its own nature, was very vnapt for the purpose: but yet before he would put hand to the worke, he prayed the Man of God to affoard his benediction to the enterprize, & to be the first to open the Earth with his holy hands. Whose request S. *Anselme* did not refuse, but for his Hosts consolation went in person to the place designed, & making his prayer for a happy successe, with a pick-axe strooke the earth three tymes, and then gaue place to others, to finish the worke. When it was not long, ere there sprung vp a most limpid and excellent water from the stony soyle, which being enclosed within a pit of a small depth, there followed after a perpetuall aboũdance from thence, inough to supply, not onely the necessityes of all those parts thereabout; but euen likewise to cure the diseases and infirmities of many, who had faithfully recourse to that succour: which thing, being once diuulged, gaue no small credit of more then human power to the B. *Anselme*, and from that tyme forwards it was worthily called, *The Bishop of Canterburies Well*.

Heere now remayned the Seruant of God, a pretty while, recollecting himselfe, and greatly attentiue to diuine contemplation and serious studies, to his most extraordinary delight; as seeming to him in a certayne manner, he was now returned to his wonted monasticall life againe: where (among other things) he finished a Booke intituled: *Cur Deus homo*, which heertofore he had begun in *England*. In those dayes was *Capua* besieged by *Roger* Duke of *Puglia*; who moued with the fame and neighbour-hood of S. *Anselme*, sent to inuite & pray him to vouchsafe to come vnto him. The holy Man went presently, and with his presence, humility, and charity, so edifyed the Duke, and gayned so the minds of the whole army vnto him, that wheresoeuer he shewed himself, he was blessed & glorifyed of euery one: in so much as many *Saracens*, being moued with his good example, & the good entertainement he gaue them, were euen ready to be conuerted to the holy Fayth: and had beene so indeed, if through diabolicall suggestion, they had not been hindred, by a Count of *Sicily*, who at the instance of Duke *Roger*, had trained, and conducted them to that Seruice.

After this, came likewise Pope *Vrban* himselfe vnto the campe, and the siege being ended, S. *Anselme* very earnestly besought him, he would please to discharge him of the dignity, & Pontificall cure, and to affoard him the fauour to let him retire againe to his ancient quiet and religious liberty: but all was in vayne, while the Pope esteemed him more worthy of a higher degree. And a litle after conducted him with him to the Councell of *Bari*, where *S. Anselme* by word of mouth, conformable to the doctrine he had written already, left the Greekish pride, and perfidiousnes much abased, & confounded, not without the vniuersall approbation of the Fathers, & most cleere confirmation of the Catholique Fayth. From thence, he returned to *Rome* with the Pope, who calling another Councell, in that Citty vpon the ensuing Feasts of *Easter*, *S. Anselme* was there also, & illustrated not a litle, the sayd assembly with his presence and authority, where with the consent of all the Prelates, and particular consolation of *S. Anselme*, was thundred forth the sentence of Excommunication, as well agaynst the Laity, that presumed to giue the Inuestitures of Bishoprikes, as agaynst the Ecclesiastiques themselues, and others, who receiued them at their hands, or durst consecrate any persons by such wayes, intruded into those dignities. The Councell being ended, *S. Anselme* hauing obtayned good leaue, departed for Lyons, with resolution to remaine there with the Archbishop *Hugo*, his most intimate friend, hauing now quite lost all hope of euer returning into *England* agayne, whiles K. *William* liued.

Newes commeth to S. Anselme, *how* K. William *was slayne, & King* Henry *had succeeded. He returnes welcome into* England: *where after some troubles passed ouer, he dyes blessedly in his Sea of* Cāterbury. Chap. 17.

SAint *Anselme* being arriued now, at *Lyons*, while he attended to his wonted exercises of vertue, and assisting the Archbishop, & that Diocesse; behold two Monks from *England* with tydings, that K. *William* vpon the second of August, being a hunting, was shot through the hart with an arrow, and had presently giuen vp the ghost. Whereat *S. Anselme* was very sory, & most bitterly lamenting affirmed, he would willingly haue giuen vp his owne life, to haue deliuered his King from so sudden, and dreadfull an end. And a litle after, arriued diuers Posts to *S. Anselme*, with letters from *K. Henry* his Successour and the Nobility of *England*, both Ecclesiasticall, and Secular, intreating him to returne backe againe with all possible diligence, for that the whole Kingdome expected him, with exceeding

ding desire, and that all publique businesses were differred, and put off vntill his comming.

Whereupon S. *Anselme* without delay, tooke his iourney towards *Normandy*, and crossing the Seas, the first thing he did, he declared to the new King, in plaine termes, what had lately been determined in the sacred Cōucel of *Rome* in the matter of inuestitures of Bishops. Whereat K. *Henry* being greatly troubled made instance to S. *Anselme* that for reuocation of such a decree, he would returne agayne vnto the Pope, called *Paschalis*, being newly elected in place of *Vrban* thē deceased: to which request S. *Anselme* made answere playnly, that it was not to be sued for, or possibly procured by any meanes; & yet notwithstanding K *Henry* vrging him, that at least for his satisfactiō he would leade with him, another Embassadour thither, whome for that purpose he determined to send to his Holynes, S. *Anselme* obeyed, and being receiued by the Pope, and the whole Court with great honour, his companion the Kings Embassadour after he had laboured in vayne for that which his Lord pretended, returned into *England* without effect, and S. *Anselme* remained in *France*, for that he heard K. *Henry* was exceedingly displeased for the ill successe of his affayres in the Court of *Rome*, and had impiously seized vpon the Archbishoprike of *Canterbury*, & despoiled S. *Anselme* of all his goods.

Howbeit after a while the same K. *Henry*, being touched with the feare of God, and true pennance, restored S. *Anselme* into the possession of the sayd Church, and very honorably receiued him againe into peace & grace. Which conuersion of his, how gratefull it was to the diuine Maiesty, did soone appeare by a glorious victory, which he got agaynst his Brother Duke *Robert*, with other personages, who had reuolted from him; through which victory K. *Henry* did remaine absolute Lord of *Normandy*. And in signe of gratitude, caused a Parlament to be called at *London*, in which, to the extraordinary consolation of S. *Anselme* there present, and of all good men, he renounced the custome of his Predecessours, concerning the Inuestiture of Churches, leauing the free disposition therof to the Pope and his Delegats, shewing him selfe heerin particularly, to be a true and obedient child of the holy Apostolique Sea.

Now S. *Anselme*, waxing dayly more, and more grieued with old age, and diuers infirmityes, especially of the stomacke, came to such weakenes, as that not being able to celebrate Masse, made himselfe to be carryed euery day to the Chnrch to heare the same, and in short

short tyme the malady increased so much, as it cleerely appeared, there was litle hope of his life. His benediction then was required by the Bishop of *Rochester*, for all that were present, as also for the King and Queene themselues, with their children, and the whole Kingdome besides: and he hauing giuen it, with much deuotion most sweetly bowed downe his head, and one of his familiars, taking the Text of the Ghospell, began to recite the Passion of our Lord, and comming to those wordes: *Vos estis, qui permansistis mecum in tentationibus meis, & ego dispono vobis, sicut disposuit mihi Pater meus, regnum, vt edatis & bibatis super mensam meam, in regno meo*; the good Archbishop, began to fetch his breath more thicke then ordinary. Whereupon the standers by, being aware of the approach of his last houre, after the due rites, and Sacraments applyed, taking him in their armes, they layd him downe, according to the manner of those tymes, vpon a Cilice, and Ashes; where he rendred his blessed soule to the Creatour, vpon Wednesday in Holy weeke, in the morning being the 21. day of Aprill, in the yeare 1109. or as others would haue it 1080. and the 13. of his Bishopricke, and the 76. of his age.

Being afterwards sockt, and reuested with his Pontificall ornaments, he was decently layd forth in the Church, and buryed with most solemne Exequies, and with the sorrow that behoued, for the losse of such, and so great a Prelate. Many other, and great miracles, besides those that we haue touched, are recounted of him, the which notwithstanding altogether with me, make him not so venerable & worthy of eternall prayse, as two only *Qualities* which he had, among others, in an excellent degree; to wit, his *Discretion*, and *Affability* with all. Most noble vertues without doubt, and such (as we haue sayd) that he aboue all other gifts, should be adorned withall, who desires to haue open, and manifest to him, the Soules and consciences of his subiects, and would seeke by due meanes, to lead them to some good point of Perfection, and Sanctity.

FINIS.

S. OTHO

S. OTHO.

THE ARGVMENT.

THE Altar deckt with Purple * did display
The fire that came from heauen which vnder lay
As in its mansion vnextinguished,
And by it selfe conseru'd, and nourish'd .
Those that Christs flock appointed are to feed,
And gouerne it, must take attentiue heed
The inward man doe with their Robes agree,
And like to that like fire do signify;
Euer conseru'd Heau'ns loue, which drawne from thence
Their nobler soules should purge, and quintessence.
This in my Rule I fostered, this my Hart
Did purify and cleanse my better part
From worldly cares, and sensuality,
And fruitefull made in acts of Charity.
My selfe of all the wretched'st I esteem'd,
And worldly ioyes, I like those Meteors deem'd
Compos'd of grosser substance, yet exceed
The starres we thinke, and greater wonder breed.
Preferment me abased, rays'd more high
Deiected more, more low in dignity.

* Sal. Iago chi vpon those vvords Num. 4. Et togent altare purpura.

THE LIFE OF S. OTHO BISHOP OF BAMBERGE.

Written by Laurence Surius.

Otho being well descended, his Father hauing left him poore, goes into Poland; *whence being sent Embassadour to the Emperour, is preferred by him to be Chancellour.* Chap. I.

THO, who was after Bishop of *Bamberge*, a Sueuian by nation (whose proper place, and Surname, is not knowne) was borne of the Count *Bartold*, and of the Countesse *Sophia* his wife; more noble of bloud, then rich in substance, & goods. Who after they had bred with diligent care, and with the help of a good Maister, brought vp this sonne, dyed; and the gouernement of the house, fell into the hands of another Sonne, whose name was *Fredericke*, at such tyme indeed, as in forraigne parts, as it happened, *Otho* was busyed at his booke. Where he hauing with good applause attended to the study of humanity, and to some part of Philosophy, and wanting sufficient meanes to proceed any further, by reason of the short allowance, which his Brother and other friends

affoar-

affoarded him, he resolued, to the end he might not be grieuous & burdensome to them, to passe ouer into *Polony*, where was as that tyme a great scarcity, and want of learned men. Heere then, for the teaching and instructing of youth, and withall likewise for his greater profit, he set vp open Schoole. And with this manner of life, comming shortly to be well knowne, not only for a pious and a learned, but euen also for a wise and discreet Man; he purchased to himselfe, besides an honest, and competent meanes to liue, much reputation, and fauour also with the principall personages of those Countryes.

There was added also to the learning and integrity of this seruant of God, a maiesty in his countenance, and such a garb in his behauiour, and so noble a dexterity in his conuersation, as that after he had in diuers occurrences handled, and negotiated affaires of no small importance, he was by the Duke of *Polony* (for as yet, there was no Alteza, or Highnes of a King) sent in weighty affaires vnto the Emperour *Henry* the fourth, his Cousin. Who was likewise so pleased with the carriage, and prudence of *Otho*, as that the Embassage being ended, with the good leaue of his Cousin he retayned him with him, with some honourable title, among his Chaplaines: and a little after, the dignity of the great Chancellour being voyd, he most graciously conferred it vpon him. In which charge, *Otho* carryed himselfe so faythfully to the Prince, and with so much courtesy and humanity towardes others, as he made a notable increase of loue, and credit with persons of all sortes.

§. Otho *is preferred by the Emperour to be Bishop of* Bamberge; *and after some difficultyes is by the Cittizens ioyfully receaued.* Chap. 2.

THERE was in those dayes introduced among Christians an abuse of much preiudice to the holy Apostolike Sea, (and I would to God, there were not as yet some reliques thereof, to be seene likewise in these our dayes) that many Princes, and especially the Emperour, vnder the name of inuestitures, bestowed the Churches at their pleasure; and when a Bishopricke was vacant at any tyme, the Chapter would send to *Cæsar*, the Pastorall staffe & ring, beseeching his Maiesty to vouchsafe to prouide them a Successour. Whence it came, that many personages, the children, & nephewes of Barons, and great Lords, vnder diuers colours of seruices done, would follow the Court of *Cæsar*, to be promoted to some Bishoprike, or other, as it chaunced to fall. Now *Robert* the Bishop of *Bamberge*, a noble Citty of *Franconia*, being then deceased, and the sacred Pledges caryed vnto Court with the wonted supplication, *Henry* answeared, he would take tyme, for the space of six months, to thinke of a new election. In the meane while in *Bamberge*, were made continuall prayers, and pennances for that effect.

The terme being ended, it was signified them by the *Emperour*, that now, he had found a sufficient Pastour for that Church, though for the present he suppressed his Name, while that good people, continued still more feruent then euer in redoubling their deuotions. And among others, on the Vigill of *Christmas day*, was a solemne procession ordayned (where none was absent) from the Cathedrall, to the Church of S. *Michael*, on the Hil, taking that glorious *Archangell* for intercessour, with the diuine Majesty, to obtayne a Prelate, of the sufficiency and goodnes, which they desired. And on the other side they sent Embassadours to *Henry*, to sollicite the expedition: & in summe neglected not any thing that concerned the happy issue of so important a busines. And the diuine Clemency, accustomed to heare the prayers of such as concurre on their parts, and manfully to set hand thereto; was pleased with the piety and industry of *Bamberge*, in putting into *Cæsars* mynd, to put the designes in execution, as soone as might be. Thereupon, sending for the foresayd Embassadours to come vnto him, he spake to them, in the manner following.

How deere to vs (*Embassadours*) your Church is, and euer hath been, from hence you may easely gather, that wee haue thought it not good to giue you a Rectour, till after a long & mature consult thereupon; and that surely with good reason: Forasmuch as the said Church, as you know, hath beene founded by our Progenitours, and adorned, and furnished of all things that seeme to appertayne to the splendour and mantenance of Christian Religion, and (which is more, and which cannot be affirmed but of few other Seas) the same ornaments, furnitures, and ancient riches, are kept very safe, and entire, vnto this day; so as reason would, for the custody, and administration of them, should be placed ouer them, not an ordinary man, but one who were sage, prudent, and zealous of the honour of God.

And

And the *Emperour* proceeding to manifest more at large, this good disposition of his, towardes the Communalty of *Bamberge*, some of the Embassadours, being wearied already with such long and tedious ambages, could not hold themselues, but they must needs ingeniously demaund of him, where, and who he was, whome his Maiesty had so destined for the gouernement.

Then *Henry* cheerefully looking about: *Behold him*, sayd he, and taking *Otho* by the hand, that was (as we sayd) of a venerable aspect, and decently clad in a Clericall habit; *This*, sayd he, *is your Lord, this is your Preist, and Bishop of Bamberge*. There could not happen to the Embassadours eares, a more strange and vnexpected thing then it. Whence being astonished, and confounded, they began priuily to looke one vpon another, and to cast there eyes from tyme to tyme on the face of *Otho*. Whereof some of *Cæsars* court being aware, who now for a long tyme, gad greedily expected to aspire to that seate and Liuing; with glaunces, nods and whispering began to stir vp the *Bambergians* to shew themselues not well satisfyed with such a nomination, and resolued not to accept it by any meanes. So as at last, with a sad countenance and free liberty, they turning themselues to *Cæsar*, sayd: We hoped your Maiesty, would haue deputed to vs, some Prelate, who had been one of the most markable, and illustrious of the Court. Now for this man, we know not eyther, who he is, or whence he came. Then *Cæsar* replyed with a seuere looke. We our selues, through long cõuersatiõ and infinite proofes haue had full, and perfect notice of this Subiect, his faythfullnes, his iudgement, and longanimity: his diligence, in small matters, and sufficiency in great, are not vnknowne to vs. Nor would we haue you to thinke but the losse of such a Minister must needes redound to the notable preiudice of our own seruice. From whence we see, as euery one may perceaue, the sincere affection we beare to your Countrey, so as we in this election so much premeditated, are not to be altered in our iudgement. And whosoeuer shall seeme to haue the boldnes to oppose this our decree, shall infallibly incurre our high displeasure.

Otho hitherto had knowne nothing of any such deliberation made: Whereupon, as one astonished with a sudden blow, falling prostrate at the Emperours feet, began to powre forth a floud of teares. The Embassadours ran readily to reare him vp. He then hauing taken a litle breath, refused the charge with might & mayne:

esteeming, & proclayming himselfe to be wholy vnworthy thereof: and affirming withall, that so high a degree became rather some other more noble, ancient, and well deseruing of the sacred crowne, then him. By occasion whereof, *Cæsar*, re-entring agayne into *Otho's* prayses, among other things, made this publique declaration, how this had beene the third Bishopricke, which the seruant of Christ had refused; how first he had offered him, that same of *Augusta*, then that of *Halberstad*, nor could euer hitherto seeme to fasten any one vpon him. From whence, very euidently appeared the modesty, the humility, and merits of such a person; through diuine dispensation reserued (as it should seeme) for the benefit and behoofe of the City of *Bamberge*. And with this, & many other Elogies, and prayses, putting the ring on his fingar, and the Pastorall staffe in his hand, so adorned he giues him to the Embassadours.

At sight whereof, with a sudaine inclination of minds, was immediately raysed a fauoutable cry, and applause of the whole multitude. The Embassadours beholding things to fall out thus, as truly from God, approaching to *S. Otho*, their Father, and Lord, saluted him cheerefully, and with Christian vertue, very reuerently adored him; When as *Henry* sayd agayne, Accept him then with a good will, and vse him with that loue and veneration, as he deserues: because I call him to witnes who knoweth all things, that I know not a man in all the world, to whom more truly, and with greater reason so ample a charge as this may be conferred, then to him. And for my part, as long as I liue, and wield this Scepter, whosoeuer shall but touch him, shall touch the very aple of myne eye. In this manner then, and by such meanes as these, came *S. Otho* to be forced to the Bishopricke, but yet full of anxiety and scruples the while, as well for other very graue respects, as also, for the controuersies sprung vp, as we sayd before, by reason of inuestitures, betweene the Roman Church, & Empire. And yet on the other side, considering, that his being now so often called to such a charge, could not choose but proceed from the diuine Wil, he feared least persisting in the negatiue, he might hap to incurre that dreadfull sentence, *Noluit benedictionem, & elongabitur ab eo.*

Amidst such streights and perplexityes as these, he finally determined with himselfe, to recurre as soone as might be, for ayde and light to the Apostolique Sea, and made an expresse vow neuer ner to admit of the Bishoprike, vnles at the instance of his flock the Pope himselfe should inuest, and consecrate him with his owne hands. With this resolution, he kept the Feast of the *Natiuity of our Lord* at *Ments* in company of *Cæsar*, and from thence, dismissing a part of the Embassadours, he stayed in Court for vrgent reasons about some fourty dayes space: Which being ended, he tooke his leaue of *Henry*; and through his expresse commandement, accompanyed to *Bamberge*, by the *Bishops* of *Augusta*, and of *Herbipolis*, & of other principall personages besides, he made his solemne entry on the day before the *Purification of the most blessed Virgin*. The Monks and Clerkes, and all the Nobility, went forth to meete him in orderly procession, with psalmes, and hymnes, and with rich ornaments and deuout reliques. Nor would the people, and meaner sort, suffer themselues to be vanquished with such offices of obsequiousnes. While euery one, leauing their shopps, & staules, ran striuing to kneele before him, and to demaund the benediction of their holy, and so long desired Pastour. In which feast, and solemnity we may not passe ouer in silence one thing, that shewes very well that euen in the Courtiers life, who will but affoard any tyme to spirituall things, may make a notable purchase of religious vertues.

S. Otho *remembring his Vow, goes to Rome, where he is consecrated Bishop by the Pope himselfe*. Chap. 3.

S. *Otho*, as we haue seene, had spent the greater, and better part of his yeares, in the seruice of secular Princes, and liued in the exteriour, a cōmon life, and without any apparent singularity in him: And yet performing, according to occasions (which want not) intense acts of temperance, and humility, and of contempt of himselfe, in short tyme he became very rich in those habits, which more gallantly adorne and deck the soule, then doe all the Mitres, and Pontificall robes set forth the body. Whereof, he gaue a most clere example in the aforesayd day of his entrance so *in Pontificalibus*. Because, that in comming to approach to *Bamberge*, as soone as he descouered a farre off the Cathedrall Church, being dedicated to S. George, he not only, according to the custome of that Bishopricke, dismounted suddenly from his horse, but also putting off his hose and shooes publiquely in the hart of winter, went bare foote and bare legg on stones, and yce through the presse of people vnto the Church, where the sharpnes of the cold, hauing (not without danger of his health) now possessed already, as it were, the vitall parts, and a hot Bath being suddenly applyed to him for present remedy, he suddenly called for cold water, when putting his legges thereinto, with one rigour, he expelled the other: and then besids the accustomed ceremonyes, hauing deuoutly made his prayers, and with the holsome signes, with his sacred hand giuen his pastorall benediction to the people, being tyred and spent, at last retyred himselfe into his lodging. After which, the first and principall care of S. *Otho*, was to render his vow, and to giue due account of his actions to the Bishop of Bishops, and generall Superintendent of the whole Church of Christ.

And though he well perceiued the danger he incurred therein of offending *Henry*, there being nothing, that more touches Princes to the quicke, then the point of *Iurisdiction*; yet for all that, preferring euer a good conscience, and a chast feare of God, before any other respect whatsoeuer, he first reduced the Clergy, and people of *Bamberge* to his opinion; shewing them the obligation that was of acknowledging the supreme power of the Pope of *Rome*. Then by letters, hauing obteined leaue of the Pope himselfe to kisse his feete, he went with an honourable traine of his followers, and familiars, and of the principall of his Church, to the Court of Rome, the Pope (who was then *Paschalis* the *Second*) then residing at *Anagni*, a Citty in *Latium*. Where *S. Otho* arriuing within the Octaues of the Ascension, after the kisse of his holy feete, very faithfully declared to the Pope, the whole order and progresse of his promotion, without cōcealing any thing of moment: and to accompany his wordes with deedes, without more a doe puts the ring and staffe at his feete, and humbly craues pardon of the offence, succeeding meerely by anothers violence, rather then of his owne inclination, demaunding withall pennance, and Canonicall censure for the same.

On the other side, the Procuratours of *Bamberge*, do neuer cease to beseech the Pope, he would daigne to confirme, or to say better, renew the election, made by *Henry*, & not to depriue their Countrey of so exemplar, and behoouefull a guide, Maister, & Supporter. To which speeches of theirs, *Paschalis* giuing a benigne answere, commaunds *S. Otho* to resume againe the deposed pledges: & he still shewing himselfe backward; The feast of the Holy Ghost (sayd

(sayd the Pope) drawing neere, we will remit the controuersy to him. And after some discourses, the Bishop, and the others returned to their lodgings, with the Apostolicall benediction, but yet with a diuerse disposition of mind, and quality of thoughts: The subiects with a firme hope of obtayning as much as they desired of the Pope, and the Prelate himselfe with a purpose to relinquish the Bishopricke by all meanes possible. And being all that night, and the day following intensly fixt in contemplating the reasons, that were of eyther part: finally pondering the malice of the tymes, the encombrances, troubles, and molestations, and daungers of the Episcopall state, the disobedience, contumacy, and insolency of the inferiours, and in summe, all the asperityes, and difficultyes of such a charge, he determined with a full and firme resolution, to reduce himselfe to a priuate life, and calling his companions and domestiques to him very plainely vnfolded to them his whole deliberation, and without delay being dispatched of the Pope, and Court, put himselfe on the way towards *Germany*.

But scarcely had he made one dayes iourney, when a Post ouertakes him from his Holynes, who calls him back. Which thing was an incredible disgust, and extreme trouble to *S. Otho*; while he prudently ghessed what was like to ensue therof. But being thẽ ouercome by the precept, and encouraged by the prayers, and exhortations of his followers, with feare and trembling he returned to the Pope agayne, and without being able to resist any longer, on the day of *Pentecost*, while the Masse was sung, with great iubiley of the *Bambergians*, and vniuersall ioy of the whole Court among other demonstrations of charity and esteeme, had likewise the priuiledge to haue caryed before *Him* and *his Successours* for euer, the Crosse and Pall, eight tymes a yeare; Whereas his Predecessours, had them caryed, but foure tymes only. Which fauour he accepted with great thankes-giuing, not so much for his owne respect, as for the loue of his Espouse, whose exaltation for the diuine seruice, was worthily most deare vnto him. But yet more glorious to *S. Otho*, and farre more fruitefull to Mankind, were the guifts that befell him in the rites of the mysticall vnction, being powred vpon him from the large and munificent hand of the *Holy Ghost*, as a vessell well disposed, and most capable of them. Thorough which, being fortifyed with new breath, and agility, and more enflamed continually to ech pious and holy worke, without suffering himselfe by any meanes to be enticed by those obiects, and allurements, which like to *Syrens* detayne a man far from his home, and residence; taking his leaue agayne of the Pope, as soone as might be, he returned back to his beloued flocke.

S. Otho *built, and founded many Monasteries, both little and great. He was hospitable, abstinent, and zealous of soules, and imployes himselfe in the conuersion of* Pomerania. Chap. 4.

BEsides the singular wisedome, which in all affaires S. *Otho* shewed, as well temporall and profane, as spirituall and Ecclesiastical; were the great testimonyes of his singular piety, and magnificence, the fifteene greater Monasteryes, and the fiue lesse, of diuers orders which in sundry places of that Prouince were erected, adorned, and founded by hym: With condition they should all remayne vnder the protection, and direct dominion of the *Cathedrall* of *Bamberge*. And in the same Cathedrall, and those other Churches of the sayd Citty, for ampliation of the diuine seruice; he increased the rents, recouered the alienated goods, reedifyed the ruyned buildings, and lastly on euery side, made very notable emprouements, being things without doubt so much more admirable, as he was more sollicitous euen at that tyme also of the interiour progresse of soules, and of the necessary prouision withall, for mayntenance of the body. Wherein expressing the figure of perfect Benignity, he spared from himselfe whatsoeuer he could, the better to supply the commodityes of others, affecting as well parsimony in priuate, as magnificence in publique, and aboue all things farre off from any shew of superfluity, and those sumptuous dishes, which vnder coulour of state and decorum, are cõmonly afforded the greater and richer Prelates.

Nor was he therefore in his dyet, or in the ordinary expences of his howse any whit scarce or miserable, but how well furnished soeuer his tables were, with a rare & noble habit of temperance he would rise oftentymes from the table with an appetite; distributing the while to the bashfull poore beggars, and to sicke folkes, the dainetyest meates which were dressed for him. And to come to some particulers in this matter: On a fasting day, there being once set before him a goodly Pickrell and well seasoned, he was not only not pleased with the dish, but shewed himselfe disgusted and

strange

ſtrange thereat. Whereupon the louing Steward, as taking compaſſion of his Maiſters extreme abſtinence, began modeſtly to exhort, and pray him to refreſh himſelfe a litle therewtih, and to enioy that bleſſing, which the common Lord had deſtined for him. But the bleſſed Biſhop, with eyes not allured and vanquiſhed with that preſent food, and eares ſhut to the prayers and enticements made him, ſayd to him: What haſt thou layd out vpon this fiſh heere? and the other anſweared, ſome two crownes. God forbid (replyed S. *Otho*) that my belly ſhould me ſo deare: Go too then, & goe thy wayes preſently, and cary it to my Ieſus (meaning by that word ſome needy, ſick, and diſeaſed perſon) as for me, that am thanks be to God, ſo ſound and able, this loafe of bread, ſhall ſuffice. Such were his delicacyes amidſt ſo much riches. Through which, and other moſt excellent qualityes of this man of God, and principally, for the great zeale, which he had of his Neighbours good, his fame being dilated through all parts, a noble occaſion was offered him of dilating of the Ghoſpell.

The Duke *Boleſlaus* ruled the *Poland* nation at that tyme, a perſonage of much valour, and ſingular piety. This man, hauing with the ayde of the *Bohemians*, and *Hungars*, ſubdued *Pomerania*, that lay drowned in Paganiſme; was much enflamed, through heauenly ſparks, to the conuerſion of that people: but as the ſame, in thoſe tymes, beſides the ſeruitude of the Idols, by nature alſo was very barbarous and fierce, the good Duke, could not find any labourers to cultiuate that land, ſo wild and ſauage as it was: and yet not ceaſing for all that, to thinke of the ſaluation of thoſe, whome the diuine Maieſty had committed to his gouernement, at laſt the perſon of the Biſhop of *Bamberge*, came into his conſideration, now liuing (as we haue ſayd) very laudably in *Polony*, with whome he was ſo well acquainted, eyther by ſight or heare ſay, as (among other gifts) he knew, he had the skill of the *Pomeranian* tongue: and promiſing himſelfe with good reaſon, all help from the charity of *S. Otho*, he beſought him by letters and meſſages, he would be pleaſed to permit him ſome little abſence from his flocke, now a long tyme ſo increaſed and inſtructed in ſound Religion; to affoard ſome part of himſelfe vnto a people drowned in Idolatry, and miſerably tyrannized by the powers of darkenes.

The prayers and perſwaſions of *Boleſlaus*, were not in vayne: Like a generous Falcon that diſcouers its prey, ſo was *S. Otho* immediatly mediately inflamed to the ſpirituall purchaſe of that Prouince; and yet diſtruſtfull of his proper forces, he recommended earneſtly the whole buſines to the diuine Goodnes, through which, though he well perceiued the vocation to be approoued; yet neuertheleſſe to proceed with the more ſtable & well gouerned deſignes, he would not ſeeme to vndertake the enterprize, though otherwiſe holy, without firſt hauing the conſent and diſpatch of the Pope of Rome. By whome being encouraged to ſo noble a Conqueſt, and prouided of neceſſary facultyes for the purpoſe, he puts himſelfe on the way; from thence paſſing through *Bohemia* into *Polony*, with three Prieſts only for his helpfull aſſiſtance, he arriued in *Pomerania*; being honourably met, in the Confines thereof, by *Chriſtiernus* Prince of thoſe Countreyes, who at the inſtance of *Boleſlaus*, againſt the will of his Wife, and Subiects, had been now already baptized.

The great labours, *and difficulties of* S. Otho, *in conuerting the People of* Pomerania : *with baptizing the VVife of* Chriſtiernus, *and* Wenceſlaus *his Sonne*. Chap. 5.

IT is no eaſy matter heere to number, much leſſe to vnfold the labours, trauailes, and toyles of *S. Otho*, while with infinite patience and ſweetnes, he ſeekes firſt to purchaſe to himſelfe the good will of the people of *Pomerania*, and then likewiſe to let them ſee the darkenes wherein they lay as buryed, through ancient errour; now awaking them with the help of the light of nature it ſelfe, to the knowledge of the Creatour; and now propoſing the Articles of the Catholike fayth vnto them, and with apt compariſons, and examples, ſhadowing and figuring the ineffable miſteryes of the moſt holy Trinity. And on the one ſide, ſhewing the conueniency and neceſſity of the Incarnation, and Paſſion of the Sonne of God; and on the other, the neceſſity of obeying the Precepts, and of imitating his actions, and in doing pennance. To which effect, the diuine Catechiſt, adding, and prouing with liuely reaſons the eternall rewardes and puniſhments propoſed for the merits of ech one, he endeauoured with all his power to roote out the fabulous opinions through diabolicall illuſion, and long courſe of tyme ſo rooted in their mindes, and withall to pull them from their impious worſhip, wicked ceremonyes, and ſacrilegious feaſts of the Idols; the which, how much more accompanyed with carnality, pa-

ſtymes

stymes, and riotousnes they were; so much stronger an arme was needefull for so hard a separation, and so bitter a diuorce.

But aboue all, was this wise proclaymer of the Ghospell made more vigilant, with the care he had of the perpetuall edification of his Neighbours, and with the gouerning not only of himselfe, but also of his companions and familiars; so as neyther in their facts, words, and carriages, might appeare any thing that might seeme to destroy with scandal, what he endeauoured to edify with doctrine: and with these, and such like meanes, S. *Otho* did proceed with the enterprize so farre, as within few dayes, came aboue seauen thousand persons to the sacred Baptisme: whereunto, for a cōplete ioy was added not long after, the wife also of *Christiernus* himselfe; and moreouer the Prince *VVenceslaus*, who was so giuen, and addicted to worldly pleasures, as it was necessary, not without exceeding trouble, to go by little & little a weeding away some foure & twenty concubines from him, and to leaue him contented with one lawful, & only Consort. For conseruation of which purchases, the seruant of God hauing erected Temples in those Prouinces, and ordayned, as much as the scarcity of subiects would permit, Pastours and Priests; he passed from thence more inward into the Countrey, where he dealt with inhabitants so inhuman, as would not endure by any meanes to be diswaded from their ancient customes; but insteed of complying with the zeale of the Messenger of Christ, did exercise their natiue fiercenes against him, with scornes iniuryes, with throwing of dirt vpon him, & rudely smiting him withall: vntill being vanquished at last through his vnheard of meekenes and holsome aduices, most humbly crauing pardon at his hands for so great pertinacity and boldnes, they accepted likewise of the sweet yoke of Christ.

Among which occupations and paynes of his, S. *Otho* not forgetting a whit his first and deerest vineyard: & fearing least through his too long absence from it, the same might hap to suffer some domage, setling affayres in those countryes the best he could, he made a progresse, as short as possibly he might vnto *Bamberge*: where the fame of his so glorious actions, hauing already arriued, he was receiued as a Prelate truly Apostolicall, and that though full sore against his will, with more exquisite honours, and greater veneration then euer: and hauing with his presence, and oportune exhortations comforted that people there, and promoted, or amended

 rather

rather, according as need required, the publique discipline; he returned very soone agayne to the tender plants of *Pomerania*. And heere encouraging such, as were running before, prouoking the slow, and confirming, and rearing vp the wauering, he attended more at ease, with due meanes, to establish the happy culture of those lands. And hauing now reduced matters to good tearmes, and being finally rich with merits, and full of benedictions, he returned agayne to his proper diocesse. Where while he attends by all manner of wayes to represent in himselfe the forme of a faythfull vicar, and seruant of Christ, there occurred to him an accident worthy of feare, and wonder, as shal appeare in the next Chapter.

After a notable accident happened, S. Otho *dismayd, desires to be discharged of the Office, and to be receaued into a Monastery: but he is denyed.* Chap. 6.

IN a Church of a certaine village, called *Buchback*, which S. *Otho* visited, he found that vnder the Aultar, within a litle chest of leade, were layd very many and most precious reliques, sealed vp. Which he not holding to be in so worthy a place, as became them, determined to translate them, some other where with more veneration, and decency to be kept by Religious persons. There being then fasts, and deuout prayers made for that intention, he returned thither, with an honourable troupe of Clercks about him, and appointed some of them to breake the seale, and to take forth the chest: but none of them daring, through their innated piety and reuerence they bare vnto it, to lay hands thereupon, he himselfe full of feruour, couragiously takes hold of the mallet, and hardly had giuen it two or three blowes, when from the chest it selfe, there flowed forth a manifest streame of bloud. The standers by being amazed at the spectacle, began suddenly to fall downe to the ground, and with teares to begge mercy of God, and succour of the Saints. The Bishop himselfe giuing ouer the enterprise, being full of confusion and feare for the matter, retires to *Bamberge*, where, eyther for chastisement of his too much confidence, or els, for matter of new crownes, being seized on by a grieuous infirmity, and desirous to be assisted in spirit (since for the body he cared not much) he caused Father *VVolfran* Abbot of S. *Michaels*, to be sent for, to come vnto him, a person of rare qualityes: and while this

this so great and faythfull freind of his sate familiarly by him, and with the hopes of heauen, and other sweet discourses, sought to mitigate his dolours; S. *Otho* one day hauing found some little truce with his malady, with an humble countenance, turning himselfe to him.

Father, sayd he, you must vnderstand, how I now for so many yeares hauing beene suddenly raysed to Prelacy, and from the noyse and vanity of the Court, being yet full of spots and dust, without passing the purgatiue way, hauing purchased the ensignes of perfection, which is, as much as to become a Doctour before one goes to Schoole. And I, though enforced in a manner vnto it by him, who had reason to command me; doe stand yet in some doubt, whether then, I made due resistance or no to such a charge: and do verily belieue, that besides those ancient remorses of conscience, these new scourges of the eternall iustice, haue thus light vpon me. And now since the common Lord, with equall benignity, seemes to punish me so, and giue me space to looke backe into my former offences: I am resolued to differ no longer the deliberation I haue often made with my selfe, to discharge me of the Pastorall office, so much aboue my feeble and weake forces, and in a priuate life to reduce me to Monasticall discipline. And since among all the congregations which I know, I find none more conformable to my designes and behoofes, then yours of S. *Michael*; I doe therefore most earnestly beseech you, Father, to vouchsafe to accept me in the name of our Sauiour Christ into your family, and to present vnto him this small sacrifice of my selfe, and being cloathed though vnworthy with your habit, to admit me into your Conuent; and ruling me in all, and in euery thing, as the other subiects, to conduct me with diuine assistance to the glorious victory of my passions, and to a full mortification of my proper will. You know well inough the bands of streight friendship & amity, which are betweene vs, and I do very well remember the charity you haue euer shewed me in all occurrences. But now assure your selfe, that in affoarding me this benefit which heere I request at your handes, you shall farre exceed all the seruices, and courtesies which you haue hitherto vouchsafed me.

Such wordes spake the Bishop, with voyce and gestures well able to demonstrate they came not from any sudden fit of passion, but from a resolute and stable purpose: and the Abbot being asto-

nished

nished at so new a demand, not to constristate the sicke man, for that tyme would by no meanes deny him, but rather with a cheerfull countenance, commending the good desire he had, made shew to accept of his prompt Obedience, reseruing the execution of the rest, to his better health. In the meane while, the feruorous Nouice, finding himselfe to be somewhat better recouered, and not seeing the houre of fullfilling his vow to come, hauing disposed as secretly as he could, the thinges belonging to him, without delay requires the habit of Religion; and makes new instance to be sent into the Monastery so conualescent and weake as he was. But the discreet Superiour on the one side being edifyed at so great humility of his; and on the other, in much suspence for the importance & quality of the busines, calling after prayer some graue & experienced men to consult, he proposed the Bishops request; and all hauing well examined the matter, did answere it to be without doubt, to the seruice of God, that a man of so eminent vertue, & behoouefull to so great a multitude, should go forwardes rather to shine on the Candlesticke of the Church, as a burning and resplendant light, then by aspiring to a priuate life to hide himselfe vnder a bushell, within Cloisters, though otherwise holy, and laudable in it selfe.

With this answeare, the Abbot being assured, and confirmed in his former iudgment, goes his wayes to S. *Otho*: who like vnto a weight that approached neerer to its center, longed so much the more for subiection, pouerty, and solitude, as the confidence was greater, which he had conceaued already of obtayning his intent; and approaching to him with due reuerence, demanded of him, if he held still his purpose to maintayne the Obedience with deeds, which he had promised him with words: and he cheerefully answearing, that for the loue of him, who to the eternall Father had obserued it to death, he was readily disposed to keep it, without exception. Then (replyed the Abbot) on behalfe of the same Lord, do I command thee to perseuere to the end vnder the charge of the administration thou hast in hand, and couragiously to go forward in the way begun to the glory of God, behoofe of the holy Church, consolation to the faythfull, the support of Widdowes, Pupills, and Orphans, and to continue thy life in good workes, & in summe, to doe what thou dost, and to execute the office thou art in, to gayne at the Prince of Pastours handes the eternall life, and reward

reward a hundred fould. Becauſe, that if we would but weigh thinges indeed with equall ballances, what Monke liues at this day vnder the Sunne, of ſo much abſtinence, and of ſo great perfection, whoſe merits and pouerty, may ſeeme to ſtand in compariſon, with the care and ſolicitude, thou haſt of ſo many ſoules, and with the ſweet diſpenſation of ſo great riches? So as thou mayſt quiet thy ſelfe, with the authority of him, whome thou haſt taken as guide and conſellour in this behalfe. And let the diuine honour and publike vtility be preferred before thyne owne particuler guſts and contentments.

With ſuch reaſons, S. *Otho* being laſtly conuinced, as an enemy of ſelfe-loue, and farre from all pertinacy, without more replyes, did bow downe his head; and putting a freſh the moſt bitter chalice of gouernement to his mouth, with new breath, and with redoubled purpoſes he began to giue himſelfe wholy to the ſpiritual and temporall help of his Neighbours.

S. Otho *was exceedingly giuen to hoſpitality. He dyed bleſſedly: And his body being buryed in the* Church *of* S. Michael, *was tranſlated afterwardes.* Chap. 7.

FOraſmuch, as among Epiſcopall parts and conditions (as hath been ſayd) S. *Otho* knew well, that Hoſpitality was one of the cheifeſt, he endeauoured to ſend before him as much corne, victualls, cloathes, and monyes, as he could poſſibly procure, by the hands of the poore, but now eſpecially, feeling himſelfe to be ſo loaden with yeares, and neere to the tearme of his life. So as like to an Oliue tree, euen ſtooping, as it were with abundance of fruites, he gaue himſelfe freely to ech ſtate and condition of mortalls. You might haue ſeene there, whole ſquadrons of Pilgrimes, very decently receaued into the chambers and lodgings of S. *Otho*. To the deſolate Widdowes, forlorne Orphans, and the needy and neceſſitous Clerks, and Monkes, ſtood his granary open day, and night, his Purſe, and Wardrobe neuer ſhut; but like a wiſe merchant, in the ſhort mart of this tranſitory tyme, he attended to barter and exchange terrene for heauenly, frayle for eternall and incorruptible ware. In ſumme, beſides the ſecret almes of ech day there was not in all thoſe partes, a Church, Conuent, Hoſpitall, or pious place of any ſort, which he viſited not, reſtored, and royally prouided of what was necessary, for the Maiesty of pure Religion, and continuation of Christian verity. And it was an admirable thing to see, how so much giuen away, and so much empting, he continually should find no bottome, as if the great Lord, and his carefull Steward, should seeme to striue togeather, the one to supply, and the other to distribute with a large hand, all manner of goodes, gold, and siluer, and what not?

Amidst such actions as these, truly worthy of the lawfull Successour of the Apostles, the blessed Man being now arriued to the end of his dayes, maturely composed the affaires of his Diocesse, and hauing made a pure and deuout confession, and after the holy Oyle, receauing with great feeling the holy Eucharist; being inuironed round with a company of Clerks, and Religious, most sweet and deare vnto him, who in that last passage came all to recommend him to their common Creatour, he peaceably yielded vp his soule, well fraught and replenished with good workes, and full of honours, and heauenly graces.

As for the mourning and great concourse of people wherewith his Exequies were celebrated, it importes not much to treate therof; while euery one may sufficiently gather how great a desire of his presence, might so louing a Father, and so vigilant a Rectour, seeme to leaue behind him. He was praysed then with a solemne Sermon by the Venerable *Embrichonus* Bishop of *Herbipolis*, and caryed vnto his Sepulcher into the Temple of S. *Michael* (while Barons, Counts, and Marquesses succeeded by turnes to conueigh the hearse) vpon the first day of Iuly, in the yeare of our Lord 1139. and of the administration of his Episcopall charge, the 37. The translation was made afterwardes vnder Pope *Clement* the III. on 89. yeare, the last of September, on which day is celebrated his memory, as eternally consecrated vnto immortality; euen by the learned penns of the noblest wits. Among which, *Iohn Trithemius* affirmes, that (besides what we haue spoken of aboue) this S. *Otho*, was no lesse in his death, then life most illustrious, and famous for many and most euident miracles.

FINIS.

S. BERNARD.

THE ARGVMENT.

THE eye, that is vnblemished, and free
From colours, their defects can better see.
Soules not forsaken, better can descry
The Worlds deceits, and note her Vanity,
He that the world abandons, this doth gaine,
Thinges dark to others are made cleare and plaine
To his vnstained soule. I well could sound
Her deep impostures by experience found,
And them display to others, whome I taught
To slight her, and to ends more noble brought:
I triumph'd ore her and her Prince, and lead
Thousandes most happy to be vanquished:
Gayning heereby eternall liberty,
And by their thraldome freed from slauery.
If thou the world wilt conquer, her contemne,
And this contempt shall gaine a Diademe.

THE LIFE OF S·BERNARD ABBOT OF CLAREVALL.

Written by three of his Monkes.

Of the Family and Parents of S. Bernard: *with a notable vision his Mother had before his birth, which gaue great hope of his future Sanctity*. Chap. I.

N the partes of *Burgundy*, is a place which is called *Fontaine*, obscure heertofore and vnknowne, but deseruedly famous and renowned, after it had so affoarded to the world, that mirour of vertue and light of Sanctity, which now to the glory of God, we beginne to describe. In that very place, was an honourable Knight, called *Tesselinus*, who according to the Euangelicall precepts, being contented with his paye, and farre from all insolency and rapine whatsoeuer, so applyed himselfe to Military discipline, as he forgot not the profession of Christ. This man had a wife, both chast and fruitfull, by name *Aletta de Monte Barro*, who amidst the familiar and transitory cares of the world, keeping her mind still fixed on eternall goodes, did increase so much in deuotion, that as many children as she brought forth into the world, (which

(which were in number some six Sonnes, and one Daughter) taking them all one by one in her armes, she suddenly offered them to Iesus; and from that tyme forwardes, as thinges made sacred, in a certaine manner, would she nurse ech one at her owne breasts, instilling into them, togeather with the milke, the feare of God, & Christian piety. And after they came to be weaned, would she feed them with grosse, and more common meates, & keep them wholy from all pampering, and childish sports, as if she had of purpose trayned them to a monasticall life. Nor was the proiect of the vertuous Mother any whit in vaine, since finally all of them, one by one (as we shall see in the progresse of the whole narration) thorough solemne vowes of Religion, came thence to be the Seruants of Christ. Of these, was *S. Bernard* borne in the third place, whose glorious merits (as they report) euen iust in a manner as of *S. Dominicke*, were through diuine ordination foretold, and prefigured ere he was borne into the World.

For as the Mother was resting one night in her bed, it seemed to her in sleep, she had a little white Dogge in her wombe, which made a great barking; wherat the poore wretch being exceedingly sad and disconsolate, demanded of a venerable Monke the true signification thereof. Who suddenly conceauing with the spirit of Prophesy, answered her: Feare not, Madame, all is well, there is an excellent Dogge, to proceed from you, which both with his barking shall faythfully guard the flocke of Christ, and with his medicinall tongue, shall heale the diuers infirmities of many and many a soule. *Aletta* being glad at such an Oracle, gaue infinite thankes therefore vnto the Creatour; and from that tyme afterwards applyed her mind with particuler diligence to bring vp that child. So as at last being deliuered of him, she was not content, as she had done with the rest, to offer him to God only with priuate and domestique ceremonyes, but in imitation of the blessed *Anna* the Mother of *Samuel*, carrying him in her armes into the Temple, with a singular affect of Charity, did dedicate him to the diuine seruice. After this, she diligently attended to the nursing and trayning him vp, and as soone as he seemed to be capable of discipline, sent him presently to the Church of *Castiglio*, vnto approued Maisters there to learne, as well good literature, as manners.

The child, as he was elected by the diuine Prouidence, and framed for high and great enterprizes, so was he likewise of a rare wit,

 and

and of an excellent inclination withall. Whence it came, that as wel in his ſtudyes in ſhort tyme, he left all his companions behind him; as alſo in ſolid vertues, he beganne to giue forth thoſe buds, which in progreſſe of tyme ſhot vp to ſuch a height of perfectiō, as they did. There was ſeene to be diſçouered in him, euen in thoſe very tender yeares of his, a meruaylous maturity in all thinges: As for examples ſake, to recommend himſelfe often to God, without omitting the while, the exerciſes of the Schoole; very ſeldome to go abroad; to keep ſilence, and modeſty at home; to ſhew himſelfe benigne and louing to all: and if any money chanced to come into his handes, he would preſently giue it freely in voluntary almes: but aboue all, he obeyed his Elders with great reuerence. With ſuch behauiour as this, the Child became moſt gratefull in the ſight of God, and Men. And euen in that very tyme, he alſo gaue forth a very notable ſigne of his Predeſtination. Becauſe, that being fallen ſicke on a tyme in his bed, through a grieuous payne of the head, there came a Witch vnto him, who promiſed him to cure him of the head-ach. But he was ſo farre off from admitting of any ſuch cure at her hands, as that not without the aſtoniſhment of all there preſent, he beganne at the firſt ſight of her, to cry out vpon her with all his might and mayne, and with a holy diſdayne very ſuddenly draue her away thence. In this manner, the chaſt Diſciple of Chriſt conſerued purity, and increaſed in learning, when through diuine reuelation, the Catholicke Fayth was both eſtabliſhed in his breaſt, and alſo an extraordinary flame of Charity, enkindled therein, as ſhall appeare more cleerely heereafter.

S. Bernard *as yet a youth, had an admirable viſion in ſleep: He ſhewes a notable example of Chaſtity. And his Mother dying, he after ſome difficultyes reſolues to follow the diuine counſayles.* Chap. 2.

ON the night of the Natiuity, while *S. Bernard* was in the Church with others attending the diuine Office, falling ſuddenly into a ſlumber, he had the vnſpeakable grace, to behold the manner by which the Sauiour and Spouſe of human generation, went forth heeretofore from the intemerate chamber of the Virgin Mary, with a firme perſwaſion, that he euen iuſt at that houre, was truly and really borne. From which ſight, it cannot be expreſſed, what iubiley, and ſpirituall ſweetenes *S. Bernard* tooke. And hence it it was, that as he had the holy Church, and all the articles proposed by it, in the highest veneration that might be; so, as long as he liued afterwards, he had a particular ioy in this solemnity, and peculiar feeling of this sacred mystery: and (as partly may be gathered in his Homelies) he did always seeme to discourse thereof with admirable gust, and a blessed fluency of conceipts and words thereupō. Through this fauour, being exceedingly confirmed, he passed ouer the first part of his age, without any rub at all, or great contradiction. But comming afterwards in the beginning of his youth, there wanted no probations, so much more grieuous, as they were full of allurements & flatteryes.

Though S. *Bernard* of himselfe, were of a tender complexion: yet was he of a good stature withall, and of lyneamēts very well in shew, and liuely withall; so as more then once he had hapned to be importunely courted, and molested by lasciuious women, but still in vayne. Because that most noble and precious iewell of Chastity, was euer kept by the holy Youth, with so much iealousy, as that he hauing one day, for a very little space, vnwarily set his eyes on a womans face; as soone as he perceiued the daunger, falling into rage with himselfe for it, in the depth of winter, immediately he stripped himselfe, and entred vp to the necke into a Poole hard by, of most cruell cold water: where with much maceration he remayned so long, till he had fully extinguished in himselfe all sinister incentiues of mind, & body.

In this meane while, *Aletta* the mother, after she had sweetly liued many yeares with her husband without iarres, and had had many Children by him, well and religiously brought vp, leauing them all aliue, came to the end of her dayes; which through the iust retribution of God, was answerable to the life she had led. For that hauing liued (as much as the band of Wedlocke, and care of the house, would suffer) in continuall abstinences, prayers, and vigills, she fell grieuously sicke, & being now through the malady brought into extremes, hauing receiued the Sacraments, with much deuotion, while the standers by were reciting the Psalter about her, she went still a long with them, with a weake voyce; and when she could do no more therewith, at least, she would follow on, with the gestures of her Countenance, and with the motion of her pale lips, vntil such tyme, as being now abandoned of all naturall heate, when rehearsing the Litanyes, they came to those wordes,

Per crucem & passionem tuam, lifting vp her hand, and making the signe of the Crosse, she happily expired. A Matrone surely most noble, truly pious, and worthy to be imitated of all those who in coniugall state, hauing the body in power of the husband, with the soule do seeke to serue and please Christ only.

S. *Bernard* being thus depriued of such a guide, began now on all sides to be continually more cruelly assaulted, then euer. The flower of his age proposed to him sensuall delights, exhorting him mainely, not to leaue things certayne, for perillous, and the present for those to come: and that heereafter when he would doe pennance, he should want no tyme in his elder age, exaggerating withal the diuine clemency, which knowes very well our human frailty; and putting him in mind moreouer of the merits of Christs passion, whreupon very safely he might build himselfe. On the other side, his freinds, and companions, who being affrighted with the difficultyes of vertue, had entred into the spacious way, inuited him no lesse thereunto, with diuers persuasions and examples. Nor was the world behind, to offer him riches, possessions, & pallaces. Besides which, the very qualityes themselues, wherewith he was endowed, of wit, of learning, and of a gratefull presence suggested to him, sundry hopes of honours, dignityes, & withal an immortall name. And all these fantasyes as so much fuell on the fire, the auncient aduersarie alwayes enkindled in him, and that so much the liuelyer as he was of a quicker discourse, and of a sharper apprehension. Who perceiuing himselfe so enuironed on all sides with such subtle nets, precipices, and snares, and iustly fearing the treasure, which he bare about him as shut vp in his breast, very suddenly determined to secure the same, and that by no other meanes, then by the counsayls of the eternall Wisedome.

S. Bernard *after many difficultyes resolues vpon Religion, and drawes an Vncle, and two younger Brothers to the same course.* Chap. 3.

THere remayned now to *S. Bernard* only, to find out how, and in what maner he might put his good purpose in effect. Wherof while he went discoursing with himselfe, the religion of the *Cistercians* came into his mind, being founded heeretofore by the venerable Abbot *Robert*, vnder the rule of *S. Benet*, with addition of some constitutions, and confirmed by the Pope, in the yeare of our

our Lord 1098. This Congregation now, as is wont to happen in beginnings, was at that tyme but of ſmall renowne, and had but one only Monaſtery, within a certaine remote wood: whereunto very few had entered, through the ſtraitneſſe of the Encloſure, and aſperity of life. But the feruent young man, and freind of the lowlynes and pouertie of Chriſt, iudged it ſtraight very apt for his deſignes, which were to ſuffer, and to be hidden, and farre off from all occaſions of vaine glory. In ſuch thoughts was *S. Bernard* much perplexed, and in great ſuſpence, and gaue beſides, diuers other ſignes of inclination to retire himſelfe, while his more domeſtique and neereſt freinds (which in ſuch occaſions are wont to be the greateſt enemyes) endeauour to diſſwade him from it, and thereby gaue him very ſhrewd encounters. They alleadged to him the delicatenes of his complexion, that could not frame to the auſterity and labours of cloyſters; they propoſed to him manie other wayes of ſeruing God, and of helping ſoules, without going ſo to ſubmit himſelfe to a perpetuall ſeruitude; and ſtuck not to put ſcruples into his head, with burying ſuch & ſuch talents in a deſart, which to the glory of God, and light of human kind were cōmitted to him: and how much better were it, that following the courſe begun of learning, and of higher ſciences in a quiet life, he ſhould become a famous Doctour, & honour to his parents, a glorie to his Countrey, and a ſuccour to the world?

With theſe, and other ſuch like reaſons his deereſt freinds went about to recall him from his purpoſe. Of all which (as the Saint manifeſted afterwardes) there was none made ſo great impreſſion with him, as the deſire and commoditie to proſecute his ſtudyes. This only reſpect did giue him a ſhrewd blow, and had euen almoſt quite ouercome him. Whence they may take faire warning, who haue had a vocation of God, and learne with what caution and cuſtody they are to keep it, and not to communicate the ſame, but to ſome perſon who is very ſpirituall and choſen of a thouſand; following heerein that wary Merchant of the Ghoſpell, who hauing diſcouered a treaſure in a field, hides the ſame, and ſells whatſeuer he poſſeſſeth to purchaſe that field: which aduertiſement not ſo fully obſerued by *S. Bernard*, had well nigh depriued him of ſo great a felicity.

But beſides the diuine Clemency, and his good nature, he was helped not a little alſo by the memory of his bleſſed Mother, who had alwayes with so many aduises and motiues incited him to perfection, and not to fall into tepidity, to the seruice of God, and not to vanity of the world, to the verity and humility of Christ, and not to the pride and swelling of secular wisedome.

With these thoughts and holesome aduises sustayned he the battayle, yet so, as the good youth went still wauering with himselfe, vntill one day taking his iourney to visite his Brothers, encamped with the Duke of Burgundy at the siege of *Grancium*, he felt himselfe so afflicted and tormented with the foresayd assaults of the spirit and sense, as that finding no rest, he retyred himselfe into a Church by the streetes side, and there with a shower of teares, and with deep sighes vnfolding his afflicted hart in the sight of him that created it, he perseuered so long in praying, and imploring help, and light from heauen, as that finally all doubt and perplexity being taken away, he felt himselfe fortifyed in the course of perfect vertue, as being now without feare of euer seuering any more, he resolued with himselfe to reduce thereunto as many as he could. Nor was his enterprize in vaine awhit, while the Highest most powerfully cooperated withall.

The first assault he gaue (being arriued to the Campe) was to his Brothers, and an Vncle of his by the Mothers side, by name *Vldricus*, a famous souldier, and very wealthy in worldly substance, and Lord of a Castle which is called *Iuiglio*. This man meeting with S. *Bernard*, and being conuinced with the spirit that spake in him, lead the way to his Nephewes. For that immediatly after him, *Bartholomew* was taken, being not able to resist the inflamed exhortations of the Saint; and in the meane while *Andrew* shewed himselfe to be somewhat difficult, but in that very instant, the Mother appeared to him (& S. *Bernard* sees her also) who with a cheerefull countenance, seemed to reioyce at those happy beginninges. At which aspect *Andrew* yielded himselfe, crying out: I see our Mother; and so he promised to S. *Bernard* to do what he would. These two were his younger Brothers.

S. Bernard *through his powerfull Eloquence, inuites and allures the rest of his Brothers to follow his example: with other notable Persons.* Chap. 4.

AFter these, the valiant Chaptaine, not doubted also to assaile his eldest Brother, by name *Guido*, though the matter were diffi-

difficult, not only for his being now in good yeares, and encombred with great affaires in the world, but euen likewise, being now marryed a good while agoe, with a Gentlewoman of a noble house, and hauing had some children by her. Neuerthelesse *S. Bernard* stucke not to set his hand, and though *Guido* at the beginning seemed to oppose, notwithstanding afterwards entring better into himselfe, and wisely considering heerein, how the affaire of his eternall saluation was handled, in being as it were wholy impossible to be happy in this and in the other life; he determined also on that very day to preferre the hope of future goodes, before the present commodities. And how much more he was encouraged the next morning, when as entring with S. *Bernard* and others into the Church, he heard those wordes of *S. Paul* recited: *Fidelis est Deus, quia qui cœpit in vobis opus bonum, ipse perficiet vsq; in diem Iesu Christi,* I remit vnto the pious Reading: for it seemes no other, but that *Guido's* ioy could be very great, in respect he heard this promise, in the very tyme of his wauering in purpose, as it were, to come from Heauen. Likewise *S. Bernard* and the rest, could not but receaue exceeding comfort heereby.

There was only one doubt yet left, whether *Guido's* wife would giue her consent, or no. And yet howsoeuer, if she denyed it, he determined with a generous and pious mind to disperse what riches he had to the poore, and labouring with his handes to liue in the state of pennance, and to maintaine himselfe and family with his owne labours. But S. *Bernard* deliuered him from that anxiety, affirming for certaine, that the Wife very soone would eyther yeild consent, or end her life. And indeed the same succeeded, for that she shewing her selfe somewhat difficult in that busines, was seized on with so grieuous and bitter an infirmity, as that acknowledging the hand of God vpon her, she resisted no longer, and permitting liberty to her husband, allowing good meanes for her Daughters maintenance, became likewise her selfe a Nunne, to the exceeding great consolation of *Guido* her Father; and in that religious course she perseuered euen to her dying day, not without the wonder of all. *Guido* in this manner being quit of all temporall cares, had leasure to attend very fully to the spirit.

It was not so easy a matter to encline *Gerard* to this, the second Brother. This man, besides that he was a braue Souldiar, was also very wise according to the world, and likewise benigne and

and beloued of all. This sudden mutation of his Brothers pleased him not awhit, he interpreted the same to a certaine mobility and leuity of mind; and in summe after he had disputed a good while, he peremptorily denyed to consent euer to alter his profession. When S. *Bernard* wholy full of fire and zeale, putting forth the finger to his side: I see well (sayth he) that tribulation only is to giue you vnderstanding. The day shall come, and that ere long, that a launce entring through this side of yours, shall set open the doore of your obstinate hart vnto the holesome counsaile, which now you will not accept from me. And so it fell out; for a little while after being encompassed by his enemyes, he tooke a blow with a launce in the same side, and being taken prisonner, and dragd through the streetes, began as one besides himselfe to cry out, *I am a Monke: I am a Cistercian Monke:* and sayd not amisse, for that he had no sooner his liberty againe, but he went to submit himself to the sweet yoke of Christ, with the great ioy of S. *Bernard*, and the rest, who most ardently thirsted after his saluation.

The *Beniamin* remayned, who was the youngest of all, by name *Ninardus*. This same did the others thinke good to leaue in the world for a stay of the house, and for the more consolation of their old Father: but he neither would be excluded of the heauenly benediction, because that *Guido* meeting him one day in the market place togeather with some other boyes: Go too *Ninardus* (sayd he vnto him) all our goods are like to fall vpon thee. To which wordes the child answered not with a childish iudgement: Belike then heauen is for you, and the earth for me: there is no equality in that partition. And so after some dayes he also dedicated himselfe to the seruice of Christ. In the meane tyme, it pleased S. *Bernard* to goe vp and downe the neighbour-places for new conquests. Going forth then in the name of our Lord, he began to preach in diuers places, of the instability of human things, of the vanity of honours, of the shortnes of pleasures, of the miseries of this life, and of the rewards and punishments of the other: and this with such an eloquence and grace, and efficacy withall, as like a deuouring flame, he transformed into himselfe what ere he met withall. And finally the matter passed so farre, as the Mothers hid their children, and Wiues their husbandes, and friends diuerted friendes from listning to the reasons and discourses of the feruorous youth, least happily against their will they might be rapt away with that impetuous

torrent

torrent of celestiall Eloquence. But for all that they could not hinder him so, but he returned to his country with a precious booty of choice men. Among whome also was *Hugo de Marcone*, a person very notable for nobility and riches, who after he had made in Religion very excellent successe, was assumpted to the Bishoprike of *Auxerre*.

S. Bernard, *and his deuout Companions retired themselues into the Monastery of Cisterce, with the Exemplar life which all lead, but chiefly* S. Bernard. Chap. 5.

THis troupe of new souldiers of Christ, assembled themselues in *Castighone*, where though in secular habit, yet liued they all in the same house in common with so much peace and concord, that as it is reported of the Primitiue Church, of all that multitude there was but one hart and soule only. And through the great veneration wherein they were with the people, there was hardly found any one, that durst approach to looke into their actions: and if perhaps any entred into their lodgings, in beholding the Fraternall vnion, and order, and distribution of tyme, and Offices, the spirituall conferences, the singing of Canonicall Houres, & other deuout exercises; they acknowledged the diuine assistance to be there without doubt, and eyther they remayned there also with the same intent, or at least departed thence compunct and ful of good desires, calling that Congregation *Thrice happy, and fortunate*.

In this manner while the domesticall affaires of some of them were in handling, they remayned in the sayd place some six mõths at least. But perceauing afterwards a manifest danger in a longer aboad there, especially for that in fine, two being miserably seduced by the Diuell, were fallen backe; it seemed good to *S. Bernard* and the others, to stay there no longer: so as all impediments being remoued or cut off, calling on the diuine assistance they repayred to the Monastery of Cisterce some fifteen years after the sayd house began. The number of these new disciples of Christ were about thirty, a very seasonable supply no doubt to that Congregation, which now already through the foresayd occasions was euen almost brought to nothing.

Whereupon, the Abbot *Stephen* who gouerned at that tyme, being *Roberts* successour, and those few which as yet were remayning with him, receaued incredible comfort, with a firme hope of a long posterity, according to a certaine reuelation had a litle before by one of those first Monkes; to whome being anxious about fayling of the Order, at the end of his life, was represented an innumerable multitude of persons, who at the fountaine neere vnto the Church were all washing their owne garments. By this meanes (through diuine grace) was *Cisterce* restored. And to this good worke was added another, to set vp at *Villeo* a place hard by, a Conuent for the wiues of as many of those Nouices as concurring piously to the promotion of the diuine seruice, had beene content to acquit their husbandes of the coniugal band, and by consequence to offer vp themselues also in Holocausts to the Creatour of all, to whose diuine Maiesty, how gratefull that sacrifice was, may well be comprehended by the notable increase, which the sayd Conuent of Nuns made in a short tyme, as well of number of subiects, as of meanes to liue.

But to returne to the Saint, as soone as he saw himselfe in the schoole of Christ, the first thing was to plant in his hart an immoueable perseuerance, in speaking within himselfe, at what tyme eyther ease inuited him, or labours deterred him: *Bernard, Bernard, to what end didst thou enter in?* And for repressing of vnprofitable appetites for the soule, because he knew well, how much the custody of senses auayled, he was so wary and diligent in the heed thereof, and especially of his eyes, as that after a whole yeare of his Nouitiate, when he went from thence, he knew not as then, whether the seelings of the chamber were painted, or of fret-worke. And though he had entred so often into the Church, where there were indeed many windowes at the vpper end, he neuer thought there had been more then one. Besides, he kept himselfe at all tymes from all leuityes and sports, and from all those things which are wont to slacken the soule. Much laughing, a thing so proper vnto man, was seldome in him; and when it was, it was without excesse, and forced as it were, vsing it sometymes, not to seeme froward in things wherin commonly others hardly could forbeare. He was moreouer exceeding sober and vigilant; refection was a torment to him; at his rising from table, he would allwayes make examen vpon what he had eaten, and if he had found he had passed the boundes in any thing, he would not let the fault be vnpunished. He had sleep in horrour, as a resemblance of death, and that

that repose which, enforced through extreme necessity, he was wont to take, was superficiall only, and so small, as to any but him, would haue giuen no refreshment at all. Whence if he saw any of the Religious to sleep vndecently, or snoring, he could hardly endure it, saying, such an one slept like a secular.

But such excesse of watchings and fastings could not chose, but bring also exceeding hurt and detriment to his health, since in progresse of tyme, his stomack together with the diminution of naturall heate, came very much to be depriued of the retentiue faculty: and the tongue and palate, the body being of so noble a temperature, thereby came so to loose the tast, as that among other things, through imprudence of him that serued, for some dayes he liued of sheeps-suet, insteed of butter, drinking some tymes very oyle insteed of water, his eyes not looking vpon it. And these vnctuous meates, he would hardly endure to be set before him, euen in tyme of conualescency: for ordinartly he fed for most part on nothing else then bread, dipt in hoat water, or some broath made of pulse, or else a little milke: and if perhappes sometymes he were fayne to tast any wine, the cup would returne from his mouth agayne, as if it had not been touched at all.

The continuation of the rare Vertues of S. Bernard: *with an example or two, of the deepe attention of his mind to heauenly things.* Chap. 6.

FRom this mortification of the flesh, though otherwise but litle rebellious or disobedient to the spirit, and by such manner of recollecting of the interiour powers, came that blessed soule of S. *Bernard* in short tyme to square it selfe, and to be purifyed in such manner, as like to a polished and lucid glasse, it receaued right well, the rayes of eternall Wisedome, and he not only purchased a most excellent habit of meditation and prayer, but euen mounted also anone to a very high degree of contemplation, by meanes whereof being abstracted from exteriour operations, and liquifyed with ineffable sweetnes, in a deep silence, he would vnite himselfe, with most chast embraces of the highest good. Besides, in the very mechanical occupations themselues, through a certayne priuiledge, he had the grace, together with the whole outward man, to attend to the worke in hand, and with interiour to deale and discourse with God, satisfying the conscience with the one, & with the other

feeding

feeding the will. For indeed S.*Bernard* was none of those, who vnder pretext of contemplation, eschew trauayle, or els for priuate gust, forgo the publique good: so as hardly with greiuous and most irksome maladies could he be drawne from the Quire, where with grauity and wonderfull modesty he would perseuere in praysing and blessing God. In the labours of the hand likewise he abhorred all liberty, or any manner of exemption at all: as if he euen but then entred into the Monastery.

Going once with the Monkes to reaping of corne, and not knowing well how to vse his sikle, he was bid to sit downe, and rest himselfe; whereat he being sad, prayed with such feruour to God, that he might not be vnprofitable, as that changing on a sudden his manner, he began to reape so readily and dexterously, as if all his life he had neuer practised any thing els. True it is, that in the exercises which required much strength of lymmes, as in carrying of burthens, in digging and deluing the ground, and other such like workes, when through his delicate complexion he was ready to sincke vnder the same, he would get himselfe to some seruices lesse difficult, but yet more abiect and vile; so recompencing in that manner the paynes and trauayle of the one, with the basenes of the other, and shewing himselfe alwayes as might be equall or rather inferiour to his companions. And these rules he did keep in thinges which were imposed by the Superiours, either to him in particuler, or to the Conuent in generall. But when the ministery was not common, and the obedience exacted no corporall application, then *S.Bernard* being abstracted from visible things he would be so absorpt in the attention of the mind, as in him all operation, and all sensitiue memory, as it were seemed quite to be extinct. To which purpose are recounted two notable examples.

The one, that he hauing as it were, all day trauayled along the Lake of *Losana*, and his companions at night discoursing therof, he demanded of them very seriously, what Lake was that they talked of?

The other example was, that he being to visit the Monkes of *Chertosa*, there was brought him in hast by a stranger or secular a steed well appoynted, and hansomly furnished, wheron the holy man being mounted, and come to the Charter-house, was hartily wellcome, and intreated with much reuerence by the seruants of God: who remayned all exceedingly edifyed with their ghest, saue only

only with the furniture of his horse, while to them it seemed, such quaintnes therein, gaue no good odour of pouerty: so as the Prior himselfe could not hold, but must needes breake a iest thereupon to one of *S. Bernards* companions, who with religious zeale soone told it to the Father: and he turning himselfe on the one side to the Priour, and on the other to the horse; made shew with great sincerity also himselfe to wonder at such trappings, ingenuously confessing, he neuer had perceaued the same. At which wordes, the good Priour in a manner remayned confounded, for hauing himselfe at first sight noted a thing, which the other well mortifyed in the sense of the eyes, and attentiue to the interiour, could not once discerne in so great a iourney, and space of tyme.

Besides which, the diuine man, not only in commodious and easy things, but euen likewise in publique mortifications was farre off from all manner of noueltyes: in so much as hauing for some yeares very secretly worne a cilice, being an austerity not commaunded by the institute, and the same by accident being discouered, he layd it suddenly aside, not to seeme singular to men, or eminent among others. And this was also the occasion, that howbeit pouerty was euer grateful to him; yet shũned he as much to be wholy careles of the exteriour habit, and to seeme vncleanely, which in a manner is wont to turne away mens eyes from one.

The very same may be sayd of the Saints learning and grauer studyes. He was wont in the fields and woods, treating with himselfe and God only, to receiue frequent lights from heauen: and in prayer and meditation to penetrate the highest Misteryes of Diuinity. Whence to his more confident and dearest freindes, with a religious iest he affirmed sometymes, he neuer had other Maysters, then Beeches and Oakes. Neuerthelesse, that the world might not thinke he had been taught miraculously, he fayled not to read, and read ouer agayne whole bookes at tymes, and in the very reading was accustomed with particuler delight and profit of spirit, to stick vpon the text and words of the sacred Scripture, with leasure ruminating vpon them, and therewith deducing rare and strange conceipts, and therewith afterwardes helping himselfe with that copy, elegancy, and dexterity, as his diuine treatises & discourses shew. And notwithstanding with much humility also, he would consider the studyes and interpretations of the Fathers and Catholique doctours, not comparing euer his opinion with theirs, but modestly allwaies submitting himselfe, and faythfully following their venerable stepps.

S. Bernard *was made Abbot of Clareuall: their temporall necessityes there, which he releiues with prayer; with the happy Conuersion of his Father & sister*. Chap. 7.

THus, this so lucid and burning lampe, being hidden and couered a good while, it pleased the diuine Prouidence, to set it so vp, that all might well participate thereof.

There is the confines of *Langres*, not farre from the riuer *Alba*, a remote place, heeretofore an infamous Den of theeues, called the *Valley of* Wormewood, eyther of the plenty of such hearbes, which grow in those parts, or for the bitter entertaynements, which the theeues were wont to giue to such as fell into their hands. In this retreat or recesse, which came afterwardes to be called *Clareuallis*, through diuine inspiration, it pleased the Abbot *Stephen* to set vp a Conuent of his. And this was the first Colony that came forth of the *Cisterce*. For this intention, the sayd Prelate made choice of S. *Bernard*, and his brothers, with some others, and at his departure declared *S. Bernard* to be Superiour, and Abbot ouer them, who had been the instrument of their conuersion. He refused the charge, but in fine humbly vndertooke the care of their soules. Nor can it be coniectured by any, the vehement desire he had rather to obey, then commaund.

S. Bernard was not now to passe into pleasures and delights: for the Monastery as then had no foundation; the lodgings but few & very streight, and but ill accommodated: the ayre intempetrate, and subiect to excessiue cold: In so much as the good family there, a tyme liued in extreme necessity, their bread was made of millet, & fetches; their cates Beech leaues sod in water. The other incommodityes, they endured as well as they might for the summer tyme, but winter approaching, being wholy without prouision for that season, *Gerrard*, who was the Procuratour, or Cellarian as they call him, went to propose the matter to the new Abbot, greiuing and lamenting that he knew no remedy to so great difficultyes.

The Saint went about to make him couragious, and to be of a good hart, but the other admitting no comfort of words; S. Bernard

nard asked him what money were needfull for the vrgent necessityes. Whereto *Gerard* answering at least Eleauen pounds: the Abbot retired himselfe to make his prayer. And behold very soone returnes the brother to aduertise him, that a woman of *Castiglion* was without at the gate, demaunding earnestly to speake with him. S. *Bernard* went forth, and she sudenly casting her selfe downe at his feet, gaue him an Almes of twelue pounds, beseeching him to recommend her husband to God, that was greiuously sicke. To whom after a short thanks-giuing. Goe thy wayes (sayd he) woman, for thou shalt find thy husband sound; as indeed, she did. And the man of God thence taking occasion very dexterously reprehended the pusillanimity of *Gerard*: and with other such like accidents which cleerely demonstrate the Fatherly care of Christ ouer his seruantes, it came to passe that the Monkes confiding in heauenly succours, molested not the Saint any more for temporall necessities, but recurred to him only for matters appertayning to spirit.

About that tyme S. *Bernard* in the night before the houre of Mattins, being gone forth to meditate, and pray in the neighbour places (as he was wont) to the end to behold and discouer thence the starres more freely: While he was there deuoutly recommending the health of the Monkes to God, and the happy progresse of the diuine seruice, being suddenly rapt forth of himselfe, he sees to descend from the mountaines so great a multitude of men of diuers habits and conditions, as the valley was not able to containe them all. Of which sight, what the true interpretation was, was easily to be judged by the multitude of those, who weary and glutted with the deceipts of the world, retired themselues from tyme to tyme to *Clareuallis*, to secure themselues there of the eternall inheritance, with the losse of the temporall.

And for the greater consolation of S. *Bernard*, of that number was his Father *Thesselin* himselfe, who becoming now both sonne and brother in spirit to those whome he was Father according to the flesh, finished the remnant of those few dayes of his pilgrimage left him, most blessedly in their company.

The daughter yet remayned, being a young woman, very richely maryed, and drowned as it were in the delights & pompes of the world: it pleased God also with the eyes of his eternall clemency to looke vpon this woman, in putting into her hart to visit the Monkes her brethren, & especially the Abbot, whose most excellent vertues so rung in the eares of men. Putting her selfe then in order, with a great trayne of seruants and ostentatiō of apparell and iewells, all gorgeous and glorious she went to *Clareuallis*: but had a farre different welcome from that she expected. For that S. *Bernard* vnderstanding the gallantry, and pompe, wherewith she came, being all enflamed with zeale, sayd; this snare of the diuel, this ruyne of soules, shall not come in my sight. *Andrew* being one of the yonger brothers, & then at the gate of the Monastery, seeing his sister so braue and gorgeously attired, with a seuere looke and bitter voyce, stucke not to call her among other things, A painted sepulcher; the others, through the example of S. *Bernard*, remayned retired, and hid from such a spectacle. Wherupon the poore wretch compunct, and wholy confounded, & melted in teares, answered, sighing deepely from her hart.

Though I be a sinner, yet Christ, he dyed for such; & because I acknowledge my selfe to be miserable, I doe therefore approach vnto the good for helpe and counsayle: if my brother despise my flesh, let not the seruant of God yet abhorre my soule. Let him come then, and commaund me, for I am ready to execute whatsoeuer he shall appoint me.

The Saint laying hold of such a promise, fayled not to come forth vnto her. And since it was not in his power to part her from her husband, at least he aduised her of the daunger she was in, by following so her senses, and exhorted her, that abandoning those vanityes, while tyme yet serued, she should attend to do pennance; and in summe, she should set continually before her eyes, for glasse and patterne, the life and manners of *Aletta* their Mother, since she had liued with her some while, and that she must needs remember her very well.

The wordes of the seruant of God were of no light moment: they enkindled in that breast as in a solid and substantiall matter, so tenacious and burning a fire of Charity, as returning home, not without the astonishement of as many as knew her, she chaunged her manners on a sudden, and the whole care of the body she turned to the dressing of the mind: she likewise her selfe attending to watchinges, prayers, fasts, and almes, and that not for a few dayes only (as commonly is wont) but with such constancy and longanimity, as that her husband himselfe now holding her in veneration,

and

and not daring to hinder the course of so great vertues, at the end of two yeares, gaue her leaue to retire, and consecrate her selfe in the Monastery of *Vilies*, whereof we haue made some mention aboue. Where the happy woman liuing to the last, with exceeding edification, shewed her selfe to be not vnworthy, either of the blessed stocke she came of, nor of the happy braunches that encompassed her round about.

The strange vocations of diuers persons, of seuerall conditions and state, to Religion, by the meanes of S. Bernard. Chap. 8.

IN the meane tyme, the Cistercian family, according to the visions, made a notable increase, and multiplyed in such manner, as in the space of few yeares, there was plenty of them through diuers Kingdomes and Prouinces. And now at this tyme the resolution of such as tooke the habit grew not (as sometymes it happens) through temporal necessities, or humane dessignes, but sprung (for the most part) from supernall and generous motiues, partly fortold, and partly also obtayned through the prayers of the Saint, as may cleerely appeare by some, for example sake, which we will heere put downe.

At the fame of the man of God, came a troupe of gallants to visit him; being all very dissolute yong men. Now, *Quinquagesima* was a tyme, when the Catholike Church, all sad, for the bitter fall of our first Parents, exhortes mankind to holsome pennance, & when euen the faythfull thēselues (O lamentable case) partly allured with sensuality, and partly quite transported with the torrent of euill custome, attend more then euer to wantonesse, feastinges, and banquets.

These Nobles, being violently set vpon the same custome, and wholy enflamed with youthfull heate, while they remayned in *Clareuallis*, went seeking a fit place somewhat neere to the Church for their marshal sports and turneaments. The thing was much displeasing to the Abbot, wherefore with instance he prayed them for the present at least to desist from such exercises, and to make him a guift of those few dayes of Carneual. The vnbridled youths stopt their eares vnto so reasonable a request, remayning stiffe in their foolish purpose; then replyed the Saint: I trust in our Lord, he will graunt what you deny me. After this, calling for a cup of Wine, he first blessed it, & then inuited the Gentlemen to pledge him, and tast of it (which he called the wine of soules.) They all drunke cheerefully thereof, some few only excepted, who tooke the inuitation in ill part, for feare some hidden power, and enchantment, as it were, might be in that wine, that might aliene their mindes from more gratefull and pleasant thinges. Nor was the suspition altogeather in vaine: for scarcely had they taken their leaue of the Abbot, and were gone out of the Monastery, when being touched and prickt with new inspirations, they began to discourse togeather of the continuall perills and foolish glory of the world. With which discourse they were so enflammed, as immediatly without more adoe, they all agreed to returne to the cloyster, and humbly demaunding admittance into Religion, they continued there couragiously, enduring many labours with much fortitude and patience: a change surely worthy of much admiratiõ; but yet no lesse marueylous are these that follow.

The Saint being once to make a peace of much importance, in going to *Mentz* a principall citty of Germany, the Archbishop of that Metropolis; vnderstanding of the approach of so great a man, sent a principall Clerke called *Mascolin* to meet him with honour, and to receaue him worthily on the way. This man arriuing to the presence of the Saint, and hauing reuerently declared to him how he came from his Lord the Archbishop to wayte vpon him, S. *Bernard* stopt, and fixing his eyes a while on the Clerke, sayd to him, he was sent by another Lord to serue him. The German was troubled at the answere, and not penetrating a whit what he meant thereby, affirmed againe, that he came being sent by the Metropolitan himselfe; the seruant of God on the contrary, replyed: You deceaue your selfe, the Lord that sent you indeed, is yet greater then he, to wit, Christ himselfe. Then finally the good man vnderstanding what he aymed at: Your Paternity thinkes perhapes (replyed he) that I intend to be a Monke? God forbid, the same as yet neuer came into my thought. Notwithstanding the Saint forbare not to rehearse againe, that by all meanes that must be which God hath disposed of him; and not what the Clerke himselfe hath thought, or not thought of. What more? He had not finished his iourney, but he resolued with himselfe to leaue the world; and a little after in company of many other honourable and learned men, gayned by the Saint in that iourney, he came to exchange his habit in the Monastery of *Clareuallis*.

A more

A more notable successe yet was that other of *Henry* brother of the King of France. This man being come to deale with the glorious Abbot, about certayne temporall affayres, the treaty being ended, desired the Monks might be assembled to salute them all together, and to recommend himselfe (as he did) vnto their prayers. With this occasion, that wise Pastour entred into some spirituall disourses with the Prince, and in the progresse of conuersation together among other things, he sayd to him: I hope Syr, you shal not dye in the state you are now in at this present; but that very soone you shall know by experience, how efficacious the intercession is which you haue requested of these poore seruants of God. Nor was it long ere the prophesy was verifyed. On that very day through diuine inspiration, *Henry* did determine to follow by the streight way the stepps of Christ, & without delay he put his purpose in effect: his family and the Nobles that accompanyed him thither, lamented him no lesse, then if that Royall youth had layne dead before them, and extended on a hearse.

But among others on *Andrew Parigino* could by no meanes brooke it, being greatly affected to *Henry*. He was euen mad with anger, and seemed to let fall from his mouth curses, banninges, and all whatsoeuer greife and rage could suggest vnto him; when *Henry* on the other side (that yet loued him well) beganne earnestly to intreate the Saint, he would seeke aboue all others to conuert this man. To which S. *Bernard* answeared: Let vs let him alone for the present, for the poore man is now full of bitternes. Nor doe you take any thought thereat; I can assure you he is yours. With these wordes *Henry* being enflamed with new hope, and greater desire began to instance anew the blessed Father to delay no longer to giue him the assault. Then S. *Bernard* replyed with a seuere countenance: What ayle you? Haue I not told you already, he his yours? The standers by hearing the discourse betwene them, and *Andrew* himselfe among the rest, who being obstinate in his mãners, and farre from changing his habit, and doing pennance; bowing downe his head (as he confessed afterwards) sayd within himselfe to the Abbot: Now I see thee very well to be a false Prophet, I know for certaine thou hast sayd one thing, and the contrary will fall out: Go to, go to, let me come to the Court once, and on my credit, the King shall vnderstand of all, and I will make thy lyes appeare to the world.

While

While this wretch makes these accounts alone with himselfe, they being in suspense, expected what would be the issue of the matter. When seeing him the day after to depart from thence without any thing done, the fayth and credit in some began to stagger, and the former conceipt which they had of the seruant of God: but our Lord permitted not the temptation to continue long; for that *Andrew* being now on his way, though his conscience began to sting him a little, yet for a while went he on cursing the Abbot, and Monastery, where he left his Maister, and wishing the whole *Clareuallis* might sinke, with as many as were in it. But these brauado's and stiffnes of his lasted that day only; for being arriued to his lodging at night, he was so inwardly gauled with such stinges, as that being not able to resist any longer, without attending so much as till day, he leapt from his bed, and speedily returned backe to *Clareuallis* agayne, where deposing the old man, with his wonted manners and fiercenes, he put on the new, to the great consolation and wonder of all.

Certaine noble Gentlemen yielded vp themselues to S. Bernard: *wherof one hauing a temptation afterwards, was happily by him quit therof.* Chap. 9

IN those dayes certaine Flemings sped very well, who besides they were of a Noble bloud, and well learned, had likewise a great desire to attend to perfection, but could not well determine what schoole was fittest for their purpose; and in this suspense of mind stood wauering, vntill S. *Bernard* about some publique affaires happened to goe into those partes of Flanders. And as his Name was now famous already, at the appearing of such a man, sprung a notable light in the mindes of those disconsolate louers of wisedome, so as without more delay they made choice of the Abbot of *Clareuallis* for Maister and Superiour, supposing he was destined thither by the diuine Prouidence for their saluation; setling and dispatching then ech one their busines, and laying aside the vayne designes, and deceiptfull hopes of the world, they went ioyfull with *S. Bernard* towardes *Burgundy*, who then likewise had finished his affaires. In which iourney there happened an accident not fit to be let passe.

It is an ordinary thing, likely in all beginners in the diuine seruice, and not yet experienced inough in desolation or substraction of grace, of grace, and ſpirituall viciſſitudes, when that guſt of ſenſible deuotion comes once to faile them, and that pleaſant light which puts them haſtily on, to looſe on a ſudden all courage quite, and to fall into puſillanimity of ſpirit, and ſadnes of hart. The occaſion therof do Wiſemen ſay to be this: the Rationall ſubſtance cannot endure to be ſtraitned, and ſome delight eyther heauenly or terren muſt be. Now the ſoules, as being rayſed aboue themſelues, with ſome taſt of ſupernall pleaſures, do eaſily renounce the viſible obiects: ſo when through diuine diſpenſation, that ioy is taken away from them, finding themſelues depriued of this alſo, and not accuſtomed to expect with patience the returnes of the new Sunne, it ſeemes to them they are neither in heauen nor earth, and are as buryed in a perpetuall night; ſo as like babes hauing loſt the breaſts they languiſh and ſigh, and become tedious, and irkeſome chiefly to themſelues.

The ſame happened on they way to one of that company called *Gaufrid*. This man being ſuddenly growne arid, and full of interiour darknes, began to bethinke himſelfe of his freinds, parents, and goods, which he had left behind, and thereby was aſſayled with ſo ſtrong a temptation, as being not able to diſſemble it in his countenance, one of his more confident and intimate freinds was aware thereof, and dexterouſly approaching to him, with ſweete and benigne ſpeach in ſecret, ſayd to him: What is the matter, *Gaufrid*? How happens this I pray you? go to, tell me, for it ſeemes to me you goe penſiue and ſad, more then ordinary? Then *Gaufrid* anſwered with a deep ſigh: Alas brother, I ſhall neuer be merry more in all my life. The other being with that word moued to pitty went ſuddenly, with fraternall zeale, to acquaint their common Father what paſſed, who vnderſtanding the daunger, began to pray for him in a Church thereby, and *Gaufrid* in the meane while being ouercome with ſadnes, repoſed his head on a ſtone, and there fell a ſleep: but long it was not ere both aroſe, the one from prayer with the grace obteyned, and the other from his ſleep with a face ſo cheerefull and ſerene, as his freind much admiring at ſo ſudayne and great a change, could not hold, but freindly vpbrayd him with what he had anſwered him a little before. Then *Gaufrid* ſayd: if I told thee before, I ſhould neuer be merry agayne, I now affirme vnto thee, I ſhall neuer be ſad more. And this ſame *Gaufrid* afterwards, in the Nouiceſhip being deſirous of the eternall ſaluation of his owne Father, recommended him to the Saint with much affect and confidence. And he sayd; doubt not, sonne, but thy Father shall be a good Religious man, and I my selfe after his death shall bury him with these armes: and so it fell out, that old man being entred into Religion, and growne very perfect in vertues, fell greiuously sick, at such tyme as S. *Bernard* was farre from *Clareuallis*, in which infirmity of his he grew dayly more sicke then other, lying in extremity for some fiue monthes continually togeather, vntill the Abbot returning, with his assistance he sweetly rendred vp his spirit in his armes, and with his owne handes buryed his body with his wonted Charity, and performing of due exequies.

Another tyme, being gone to *Chalon* in *Champayne* to deale with the Bishop of that Citty, he thence lead with him at his returne a good number of excellent subiects: and such manner of purchases with the help of the diuine hand he made happily from tyme to tyme. Besides which, there wanted not daily many, that being allured by his Name, and glutted with the deceipts of the world, came voluntary of their owne accord to submit themselues to the obedience of so great a guide. Whence no wonder is it, that from the garrison of *Clareuallis*, should be sent after (as we haue sayd) so fit supplyes, as there did, to so many partes of Europe.

S. Bernard *deuinely admonished, changes his stricter hand vpon his Nouices, to a milder way, with the good fruit that came thereof.* Chap. 10.

IT remaynes now to see, what manner the diuine man tooke in guiding and gouerning the Soules, recommended and committed to his care by the Prince of Pastours. It is then to be vnderstood, that in the first yeares of his Prelacy, in measuring others feruour by his owne, he was something more rigid and seuere, then good and moderate gouernement would seeme to beare. For that in receiuing of Nouices into the Conuent, he was wont to bid them (among other things) by way of Enigma, to leaue the body without, and to enter only with the spirit. Through which saying of his, some of the simpler of them, remayned so astonished, and terrified therewith, as they were after not able to vnderstand the sense and meaning of those wordes, though the Saint himselfe explayned the same. In the confessions which he heard of his Monks, with a bitter countenance he abhorred any manner of defect; esteeming euery

light,

light fault in Religious, as a mortall sinne. In his Sermons, or as we say Homilyes rather, in the speculatiue, he often soared so high, as the hearers vnderstanding, would loose the sight of him: and insteed of being fed and refreshed, would come to be dry and arid. And for the morall, he required so curious & exact perfection of all, as the poore disciples, besides hope of gayning it, came to loose the desire & will of procuring it.

With these and other such proceedinges, the greater part of the Monkes, especially of the yonger of them were soone oppressed with a certaine sadnes and timidity withall; which both tooke away deuotion, and hindred their profit in solid vertues. Among which inconueniences was yet this good besides, that the Monks through the great opinion they had of their common Father, would lay the whole fault thereof, partly on their owne tepidity, and partly also on their poore wit, and small capacity, without euer once complayning of the Abbot, or opposing any thing which he sayd, or diminishing awhit the reuerence they bare him. It pleased God this humility of the subiects should get the vper hand vpon the Superiour: because, that he being lastly ouercome and compunct in a manner at so much submission and modesty of theirs, began to assume to himselfe the occasion of losse, and to say within himselfe. O *Bernard*, how much better were it for thee to attend to the amendement of thyne owne imperfections, then so to disquiet with too much seuerity and importune discourses the soules more timorous of God, and more religious then thee? Now, are not these seruants of Christ, better able to walke with their simplicity, then with thy indiscretion? And to learne much better the spirituall doctrine, in one only meditation, in dealing with the Highest Wisedome, then by all the preachinges and exhortations thou art able to make them? Learne then at last, that the Abbot *Stephen* hath layd a pack-sadle on an Oxes backe, & that this gouerning of others is not thy talent.

With these thoughtes, the man of God began to enter into so great a bitternes and hatred of his actions, as he determined to retyre himselfe more then euer, and to abstaine from all pastorall functions, what possibly he might, vntill such tyme as had some cleere signe of the diuine will: nor was his expectation awhit in vaine, because it was not long, but there appeared to him by night a little child, cloathed all with eternall light, expressely commanding him, he should desist to propose vnto him, what his hart seemed to dictate to him, since it was not he that spake to them, but the Holy Ghost discoursing by his mouth. And togeather with an inestimable guift, besides, of a sweet & discreet maturity, whence he might learne to compassionate the weake, to temper himselfe to the capacity of the rude, and to condescend to ech what he might well do with the safety of Monasticall discipline.

Heereupon the rigourous Abbot, in this point being changed as it were into another man, began with extraordinary tendernes, and solicitude to preuent the necessityes of ech one, and not only of the soules, but euen also of the bodyes, prouiding as much as possibly he might, that euery one being free, and deliuered from temporall troubles and molestations, might attend with the whole mind to the purchase of vertues, and to the diuine seruice. Howsoeuer yet to himselfe only, and his owne person, the man of God, not altered awhit his former customes, for that indeed in him (as is signifyed already) the appetite was naturally much subiect to reason, and had no need through force of chastisements & scourges to reduce it to seruitude. Whence came the flesh to be a great deale more weakned in him, and afflicted with sundry infirmities: in so much as the Phisitians were astonished, how the Holy Abbot amidst so many dolours, could attend to occupations of any sort; and resembled him iust to a Lambe being put to the plough: & he himselfe also at the latter end of his age, was finally aware thereof and accused himselfe for excesse of maceration of the body, and for destroying his complexion with austerityes, enfeebling the organs of the Holy Ghost, and consequently for hindering on his part the greater glory of the diuine goodnes.

But for these new proceedings of his which we spake of, it cannot be expressed, to what edification & publique commodity they redounded. Because (which are the effects of knowne loue) there sprung very suddenly a noble strife and contention, betweene the fatherly indulgence of the Maister, and generous feruour of the disciples, being all (for the most part) well descended; so as by how much he shewed himselfe to them to be a lesse strict exactour, so became they ordinarily more rigid censurers of themselues, extending themselues to the perfect obseruance of vowes and rule, not leauing a defect vnpunished, and holding the allurements and enticements of sensuality farre off from them. And the matter procee-

ded

ded so farre indeed, as not without some manifest perill of life, they went about in diuers kinds to take away all tast and relish of meate and drinke, as seeming to them a thing vnlawful, that he who hath layd vp his treasures and delights in heauen, should take any gust or pleasure in terrene things. And they were so rooted in such an opinion, as hardly with sundry examples and reasons, and with the authorityes of the sacred Scriptures themselues, could they be brought to vnderstand, that ech creature was good, being vsed in tyme and place, and with due moderation. Note this finally, they left that pernicious errour, but yet they wanted not matter of mortification. First the diuine offices were celebrated with greatest attention, and that for a good space of the day, and night. Moreouer the Monastery as yet not hauing any manner of rents, their holy pouerty was heere so much the more easy and familiar vnto them, as it was more straitly embraced and cherished of ech one. Heerreto was added the straitnes and incommodity of the dwelling, which while they sought to remedy, their continuall labour of the hands at certaine houres appointed, affoarded them no leasure for slouth and idlenes.

The sage and prudent gouernement of S. Bernard, *in guiding his Monkes: with his enflamed Charity to his Neighbour*. Chap. 11.

Among all the labours and trauailes of these blessed men, as there were many things of excellent example: yet was there none of greater edification to the beholders, then the continuall recollection and silence of so many seruants of God; so as, within the same habitation was ioyntly to be seene a noyse of a multitude, and a silence of a solitude, and that surely not without cause. For that as a man which is solitary, if he be inwardly vnruly and distracted, makes of his hart a very Inne or Market-place; so a number of persons well disciplined and composed, through meanes of good order and custody of the senses, represents in the thickest concourse of people a very desert or hermitage. This continuall discipline and custody of the monks, was to them an exceding help for the vnion with God. Whereto also they approached so much the neerer, as they had allwayes more liuely aud admirable examples of all Christian vertue before their eyes, in the person and actions of the holy Abbot. In whom was seene so burning a Charity, as he neuer pretended or wished ought, then the honour of God, and saluation of soules; procuring euer the one and other, with the forme and manner of his life, with heauenly conuersation, with prayers, with the labours of writing, and of interpreting the diuine Scriptures, and finally as occasion serued, with priuate and publique discourses.

For eloquence, it was a thing in the blessed man more Angelicall then human, with so much sagacity would he discerne the peccant humours of men; with so much dexterity accommodated himselfe to their wits, docility, and manners. He would deale with the country people, as if he had continually been bred vp in a village: with the Nobles he kept all the points of good breeding: with the Ideots he would vse comparisons and conceipts of material and palpable things: with the learned and Sophisters he knew well in his tyme, to stand vpon subtilityes and acumens: and in summe had a great store and copious variety of bayts and hookes proportionate to the gust, forces, and nature of ech one. To this so excellent prudence of his in practise, and so happy and rare a faculty of speaking, was adioyned another guift and priuiledge, indeed not afforded to many, to proue when need required his doctrine, with frequent, and great, and those euident Miracles. Whereof, besides what already hath been touched (not to go forth heere from our purpose) we shall discourse with our wonted breuity in its place.

But with the ardent Charity of the Saint, we spake of, he gaue vs likewise a most cleere demonstration, in the sorrow and compassion he felt for the peruersenes, and fault of his Neighbours, especially of such as he had vnder his gouernement: which in so great diuersity of nations and temperatures, may not seeme very strange that some disorder now and then should fall out; and that so much the rather, as the Religious state supposeth men not allready to be perfect, but studious, and (so we may euen say) scholers of perfection, in as much as ech discipline and art (as the Philosopher sayd) is in erring learned. In such occurrences then, the good Prelate, though touched in the soule with the sharpest stings: yet neuerthelesse with familiar countenance and paternall grauity withall, would not hold in secret from rebuking the delinquent; who coming heereby to acknowledge the fault, and to shew forth true pennance, the man of God contented with the humble satisfaction, would comfort him, and proceed no further. And when the guilty shewed himselfe stiffe, and gaue a harsh answeare, he would suddenly

denly cease to striue or contend with him, not to put in some sort his pastorall authority in daunger. But leauing to the disciple new space to acknowledge his errour, with occasion he would returne agayne afterwardes to the same office of louing correction; or else when necessity required, he would betake himselfe to the counsel of the Scripture, which aduiseth, the foolish man not to be corrected with wordes. And when this last remedy at any tyme proued vnprofitable, it cannot be expressed what affliction and corrasiue the blessed Soule, would take thereat.

And if any perhappes should wish him not to grieue so much at it, since he had fully satisfyed his duty in the sight of God, & that he could by no meanes doe any more with one, that through obstinacy would needes perish; the amorous Rectour would answere sighing, how these nor infinite reasons could quiet him, in beholding him as dead before his eyes whome he loued so much: & you would haue me (sayth he) to feele no griefe at so ill successe, as if in this reprehension and rebuke, I had for scope only the sauing of myne owne soule, and not rather the saluation also of that of my beloued? And what Mother is there, that howbeit on her part she haue vsed all care and diligence in her childs infirmity, if she see it dead, who can choose but lament and bewayle the same, considering the while the paines she hath taken for it in vaine?

Such then were the bowells of this true follower of Christ, whence it would happen likewise, that if he had denyed any thing at the first to any indiscreet and importunate suiter, he could by no meanes deny him the second tyme. Forasmuch as euen by naturall instinct, his hart would not serue him to behould any one contristate and afflicted, so as he neuer despised or made light reckoning of the trouble and perturbation of any one tempted: and howbeit in its tyme he could shew, that he sought rather the pleasure of God, then that of men, and preferred truth and iustice before any other respect whatsoeuer; yet did he all with such regard, and so much circumspection, as euen to such as seemed offended with him there wanted not matter to remaine well satisfyed. Whence sometymes it happened, that such as these would become afterwardes more deuoute, and affected to the man of God, then euer.

Diuers examples of the meekenes and patience of S. Bernard*: and how the Monastery of* Clareuallis *flourished by him founded.* Chap. 12.

IT may not seeme strange, that so much piety to Rationall creatures should seeme to lodge in that sacred breast, since he wanted not tendernes and affection also to the very Beasts themselues. It fell out sometymes he should meet on the way with Hares hoatly pursued by the houndes euen at the heeles; or els some Fowle flying from the hawke, which the blessed Man beholding, would straight deliuer them from the present danger with the signe of the Crosse, signifying to the hunters (as indeed it happened) that they pursued them in vaine. From this so burning a furnace of Charity, with reason proceeded that refined gold of his solid Patience, which he truly made manifest in the continuall tribulations, scourges, & infirmities, wherein he was proued by our Lord, from the beginning of his blessed conuersion vnto his last breath; in so much as his life was esteemed by such as familiarly conuersed with him, to be a lingring death, except only in occurrences of some great vniuersal benefit. For in such necessity through diuine dispensation he would seeme to haue gotten new forces, and extraordinary vigour. And euen with men also (though perhaps not so often) he had sufficient occasions to shew himselfe armed with inuincible sufferance and constancy.

He would speake as well through experience, as speculation, very learnedly of this most excellent vertue, and was wont to distinguish the subiect thereof into three manner of offences, to wit, of honour, of goods, and of the person: according to this diuision, let vs see briefely how he behaued himselfe in effect.

The great seruant of God had written on a tyme, to a Bishop being a principall Consailour in the Court, intreating him to giue certaine aduices and admonishmentes in a thing about some matters that went not well. Whereat the Bishop being strangely offended, wrote back a letter agayne to the most deuout S. *Bernard*, dealing with him at the very beginning as with an impious and wicked blasphemer. To which so sharp and bitter reproach, answered the seruant of Christ with these wordes: I cannot beleeue now, I haue the spirit of blasphemy in me, nor was it euer any intention of myne to speake ill of others, and especially of my soueraigne Prince. And this Answere of his, he afterwards accõpanyed also with actions so louing, and with so much obseruance towards him, who had so wronged him, as he gayned him at last, and made him his greatest freind.

After the enterprise of *Sozia*, which vnder the conduct of *Lewes* King of France, through wicked perfidiousnes of the Grecian Emperour, had taken but ill successe, there were some that traduced the fame of *S. Bernard*, as who had beene the principall authour of that expedition. Whereunto being not able to giue a particuler account to euery one of his motiues, and of what had passed in the voyage, at least he prayed often for them all, being a great deale more sorrowful for their sinne, then for his proper infamy: & being not able to suppresse such murmurs reioyced at least, that those poysonous shafts of the slanderous ignorant, were aymed all at himselfe (who did little respect them,) and much reioyced that the diuine Maiesty and Prouidence, was come to be entire, and vntouched by those impious people.

There were once 600. markes of siluer intercepted by the way from the seruants of the man of God, being magnificently assigned by the Abbot of *Farco*, to the behoofe and benefit of the Order. To which newes the Saint replyed with a cheerefull countenance: Blessed be God who hath deliuered vs from such a burthen: and he truly who hath taken away the money, in some sort deserues to be excused, since such a summe might well giue a shrewd temptation. The same tenour he kept of a serene mind, without contention or strife at all, when there were taken from him, partly through deceit, and partly by force about some ten Monasteries, or places at least very apt to erect foundations for them.

A certaine Regular of another Monastery being tempted, and not sound in his vocation; hauing read some spirituall treatises of S. *Bernard*, went his wayes to *Clareuallis* to make instance vnto him, to receaue him among his: to whome the blessed Man sweetly answering, wished him to returne, not seeming good to him for iust respects to yield to his request. Why haue you then (replyed the wretch) Father, so extolled Perfection in your writinges, if you will not succour and help him, who desires the same? And being vrged by the infernal spirit, added: Now then if I had those books in my hands, I would surely rent them in a thousand peeces. To this, the Man of God answered: I do verily thinke, sayd he, that in none of them thou shalt find, Thou mayst not be perfect in thy cloyster: the amendement of manners, change not of places (if I well remember) I haue proposed, and commended in my bookes. Then went that frantique man quite out of his wits, and lifting vp suddenly his most sacrilegious hand, he gaue so huge a cuffe on the eare to the holy Abbot, that his cheeke was presently swolne: wherat with reason the standers by being incensed began to rise vp to handle the Wretch as he deserued; but soone the Seruant of God preuented the same, exclayming and coniuring them by the name of Christ, not to touch him, but warily to lead him away, procuring by all meanes possible, he should take no harme. And thus the wretch all pale, and trembling escaped thence without the least punishment. Moreouer this defendour of the Truth, and promoter of the diuine seruice, wanted not his emulous, and persecutours, though he, through the eminence of his qualityes, and glory of his wordes and deedes, had very much ouercome their enuy.

With such a pest of men, the louer of Christ vsed this manner of proceeding: first according to the precept of the Ghospell, he would make feruent prayer for them; after that with might and mayne he sought to extinguish that malignant passion with all manner of submission, and good offices; in rendering benefits for iniuryes, honour and reuerence, for contempt and affronts, as he who had their saluation as deere as his owne, and felt particuler torment, at the scandall of those, to whome he had giuen no occasion at all: and the malice of others did excruciate him more, then his conscience seemed to satisfy him, it seeming a matter too difficult for him to cure a malady, whose origine he could not discouer: and whensoeuer he was able to come to the knowledge thereof, he tooke no greater pleasure then to roote it out, although he were thereby to haue his handes all mangled and bloudy.

The most holy Abbot was arriued to such a point of the loue of God, and of his Neighbour, through the continuall meditation of the life and passion of Christ, being truly become the forme and example of the flocke, which he had in charge, as that now with great reason was the good odour of *Clareuallis* spread, and dilated through out all Christendome; and in all partes (as we sayd aboue) with cost and diligence were the grafts of this happy plant both craued, and procured; nor were there only Monasteryes of S. *Bernard* founded heere and there, but euen whole Conuents likewise

of

of other families, came voluntarily to submit themselues vnto his obedience, and to conforme themselues with all study to the rites and profession of the *Cisterce*, yea euen he himselfe whose principall care was (as we sayd) to remaine hidden and vnknowne in that corner, and valley, was yet very suddenly more highly placed by the diuine hand, in the light, and sight of men, and obliged to dispense to the benefit of the world, the treasures and graces which he heaped vp togeather in his Cell. Whence Schismatikes were reconciled to the Roman Church, Heretikes publikely conuinced, and Catholikes promoted, and established in peace.

A Schisme in the Church ariuing about the election of a Pope, was happily ended through the wisedome of S. Bernard. Chap. 13.

THe first achiuement the Saint happened to make for the good of all christendome, tooke occasion from the Schisme of *Pierlonio* the Roman, who after the death of *Honorius*, with euill practises, making himselfe a false Pope, and taking the name of *Anaclete*, opposed himselfe to the true and canonically elected Pope *Innocent*; in which so scandalous a diuision, both the one and the other endeauouring as well with messages as letters to draw whole Kingdomes and Christian nations to their obedience, the world was put into a great confusion and perplexity, being as yet not able to discerne which of these two fornamed Popes they were to acknowledge and adore for lawfull Successour of *S. Peter*, and vicar generall of Christ. Vpon this then so important an article were assembled in diuers parties of Europe nationall Synods, and particulerly in France was called the Councell in the Land of *Tampes*, where to be able with the more light & more fauourable assistance of the holy Ghost to decide so great a difficulty, it seemed good to the King himselfe, and the more principall Bishops, that aboue all, the Abbot of *Clareuallis* should be called thereto, so great was the conceipt had euen at that tyme of the wisedome & spirit that spake by him.

Being inuited then on behalfe of the King, and exhorted withall by the other Abbots of his Order (to whome he was euer most obedient) he went his wayes thither, wholy full of feare and trembling, considering the waight and danger, and the other qualityes of the busines. And yet he felt notwithstāding great comfort in a vision which he had on his way by night, wherein was represented to him a very great assembly of Ecclesiasticall persons, who with sweet harmony praysed and glorifyed God: from whence he conceaued firme hope, that soone after would follow the desired vnion and concord of the Christian people. When he came then to the place designed, and that the Councell was opened, the Fastes and deuout Processions according to Apostolicall custome being celebrated, in the same first Session, with iudgment and consent resolution was made, that the whole controuersy should be remitted to *S. Bernard*, the seruant of God, and nothing should be done therein but what he determined. Which charge truly as vntolerable, the man of God refused with great modesty, but won at last through the prayers and authority of that holy multitude, he accepted the same, and buckles himselfe to the enterprise, so much more stout and confident in God, as he was more diffident and weake in himselfe. So as inuoking the ayde of Heauen, & making a most exact inquisition and examine, first of the manner and order of Election, then also of the qualities and merits of the Electours, as of both the elected Popes themselues, he securely nominated & declared *Innocent* for the chiefe and true Pastour; to which proposition was not one in the whole Councell which opposed a whit, but suddenly singing a ioyful Hymne with the accustomed prayers and thankesgiuings, they all with one accord subscribed to the sayd declaration.

In the meane tyme *Innocent*, being not able to resist the power and fury of the adursaryes, going forth of *Rome*, and receaued with due honour & reuerence of all *Tuscany*, he came into *France*; and the glorious Abbot with the same greatnes of courage passed ouer into England, where King *Henry* through the persuasion of some Prelates, declared and shewed himselfe very backward and hard to accept of *Innocent*. But the venerable Abbot after many reasons alleadged in vayne, at last full of zeale & fortitude sayd to him. What feares your highnes? doubt you to commit synne with affording obedience to *Innocent*? Go to then, do but thinke as you ought to doe, to render accompt to God for your other synnes, and doe you leaue this to me, and I will take it vpon my charge. With such an offer made, that mighty King without more adoe, was satisfyed, and was so assured thereof, as he determined to goe forth of his kindome to goe meete, and humbly receaue *Innocent*, who

through

through *Prouence* and *Burgundy* being come to *Chartres*, *Henry* came thither to kisse his feet, who with great common iubiley did giue him the Apostolicall benediction.

While many matters touching the diuine seruice, and the holy Church, were there handled and defined in the sayd place: behold the Popes Nuntio's to arriue thither from *Germany* with letters frõ those Lords, and those Countryes, full of affectious prayers, that his Holines would daigne so much as to comfort those Northerne parts with his presence, since now all, through the example of *France* and *England*, acknowledged him for supreme guide, and head of the Church militant. But the Pope so soone could not affoard himselfe to those nations, being with so much deuotion cõtinually entertayned and desired by the Cittyes of *France*, through which hauing made his progresse a while, he intimated a Councell in *Rhems*, where likewise hauing ordayned many things to the honour of God, he after with many solemne ceremonyes at the instance of King *Lodouik* the Father, crowned and annointed *Lodouike* the sonne, in the place of *Philip* his elder brother deceased.

In these and other actions, the Pope would neuer suffer the glorious Abbot of *Clareuallis* to depart from his side, yea diuers supplications of moment were presented vnto him, and he would afterwardes propose them in the consistory, where *S. Bernard* was forced to be present, and to sit with Cardinalls themselues, vndertaking the protection of the opppressed, and shewing continually fauour to what was honest & iust: after which the Councell brake vp, and the Pope going to meet with the Emperour *Lotharius* at *Liege*, was entertayned with much solemnity and great veneration. But al that ioy was changed very soone into sadnes and bitternes: because while it seemed to *Lotharius* he had a rare oportunity without trouble and difficulty to strayten the Pope, and draw him to his designes; he began to make suite to recouer agayne the inuestitures of Bishopriques taken away heeretofore from the hands of *Henry* his Predecessour.

Innocent with his whole Court being strooken with so harsh a proposition and so vnexpected, grew pale thereat, and stood as a man wholy voyd of counsayle, as seeming to him he met in *Liege* with a greater checke, then formerly in *Rome* it selfe: when the venerable Abbot with freedome of mind and meruaylous liberty counterposed himselfe as a solid wall to the demaund & pretension of the Emperour, and so well disswaded and discoursed, as he soone drew him from that couetous and ambitious thought. An exployt, surely, of a poore Monke truely glorious, and hitherto vnheard of; howbeyt perhapps for so happy a successe, may some prayse also be giuen vnto those tymes, wherein commonly the Signors and Potentates of Christendome applyed themselues of their owne accord, or easily at least were brought to exalt & propagate the splendour and authority of the Apostolique Sea; whereas at this day (O vnworthy spectacle) it seemes as all were striuing to abate the same, to weaken, and euen to extinguish it quite. But heere let vs silence all odious and vnprofitable complaints.

Troubles arising in the Church through the faction of the Antipope, were by S. Bernard *pacifyed, in fauour of the true Pope: with the miserable end of a cheife Party of the Schisme.* Chap. 14.

INnocent being thus freed by meanes of S. *Bernard* from the anxiety he was in, and hauing taken moreouer a firme purpose and a inuiolable promise of *Lotharius* to come with his army to *Rome*, as soone as possibly he might, to quiet the tumults there, and to place him in the pontificall Throne, tooke his leaue of the Church of France, and ioyfully went towardes Italy, making his iourney through *Burgundy*, and by the way was pleased to visit, and take *Clareuallis* for his Inne, where receiuing much consolation of the voluntary pouerty and abstinence, & religious conuersation of the Monks, he prosecuted his iourney, and arriuing at *Rome*, found *Lotharius* there ready with his army, by whom being brought through force into the pallace of S. *Iohn Lateran* (being the ordinary residence in those dayes of the Popes of *Rome*) yet for all that, had he not the desired contentment to behold things pacifyed and quiet. Because the Anti-pope being obdurate in malice, and continually accompanyed with armed men, kept himselfe in hold, and allwayes well fortifyed in Towers, and more eminent places of the Citty: from whence with sudden incursions and stratagems without euer entring into open battaile, or once seeking to come to a parley with *Lotharius*, he neuer left infesting both day and night the freinds and defenders of the Pope.

Whereupon the Emperout being now growne weary of the excesse, charge, and small fruite, returned into *Almany* agayne: and

Innocent

Innocent fynding no better remedy for so great mischeifes, went out of *Rome* the second tyme, and assembling togeather another solemne Councel in the Citty of *Pisa,* among other things publiquely declared *Pierlonio* excommunicate: of which censure, the miserable man was neuer absolued. Heere also S. *Bernard,* through obedience assisted the cheife Bishop, and was not only a helper and partaker of the whole affayres and counsells therein, but may be sayd more an arbiter and vmpier in the busynes. Which affayres being once dispatched, it seemed good to the Pope to send him to *Millan,* where the poyson of the Anti-pope hauing got in, the whole people were found to be in a most inextricable trouble and discord among themselues. Nor was heere likewise the arriuall of the man of God in vayne. He soone reunited the whole Citty agayne, and reduced it to the deuotiō of the true Pope. From hence passing ouer the Alpes, he returned to *Clareuallis,* and being receaued by the Monks there with infinite iubiley, at their instance transferred he the Monastery into a more ample situation; wherof the fame being spread through out, there immediatly concurred so great almes from Princes and Prelates, and from other deuout persons, as in very short space, the building adorned withall commodityes was brought to perfection to the great increase of the diuine seruice.

At the same tyme the Country of *Gascony,* and especially the Chuch of *Bourdeaux* was fallen as it were into some afflictions and calamityes, from whence the city of *Milan* had beene deliuered but a little before. Of the e mischiefs *Gerard* Bishop of *Angolesme* was the principall occasione who with ambitious promises hauing gotten of the Antipope the, Legacy of *Gascony,* had drawne to their wicked designes not only a good part of the Cleargy, but euen many also of the Nobles, yea the Prince himselfe & Lord of those Countreys, called Count *VVilliam,* through whose forces, and other ill practises of his owne, he had brought thinges into those tearmes, as that against all those that would not consent and subscribe to the election of *Anaclete,* they openly proceeded with banishments, confiscation of goods, and with other inuentions, and examples of fierce and barbarous cruelty.

One of the chiefe of those that were persecuted, was *VVilliam* Bishop of *Poytiers,* a man well qualifyed and exceeding constant in defence of the Catholike Religion. This man with many iniuryes was expelled from his Church, and a Schismaticall and wicked one

put

put into his place. The same happened in the Diocesse of *Limoges*, where insteed of a Catholicke Prelate, was placed one Abbot *Ranulfus*, who through diuine iudgment, payed full soone the punishment of his impious boldnes, since in a plaine and euen way being fallen from his horse, he pitcht his head so shrewdly on a stone, (which lay in the way) that dashing out his braynes, he dyed suddenly.

S. Bernard *hauing excommunicated Duke* William, *he submits himselfe: with the iust iudgement of God, shewed on the schismaticall Bishop of* Angolesme. Chap. 15.

AS soone as *Gaufrid* Bishop of *Chartres* had notice of so great disorders and inconueniences, to whom the Legacy, and euen spirituall gouernement of *Gascony* was committed by *Innocent*, he was hartily sorry for it, and layng other busynes asyde, determined to succour those Churches as soone as he could, which were in extreme daunger; and for that he knew well how noble an instrument of the diuine prouidence the Abbot of *Clareuallis* was for such effect, he intreated him very earnestly to accompany and assist him in such an enterprize, And the man of God made no resistance thereunto. But only required, they might passe by the way of *Nantes*, where *Ermengarda* the Countesse had founded a Conuent of his Monks, and it was necessary for him to passe that way, to giue order (as he would quickly doe) to the affayres belonging to the sayd Monastery. *Gaufrid* and *S. Bernard* then put themselues on the way with an honourable trayne of Prelates, and other Catholiques: and the matters being dispatched which were to be done in the Citty of *Nantes*, they entred into the cõfines of *Gascony*, where *Gerard* already with consent of the Count *William*, had intruded himselfe into the administration of *Bourdeaux*, and possessed the two Churches at once, of *Bourdeaux*, and *Angolesme*.

Now the Count vnderstanding of the comming of the Bishop of *Chartres*, and of the Blessed *Bernard*, as also of other Bishops and Religious with him, to treate with him in the affaires of Ecclesiasticall matters, he thought it not fit for many respects to refuse that parly. They were all then assembled togeather by agreement in a place which was named *Pertinaco*, whereby the Seruants of God had fit oportunity to expresse their mindes to the full, and it was proposed

proposed (among other thinges) how vnseemely it was, that all France being now at the deuotion of Pope *Innocent*, *Gascony* should only diuide her selfe from the common communion and accord, & cause so great, and so miserable a separation and defection in the people of God: how he could not but know, that the Church of Christ is but one only, and whatsoeuer out of it, as found out of the Arke of *Noe*, must of necessity sincke and perish. They likewise reduced to his memory the dreadfull euent of *Dathan* & *Abiron*, who for no other cause, then for making disunion, were swallowed vp aliue in the earth. To this they added other examples of manifest vengeance and wrath of God against seditious persons and Schismatiques. Count *VVilliam* being moued with these exhortations & menaces, partly became flexible thereunto, offering himselfe to accept *Innocent* for lawfull Pope; and partly shewed himselfe obstinate and hard, being not willing by any meanes to restore the Catholike Bishops againe so violently deposed, and sent into banishment, and that not so much through occasion of the publique cause, as for some particuler grudges which he had against them.

This article was disputed a good while in two assemblyes, & the second tyme S. *Bernard* perceauing, that nothing could be concluded by way of wordes, he straight recurred to more efficacious and potent meanes, as in such occasions he was wont to do. Wherfore breaking off the discourse, he goes directly to the Altar, and prepares himselfe for Masse. Those only entred in, who were not forbid to assist at that dreadfull sacrifice, while the Count with others being seuered from the Catholike communion, stood without at the gate. When the Priest of God, hauing finished the whole consecration, and giuen the Pax to the people, not now as a man, but as one of the spirits of the heauenly squadron, holding the most holy Sacrament ouer the Paten with flaming countenance and burning eyes, not with a supplant visage, but with a power more then humane, going forth of the Temple, with a terrible voyce, thus thundred to the Count: Haue we not intreated you, and you despised vs? Besides, haue not this multitude of Gods seruants coniured thee, and yet hast thou made no account thereof? Behold the Virgins sonne is come into thy sight, being the head and Lord of the Church which thou dost persecute. Behould thy Iudge into whose handes that soule of thyne is sure to fall. And now wilt thou seeme to contemne him likewise? Wilt thou also affront his

his person, as thou hast his Seruantes?

At such a sight, and such words withal, the standers by being astonished and much amazed, began to inuocate the diuine succours: but the Count himselfe perceauing the Priest to come towardes him with the most sacred body of Christ in his hand, being ful of sudden horrour and trembling, fell flat to the ground, and presentlyraysed vp by his Guard, fell downe againe, with quiuering nerues, without speaking a word, or lifting vp the eyes: but only with deep sighes, by the mouth and beard he put forth both foame & spittle, as he had been in a Epilepsy. Then the Seruant of Christ approaching vnto him, and touching him with his foot, commanded him to stand vp, and heare the diuine Sentence, in the tenour following: Let the Bishop of *Poytiers* come hither into this place, whome thou hast banished from his Sea: Goe thy wayes to him, & with the holy kisse hauing giuen the peace, doe thou thy selfe restore him againe into his Church, & satisfying our Lord God, giue honour to the good Prelate for the iniuries & affrōts thou hast done him. Moreouer in thy whole dominion do thou then regather and recall againe into a true vnion all those who are now in discord & diuision: Submit thy selfe to Pope *Innocent*, & as the other are obedient to him, so do thou also affoard due obedience to his Holynes, elected by the diuine Maiesty.

The Count hearing this, and being conuinced and confounded, as well through the worke of the holy Ghost, as with the presence of the sacred mysteries, he neyther could, nor durst answere a word, but seeing the Bishop of *Poytiers* present, went speedily to salute him, and receaue him with imbraces and signes of loue and peace, and without delay conducted him, and restored him to his Episcopall seate againe, with the same hand wherewith he had deposed him, and thrust him out. After this the holy Abbot oftentymes looked more sweetly & more familiarly on the Count, aduising him to beware henceforth of so impious and temerarious actions, and neuer more to prouoke the anger of God. Nor were the admonitions cast into the wind, since that Prince not only abstayned for euer after from troubling the Ecclesiasticall vnion and tranquility, but euen rather in processe of tyme, arriued to the termes of most excellent vertue & Christian charity, as the things that are written of him do sufficiently declare.

In this manner were matters in *Gascony* well pacifyed, saue only

only the Bishop of *Angolesme* continued still fixed in malice. Who yet soone after, through the iust iudgement of God was found dead one morning in his bed, with a terrible swelling, without confession, and the last rites. And though for that tyme, through the help of his deerest friends he was buryed in the Church, yet after notwithstanding by order of the Bishop of *Chartres*, were his execrable bones taken out of the sepulcher, & cast forth to the fowles of the ayre, and the rauenous beasts. Nor ceased heere the punishment, for as much as euen his Nephewes also with the whole race and kindred of the sayd deceased, being afterwardes banished out their countrey, went wandring into diuers partes, infamous and miserable.

S. Bernard *is sent for to* Rome *againe by the Pope, to pacify the troubles there, with his ioyfull reception of all the Faythfull.* Chap. 16.

IN the meane tyme *S. Bernard* hauing brought so noble an enterprise to a wished end, with the exceeding consolation of his Monkes, returned to *Clareuallis*. Where while he was so farre remoued from worldly contemplation of diuine thinges, and for the help also of others, being seriously occupyed in expounding of the Canticles of *Salomon*; behold new Letters, and Couriers from the Pope, who after the Councell of *Pisa* being returned to *Rome*, was yet busying himselfe to allay the tumults, & to reduce that Church the Mother of all Churches, to some tolerable state at least: but finding euery houre new obstacles, as well from *Pierlonio* himselfe within the citty, as without from *Roger* King of *Sicily*, who for priuate designes of his, did secretly fauour the Antipope and Schisme, he resolued to call the Abbot of *Clareuallis* once more for help and counsaile, hauing knowne already by so many proofes of what auaile in such difficultyes was the valour, and prudence, and sanctity of the man of God.

He sends him Messingers then with Apostolicall breifs, and in the same matter, many Cardinalls likewise wrote vnto him, he would be pleased once more to come to the Citty of *Rome*. Wherupon S. *Bernard* though loth to leaue his study and Cell, yet preferring prompt obedience before any iust respect whatsoeuer, prepares himselfe for the iourney, and causing his Monkes to be assembled togeather from diuers partes, after he had a good while sent forth deep sighs and sobs from his breast, at last tooke his leaue of them in this manner: You see, Brethren, into how great disorders, and tribulations the Church of God is now brought. And to say truly, the followers of *Pierlonio* are now, as it were throughout, by the diuine grace pulled away from that feygned Head, and so pestiferous a sect. And euen in *Rome* also a great part of the Cleargy & Nobility in their harts do follow *Innocent*, though otherwise through feare of some more potent, and of the common people withall corrupted by the Antipope, they dare not openly shew forth what they haue more secretly layd vp in their breasts. So as the West being now subdued, we may say, there remaines but one Nation only to be vanquished and ouercome: if you make but prayer with spirituall Iubily, *Iericho* shall euen fall to the ground, and you but lifting vp your handes with *Moyses*, *Amalech* be put to flight. *Iosue* victorious in the battaile, to haue full space of a complete victory very bloudy, commands the Sunne to stay its course, and is obeyed. And you likewise seeing vs, in the heate of the battaile, cease you not to affoard vs your ayde and succour with feruent prayers: and in the meane tyme, be you firme in the way begun, and holy purposes made; and howbeit in your selues, you be not conscious of any great cryme, yet beware you esteeme not your selues in your owne iudgement to be innocent and iust, since to iustify, and iudge the cõscience, appertaines to God only: yea, by how much a man is more forward in perfection, so much the lesse presumes he of the strait & rigourous account of the diuine iustice. On the other side make you no reckoning of humane iudgements, eyther of your selues or others, but so keep you vnder the feare of God, that neither you, in iudging by him, come to dash vpon some rocke of pride or vanity. You are to attend to an exact and continuall search into your selues, and of your selues; which doing, yet shall you alwaies repute your selues to be vnprofitable seruants, as our Lord commands. It behoues me to go, whither the chiefe Pastour appoints me; and since all this trauaile is vndertaken by me, purely for the seruice and glory of the diuine goodnes, I shall not fayle to beseech the same with much confidence, to take you into his custody and protection.

After these words, being accompanyed with aboundance of teares and deuout desires of that pious congregation, he puts himselfe on the way towardes *Rome*, and being receaued, wheresoeuer

euer he passed as a man from heauen, with his arriuall he brought extraordinary ioy and comfort to the Pope, with all Catholiques. And without delay endeauouring with diligence to find out, whence so long obstinacy of the cōtrary faction proceeded, he soone came to vnderstand, how the Clergy though stung in conscience, yet through feare of loosing the benefices obteyned of the Antipope durst not forsake him: besides which, the respect they had of a vaine constancy and foolish reputation, filled their mynds with a cloud of obscurity; but for the popular sort, being likewise deceiued partly through couetousnes, and partly with a false religion, held it a great scorne, and iniquity to breake the oath of fidelity once giuen to *Pierlonio*.

S. Bernard *endeuoured in vayne to withdraw the king of* Sicily, *from the part of the Anti-pope; through whose death peace was restored to the Church agayne*. Chap. 17.

FRom these errours S. *Bernard* did endeauour, and not without fruite, to deliuer that blind people, when the Embassadours of *Roger* King of Sicily arriued at *Rome*, who with a dissembling zeale of the common good, made shew of being desirous to enforme himselfe fully of the truth, and to become arbiter of so great and pertinacious discords, though in secret (as we sayd) he were held to be a fautour of the peruerse faction, and therefore craftily required *Anaclet*, to send him *Peter* of *Pisa*, a most wise and eloquent man on his behalfe, and made instance to *Innocent* for the Abbot of *Clareuallis*, that these two as aduocates being to argue and plead in his presence, might giue him true notice of all, hoping by this meanes the lowlynes and simplicity of one poore Monke might be ouerborne and opprest, through the eloquence and cunning of that famous Doctour.

The sayd King was very potent, and was at that tyme with a puissant army in the kingdome of *Naples*, so as the Embassadours had no great difficulty to obtayne at *Rome* what they would. But through diuine disposition the matter had a farre different euent from that which the King thought of. Because that *Peter* and S. *Bernard* being arriued at his Court, after they had discoursed apart with him, and the principall Officers, there was finally deputed a certaine day to both the Procuratours togeather for publique audience

dience. Now what successe was to follow of this duell, a certaine battayle fought betweene the sayd King, and the Duke *Ranulphus*, who was a Prince, and a very vertuous Catholike, gaue no small demonstration at that tyme. S. *Bernard*, with Charity had endeuoured to hinder the sayd conflict, and to make peace betweene the two Christian armyes; and to *Roger* had manifestly threatned and foretold, that if he fought he should loose the battayle. But he finding himselfe to haue much odds, and aduantage ouer *Ranulphus* in number and forces, with haughtynes and pride contemning the aduises and protestations of the man of God, would needs by all meanes encounter and set vpon him, neer vnto the Citty of *Salerno*: where, with the astonishment of all, there suddenly entring a feare into the campe, he was vanquished by the Dukes army, routed, and put to flight. And yet notwithstanding hauing reassembled together the vnhappy remainder, and with new succours made vp a Royall army agayne; he presents himselfe in Councell and Tribunall on the day assigned for the dispute, hauing first in priuate, with great promises and large offers set the Pisan Doctour on fire to purchase himselfe hononr, in sustayning the cause of Pope *Anaclete*, and in that assembly of noble and learned men to stop the mouth of the French Abbot.

Peter then full of vayne hopes, and of high thoughts, appeared in the Court, where with much eloquence, and great memory and art, depainting forth first the fact, with handsome coulours, then alleadging and interpreting in his manner the decrees and Canons, he endeuoured to proue how the election of *Anaclete* had been most sincere and legitimate. On the contraty the holy man hauing heard the Oratour with much patience, began his discourse with great humility and modesty, and by little and little grew into so great vehemency and liberty of heauenly spirit, and with such pregnancy of reasons, and weight of Scriptures, and variety of examples, and comparisons, so defeated the foundations, and discouered the falshoods of the aduersary, as not only almost all the auditory then remained perswaded, but euen the Aduocate *Anaclete* himselfe of being conuinced with the truth, and returned to himselfe, repented he had euer vndertaken the protection of the wicked and false Pope; and being afterwards further assisted with the priuate exhortations of the seruant of Christ, fayled not to reconcile himselfe to *Innocent*.

But *Roger*, howbeit he could now pretend no ignorance, yet being

being ouerwhelmed with diuers passions, could neuer be brought to the sayd demonstrations and acts, which in a matter of so great importance ought publiquely to be done. Whence S. *Bernard* being satisfyed with his owne conscience, and remitting the rest to the diuine Iustice, returned back to *Rome*, and renewed agayne the interrupted labour of reducing the soules to the obedience of the Pope, & vnion of the Church, which till that time had been eyther seduced through opinion, or enchayned by malice. For so great a hurt and notorious a scandal, *S. Bernard* was exceedingly afflicted: but it pleased the diuine goodnes soone to deliuer him from that greife through the death of *Pierlonio:* who being seized with a pestilent malady, though he had three dayes space, to acknowledge his offences, yet obdurate & impenitent, he passed to render accompt to the eternall Iudge of his misdeed.

Being dead, his followers did presently substitute, and set vp an other Anti-pope, who yet being conscious of his owne weakenes, and the dangers which hung ouer his head; went by night to seeke out S. *Bernard*, who hauing louingly reprehended him, and made him to lay downe the ornaments vsurped, led him with his owne hands to the feete of *Innocent*, from whom benignly receiuing absolution, he was admitted into grace. And from thence began the Pope to giue dispatches without disturbance, to attend to reformation, and to take away the abuses introduced in tyme of the discord. For so ioyfull successe next vnto God, they all gaue the glory and honour to the Abbot of *Clareuallis*, & not without reason, since trauayling in the enterprise, into diuerse parts of the world, for more then seauen yeares togeather, finally in the Citty of *Rome* with the diuine helpe most happily concluded the same.

But the true disciple of Christ being not able to endure the human prayses, applauses, & the extraordinary veneration wherein he was held of the whole Court and Citty, within the tearme of fiue dayes and no more, hauing got leaue of the Pope with all importunity, he suddenly went his wayes towards *Clareuallis*. And forasmuch as his Holines required some of his Monks to inhabite neere to *Rome*, he made choyce of them, and sent them at that tyme vnder the care of one *Bernard* of *Pisa* a good Religious man, & a person much honoured in the world, who not long after, *Innocent* being dead and his successours *Celestin* and *Lucius*, was with much approbation made Pope, by a new name, called *Eugenius*, and to him

him S. *Bernard* wrote those most learned bookes *Of Consideration*. In this manner then did *S. Bernard* cary himselfe in repayring the torne coate of our Lord, and reuniting to their head the members of the Church, with most wicked example so seuered and disioyned. And no lesse vigilancy and sollicitude shewed he in oppressing and rooting out heresyes, which discouered themselues in his tyme as shall presently appeare.

S. Bernard *refutes and confounds* Abaylard, *a famous Heretike: with other heresyes arising at that tyme*. Chap. 18.

THere flourished in those dayes, with great fame of much knowledge, one *Peter Abaylard*, a person of an exceeding sharpe wit, but proud and haughty withall. This man (as it happens often with the proud) being deceaued by the Father of lying; began to disperse writings, full of new doctrine, and of pestiferous opinions: wherof S. *Bernard* hauing notice, through his accustomed goodnes and benignity, performed the office towards him of fraternall charity; endeuouring that without preiudice and infamy of the writer, those blasphemyes might be amended. And truly *Peter* himselfe for the present, through the words and Charity of the Saint shewed himselfe to be so changed and compunct, as he promised to remit al to his censure and correction. But a little after, being vanquished through the blind loue & vaine persuasion of himselfe, he not only brake his word, but euen also taking his aduantage of the tyme, he went to the Bishop of *Sans*, in whose Church was presently a great Councell assembled, and before him very insolently complayned of the Abbot of *Clareuallis*, as of a slaunderer, and detractour, and made instance, the Councell being opened he might be cyted to yield account of the obiections and calumnies giuen out against his bookes, shewing himselfe to be prompt and ready to defend in publique whatsoeuer was contayned therin. Nor did the Bishop refuse him: the tyme being come, he cites the Man of God to the Synod to iustify the sayd oppositiõs. There came likewise thither *Peter* full of pride, founding himselfe in sillogismes, and his dialectical art: but well it appeares how vayne human meanes are against the diuine power. Because, the designed day being come for discussion of those articles, S. *Bernard* in the presence of all those venerable Prelates and Doctours, produced the volumes of *Abaylard*, and with very

very strong reasons and cleere testimonyes of Scripture and holy Fathers, went manifesting and refuting one by one, all the propositions, which digressed from fayth, and the Apostolique traditions. And such was the spirit, which in that Session also spake in the mouth of S. *Bernard*, as that *Abaylard* loosing in a moment his memory and discourse, full of shame and confusion with the wonder of all was strooken dumbe. There was giuen him space notwithstanding, and election, eyther to deny those writings, or humbly to amend himselfe, or els to answere (if he coud) to the obiections made. But he very hard to repent himselfe, to gaine (as they say) more tyme, resolued with himselfe to appeale to the Sea of *Rome*, howbeit, that sacred Congregation stucke not to reproue the doctrine, though forbore the person: and a little after came the sentence of the Pope, which declaring *Abaylard* to be a manifest heretike, condemned him to silence, and his workes to the fire.

This disorder being thus remedyed, after some yeares againe there appeared another, through the fault of *VVilliam Porretta* Bishop of *Poytiers*, a man much versed in the diuine Scriptures, but temerarious & arrogant, in so much as he had the boldnes to medle with the mystery of the most holy Trinity, with many capriches & subtlityes neuer heard of before, and that with so much the greater common perill, as he was more pregnant and dexterous, to couer the senses with artificious and obscure wordes; in such sort, as the poyson had much spread it selfe before any could easily perceaue it. To these snares S. *Bernard* did most valorously oppose himselfe in the Councell of *Rhemes* celebrated by Pope *Eugenius*, wherein disputing continually for two dayes togeather against those impious dogma's, what with quoating and comparing places one with another dispersed and disioyned heere and there, with determining of equiuocations, distinguishing ambiguityes, inserting of consequēces, and deducing of corolaryes; he draue out of darknes & caues, that whole antiquity, and exposed it so to the light, as there remayned no more any place for doubt.

And because notwithstanding all this diligence, some fauourers of *VVilliam* hindred that the processe could not he finished against him; *S. Bernard* with his great authority, caused a congregation to be assembled of purpose, where with the consent and subscription of the Fathers of ten Prouinces, and of very many Bishops and Abbots, he framed, and added a new symbole, as opposite to the noueltyes of *VVilliam*, & with such means very easily wrought that these peruerse opinions should be vtterly prohibited, though no chastisement otherwise were inflicted on the Authour, since he was in the mind to enter into that dispute with this condition and ptotestation, that in case his sayinges were not excepted and approued by the sacred Councell, he would be ready without pertinacity at all, to reuoke them quite, and so being demanded if he gaue his consent to the sayd condemnation, answered: Yea, and in full session retracting and detesting the errours, he obtayned mercy.

No lesse horrible and pernicious, about the same yeares, was the impiety of a certaine Precursour of *Martin Luther*, called *Henry*, a most vile Apostata also, and euen possessed wholy with the like spirit of blasphemy; so as he doubted not to open his sacrilegious mouth against heauen, to discouer himselfe to be the enemy of Christ, to assaile, and to his power to destroy the Sacramentes and Ordinations, and the ancient rites of the ecclesiasticall Hierarchy. And as he had a good tongue, and knew well how to handle the people, and entice men to licencious liberty, he made such progresse in some parts of *Gasceny*, as now at last heere and there were Pastours to be seene without flockes, people without Priestes, Priests without due veneration, & finally Christiás without Christ himselfe. To children there was none to open the gate of holy Baptisme; the offeringes and suffrages of the dead were come into derision; the inuocation of Saintes, Excommunications, Pilgrimages, the building of Churches, the keeping of Fasts, the consecration of Oyle, and summarily all the institutes and traditions of the Apostolike discipline were had in great despite and abominatiõ.

At such vnhappy newes, a Legat being sent from *Rome* to those partes, in passing by *Clareuallis*, lead *S. Bernard* along with him, who being receaued by those people, with incredibie deuotion, he began to fructify among them, abiding particulerly in the citty of *Tholouse*: and euen in those very places, where the Minister of the Diuell had made his most abode, and done most hurt, there *S. Bernard* being assisted by the right hand of God, with Sermons, and preachinges, & with euident miracles besides, in a very few dayes made a notable purchase, in catechising the rude, confirming the doubtfull, reducing the erring, resisting & repressing the authours and instruments of the malignity: in so much as in very deed they durst not appeare before him, much lesse oppose and stand against

him.

him. *Henry* himselfe at the arriuall of the Legate, fled presently away, & after he had hid himselfe heere and there for a good while, was at last apprehended and bound, and so deliuered into the hands of the Bishop of *Tholouse*.

Thus was remedy put to the infernall pest, which otherwise had spread and dilated it selfe through all those Prouinces.

S. Bernard *settles peace and concord among Princes and States, and particularly betweene the City of* Mets, *and the neigbour Countryes.* Chap. 19.

FRom such paynes and trauailes, suffered by the Labourer of Christ, in curing and recouering of Heretikes, may euery one imagine how much care and study he employed in preseruing and helping Catholikes. So as, it would be ouer long and tedious to recount how many great Princes, and other persons of ech state & quality, he instructed with great patience in Christian vertues, and from the vanityes of the world conuerted to the loue of heauenly thinges. How many Churches at variance and discord with their Pastours, how many Chapters and Colledges not without most grieuous scandall disunited from their head and in themselues, with his sweetnes and authority hath he reduced to peace and amity? To how many afflicted and distressed soules hath he giuen counsayle, succour, and comfort? How many fires already kindled of open warre betweene mighty Lords, and neighbour-people with like zeale and prudence hath he extinguished?

To which purpose, we are by no meanes to passe ouer in silence, the accord which he concluded with so great trauaile betweene the inhabitants of *Mets* in *Lorayn*, and some Neighbour-Princes thereabouts, by whom that noble City being prouocked with some iniuryes, sent forth to reuenge the same a great number of Citizens in armes, but with ill successe, because they being taken on the sudden through the exceeding disaduantage of the place betweene the straits of *Montefred* and *Mosella* a famous riuer, & assailed by the enemy, though inferiour in number, and put to flight, were about two thousand of them lost, partly by sword, partly in the waters, partly also by their owne confusion smoothered and crushed to death in the presse. Whence the Princes on the other side being rich with the spoiles, and proud of the victory, returned home with triumph. Nor yet lost the citty a whit of courage, while they ſeemed to be vãquiſhed more through inequality of the place, then by the valour and skill of the aduerſaries.

They prepared then anew on all ſides, and doubtles there hung a cruell mortality, and a miſerable waſt ouer all thoſe countryes. When the Metropolitan Archbiſhop of *Treuers*, for the fatherly care & ſollicitude he had of his people, after he had tryed many meanes in vayne, he recurred for the laſt refuge to S. *Bernard* the great ſeruant of Chriſt; and being come to *Clareuallis* in perſon, proſtrating himſelfe very humbly at the feete not only of him, but of all the Monks alſo, beſought & coniured him withall to vouchſafe to apply ſome remedy to ſo great miſcheifs and euills, ſince for ſuch an office of piety in the world beſides, was no other perſon found to be ſufficient.

S. *Bernard* at that tyme approached neere to the end of his dayes and being ouercharged as well with old age, as infirmityes, kept his bed; yet notwithſtanding moſt benignly promiſed his help, and (as we haue ſayd aboue, is wont to happen in like caſes) his forces being ſuddainly recouered for this affayre, he went his wayes in company of the Archbiſhop. When they arriued, they found the two oppoſite armyes, who attending on the banck ſide of the riuer, were expecting an occaſion to come to a freſh battayle.

From ſo great a hazard, and ſo much hurt, ſought S. *Bernard* with prayers and exhortations to deliuer the Chriſtian armies; but wordes auayling litle, with the efficacious force of ſtupendious miracles, he filled thoſe fierce and obdurate harts with ſuch religion and horrour, as being finally mollifyed like wax, were all the controuerſyes by common conſent remitted to the arbitrement of the man of God. Whereupon he hauing brought the Procuratour of ech part vnder publique ſafe conduct, to a Parley in an iland of the Riuer, hauing now well vnderſtood the beginning of the ſtrifes betwene them, preſcribed them conditions and articles of peace, the which without rigour were accepted, and in ſigne of accord, the Procuratours gaue ech other their hands, with louing imbraces, and thoſe dark cloudes, and dreadfull lightnings of warre, were ſoone turned into a goodly calme of tranquility and concord.

And ſince we haue already often made mention of Miracles of the Saint, and ſometymes alſo according to occurrences declared ſome of them; you muſt vnderſtand, this matter affoards an infinite ſtore of narrations; foraſmuch as among other Authours the venerable

rable *Gaufrid* Monk of *Clareuallis*, who was companion & Secretary of *S. Bernard*, affirmes for certaine and notorious, that in a village of *Constance*, called *Dominge*, in one and the selfe same day, with the only imposition of hands, in presence of a multitude of spectatours, he gaue sight to eleuen blind, healed ten maymed, and eyghteene cripples: and in *Colonia Agrippina* in three dayes he reared twelue cripples, cured two lame, gaue speach to three dumbe, and hearing vnto ten deafe men. So as certaine pious men hauing begun to note downe all such wonders of his, being after oppressed with the multitude of them, and not being able with the pen, to set downe the store of effects in that kind, very soone gaue ouer the enterprize. Neuerthelesse there remaynes yet a faythfull and distinct memory of so many of them, as to goe about to set them heere downe one by one, would be a thing too prolix and far off from our scope. We therefore making choyce (according to our custome) of the more notable and of greater edification, shall reduce them to fiue heads; that is, to the grace of Cures; to power vpon deuills; to visions or apparitions; to the spirit of Prophesy; and to efficacy of prayer: which, though indeed it may be sayd, to run through all the other species, notwithstanding for that it wants not proprietyes also of its owne, we haue thought good to put it downe by it selfe a part; yea & taking beginning from thence, we shall tell what happened to *S. Bernard*, concerning one of his Monks lesse mortifyed, and lesse perfect then the rest.

The Iudgment of God, shewed vpon one, approaching to receiue the Sacrament at S. Bernards *hands, without due preparation: with diuers other Miracles besides.* Chap. 20.

THere was a Monk, that for a secret fault being suspended from the participation of the diuine misteryes, and beholding all the others to communicate on a very solemne Feast; the wretch for feare of shame and infamy, boldly also approacheth to the hands of the holy Pastour. Who not willing to expell him thence, the occasion being (as it was sayd) secret and vnknowne, turning himselfe to God from the bottome of his hart, he besought him to put remedy for such and so great a presumption, and heerewith ministred to him also the Bread of Angells, as to the rest. But behold the hoast being receiued into his mouth, he could by no meanes let it down, though he ſtriued neuer ſo much to ſwallow it. Wherupon being wholy anxious and trembling, he kept it encloſed within his palat, vntill ſuch tyme, as the Communion being paſt, with an humble ſigne he drew the man of God apart, and being proſtrate at his feet with many teares declared to him what he ſuffered, & opening his mouth ſhewed him the hoaſt it ſelſe. When the good Father reprehending him for it, as it behoued, went about to reconcile him againe, and the Penitent ſuddenly hauing receiued abſolution without any difficulty ſwallowed the hauenly food.

Another entring a freſh into *Clareuallis*, to doe penance there of his life very diſſolutly led in the world; found himſelfe to be aride and exceeding indeuout, while his companions with many teares, were cleanſing themſelues of their paſſed crymes. Being moued with this example to enter into himſelfe, and trying in vayne to imitate them, he recurred with moſt inward affect of hart to the holy Abbot: who yeilding to ſo honeſt and pious a demaund, obtayned him from heauen ſuch aboundance of teares, as from that houre the good diſciple was neuer ſeene to be with dry eyes, and cheekes not dewed with teares. The like power though in a baſer ſubiect ſhewed the ſeruant of Chriſt with his prayers, once eſpecially among other tymes, when he returned from the Citty of *Chalon*. There was then a cruell winter and moſt bitter cold, ſo as allmoſt all thoſe of his company being ſhrewdly pinched with the weather, and buſyed in defending themſelues from the ayre (as it happens in that caſe) making much haſt, heedleſly left him behind with two only in his company, one of which by chaunce alighting, his horſe brake away from him in the open fieldes (as the Camel once eſcaped from *S. Antony* in the deſerts) without commodity of catching him againe in haſt, when the venerable Abbot turning to him that was left with him, ſayd let vs pray. And kneeling on the ground ſcarcely had they finiſhed a *Pater Noſter*, when behold the vnruly beaſt, with all gentlenes returning back, ſtood quietly at the feete of S. *Bernard*, and thus he who had loſt him recouered him againe. A great expedition ſurely in regayning him ſo, but this other which followes was nothing inferiour.

S. *Bernard* in the Court of the yong King *Lewes*, negotiated a peace of moment, and ſecretly had the *Queene* his oppoſit therein, though otherwiſe openly ſhe ſhewed her ſelfe to be deuoted to him.

This

This Lady was held to be barren, hauing now liued many yeares with her husband without issue, for which she with the whole Court, was exceedingly afflicted. Now she one day with the holy Abbot lamenting her selfe for such a disaster, with this opportunity he fayld not to aduise her, that if she would be comforted in her desire, she should cease to hinder the peace in treaty: which she did, and soone after the accord very happily succeeded. Then *Lewes* through suggestion of his wife, put *S. Bernard* in mind of the promise made, and he faythfully acknowledged it; recommending the matter so feruently to God, as the *Queene* at the yeares end was brought to bed, with the extraordinasy ioy as well priuate as publique. That effect also was held very memorable, which now we shall tell.

S. *Bernard* being ready to depart the second tyme from *Rome*, procured with the Popes consent, some Relikes of Saints to carry with him; and visiting Churches for that end, he was offered by the *Grecian* Monks the entire head of S. *Cæsarius* Martyr. But he of innated modesty, hauing respect as not willing to depriue those Religious of so noble a treasure, was content to accept as a fauour one tooth only. The Monks then endeauour to pull it forth, and being not able with their hands, they brake two kniues about it, without profitting a whit: it is fit (sayd S. *Bernard*) we pray to the glorious Martyr, he would vouchsafe to doe vs this fauour: he prayed vnto him, and after reuerently approaching to the sacred skull, without any difficulty he tooke out one, with two of his fingars, which before could not be stirred with the force of instruments. I will finish this part with the first of all the miracles which S. *Bernard* wrought.

The venerable Abbot, returned from a certaine Monastery called *Three fountaynes*, which was in truth the first which he founded, & behold a Messenger in hast, comes running on the way very anxious, acquainting him how in a Castle at hand, by name *Firmita*, a kinsman of his called *Guisbert*, lay in extreme daunger of death, hauing lost his speach before he was able to be confessed. This same was a noble & rich man, & withall a great vsurper of others goods, and of a very ill conscience. Whence through the iust iudgment of God, he was ready to depart this life without the viatique. At which tydings *S. Bernard* as soone as he had commodity of a Church did celebrate the Masse, and prayd for him, and at the same hower

(as

(as was knowne afterwards in reckoning the tymes) *Guisbert* returning into himselfe, brake silence, and began with teares to bewayle his sinnes: but scarcely had *S. Bernard* finished the Masse, but he fell dumb againe, and presently thereupon arriued *S. Bernard* with *Gerard* his brother, & *Galdricus* their vncle: and much instance being made to the Abbot by the freinds and kindred that he would be pleased to pray for the sicke man; lifting vp his mind to God, and touched by the holy Ghost, he answered with all libety: you know how much euill this man hath done, and how much he holds of other mens goods; let him, and his children make restitution, and renounce the wicked customes introduced, and satisfy the wrongs he hath done to the poore, and so doing, he shall dye like a Christian.

The standers by were all astonished at these wordes, and at so firme a promise, not knowing yet the mighty power which God communicated to *S. Bernard*; and the brother and vncle were more affrighted then the rest, for feare least being deceiued by some illusion or craft of the enemy, he proceeded too farre to vndertake so much. But immediately the successe shewed the contrary: for that due restitution being made by the Gentleman and his sonnes; that tongue so tyed before began suddenly to be vnlosed, and *Guisbert* being confessed with much contrition, not ceasing euer to kisse the Abbots hands, deuoutly receiued the most holy Eucharist, and adioyning thereunto the holy Oyle, with all the other ceremonyes that belong to that tyme, the night following, with great edification of all, and all with much hope of eternall saluation, he dyed.

In testimony of the Catholike fayth, S. Bernard *cures all the sicke and infirme, with holy bread: and miraculously heales one afflicted with the Palsey*. Chap. 21.

LEt vs now come to his Cures: of which so great a number, we will take two examples only, which to euery right iudgment may suffice for a thousand. When the man of God went his wayes into the parts of *Tholouse*, to oppose (as we sayd) against the impious endeauours of *Henry* the *Apostata*, it chanced that he preached in a certayne place called *Sarlat*: the sermon being ended, those good people came and brought him bread to blesse, which he lifting vp his hand, and making the signe of the Crosse in the name of God blessing

blessing it, sayd: By this shall you see, my Children, how true are the thinges which we instruct you in, and how false those which our aduersaryes seeke to let you vnderstand; to wit, if your sicke with tasting of this bread shall be all cured or no. At his word remayned the Bishop of *Chartres* there present in some suspence, and with good zeale fearing the proposition might be too vniuersall, modifyed the same with adding to the hearers: you must vnderstand, they shall be cured in tasting therof with a good fayth; When the holy Father confiding and secure of the diuine power replyed bouldly: My Lord, I speake not in that manner, nor do not add any such condition thereunto, but I say in truth, and as the wordes sound, That as many sicke as tast therof, shallbe all freed of their infirmityes, to the end at least that hence all men, may come to acknowledge vs to be the vndoubted, and true Embassadour of the eternall God. According to the word the effect followed, as many as did eate of that bread, were all cured without exception: wherof the same flew on a sudden through all the prouince, and so great was the concourse of people desirous to see and adore the seruant of Christ, as that in his returne from *Sarlat* to *Tholouse*, to shunne the presse, and to haue passage, it behoued him to turne out of the way with all secrecy.

At the very same tyme, and in the selfe same Countryes, there lay in the Colledge of the Clarks of *S. Saturninus*, one sicke of the palsey that was incurable, called also by the name of *Bernard*, so pined therewith and worne away as he seemed daily euen ready to giue vp the Ghost. The Abbot of *Clareuallis*, was besought now by the Superiour & by the others of that place, that he would daigne to go & see that miserable wretch: The Man of God did so, he went in hast, and benignely comforted the sicke man, & hauing giuen him the wonted benediction, he went forth of the Cell with particular desire, that the diuine Clemency in confirmation of the Catholike doctrine, and confusion of the obstinate, would affoard some notable demonstration, in this mans extreme and euident perill Our Lord accepted the good will of his seruant. He had hardly departed thence, when he saw himselfe ouertaken by the Clarke; Who feeling his nerues on a sudden restored to him, and his ioynts confirmed, slipping out of his bed, followed the Abbot apace, vntill ouertaking him, at last he casts himselfe at his feet, kissing thē with much deuotion, and with affectuous thankesgiuing. Whereupon by chaunce, one of his Collegues meeting with him, who had left him the other day neere death, and with one foote in the graue, he was filled with so great horrour, as he was ready to fly from him, as it were from a Ghost; nor to stay vntil he were certifyed, & secured by diuers of the truth.

The same had happened doubtlesse to many others besides; but the fame of the admirable successe being sudenly spread, tooke away all suspition quite; and the people with the Bishop and Apostolicall Legate, came striuing to behold and enioy so new a spectacle; and after went altogeather into the Church, to giue due prayses to Almighty God, through whose power he atcheiued al these things; the Clarke himselfe going before all, singing with full voyce togeather with the rest: Who being afterwards no lesse sollicitous for his spirituall health, then glad of his corporall, not only very willingly accompanyed the Saint to *Clareuallis*, but likewise submitting himselfe to his Obedience, tooke there the habit of Cisterce, & giuing good demonstration of prudence, and of Religion; was sent backe agayne by the glorious Father into his Countrey, with title of Abbot of the Monastery called *Valdacque*. This fact likewise was very famous, and stopt the mouths of all the Heretikes thereabouts.

S. Bernard *dispossesseth two women very grieuously infected with euill Spiritts, in the Citty of Milan.* Chap. 22.

LEt vs now passe to the power and command which the Saint had ouer wicked spirits; and in this so ample a subiect, we wil set downe likewise two only examples therof, which shall serue for sufficient coniecture, and consideration of the rest, being able otherwise to say truly, that no person obsessed, or possessed through secret pacts, by those malignant and vncleane Substances, appeared euer before *S. Bernard* for help, that was not quit and deliuered from the infernall tyranny. And though on euery side, and at all tymes, there were occasions to vse the exorcismes of the Church, notwithstanding during the schisme of *Pierlonio*, it seemes the aduersary of humane kind, had through diuine iudgment obtayned particuler licence in the citty of *Milan*, to seduce (as we sayd aboue) the followers and ministers of the Antipope.

Heere then besides many other signes, wrought through diuine power by meanes of this feruent Labourer: one morning as he was celebrating

celebrating Masse in the Church of S. *Ambrose*, with an exceeding great concourse of people, there was presented to him by her parents a little Girle of tend r age, in whome the Diuell most tyrannically raigned, and he was prayed with great instance to take pitty of that vnhappy Wretch, and deliuer her from so cruell torments, which appeared by the shreekes and cryes she gaue, and in her coũtenance and in all the partes of her body, with the exceeding horrour of the standers by. The tender hart of the good Priest was moued with these prayers, and such a spectacle: who sitting neere to the Altar, while the Quire was singing, called for the Patten whereon he was to make the Offertory, and with his fingar distilling some droppes of water thereon, he gaue it to the possessed person to drinke, and immediatly the Diuell not able to suffer that sacred Antidote, and that blessed effusion, by meanes of a foule and nauseous vomit, very hastily departed, and the Girle with infinit applause and admiration of the people was restored to her Parents safe and secure.

After this, vpon another day, in the selfe same place & houre, was a gentlewoman of mature age brought thither by many with mayne strength, in whose breast now for many yeares Sathan had remayned, and so disfigured and deformed her, as that being depriued of hearing, sight, and speach, in putting forth the tongue, like an Elephants truncke seemed rather a Monster then a woman; besides which, the face all soyled and vgly to see, with a stincking breath withal, shewed well the quality of the Ghest that kept possession. Being brought then into the presence of the Saint, he knew at first sight, through diuine permission, that enemy was of an euill and cruell race, and so inueterate and settled in her, as he would not easily be got forth of so gratefull, and so ancient a dominion. Then the seruant of Christ, turning to the people which were there in great number, bad them all to pray very attentiuely, & commanded the Clerkes to hold the Woman there as firme and immoueable as they could: but she with diuellish force resisting and kicking withall, with her foot came to strike the Priest himselfe, who not regarding the same, entred into the consecration in such manner, as looke how many signes of the Crosse he made vpon the hoast, so many in turning himselfe he made vpon the possessed person, with the incredible rage, and dolour of that fiend, as by the gnashing of teeth, and sundry, and those strange, gestures and roaringes and ſtruglinges ſhe made, moſt manifeſtly appeared.

After which the *Pater noſter* being ſayd, the Prieſt began againe to giue a more ſhrewd aſſault to the aduerſary, with likewiſe holding the Paten, with the body it ſelfe of our Lord ouer the Matrons head, and ſayng: Behold heere, O wicked ſpirit, thy iudge; behold the ſupreme power, now reſiſt, if thou canſt; behold him, who being to ſuffer for our ſaluation, affirmed that then the Prince of this world was to be baniſhed hence; heere is that ſacred body, which being taken from the body of a holy Virgin, extended on the Croſſe, put into a Sepulcher, and riſen from death, aſcended triumphant into heauen. So then in the power of this Maieſty, O malignant ſpirit, I do commaund thee to leaue this his ſeruant, & not dare to moleſt her more. That ſayd, and the hoaſt (according to the vſe) being deuided into three partes, he gaue the Pax to the Monſter: which peace and health diffuſed by him, through all the congregatiõ with particuler influence did euen penetrate into the ſoule and body of the poſſeſſed, becauſe the vniuſt and pertinacious poſſeſſour went forth immediatly from her, declaring thereby of what efficacy and value the Sacrament of the Altar is, eſpecially being handled with the purity and fayth it deſerues. And it may be well belieued with good reaſon, that this Diuell with whome ſo much tampering was vſed, was one of the cheifeſt of the Helliſh ſquadrons, ſince others of a lower rancke not only vſed to fly away very fearefully from the coniurations vſed, and preſence of the ſeruant of Chriſt; but euen alſo from his Stole, though he himſelfe had byn diſtant farre off, as from an obiect intollerable to him, and a moſt grieuous puniſhment. Such, and ſo great was the ſanctity of S. *Bernard*.

S. Bernard *with prayers deliuers a ſoule from paynes: with other notable Viſions beſides, that happened to him.* Chap. 23.

IT followes now that we touch ſomething of the Viſions, in which, either he appeared to others, or others appeared to him. And be that the firſt, which himſelfe afterwards was wont to tell vnto others. A certaine Monke of a good intention but of harſh conuerſation, and leſſe compaſſionate to his neighbours then he ought to haue beene, in the Monaſtery of *Clareuallis* came to the end of his dayes, and a little after appeared to the holy Abbot with ſad countenance

tenance and a miserable habit, signifying that matters went not very well with him. Being asked the particuler, he added with dolourous accents, that he was giuen vp into the power of huge, and cruel Elfes; he had scarcely sayd so much, when being pushed with a fury, and chased away from the face of the seruant of God, he suddenly vanished. Then the Saint with a sigh and compassion as behoued, sayd, calling after him with a loud voice: I command thee in the name of the Highest, to returne to me againe within few dayes, to tell me how thou farest. From hence applying himselfe to help that soule with prayers and sacrifices, he neuer gaue ouer vntill such tyme as the dead himselfe appearing once more according to the precept giuen him, did comfort him with the happy newes of his deliuery.

S. Bernard found himselfe on a certaine tyme in a strange manner to be grieued and oppressed with an excesse of cold humors, so as a gush of fleame continually running from him, soone brought that body, nigh worne and spent already, to a manifest point of death. His children and other Deuotes doe gather about him, as it were to prepare the exequyes, and he being in excesse of mind, seemes to himselfe to be brought vnto the Tribunall of Christ, where the ancient aduersary was likwise present most outragiously accusing him. The accusation ended, and space giuen to the seruant of Christ to plead & defend himselfe, not shewing the while any signe of perturbation at all, thus answered: I do confesse I am not worthy of eternall glory, nor of the heauenly kingdome; but my Lord who possesseth the same by a double title, that is, by paternall inheritance, and painefull purchase, contenting himselfe with the one of the two titles, of the other makes a liberall guift to me, and in vertue of this deuotion, I doe with reason aspire thereunto. At which answere the enemy was confounded, that forme of iudgement and tribunall vanished, and the man of God without any more returned to himselfe againe.

Another tyme he beheld himselfe at the Sea side, expecting a ship to passe ouer, the ship came & approached to him: but being to leape therinto, it suddenly gaue backe; so did it thrice togeather, and at last leauing him on the shore, it went away without returning any more: so as S. *Bernard* easily gathered, that the houre of his passage was not yet come, notwithstanding his dolours continued so much more sharp and irksome, as he had lesse hope to be haſtily rid thereof. Now it happened in the euening, that all the other Monkes going according to cuſtome to the leſſon which was made of the collations of the ancient Fathers, the two only aſſiſtants of the Abbot remayned there, and he being continually more afflicted and tormented with the malady, bad one of them to go into the Church to pray for him. There were three Altars in the ſayd Church, one of the Bleſſed Virgin, and at the ſides thereof two others, to wit, of S. *Laurence*, and of S. *Benet*; making prayer then at all three, euen at the inſtant the glorious Mother of God accompanyed with thoſe two Saints, with ſuch a ſuauity and ſerenity, as may rather be imagined then deſcribed, entred into the ſicke mans Cell, ſo maniſeſtly, as he, with full and perfect knowledge could eaſily diſtinguiſh ech perſon. Thence ſhe approaching to him, and touching ſofty all the places of the paines, immediatly all malignant qualityes vaniſhed, that rhewmatique ſpring in the ſame moment being quite dyed vp, whence grew the dolours.

Diuers examples where S. Bernard *in his life tyme appeared to many, remayning in places farre remote.* Chap. 24.

THe foreſayd apparitions were made by others vnto *S. Bernard*: now follow ſome of him to others, of which number one was to brother *Robert* of the order of Ciſterce. This man at ſuch tyme as the venerable Abbot remayned in the Citty of *Rome*, fell deadly ſick at *Clareuallis*. In that ſtate appeared to him a yonge man like to the infirmarian, commaunding him to goe along with him, and ſo doing he was ſtreight conducted to the top of a high mountayne where Chriſt was encompaſſed round with Angells, who ſayd to his guide: looke well to that man there; and withall he put a meſſage into the ſickmans hart to deliuer the Conuent of *Clareuallis*. The morning being come, he ſits vpright in his bed, whome euery one held to be quite dead, and calling for Don *Gaudfrid* as then Priour, that was afterwardes Biſhop of *Langres*, among other things ſayd cleerely to him: Our Lord commaunds you to erect great buildings to contayne the multitude of people, which he is to ſend you, and for the ſame end giue order that our Brothers who haue care of the poſſeſſions and tenements be mindfull of modeſty, and endeauour to giue good example to ſeculars, for wo be to him, through whoſe default any one ſhould come to fall. From hence

twenty

twenty dayes being passed, the sicke man still remayning quite forsaken of the Phisitians, S. *Bernard* appeared to him in his cell in spirit, paternally visiting him, sung there the mattyns with a good number of brothers, and passed all that night with him: and the morning being come, *Robert* without any more adoe, arose vp sound, and faithfully recounted the manner how he escaped so great a daunger. A notable euent surely; but this other is no lesse worthy of memory.

The seruant of God lay sicke in *Clareuallis*, more worne and decayd with labours and infirmityes, then yeares; howbeyt he ceased not to attend to the gouernement of his Monkes, and to feed them with the word of God, and to rise likewise euery day to celebrate Masse, which he neuer omitted but of meere necessity, reuiuing his afflicted members with the feruour of spirit. In this while it so happened, that he was fayne to send some person of quality into some more remote parts of *Germany* about matters of importance. For which enterprise a German Monke was elected, by name *Henry*, whom with many other subiects the same holy Father some six yeares before in his returne from *Constance*, had induced to the diuine seruice. This man entring into so long a voyage, especially in the midst of winter, as one with reason indeed feared many disasters, and aboue all he doubted, least the venerable Abbot might come to dye in the meane tyme, and he remayne defrauded and depriued of his last benediction. But the holy Father blessing him for the present and saying: Goe thy wayes in Gods name, for thou shalt returne safe, and shalt further find me as thou desirest: and so sent him away full of comfort.

Being arriued in the territory of *Strasburge*, as he was passing ouer a riuer all frozen with Ice, his beast stumbled, and he without remedy fell quite ouer head and eares in the water. What could the poore wretch doe heere being plundged beneath in the waters, aboue couered with Ice, & both back and sides being dashed with the current? He had surely no comfort but meerely the promise of the holy Father, by whom indeed he was not deceiued. Because in that agony he saw him before him, and was so full of consolation withall, that now he felt not the violence of the riuer, nor any difficulty of breathing, nor finally feare, nor any manner of disease at all. Heereupon forsaking the beast he was on, through diuine power, he found himselfe to be pushed softly against the

streame

ſtreame without any force of his to the ſame breach, which with his fall he had made, where taking hold with his hands on the edge of the Ice he eſcaped; he returned very ſafe and ſound to *Clareuallis*, and for a full accompliſhment of ioy and contentment, had the wiſhed fauour to ſee his moſt deere and deſired Maiſter againe, to whom he ſhewed himſelfe very gratefull and obſequious, not only as long as he liued, but euen alſo after the death of S. *Bernard* in frequenting his ſepulcher, and there moſt deuoutly making his prayers.

Surely a large matter of diſcourſe for him that would compare this with other ſuch like meruayles. But let vs, leauing this artificiouſnes to Oratours, content our ſelues with the naked & ſimple truth. Beſides what hath been ſayd, it is alſo reported for a thing moſt certaine, that the vigilant Prelate in the gouernement of his order through diuers Monaſteryes very farre aſunder and remote from him, gaue many commiſſions and precepts of things, which through human meanes he could no wayes come to vnderſtand, in ſo much as though abſent in perſon, notwithſtanding (as it is read likewiſe of S. *Benet*, and other ſeruants of God) with the ſpirit he ſeemed to be preſent at the actions and proceedings of his Monkes. The which reuelations albeit Deuines aſcribe to the gift of Prophecy; yet we reſtrayning the ſenſe of this word, and applying it only vnto preſage and prediction of future things, ſhall demonſtrate, that to S. *Bernard* alſo (among other titles) this ſame ſo precious a guift was not wanting.

Some examples of the admirable guift of Prophecy, and diſcretion of ſpirit in S. Bernard. Chap. 25.

THat troupe of choice young men, which, as at the beginning we mentioned, S. *Bernard* in the citty of *Chalon* purchaſed to our Lord, were almoſt all of them in worldly wiſedome the diſciples of one *Stephen* of *Vitreo*, a perſon very famous in thoſe dayes and Country thereabouts. Now being come to *Clareuallis*, while they were yet kept by the man of God in an Inne, as it were in their firſt probation, and inſtructed by litle and litle in the rules of the diuine ſeruice, comes in *Stephen* of *Vitreo*, beyond all expectation, and demaunds to be likewiſe receiued into monaſticall diſcipline. It is the manner of thoſe who haue newly left and forſaken the ſecular

cular hopes and affayres, to feele incredible iubiley of hart, when they behold some others to doe the like; whether it be, through that new zeale which the beginning of spirit subministred to them; or els for that they take delight to haue their election approued by the iudgment and example of many: so as at the vnlooked for appearing of no ordinary subiect, but euen of their owne so famous a Maister, it cannot be told what great contentment those good Brothers tooke, and what ioy they made both priuate and publike. But the mind and iudgment of the wise Abbot in this point was so farre otherwise. Who by diuine aduise knowing suddenly the quality of his vocation, first sighing held his peace, then in the presence of all, he sayd: This man is sent hither by the euill spirit, he comes without a companion, and without a companion he shall goe his wayes againe. At this speach of his, they were astonished and amazed, who euen now could not containe themselues for ioy: neuerthelesse not to scandalize those tender plants S. *Bernard* was content to admit *Stephen* vpon tryall, especially making large promises to obserue very punctually the rule, and to execute with all promptnes whatsoeuer should be ordayned him. But it was not long ere being ouercome with the tediousnes of silence and of solitude, being affrighted with the rigour of the obseruance, & weary of the exercises, and mentall labours, he was seene to be drawne forth of the Oratory by a vile Black-more, as heeretofore was that Monke of *Cassin* From hence after some six monthes were passed, repenting himselfe of the good begun, he endeauours to attempt, and to stirre vp others, according to the manner of Religious men ill grounded & mutable; who being resolued to leaue the banners of Christ, and to returne to the leekes of Ægypt, thinke to couer their shame with the multitude of companions, and to diminish the infamy by communicating the fault: but neither he, nor he that set him a worke could effect the same. Because all those soules, through the preseruatiue infused into them by the faythfull & prudent Steward, still remayned where they were, firme and immoueable, and according to the protestation of the holy Pastour, that vnhappy *Stephen de Vitreo* did but trauaile in vayne. He entred alone, and alone went forth againe. Nor was the prophesy which followes much vnlike.

Three yong men hauing taken the habit together in *Clareuallis* one of them through instigation of the deuill, within a litle while after returned to his vomit againe. Whereupon the Fathers being so much more anxious for the health of the other two, in their presence treated of this matter with the holy Abbot. Then he looking in the face of both those Nouices, answeared plainely: This man shall neuer haue temptations of moment. That other shall haue many, but shall finally preuayle. The one then with a prosperous gale went allwayes forward in religion. The other being encompassed with tribulations, and assayled with perillous assaults, after he had wauered more then once, and turned his back as it were, yet being sustayned by diuine grace, and through the memory of the Saints promises, victorious at last was crowned with perseuerance. Of these kind of Oracles this same that followes was so much more famous, as it was published vpon a greater occasion, and in a place more notable, and with persons more illustrious.

Lewes the old King *France*, being greiuously offended with some Bishops of that kindome, suffered himselfe to be led so farre into passion, as to expell them by force from their Churches and Cittyes. Whereupon S. *Bernard*, wrote many letters to him to appease him, whose coppyes are yet kept to this day. It chaunced the while, the seruant of Christ being present, that many of those Bishops, to mollify the Kings mind prostrate with all humility on the ground, and imbracing his feet, were not all able to moue him to pitty. The man of God touched with this spectacle, and full of a holy zeale stuck not the day following to giue a free and stout reprehension to the King himselfe, for hauing in that manner despised the submission, and prayers of the Preists of Christ, and clearely made protestation of that which was reuealed to him, that night. This thy obstinacy shall cost thee the death of *Philip* thy eldest sonne, and sworne Prince. I haue seene thee, in company of thy yonger sonne fall prostrate at the feete of those Bishops, whom but yesterday thou madest so small accompt of: Collecting thence, that soone thou shalt loose *Philip*, and for substitution of this other, thou shalt sue to the Prelates, whome now thou vsest so hardly. Which was not long ere it came to passe. *Philip* dyed, and the Father being humbled, wrought by al meanes with the Ecclesiasticall state, that *Lewes* the second borne might be accepted for Successour, and be annoynted with accustomed ceremonyes. And so much may suffice of matters sayd or done by this admirable man aboue all force or terme of nature: of which subiect notwithstanding, though perhaps happs by vs too ſparingly and ſcantly handled, yet it is much harder for vs to find an end, then how to beginne.

The great Humility of S. Bernard *in auoyding worldly prayſes and honours, and the pious shift he vſed to acquite himſelfe thereof.* Chap. 26.

OF all that which we haue hitherto written, or left vntouched, two things doe moſt aſtoniſh me. The one how S. *Bernard* amidſt ſo great variety of vniuerſall buſineſſes mainetayned himſelfe allwayes as Lord and Maiſter of himſelfe, without neglecting euer the cuſtody of his hart, and continuall examine of his actions; and alwayes walking therein ſo vigilant and prouident, as if euen then from the ſhade of the Nouiciate he had paſt forth into the duſt, & ſunne of Chriſtian warfarre. The other wonder is, how among ſo many fauours from heauen, and applauſes of men, he neuer abandoned the confines and center of holy Humility; and this ſeems to me to be the principall cauſe why continually from the diuine hand were ſhowred vpon him ſo excellent guifts, and ſo rare and incōparable graces: becauſe that euen as there is nothing which of its part, more dryes vp the fountaines of the diuine benignity, then Pride and Arrogancy, in whoſe company Ingratitude goes hand in hand: ſo is there not a nearer and more apt diſpoſition, to become capable of that ſouueraigne liberality, then Modeſty, and to thinke humbly of ones ſelfe. With which as we ſee alſo in human thinges, a deuout will, and a ſolicitous care of thankeſ-giuing goe commonly vnited. The great ſeruant of God would diſcourſe highly, as well of this as of other heroicall vertues, and among other celeſtiall ſentences he was wont to vtter, he would ſay: The true humble man deſires not to be held for humble, but vile and abiect, and that ſurely with reaſon, ſince to the magnanimity of the Gentils correſponds, though in a more eminent degree, the humility of Chriſtians, whoſe property is to hide and conceale their owne prayſes as much as may be: though humility outwardly be obſcure and neglected, yet inwardly being quaint and well deckt, it ſhines ſo after, as all, eyther firſt or laſt, in fixing their eyes thereon, doe admire it without end. But how S. *Bernard* deſpiſed from the hart to be prized & reuerenced of the world, may be manifeſtly known by that which I ſhall tell.

Perceauing before hand, how they went about to make him

 a Bia Bishop, he very dexterously procured that the other Abbots of his Order, vnto whome (as hath beene sayd aboue) he had made profession to owe obedience, should obtaine an Apostolicall Breue, wherein it should be commanded them, that if it happened, the Man of God were requested of their Congregation for any Prelacy forth thereof, they might deny it by all meanes, and not seeme at the petition of others to despoyle themselues of such a guide, and so great a Pastour. And this preseruatiue of his, was very efficacious, because that S. *Bernard* indeed with full consent of all the Cittizens & Clergy was first chosen Bishop of *Langres*, then of *Chalon*, anone of *Rhemes*, and of most noble Cittyes in *France* & *Flanders*. Moreouer also in *Italy* he was required for Archbishop of *Milan*, and of *Genua*: and from all these Cõmunityes and Republiques had come Embassadours for the same effect. With whom to diminish the opinion of sanctity, which is wont to grow of such refusalls; the seruant of Christ would answere no more, but that he was not of his owne power, but subiect wholy to the Cistercian Abbots; they might goe vnto them, and he would doe what they should determine. So as remitting all to those Fathers, they without respect through common accord gaue allwayes a precise and peremtory repulse.

The great Honours affoarded S. Bernard *by all sorts of people: with the most blessed end he made.* Chap. 27.

THus had S. *Bernard* fully his intent to put off the marks and Ensignes of Honours, but yet could not with this so escape and free himselfe from the glory of them, which like the shadow (according to the ancient Prouerbe) followes men flying, & men following it, flyes. Because notwithstanding all the repugnance he could make, and felt therein, he was allwayes in such credit and reputation, as it may securely be affirmed, that the maiesty of one poore and simple Abbot seemed to paralell with the crest and altitude of any degree, title, and dignity whatsoeuer. And peraduenture when the ancient and moderne historyes be all turned ouer, there shall not be found any, who yet liuing in mortall flesh was so much reuerenced in presence, and renowned so in absence: forasmuch as not only priuate persons, or some Communityes, but euen Kings, Princes, and Popes also would recurre to him in their greatest difficultyes, to him put their strifes and controuersyes of

most

most importance to compromise: and finally from him expected nothing, but succour, iustice, and truth. Nor only from neighbour Prouinces, but euen from the furthest parts of *Europe*, as from the vtmost confines of *Spayne*, *Ireland*, *Denmarke*, *Sueueland* receiued he Letters full of reuerence, and louing presents also, in signe of memory and deuotion.

Wheresoeuer he went, he was reuerenced of all, as sent from Paradise, and with great fayth the infirme, and afflicted with any calamity soeuer, were presented to him for succour. Bread & water by him blessed, were kept as certaine Antidotes against all euills, and with great industry were sought for from the furthest parts. The shreds of his garments, or whatsoeuer he had worne, were held for holsome, and venerable Reliques. It cannot be expressed what concourse and multitudes of people there were, wheresoeuer he was, or went any way. He could not appeare in *Rome*, but the people and Court would be about him. In *Milan* and in other places of *Lombardy*, he was constrayned for the great presse to shut vp himselfe in his Inne, and to be seen by the people at grates and windowes to giue them his benediction. In passing ouer the Alpes, when he went, or returned from *Rome*, whole troupes and familyes of shepheards and swaynes, would descend from those rocks and tops of mountaynes to meete him, crying out aloud a farre off, and climbing vp the clifts, & shewing themselues on the highest places there to haue his benediction, and from thence retire them agayne vnto their Cotages, making great ioy and vaunts for being worthy to behold that angelicall face, and for their good to haue the Saints right hand extended so vpon them.

In the Citty of *Spire*, the Man of God hauing wrought some notable wonders, there came so great a multitude of people about him, as *Conrade* himselfe King of the *Romans*, was forced to lay off his robe, to carry him with his owne armes out of the Church for feare he might be oppressed and smothered in the croud. And when he passed into *Mets* for the pacification we mentioned aboue, he was one day among others enuironed by such number of people, as it was needfull for his followers to embarque him with great dexterity in the riuer of *Mosella*, and there in resemblance of the Sauiour of the world, he ceased not to exhort and assist the people. And this was the last of the publike actions of S. *Bernard*.

For that peace, being made in that Prouince, and the minds of men reconciled among themſelues, returning to *Clareuallis* he felt himſelfe to grow ſicke of a mortall infirmity, wherein yet euery day he approached to the end of this life, with ſo much ſweetenes of ſpirit, as if now already ſayling in the port, by little & little, he were taking downe the tacklings, and ſtriking ſayle. And because the Monkes with teares and prayers beſought the diuine Maieſty, not to take away their louing Maiſter from them, he tenderly complayned with them, for prolonging by that meanes his exile, and depriuing him of the deſired ſight of his Redeemer and Lord: finally he became ſo feeble of his ſtomacke, through fayling of the natural heate, as that bleſſed ſoule being not able longer to vphold and gouerne the worne and decayd members, flew directly to those manſions of heauen, whereon he had euer his eye fixed, on the 20. day of Auguſt, in the yeare of our Lord 1153. leauing by his meanes founded more then 160. Monaſteryes of the family of Ciſterce, among which, in the Conuent only of *Clareuallis* liued 770. ſeruants Chriſt. He was depoſed ſome two dayes after his departure, with a litle caſe on his breaſt, wherein the Reliques of S. *Thadeus* the Apoſtle were conteyned, being ſent him that very yeare from *Hieruſalem*, the man of God ſo ordayning it, with hope and intention to be vnited with the Apoſtle in the day of the Reſurrection.

The mourning and concourſe of people at ſo dolorous a newes; the preparation of the Exequies which followed; the interceſſions made at his shrine, were a matter more eaſy for the pious and prudent Reader to imagine, then for vs to deſcribe. The holy Father (as his moſt ſweet writinges demonſtrate) had a perpetuall and moſt ſingular deuotion towardes the moſt bleſſed Virgin, the Mother of God. In ſo much, as with reaſon it is belieued, how from that inexhauſtible treaſure of celeſtiall riches, he drew the talents and graces, which made him ſo graue and compoſed in his perſon, ſo acceptable to the diuine Maieſty, ſo helpfull, ſo wiſe, and admirable to the world.

FINIS.

THE ARGVMENT.

PHysitians say, Diseases faster grow
Whose mouing causes our complexions feed:
Whome most we trust, most dangerous is the Foe,
Spite is more fell, attyrd in freindships weed;
And sooner it procures our ouerthrow,
Then that which doth from open foes proceed.
For armes, or lawes, or friends preuent the one,
The other God himselfe must shield, or none.
More dangerous are allurements which we loue,
And with our perills do like serpents warme:
Worldly delights, neglecting those aboue,
Because most present, most our soules do harme.
This I discouering plainely, euer stroue
To free my selfe, and others from the charme
Of that Enchauntresse, whose endearments bring
Eternall griefe, paines euer torturing.

THE LIFE OF S. HVGH BISHOP OF LINCOLNE.

The Parentage and Minority of S. Hugh: *with his Vocation, & entrance into the Charter-house at* Grenoble. Chap. I.

He blessed *Hugh*, whose life and manners we take in hand, was nobly borne in the partes of *Burgundy*. His Father was a valiant Captaine, fearing God, and liuing well contented with his Pay. There was not farre off from a Castle of his, a Monastery of Canon-Regulars, to whome he was much deuoted. Heere as soone as he was depriued of his Wife, he placed his sonne, who was about some eight yeares old, that from his tender yeares, vnder spirituall standarts, he might accustome himselfe vnto Christian warfarre. S. *Hugh* was very willingly receaued by those good Fathers, and put ouer to a venerable old man, who was to instruct him in learning, and religious discipline. This man with a reuerent grauity, first premonished him to beware of licencious & light sports, and to endeauour to anticipate the benefit of tyme, with maturity of manners, and sometymes would say vnto him: *Hugh, I trayne thee vp for Christ, these sportes become thee not.* And his admonitiōs were not in vaine: the holy Ghost found such disposition in him of wit and

and purity, as he was soone replenished with wisedome, and vnderstanding, whence in short tyme, he came to be very gratefull to God, and most deare to men. In the meane while, the Knight his Father touched with heauenly inspiration, leauing the world, retyred himselfe into the same Monastery, and there attended to the seruice of God vnto his liues end.

But S. *Hugh*, as soone as he arriued to the nineteenth yeare of his age, at the instance of the whole Conuent, hauing taken all the holy Orders, except Priesthood, was applyed by Superiours to the help of a certaine Parish, in which office he bare himselfe in such sort, as euery one framed a high conceit of his sanctity & prudence: but our Lord willing to lead him to a life of stricter obseruance, & of greater merit, disposed that his Priour, going for deuotion as he was wont, to visit the *Charter house* of *Grenoble*, tooke *S. Hugh* in his company, who making his prayer, and now entred in the Cloister, in beholding partly the solitude and silence, partly also the semblance and manners of the Monkes, felt immediatly such an ardent desire of passing vnto the same Rule to enkindle in his breast, as not being able by any meanes to conceale, or endure the flame, he began presently to make secret practises, and to intreate the Fathers one by one to vouchsafe to admit him into their Institute.

His Priour was aware heereof, and calling him aside with dolourous sighes and teares in his eyes: O my beloued Sonne (sayd he) I see well now, and perceaue too well, I haue brought thee hither to my great mishap, and the irreparable losse of my whole flocke. And as soone as they returned home againe, he discouered all to the Chanons, and especially to the Father of *S. Hugh*, intreating him with great feeling, to put some remedy to so great a crosse. This being once vnderstood, they runne presently to the younge man, and more fully informed themselues of the nouelty from his owne mouth, and finally pressed him so hard, as they made him to promise with an Oath, that he would not forsake them. To which purpose, by how much *S. Hugh* condescended against his will, so much more troublesome and sharpe prickes of conscience, and scuples felt he in himself: on the one side, the touches of a more high vocation ceased not to molest him, and with reason feared he to constristate the holy Ghost, in resisting so: on the other, he was opposed against by fraternall charity, and the promise he had made with an oath. S. *Hugh* being assaulted a good while with this contrariety

trariety of spirits, aftet many prayers and considerations, was satisfyed at last, that he was not tyed to the obseruance of his word and promise, which hindered him from the gteater seruice of God, and his own perfection. With this resolution being now returned very quiet againe to the *Charter-house*, he did so efficaciously a new expresse his desires, as those Religious men admiring so constant a feruour of his, without more delay admitted him.

S. Hugh *is made Priest; then Procuratour of the house of* Grenoble; *and lastly sent for into* England *by the King there.* Chap. 2.

THe souldier of Christ, being now entred into a new warre, beginnes to feele new battailes, all which notwithstanding through diuine succour to him, were a subiect to him of glorious triumphes. Especially he was molested day and night by the concupiscible part, neuerthelesse to conserue his Virginity, he ceased not to macerate his flesh with abstinences, vigils, scourges, & other mortifications; yet sometymes refreshed with consolations againe, and with heauenly sweetnes, with which meanes, and with humble and continuall prayer, at last the fiery shafts of the enemy were quite extinguished. Amidst these labours, the tyme of Priesthood approaching, a venerable old man (whome *S. Hugh* according to the custome of the Order, through charity & submission deuoutly serued) demanded of him, if he were willing to be a Priest or no? Whereunto he hauing sincerely answered, that for his part there was nothing in the world he desired more; to whome the old man replying with a seuere countenance. And how darest thou aspire to a degree whereto none, how holy soeuer, but through constraint is worthily aduanced? At this teprehension *S. Hugh* being terrifyed falling flat on the ground, with teares in his eyes, suddenly craued pardon; at which humility of his, the Maister being tender, and touched with the spirit of prophecy sayd: Rise vp my sonne, rise vp, do not trouble thy selfe, I know very well with what effect, and with what intention thou vtteredst such wordes: and I tell thee moreouer, and affirme it to thee without all doubt, that ere long, thou shalt be a Priest, and within a certaine tyme after shalt thou be a Bishop also. At which presage of his, the good disciple ful of blushing, and confusion held his peace, and a little after being promoted to the dignity of the Altar, prepared himselfe with most exact

exact diligence to the sacrifice, and with the same continuing to celebrate, not only slackened not, but augmented his spirituall exercises, and his accustomed mortifications, whence he tooke such a weaknes of stomacke, as euer after afflicted him sorely; for the obligation of the rule, and the publike assemblies of the Quire, the Chapter, and the like, was he euer the first, endeauouring in all thinges, yea euen in the least, to edify as many, as conuersed with him.

In this manner, hauing passed in his priuate Cell, and priestly ministery about ten yeares, the principall Procuratourship of the house, being a charge amongst those Religious of no light importance, was by Superiours imposed vpon him, and which to S. *Hugh* layd open a new field to exercise his excellent Vertues in. Because he vnderstanding very well, how from his care and vigilancy, depended the Religious quiet, and contemplatiue life of the others, abandoning quite for the loue of Christ his owne consolations, attended with extraordinary care, vnto all the partes of Oeconomy, and of a perfect Steward, making prouisions in good tymes, preuenting the necessityes of euery one, and especially of the sicke; surueying, and reuiewing the accounts of the Officialls and Factours, improuing continually the possessions, defending and conseruing the rights and rents, and all in such manner, and with that maturity, as well gaue the world to vnderstand, how farre he was from all particuler interest.

For these so rare qualityes, in short tyme his fame was spread euen to the remotest Countreyes,; and *Henry* the second King of *England*, who in those dayes, was vpon founding a Monastery of *Carthusians* at *VVhitam*, & through the ill condition of that neighbourhood, could not bring the matter to any good passe: after he had with small fruite applyed two Priours of the Order vpon the enterprise; being finally moued with the constant relation of the worth, and sanctity of S. *Hugh*, not fayled to send in post, to that end, very honourable personages to the aforesayd *Charterhouse* of *Grenoble* (and among them *Reginald* Bishop of *Bath*) to require him for this office. To which purpose, those Fathers being assembled togeather, there followed an earnest dispute among them, while to some it seemed not iust or reasonable, for any ones sake whosoeuer to depriue their owne house of so firme a propp, & others iudging on the contrary, & with liuely reasons demonstrating, how it became not Christian charity, and the Euangelicall profession, to haue the eye fixed vpon the commodityes only of one family, and to keep that vertue enclosed in so little a space, which might be extended for the benefit and saluation of foraine nations, with the great augmentation of the diuine glory.

Among such contentions had for a while, to and fro, of no light moment, that Part preuayled at last which would the publike and vniuersall, should be preferred before the priuate; and that they ought not, with so harsh a repulse prouoke the displeasure of so great a King. In this manner S. *Hugh*, being otherwise an enemy to Prelacy, and who protested himselfe to be wholy insufficient for such a charge, was by Superiours constrained to take it vpon him: and not without much teares, departing from his deere Cloister in company of the sayd Embassadours, he arriued safe & sound at the coasts of *England*. From thence without going to the Court, trauayling by the neerest way to *VVhittam*, the first thing he endeauoured to do, was with a cheerfull countenance, and with fit exhortations to comfort those few afflicted Monks whom he found there: and being afterwards sent for by letters vnto the Kings presence, through diuine fauour he had such grace in the eyes of that Maiesty, as that after diuers discourses thereof, he brought away both for the present and future necessities, a very large prouision of all thinges; and besides could tell how to vse such dexterity with that people, and so to purchase their loue and good opinion, as that from harsh, contumacious, and froward, in short tyme they became very gentle, obedient and tractable: whereby very easily both the Church became more enriched through diuine offices, & the house to be the better accommodated for the sustentation of the Monkes, and for the splendour and ornament of the place the fabricque to be finished; while S. *Hugh* laboured thereat with his owne handes, and carrying, for example and publique edification, stones & morter on his shoulders: in so much, as many seculars being inuited, partly by his sweet and sanctifyed manners, & partly also through a gust of a retyred life, and of the commodity of the buildings there, abandoning the cares of the world, and renouncing the proper liberty, came thither to consecrate themselues vnto God, & by vow to oblige themselues vnto monasticall discipline.

The King with his whole army at Sea, is deliuered, by commending himselfe to the prayers of S. Hugh. Chap. 3.

THe king of *England*, tooke no small cōfort at these proceedings, he reioyced much, in that he was not deceiued awhit in his iudgment in the election of such a one. And (as he was a wise and prudent King) hauing very often familiar and long discourses with the Priour, the more he diued into him, the greater esteeme made he, not only of his prudence, but of his piety and perfection also, holding it a great happynes, to haue such a man in his Kingdome, and placing a good part of his hopes in his deuout intercessions & suffrages: as among other tymes, he cleerely shewed, when as returning with a great Army, from the enterprize of *France*, he was suddenly assayled with so cruell a tempest, as the fury of the winds illuding all the art of the Mariners; they all betooke themselues, as many as were with him, according to custome, to vowes and prayers; and the King notwithstanding perceauing the waues to grow more rough, brake forth at last into these words: O if my good *Hugh* of the *Charter-howse*, were now aware of this, & would make feruēt prayer for vs, as he was wont, the diuine mercy would not be so slow to our succour. And a little after, with other sighes he gaue not ouer, but added: O blessed God, whom the Priour of *VVhittam* truly serues, vouchsafe through the merits and intercession of thy faythfull seruant, with the eye of pitty, to reguard our distresse, and afflictions. And behold the inuocation was scarcely finished, but a calme began, in such sort, as the whole company, with as many as sayled with them, yeilding thanks without end to the diuine Clemency, very happily arriued at the wished port.

The newes whereof on a sudden flew into all parts, and the name of S. *Hugh*, grew to be in so great veneration, as *Henry* had not in his whole kingdome besides, a man he esteemed more, nor in whom he reposed more confidence: and the number of those Religious went multiplying euery day more & more; in the manage & instruction of whom, S. *Hugh* shewed very well, how excellent a guift he had in gouernement. Because, that pursuing his ancient thoughts, the first thing he endeuoured effectually, was that men might know cleerely, that nothing was more deer vnto him, then the quiet and consolation of euery one. To works (as need was) he adioyned words, and efficacious and discreet aduises. But aboue all things he pressed them, through the example of his owne manners; being so habituated in treating with God, as his familiars also in his sleep, should heare him vnawares to pray, & say his Psalter. He was besides, as much as publike occasions permitted him, much giuen to sacred reading, and was wont to say, how the diuines Scriptures to all Religious, and especiall to such as leade a more solitary life, are delights in peace, armes in warre, foode in tyme of famine, and a medecine in infirmity: so as, when according to the custome of the Order, he eate alone, he had allwayes, on a litle table, the scripture open before him, or some holy Doctour: though otherwise, he was so diligent in the custody of his senses, as when he happened on holy dayes to take his refection with the rest, he would neuer hold his eyes from the table cloth, his eares from the pulpit, and his mind from God. This holy man was exceeding carefull, that, for his sake or any of his, no person should receiue any agreiuance and scandall.

And to this purpose, we may not conceale, how the King hauing taken from a certaine rich Monastery, and well furnished with bookes, the new and old Testament, written by those Regulars, with great labour and diligence, and bestowed it on the Fathers of *VVhittam*, as yet not well prouided of such necessaryes: as soone as S. *Hugh* had knowledge therof, from one of the aforesaid Monastery, he answeared with a sad cheer: thus stands the matter then. The King would haue depriued your Church of your labours and trauayles, so fruitefull, to accommodate and enrich vs by such meanes. We cry you mercy with all our harts for the losse you haue sustayned for our sake, though in truth til now we were neuer made acquainted therewith. Take yee then the Booke agayne, and if your Fathers will not receaue it, I will without more ado, restore it my selfe, to the party that caused it to be brought hither. And further, if they be willing to accept the same, I will cause the matter to be kept secret by all meanes. This modesty of his pleased them exceedingly, and as they remayned much edifyed thereat, so they came to contract a great frendship with the Family of *VVhittam*.

S. Hugh

S. Hugh *is made Bishop of* Lincolne, *and how stoutly he demeanes himself in his Pastorall charge.* Chap. 4.

NOw approached the tyme, destined by the diuine prouidence, for the exaltation of his faythfull and wise seruant. The Sea of the Citty of *Lincolne* had now beene vacant for some eighteene years, and those of the Chapter being moued at the losse which the flocke suffered so without a Pastour, laying finally aside the strifes and contentions risen amongst them, resolued with the approbation of the Metropolitan of *Canterbury*, to goe a sufficient number of them to the Court of the King, vnder whose protection, and superintendency, the election being celebrated with wonted ceremonyes, they agreed vpon the person of the Priour of *VVhittam*: whereat *Henry*, being extraordinarily ioyfull, sent the newes thereof presently to *S. Hugh*, as he thought most ioyfull tydinges. There also arriued together, the letters and messages of the Archbishop himselfe, who congratulating with him for such a dignity, did liuely exhort him not to resist so honourable a iudgment of the Canons, and so manifest a signe of the diuine will. His freinds likewise generally encouraged him to it, with reasons and importunityes.

But *S. Hugh*, now experienced in the chast gouernment of soules, weighed all things with a more iust ballance, and who knew very well, how great temerity it was, in a stormy sea to take voluntarily in charge with so much hazard a barke repleate with the bloud of Christ, with might and mayne endeuoured to withdraw himselfe from the enterprise: alleadging besides his owne insufficiency, the election to be likewise inualid, as well for being prosecuted forth of the Diocesse, and practized with the fauour and authority of the King & Archbishop, as for that the voyce of the Priour of the great *Charterhouse* was not concurring thereto, without whose approbation, he could by no meanes accept such a charge.

These and many other things of like tenour, the man of God replyed: hoping the Electours eyther mooued through equity, or disdaining the repulse, would easily turne the designes to the other part. But through diuine dispensation he remayned much deceiued of his conceit. Because the same humility wherewith he thought himselfe vnworthy of such a manage, & the earnest instance which

he

he made, that it might be transferred vpon some other, inflamed the Chanons to extoll and aduance so great submission, & so great vertue; so as to take away from *S. Hugh* all excuses and occasions, being a new assembled togeather in the same Citty & Cathedrall Church of *Lincolne*, with like consent they ratifyed the decree as at first, and besides sending for that purpose vnto the great Charter-house of persons of quality, they brought backe in ample forme, not leaue only, but so expresse command, as for S. *Hugh* there was no euasion.

With this dispach went all the fauourers of that creation very glad and triumphant to the Monastery, and taking the sad and sorrowfull Priour from his Cell, they lead him with great ioy to the Cathedrall Church. In which act appeared very well how great a friend he was of pouerty both of body and mind, because being not able to hinder so noble a concourse, which came to accompany him, reteyning at least in himselfe, the desired lowlynes, he would neuer permit some few cōmodityes of his, for his owne vse, should be carryed by any: but rather putting them behind him on the cropper of his horse would needes conuay them himselfe publiquely to the Bishops lodgings, and by no meanes before consecration; he would admit eyther title of Prelacy, Pontifical robes, or attendance of seruants.

Finally being afterwards annoynted, and placed with solemne rites, in the Pontifical Throne, he felt himselfe as a choyce and disposed vessell, to be replenished with so great a plenty of celestiall gifts, and particularly of the spirit of fortitude, as from that tyme he made a purpose to spare no labours, to shun no perills, nor yeild to intreaty or threats, where the diuine glory, or good of the Church might take place: and for this very respect, he liked not those rich Presents, with the fresh gratulations sent vnto him from the king; and so it was necessary for him to make such a resolution. Because there passed not many dayes, but that the King Raungers of the forest (so they call in those countryes, the ouerseers of the forests and of the chaces of the kings) relying on their fauour in Court, and on the custome now vsurpt a good while, vpon light occasion layd hands vpon a Clerk, and condemned him in a good summe of mony. Whereof S. *Hugh* being fully enformed, with reason (sayd he) these people are called Foresters, as it were standing forth of the kingdome of God. Heerupon calling to a Consult, certaine excellent Doctours, and such as feared God (whereof, from the tyme he was

was first assumpted to the Chayre, he had made prouision with good care) and by the common opinion of all, hauing giuen due premonishments already to the delinquents, he courageously proceeded to excommunicate the head of that company.

K. *Henry* tooke this act of the Bishop very bitterly; but yet to satisfy himselfe better of his disposition, dissembling the matter for the present, he requested of him by messengers and letters in post, a Prebendary then vacant in the Diocesse of *Lincolne*, in fauour of a certaine Courtier; while some freinds of S. *Hugh* laboured it much, that he might take occasion thereby to mittigate the anger of the King, & to returne into grace with him: but the souldiour of Christ, hauing read the petition, sayd: These vacant places are not to be conferred vpon Courtiers, but to Ecclesiastikes rather. The Kings Maiesty wants not meanes to reward his seruants: nor is it iust, to depriue such of their rents, who serue the king of heauen, to bestow them on those, who wayte vpon the Princes of the earth. With this answere he dispacht away the messengers of K. *Henry*, & being intreated at least graciously to absolue the Raunger, he could not be brought therunto.

Vnto such, and so open contradictions of the Bishop, the King being accustomed to be obeyed as a becke, brake his patience at last, and sending for him, after the vpbreading him with so many graces & fauours don him, he cōplayned bitterly for so hard a measure from him. And the venerable Bishop, being not troubled any thing thereat, with a graue and sweet countenance withall, demonstrated to him, how in the whole affayre he had regard, next to the seruice of God, principally to his eternall saluation: which incurred manifest danger, when through his occasion, eyther the oppressours of the Church remayned vnpunished, or sacred benefices were rashly bestowed. And briefly S. *Hugh* could so wisely iustify that fact, as the King being a man otherwise discreet, and a freind of iustice, remayned satisfyed, and restored the blessed man into his ancient freindship agayne. After this the Raunger shewing himselfe sorowfull and penitent for his ill deportments; S. *Hugh* gaue him, not without the publike chasticement of the verge appointed by the *Canons*, the desired absolution, and further assisted him in spirit: in so much as of a troublesome aduersary, he had him euer after a freind much deuoted to him, and in busynesses occurring a most faythfull sollicitour. With the same courage of mind S.

Hugh endeuoured, to extirpate many inueterated abuses from that administration; among which was that very markable which we shall speake of in the next Chapter.

S. Hugh *reformes certaine abuses*: K. Henry *dyes the while, and* K. Richard *succeeds, which some passages besides*. Chap. 5.

THe Clergy was wont euery yeare, to present the King with a precious Mantle, at the charge of the people; and the care of going heere and there, to make the collection, the Clergy had taken vpon them, reteyning afterwards, and diuiding among them as it were for their paynes, those moneyes which amounted ouer and aboue: and that to the extreame disgrace of their Order, and most greiuous scandall of the people. The new Pastour, could by no meanes endure this custome amongst them: and hauing efficaciously made the Preists, to acknowledge the shame, and impiety thereof, he likewise obteyned from K. *Henry* authentique Patents, wherein he renounced such a guift, and ech right, which vpon any apparence he might pretend thereunto. The Magistrats & Ecclesiasticall Iudges, in criminall causes touching that Court, were wont to condemne the delinquents for the most part, in mony: whence it followed the rich not caring much for such penaltyes, perseuered most impudently in their sinnes. S. *Hugh* therefore opposed himselfe maynly against this inconuenience, by changing the losse of mony into corporall afflictions, or into publike notes of infamy, or els when the case required it, also into excommunications; the which thunder as we shall presently see, came neuer from the hands of the Saint without admirable effects.

K. *Henry* in the meane while, after diuerse trauailes of mind & body, departed this life, with much hope and many signes of predestination. There succeeded him *Richard* his sonne: who by how much he shewed himselfe lesse propitious and freindly to *S. Hugh*, so much greater and more ample a field he gaue him of exercise, & of glory. This King imitating his *Auncestours*, passed ouer to the warre in *Fraunce*, and in processe of tyme, as it happens, the Paymaisters of the Campe being out of money, he resolued to send back the Archbishop of *Canterbury* whom he had then with him, into *England*; that by the fauour and help of the Clergy, he might seeke to get from his subiects the greatest quantity of mony he could posſibly procure. The Archbiſhop obeyed, and calling an aſſembly in a fit place, he found none that openly durſt oppoſe, but the Biſhop of *Lincolne*: who deteſting the impious contentions betweene Chriſtian Princes (eſpecially at ſuch tymes, when the warres of *Egypt*, and enterpriſe of the *Holy-land*, waxed hoate) demonſtrated with ſolid grounds, how vnlawfull it was, without very iuſt and vrgent neceſſity, to ſquize the ſubſtance of the poore afflicted ſubiects.

To this voyce of his, conſented, though but timerouſly, another Biſhop only, whoſe name is not expreſſed. For all the reſt, they ſtriued to pleaſe the King. Who being certifyed by the Archbiſhop of what happened in the ſaid Congregation, was ſo troubled thereat, and enflamed with rage, as that ſuddenly he gaue order to a principall Officer, as he loued his life, with a ſufficient preparation without delay, he ſhould vtterly ruyne and deſtroy both thoſe obſtinate and rebellious Biſhops. The Cōmiſſary was not ſlack in obeying. But the matter ſucceeded not ſo happily with one, as with the other. Becauſe the timerous Biſhop, at the firſt noyſe of the Court, abandoned his Church, and the ſacred goods without reſiſtance were all confiſcated. But the bleſſed Biſhop, vpon the approach of that profane and rauenous troupe, calling on the diuine aſſiſtance, prepares for Excommunication, & cauſed all the Pariſhes to ring their bells, with ſuch confidence, and with ſuch a preſence of vndaunted courage, as the Courtiers who held him a Saint and fauourer of God, being terrifyed and confounded, returned backe without doing any thing. And ſome few dayes after being paſſed ouer, the other Paſtour at the interceſſion of his friends, was recalled from baniſhment, and the King by this tyme being returned from *France*, he went very ſuppliantly to meet with him, and with teares to aske him pardon, and with humble promiſes not to contradict any more. But the diſpoſition of S. *Hugh* was quite otherwiſe, as ſhall appeare in the next Chapter.

How S. Hugh *admoniſhed* King Richard *of his abuſes: and what effect the admoniſhment tooke.* Chap. 6.

S. *Hugh* putting his confidence in iuſtice & reaſon, remayned ſtill immoueable in his reſidence, the Court being eſpecially at that tyme farre off: but afterwardes bethinking himſelfe of the precipitous nature of the Prince, and the ill offices he had done already, and which anew were like to be done by him, and how at last, the fury would come to fall vpon his poore people; laying aside all feare, and all respect of death or affronts, he determined to goe in person to the Kinges presence, and to pacify him by those meanes which were conuenient to the diuine glory, and quality of the tymes. With the ayde of prayer then, putting himselfe on the way, he was no sooner come to his iourneyes end, but some of his principall friendes, and zealous of the honour of God, came to meet him, intreating him most earnestly, and coniuring him withall, that by no meanes he would appeare before the King, nor giue him occasion to renew in him, the slaughters, and cruelties heeretofore happening, with so much infamy of the Kingdome in the person of the glorious Martyr S. *Thomas* Archbishop of *Canterbury*.

These and other thinges to this purpose, with much affect represented those vertuous men, wherewith while S. *Hugh* was nothing moued, one that loued him more tenderly then the rest, neuer left intreating him, he would be pleased at least, to stay vntill such tyme, as he might preoccupy the mind of K. *Richard*, with fit offices, and so dispose him with prayers & reasons, as he might not looke awry vpon him. To such an offer, the Bishop answered, full of vndaunted courage and fraternall charity: Would you then, to saue my selfe, I put thee and all thy family in hazard? And what greater gust could my enemyes haue, then to take occasion to calumniate thee as partiall to me, and enemy of the Crowne? That sayd, without more ado, he passed into the Kinges lodgings, and finding him by chance hearing of Masse, in his Chappell, he approached to him with a cheerfull countenance, and demanded of him (according to the vse of that Country) the holy kisse of vnion and loue. And the King disdainefully answering: No, thou deseruest it not; yea but I doe, answered S. *Hugh*, and that especially after so long a iourney: and withall taking him pleasantly by the Robe, endeauours to hang on him with so great ingenuity, as K. *Richard* changing his bitternes to a sweet countenance, was won at last, and kissed him.

At such a sight, the Prelates and Barons standing by, remayned astonished. And so the Masse went on: and in the meane tyme the seruant of Christ, without putting himselfe into the company, or taking vp a seate among the Bishops, most humbly betooke himselfe to a meaner place. The King noted the act, and arguing from

from thence, how S. *Hugh* was as litle in his owne eyes, as magnanimous and great in common causes, began to hold him in so great veneration, as that euen at that tyme, the Deacon coming according to custome, to present him the *Pax*, he commaunded in signe of reuerence, it should be giuen first to the Lord of *Lincolne*.

The Masse being ended, S. *Hugh* resoluing to giue K. *Richard* a fraternall admonishment, for the more decency, and liberty, he sweetely tooke him behind the Aultar, and there being both set downe together, with a gratefull aspect began to examine him, saying: how is it with your conscience? Now you are of our parish, and we are to render a streight accompt of you before the dreadful Iudge. My conscience (answeared the King) reprehends me of nothing, saue only, that I cannot beare any good will to such as stand but ill affected to my Kingdome. Then S. *Hugh* with a great vehemency sayd: what is this thou sayst? And is it not true, that thou goest euery day without feare imposing new greiuances vpon thy people, oppressing the poore, afflicting the innocent? And moreouer the publique fame runs, that thou keepest no fayth, nor the Sacrement of Matrimony. And thinkest thou these to be matters of no moment? At this voyce of the Bishop, or rather of the Holy Ghost which spake in him, the King being terrifyed, was fayne to hold his peace. Whereupon with like fortitude, S. *Hugh* reproued him of diuers faults, which the King endeuoured partly with excuses to purge himselfe, and partly craued pardon, with purpose of amending his life.

S. *Hugh* hauing giuen this admonition in secret, gaue after accompt in publike, of the iust motiues that moued him to take, in matter of new tributes, the protection of the multitude committed to him, and spake in such manner, as not only the rest of the auditory, but euen *Richard* himselfe remayned satisfyed, holding it for a great happynes, that the tax went no further. S. *Hugh* taking afterwards, a courteous leaue, returned back vndaunted to his flock: and *Richard* turning himselfe to his followers, sayd, that if al the Bishops were like to this mã, no power could preuayle any wayes vpõ them: to which opinion they all agreed with one consent, because S. *Hugh* through his frequent victoryes so got, was by a surname called, *The mallet of the King*. And if for the seruice of God, he shewed himselfe so couragious and bold, it may easily be gathered, how immoueable he remayned in like encounters with other persons of

 meaner

meaner ranck, and with the ordinary sort, as appeares in the next Chapter.

How stoutly S. Hugh *carryed himselfe to all sortes, to the greater honour of God.* Chap. 7.

IT chaunced to S. *Hugh* more then once, in sundry places, to be barehead, among speares and naked swordes, reprehending the armed themselues, like a Lyon, of their impious and wicked indeauours, they remayning amazed and astonished the while at so great a freedome. Vpon a tyme he met on the way with a company of Sergeants & catchpoles leading a malefactour to death: & being moued with the prayers of the vnhappy wretch, who in that necessity most earnestly recommended himselfe vnto him, he gaue order presently to the Ministers to vnloose him, alleadging that where the Bishop was present with the faythfull people, there was the Church, & that the liuing stones deserued no lesse priuiledge and exemption then the dead. The enterprise was not in vaine, though otherwise perhaps more worthy of applause, then imitation and practise. The officers being moued at the maiesty of the Prelate, making some protestations only for feare of the King, left the guilty wholy free, and infinitly obliged to him, who beyond all hope had giuen him his life.

Of this so great a hart, and couragious constancy of *S. Hugh*, if one seeke into the causes, besides the vnction of the holy Ghost, there may many be brought. And among these the naturall generosity of the man, inflamed also from tyme to tyme with the instigations of his old Father by vs named aboue, and the two naturall brothers of his, braue Souldiours, and valiant Champions of the Catholike Church. These men would come sometymes to visit him at *Lincolne*, and by letters as occasion serued, would exhort him allwayes to stand firme in his purpose, and not to yield awhit, eyther to the headlong multitude, or furious Tyrants. And gaue him moreouer to vnderstand, they had rather see him dead, then for any terrour to commit any thing vnworthy the Episcopall degree, and honour of his family. Besides which, S. *Hugh* helped himselfe much, with his frequent reading the liues of the glorious Martyrs, and Confessours of Christ, especially of such as for defence of the diuine worship, & of the sacred Constitutions, haue promptly exposed

exposed themselues to all punishments. And then from his dayly sacrifices the while what comfort he felt, is a thing not easily to told: in which mistery he was so diligent, as he preferred it before all other thinges whatsoeuer; and was so grounded in that verity, as it seemed in some manner he had some cleare euidence therof, as appeared in a case which followes, in a village of those parts.

Where a certaine Preist, of very dissolute manners, hauing no feare at all to celebrate that diuine Sacrament, and to handle with his impure handes the dreadfull King of Maiesty, as he came to the breaking of the consecrated Hoast, saw manifestly the most holy bloud to proceed, and fall from thence: at which sight being affrighted & contrite, he tooke dexterously the precious liquour in the Chalice, and changing his manners, gaue himselfe to sharp penance in so much as euery one was astonished. By this occasion the miracle came to be diuulged, & the Preist himselfe to giue God the glory, gaue publique account thereof, in shewing also the bloud it selfe to euery one that was desirous to be better satisfyed in the matter. It happened, that the Bishop of *Lincolne*, for certaine affaires of his, was to passe that way, and with that occasion it pleased him to vnderstand and confer some spirituall thinges with the Priest, the fame of whose strange mutation and singular austerity of life, ran euery where: falling then into diuers discourses with him, among the rest the good man gaue account and information to the Bishop of the beginning of his conuersion, intreating him withall he would be pleased to contemplate with his eyes that venerable relique it selfe; which S. *Hugh* not only refused to do, alleadging the certainty therof had need of no such probation, but euen reprehended such of his family, accepting the inuitation, of little fayth, & too much curiosity. And it is a thing well knowne, that in recompence as it were of so great a stedfastnes, the Sauiour himselfe, in the sight of some Religious men appeared many tymes in the Hoast in forme of a most beautifull child vnto S. *Hugh* himselfe, while he celebrated the Masse.

Besides this, the Blessed Man tooke great spirituall forces, from the liuely and more then human conceits of the holy Psalter: wherein what gust he receaued, and how obseruant he was of the tymes and determinate houres of the diuine Office, may in part be gathered at least, by that which we shall speake in the next Chapter.

The

The good successe S. Hugh *had, through his deuotion to the Canonicall Houres: and how dreadfull his Ecclesiasticall Censures were.* Chap. 8.

VVHile S. *Hugh*, was trauayling on the way, vpon publike affayres, with some Prelates and other Ecclesiasticall persons; he chaunced to arriue vnlooked for, at a certaine place much infested with men distracted of their witts. His companions being aduertised of the daunger, full of dread, consulted with themselues what to doe, and resolued at last, to passe those wayes by darke, & with all the secrecy that might be. With this resolution remayning in the Iune, about midnight they rise, and their horses being made ready in hast, they go to the Bishop of *Lincolnes* chamber, who was now euen ready to say his Mattyns, and with much instance, they sollicite him, to prouide for his safety by the opportunity of the darkenes. And he answered, What should I goe hence without saying of my Mattins? Then they replyed, there would be tyme inough for that afterwards, since the present necessity affoarded no delay, and they had need to go away suddenly, if they would not be taken by those Beadlams.

Then *S. Hugh* with his Breuiary in hand, Stay they that will stay, and feare that list to feare, sayd he, for my part I am determined not to go forth, till first I haue payd this duty. And so performed it, saying his Office with ease and attention: And after that, with his family, getting commodiously on horsebacke, he met with no misaduenture at all: whereas those wary and cautious people in taxing him for superstitious and improuident, so preferring human respects before the diuine glory fell (as it often falls out) into the same net they so carefully shunned.

To all these so efficacious and potent helpes, he added another surely of an excellent vertue. He retired himselfe at least once a yeare, to the Cloyster of his beloued *VVhittam*, & there vnder the common Rule, without any other difference, but only the sacred ring on his fingar, he attended all the vacant tyme he had, as from a high tower, to suruay the vanities of human thinges, the shortnes of life, and immense greatnes of eternall Beatitude. And casting his eyes withall vpon the infinite difficulties of spirituall gouernement, and the horrible precipice wheron all Prelacyes stand; and as at the beginning he had auoyded with all his power the Episcopal digni-

ty

ty, so many tymes afterwards he sent letters and agents to his Holynes, beseeching him with much importunity to be disburdened of the administration, and restored to his Order, from whence he was taken against his will.

But since his supplications were not only not heard, but euen the Sollicitours themselues came backe sometymes very shrewdly checkt from the Vicar of Christ, & rather other cares for the vniuersall good imposed vpon him; *S. Hugh* being enforced to obey, prepared himselfe for new labours, and new battells, nourishing still with the foresayd meanes in his breast, a burning desire of satisfying the highest in all things. Whereby in difficult enterprizes, were equally matched in him a security of mind, and such a confidence, as that amidst the greatest difficultyes of all, yea euen the daungers of death it selfe, neyther lost he the peace of his soule, nor the conuenient repose of his body. So as being one night for some graue accidents transported in imagination, into diuerse thoughts, which tormented him without fruite, after he had thus roued with his fantasy a pretty while, at last was aware thereof, and smiting his breast with a deepe sigh, be began to reprehend himselfe sharply, for not suddenly remitting all anxieties vnto the diuine Prouidence, but being troubled and grieued for thinges so happening, as if the direction of them had depended on his owne knowledge and care: and scarcely was the day come, but calling for a Confessour, he declared that sinne with much contrition, and surely not without reason, especially the hand of the Highest so concurring with him, by wonderfull effects, as well in other actions as particularly in Censures: Wherof some euents which happened in this matter, will purchase a firme beliefe. Certaine rebellious and contumacious fellowes being by him giuen ouer vnto the power of the Diuell, vanished immediatly, nor were euer seene more.

A Souldier, who at the instigation of his wife, vniustly vsurped the goods of another, and being often reprehended for it by the holy Bishop, with diuers pretexts and falshoods still couered the same: this man being excommunicated by him one day, was on the next night following strangled by the infernall enemy: and yet for all that, another pursuing the same vniust suite, being gone to bed well fed & merry, continuing sleep with death, payd the fee of his iniquity.

A Deacon for hauing calumniated others of high treason against his Maiesty, being worthily condemned by the Bishop, by diuers colours and policyes vsed, obteyned the absolution therof from the *Metropolitan* himselfe, which *S. Hugh* knowing to be vayne, and surreptitious, stucke not to renew the Censure; and to the end it might appeare which of the two, was the true sentence, it pleased God, that the Deacon within few dayes after, most miserably ended his dayes. A certayne yong woman, who in presence, & agaynst the reprehension of the Bishop ceased not to spit in her husbands face, being stifled by a Diuell, very sudenly expired.

A vertuous Clerke, through the faction of the more potent, being quite depriued of his right which he had in a Church, after he had without any profit at all, gone to suite a good while both at home in his Country, and at Rome abroad, and consumed his substance therein, tooke finally resolution to recurre to the Bishop of *Lincolne*: who being well informed of the cause, and mooued to pitty vpon the trauayles of the suppliant, resolued through diuine instinct, no doubt, to thunder against all those wicked & sacrilegious men, although they were not of his owne iurisdiction. An admirable thing. The bolt was no sooner shot, but some of the impious company, hauing lost their senses became furious; others ended their life vnprouided; others lost their eyes with excessiue torments; and finally, the Heauenly vengeance ceased not, vntill such tyme as the Client of *S. Hugh*, was restored to his Benefice againe. This also, was of much consideration which I shall presently tell you.

Seauen of the Kings Court, hauing by stealth taken out a thiefe from the holy Church-yard whither for feare of iustice he had fled to saue himselfe, without the Bishops consent, hung him vp. The seruant of God resented the matter as was fit, and with his wonted armes chastized them straight. And they from others example likewise fearing the worst, very sorrowfull and compunct, cast themselues at his feet all crauing pardon of him, one excepted; and hauing obteyned the same, vpon condition, that among other satisfactions, being halfe naked (it being then winter) they should carry on their shoulders the man that was hanged for a good distance vnto the said Church-yard, whence so temerariously they had taken him forth, and there bury him with their owne hands. So did the six penitents, not without publike scorne and a great deale of trouble the while, and had no other hurt, that ensued thereon. When lo, the seauenth proud and pertinacious wretch, after seauen yeares, came also at last

last, to prostrate himselfe in the sight of the Bishop, declaring to him a strange story of the hurts and domages befallen him in this while, as well in his honour, as in his goods and person besides, and hartily craued absolution at his hands, for mitigation at least, if not an end of so great miseryes. The conuersion & supplication was not in vaine. when S. *Hugh* not to add affliction to affliction, absolued him with a light pennance, and restored him agayne to the Communion of the faythfull.

The sweet manner of behauiour which S. Hugh *carryed towards all: VVith his Charity, and Prudence in the manage of things.* Chap. 9.

IN these and such like affayres touching the honour of God, and Ecclesiasticall immunityes, S. *Hugh* would shew so much rigour and seuerity, as may seeme perhaps to be attributed, to a certaine asperity or harshnes of mind, and rusticity of manners, if otherwise he had not alwayes vsed much humanity, & still reteyned the wonted bowels of Mercy. At Table, and Feasts, he shewed himselfe very soberly pleasant and merry, & would exhort his friends to the same cheerefulnes, with giuing thankes to the giuer of all good. As for banquets, sports, and musicke, if he could not auoid them sometymes, he would make vse of them, eyther to refresh himselfe, for new trauayls, or for a tast of celestiall delights. Not only, in the publike preaching of the Word, but euen also in familiar conuersation, would he loose no occasion, most sweetly to allure men vnto solid vertues, and through their amendment, very manifestly appeared the profit thereof. His conceipts were efficacious and liuely, and fitly accommodated to each condition and quality of persons. Of which kind, may serue as a certayne patterne, that with diuers demonstrations he would giue Religious to vnderstand the necessity they haue, of fighting continually with themselues, and ascending alwayes to the top of perfection. Vnto seculars, & especially to such as traffike, aboue all things would he inculcate faith and truth in all things, without which of necessity all human commerce must vtterly perish. The women, he was wont to incite to diuine Loue, in putting them in mind particularly of the singular priuiledge, & the inestimable fauour done to that sexe, by the soueraigne Maiesty, in vouchsafing to take flesh and become the sonne of a woman: and whereas man had neuer the honour to be called the Father of God, a woman yet hath had the grace, & preheminence to be named the Mother of God.

In this manner, he stirred vp alwayes mortals from slouth and tepidity, and was most vigilant in encountring with the first origines of discords, and maintayning peace, as well in priuate as in publique; hauing among other guifts so great a iudgment and light touching the point of equity, as that not only neere at hand, but also from remote countryes, and euen from *Rome* it selfe (as we insinuated aboue) there came controuersyes delegated to him, of no light importance. He was wonderfully beloued and reuerenced by his Chanons, though for their sakes he would not swarue from righteousnes; and with his prudence, and sweetnes he knew how to manage them so, as he neuer pretended any thing from the Chapter, which he obtayned not at last; he had likewise very admirable successe in the highest affaires of the Kingdome, and among other his actions, was remarkeable that peace, which he concluded betweene King *Philip* of *France*, and *Iohn* King of *England*, being the immediate successour of his brother *Richard*, who in punishment of the troubles brought vnto Ecclesiasticall persons, within a few yeares of his Crowne, was miserably slaine in battaile.

And to the purpose of this pacification of his, it seemes not good to passe ouer in silence, how S. *Hugh* returning from *Normandy*, with the accord established, happened by the way to lodge in a Monastery of his *Carthusians*, called *Arneria*: and some of those Fathers familiarly crauing he would make some particuler relation of the sayd expedition, and quality of the articles; Saint *Hugh* mortifying such a will in them, sayd: *These secular businesses may well be declared by Bishops indeed, but should not be curiously enquired into by Monks.* So tenacious was he at all times of Monasticall discipline & of chast silence. This also was a matter of much edification, in this great Prelate, that hauing lost (as we haue sayd) through excessiue abstinence all appetite, was vexed with most bitter gripes of the cholike, yet fayled he not for all that, to employ himselfe when need was, with a most exact diligence, in consecrating, or rehallowing of Churches, and administring the Sacraments, especially of Confirmation & of Order, obseruing euer the Catholike rites in al things, & beginning sometimes before day, perseuering therin some houres of the night following without any refection at all. He spared not to bestow a good part of his tyme, in informing himselfe of the behauiours

hauiours of the people and Clergy, of the necessityes of the poore to relieue them, in & visiting and louingly comforting the sicke.

But though he shewed himselfe most pittyfull and beneficiall to all, yet felt he a singular tendernes of affect towardes the infected with leaprosy: he would goe into their Hospitalls in person, and after that in common he had giuen benigne consolations and fatherly aduises to that wretched people, he would approach to ech one in particular, and humbly inclining himselfe vnto them, he abhorred not to kisse their loathsome vlcers, and lastly refreshed them with conuenient almes. The Chauncellour of *Lincolne*, called *VVilliam* one day was present at such a spectacle, who being first astonished at so great humility, and afterwards doubting some vaine glory in the Bishop, began to tempt him, with saying: S. *Martin* with a kisse only cured the leaprous, but you, me thinks, doe not so. To which iest of his, S. *Hugh* made answere: S. *Martins* kisse cured the leaprous in flesh, but the kisse of the leaprous euen cures my soule. He was wont also, most ordinarily to wash secretly the feet of thirteen poore folkes, and to serue them at table. And finally his workes of piety were so notable and famous, as he was vniuersally called the Father of Mercyes; and euen sucking Babes, as it were, through naurall instinct would stretch forth their little armes to call, and imbrace him.

How S. Hugh *addicts himselfe to bury the dead: with a strange prognosticate of his owne death.* Chap. 10.

VVHat meruayle is it, that *S. Hugh* should shew such clemency and compassion to the liuing, who vsed such Charity and sollicitude towards the dead, and that not only to their soules, but euen likewise to their corps; he no sooner vnderstood that there lay heere or there any body vnburyed, but setting, as a new *Tobyas*, all other businesses aside, he would goe thither in hast, and with due exequyes, according to the condition of ech one he would commit them to the earth. And he was so giuen to this holy occupation, as that being sometymes inuited by the King himselfe vnto dynner, he would let him expect some whole howers together, vntill his worke were finished: and while the messengers came in one after another, to sollicite him, with saying, the King yet differred his dynner for his sake, and remayned still

 fasting,

fasting, S. *Hugh* freely would answere: Why doth he expect me? For better it were an earthly King should eate without me, then for me to consent that the commaundement of the King of Heauen should be contemned. My food is to fullfill the will of the eternall Father.

It happened one day, that he buryed a most stincking & corrupt corps of a drunken and dissolute sinner, to which none durst approach without stopping the nose; and yet *S. Hugh* went about to handle him without any auersion at all, vntill he had layd him and couered him with earth: the standers by being amazed therat demanded of him, whether he felt not any noysomnes or loathing from the corrupt corps, and he answering, that he felt no offensiuenes thereat, and how they were deceaued with their owne imagination; being full with new wonder, they ceased not to glorify the diuine Goodnes in his Seruant.

Newes being brought him one day, of the death of a bitter persecutour of his, he suddenly puts himselfe in order to goe vnto that house of mourning, and to be present at the hearse: and being told for certaine, there were traynes layd for him on the way, and therefore by no meanes he should go thither: I deserue well, indeed, answered he, to haue fetters at my feet, and bolts on my legges, if I should once but neglect such a visit. And so causing the rest of his trayne, to stay behind, he went thither but with two only familiars of his, and there arriued without any stop or hinderance at all, and procuring a decent funerall for him that hated him so much, and placing the body in a vault, he returned home agayne replete with ioy and merits.

How acceptable these and the like exercises of *S. Hugh*, were in the sight of God, was euen manifested also in this present life, with the precious guifts of healing infirmityes, and expelling the wicked spirits, and quenching flames. In the meane while, from his indispositions, from his trauailes, and yeares, *S. Hugh* continually feeling himselfe to decay, attended with more feruour then euer, to prepare himselfe for that passage, whereto in this short & vncertaine course of mortality, all the cares and studyes of men, should be most intent and fixed. A notable presage of the end of this Saint approaching, were the actions of a certaine Swan of an extraordinary greatnes, which on the selfe same day whereon S. *Hugh* being created Bishop entred into *Lincolne*, was now likewise

wise come from parts farre remote vnto a certaine Castle, whither the Bishop afterwards resorted sometymes for honest recreation: and when he arriued at any tyme, that white bird would immediately fly to receiue him: and where to others it shewed it selfe very shye, and coy; to the Bishop only it would be most domestike, and giue forth infinite shewes of welcome; it would take meate from his hand; it would thrust, as in a poole, the head and neck, within those large and ample sleeues of his, and not contented therewith, leauing the fresh waters, and its accustomed haunts, would stand all night a watching, and keeping centinell at his chamber doore. Moreouer it had taken vp a custome, as often as the Bishop was to retyre thither, to be very iocund, to cry out, and flap with the wings, in so much as the keepers of the castle, as they had been aduertized by some harbinger, would be accited thereby to prepare the chambers, and to put all things in order against his coming. Now the last tyme that S. *Hugh* came thither, the amourous Swan leauing its accustomed dalliances, would so hide it selfe, with the head drooping, and with other signes of sadnes, and frowardly sequestring it selfe from his sight, which it was neuer to behold more; as the seruants were fayne to take it, and bring it in by force. And thus much of this new prognosticate.

The death and funeralls of the Venerable Bishop, not without some miracles accompanying the same. Chap. 11.

IN those dayes was assembled at *Lincolne*, a most famous nationall Councell: and S. *Hugh* being then in the City of *London*, vpon vrgent occasion, with purpose to hye himselfe as soone as possibly he could to the sayd Assembly, being there ouertaken by a suden & vehement feuer, was forced to keep his bed; and yet in despite of the disease, re-enforcing his prayers vnto God, and to the most blessed Virgin, and deuout colloquyes with his Angell Guardian, and with the Citizens of *Heauen*; he ceased not withall to afford gratefull audience, with holsome admonitions to as many as came to visit him. Being admonished to make his will: It greiues mee (said he) for this custome of making wils, introduced into the clergy. I neuer had, nor haue at this present any thing, that is not wholy of my Church: and yet that the Fiscall may not lay hand thereon, let all be distributed to the poore, as soone as may be, whatsoeuer

may

may seeme to others I possesse. Heereupon the Feast of *S. Mathew* being come, wherein he remembred he was consecrated Bishop; he caused the celestiall Viatique, and the Sacrament of Extreme vnction also to be ministred to him, as thinking very probably, that immediately he was to depart: but it pleased our Lord to differre the same, vntill the 17. day of the next moneth, in which space he ceased not from deuotious for himselfe, and exhortations for others; and moreouer with the spirit of Prophecy, very cleerely foretold, the great disasters, which soone after, were to happen to that Kingdome, and particulerly to the Clergy.

The foresayd terme being afterwards arriued, the holy Bishop being interiourly certifyed of his departure, caused besides his Chaplyns some Monks and Preists to be called to assist him, and seeing them all to weep bitterly, he sought with interrupted speeches, but graue and affectuous withall to comfort them, and laying his right hand vpon ech one, he recommended them to the diuine custody. And now his feeble voyce began quite to fayle, when he willed, that the flore being swept, a crosse of hallowed ashes should be formed thereon, and that a seruice should be sayd in manner of a Quier, whereat being present with great attention, as soone as he came to that verse of the 90. Psalme: *Clamabit ad me & ego exaudiui eum, cum ipso sum in tribulatione*, causing himselfe to be lifted from his bed, he stretched his withered and frozen members (being mindfull of the Passion of Christ) vpon the sayd Crosse, and presently beginning the Canticle of *Simeon* very happily expired, in the yeare of our Lord 1200. of his age 60. and of his Episcopall charge the 15.

In this manner it pleased the Prince of Pastours, to put an end to the trauailes of his most faythfull Coadiutour, of whose passage into heauen some persons worthy of credit haue had vndoubted reuelation. The body being spiced with Balme and other odours, was in pontificall habit exposed in a Coffin ready to be carryed, according to the order left by him, vnto his Church: but through the infinite concourse of people, which pressed in, to touch or at least to behold more neere that sacred Treasure; there succeeding by turnes very Honourable personnages to carry the corps, the way became to be so taken vp, and stopt the while, as it was there fayne to stay for no lesse then six dayes. In approaching to *Lincolne*, the two Kinges *Iohn* of *England*, and *VVilliam* of *Scotland*, who

who then were present, came forth to meet them with a most noble trayne, and both being desirous to submit their shoulders to the venerable Beer, the *Scottish* King among others (who loued him deerely) powred forth a floud of teares. After that, in the Cathedrall were the solemne exequies celebrated, with the pompe that became both the dignity of the deceased, & the quality of the standers by, among which two crowned heads, three Archbishops, fourteene Bishops, more then a hundred Abbots, very many Earles and Barons, drew the eyes of the people vpon them; the diuine Prouidence so disposing, that the promptnes and perseuerance of S. *Hugh* in taking so great care to bury the bodyes of others, was thus recompenced with so magnificent and glorious a Sepulture. To this were added for greater splendour, new & famous miracles, which to recount throughout, were a thing too long: it may suffice for example only to add heere also, that within few dayes at his monument, were cured six Palsey men, three blind receaued their sight, and two dumbe men recouered their speach. Moreouer the deposition, customes, and heroicall prowesse of the Saint, were afterwards not only celebrated with a liuely voice, by that age, but by many Writers also registred with a faythfull pen, to the glory of God, the memory of him, and the noble example, & incitement to posterity.

FINIS.

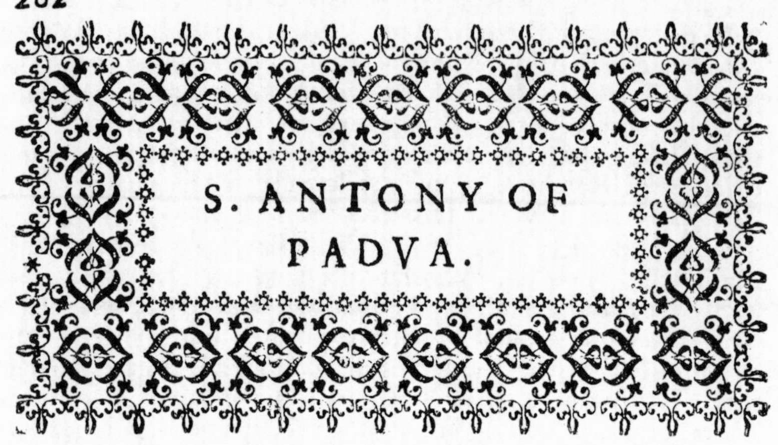

S. ANTONY OF PADVA.

THE ARGVMENT.

RIch *LVSITANIA*, yields thee vitall ayre,
And first of others shines with such a gemme
Thy countreyes Father; thou dost her prepare,
Thou dost dispose her vnto Heaun's diademe
By doctrine and example; they declare
How gratefull was such charity to them.
Thou *Solons* doctrine well dost ouerthrow,
Shewing the Countrey to her brood may owe.
Padua adopts thee hers, whose spacious Fanes
Could not containe thy happy audience:
The larger fields, and open spreading plaines,
Did seeme prepard for such a confluence:
Thy heauenly doctrine sweetly entertaines
The hearers, charm'd with golden eloquence.
A second *Orpheus*, whose commanding Lyre
Euen senselesse thinges do follow, and admire.

THE LIFE OF S. ANTONY OF PADVA.

Taken forth of Laurence Surius.

Of the family and youthfull age of S. Antony: *and how he became be of the family of the Chanons-Regular.* Chap. I.

HE marueilous Mysteries of the diuine prouidence, are discouered as it were, through the whole pilgrimage of S. *Antony*, commonly called of *Padua*; and so much more worthy to be renowned by the world, as through the sollicitous cooperation of this most noble Confessour, they are seene to be accompanyed with the cleere examples of an Apostolicall spirit, and of ech Christian vertue. The blessed man was borne in the famous Metropolis of *Portugal*, which is called *Lisbon, K. Alphonsus* raigning in those partes the second of that name, in the yeare of our Lord 1195. His Father was called *Martin Boglion*, his Mother *Mary Tauera*, both of ancient and very honourable families, dwelling right ouer against the great Church dedicated to the Mother of God, wherein the Reliques of the glorious Martyr S. *Vincent* are kept with much veneration. From so noble a couple, in the flower of their youth sprung forth this blessed Bud, and in Baptisme was named *Hernando*.

In the first rudiments of learning and Christian manners, he was with diligence instructed by the Priestes of the sayd great Church; so as an exact education being added to an excellent inclination, vnder the protection of the most Blessed Virgin Mary, and that most inuincible Martyr, he came very soone to bring forth most euident signes of his future greatnes: because, as it is likewise reported of some others elected of God in their childish age, being farre off from childish thoughtes, he tooke pleasure in imitation of his Parents, to frequent holy places, and to distribute almes to the poore, as he was able, that saying of *Iob* well suiting with him: *Ab infantia mea, creuit mecum miseratio.* With these passages of his childish innocency, being come to the dangerous & ticklish point of youth in choice of an estate of life, he felt himselfe not a little to be allured by sensuality, with enticements of flatteryes: but preserued doubtles by the diuine Mercy, very generously withdrew his foot, resolued to follow by the sharp way, the guide of reason, and splendour of honesty.

And to secure himselfe the better, with perseuerance, with a voluntary holocaust he dedicated himselfe to our Sauiour Iesus Christ, in the Monastery of S. *Vincent* of the Chanons-Regular: which Monastery howbeit scituate forth of *Lisbone*, yet was it not so farre, but many, as it happens some for loue, some for curiosity, came to visit the new souldiour of Christ: whence he perceauing himselfe to be disturbed in his deuout exercises, obtayned with much difficulty to be remoued from thence, some three dayes iourney, into the Monastery of the *Holy Crosse* of *Conimbria*, where yet to this day that Order flourisheth, to the great benefit and ornament of that Citty. Heere the feruorous disciple of Christ, besides the learning and diligent obseruing the holy Ceremonyes, so imployed himselfe in the grauer studyes, as he alwayes reserued the better part of his tyme and trauaile for spirit: nor suffered he (as often it fals out with they vnaduised) the vehemency of speculation should come to oppresse or diminish deuotion, but with a sage temper, helping himselfe with the sacred Scriptures, partly for finding out of deep senses, partly to enflame himselfe with diuine loue, and making no lesse often acts of the Will, then of the Vnderstanding, he arriued within a little while, to so high a degree of perfection, as he had no greater thirst, then to spend his bloud for

the

the Catholicke fayth. And in this so laudable a desire of his, he became much more confirmed, through the occasion we shall presently declare.

The occasion that moued S. Antony *to endeauour to change his Rule, and what it was.* Chap. 2.

THe venerable Family of Fryars, which through Christian humility doe call themselues *Minours*, was by the Eternall Pastour newly founded, to the help and reduction of wandering soules. The head of these was the most blessed *Francis* of *Assisium*, who with the approbation of the Sea Apostolike, and with the example and profit of his holy manners and speaches, trauayling into diuers Countryes, and especially into the vtmost confines of *Spayne*, had with admirable increase spread his name, and ministery, by the many residences of his children. And by this way had sought with all industry to prouide for the extreme necessityes of the afflicted Christianity. After this being not able to suffer the other so great a part of the world to be seduced by the fabulous lyes of the Mahumetan perfidiousnes, he very freely determining to bring, to his power, some light and succour to those miserable nations; and when he should be able to profit no more, with a glorious end at least, to lay downe his life, in confirmation of the Ghospell.

Into which enterprize hauing put himselfe more then once, but through diuers impediments, being not able euer to prosecute any thing; at last, assembling together, two squadrons of choyce workemen, with one of Eleuen, he himselfe passed from *Ancona* into *Egipt*, where vnder *Damiata*, the Christian army was encamped against the *Saracens*: the other of Six, he sent vnder *Fryer Vitalis* an *Italian*, into the land of *Granata*, and of *Andaluzia*, being tiranically handled by *Miramolinus* King of *Morocco*, a great vpholder of the name and sect of *Mahomet*. These two expeditions concerning the litle fruit they wrought, with those blind and obstinate people, had in a manner the same successe: but for the dealing with Apostolicall persons they were farre different. Because S. *Francis* passing boldly from the Christian tents, vnto those of the *Saracens*, was by the *Soldan* (though for that tyme he resolued not to accept the Ghospell) more then once, yet graciously heard, and with diuers courtesyes and fauours much honoured and entertayned, not without the infinite wonder of the ſtanders by.

But the troupe, which vnder *Vitalis* went into the Weſt, by his order continued their way, and with incredible fortitude preaching the truth of Chriſt, and accuſing the vanity of the falſe Prophet, not only in *Seuill* of *Andaluzia*, but euen alſo in the City of *Marocco* it ſelfe, and in *Affrica*, and confirming their doctrine with workes aboue nature, they were firſt ſcorn'd, pelted, & ouerwhelmed by the people, with ſtones, cudgells, and priſons: and afterwards by *Miramolinus* himſelfe (to reuenge the iniuryes of his *Mahomet* with his owne hands) very cruelly ſlayne through the ſtrokes of a Semiter, in the preſence of his people. Whoſe bones now renowned with new and euident miracles, being diligently gathered by the meanes of the *Infant Don Pedro*, the King of *Portugals* Brother (who was very acceptable at that tyme in *Marocco* to *Miramolinus* himſelfe) and decently conuayed to the Church of the holy Croſſe of *Conimbria*, cauſed in that deuout people, diuerſe motions of Chriſtian piety, but in the Chanon *Don Hernando*, through holy emulation increaſed ſo the thirſt of Martyrdome, as he could find no reſt by day or night; and he was much more rouzed vp, being taken with the triumphall palmes of thoſe valorous Champions, thẽ was *Themiſtocles* awakened from ſleepe through the Tropheyes of that other *Athenian* there. In fine, the enkindled flames of charity at this ſpectacle increaſed ſo in him, as *Hernando* being not able to contayne the ſame, with full reſolution, determined to paſſe likewiſe ouer himſelfe into *Mauritania*, and preaching couragiouſly the fayth of Chriſt, to purchaſe to himſelfe, a precious death for the glory of Chriſt, and ſaluation of Soules.

Now by this tyme, he was made Preiſt, and had arriued to the age of 26. yeares. He was for his ſingular vertue and rare talents, ſo deere to his whole Congregation, as diffiding wholy to get leaue of the Abbot for ſuch an enterprize, concealing his purpoſe vnder the pretext of chooſing a more auſtere and ſtrict rule, he determined to paſſe into the new religion of the Fryars Minors, holding for certaine, that thence he might more eaſily compaſſe his deſired enterprize. Wherefore making very feruent prayers thereupon, at laſt he found out this way to execute his deſigne which followes in the next Chapter.

S. Anto-

S. Antony *is admitted into the Conuent of the Fryars Minors, where he pursues his intent, but all in vayne.* Chap. 3.

AMong other Conuents of S. *Francis*, dispersed through the kingdome of *Portugall*, there was a litle one vnder the protection of S. *Antony the Great*, without the walls of *Conimbria*, where those Fathers philosophizing rather with life and manners, then with questions and disputes, gaue themselues to let the world vnderstand the vanity of things present, and solid hopes of voluntary pouerty. Some two of this Conuent, from tyme to tyme, were wont to come to the sumptuous and rich Monastery of the holy *Crosse*, according to their institute, very humbly to craue Almes: So as *Don Hernando*, taking them one day aside, with a liuely affect of Charity vnfolded vnto them, as to two Angells of Paradise, his holy purpose, and besought them, keeping it secret where need was, to deale with their Superiours, about his admission into their Order, but yet with expresse condition to send him by obedience, as soone as may be vnto the land of the *Moores*, to worke some fruit in the conuersion of *Gentils*. Euen from that tyme, was the name of *Hernando* famous for learning and goodnes; so as the *Fryars Minors*, tooke it to be no small fauour so to enrich themselues with such a purchase. Wherefore the busynes being concluded on their parts; on the other *Don Hernando* began to craue humble licence of his Prelates, who made a very strong resistance for a tyme; but his prayers were so continuall and vehement as they finally preuayled. So as deuoutly taking the habit of *S. Francis* from the *Minors* in their Cloyster, he went his wayes thence with such displeasure of the Chanons, as he heard at his going forth, such a bitter taunt in the way of iest cast forth by one of them, as this: *Goe your wayes now, perhaps you will be a Saint in that Religion*. At which words (sayd he) with a cheerefull countenance: *VVhen that shall be, I beleiue you will giue praise and thanks to the Redeemer for it*.

In this manner passing into a new habitation and institute; the first thing he did, was to lay aside all secular habits, and quite to forget his fathers house, & to be also himselfe the more vnknowne, and quite forgotten of the world, from the title of that litle Church, or to say better, Oratory of the *Minors*, in changing his name, he caused himselfe to be called *Fryar Antony*. From thence renewing

his

his supplications to God, and his Superiours, and preparing himselfe continually with fit meditations, to each cruelty of punishments that might be, it was not long ere he was sent into the desired parts of *Marocco*; where as in a most certaine field of battayle, he hoped to obteyne by dying for Christ, a glorious victory.

But soone appeared very euident signes of the inscrutable disposition of our Lord; who accepting herein the good will of his seruát, had preordeyned him for other labours, and to other merits. Because, that in the very beginning of his departure, being oppressed with a greiuous malady, he was constreyned for the most of that winter to keepe his bed. Where, though after many profers and endeuours made in vayne, he coniectured, the diuine Maiesty was no wayes propitious to his purposes; yet by the beginning of the next yeare, hauing scarcely recouered any forces, he valiantly began afresh to make proofe of himselfe, and to sayle towards *Affrick*. But the barke had hardly hoysed sayle & departed from the hauen, when behold a contrary storme of the South-west winds, by force, transported the Mariners to *Messina* of the Iland of *Sicily*.

This aduenture gaue S. *Anthony* much more matter to reflect vpon the interpretation of the diuine will, and had yet a more euident signe therof. As soone as he landed he vnderstood by the *Fryars Minors* there resident, how of late a generall Chapter was intimated of the Order, at *Assisium*, and therefore it apperteyned to him also, as a Preist, not hindered by any lawfull cause to goe thither. Through this citation ioyned with passed accidents, he came to be satisfyed, it was not the diuine pleasure he should aspire to preach to the Mahometans or Gentils. From which barre of exclusion, the wary Merchant went about to make a double profit, one of his owne confusion, accusing himselfe of too much boldnes, and presumption in himselfe; the other of a stable purpose, to suffer himselfe heereafter to be wholy guided by the Creatour, by meanes of his Ministers, without making choyce on his owne head, of this or that manner of procuring the diuine glory. And withall, since it was not permitted him to expose himselfe for the holy fayth, vnto the fury of the people, to the cruelty of Tyrants, to the scourges & kniues of the mercyles hangmen, he determined to offer vp himselfe, another way to Christ, in a liuing hoast, vpon the aultar of Religious iustice, by mortifying the flesh with whips, fastings, prayers, and vigils, slaying and annihilating the will and vnderstanding,

ſtanding, with perfect obedience, and full contempt of priuate reſpect.

How S. Antony *goes hiding his talents for humility ſake, and is vnknowne to men*. Chap. 4.

S. *Antony* going with ſuch deſignes in his breaſt vnto the Congregation of *Aſſiſium*, ſince by reaſon of his celebrating of Maſſe euery day, and reciting the canonicall howers, his Prieſtly dignity could not be hidden, he endeauoured at leaſt with all care to conceale the nobility of his bloud, the force of his wit, and the variety of learning which he had; which ſo cunningly he did, as with the whole Chapter, he remayned in opinion of an Idiot or ſimple man, and not apt, eyther for ſubtilityes of ſpeculatiue learning, or manage of practicall matters. Whence it followed, that the aſſembly being diſſolued, while diſtribution of ſubiects (according to the vſe) was made, and the Superiours requiring to haue ſome this, ſome that man, along with them vnto their reſidences, S. *Antony* remayned alone without being required or requeſted of any. Meane while the diuine man exceedingly reioyced, in beholding himſelfe, in imitation of his great Maiſter and Sauiour Ieſus, without fault of his to be ſlighted and neglected of all. Yea rather to make continually more intenſe acts of Chriſtian humility, approaching with great humility and ſubmiſſion to the Miniſter of the Prouince of *Romania*, called *Fryar Gratianus*, he did reuerently beſeech him, he would daigne to intreat Father Generall, he might take him to him, to inſtruct him with other Nouices, in the ceremonyes and obſeruances of the Order.

Nor was the petition made in vayne. For *Fryar Gratian* being moued with the modeſty and ſolitude of the perſon, come thither from parts ſo remote; tooke him benignly along with him, vnto his owne Dioceſſe, and a little after, at his new inſtance permitted him to retire himſelfe into the hermitage of *Monte Paulo*, with ſome others. Where *S. Anthony* being prouided of a narrow Cell, in faſting with bread and water, and perſeuering in holy contemplations, and manfully reſiſting the temptations of the Diuell, prepared himſelfe vnwittingly, vnto the admirable exploits and enterprizes, which for the benefit of Chriſtendome, God was pleaſed to worke by his meanes. Being afterwards called from the deſerts to the Conuents, he departed not awhit from his firme deliberations, to vse and cause himselfe to be dealt with by others, as the meanest & most abiect of all: whence the tyme which he had spare frō the aultar & Quire, he spent cheerfully in sweeping the house, in seruing in the kitchim, and in doing such offices, which ordinarily are held in most scorne, and are most abhorted of human pride. And in such ministeryes, he continued hiding, shrouding, and concealing himselfe from mortall eyes; when it pleased him at last, who beholds the hidden things, to his eternall glory, and saluation of many people & nations, to manifest him to the world, with the occasion following.

How S. Antony *is discouered by his talents, to be singular, and is declared Preacher.* Chap. 5.

IT was now the tyme of Ecclesiasticall Ordinations; and therefore Father Guardian hauing destined some Fryars to the City of *Forli*, he thought good to lead them thither in person himselfe, & would needs haue S. *Antony* also along with him being Priest already, as we haue sayd; and as reason dictats vnto vs, and the Portugall Chronicles themselues doe cleerely demonstrate, howsoeuer more moderne Authours being mooued by one ambiguous word only of *Surius*, haue after affirmed, that *S. Anthony* went thither to be enrolled with the others into the sacred warfare. With this family then, for the same effect, went some Dominicans a long likewise: a Religion instituted as it were, by the eternall Father at the same tyme of the Franciscans, for the greater help of the Catholicke Church, and for supply, of men for the continuall preaching of the word of God.

These two companyes, though diuerse in habit and meanes, yet in will and end very conformable, being come to *Forli*, were lodged both in the same place: and not for to giue ouer their spirituall exercises, the houre of their conferences arriued, the Guardian of the Minours made great instance to the Father of the Preachers, that according to their institute they would be pleased, for the common consolation to discourse something of matters concerning the diuine seruice, and for the purchase of vertues. Whereof those vertuous Fathers excusing themselues, through the shortnes of tyme, & wearynes of the iourney; the Guardian being doubtlesse touched

with

with some hidden inspiration from Heauen, contrary to the opinion of all, turned himselfe to S. *Antony*, and suddenly imposed vpon him to make them a Homily, and to say something of edification. To which precept the seruant of Christ very modestly opposed a while, but the Superiour and the rest vrging him to it, at last not to breake with Obedience, recommending himselfe to God, he began to discourse, but rudely at the beginning, and without any shew of learning in him; but in the progresse of the discourse, the Holy Ghost without doubt, so guiding his tongue and hart, ere he was aware, he entred into so great a variety of allegations of the diuine Scripture, into so great sublimenesse of mystical senses, & aboue al, into so great an accesse and ardour of charity (which euen cast forth flames from his countenance and gesture) as all the Auditours remayned partly inflamed with heauenly affects, partly also astonished with wonder, as of a man that knew no more then his Breuiary, that neuer handled as it were any bookes, and from whose mouth scarcely euer came forth any Latin word.

But he, to whome, as well the memory, as also the creature it selfe, serued as a Booke layd open, and in so long an intermission of study and reading, had yet neuer fayled from treating familiarly with the benigne Giuer of Wisdome, gaue forth to vnderstand in that act, how much richer are the treasures of the mystical & sweet, then the scholasticall and sterile Theology. Besides their astonishment at this so sudden an eloquence; such indeed as all confessed they had neuer heard the like; they had a singular esteeme & consideration at his so rare humility, since whereas others, hauing scarce got a smatch in learning, can hardly conteyne the vnbridled will from appearing in Pulpits, and hunting after vayne prayse and applause of the people: he though very well instructed already, with infused and purchased learning, and besides endued by nature, with those parts which are required in a Christian Oratour, had euer held his peace, & was euer more willing to heare then speake, and striued as much to abase himselfe, as others doe to procure high degrees, and to be notable and famous in the world.

It was not long ere the Blessed Father S. *Francis* had newes thereof, who tooke extraordinary contentment therein, and gaue infinite thankes therefore to the diuine Goodnes. And howbeit he might without more adoe haue deputed S. *Antony* vnto the holy Function of Preaching, as who had beene well studyed already of himselfe

himselfe; yet by reason of his so long intermission now from his said studyes, and not to giue matter of murmure vnto others, he determined to make him renew and refine his mystical Theology, vnder the direction of the Abbot of *S. Andrew* in *Vercells*, a man very famous in those dayes for learning and sanctity, and who among other signes of profound Science, had lately translated the workes of *S. Denys Areopagita*, out of Greeke into Latin, and illustrated the same also with his explications and comments. *S. Antony* then being recōmended to this Doctour, with another English Fryar called *Adam de Marisco*, within the space of a yeare, they both made such profit in the knowledge of celestiall things, and arriued to such a height and eleuation of mind, as it seemed to the sayd Maister, he had two Angells in his howse, and that he had learned of them rather then they of him. With this so happy successe, S. *Francis* was more confirmed in his opinion already conceiued of S. *Anthony*, and with great hope, of much profit to the world, declared him Preacher, & commaunded him very confidently henceforth to apply himselfe to the ministery of the Word or God.

How S. Antony *mollifyed a Tyrant with his sharpe reprehension, and brought him to reason.* Chap. 6.

THis excellency of preaching, was not only discouered in the blessed disciple of Christ; but as true humility is capable of all graces, and mother of all vertues, he shewed himselfe very soone, how exceeding sufficient he was for confessions, and apt withall for disputations against Heretikes, and for Scholastical chayres, & for writing of bookes very profitable for the whole posterity: and (being a thing very hardly to be coupled with such talents) he shewed likewise no small skill and dexterity in gouernment. To all which prerogatiues, as by an irrefragable seale and patent, the diuine Clemency had annexed the spirit of Prophecy, with the priuiledge of frequent and manifest miracles. Of ech one of which guifts according to our purpose, we shall declare the cheife of them with breuity.

And first, for his preaching, we must know, there was so burning a zeale of the glory of God, and the saluation of men, planted by such solid and deep rootes in the soule of this louer of Christ, as that being suddenly pushed forth of his stand, like a generous steed

steed, he began to discurre through villages, Boroughes, castles, and Cittyes, leauing steps imprinted of holy customes on all sides, and exciting miserable mortalls, from base and terrene cares, to high and celestiall thoughts. And this his zeale of Charity, he endeauoured allwayes to keepe liuely and flaming, with the breath of prayer, and with matter of consideration, keeping also it from all humidity of sensuall pleasures or disordinate affections. Whence followed among others, two inestimable aduantages, to wit, a great credit with the auditory, and a singular energy of discourse: the one of which conditions, more auayles to perswade with, then all the artificiousnes, and figures of Rethoricall art that may be: the other how behouefull for a Teacher of truth, and Embassadour of the King of Heauen, may be easely comprehended of euery one.

By this meanes he came to be free and rid of those bands, which are wont to inueagle the mind, or restrayne and tye the tongue of others. So as neyther the force, nor malignity of the Mighty was able to dismay him, nor flatteryes or offers of freinds to bow him, nor the winds of popular applause to puffe him vp. Without all exception of persons, as well in publike according to occasions, as in priuate, the magnanimous Interpreter and Messenger of Christ, ceased not to hammer & breake the wils growne obdurate in vices, and that with a presence of a couragious hart, as that many famous Preachers, who came to heare him would euen tremble; and some amazed at the lightning and flashes he sent from him, would couer their face; others agayne, through doubt of some perilous accident, would retyre themselues. Which thinges to be no whit exaggerated, nor feigned may sufficiently be seen by that, which happened to him, with that famous Tyrant *Ezelinus*, of the Citty of *Padua*, and of a great part of *Marca Treuisana*.

This man vnder a rationall figure, hauing the hart of a Beare, and Tigre, seemed to thirst for nothing more then human bloud. Perfidiousnes and impiety both, were in him as conuerted into nature: robberyes, rapines, destructions through fire & sword, were euen sports and recreations to him, and (as to the Captayns of mischiefs it happens) he was allwayes wayted on by Souldiours and Sergeants, neyther in auarice, nor cruelty, nor lust much inferiour to him. Now this bloudy wretch, only to terrifye the people, without cause, made many noble Cittizens, to be slayne in *Verona*. *Saint Antony* tooke such sorrow, and indignation thereat, as that going boldly into the presence of that monster, and those Sergeants of his, began with a loud voyce to cry out against him, saying: *VVhen wilt thou cease, thou fierce Tyrant, and rauenous Dog, to sheed so the bloud of innocent Christians? VVhen wilt thou termine or mitigate euer this so great inhumanity? Know then, there hangs a dreadfull punishment of the diuine Iustice vpon thee which shall not leaue vnpunished the homicides, the robberyes, the extorsions, and wicked slaughters thou committest.*

These thinges the Seruant of God vpbrayded him with to his face, first in generall, and then after in particuler, descending into circumstances, with so much vehemency of spirit, with so much sparckling of the eyes, & feruour withal, and with so much weight and liberty of speach, as that most rauenous Wolfe became now of a sudden a most meeke Lambe, & in the presence of as many as were there, pulling off his girdle with his owne handes, & putting it about his necke, cast himselfe at his feet, very humbly crauing pardon, both of God and him, and offering himselfe most ready to performe whatsoeuer pennance the Venerable Father should impose vpon him. Whereupon the Blessed *Antony* being somewhat pacifyed, and the penitent confirmed with sweet admonitions in his good purposes, not only without any hurt at all, but rather with a great deale of reputation and honour, and grace withal, came from him: the people remayning the while much admiring, and amazed beyond measure, how *Ezelinus* at the first sound of such rebukes and reprehensions, had not caused him to be hewed in peeces, and cast forth to the beasts with a looke only. To take away the wonder, he yet wholy confounded, and euen pale for feare, sayd: Let it not seeme strange to you my Maisters, what heere I haue done, because while that same Religious man spake in that manner, I manifestly saw most liuely rayes of diuine splendour to come from his face, which so dazeled me, & filled me with such feare, that euen doubtles me thought, I should euen haue beene swallowed into hell. These wordes indeed *Ezelinus* spake, and such feelings he shewed for the present: but as the promises proceeded from seruile feare, & not for the loue of vertue, after a short remorse, returned the Barbarous wretch to his former custome, accusing himselfe for hauing yielded so basely, to the boldnes and menaces of a presumptuous Fryer, and perhaps also a dissembler and hypocrite. Yet neuerthelesse, remained that more then humaine countenance so engrauen in his memory, and that Maiesty, wherewith he was terrifyed,

as

as to him it seemed very hard to belieue, that without some heauenly concourse, and the hidden merites of so couragious a reprehender, so strange and vnusuall a thing should befall him.

After the Tyrant had beene thus perplexed in mind a prety while, wauering in himselfe, he resolued at last to cleare himselfe in that point of the goodnes & sincerity of the Fryer, with the touchstone as followes. Taking then forth of his treasury a rich Iewell, he gaue it to some Ruffians of his, to carry it to S. *Antony* on his behalfe, with faire and amorous speaches, but with expresse order, that if he accepted the same, as a false & couetous man, they should suddenly hew him to peeces: and if he should refuse it, they should with all respect abstaine, as from a person truly holy and acceptable to God; nor for whatsoeuer he should say vnto them, they should take any reuenge vpon him, but without any reply at all returne backe againe. With such commission those Ruffians being come to S. *Antony*, and intreating him with the greatest courtesy they could, to accept of that small charity, which *Ezelinus* sent him, and to remember him only in his deuout prayers; by so liuely experience they presently knew what he was, since with a seuere looke & shew of anger, he thus answered to the message: God forbid, I receaue in signe of liberality the very bloud of the poore of Christ: for which shall *Ezelinus*, ere he be aware thereof, make an exact accompt to the diuine iustice: and get you hence also without delay, least through your iniquityes eyther the howse ouerwhelme vs with a sudden ruine, or the earth come to swallow vs vp with a horrible rupture.

Whereat those miserable wretches, with bowing downe the head, went silently and fearefully away to giue account to their wicked maister of the whole successe; who being cleared in this manner of the suspitions falsely conceaued by him, touching the seruant of God, from that tyme forwards held him in the esteeme he ought, and gaue order to his souldiers, they should let him say of him what he listed himselfe: and though the Tyrant, through his inueterate custome in sinning, was neuer conuerted from his lewd wayes, yet certaine it is, that the memory of S. *Antony* serued him often tymes for a bridle, and through feare and reuerence of so great a man, he forbare afterwardes to commit many outrages, which he had otherwise effected without respect. These then and the like assaults, the couragious Champion of Christ, would not fayle to make at any tyme when need required. Though indeed no merueyl it be, that for the defence of the truth, he ſhould not feare the face of any man how angry ſoeuer, who with ſo much deſire heretofore had ſought to drinke of the chalice of the paſſion.

The excellent guifts, and talents of S. Antony, *eſpecially neceſſary to ſo notable a preacher, as he was.* Chap. 7.

LEt no man thinke by the former Chapter, that S. *Antony* ſhewed himſelfe to be ſo rigorous and terrible to all. He wanted not iudgment to diſcerne the difference of his Auditours, nor skill and practize to deale with the rich, with the poore, with the noble and ignoble, according to the capacity, and nature, and ſtate of ech one. And howbeyt the principall foundation of his preaching was placed, as we haue ſayd, in frequent prayer, and continuall abnegation of himſelfe; neuertheleſſe he tooke light and nouriſhment of ſound and ſincere knowledge from the auncient Doctours, ſacred Councells, and diuine Scriptures, wherein he was ſo verſed and dexterous, as it is affirmed for certaine, that when by any misfortune, they might hap to be loſt, he alone from the Cabinet of his memoty, was ſufficient to recouer them agayne, as heeretofore *Eſdras* had done, and to put them faythfully in writing.

Wherof among other perſons of authority, *Gregory* the *Ninth* his Holynes, gaue truely a moſt cleere and graue teſtimony; for that S. *Antony* being come to the Court of *Rome* (for this likewiſe was a notable exployt of his) to oppoſe the deſignes and endeuours of Fryar *Elias*, and of others, who ſought to wreſt the Rule, and enlarge the Religious diſcipline, he not only laboured efficaciouſly in this matter, but preached alſo to the Court, and people of *Rome*, in diuers places and tymes, with ſo great abundance of true and profund conceipts, with ſuch ſubtilityes, and art in diſcouering the origens and cauſes of vices, and in appling apt remedyes to each one, and with ſuch ſharpe and ſound interpretations of the Pſalmes and the Prophets, and of all hiſtoryes & Oracles, and diuine precepts, as the Pope himſelfe being aſtoniſhed, beſides infinite other prayſes afforded him, with a Pontificall ſpirit daigned to call him, *The Arke of the Teſtament*. There were added to theſe ſo rare guifts of a Chriſtian Oratour, a dignity of aſpect, a grace in his geſtures, a ſweetenes and cleernes of voyce, and all in ſo eminent a degree, as he ſeemed to be an organ for honeſt delectation, and for a hole-ſome mouing of ſoules, framed by the hand of God himſelfe. And that which more increaſed the wonder, was ſo great a variety, quaintnes, and propriety in the Italian tongue, in a man trayned vp in Prouinces ſo remote, and come into *Italy* being of yeares ſo mature, and ſo late brought forth to the light of the world, and to the eminency of Pulpits.

Whence it is not very eaſy to explicate the concourſe of people of all conditions, that aſſembled together at the ſound of that celeſtiall harmony and diuine Trumpet: in ſhutting vp their ſhopps, leauing their traffikes in the market places, and the noyſes of the Pallace, and taking vp places before day at the ſacred audience, with ſuch haſt and ſtrife withall, as many tymes the ſeruant of God was conſtreyned to abandon the Churches and Cittyes, and goe forth into the ſpacious playnes, and there from the higher bancks to breake the bread of the diuine word vnto the hungry multitude. And he howbeyt corpulent by nature, and much ſubiect to ſweating, and diuers infirmityes, left not for all that, to expoſe himſelfe with great promptnes, and without ſparing any labour, or trouble where the greateſt need was, & hope of a more certaine & copious harueſt.

Now who were able to ſet downe what fruite followed, to the glory of our Lord and ſaluation of men? Who could number the rancours and enmityes depoſed, the reſtitutions made, the Concubines forſaken, the proceſſions, diſciplines, faſts, the pious works both common and particuler inſtituted for behoofe of body & ſoule? Many contemning the vanity of the world, though rich and potent otherwiſe, eyther dedicated themſelues to the diuine ſeruice in Religion, or the better to aſſure their conſcience, very freely ſubiected their whole ſubſtance and their life it ſelfe, vnto the diſpoſe of the faythfull ſeruant of Chriſt; the good and faythfull through his diſcourſes would depart from him very full of conſolation of new courage and purpoſe afreſh. The ſinners chaſing away darknes and ſleep, aſtoniſhed at the diuine prouidence, acknowledging their perilous eſtate, and the greiuouſnes of their ſynnes, as wounted Harts to the fountayne, ſo ran they to the tribunall of Confeſſours, with teares and ſighs.

How S. Antony *mountes into the Chayre of Theology, and was the first of his Order, that read in those Schooles.* Chap. 8.

VVE may not seeme to passe ouer in silence, how 22. Theeues being accustomed to rob and murder trauaylours in a certaine thick and obscure forest, and then after vnknowne in the City, to appeare in the habit of Honourable persons, being lastly moued with the fame, which ran euery where of the Angelicall preaching of S. *Anthony*, resolued to goe all at once to heare him. And found the report of him to be nothing false, but rather remayned so mollifyed and softned, at his fyery speaches, as the sermon being hardly finished, they went al one after another, to cast themselues at the feet of the Preacher, with most humble confession, crauing absoluion at his hands, and promising amendment. Of whome being graciously heard, and with fatherly admonitions being encouraged and instructed, they retired themselues to performe the pennances imposed vpon them.

By which example, may easely be estimated without more ado, how great, and how vnusuall effects, that instrument of the diuine goodnes occasioned in the harts of men. So as S. *Bonauenture* in the second translation of the Saint, which was some thirty two yeares after his death, finding that happy tongue, through the diuine will, wholy fresh and red, with good reason exclaymed: *O tongue, which hast euer blessed God, and taught others to blesse him likewise, it appeares now manifestly of what merit thou wast before our Lord*: and so kissing it deuoutly he placed it in a decent Reliquary, for that purpose. But returning to the matter of the spirituall purchase, and most burning zeale of S. *Antony*. It is surely a merueilous thing, how the man of God, notwithstanding the occupation of the pulpit, and other trauayls of no light importance, employed himselfe very willingly in hearing confessions, and with so much prudence, and longanimity applyed himselfe to looke into, and to cure the wounds of soules, as sometymes from morning to late in the eueuing, he had no tyme to restore his weary and afflicted body eyther with meate, or repose at all.

The Heretikes moreouer and the Heresiarks being manifestly conuinced by the wisedome and spirit that spake in him, were constreyned opēly eyther with base silence to confesse their perfidiousnes, or with wholesome compunction to accept the truth. Though indeed

indeed he combated against such a plague, not only from aloft with long and continued speaches, but euen also in meetings and assemblyes in schooles, with syllogismes and distinctions, and with other arts which Logick teaches. Which perticularly is seen in the Citties of *Arimini*, *Millan*, & *Tholouse*. From which things grew also another effect of no small consideration, as well for the common benefit of all Christendome, as for the especiall increase and reputation of the *Fryars Minors*.

The sayd Religion, as we mentioned, was lately founded by the most Blessed *Father S. Francis*, in profession and spirit, rather of Christian pouerty and humility, then of erudition or learning. Which though they were not despised, or in contempt with him, yet was he very circumspect and cautious in admitting them into his Institute, being desirous that his Fryars should preach rather with example and good works, then with precepts, and words: nor lightly would he giue them leaue to study, as fearing not without good reason, least through weakenes of humane nature, much reading might extinguish deuotion, and the wind of curiosity destroy the building of Charity. From this caution of the holy Father, and simplicity which commonly appeared in his children, sprang vp an vniuersal opinion in the world, that the Fryars were certainely but silly, and good men only; but ignorant meerly and litle apt for discouering the deceipts of the auncient aduersary, and iudging the quality of synnes, or distinguishing between leaprosy and leaprosy, and by consequence vnable to cooperate with the diuine prouidence in the conducting of soules.

Now some Fathers being desirous to cancell this note, as zealous of the fame of their Order, and of the glory of Christ, made great instance vnto the Blessed *Antony*, he would take the paynes to read and explicate the more grauer sciences, and set vp in the Religion of the *Minors* a Schoole also, whence as from a noble and perpetuall Seminary, might issue from tyme to tyme sufficient workemen for the Vinyard of our Lord. To which so honest requestes, howbeit otherwise he would willingly haue condescended, yet hauing some notice of the mind of his common Father and Superiour, he could neuer be brought to accept the enterprise, vntill such tyme, as he had expresse faculty and commission from him, with a letter of the tenour following: To his most deere Brother *Antony*, *Fryar Francis* sends greeting. I am content that you read Diuinity to the

the Fryars, but in such sort, that (according to the aduise of the Rule) neither in you or them, the spirit of holy Prayer may be extinguished.

Heereby, all excuse being taken away, S. *Antony* did at last begin to satisfy the continuall desires of the Fryars, and he was the first, who in that venerable Family euer held the Chayre; beginning in *Mompelier* in *France*, and prosecuting afterwardes in *Bologna*, and then in *Padua*. To which Citty, whether it were for the clemency of the ayre, or for the humanity and disposition of the inhabitants, he bare very speciall affection: and with this his new labour of interpreting the diuine mysteries, he came both to illustrate the Order of *Minours*, and to affoard the militant Church a fit supply of the choicest souldiours. Amidst these so noble and fruitefull cares of his, the Seruant of Christ, could not also auoyd that same of gouerning others, in diuers degrees, and places of *France*, and *Italy*, where he was (according to the institute of the Order) both Guardian and Minister. In which dignityes, howbeit he shewed affability, and such iudgment, as he was both reuerenced and beloued of his subiects: yet to the end he might more readily attend to spirituall workes, and for the greater common good, it seemed well to Pope *Gregory* the IX. through singular priuiledge, to discharge him of all superintendency of Conuents, or of Prouinces, which do necessarily bring with them diuers distractions and thoughts of temporall matters. And besids the office of confessing, conuersing with the Neighbours, and preaching, the same Pope would haue him to put his sermons into writing, that the profit might not only deriue to the present and liuing, but euen also to the absent, and posterity. Whereupon retyring himselfe a new into the Citty of *Padua*, being a place for diuers occasiōs very apt for al exercise of learning, he went forward in putting those bookes to writing, which are now read in print, & which to the studious of christian eloquence, serue as a copious and rich storehouse for any subiect whatsoeuer.

A certaine Prophesy of S. Antony *fullfilled, of one* Philip *a Martyr of Christ.* Chap. 9.

HItherto we haue spoken of the actions of the Saint, which are imitable of ech religious person. It remaynes now to touch some thing of the more admirable. And to begin with prophecy.

whereof two no lesse certaine then famous predictions, sufficienly declare, how much this so precious a gemme shined in the blessed S. *Antony*. There being a woman at *Assisium* now ready to be brought to bed, she deuoutly recommended her selfe to his intercession, who for charityes sake had been to visit her. To which request, through the hidden instinct of God, he manifestly answered forthwith, she should be of good cheere, that she should haue a happy labour, and haue a sonne, and that which more imported, he was destine by diuine prouidence, first, to be a glasse of vertue in the Religion of *S. Francis*, and then also with effusion of his bloud, and great torments, for Christ should purchase a palme of a glorious martyrdome. There was nothing of all this that infallibly fell not out. The happy Babe was borne without hurt of it selfe or mother, and in the sacred Baptisme, tooke the name of *Philip*. And passing his first yeares in Angelical purity, of his owne election became a *Fryar Minour*. Hence fortifying himselfe in the loue and feare of the eternall God, through a heauenly inspiration, was moued to the pilgrimage of the holy Land, and arriued at *Azotus*, euen iust at the tyme, when that Citty, was by treason taken by the *Saracens*, and the Christians that were there, to the number of two thousand, were all publiquely condemned to death.

Through which so cruell a sentence, *Philip* fearing least some being affrighted might come to abandon the holy fayth, requested as a fauour at the ministers hands of the *Souldan* there (and obtayned it without difficulty) to be the last executed of all. Whence the *Mahumetans* being brought into some hope, that he would renoũce in the meane tyme; found themselues at last to be far deceaued of their expectation. Because the cruell spectacle being now begun, *Philip* endeauoured with all feruour & fortitude of mind to comfort all the Christians, to suffer freely, speaking aloud, he had a reuelation of our Lord, that he was to enter that day into the kingdome of Heauen, with more then a thousand Martyrs; through which so high a promise these faythfull people being exceedingly comforted, did voluntarily, yea euen cheerfully present their bare necks, to the sword of the bloudy Executioner.

Which thing the *Souldan* noting (who beyond measure abhorred the name of Christ) entered into such a fury, as he suddenly commaunded, that with all the sortes of most exquisite tormentes that might be, should his temerity and boldnes be punished, that durst so disswade from the worship of the Great *Mahomet*. Whereupon a troupe of hangmen, assailing *Philip* without more ado, and in the sight of the whole company of Christians, went first to cut of his fingars ioynt by ioynt, in which so sharp and prolix a torment, he neuer ceasing to exhort and enflame the Christians, in such wise as neyther being enforced with menaces, nor won with flatteryes, they all cryed out, with one accord, they would follow by all meanes the stepes, and counsails of the couragious *Philip*. The *Souldan* continually more enraged, caused him to be fleaed aliue to the nauell, and afterwards that blessed tongue to be cut out, whereof being depriued & torne in all parts, he ceased not for all that with signes and gestures, and much more with example to enflame those sacred victimes, vntill such tyme as he was beheaded with them, and that alltogether ascended to the eternall Country, leauing euen to their enemyes behind, an euident signe of their felicity, since the bodyes being kept a good while, in the same place vnburied & vncouered did not only not giue forth the least ill sauour, but rather yeilded a most sweet odour. And in this sort came that to effect which had now for so many yeares before, without all doubt, or ambiguity at all, already beene prophesyed by S. *Antony*.

Another example of S. Antonyes *prophesyes, which happened in another Martyr*. Chap. 10.

NO lesse memorable then the former, was a certaine reuelation, which S. *Antony* manifested cleerely being Guardian at that tyme in the confines of *Aquitan*, in a Citty, which being in a more high place, the Frenchmen called *Le Puy*, and the vulgar Italian *Val Poggio*, and was auncientl by the Latins called *Anicium*. In this Citty among other Inhabitants, was a certaine Notary, very Catholike in fayth, the worldly in his dealinges, and more practized in taking of Suretyships, then discerning of spirits, more aquainted with plying the Iudges, and Aduocats, then frequenting of Churches and Sacraments. And yet S. *Antony* on a tyme, meeting him one the way, with a low duck, & vncouering of the head, made him an extraordinary reuerence and obeysance. Which thing the Notary, being guilty of his owne quality, and not tyed through any freindship to the poore Fryar; at first attributed the same to errour or simplicity, afterwards perceiuing him to persist in in the ſayd obſeruance, when he ſaw him a farre of, endeuoured to ſhunne him. But meeting full on a tyme where he could not auoyd him, and the *Fryar* ſaluting him againe with the accuſtomed, or rather with greater ſigne of honour then euer, he holding the ſame as an act of ſcorne and deriſion towards him, began with anger, euen grinding his teeth, and drawing out his ſword withall, and to cry out, ſaying: If thou hadſt not been a Fryar, I had now a good while ſince euen thruſt this ſame in thy ſides.

But tell me, thou rude, baſe, and errant Iacke: What is the matter thou ſcoffes me thus to my face? To whome the ſeruant of Chriſt anſwered with all ſubmiſſion; Brother, trouble not your ſelfe, I do reuerence you with my hart, and do honour you withall fidelity that may be: the reaſon is, for that I hauing greatly deſired, & begged as a fauour of our Lord, to ſpend my bloud in his holy ſeruice, haue neuer been worthy, nor hath he byn pleaſed to heare my ſuite. But indeed of you, he hath reuealed to me, that you ſhal one day dye a Martyr; Whence I am conſtrayned with a ſweet enuy, to hold you in the eſteeme and regard I doe: and doe moſt affectuouſly intreate you, that when you ſhall come to that glorious conflict, you would be mindfull of me poore wretched ſinner. At which words the Notary being pacifyed, conuerting choler into laughter, went his wayes ieſting at the matter. Nor long it was, but the effect did really ſucceed.

Becauſe the Biſhop of that Citty, preparing himſelfe to go vnto the holy Sepulcher, the Notary being touched with ſupernall motiues, reſolued to accompany him thither, as he did. And being arriued at *Paleſtine* poſſeſſed by the *Saracens*, the Biſhop happened to fall into diſpute, of matters concerning the holy Fayth. In which conflict thoſe barbarous people ſhewing themſelues very bold and inſolent, againſt the honour of Chriſt, and the Biſhop being timorous in defending the ſame, and in oppoſing their blaſphemyes; the Notary could by no meanes brooke ſuch indignities, but couragiouſly entred into the quarrell, & without any reſpect awhit indeauoured to diſcouer & accuſe the vanity, fraud, & ambitions of their wicked Mayſter whome they adored: wherupon the *Mahumetans* being all enraged tooke the Notary, & for the ſpace of three continuall dayes, hauing ſatiated their greedy deſires, with mangling and ſcourging the victorious warrier of Chriſt, at laſt they led him to death: and he remembring very well, what had been told to

him

him by *S. Antony*, declared it to the Christians about him, and with infinite consolation, stretching forth his neck, to the seruants of impiety, and washing his stole anew in the bloud of the Lambe, went immaculate to the heauenly banquet. And thus, with the stupour, and amazement of all, came the Oracle to be verifyed.

Of sundry apparitions of S. Antony, *made in his owne person, vpon seuerall occasions.* Chap. 11.

THe apparitions of God, made to S *Antony*, & of him to others, are worthy of eternall memory. Being one day receaued as a Ghest, by a certayne Knight, no lesse deuout then illustrious, he had a lodging appointed him, farre from noyse, where he might the better attend to study, and contemplation. Now, while the Knight passes in the night by the house, he sees a most bright splendour to proceed from that chamber, whereat merueiling much, he secretly approches to the doore, and looking through the key hole, beholds vpon an open booke before S. *Antony*, a child of a celestiall beauty; who sending forth rayes more bright then the Sunne, threw himselfe tenderly about the necke of the blessed man, and imbraced him without end, and S. *Antony* likewise him, with ineffable ioy and affection. Amidst these chast imbraces the most sweet Babe shewed him how his Host was standing at the doore, & beheld al things remayning in a rapt. S. *Antony* not enuyed him so happy a sight, letting him enioy it at his pleasure, vntill such tyme as the glorious child did vanish away, when lastly he opened the doore, and with a thousand prayers coniured him to keep the matter in secret vntill his death. So promised the Knight and obserued the same: and as soone as the Seruant of Christ was quit of the bandes of his body, he vnloosed the same of silence, and began to proclayme the aforesayd spectacle, and to affirme it with oaths and teares togeather, with so much gust as he could neuer be satisfyed with recounting it. And hence it is, that the images of the Saint, are seene so depainted with a child in his armes, sitting on a booke, for a difference of others of his Order. In this manner was *S. Antony* among other tymes, as then made worthy of the presence of our Sauiour.

And he also, as we sayd more then once, affoarded himselfe in seuerall places, vnto diuers persons at once, and that allwayes eyther

eyther for the diuine seruice, or for edification, and the helpe of neighbours: as particulerly happened to him in *France*, while he was preaching first in *Mompelier*, in the great Church, after in *Limoges* in *S. Peters*, which they call of the *Quadrino*. Because S. *Antony* being in the pulpit, and remembring suddainely, he had forgot to substitute one in the Quire of the Conuent, who should supply his part, that belonged to him; suddenly by diuine power, not fayling neyther the people assembled, nor pulpit, was present with his Fryars to sing his Lesson, and Antiphone.

At other tymes his Father being falsely accused in *Lisbone*, for intercepting the monyes of the Fiscall, and then agayne for killing a yonge man, which by certaine wicked men, was of purpose put into his garden with many signes of bloud vpon him, S. *Antony* in the meane while being certifyed by diuiue reuelation of what had happened at both tymes, from places and Prouinces most remote, was found to be present in the same moment in the Citty of *Lisbone*; and as for the monyes he made the Magistrates to vnderstand, that the Kings Treasurers, though fully satisfyed heertofore, yet maliciously had denyed the receipt thereof, and acquittances giuen. For the homicide, it pleased him to demaund it publiquely of the dead himselfe, whether his Father (though sentenced already for it) were guilty of the said wickednes: whereto hauing answered no, without the vrging of S. *Antony* to name the malefactours, he demaunded absolution of the seruant of God, for a certayn excommunication he had formerly incurred, and intercession for his synnes; which hauing obtayned in the sight of all the multitude, he fell downe dead into the sepulcher agayne. And thus S. *Antony* conserued his innocent Father in his goods, honours, and life.

Moreouer, the seruant of Christ, was wont to shew himselfe cleerly in the night in sleep, to some inueterated in sensuality, and other vices, who for feare or shame durst not to lay open their enormious synnes to the Priest, and vpbrayding them their of crymes, and circumstances thereof, now to admonish them with sweetnes, and now to constreyne them with seuerity and menaces, to repayre to this or that Confessour, as he esteemed most for the purpose, & so with the Sacrament of penance they had tyme, to deliuer themselues from the power of the diuell: which euen the penitents themselues related afterwards, not without the great meruayl of euery one. So as neyther in this alſo may the bleſſed S. *Antony* be accompted inferiour to *S. Nicholas*, to S. *Ambroſe*, to S. *Francis*, and others, of whom it is read, how they had the ſame very fauours from the Almighty in diuerſe occurrences. And ſince we haue newly made mention of penitents, we may not fold vp in ſilence, how efficacious the words of S. *Antony* were concerning that holſome Sacrament.

Other notable examples, of the efficacy of S. Antonyes *preaching, not without manifeſt miracles.* Chap. 12.

A Certaine Cittizen of *Padua* by name *Leonard*, confeſſing vnto him, among other iniquityes diſcouered, being very contrite, that he kickt his Mother on the belly ſo hard, as he threw her to the ground. For which the Saint reprehending him moſt grieuouſly, in proceſſe of diſcourſe ſayd to him: How that foot which had had the boldnes to ſtrike the belly, whence he came forth, deſerued to be cut off. The wordes were not ſpoken to a deafe man: the abſolution receaued, *Leonard* goes his wayes home, and interpreting the ſillables as they ſounded, taking a hatchet really in hand, he cut off his foot, and preſently being ſeiſed with a mortall ſooning, began to cry out aloud; to theſe cryes the vnfortunate Mother full of feare came ſuddenly in, the Chirurgians are ſent for, the wound is ſwathed with little hope of remedy or cure, the neighbours run in, one cryes, another weepes, all are aſtoniſhed.

The wofull woman, ſcarcely yet recouering breath, goes her wayes with her haire diſheueled to the Saint, and with womaniſh plaints, & bitter ſobs, charges him with the death of her deare ſonne. The Bleſſed *Antony*, with the newes thereof remayned extremely diſconſolate and afflicted, and not content to haue diſcharged himſelfe with iuſt excuſes, he went immediatly to the lodging of that ſimple man, and there ſending vp enflamed prayers to God, he tooke vp the foot cut off, and laying it to the ſtump of the legge, with the benediction of God ſo vnited the ſame, as the yonge man without griefe or ſcarre remayned ſafe and ſound. The fame of ſo great a miracle dilated it ſelfe throughout, and thankes were rendred to the diuine goodnes on all ſides. Theſe and other ſuch like thinges befell *S. Antony* in Confeſſions.

But turne we now to his Preaching againe, we may not let paſſe,

passe, how the *Crusado* for the holy Land being proclaymed, vnder *Gregory* the IX. and a most ample Iubiley published for such an intention in *Rome*, there assembled together an infinite number of people from all parts of Christendome, as Greeks, French, Almans, Spaniards, English, and of other nations: by all which, the blessed S. *Antony* was heard to preach at once, ech one in their proper language, as in the City of *Hierusalem* heeretofore the Apostles were heard on the solemne day of Pentecost; that supernaturall effect being renewed, with the astonishment of as many as heard the same.

In *Arimini*, the Citty being full of Heretikes, S. *Antony* endeuoured cheifly, and not without much trauayle to reduce the Heresiarcke *Bonuillus*, or (as some would haue it) *Bonellus* to a better mind, who for thirty yeares continualliy had persecuted the Church of Christ: and after his amendment, notwithstanding many others yet remayning most peruerse in their obstinacy, and shutting their ears vnto the truth, after that S. *Antony* with many prayers in vayne, had inuited them to a Sermon, there being a great number of them as then forth of the wals, where the riuer called *Marechia* discharges it selfe into the Sea; with great cõfidence in our Lord, he begins to call the Fishes vnto the word of God, since men of reason & redeemed with his precious bloud, would by no meanes seeme to harken to him. And incredible thing had it not been euident: he had scarce giuen forth the commaund, when an innumerable multitude of fishes of sundry formes and bignes, were seene to appeare on the waters of the Sea and riuer, which euen of their owne accord came in by sholes, and with heads erected accommodating themselues to listen to him; in so much as the lesser put themselues neer to the bancks side, and then the greater and bigger in order, with so goodly and fayre a dispose, as a more pleasing sight could not be seen.

To these squadrons so well ordered, the blessed S. *Antony* lifting vp his voyce began to vnfold vnto them the benefits vouchsafed them from the Creatour, the guift of swiftnes and colours, and of their beauty in particuler; the medicine subministred from them by *Toby*; the tribute, and food of our Lord himselfe: the mistery of the Resurrection represented in the Prophet *Ionas*. For which reasons with many others besides did S. *Antony* exhort them to yeild God thanks. To which aduise of his those Marine troups, since they could not by words, with sundry motions at least did signify their obedience, stooping with the head, sporting with iubily and

and shewing a will to honour the messenger of Christ. Nor would they depart from the place, vntil they were liceced thence, through his holy benediction. And so in the meane tyme the concourse of spectatours being now continually growne greater; the man of God taking then occasion, vpbrayded those obstinate and peruerse men of their malice and impiety, since in acknowledging the high Creatour, admitting so his holy law, they would so manifestly suffer themselues to be vanquished by beasts; whereupon the Heretikes at last remayned confounded, and the Catholikes continually more confirmed, in the holy doctrine and veneration of the Sea Apostolike.

Other miracles which S. Antony *wrought in the sight of Heretikes, to the conuersion of many, and confusion of others.* Chap. 13.

MOst famous was that which happened in the exequyes of a certaine publike Vsurer, now buryed allready: at which exequyes, it belonging to the blessed S. *Antony* to make the sermon, he tooke for text that saying of our Sauiour: *Vbi est thesaurus tuus, ibi est & cor tuum.* To which purpose with accustomed liberty he inueighed against the disordinate loue of gold and siluer, and weighed the inestimable domages which grow from thence: finally to let them see with their eyes themselues the truth of that sentence, turning himselfe to the neerest parents of the dead: Go your wayes (sayd he) by and by, to the chest of the miserable wretch, and there within shall you find his very hart it selfe: which they did without contradiction, and to the great terrour of them, and of the whole land, in the midst of his monyes they found the said hart, as yet not wholy cold. We shall now ad another of no terrour awhit, but of meere consolation.

S. Anthony being Custos at *Limoges*, after he had passed through *France* still preaching heere and there, chaunced to discourse with the inhabitants of *Burges*. But the presse was so great of such as came to heare him, as that the Canons of the Church, putting themselues in procession with the whole Auditory, went forth of the gates of the towne, into the open fields: where while the man of God puts himselfe to discourse in an eminent place, behold there gathered togeather very blacke clouds in the ayre, which threatned a terrible tẽpest; for feare wherof the people flying from thence & beginning to shift for themselue, S. *Antony* sayd with a loud voyce: Bee of good cheere my maysters; stirre not a foot, there shall not a drop of water light vpon any of you. The people obeyed: and behold suddenly a mighty storme of hayle and rayne to fall from heauen, which enuironing the Auditory as a wall, did not wet the breadth of a palme in the whole circuit, but left the people dry & vntouched. Whence followed many prayses vnto God, and extraordinary credit and reuerence to *S. Antony*.

And now to speake something likewise of meruails succeeding in his disputations with Heretikes: It is reported for certayne, how the diuine man being at *Arimini* on a tyme, or as others would haue it, in the Citty of *Tholouse*, a malapert minister of Sathan, of the Sect of *Berengarius*, being not able to maintayne himselfe in a controuersy of the most holy Sacrament, agaynst the reasons alleadged by *S. Anthony*, sayd finally vnto him. Thou confoundest me with words, as more learned then I; but not because they haue more foundation of truth. But let vs come to some more cleere experiences in effect; Whence I may be certifyed indeed, that God is really present in the consecrated host, and I promise and sweare vnto you (when it shall succeed) that I will confesse to be vanquished, and belieue this article, in the manner as you teach it.

S. Anthony accepts the condition, nor doubts awhit to put the quality of the tryall to his owne choice. Let vs do it then in this manner replyed the Heretike. This day will I beginne to keep my Mule without meate, & after three dayes againe shall I bring him forth so hungry into the market place, togeather with a pecke of oats for the purpose. And at the same tyme thou likewise come thither with thy azime or host, and if the beast in presence of the one and other shall forbeare to eate the oats, and turne to bow vnto thy bread, I am content also to adore the same, without more adoe. In the name of God sayd *S. Antony* let the matter be published through the Citty. The third day being come, both parties repayre to the market place, with such a thronge of people as euery one may iudge. Heere *S. Anthony* sacrificeth vpon an Altar set vp for the purpose, and before he communicates, conuerting himselfe to the principall Cittizens, with lighted torches about him, holding the Host in his hand replenished with fayth, turnes to the brute beast, which now was feeding the oats, & commands him in power of that God there present, that leauing the prouander now taken out

 of

of the ſacke, & ſet before him, to come preſently to his Creatour, and acknowledge and adore him in the ſayd Hoſt.

The Prieſt had ſcarcely ended theſe wordes, when the Mule deſpiſing the prouander, with headbowing, humbly approaching to the moſt holy ſacrament kneeld downe to adore it, to the infinit iubiley of the good, and holeſome conuerſion of that wretched Sacramentary. In this manner was a very ſtrange experiment brought to paſſe, vnworthy indeed of ſo high a myſtery; but yet nothing preiudiciall, nor perilous to the life of *S. Antony*.

How S. Antony *eſcaped the treacheryes of his enemyes by ſecret poyſon, and of the opinion he gayned with all men.* Chap. 14.

SOme others of the ſame kind with the former, found out another more wicked proofe, and by ſo much more dangerous, as more hidden; who being not wone with the former paſſage, but more exaſperated rather with the ſayd miracle, determined with poyſon to murder the ſeruant of Chriſt. Inuiting him therefore to dinner (whither he refuſed not to goe, being deſirous to help any manner of wayes) vnder colour of charity, they preſent him with poyſoned meat; which fraud being ſuddenly knowne in ſpirit, he reprehended them with loue & grauity for ſuch impiety: but thoſe obſtinate and peruerſe men, inſteed of being compunct, and penitent therat, vnto their hidden deceits added a maniſeſt impudency, and boldly thereupon began to ſay: How Chriſt had promiſed his faythfull Diſciples, that neyther the poyſonous, nor fatall drinkes, ſhould ſeeme to hurt them. Whence if he would but taſt thereof, he ſhould ſoone doubtleſſe confeſſe that ſaying of the Ghoſpell to be falſe. At which wordes *S. Antony* recollecting himſelfe, and on the one ſide; holding the taking of ſuch food were a meere tempting of him that had reuealed the danger vnto him; and fearing on the other, through the wicked diſpoſition of thoſe Calumniatours to occaſion ſome diſcredit to the ſacred Scripture, was reſolued at laſt to eate, and drinke the ſame without exception, if they would promiſe to returne to the Catholik fayth, when as he ſhould receaue no hurt thereby. To which condition they yielding aſſent, his word was performed, as well without the hurt of his perſon, as with the glorious purchaſe of thoſe mindes ſeduced.

Theſe, and many other thinges, which for breuity we let paſſe were

were wrought by the Blessed *Anthony* in the name of Christ, beyond all course & compasse of humane power: which being matched with a singular innocency of manners, and with a solid, liuely and enflamed eloquence, may not seeme strange they should fructifye so much, not only in the harts of the meaner and poorer sort (which ordinarily is wont, very willingly to accept the word of God, & without difficulty to rayse the affect from visible things) but euen also in the minds of the rich and potent; who so rarely imbrace the seed of the Ghospell, and be so hardly weaned from false delights, and designes, to aspire with paynes, mortifications, and almes to the future felicity. And yet many of this condition rendred themselues to the battayls of this great Captayne, and committed wholy to his discretion and gouernement (as we sayd) both their goods and liues.

Among which, a principall Baron of *Padua*, being called *Tisone Campo San Pietro*, may not seeme to be reckoned in the last place. This man after he had serued long in the warres, wherein he had beene a chiefe Commander, retyring himselfe to his house, and laying his armes aside, at the intreaty of the Blessed *Antony*, with the good example of the whole Citty, gaue himselfe to spirit; and conceauing feruour and zeale to help his subiects, obtayned of the Blessed Father to vouchsafe to come into the Land of *Campo S. Pietro* (from whose dominion, tooke the noble family of the *Tisons* that name) to cultiuate & instruct the rude people there in Christiā Religion, and in the feare of God. Which S. *Antony* refused not, especially for that there was in that place a little Conuent of Minours, that was maintayned by the almes of *Tisone* himselfe. True it is, that *S. Antony* being arriued there, to remaine more retyred, would not abide continually, neither among the Fryars, nor lesse in the Pallace of his Host, but vnder a Nut-tree of an vnmeasurable greatnes, from whose truncke grew forth six great branches in manner of a crowne, causing three litle Cells to be set vp, one for himselfe, and the other for two Fryars and companions of his (in which worke *Tisone* himselfe with singular piety did labour with his owne hands) whence *S. Antony* was wont after his exercises of prayer and contemplation, to preach vnto the people; which assembled to that heauenly food, from the neighbour countryes thereabout; but yet descending at the howers of refection and rest, he remayned in the Conuent.

Amidst

Amidst these things the diuine man, although by his old Institute he shunned, and had all worldly glory in much horrour; yet through the greatnes of his merits, he was arriued to that veneration with the people, that euen peeces of his poore cassock were secretly cut off for deuout Reliques; & when the word *Saint* was but named, for excellency sake it was cōmonly vnderstood of him. And yet he notwithstanding continued in austerityes, macerations, & vigils, not that his flesh now tamed and subdued allready, had need thereof; but to afford therein a perpetuall example, and edification to seculars. Who ordinarily not hauing iust weights to ballance the integrity of vertues, are wont, and accustomed to valew and prize perfection, by the exteriour afflictions and penances they discouer in Religious.

The Death of S. Antony, *with the sequels thereof: and his speedy Canonization.* Chap. 15.

VVIth such manner of strictnes of life accompanyed (as we haue sayd) with an extraordinary weake complexion, and many labours, and trauayls withall, came the seruant of Christ to be so feeble, as being surprized in *Campo San Pietro* with a greeuous infirmity, he soone, and directly told it likewise to one about him, that he was now arriued to the terme of his short dayes, and hoped ere long to go, & enioy those places without terme or measure of tyme. And withall not to be troublesome in his cure, either to that small Oratory of Minors, or the lay Families there, though he were with the most affectuous prayers that might be, coniured by all to abide with them, yet causing himselfe to be layd in a Countrey cart, he went to *Padua*. And considering that in the Monastery of *Sancta Maria Maior,* within the wals, he should too much be molested with visits, he diuerted to another place, which is called *Arcella*, of *Franciscans* indeed, but yet somwhat forth of the Citty.

Heere now being oppressed with the malady, with all deuotion he receiued the holsome Sacraments, and with hands ioyned together, and lifted vp, not without extraordinary feeling he recited the seauen Penitentiall psalmes, and a deuout hymne to the most Blessed Virgin, whose protection with particuler seruice he had allwayes sought to rely vpon. From thenceforth he begins suddenly to lift vp his eyes, and to fix them on heauen; & being

being demaunded what he looked vpon? I behold, sayd he, my Lord Iesus Christ: and after a short repose, among a thousand benedictions and pious teares of his deerest freinds, he yeilded vp his spirit to the Creatour, with all the tranquility and serenity that might be, in the yeare of our Lord 1231. and the 13. of the month of Iune, on a Friday, he being then but 36. yeares of age, whereof 15. he had spent in his Fathers house, two in *S. Vincents* of *Lisbone*, 9. at the holy Crosse of *Conimbria*, and about some 10. in the Order of *S. Francis*

After the passage, that blessed flesh, which through euill vsage, was before so horrid to see, so rugged, dry, and wrincked to be touched, became in a moment so white, soft, and plump, as if it had been of a tender and delicat child. His beloued freind & maister the Abbot of *Vercells*, whom we mentioned aboue, at that tyme, was much afflicted, with a disease of the throat. And euen loe, the same day, when S. *Antony* dyed, being in his chamber alone at prayer, he saw him suddenly to appeare before him; and after mutuall salutation, & imbraces: Behold (sayd he) my Lord Abbot, hauing left my Asse at *Padua*, how I goe in hast to my Country. And saying so, with a light touch only, he cured his throat, and so vanished. But the Abbot stedfastly beleiuing, that *S. Antony* was really passed by to *Lisbone*, going forth of his chamber, began to enquire of his familiars, where he was; from whom not gathering any thing, at last returned into himselfe, and coniectured by that vision the happy departure of the man of God: whereupon, making new diligence by letters, he found the encounter of howers and moments to be iust the same, as he himselfe did afterwards testify.

In the meane while the Fryars of *Arcella*, fearing some tumultuous concourse would be at the body, endeuoured to keep the departure of the seruant of Christ very secret, but in vayne. Because the very innocent boyes, through hidden instigation of the spirit, began in many troups to goe crying through the countryes: The holy Father is dead, the Saint is dead. With which voyce the people being awaked, on a sudden they shut vp their shopps, and laying all other businesse aside, put themselues in armes, with great effusion of bloud, while one part stood for retayning the sacred treasure in *Arcella*, and the other to conueigh him into the Citty: but after many and perilous bickeringes betweene them, by the humble prayers of the Fryars, & the authority of the Magistrates it was obtayned, that as himselfe being neere to death had requested, he should be carryed to the Church of *Sancta Maria Maior*, and so he was accompanyed thither by the Bishop, the Clergy, and by persons of quality in good order, with such aboundance of lightes, as the whole City seemed to be on fire.

Heere the high Masse being sung by the Bishop, began continually new and stupendious miracles to manifest themselues in diuers infirmityes of soules and bodyes. To which fame, with incredible feruour, continued a long tyme, whole troupes of Pilgrims to resort thither, not only of those confines, but of *Italy* also, and as it were of all *Europe*, with such a number of large guifts, and precious offeringes, as they were fayne to appoint chamberlaines and keepers for the custody of them, of the chiefest, & most honourable persons of *Padua*. With the help whereof, and with that moreouer which the Citty it selfe adioyned thereto, changing the title of the Temple (which was first of *Iuno*, & after of the Blessed Virgin *Mary*) in honour and inuocation of the Saint, was built in the same place, one of the magnificent and sumptuous Churches of Christendome. *Lisbone* it selfe being the natiue Countrey of the Saint, concurred in a manner with the deuotions of the *Paduans*, in making by command of the King, of one part of the House, where he was borne, a fayre little Church as we sayd, and of the other a Hall, where the Ancients with the Senate, vnto this present day, are wont to assemble to deale about matters of the Common wealth.

But aboue all, Pope *Gregory* the IX. himselfe, who before in *Rome* had with so choyce an Elogy commended the doctrine of the seruant of God, concurred to the exalting of his glorious memory. So as scarcely had a moneth passed ouer from the death, or to say better, from the natiuity of S. *Antony*, but causing a most exact inquisition to be made of his life, and miracles, with the high approbation of all the Cardinalls, and Prelats of the holy Church, he canonized him solemnly, and enrolled him among those spirits, who arriued in the eternall country, doe securely enioy the beatificall vision of God, there making intercession for others, who being on the way, are yet doubtfull continually of their progresse and tearme. Through which iudgment and approbation of the Sea Apostolike, was enflamed in all Christendome, a new desire to accumulate honours vpon the sacred depositum, & a liuely fayth in presenting supplications to that glorious soule: the *Paduans* yet in this

this part ſhewing themſelues moſt remarkable of all; who being conſtant in their auncient piety, follow in celebrating euery yeare the day of the depoſition of the Saint, with moſt exquiſite pompes, pſalmes, panygeriques, & other triumphs, truly belonging to the immortall merits of the noble Confeſſour of Chriſt, and particuler protection he affords that famous Citty: whence he renouncing in a manner his proper Country, hath been pleaſed to accept, the perpetuall ſweet Surname of *Padua*.

FINIS.

S. THOMAS OF AQVINE.

THE ARGVMENT.

THe * Tree that beares the dainty *Cyprian* flower,
Vnles oft prun'd by skillfull workemans art,
Growes wild & fruitlesse: *Loue* doth loose his power
And vigorous force, vnlesse our Soules do dart,
And force it oft, with often acts on high;
Or feeble soone it growes, and soone doth dye.
The smiling leaues ech other seeme to kisse:
Giue heau'n thy *Loue*; *Loue* shall from thence descend,
Cropt, bruiz'd, distill'd more sweet by farre it is:
Troubles make ours more gratefull in the end,
And oppositions nobly borne away,
Crowne our afflictions with a nobler Bay.
Oppos'd by Friends their force I ouerbore;
My wish at last obtayning to enioy,
Heau'ns *Loue* I found in me augmented more,
While more to gaine it, I my *Loue* employ:
By painefull acts this Passion I dilate,
And keep my soule by weaknesse in her state.

* An allusiõ to the Rose called in Hebrevv, Loues shaddovv. Cant. 2.

THE LIFE OF S. THOMAS OF AQVINE.

Written by the Reuerend Fathers Preachers.

Of the Parents, and education of S. Thomas: *with the signes of his future greatnes.* Chap. I.

SAINT THOMAS Doctour, for the excellency of his learning, surnamed the *Angelicall*, was borne in the Citty of *Aquinas*, in the yeare of our Lord, 1224. His Father was *Landolphus* Count of the sayd Citty of *Aquinas*: his Mother *Theodora*, daughter of the Count of *Thean*, being both of a noble and illustrious house. The birth not only of the Saint, but also his Religion was foretould by a venerable Hermit, who liued in those Countreyes, called *Bonus*; who visiting *Theodora* neere her childbirth, saluted her, saying: *Be ioyfull Lady, for you shall shortly haue a sonne, who for his singular qualities, shall be renowned through the world, and shall take the habit you see heere depainted*: It was euen the habit of S. *Dominicke*, the which, at the foot of the Mother of God, in a little image, he wore for deuotion hanging about his necke. *Theodora* answered: *Gods will be done*. After which, the child being borne into the world, and called in sacred Baptisme by the name of *Thomas*, soone gaue very manifest signes of the learning and sanctity which in tyme were to shine in him. Because on a day while the Nurse was making him a bath, he snatching vp of his owne accord a peece of paper from the ground, held it fast in the hand, and the Nurse going about to take it away, he began to cry, and to be so troubled at it, as for a last remedy she was feigne to wash him, with the same in his hand.

Wherefore the mother being aduertised, to cleere and satisfy her selfe the better of the matter, opened his hand by force, and taking away the paper from him, they found there written the salutation of the Archangell *Gabriel* to the Virgin Mary, and that with so much more wonder of theirs, and of all the standers by, as they could lesse coniecture, how such a writing could come into his handes. The little Child in the meane tyme, with signes neuer ceased to reach after it, and to cry and sob for the same, vntill to quiet him they were forced to yield it him againe: and he not to haue it taken away any more, putting it in his mouth, on a sudden swallowed it vp. This same, as we say, was held of the wise, and of men of good vnderstanding, for a great and certaine presage of celestiall knowledge, and of the rare vertues, which in progresse of tyme were to ripen in *Thomas*: it being not likely that a chlid in the swath-bands, without diuine operation could be so enamoured with the words, which were the beginning and fountayne of all the mysteryes of the new law, and of Christian piety.

Nor this signe only of future fruites, was seen in that noble bud, but as often as a booke, or ought els but like to a booke, was presented to his sight, with childish endeauour he would reach after it, and take it in his hand, turning it vp and downe, and looking on it without end; so as to comforte him, when need was, and to still him and dry his teares, there was no more efficacious way, then to put a paper or booke into his hands, to play withall. Amidst such hopes, being now arriued to fiue yeares old, that he might be the better conserued in purity and vertuous manners, he was according to the laudable customes of those tymes giuen to the venerable Monks of *Monte Cassino*, to be trayned vp: vnder whose care were likewise many children of Lords and Princes besides. Nor had the Maister any difficulty at all, to direct this happy plant vnto immortall and diuine things; since the child of his owne accord, shewing himselfe to be aliened from base thoughts, and from all curiosity whatsoeuer, did euen tyre him with high and profound questi-

questions, whereof one was, to demaund often, what God was? Besides that, keeping himselfe from company of the lesse modest & deuout, he would voluntarily recollect himselfe, with the wiser & more prudent sort, and more addicted to spirit: yea it is affirmed for certaine, that euen at that tyme, he would spend two houres of the day, in sundry deuotions, and yet not fayle to be at schoole, or to do whatsoeuer the Maister appointed him besides. In breife, out-stripping his yeares by many degrees, with his iudgement he became a patterne of industry, of obedience, and of all goodnes.

Whereupon the Abbot of *Monte Cassino*, for feare least Count *Landolph* & *Theodora*, should transferre him from the arts of peace, to those of warre, as they had allready done with the other two elder sonnes of theirs, very instantly perswaded them, that they would not smother such a wit in the tumultuous exercises, & occupations of chiualry, and depriue the world, and the Church of so great a help, as such beginnings without doubt seemed to promise them. Great was the authority of the Abbot with all men, nor lesse efficacious were the reasons alleadged by him. *Thomas* his age (which as yet not passed ten yeares) afforded a large field for great designes. The neighbour Citty of *Naples*, being the auncient and gracious receptable (as *Strabo* testifyes) of sublimer witts, and of the liberall arts, being in loue with so great a Student, seemed as it were, ambitiously to stretch forth the armes, to inuite and entertayne him.

All these occasions, through diuine disposition concurred together, to mantayne *Thomas* so studious of speculation and learning: so as being conueighed from the Country to the Metropolis, & from grāmer to the grauer studyes, vnder famous Doctours, he studyed the Mathematikes, Logike, and Philosopy, with such profit as in short tyme, his name began to resound through the whole Vniuersity, extolling with the lustre of his Bloud, and splendour of his parents, the singular qualityes and rare ornaments of his person. At which glory afforded him, was yet the wise and chast youth not puffed vp a whit, but rather endeuoured he with all force, to stand firme in the knowledge and meane esteeme of himselfe, and amidst what varieties so euer of human accidents, to hold his intention fixed and centered in God only: and by how much more knowledge he got of the Creatour by the meanes of creatures, and from Tyme learned Eternity, & from transitory things the stable and

and eternall, so much greater desire was enkindled in him, to sequester himselfe from the vulgar, and with a generous contempt of the world, of purpose to attend to the contemplation of the first cause, & to cultiuate wholy that part of himselfe, which he knew to be more worthy, and more like vnto God. Such was the end & scope of the good youth, but in the election of the meane, he could not yet resolue, but remayned in the same perplexity, vntill a cleare day was added to the vncertaine light of the passed inspirations, through the occasions we shall presently declare.

How S. Thomas *enters into the Family of the* Dominicans; *and how he beares himselues therein.* Chap. 2.

THe sacred Order of the Fryars Preachers, now flourished in those dayes, that was founded by the glorious Father S. *Dominicke*, and there were, euen at that tyme also, as euer after haue been, many men of excellent learning and singular vertue amongst them. Now S. *Thomas* hauing friendship with one of these, namely with *Iohn* of *S. Iulian*, began ingenuously to conferre with him of his studyes and labours. Whereupon being often present at his disputes, & discourses, and of others of the same Family, he came by little and little to affectionate himselfe to their Institute, while it seemed to him, he could no wayes better imploy the talents he had from God, then in the company of men wholy giuen to the extirpation of Heresies, and defence, and exaltation of the Catholike Fayth. But perhapps the better to examine his spirit, or not to trust to much too himselfe, he differred (as the vse is) his resolution yet longer. When *Iohn* easily perceiuing what the noble youth reuolued in mind, he determined to spurre him on, & with good opportunity sayd to him one day: It seemes to me *Thomas*, when I cast myne eyes vpon thee, and thy labours, and trauayles, thou aspirest to no vayne, or transitory rewards: but if thou wilt attayne thy purpose, Know assuredly my Sonne, that perfect wisdome and true felicity, is not got amidst the distractions, intrications, & labyrinths of the world. The recollection of the soule, and the repose and solitude, which are found in Religious, is the next disposition to apprehend the truth with, and to receiue continually new rayes and influences from heauen. This way, as you well know, haue the greatest lights of Christendome held; who sequestring themselues from busynesses and

and perturbations, & cares, haue attended to Philosophize in good earnest, nor haue reguarded any more the peoples tatlings, then the bawling of so many Curres. Wherefore do thou also with like examples not fayle to disentangle thy selfe. This habit heere now expects thee a good while, and if thou resoluest but to accept the same, my mind giues me, nor am I a whit deceiued, that by thy meanes our Lord will worke some notable exployt.

Such was the first assault and battery which *Iohn* gaue him, and not in vayne. Since that finding now at first the walls to be shaken with this discourse, he proceeded on to leuell them with the earth, and to take all obstacles quite away: and S. *Thomas* easily conuinced, gaue vp the hold, saying: Father, I would not haue you thinke me to be so cold, and so poore a louer of the chiefest good, as that the peoples talke, or any other respect whatsoeuer, should put me off, from following it with all my forces. Your exhortation, hath not found me alienated awhit, from such manner of designes, since now already I haue thought with my selfe long since, to retire me. And now only to resolue of the place, I had need of some louing direction, and prudent counsayle. To which office of charity, since it hath pleased our Lord to make vse of your person, assure your selfe I receiue your words, as come from the Holy Ghost. Whence I pray, let there be no delay made: Doe you deale with the Superiours, for I will not depart hence, til the busynes be concluded. *Iohn* could haue wished for no better newes. Soone shall you be satisfyed, replyed he then; and going in hast to the Priour, without any difficulty, but rather with a great deale of ioy of the whole Conuent, he brought the busynes begun, to a very good passe; and *Thomas* was put into the habit, with the due ceremonyes, being then of seauenteene yeares of age.

Now seeing himselfe, to be thus shut vp in the Monastery, & esteeming himselfe to be sufficiently fenced against the clamours of his freinds, and Citty: considering the state he had entered into, he began to frame his life, according to the obligement of his vocation; holding it a great scorne if after the leauing of such hopes in the world, he should not so carry himselfe in Religion, as euery one should not rest satisfyed of the course he had vndertaken. Then partly through the internall motiues, which he felt in his breast, partly the exteriour examples & aduices of the Fathers with whom he liued, he went on more encouraged euery day, not to forslow any thing, that might any wayes promote him to the top of perfe-ction, which he had proposed to himselfe. And howbeyt in ech vertue through diuine grace, and with the continual vse of prayer, he laboured to become excellent, yet with particuler application he endeuoured to goe forward in holy humility, as well for acknowledging it to be the Mother of all good, as also in seeing an extraordinary necessity imposed vpon him, to shew forth himselfe more meeke and humble to all, by how much the ornaments and habilityes he had receiued from God, were more apt to moue enuy, and to make him more haughty and proud. And forasmuch as he well knew, there was no more direct, and speedy way for the aforesaid vertue, then the perpetuall subiection and mortification of the proper will & iudgment, he gaue himselfe to obserue obedience aboue all things: and euen from the first beginning so ordered he, & composed the mind, as that neither in words nor deeds, would he once digresse from the Superiours dictamens, nor from the orders, and rules of his Religion: and therefore he attended to read them, as he might euery moment without difficulty be putting them in practise. Besides which, knowing how important sobriety and abstinence were to restrayne passions, and to conserue the vnderstanding cleere, and quick-sighted, he determined to giue no place to superfluous nourishment & sleep; whence, eyther the flesh might kick through too much pampering, or the mind be ouercast with fumes and vapours. Finally, he euer abhorred all idlenes, not suffering any houre vnfruitfully to passe away, and leauing withall, as litle place as might be to the temptations, and subtilityes of the ancient Enemy.

Theodora the Mother beares of S. Thomas *his entry into Religion; & labours to draw him from it, by all meanes possible.* Chap. 3.

IN the meane tyme Count *Landolph* dyed, after he had suffered many troubles and losses, for defence of the Sea Apostolike, by *Frederick* the Emperour: who being now with his army in *Tuscany*, vnderstanding of the death of the Count, sent for his two eldest sonnes, the one called *Arnold*, the other by the name of his Father, *Landolph*; and vnder the shew of honourable seruice in warre, kept them for hostages, that in defending the cause, and part of the Pope, they might not follow their Fathers steps. The widdow *Theodora* being

being now in these tearmes in the City of *Aquinas*, had newes of the election of life, which her sonne *Thomas* had made in *Naples*; and remembring withal the prophesy of the good Hermit, she endeuoured to satisfy her selfe, with what the diuine prouidence had ordayned: yea she began to render thanks to God for it, as became a Christian, and vertuous woman; but was enflamed notwithstanding with such a burning desire, to behold and imbrace her desired sonne, as without delay she trauailed to *Naples*, with the mind (as the writers say) to examine the counsails of the young man, and that if she found them to be reasonable, and well grounded, to encourage him to perseuer in the diuine seruice, rather then to alienate or diuert him any manner of wayes.

Neuerthelesse, the Dominican Fathers, not to expose so new and worthy a subiect to the hazard of his vocation, vnderstanding of the Countesse comming, made hast to send him to *Rome*; from thence to passe vnto *Paris*. When *Theodora* had notice thereof, it cannot easily be expressed what anger and disdayne she conceiued for it, and laying all other thoughts aside, she posted to *Rome*; and not finding her deere pledge there neyther, she presently wrytes to her sonnes in the Campe, to send forth assoone as may be, to way-lay the Roman passage, and apprehending their Brother on his way to *France* in a Fryars habit, by any meanes to send him to her. This message to those Souldyers (who as yet had heard nothing of the newes of S. *Thomas*) was both sudden, and vngratefull to them. They being no lesse enflamed with choler then the Mother was, with the Emperours consent, they went scouring the Country with a good band, vntill by diuine permission, they found the Pilgrim, through wearines of the iourney sat downe with fowre others, at a cleere fountayne somewhat neere the Bourge of *Aquapendente*, and running furiously vpon him, first they tryed to pull away his habit, by force; but that not becoming them to doe, they tooke him lastly, and sent him bound to his Mother: who receiuing him with sighs and sobs, caused him to be carryed for the present to *Rocca secca* (a place that was seated, on the top of a hill neere to *Aquinas*) to see if heereafter, with more leasure, she might draw him to her designes.

This boldnes of *Theodora*, and of her elder Sonnes, with reason displeased the Pope, when he heard the same from the Fathers of S. *Dominicke*, and would surely haue proceeded against them with censures & excommunications, if the sayd Religious for auoyding scandall, and to shew themselues rather to be friends of peace, had not pacifyed the matter, in leauing all to the diuine iustice. But *Theodora* yet not contented with what she had done, being returned to her countrey, beginns afresh to lay a cruell assault against S. *Thomas*, saying among other thinges, that which followes: When thy Father of happy memory, and I thy vnfortunate Mother first sent thee to *Monte Cassino*, and afterwardes to study at *Naples*, we had verily thought, that the conuersation of such, euen so held in esteeme for sanctity and learning, as the Fathers of *S. Benet* were, and the others of *S. Dominicke*, would haue bred and nourished in thee nothing but piety and reuerence due to a Mother, at least humanity and discretion, to be shewed of right to euery one: but now with these deportements of thyne, thou makest me doubt that these new Orders insteed of meeknes and ciuility do but teach men to put on the habit of fiercenes & cruelty: yet when I am present at their preachinges, I do heare them commend both with reasons, and with authority of sacred Scriptures, the obseruance, and honour due vnto Father and Mother, and the care which euery one ought to haue of their domestiques. If these moderne Deuines, to purchase in publique an opinion of sanctity, and in secret to attend to their priuate interests, do but celebrate Mercy in the Pulpit, and in their Cell approue inhumane, rigours, and of harsh manners, and if so it be with them; then surely it is to be thought a goodly sanctity to lye so in the Pulpit, to deceaue the Auditours, & with trim and colourable speaches of piety to inueagle and entice the vnwary youth, to make them afterwardes in Cloysters, to become very sauage and brutish, arming them, and setting them on against their owne Mothers, sometymes more iust and timourous of God, then euen the Preachers themselues.

And likewise if it be true, as I haue alwayes vnderstood, that to haue respect to Parents, both by diuine Law and naturall instinct, be straightly imposed on euery man; what excuse canst thou seeme to alleadge, my Sonne, for not casting thyne eyes hitherto, on so great calamityes, as now haue partly happened to me, and partly also, are likely to arriue anew, and euen hang ouer my head? Tell me? Where is thy Father, who hath left me a Widdow, surcharged so with yeares, amidst so grieuous stormes & aduersities? Where are thy Brothers, who being accused for being too fauourable, and followers of the Pope, are violently detayned by *Cesar*? Yet so great losse, and miseries might in some manner be suffered by me, if there were but any hope yet left vs of better. But these differences which raigne so betweene the Emperour and the Pope, and the sinister conceit, wherein we are with the most potent and stronger part; alas, how I feare it will redound at last, to an vtter ruine of our house, and our whole Citty. One comfort only remayned vnto me, in thy person, while thy wisedome and rare partes seemed to promise me, they would shortly rayse thee to so high an estate and dignity, as thou only mighst suffice to remedy all these losses and perills. But most vnhappy we, that euen we applyed thee to study and deuotion, while now thou art become an idle spectatour only of the calamityes, and troubles of thy disconsolate Mother, Brothers, Parents and Friends, and lastly of the flames and ashes of all the afflicted countrey. To which I see well thou art likely to giue vs some goodly succour surely, with those horrid garments I see vpon thee, and with thy flying so, into the dens of *France*, there to reioyce thee, and to laugh at our death and Exequies.

The Answere of S. Thomas *to his Lady Mother.* Chap. 4.

THese words *Theodora* accompanyed with weeping, and anger withall, but yet not entring into menaces, hoping that her Sonne being mooued to pitty would be able to make no more resistance against her. But he being resolute and firme as a tower, did seeke indeed to comfort her, but as farre as duty would and no further, and gaue her accompt of his doings in the manner following. If so many ruines as you say Madame, are like to befall our house, neyther you nor I can tell which way to remedy them, since for the future it rests in the hands, and will of God. Nor to me appeares, we are to expect so much euill frō the diuine Goodnes: & if in very deed our sinnes, and those of our Country seeme to merit the same, what better meane can I take, to pacify the Heauenly wrath, then to dispoyle me of my selfe, and to offer me vp as a full and perfect Holocaust to his Eternall Maiesty? If I should haue remayned with you in the world, or now returne to it a new, what should I doe but increase with my presence your misfortunes, laments, & woes? And is it possible that our Citty should be reduced into so il tearmes, as that the only safety thereof, should be founded in a poore youth, of little knowledge and of no experience at all? And yet when necessity shall require it, I shall be ready to succour it with my life and bloud.

But where are the flames? where the fires you exaggerate so much? For my part I do see none present, nor do I know whence they are like to come. And if indeed (as I sayd) they were to be feared so, for our owne sinnes; it rests not in my power but in Gods only, to exempt vs from them. And when you would rely on human succours, haue you not other Sonnes, as more auncient in yeares, so of much more prudence and worth then I? Are they not continually with the person of the Emperour? Who, supposing he haue some suspition of our bloud, yet will it be no hard matter, for them with their seruice and loyalty (which is wont to soften & relent euen Beares and Lyons) to pacify him so, that his ill conceipt may turne to a good opinion agayne, and his hatred be conuerted into grace and protection. Nor would I haue you say heere, Madame, that I am quite depriued of affection and of common sense, and that from the Seruants of God I haue learned to be inhuman & sauage: these are but fables meerly. I contemne not your sighes, I take no pleasure (as you please to say) in your tribulations and afflictions. God calls me another way, him must I needs obey rather then men: and you consider not the great danger, the while, you put me into, through your so obstinately opposing his holy will. And since you tearme me hard and sauage, for sequestring my selfe from the snares of the world, what manner of loue shall I call yours? how pious, how benigne, how motherly, so to pull me from the midst of the hauen of tranquility, to expose me to the raging winds and furious tempests of the world? But in summe, you deceiue your selfe Madame, if you thinke with your artificiousnes to draw a soule into basenes and mire, that hauing through the grace of God already tasted some fruite of the spirit and true vertues, hath now at last in scorne and loathing what pleasures soeuer the sense and flesh can promise. And well may you with violence retayne this body of mine with you, and make it consume in prison: but that euer the mind should be aliened from Religion, and should lay aside this poore habit, and courser garments, while I breath you shall neuer obtayne the same.

The

The perswasions vsed by S. Thomas *his sisters. His answere to them, and what followed thereof.* Chap. 5.

VVIth this so free discourse of *S. Thomas*, the Mother now satisfyed, that by way of perswasions, or prayers, she should profit but little; so as being much exasperated therat, with an angry contenance she betakes her selfe to protestations & threats: but finding him continually more constant and impregnable, very sad and heauy she parts from him, leauing him still shut vp in the Rock with a good guard. A litle after to see if the enterprise would succeed better with others, she commaund two daughters of hers of sharp wits, and of excellent speach to goe vnto him, and to try by all meanes to bow that obdurate hart. Nor stayd they awhit (as the human Nature is more prompt to the execution of euill then good) to make tryall with all industry that might be. Apparelled then very sumptuously, and with the most gorgeous ornaments they had, they went both of purpose to see him, shewing themselues with amourous lookes, and premeditated words, to meruayle much, how he could once let such a folly enter into his head, and by whom he had been so deceiued, and induced, as to forget his greatnes so much, and the splendour of his so illustrious and ancient a Family, of so many and so famous Predecessours of his. He should consider a litle, if the habits and habitations of the meane, base, and obscure people, become persons of so noble bloud: if it were sufferable, that a yonge man elected by God, for high enterprises and affayres, to gouerne states, to rule vassalls, with so much dishonour of him, and his freinds and parents, should goe hide and bury himselfe in cloisters. And therefore by all meanes, he should chaunge his mind, and turne the same, to take to himselfe some noble and bewtifull Spouse, to liue (as men of iudgment doe) according to decorum, and to procure by all meanes, the greatnes & glory of the house of *Aquinas*, for these were atcheiuements worthy of him.

At which suggestions of theirs S. *Thomas* fetching a deep sigh: Cease, answered he, from such vanityes, for you are not to deale heere with a Reed, to be shaken with euery wind, but with a Religious man and seruant of Christ. The noble bloud you so much vaunt of, if not accompanyed with solid vertues and diuine grace,

in

is no more then a foolish fantasy? And where the goodnes & friendship of God is found, what need is there of nobility of birth? As for the exteriour habit, I haue a great deale more occasion to see you, or rather to bewayle you, to behold you so braue and gallant as you be. And know you not how this quaint workeman-ship of yours, springs but from the diuell, & serues for nothing else, but to put the honesty of body and soule in hazard? And much better is it, vnder a poore, and course mantle, to couer a candid and pure spirit, then with superfluous ornaments of the body to shew a mind not so Christian or modest as it ought? And it appeares, Sisters, you regard not so much the eyes of Christ, as those of men. And this perhapps were a lesse euill, if together with humane arts heere, were not mingled also the diabolicall. You see not the spots which by this mãner, you put vpon the soule, & thinke belike, you wretches as you are, with your silks, gold, and iewells, to deceiue the sight of the most holy Trinity, and of all the heauenly Court. And what suppose you at last to deriue from terrene loue, but a perpetuall succession of sorowes and troubles?

Looke vpon our Mother, in what torments she is now, & how vnhappy a life she confesseth she leades. Let her goe on, forsooth, gathering the sweete fruites of the world, and do you follow her likewise if you will, hauing still before your eyes the continuall punishments she hath, and the infinit dolours she feeles. These are the gaynes your worldly industryes procure you. To this finally, doe those dressings of the body point; to those proud thoughts of vayne glory, of vayne nobility, of vayne honour. I would to God, he would so open your eyes a litle, as that transcending the heauens and starres, they might penetrate into the inmost bowers of the blessed spirits, where you should behold, very liuely tragedyes of your perdition, and folly, most perfectly represented. And if in that fortunate number, were some of our Auncestours to be found, whose fame you seeme to extol so much, whence thinke you, would they receiue a more gratefull and sweete spectacle, eyther of me, that labour withall my forces to imitate them, and who therefore treading vnder foot all mortall care, and contemning all human reputation, & guirt with this habit to be able more freely to follow their stepps; thẽ of you, who forgetting their examples, do spend the time in chats, & attend to flesh, without any reckoning of the soule, and doe seeme to giue your selues to nothing els, then to kindle

your

your selues an euerlasting fire?

With this discourse accompanyed with truth & spirit, S. *Thomas* did so mortify the boldnes of his Sisters, as for shame they held their peace. And the one of them being touched with particuler feeling, afterwards continued a good life, and holy conuersation, vntill such tyme as moued by God, imitating her Brother she made a vow of Religion, and being reclused in a monastery of the Nunnes of *S. Benet* of *Capua*, laudably perseuered therein vnto her death. But S. *Thomas* in the meane tyme making a vertue of necessity, & a Cell of his prison, spent the tyme in prayer and study as he was wont, esteeming it to be no small happynes to him in those persecutions, to see occasions cut off, of wandering abroad, heere and there, & the distractions, which a more free, and common life would bring with them.

How S. Thomas *is prouoked by his Brothers agayne; then tempted by a woman; and lastly escapes out of prison*. Chap. 6.

S. *Thomas* continued not long thus quiet and secure, because *Frederick* the Emperour, being passed with his army into *Puglia*; the two Brothers, of whom we haue aboue made mention, vpon that occasion came to *Rocca secca*, renewing their auncient purpose, of diuerting S. *Thomas*, by all meanes possible, from his way begun: and since that neyther with terrours, nor flatteryes they could preuayle with him, being enflamed with rage, they doubted not furiously to teare off the sacred weed from his back, and leauing him so halfe naked in the place, they departed thence full of wrath and indignation. Then the disciple of Christ, taking compassion of their youthfull errour, & praying most earnestly for those soules, endeuoured to peece vp agayne the torne habit, the best he could with his owne hands, and thanking God for the victory obtayned, now returned agayne to his wonted occupations; when besides all expectation, he was surprized with a new assault, more fierce then euer; a wanton woman, set on by the Brothers, and brought in of purpose to tempt him: But he, as one that knew well the daunger of such manner of battayles, snatching suddenly a brand out of the fire, chased away that monster from his chamber, and shutting fast the doore, at the same instant drew a Crosse on the wal with the same stick, before which hauing prostrated himselfe, most

 humbly

humbly besought he our Lord, that if by chance that hellish sight had left in his imagination any manner of blot whatsoeuer, he would vouchsafe of his infinite mercy to take it away quite, and to graunt him besides so much help and fauour, as he might be able very perfectly to preserue his chastity to his death, which in Religion he had deuoutly promised.

The diuine eares were not deafe, vnto so iust & feruent prayers. The Champion of Christ thereupon being growne very weary, fell into a short sleepe: when two Angells from heauen appeared to him, telling him his prayers were heard, & for a testimony thereof, they guirded his loynes with a belt, so strongly, as that through payne therof crying out aloud, it made his keepers to enter into him, to whom notwithstanding he would not discouer what had happened, as neyther reuealed he it afterwards to any others, vntill the article of his death, when it seemed to him, he was then obliged in cōscience not to bury so cleere an act of the diuine goodnesse in perpetuall obliuion. But after that accident, if some great necessity for the glory of God or behoof of the neighbours required it not, he kept himselfe wholy from all couersation with women, as from basiliskes, and serpents.

For two whole yeares he had now been shut vp in that prison, at the end whereof *Theodora*, being now growne weary, & partly also being gauled with touches of her conscience, calling for some of the Fathers Preachers vnto her, she secretly gaue order to them to come at a certaine houre of the night, vnto the foot of the wall against the chamber of S. *Thomas*, and that he descending by a cord from the window, or a false ladder, they might carry him away in the name of God. The occasion of this secrecy was, as well the feare of offending her other Sonnes, if without their consentes he had been openly let goe, as the respect of her owne reputation, which seemed to be in danger, if after so many contentions, and so much adoe, her sage practizes should manifestly be vanquished at last, by the constancy and reasons of a youth only. For this enterprize *Iohn* of *S. Iulian* was chosen, whome we mentioned aboue, being the deer father & Maister of S. *Thomas*, & who heretofore truly was wont by the tacite consent of *Theodora* to visit him in prison. By this man, and other his companions being led away to *Naples*, not without the common Iubiley of all, from thence they sent him to *Rome*, by order of Superiours, and from *Rome* in company of the Generall of the *Dominicans* he went to *Paris*; and from thence agaiue within few mouthes, being sent to *Colen*, he began with great contentment, to heare *Albertus Magnus*, holding it to be no small happynes to him to haue met with so famous and excellent a Maister, and with so cleere a glasse of all religious vertues.

S. Thomas *is graduated, and made Maister of the Chayre: and how he caryes himselfe therein.* Chap. 7.

BY occasion of such a Doctour, S. *Thomas* gaue himselfe to heape vp new treasures of wisedome, and to attend the better to so noble a purchase. He imposed on himselfe in the meane tyme, a Pithagorean silence, in so much as he was come into contempt for the same with the rest of his fellowes in the schoole, & was brought into such a conceipt amongst them of a slow and grosse capacity, as by a surname they called him the *dumbe Oxe*. But the diuine Prouicence suffered not so rare a light of wit, should be hidden long. It came into the mind, to some of the more curious, with diuers demands to tempt the vnknowne learning of the youth, & to breake in some sort that pertinacious silence of his. There was explicated at that tyme in Schooles the booke of S. *Denys Areopagita, de Diuinis nominibus*, a very high matter, and full of deep mysteryes. Vpon the lessons S. *Thomas* then being cunningly examined by more thē one he gaue such accompt thereof beyond all expectation, both by his pen, and by word of mouth, that *Albertus* would needs oppose, and proue him also; ordayning in the first disputations, he should be *Respondent* in very difficult questions.

This did *S. Thomas* refuse at first, of his innated modesty. But *Albertus* continually making more instance, he thought good, to resist no longer: and recommending himselfe first very humbly to our Lord God as he was wont, he answered after, with such acumen of wit, and with so much dexterity withall, as that *Albertus* being full of astonishment exclaymed at last: *Thomas, thou seemest to me rather a Moderatour, then a meere Respondent*. And thereupon turning to the Auditory. *My Maysters* (sayd he) *you call him a dumbe Oxe, but certainely he shall one day giue forth such lowings, as shall be heard throughout the whole world*. With his so cleere a testimony made so publiquely of him, it was not possible for him any more, to remayne eyther retired or silent; but yet he alwayes conserued himselfe farre from any arrogancy at all: whence he came every day to be so much the more admirable to all, and was by vniuersall consent held no lesse then a Saint. Thus being in *Colen* for some tyme, he was by the instance of *Albertus Magnus*, recalled to *Paris* by the Generall of the order, there to take the degree of Bachelour vpon him. To which degree being promoted against his will, they applyed him presently to expound the Maister of *Sentences*; wherein (hauing kept for this intention very strict vigils, and fasts, and made his prayer) he came off with it in such manner, as that the Rectour of the Studyes, determined very soone to make him a Maister in Theology, with all the solemnity that might be.

S. *Thomas* vnderstanding thereof, and esteeming himselfe very farre vnworthy of that name, began afresh to find excuses, and to alleadge particulerly his age, which as yet had not finished the thirtith yeare, yet for all that he was fayne to obey. And in such extremity of his, recurring (according to custome) to the armes of prayer, he begins to craue the succour of the Almighty God; vntill such tyme as being once perplexed, among other things, about the Theme he should take in that publike act, a venerable old man appeared to him in sleep, and sayd to him: What aylest thou *Thomas*, that thou weepest, and so afflictest thy selfe in this manner? He answered, they enforce me to take the name & office of Maister vpon me, wherto I know my selfe, to be insufficient: and being among other things at the beginning to make a discourse, I know not what Theme to take. Then, replyed the old man: Be of good cheer my Sonne: It is the will of God that thou accept the degree. For Theme thou shalt take that verse of the Psalme, *Rigans montes de superioribus suis, & de fructu operum tuorum satiabitur terra*. That sayd, the old man vanished, and *S. Thomas* yielded many thanks to God, for being so benignly comforted by his immense goodnes. Being now made Maister, he went forward in explicating the sacred Theology with great applause, hauing alwayes an eye to the profit, & capacity of the schollers, rather then to his owne reputatiō or proper gust. In his manner of interpreting he had an easy, cleere, and distinct methode. He fled new opinions, and the vnusuall manner of phrases and words. In disputes, he kept himselfe from moderate contentions, and extrauagant acts or clamors, maturely yeilding to others obstinacyes or pertinacityes, and choosing rather for the glory of God, and edification of the Neighbour, to appeare

sometymes

ſometymes leſſe learned, then little modeſt. Whereſoeuer he read, but eſpecially in *Paris*, and in *Rome*, he had alwayes his Schoole very flouriſhing, both for number and quality of hearers, Doctours, Biſhops, Cardinals: and it is a notable thing, that with all the credit and authority he had gotten, yet neuer ſlacked he his dilgence, being otherwiſe one of ſo great a naturall wit, as he had few his equalls, and of ſo happy a memory withal, that in a manner, as often as he had but once ſeene any thing, he would faythfully retayne it for euer; and of ſuch vigour of mind, as that which is recounted of ſome Ancients for ſo admirable a thing, he would yet doe more in dictating, in diuers matters, vnto three or foure Scribes at once, & yet that rich floud of wiſedome would neuer be diminiſhed.

Of S. Thomas *his Speculations in ſtudyes: with his Rapts, and Extaſies in Spirit*. Chap. 8.

IT would be too long, and a ſuperfluous thing to make heere a Catalogue of his workes ſo many, and of ſo great note, wherwith he confirmed the Catholike fayth, & rooted out, and oppreſt many hereſies, partly increaſed already, and partly new growne vp: ech ſtate and quality of perſons he would inſtruct with holſom aduiſes and precepts, and finally illuſtrated the ſacred Thology, and brought it againe to its ancient dignity, reducing and ſubmitting all other ſciences to its Empire, which through the fault of ſome impious Sophiſters ſeemed heeretofore to diſſent and rebell from it. But as he would touch the point in euery matter, ſo he ſeemed to haue a ſpeciall grace, in treating of the moſt excellent Sacrament of the Altar, and not only in Proſe, but in Latin rime alſo, according to the cuſtomes of thoſe tymes; in ſo much as for the eminent doctrine and piety contayned therin, the Catholike Church euen to this day, ſinges no other Office, or Maſſe on the day of the great ſolemnity of *Corpus Chriſti*, then that which he compoſed, at the inſtance of Pope *Vrban* the IV.

And it is moſt certaine, that in *Naples*, being once much eleuated in mind, and preſent in perſon before a Crucifix, our Lord ſpake to him in that image: *VVell haſt thou written of me, Thomas; VVhat reward then wouldst thou haue? VVhen he anſwered: ſurely nothing, O Lord, but thyne owne ſelfe*. Two notable parts concurred in the glorious Doctour, which are hardly coupled together; as quicknes in apprehension, and patience in speculation. Forasmuch as he not only acutely penetrated and distinguished at once, but would also diue into the deeper inuestigations, as that very often he would come to loose his senses. When on a tyme, being in such an abstraction, a cole of fire, lighting on his leg, and agayne the flame of the candell, which studying he held in his hand, euen touching his flesh, a prety while, he stirred not awhit, nor was moued any more thereat then a meere stone.

That same likewise was memorable, which happened to him, at a Feast with *S. Lewys* King of *France*, at such tyme as he wrot that noble Summe against the Gentils: in which matter he was then so absorpt, as that amidst the Royall dishes of the King, forgetting himselfe and the standers by, he suddenly cryed out: *The Manichies are conuinced*; and seeming to him, that he was in his Cell, called to *Fryar Reginald* his companion, to dictate to him as he was wont. But after awaked by the Dominican Priour who sate by him and crauing pardon with some confusion, he was comforted and excused by the wise King, at whose beck one was suddenly called that might faythfully note those new conceipts. Nor lesse memorable was the excesse, which he suffred towards the end of his life, remayning in the Castle of his *Sister*, where he was for three dayes abstract, as it were, from his body, and returning on the last to himselfe agayne, he confessed to the aforesayd *Reginald* (but vnder the seale of a secret, vntill his death) that he had notice of more things and of more excellent misteryes in that space only, then euer he had in all the labours, & watches he had endured till that tyme.

And surely is it not to be past ouer in silence, that he being adorned with so great guifts by nature, and besides that, so great a freind to labour, yet to make new profit euery day in sciences, he depended so much on God, as that before his entring vnto study, he would allwayes recommend himselfe very ardently to the eternall wisedome, as if he had expected all successe from heauen only, and by no other wayes. An industry truly, very worthy to be imitated of ech Student: Because that such as without hauing recourse to God more then so, do confide & in their proper guifts, by how much they goe forward, and proceed in learning, so much are they puffed vp in their soules; in such wise, as being thence blinded whence they might haue had light, they stumble themselues, and draw others withall into their miserable errours and pe-

pestife-

pestiferous opinions. But the Angelicall Doctour (as I sayd) did quite the contrary, nor was he deceiued awhit of his hope: since many conclusions, being otherwise doubtfull and obscure, by this only way he drew forth from the deep abysse (as they say) of truth, as we shall cleerely make appeare by the example following.

The Saint explicated the oracles of *Esay*, and being come vnto a passage, whence by human help he could no wayes acquit himselfe; according to his vse he recurred to diuine, and gaue himselfe to fast and pray for that intention, so many dayes (taking besides *S. Peter* and *S. Paul* for intercessours) as that those glorious Apostles at last one night appeared to him in his Cell, and there sweetly conferring with him, a prety while, put light into him, and so quit him of al perplexity. In the meane tyme, *Fryar Reginald* was in the ante-chāber as he was wont, and though he heard the voyces, yet nothing vnderstood what they sayd. The vision then being vanished; S. *Thomas* called him in to write, and dictated the whole declaration to him, so largely, and without stop, as if he had been taking it forth of another booke in order. The dictates being ended; *Reginald*, who had heard confusedly the murmure aforesaid, did most ardently thirst, to haue a distinct notice thereof, and therefore lying prostrate on the earth, besought him not to hide or conceale it from him, and that with so much affect, and with so great instance withall, as the seruant of God (vnder the condition and seale as before) ingenuously discouered it to him.

Besides that, this so frequent prayer auailed him much, to maintayne his spirit alwayes very cheerefull and fresh, which of its nature with much speculation is wont to be arid and dry. Howbeit the holy man togeather with the assiduity of prayer, would vse also other potent and generous remedyes. Whereof the principall was, to approach to the fōtaine of all graces, the sacred Eucharist; wherto he was so deuout, that besides his saying euery day Masse, he would afterwards humbly serue another. And as in preparing himselfe to that banket of the Angells, he would add particuler study and attention; so after in rendring of thankes, he would suddenly be rapt into extasies, and being liquefyed in celestial sweetnesses, ere he were once aware thereof, would be wholy bathed in teares. He was exceeding sollicitous moreouer, in procuring the protection and fauour of the Saints, and especially of the glorious Virgin and Martyr *Agnes*, whose reliques he had alwayes hanging at his breast with

with so much fayth, as that one day touching *Fryar Reginald* therewith being dangerously sicke, he recouered him straight. He was wont also at tymes to help himselfe, with the reading affectuous & morall bookes, especially the Collations of *Cassian*; wherein he knew likewise the Patriarke S. *Dominicke* to be exceedingly versed, and to haue gathered thence incomparable helps for discretion of spirits, and solid vertues.

By which meanes, in so great an abundance of heauenly guifts, how he kept himselfe humble, and magnanimous both, through his whole life (being qualities not so disioyned from themselues, as some thinke, but deere companions rather, and indiuiduall Sisters) may be easily gathered, by the acts that immediately follow.

Some notable Acts of Humility of S. Thomas, *with the like; and particularly his deuotion for the soules in Purgatory.* Chap. 9.

SAint *Thamas* now ripe for glory and age, by this tyme passed to the Cloysters of *Bologna*, addicting himselfe to most deep considerations: when a certaine Fryar, new come from forren parts, & hauing leaue of the Priour, to goe forth into the Citty for some businesse with the first Companion he could meete with, by chaunce lighted on *S. Thomas*, not knowing him by sight, and willed him in behalfe of the Superiour, to goe a long with him: at which voyce, the Imitatour of Christ, as sent from an Oracle, not only obeyed without delay, but also being after not able to go so fast as the other, through a lame legge which he had, with incredible patience he suffered some rebukes for the same; vntill such tyme as being aduised by Seculars of the person whome he intreated so ill, being wholy confounded thereat, and excusing himselfe of his ignorance, very humbly craued pardon of him for it. Whereupon *S. Thomas* being demaunded of the same Gentlemen, wherefore he had so abased himselfe, he made answere with a graue countenance: *Religion* (forsooth) *consists in Obedience, and obedience for one man to submit himselfe to another for God, since God himselfe for our sake would subiect himselfe to Man.*

From another thing, we may likewise gather, the loue which the Saint had of his owne proper subiection; Which is, that he not only, in his owne Order, abstayned alwayes from Prelacy and gouernement, but euen likewise abroad, being called by Pope *Clement* the

the IV. to the Archbishopricke of *Naples*, he so refused the same, as he supplicated withall, and as much as he durst tooke hold of the chiefe Bishop, beseeching him not to offer him any dignityes. What shall we say then of the regard and caution he had, not to attribute any good to himselfe? In so much as to the honour of Christ, and for the help of soules, vpon good occasion he confessed sincerely, being then of good yeares, amidst so much celebrity and humane prayses, so many Magistrall Chayres, so many Preachinges, lessons, disputes and so many publique Acts maintayned, and so great variety of compositions and labours, he had neuer felt in his soule the least gust, or complacence of Vaine-glory.

From this so chast a loue and feare of God, and from this care which the Seruant of Christ had of himself, sprung the fruit which he wrought with others; and from his conuersation in Heauen, followed his dealing securely with men. In his preachinges (as we haue sayd also of his Lessons) he attended more vnto profit, then pompe; he attempered himselfe to the reach of the people, and aboue all, conformed his life with his wordes. Whence he came to be heard with so great concourse, veneration, and silence, as he had beene an Angell descended from Paradise. And sometymes our Lord God would concurre with euident miracles, as it happened once on an Easter day in the Citty of *Rome* at S. *Peters*, where he descending from the Pulpit, a certaine woman, now troubled and afflicted a long tyme with an incurable fluxe of bloud, approached vnto him in a presse of people, and touching him by the hemme of his Cloake with much fayth, she was immediatly made sound, and as strong as euer.

His priuate discourses also were of marueilous efficacay, wherin he studyed alwayes to insert vpon good occasions, some thing of edification, and if perhaps in any graue matter, it were needfull to perswade, or to examine out the truth of any thing with reasons, there was hardly found any that were able to make resistance against him, as may easily appeare by the action following. Being once present at the feast of the Natiuity, for certaine occurrences, with the Cardinall *Riccardo*, at *Molara*, a place somewhat neare to *Rome*, there met also by good happe two *Iewes*, by how much richer in substance and more learned in the ancient Law, so much the more were they addicted to flesh, and more obstinate in their perfidiousnes. Hauing taken in hand then to treat with those two soules at the instance of the Cardinall, after an encounter had, with a long dispute, he conuinced them in such sort, that hauing both by accord taken the space of a night to thinke vpon it (while he in the meane tyme was praying for them) at last they yielded, and the infant Iesus now corporally borne in a vile manner, was spiritually borne anew in their hartes. So as repenting themselues of their life past, and comming forth of darknes into a cleare light, they were both baptized with the common ioy and gladnes of all.

This singular Man had a notable zeale of the saluation of all; but yet notwithstanding his familiar freindshipps were restrayned to few. One of his deerest and beloued was, the Seraphicall S. *Bonauenture*; & to this purpose it is recounted, that going once to visit him, at such tyme as the Saint was writing the life of S. *Francis*, finding him in an extasy, and with the body eleuated in the ayre; he stopt awhile, and turning to his companion sayd: *Let vs suffer one Saint to work for another*. One quality also was seen in him, very proper for perfect men, that he being so rigid & seuere to himselfe, was yet exceeding benigne and mercifull to those, that synned out of human frailty, in taking compassion vpon their defects, yea weeping also alike for them, as they were his owne. And besides had a pious and officious memory of the faythfull departed, so as his *Sister*, once being dead appeared to him in *Paris*, crauing succour at his hands to be deliuered from Purgatory. And he as well by himselfe as others, afforded such helps, and suffrages togeather, as a litle after he being in *Rome*, she returned to him, to let him vnderstand, that now she was quit of her paynes, & for euer blessed, beholding the face of God. Vpon this occasion, S. *Thomas* required of her some newes likewise of his of two Brothers, both deceased: & she answeared, that *Landulph* continued yet in Purgatory, but *Arnold* reioyced now in heauen; and thou soone shalt be also in our company, but with a great deale more glory, for thy labours endured in the seruice of the holy Church.

The death of S. Thomas, *with his funeralls, and what happened thereupon.* Chap. 10.

AS this great Seruant of God, had so much charity towards euery one, so he was ordinarily esteemed and loued by as many as knew him, but especially he was gratefull and acceptable, to three seuerall holy Popes, *Clement* the IV. *Vrban* the IV. & *Gregory* the X. The first whereof, as hath been sayd, endeuoured in vayne to make him Archbishop of *Naples*: the second helped himselfe much by him in writing things of great importance, and especially in confuting the errours of the Greeks: the third hauing intimated a Councell at *Lyons* in *France* for weighty necessityes of the Catholike Church, among the cheife, called for S. *Thomas* thither; and heerewith, not thinking thereof, he hastened his end, and the reward of his labours. Because being then at *Naples*, not wel disposed for health, to obey the Pope, he put himselfe on the iourney without delay: and being arriued at S. *Seuerine* a Castle of his Sisters, there fell sick. From thence, being yet not well recouered, sustayning the weakenes of his body with the forces of the mind, against the will of his deerest freinds, he went forwards, vntill such tyme as he fell into a relapse at *Fossa-noua*, a place of the *Cistercians* in the Diocesse of *Piperno*, in so much as he felt (and so told Fryar *Reginald* in secret) that now approached his last day.

Heere he was receaued by the Abbot, and the other Monkes with the greatest Charity that might be, who the more they laboured in curing and seruing him, in carrying among other things some fuell from the wood, on their owne shoulders, being then the tyme of winter, so much more was the sicke man sorry and troubled, to haue them suffer so much for his sake, saying with great feeling: *And who am I, that the seruants of Christ, should trauaile so much for me?* Nor would he likewise in that space be found to be idle, because at the instance of some of them, who desired some yssue of his noble wit, he briefely expounded the Canticles of *Salomon*, foreseeing his passage out of this life, and aspiring vnto the Eternall Canticles. And for that now his forces began to fayle him, he deuoutly required the most holy Sacrament of the Eucharist, which being brought by the Abbot, withall the Conuent, though now reduced to extremes, yet he leaped from his bed, and cast himselfe on the ground with many teares.

Being afterwards demaunded (according to custome) if he belieued indeed the true Sonne of God, for our saluation borne of the Virgin, dead on the Crosse, and then risen agayne, to be contayned in the sacred Host, with a cleere and confident voyce he sayd: *I wholy beleiue it, or rather more then certainely I know, this to be* IESVS CHRIST *true God, and true man, the Sonne of the eternall Father, and of the Virgin Mother. And as I beleiue it with a pure hart, so doe I also with sincere mouth confesse the same.*

That sayd, very reuerently he receiued the Viatique, and the day following he craued the extreme Vnction, remayning allwayes in his perfect iudgment, so as himselfe did answere very punctually to euery thing: and finally with hands vnited & lifted vp to heauen-wards, recommending his spirit to the Creatour, he happily departed, in the morning on the seauenth day of March, in the yeare of our Lord 1274. which was of his vocation the 32. & the 50. of his life. At this his passage, besides the *Cistertians*, were present many Dominicans and Franciscans, being come at that tyme to visit him from sundry Monasteryes. The Bishop of *Terracina*, likewise was there present. But the Nephew of the Saint, running thither at the report of his danger, now finding him departed this life, and being not able to enter into the Monastery, obteyned with much prayers, the sacred corps might be exposed at the gate that he might behold the same. Heere arose a great and vniuersall playnt for the losse of such a personage. Yea the writers doe affirme for certaine, that the beast it selfe which he was wont to ride on, breaking the halter by force wherewith he was tyed, ran thither at the same tyme also, to the Beere or hearse, and there in the presence of all, falling to the earth, fell suddenly dead. Whereat the standers by being astonished did glorify God, and carrying the body into the Church of S. *Thomas*, with such and so great veneration they buryed it, as cannot easely be xepressed, and that before the high aultar. He was of complexion very corpulent, though he were so strict an obseruer of fasts and abstinence. He was of a very delicate flesh, sensitiue, and conuenient for the most excellent temperature of his organs; of stature straight and tall; of the colour of wheat; of eyes most modest; for strength robustuous, his head somwhat great, and bald in diuers parts.

Of two notable presages of S. Thomas *his death before hand.* Chap. IX.

SOme notable signes did prognosticate the death of this our Saint. Because, he lying at *Naples*, so indisposed as he was at first, before his departure to the Councell, a most bright starre was seene by two honourable persons of the house of *Coppa*, who were then with him,

him, to enter in by the window, and to rest a good while vpon the Saints head. Besides this, some three dayes before his death, appeared a Comet ouer his Inne at *Fossa-noua*, and when he gaue vp the ghost the same vanished away. Moreouer at the very same houre that he was in his passage, a Dominican Father of great vertue, by name *Fryar Paul Aquilin*, in the Conuent of *Naples*, saw in his sleep, how S. *Thomas* reading in the same Citty vnto a great Auditory, *S. Paul* entred into the Schoole, with a great troupe of Saints in his company, and the Angelicall Doctour being willing to descend from the chayre, the Apostle commanded him to proceed in his lesson: and at last demaunding of the same Apostle, whether he had penetrated the sense of his Epistles or no; he answered: Very well truly, as much as humane vnderstanding in a mortall body can possibly arriue to. But I will lead thee into a place, where thou shalt vnderstand them much better: and heerewith taking him by the garment he lead him out of the Schoole. And *Fryar Paul* began to cry out with a loud voyce: Help Brothers help, because *Fryar Thomas* is taken away. At which cryes of his, many in hast running in, & requiring wherefore, he declared vnto them the whole vision in order. The houre was noted, and diligent inquisition being made thereupon, it was found, that at that very instant the blessed soule departed from the body.

Many miracles afterwards of health, and of other supernaturall effects, ensued to the perpetuall prayse and exaltation of the Saint, which would be too long & superfluous to relate in this place. But howbeyt by such euents, is discouered in a manner the greatnes of the merits and rewards of the man of God; yet more euident testimony therof, gaue another vision, which *Fryar Albert* a Dominicã of *Brescia* had afterwards, being a man very famous alike both in sanctity and learning. This man being giuen to the doctrine of *S. Thomas*, and much deuoted to his diuine vertues, had now a great while desired to know, what degree of glory he was to haue in Heauen. With this ardent desire, being once in prayer with teares, before an Aultar of the most Blessed Virgin, after many enflamed sighs and feruent prayers, there appeared at last two persons vnto him, no lesse venerable in aspect, then for ornament and splendour admirable; the one in *Pontificalibus*, with a Miter on his head, another with the habit of the Dominican Fathers, with two very rich chaines about their neckes, one of gold, the other of siluer, and a

Carbuncle on the breaſt, which with its rayes did illumine the whole Church. The reſt of the garments beſides were powdred & beſet with moſt noble Pearles, Diamonds and Rubyes.

Then he in the miter ſayd: Brother *Albert*, what lookeſt thou on? I am *Auguſtine*, the Doctour of the Church, ſent hither to let thee vnderſtand the glory of *Thomas* of *Aquine*, who is now heere preſent with me, in following the Apoſtolicall traditions, and illuſtrating the Church of Chriſt. That ſame ſo reſplendant iewel which thou ſeeſt at his breaſt ſignifyes a moſt right intentiõ, which he hath had continually in teaching and defending the Catholike fayth. Thoſe other pretious ſtones heere and there, do ſhew the multitude and variety of bookes he hath written, and put to light for the help of ſoules. In ſumme we are both equall in the eſſential of glory; for the reſt he exceeds me in virginall purity, and I him in Pontificall Excellency: which ſaying they vaniſhed away. Of this ſingular chaſtity of the holy Doctour, beſydes what hath been ſayd allready, there appeared very euident ſignes thereof in his funeralls.

Of the diuers tranſlations made of the holy Body of S. *Thoma, and where it reſted at laſt.* Chap. 12.

A Litle after the corps of S. *Thomas* was enterred, the Abbot of *Foſſa-noua* with others of the Conuent, fearing that ſuch a treaſure would be taken away from them, eſpecially ſince *Fryar Reginald*, by Notary, & witneſſes now had conſigned him as *in depoſito*; in the midſt of the night, they ſecretly conueighed him into the Chapell of S. *Steuen*. But *S. Thomas* appeared to the Superiour in ſleepe, threatning him much, if he carryed it not backe, into the place agayne. Whereupon being terrifyed, he went with ſome lay men vnto the ſayd Chapell of S. *Steuen*, opened the ſepulcher, from whence proceeded an odour ſo fragrant, as preſently drew thither all the reſt of the Monks, in whoſe preſence, that chaſt lodging of the holy Ghoſt, was found to be wholy and throughout entire, together with the garments. Being a thing ſomuch the more to be wondred at, as the place was more humid, and the body (as hath been ſayd) more full and corpulent. Repleniſhed then with all conſolation and meruaile atonce, they honourably conueighed him back where he was at firſt. And the day following hauing a ſcruple

scruple to sing the Masse of the dead for him, through diuine instinct they celebrated Masse, of a Confessour not Bishop.

This first ranslation was made 7. monthes after his death: he afterwards was chaunged agayne more then once, while the same fragrancy continued still as before, as well to make he sepulcher more magnificent, as also to affoard others some part of the holy Reliques. One of his hands was graunted to his Sister, in whose Oratory remayning awhile, it was carryed to *Salerno*. The head was giuen to the Fryars Preachers of *Pipern*. It being after vnderstood that a wicked man went about to rob and to sell away the rest, the Count of *Fondi* preuented it, by taking it into his owne custody, & after that at the instance of his wife (who was therefore in sleepe very greiuously reprehended by the Saint) he consigned it to the conuent of Preachers, in the same Citty of *Fondi*.

The Monkes of *Fossa-noua* resented the iniury, and for the same hauing made many tymes complaints to the Sea Apostolike, Pope *Vrban* the V. at last to put an end to so great quarells and contentions, caused it to be transported from *Fondi* to *Thoulouse* in *France* to the end that Vniuersity (there newly founded by the Pope) might continually prosper vnder the shaddow of such a Protectour. And this last Translation, was the most noble and solemne of all, as well for that now after a full and exact information, he was canonized by Pope *Iohn* the XXII. as also for the great number of miracles, which in that Translation there followed anew. The greater part of the Bishops there, and *Lewis* Duke of *Angiou*, being the Brother of the King of *France*, with an infinite number of people, came to meet with, and receaue the sacred Pledge; by all which with great preparation and exquisite pompe, it was decently reposed at *Thoulouse* in the yeare of our Lord 1370. It hath preserued that Citty euen to these dayes from many perills of body and soule.

FINIS.

B. ANDREW. B.

THE ARGVMENT.

THE very Starre that's placed neere the Line
That parts vs from the other *Hemisphere*,
Through interposed vapours cleare doth shine,
When in our *Zenith* dimme it doth appeare:
Blinded, we slight heau'ns ioyes, which we might gaine
As well as earth, and with an equall paine.
I this perceyu'd, and learn't to rayse my hart,
And farre aboue such fain'd contents to soare;
I with the World, and with * the Wolfe did part,
And tooke the *Lambe*, whome I contem'd before:
And borne by zealous loue ascend the skies
In fiery Carre, to * my *Elias* flyes.

* His Mothers dream &c.

* This Saint a Carmelite.

THE LIFE OF B. ANDREVV BISHOP OF FESVLA.

Written by *Francis* his Successour, and others.

Of the Parents of B. Andrew: *with the miraculous presage of his Birth, and first beginnings.* Chap. I.

MONG the noble families of the renowned Citty of *Florence*, is *Corsina* worthily named for one, spread as we find, in other parts of *Italy*. Of this bloud *Nicolas* and *Peregrina*, being conioyned togeather with the holy band of Matrimony, as they were both timorous and fearing God, and much frequenting Churches, & the sacred offices, had a great desire to offer vp, to the high Creatour, and the most B. Virgin, the first-borne of their Progeny, to imitate in this point also, the piety of the ancient Patriarks, so much celebrated in sacred Scriptures. Nor did any thing hinder them from fullfilling their vow then sterility, or want of fruit to present: from which being deliuered through the intercession of the same Virgin they at last had a sonne, in Baptisme called by the name of *Andrew*, for being borne on the feast of that glorious Apostle. But the day before his natiuity, for a cleare presage, as it were of thinges to come; it seemed to the Mother in sleep, that she was deliuered of a Wolfe, which turning into the Church, was by little and little transformed into a Lambe. At which apparition, though *Peregrina* remayned in ſome feare, yet made ſhe no kind of demonſtration thereof, but kept it ſecret vntill the tyme we ſhall ſpeake of anone.

In the meane tyme, the faythfull parents trayned vp the child in learning, and much more in manners, with that care, as was fit for the yſſue now dedicated already to the ſeruice of the Queene of Angells. But ſoone might be gathered in him without doubt, how prone to ech vice is human kind, without the partiouler ayde and ſtay of celeſtiall grace. Scarcely was he arriued to the vſe of reaſon, when being enflamed within, by the ardours of concupiſcence, and by the incentiues of the falſe Angell, and outwardly allured by ſenſible obiects, and lewd companyes; he began, from the ſtraight and direct way of ſaluation, to bend to the ſpacious and large way of perdition, to abhorre vertue, to fly his ſtudyes, to ſerue the belly, and diſhoneſt pleaſures, to follow the diſſolute, to giue himſelfe to pompes, to handle partly cards and dice; & partly alſo his ſword, and armes prohibited, to moue often quarells, and to challenge now this man, and now that into the field, to waſt the goods of his family, and to put himſelfe continually into dangers both of body and ſoule.

Theſe manners of his euen pierced the Parents to the hart, ſeeming very vnfit for one, ſo conceiued through prayers, & brought vp for the ſeruice of the Mother of God. In the meane while they ſought, now with allurements, and now with menaces, and agayne with reaſons, to pull him back from the precipices he ran into, without ſtay, but all in vayne. The fierce youth had now ſhaken off the yoke, he champed the bridle, he ſcorned the rod, & finally became euery day more rebellious, and refractary then other. Yet for all this the diuine Clemency, would not ſuffer ſo ill a bud of ſo good rootes ſhould eternally periſh, but through meanes vnexpected reformed him on a ſudden, in the height of his debauſhments. Becauſe hauing once among other tymes, anſwered not only with contempt and contumacy to the holſome aduiſes of them that loued him ſo deerely, but euen alſo with iniuryes and outrages very impiouſly turning his back towardes them; *Peregrina* remembring her ancient dreame: Thou art ſurely (ſayd ſhe to him) that infamous wolfe, which in viſion I ſeemed to bring forth into the world, when thou waſt borne.

At the sound of which words, B. *Andrew*, as awaked through diuine operation, as it were from a deepe letargy, and returning to himselfe, stood still, and with voyce and countenance altered, turning himselfe to *Peregrina*: I beseech you, sweet Mother (replyed he) not to hide from me longer that monstruous prodigy, which you now intimated to me: whence howbeyt on the one side I find my selfe terrifyed & astonished as stroke with a thunderbolt, yet me thinkes on the other, I doe feele my selfe to burne with so ardent desire, to know the full truth, as I shall neuer be at rest, vntill you giue me a faythfull and distinct notice thereof.

Then the disconsolate Matron, being moued from the bottome of her hart, and now brought into some hope of amendment in her Sonne: Know thou, sayd she, my beloued Sonne, that after my espousals I liued many yeares without yssue, but with so great desire thereof, that to obtayne the same I promised and obliged, with solemne vow to the seruice of the diuine Maiesty and to his most holy Mother, the first Sonne that should spring from my wombe. Thy Father also concurred in the same vow with me, and with the same deliberation which I did. Nor was the remedy in vayne. The Conception followed, & now being neare to those pangs of child-birth, I dreamed I was deliuered of a Beast, which entring into the Temple in the figure of a wolfe, was changed into that of a lambe. The day following wast thou brought forth into the world. What thou hitherto hast shewed thy selfe to the world, thou knowst very well, and that surely no rational creature, but a sauage & rauenous wild beast. It were now high tyme thou conuertedst thy selfe, and helpedst vs in good order, to repay what we owe as debtours for thee. For neyther to *Nicolas*, nor *Peregrina* wast thou borne, but rather to the Virgin Mary. Awake then my Hart now, once at last, nor goe thou on so blotting that victime, that should liuing and cleane be presented to the highest. By these, & such other words, full of iust disdayne, and of most tender affect, through diuine power, that stony breast, was mollifyed and compunct at last, who casting his eyes with horrour on his actions past, became on a sudden to be a bitter accuser of himselfe. And finding no other remedy, then to humble himselfe, to craue pardon, and to procure aduocates, he went the next day to the Carmelites, being a Family by an ancient Institute applyed to the honour of the most Blessed Virgin. Heere then being prostrate before her Aultar, as well for shame of his offences as feare of the punishments, with a blush and palenes enterchangeably, going and comming in his countenance, without motion of his lipps, and with deep sighes, he remayned a good while begging of succour, and mercy at her hands.

B. Andrew *is conuerted frō his loose life, and enters into Religion.* Chap. 2.

VVHyle B. *Andrew* was in that agony aforesaid, he was let see by diuine power, his debts to haue gone so farre, & growne to be so great, as there was no way to be acquit of them, but to change himself, & to leaue the world; & to deale with some creditour, so exact and rigid on the one side, who should sift out al what possible he might, without leauing a dram; and so magnanimous and courteous on the other, that for so vnequall a payment, should giue not only a full acquittance, but an Eternity moreouer. The contrite yong man was not backward awhit to these heauenly consayls. He goes in all hast to Father *Hierome Migorato* Prouinciall of the Order, and beseeches him on his knees, he would be pleased to accept him into the number of his subiects, he being most resolute to leaue the world, & promptly to follow the Euangelical cōsails.

With this short manner of speach, so accorded his gestures and actions withall, as left no place of sinister suspitions to any. The holy and discreet Superiour notwithstanding, regarding the qualityes of so noble and delicate a subiect, partly to assure himselfe the better of his vocation, and partly also to auoyd all scandall; giuing good words for that tyme to the suiter, sends by an expresse messenger to certify *Nicolas Corsino*, & *Peregrina* his wife, how their Sonne *Andrew* had made great instance for Religion, and the habit. More ioyfull tydings could not possibly arriue to the eares of the good and truly Christian couple. But both full of ioy and iubiley alike giue infinite thankes therefore to the diuine goodnes: after which without delay they went both togeaher vnto the Conuent, where the feruorous Penitent anew, was set to prayer at the same Aultar as before. With this opportunity they likewise falling on their knees, being quiet, and all of one accord made the desired oblation of him, and so performed their vow. From thence the holy busynes being concluded with the Prouinciall, the Father and Mother being wholy replenished with consolation, returned home againe;

agayne, while the sonne so altered now and quite transformed with the singular content and edification of the Fryars, remayned in the Monastery; nor cared he awhit to change his name, while to him it seemed the name of *Andrew*, would be a sufficient incitement for him to loue and embrace the Crosse of our Lord Christ. And he conuerted his thoughts & applyed his whole mind by all meanes possible to suppresse the vices which infested him most, and particulerly pride, and a vayne esteeme of himselfe.

In which battayle besides the actions which he did of his owne accord, in submitting himselfe to others, and flying all shew and demonstration of vanity, he was much furthered likewise by maisters skillfull in that Religious list. Who exercised him in those occupations point by point, which were most accommodate to abate pride, and to subdue the appetite of disordinate excellency. So as they deputed him to the vile seruices of the kitchin, to wash the dishes, to sweep the house, to cary away the dust, to serue & wayte at the porch; which things he discharged with so great simplicity and feruour, as they were all astonished thereat, and he remayned euery day more confirmed, then other in his good purposes.

How B. Andrew *was tempted by a kinsman of his, to leaue his vocation, but in vayne.* Chap. 3.

TO come now to some particular of the soundnesse of his vocation; he hauing one day the care of the Gate, while the rest were at dinner, behold on a sudden, there arriued thither, a Gentleman a kinsman of his, with a good trayne with him, very rich and gallant, but exceeding subtile and practical in the world. Who being let in, when he saw the seruant of God with keyes in his hand, so meagre in the face, and so poorely clad; discouering at once both wonder and scorne, with a voyce full fraught of disdayne: Is it possible (sayd he) this same should be that *Andrew Corsino*, who but euen the other day flourished so among the noblest, and gallantest of our youth, of so royall aspect, of sumptuous apparell, and of so great acquaintances of all? What madnes or what desperation, most deere Brother, hath brought thee into this Cloyster, to loose thy best & fayrest years, and to denigrate with so base a habit and abiect seruitude, the tytles and splendour of thy family? Re-enter agayne into thy selfe; Thinke on the irreparable losse thou incurrest, and that while thou art as yet, but new in the rule, and mayst without note of leuity, resume agayne to thy selfe, the passed course of thy happy life: Breake off these bands, and render thy selfe to thy sweet companions agayne, to thy deare bloud, and particularly to me, who thou knowest how deerely hath euer loued thee. And if some respect peraduenture of Fathers or Mothers superstition doth retayne thee from going hence directly vnto their house, stay with me vntill such tyme as things be accommodated betweene you, there shall be no diuision or difference betweene vs two. We will be all one, thou shalt euer dispose of my Wardrob, seruants, and rents with the same security as of thine owne. But if perhapps certayne gusts allure thee, which these Saints and precise Hypocrites tell thee are found in that solitary and extrauagant life; make this accompt, (as so it is likewise their owne doctrine too) that after a little hony shall follow a great deale of gaul. The memory of the commodityes and hopes so left shall vex thee, vnprofitable repentances shall gaul thee, and the rage of persecutions, infirmityes of the body, and bitternes of mynd shall torment thee; and when there is nothing els, thou shalt euen cary thy selfe with thee, nor with the flying world, hast thou layd away thy flesh: whence the more continuall the wills are that do spring from thence (especially of thinges that are wholy forbidden vs) so much more shalt thou find thy selfe to be suspended, and strangled as it were amidst the incentiues of thy appetit, & impossibility to quench them. Wherupon of necessity, eyther thou must needes dye of sadnes, or prolong thy dayes in infinite dolours, or abandon thy profession with eternall infamy.

Remember, how the lyllies flourish not alwayes, nor the leaues are euer greene: Let so many others be a warning and example to thee, who eyther in Cloysters being forlorne of al, in their greatest necessity, haue finished their dayes vpon straw, or after many yeares of Religion, being vanquished with the labour & tediousnes thereof, and lastly turned backe from Religion, are at this day to their endles reproach, now pointed at in the Citty. So as now while matters are yet but fresh and entiere, doe thou looke to, & prouide for thy selfe; and throwing away in good houre these keyes and raggs of thine, come along with me without delay. And belieue me, from others thou shalt receiue but wordes only; but deeds at my hands thou shalt really find, who vaunt my selfe, that I will be to thee no feigned Fryar, but a true friend, and louing kinsman to my liues end

end. Therefore (deereſt Nephew) let me preadmoniſh thee of theſe future euents, and ſeeke with all thy diligence to preuent them; and returne agayne to thy moſt louing Companions, who will exceedingly reioyce at thy preſence.

With theſe, and other ſuch like fiery darts, was the fayth and conſtancy of *B. Andrew* aſſayled this day. In which conflict he defending himſelfe with the ſigne of the Croſſe, and reſolute ſilence, ſtood as firme as a tower, in ſuch ſort as the domeſticall enemy, being aſtoniſhed at ſuch fortitude, and confounded at his proofes ſo deluded, departed without more ado. It is held indeed by many with probable coniectures, that ſome ſpirit of Hell, had appeared in the figure of that Gentleman, but whether the Diuell or ſome Miniſter of his (for euen alſo among the Children of *Adam* there want not ſuch) it is manifeſt, that with ſuch aſſaults, he wrought no other effect, then to affoard to the new Souldier of Chriſt both matter & occaſion of a noble fight, and of a glorious victory. Hence taking more courage and new vigour, and after many other experiences, *B. Andrew* being admitted with ſolemne ceremonyes into the body of Religion, he gaue himſelfe together with the ſtudy of perfection, to the purchaſe alſo of ſciences: with particuler caution, that the vehemency and aſſiduity of ſpeculation (as happens but too often) conſume not, or quite extinguiſh the oyle of deuotion, and the ardour of ſpirit.

Of the zeale of ſoules, which B. Andrew *had, and how he conuerted a Kinſman of his from a lewd life.* Chap. 4.

B. *Andrew* had yet reguard to the age he was of, & to the ſtrength and liuely temperature of his complexion: and aboue all things, held it a great baſenes, & a barbarous ingratitude to abandon Chriſt in his paſſion, and to haue no will to taſt of the chalice, which the heauēly Phiſitian ſo benignly for vs would firſt be prouing himſelf. So as beſides the continuall guard & cuſtody of the hart, beſids the familiarity with God, by the meanes of holy prayer, beſides the frequent interiour acts of humility and of charity, he left not alſo at tymes to macerate the body with abſtinences, vigils, and ſharp labours. He wore on his bare fleſh a cruell cilice, he made frequent diſciplines, he kept moſt exact and entire ſilence, at due howers, he faſted (beſides other obſeruances of the order) in bread & water for three dayes of the weeke; would take euery occasion to serue and obey ech one, euen the least of all. He would goe forth with a wallet on his back, to beg from doore to doore, especially *In via maggia*, a Way so called, where many of his noble freinds, kindred, and acquaintance were assembled together; reioycing not a litle to labour in so base an occupation for sustenance of the Monks, And much more for hauing by that meanes frequent occasion to be mocked, scorned, and iniured not only by those, who call holy mendicity, a lazy and Gipsian life, but euen also by such that through his appearing so in that habit, with a foolish pride reputed themselues to be much disparaged and digraced by him.

Vnto this loue of purity, and contempt of himselfe, and of true pennance indeed, and voluntary pouerty, was added an inflamed desire, and zeale of saluation of soules, whereto he attended not only with feruent prayers, and good examples of life, but also as occasion serued, with exhortations, counsailes and aduises. And the Eternall Goodnes also sometymes fayled not to concurre thereto with diuine workes: as it happened perticulary in the conuersion of a kinsman of his, by name *Iohn Corsino*. Which fel out, as followes.

This man being afflicted with a most troublesome disease of the Wolfe, the lesse hope he had to be cured thereof, so much sought he out solaces and allurements to diuert the thought thereof; and among other thinges gaue place to vnlawfull games, with such a number of debauched people, as his house at last was become a publique house of mis-rule, and was commonly called the *Dicing-house*. The Blessed *Andrew* not brooking so hellish an errour, to so great an infamy of the name of *Corsino*, and so grieuous a scandall to the whole Citty: First calling vpon diuine succour (as he was wont) he went at a fit hower to visit the sick patient; & after mutuall salutation and demaunds had between them, which in such encounters are vsuall with those of the best breeding, with a liuely fayth and a louely face he sayes to him: If thou wouldst but doe as I would haue thee, *Iohn*, I doe heere promise thee with the grace of God, to deliuer thee suddenly of this soare, which seemes so incurable, and from the snares and deceipts of thine enemyes, that so persecute thee. To this promise of his the sick man, though he could hardly afford any credit, yet for the great desire he had to be rid of his paynes, did offer himselfe very prompt and ready to any thing that B. *Andrew* should please to commaund him.

Then

Then answered the seruant of Christ: I will haue thee the first thing thou dost, to relinquish this ill practise and conuersation of Gamesters; and after that, for eight dayes, that thou attend to Fasting, and to recommend thy selfe hartily to the most Blessed Virgin. The conditions seemed hard to *Iohn*, and yet notwithstanding to make some tryall thereof, vsing some violence to himselfe, he dismissed and abandonned the euill companyes, and with abstinence and prayer, made the Mother of God so propitious to him, as not without the amazement of the whole Citty, and his infinite ioy, he was cured, both of the Vlcer, which deuoured his flesh, and of the greedy appetites, which vnder a false shadow of good, consumed his sensuall and vnwary soule. Such then were the actes which B. *Andrew* practised with his neighbour, full of simplicity & truth; by whose meanes we may well beleeue, that many others at that tyme, were weaned from vices, and confirmed in vertue.

How B. Andrew *was made Preist, and then Superiour: and of the guift of Prophesy, which he shewed in a particuler euent.* Chap. 5.

THough the modesty & submission of the Blessed *Andrew* were now already well knowne, he had notwithstanding new commodity to manifest, with a noble document, how much he sought to please God only, and how be abhord all worldly glory.

It was in tymes past, and is yet to this day, a custome in *Florence*, as in other places of Christendome also, to make feasts at the first Masse of a new Preist, with musique, pompes, and banquetes: which demonstrations of ioy and gladnes, as they are not to be blamed, while they are kept with in the bounds of a moderate festiuity; so when they exceed the same, there is much danger incurred, least Christiá ceremonyes degenerate into gentil, & prophane, and that in operations of the spirit, and mind, the flesh and belly may intrude themselues; and finally least in the seruice and worship due to God only, the diuell (a fearefull thing) should haue his part therein. Now the Blessed *Andrew*, hauing passed ouer allready the gulf of youth, and not being able to resist Superiours, that he might not be promoted vnto sacred Orders; as soone as he knew the matter to be diuulged, and how the *Corsinoes* striued to celebrate the *Primitiæ* of his Priesthood, with exquisite musique, rich hangings, and sumptous banquetes; recollecting himselfe a litle, and consi-

considering such pompes were not any thing conformable with his profession, and worthily fearing some manner of abuse therein, with leaue of the Prelate, retired himselfe into a Conuent, which is called by the name of the *Sylua*, some seauen miles forth of the Citty; and heere as without all noyse, so with extraordinary spirituall sweetenes, he offered his first sacrifice to the most holy Trinity, which how gratefull and acceptable it was, the Emperesse of Heauē her selfe did testify, who ouer that same vnbloudy hoast, appeared to B. *Andrew* encompassed with a troupe of Angells, and with the words of *Esay* the Prophet very plainely sayd to him: *Seruus meus es tu, & in te gloriabor*. Which sayd, by little and little mounting aloft, she vanished quite.

With which fauours, the prudent man not puffed vp awhit, but rather attending to abase himselfe, and to acknowledge all good to proceed from the meere benignity of the highest, became euery day more worthy, and more capable of new graces. So as a little after the aforesayd vision, being sent to *Paris*, to giue himselfe more exactly to his studyes, and thence afterwardes in his returne into Italy passing by *Auignon*, where the Cardinall *Corsino* his neere kinsman was, while there he entertayned himselfe for some space, he gaue sight to a blind man, who in the Church porch according to custome was publikely begging an Almes. From thence being come into *Florence*, he deliuered one Fryar *Ventura* a *Carmelite* from a dropsy.

And to the end that B. *Andrew* might not seeme to want the guift of prophesy also; euen much about that tyme, being intreated by a freind to baptize an infant, which had beene newly borne into the world, he did it louingly, and in taking him out of the sacred Font, had a reuelation from heauen of the vnhappy successe, which that poore creature was to haue. Whereupon being moued to compassion, and being not able to hold from weeping, he was demaunded by the Gossipe, what made him to weep so. Then B. *Andrew* though vnwillingly made answere: Know then, how this Child is come into the world to the totall destruction of himselfe and his howse. Of which prediction as then the secular made but litle reckoning, but saw it at last to be too true. Because the Child in progresse of yeares being giuen to an ill life, and euen loaden with crymes and wickednes, at last with some men of ill demeanour conspired against his countrey, and the conspiracy discouered, the miserable

miserable wretch by the hāds of a hangman finished his dayes, with a due punishment, and the vtter ruyne of his Family.

The excellent tallent, and manner, which B. Andrew *had, in gouernement.* Chap. 6.

THough B. *Andrew* endeauoured what he could, to keep himselfe from the eyes of mortall men obscure, and vnknowne; notwithstanding being now come into a singular opinion & fame of sanctity, he was chosen by the Pouinciall Chapter of the *Carmelit* Fathers to be Superiour of the Conuent of *Florence*; to which charge, he maynly opposed himselfe: but yet the common consent of the Electours preuailed, and the authority of him who of obedience might impose it vpon him. In which office, he let the world to vnderstand cleerely, that it is not, as others thinke, that much spirit, and good gouernement be incompatible in the same person. B. *Andrew* through the habit of prayer and of other vertues now already confirmed in him, conseruing that which he had so purchased for himselfe continually (without loosing yet awhit of his authority) the least of all; and not affecting preeminencyes nor titles, but endeuouring with all possible diligence, that such as were vnder his care, should, wholy free from all temporall sollicitude, attend to God only, wherein without doubt consists the true and essenciall fruite of the religious and monastical life; since otherwise for a man to be shut vp in Cloysters, and to thinke continually of meat, drinke, and cloth, and other such like necessityes, is not formally to abandon the world, but materially to change the dwelling only; nor is it to leaue the old habits, but only to alter the objects; and it is euen the same to be drowned in the Hauen, as in the wide Ocean, as much to be loaden and oppressed with iron as with lead. Whereas on the contrary the mind being discharged of terren thoughts, like a dry feather flyes lighlty aloft; and then spirituall exercises do neuer tire, when the frayle nature neuer wants its due and conuenient sustenance.

Which charge, for that it singularly belonges to him that gouernes others in the diuine seruice; hence it is that Prelates and Princes, are worthily called and sayd to be honourable seruants; & for want of this sollicitude and prouidence, murmurs and scandalls doe openly follow, and finally vnhappy propriations, the certaine pest, and vtter ruine of Congregations and Orders. Which thing the man of God, well foreseeing, did not only heare benignely, but euen preuented the honest suites, and necessityes of his Monkes: whence after would appeare that it was no hard matter to exact the rule and discipline of euery one; while to all it was manifest and cleere, that he being wholy attentiue to the weale publike, had no reguard to his particular interests, gusts, or greatnesses. In summe, he in that Superintendency of his gaue such proofe of the talent he had, in dealing with, and guiding men, as that euen both heauen and earth might seeme to haue accorded togeather to exalt him, with the occasion that followes.

How B. Andrew, *was miraculously elected Bishop of* Fesula. Chap. 7.

IN those dayes, *Fuligno* the Lord Bishop of *Fesula*, a most noble Citty neere to *Florence*, though now quite destroyed as it were, dyed. Whereupon the Canons and the rest, to whome belonged the nomination of a new Pastour, being assembled togeather in the name of God, and mooued through the constant fame that resounded euery where of the name of *B. Andrew* preferred him before any other, that might be destined to that Chayre. The newes wherof, was speedily brought to the Man of God. But knowing well the greatnes of the weight, and esteeming it farre too burdensome for his shoulders, he retired himselfe from his Conuent, into the Monastery of *Carthusians*, a little out of *Florence*: & there hid himselfe in such wise, as the *Fesulans* hauing sought him through the Citty and Prouince, were resolued at last to come to a new election.

But to the end it might euidently appeare, how that tytle was reserued by the diuine Prouidence, to no other then *B. Andrew*: behold while the Assembly was ready to enter into the Scrutiny, a Child there present, cryed out with a lowd voyce, saying: *Elegit Deus Andream in sacerdotem sibi*, who is now in the Charterhowse, making his prayer; there shal you certainely find him out. At which voyce those of the Councell being astonished, without more adoe confirming the former election sent immediately messengers to the *Carthusian* Fathers, beseeching them very earnestly to worke so, as their Bishop, with so marueilous an vnion chosen of men, and with a greater wonder approued of God, might accept now at last the enterprise, whereto with so cleere and euident signes, he was

called

called so by the high Rectour and *Ruler* of all. And euen iust at that tyme, while this passed in *Florence*, there appeared to B. *Andrew* then, being in deepe contemplation, another Child in a white garment, which openly declared to him, the will of God to be, that he should goe forth to that charge, nor feare the while, any danger, nor fly the trauayle. By this declaration the seruant of God being finally assured, and arysing from his Oratory went to meet with the messengers of *Fesula* that sought for him; and taking a sweet leaue with a thousand thanks of his Hosts, he went cheerfully to his diocesse, being then some 58. yeares of age, & through diuine fauour completly answered to the great expectation which all had already conceiued of him.

How B. Andrew, *demeaned himselfe in his Bishoprike: and how charitable he was to the poore.* Chap. 8.

OVr B. *Andrew* knowing both by learning and experience, that the office of a good Prelate consists, in feeding the subiects as well with example as with the word; and also in temporall necessity with meate and drinke: first of all he reteyned his ancient maxime in preaching Christ aboue all, with works. So as he endeauoured to shew himselfe continually a Maister of all disordinate passions, to restrayne sensuality, and to macerate the body with abstinencyes, and with wearing on his bare flesh, not sackcloth and cilices now as he was wont to doe, but an iron chayne; to sleep, insteed of a matteresse, vpon hurdles, to fly all banquettings, to beware as much as possibly he might from discoursing with women, to shut his ears to flatterers, to trample on vayne confidence or esteeme of himselfe, not to remit the study of meditation, to walke alwayes in the presence of God, & to acknowledge him with amorous affects in all creatures; whence afterwardes deriued that charity of his towardes his neighbour, and that so tender cōpassion on the afflicted and distressed, as that in hearing their calamities he could not hould from teares; and none had recourse to him for comfort or succour, but he indeauoured by all meanes to send them away both comforted and contented. Yea following the stepps of the great S. *Gregory* he would haue an exact catalogue with him of all the poore, especially of the shamefast, and continued to susteyne them with all possible secrecy.

With which humanity and bounty of his, how much the Giuer of al good was pleased, very manifestly appeared in tyme of a cruel Dearth, wherewith the people of *Fesula* being much tormented & oppressed, not finding on earth any refuge more fit and opportune then the benignity of their Bishop, they came running in troupes vnto him, and he shut not vp his coffers, or dispense from any: in so much as hauing one day very liberally distributed what bread was in the house, and now beggars continually comming in, he commanded more bread to be giuen vnto them; and his seruants knowing very well, there was not so much as a loafe left, they endeauoured to certify the Maister therof, who notwithstanding perseuering in calling for it, and bidding them earnestly to seeke yet better; they not to seeme contumacious, though against their wils, turning backe, found to their extreme wonder a great quantity of loaues, and with great ioy brought them to the man of God. Which presently he deuided among the hungry, imitating in this also, the mercy, and representing the infinite power of the Sauiour. Besides this, he was wont truly, in memory of our sayd Redeemer and Lord, the singular Maister of holy humility, to wash euery Thursday with his owne handes the feet of some poore folkes, wherin he felt particuler gust and consolation.

Now it happened once, that among those Beggars, was called in one, who had his legs in a loatsome manner very soare and corrupted, who as he was well bred and modest, began to resist the admirable man, not suffering by all meanes he should wash his feet: and B. *Andrew* demanding wherefore? The other answered: My leges are so soare and putrifyed, as I haue good cause to feare, they will turne a Prelats stomake, and breed a loathing. Then answered the Saint, haue confidence my sonne in our Lord Iesus Christ, & so hauing sayd, he powred out the water into the vessel straight, and sets himselfe to wash his feet. A wonderfull thing, scarcely had he finished to wipe that happy man, but his feet were made cleane, and his soares cured. Such was B. *Andrews* care & diligence of the corporall necessityes of his flocke, and vpon these foundations of well knowne goodnes, did after securely arise the celestiall building of soules: because he had gotten so much credit and authority with those carriages of his; as to reclayme and pull away ill liuers from their lewd life, one word or becke of his, had more moment with it, then the longe and premeditated disswasions of others.

How

How B. Andrew reconciled most deadly emnityes and debates; and how his death was miraculously foretould him. Chap. 9.

THough B. Andrew had great efficacy with him, in ech kind of spirituall remedyes, yet shewed he to haue a particuler talent in contracting honest friendships, in taking vp quarells, in composing controuersies, and so much the more willingly laboured he in these thinges, as the Holy Ghost had giuen him to vnderstand, that in mutuall fraternall loue, consists the whole summe of the Christian Law. The honourable fame now of all these noble actions dilating it selfe, through all parts, Pope Vrban the V. tooke particuler contentment therat, and for some dayes, gaue a large field vnto so eminent vertue to exercise it selfe in. The Citty of Bologna in those dayes was enflamed with perilous tumults and discordes, nor was there any remedy of that euill to be found, through the inueterated hatreds, disordinate passions, and obstinate pertinacity of the partyes. The common Pastour being worthily anxious and sollicitous for it, after many cares and diligences in vayne vsed about the same, resolued with himselfe to make vse of the person of the Bishop of Fesula for that busines, and with an ample power sent him as his Nuntius to the Bolognians: nor was he awhit deceaued in his opinion, because B. Andrew being arriued thither, began immediatly to mitigate the exasperated woundes of their mindes, and with the didiuine help, had so lucky and dexterous a hand, as he shortly recouered them, reducing the nobility and people, without new noyse to a desired peace and tranquility. And some few more stiff and obstinate then the rest, by diuine iudgment being strook with a greiuous and sudden infirmity, and agayne through the merits of the Saint deliuered thereof, did willingly yield themselues likewise, and he with the like contentment of Citizens and Pope Vrban also, and with the vniuersall applause of all Italy, returned home agayne to his residence. Where besides the mayntayning and nourishing as we haue sayd, with great charity, the bodyes and soules committed to him, he tooke likewise particuler accompt of the sacred buildinges; and among other restaurations sumptuously repayred the Cathedral Church, which was euen threatning ruine.

With these passages being arriued to the 71. yeare of his age, while he was celebrating solemne Masse on the most happy night

of

of the Natiuity, the Virgin Mother of God appeared to him anew, and saluted him truly with the good tyme, aduertising him withall, on the *Epiphany* he should be loosed from the mortall prison, & led to the supernall Hierusalem, to enioy euen face to face the eternall word, whom with such fayth and feruour he had now serued for so many yeares.

At this newes *B. Andrew* felt incredible content. So as where before, through continuall pennances, he was pale and meagre in the face, from that tyme, his vitall spirits dilating themselues, his countenance began to waxe ruddy as a Seraphim; shewing a marueilous serenity to all, communicating with infinite iubiley to his dearest friends so blessed a reuelation, and aboue all preparing himselfe with extraordinary diligence for the eternall banquet; nor was the terme awhit differred him. The sixth day of Ianuary being come of the yeare following 1373. the affaires of his Bishoprike and conscience being well composed, & leauing most holy aduertisements and examples to his family, he flew the straightest way to the heauenly Countrey. Which, besides the certainty which the splendour appearing about his bed gaue while he passed, and a most sweet odour which the spirit, being departed, those sacred members sent forth, was manifested also by some visions and predictions worthy of credit. Which truly, with many other workes besides aboue nature, succeeding at his sepulcher, not only immediatly, but also many yeares after his death, I doe heere forbeare to relate, as well for being sufficiently already recounted by graue Authours, partly also for that my purpose was, and is still, as I haue sayd aboue, to propose to Readers in these venerable memories, not admirable thinges so much, as the imitable, through the grace of our Lord Iesus Christ. To whome with the Father, and with the Holy Ghost, be prayse, honour, and glory for all eternity.

FINIS.

B. LAV-

B.LAV. IVSTINIAN.

THE ARGVMENT.

BY wonders freed, when *Iacobs* ofspring went
From land that *Nile* feeds with his excrement,
Leau'n cloudes * (as Iewes auerre) themselues engage
Them to defend in their long pilgrimage.
One plac't below supports the numerous thronge,
As Nurse the child, or Eagle beares her yonge:
One set direct betwixt them, and the heate,
Foure on all sides ech one hath seuerall seate.
An Harbinger the last, before doth goe
Serpents to kill, and make the mountaines low.
Our Saint their generall office doth supply,
Prostrate to all with true humility.
Greater himselfe, great weight his shoulders beare;
(How great's the flocke, so great's the Sheepheards care)
His Towring soule doth to the skeys ascend
And makes the Heau'n to him, and his a friend.
He on ech side is watchfull, ready still
T'oppose their foes, and saue his charge from ill.
Thinges yet conceald his piercing eye could view,
And meet with dangers that were to ensue.
He (the worlds Sunne) contem'd the world, but stroue
That this contempt might shew the world his loue.

* The Iewish Rabbins Num 10. Paraphr. Can. 2.

THE LIFE OF B: LAVRENCE IVSTINIAN THE FIRST PATRIARKE OF *VENICE*.

Written by the Honourable *Leonard Iustinian*.

Of the parentage, infancy, & minority of B. Laurence: *and what a strange vocation he had*. Chap. I.

LESSED LAVRENCE was borne in the Citty of *Venice*, of the Magnifico *Bernardo Iustiniano*, and of Quirina his wife (both of a high and noble linage) in the yeare of our Lord 1380. He was left a child, with other Brothers of his by his Father, who dyed very soone. His heauy and disconsolate Mother being yet but yong, macerating her body, as well with fastings and vigils, as with a sharp cilice and a brazen girdle, kept viduall state, not without a prosperous and perpetuall fame of purity: nor attended she with lesse sollicitude in the meane tyme, in bringing vp her children in learning, and that which more imports in in Christian manners: and though they all gaue much hope, not to degenerate awhit from their Ancestours, notwithstãding a particuler towardnes of a great spirit, and generous thoughts went discouering it selfe, in the B. *Laurence*; since that in those his first yeares, scorning and loathing the sports, and other leuityes, which are permitted to that age, with a certaine sage maturity, he conuersed with men of stedder iudgments, and of thinges indeed not childish; in so much as this manner of proceeding of his, was attributed by some to an ouermuch desire of greatnes of glory. Yea his owne Mother, fearing he would giue vp himselfe as a prey to Ambition, (as most commonly the nobler wits are wont) of purpose sayd to him on a tyme: Goe to, *Laurence*, leaue this manner of thyne, this thy pride euen sauours of Hell. Whereto he smiling, merily made answere: Doubt not Madame, you shall yet see me a great seruant of God. Nor was the prediction awhit in vayne, because he being now come to nineteen years of age, when as man commonly stands vpon the point of taking the good, or ill bent; in vision there appeared to him a woman more bright then the Sunne, who with a pleasing and gratefull countenance spake to him in this sort.

My beloued youth, why distracts thou thy hart into diuers parts, and seekest rest forth of thy selfe, now in this thing, and now in that? Looke what thou wishest for, is in my handes, and I promise to affoard it thee, if thou wilt take me to thy Spouse. At which wordes *B. Laurence* being at first astonished, and taking after more courage, to demand her name, and what her condition was, the Virgin replyed: I am the Wisedome of God, who for reforming the world heeretofore haue taken mortall flesh. Which the happy *Louer* hearing, soone yielded his assent; and she reaching him a chast kisse of peace, very suddenly vanished. At this vision now B. *Laurence* being stirred vp to new cares, & feeling vnwonted flames of fire to burne within his breast, yet could not fully interprete the inuitation made him, nor to which to betake himselfe aboue others. It is true, that inwardly he found himselfe to be much enclined to a religious and perfect life; but as yet not trusting to his owne iudgment, he went for counsaile to a certaine Cousin of his Mother, called *Marinus*, who leading a monasticall life in S. *Georges* of *Alga*, of the Congregation of *Celestines*, was held in great opinion of learning and sanctity.

He now vnderstanding the inspiration and motiues of the yong man more maturely to examine the whole, exhorted him first ere he entred into Religion, or changed the habit, he would secretly make some experience, what he were able to suffer in a strict life. To which aduice *B. Laurence* did very promptly obey, and among other industryes, began insteed of a soft and downy bedde, to ly in the night vpon crabby and knotty wood. And with all to make his accompts the better, he endeauours of purpose one day, to contemplate on the one side Magistracyes, Honours, Wiues, Children, riches, sundry sorts of pastimes and sports, and all the pleasure besides which the world may afford; and on the other, abstinencyes, fasts, vigills, pouerty, incommodityes, heat & cold, the abnegation of himselfe, with perpetuall seruitude, and other difficultyes besides, which present themselues in the narrow way of more perfect vertue, and diuine seruice.

Heereupon as an Arbitour placed betweene two troupes of obiectes, demanded he accompt of himselfe, saying: Now consider well *Laurence*, what thou hast to do: Dost thou thinke thou canst endure these austerityes, and despise those commodityes? Whereupon standing in suspense and contention within himselfe, at last casting his eyes vpon a Crosse of Christ: Thou art (sayd he) my hope, O Lord, in this tree is found comfort and strength for all, a secure & safe refuge for all. And without doubting any more, he determined by all meanes to follow the internall voyce, and counsayles of the Chiefe Pastour.

Of the singular vertues of B. Laurence, *and particulerly of his Fortitude in suffering the paynes of the body.* Chap. 2.

IT cannot easily be explicated, how much feruour and spirit was augmented in that blessed soule from that so free and well grounded resolution which B. *Laurence* made. Which howbeyt he laboured to hide by all meanes possible: yet could he not so do, but those of the howse, especially his Mother must needes find it out. Whereupon she, though vertuous and deuout, yet tender and anxious for her deer sonne, fearing least through violence of nature, he might come to be transported vnto some hardy enterprize beyond his forces, she determined vpon agreement with others, to ty him, as soone as might be, with the bands of Matrimony. So as hauing practically proceeded therein without delay, she soone

found

found out, and offered him a beautyfull, noble, and rich ſpouſe. But the holy youth being aware of the temptation, and conſpiracy of his freinds, would deterre no longer, to rid himſelfe of the danger, and to conuey himſelfe as ſecretly as he could, vnto S. *Georges*: where taking the habit of Religion, he manfully began to enter into the battayle, againſt the inuiſible Enemy.

The firſt aſſault then, he gaue to Senſuality, depriuing himſelfe of all wantonnes, and diſports. To hungar he gaue but that only, which euen the vtmoſt neceſſity required. Thirſt he did tolerate, in ſuch ſort, as that neyther for the vehemency of heates, nor wearines of the iourneys he made, or other labours whatſoeuer, nor for any indiſpoſition of body, would he euer call for drinke. But rather if ſometymes, he were inuited therunto, he was wont to anſwere: how then Brothers ſhal we be able to endure the fire of Purgatory, if we cannot ſuffer this litle thirſt? At the vigils at night, and mattyns, he was the firſt in coming thither, & the laſt to depart from thence: for that, it being the cuſtome of others, to returne to bed againe vntill the riſing of the Sunne; the B. *Laurence* would neuer goe out of the Church, vntill the hower of prime. He would neuer approch to the fire, not ſo much as in the hart of winter: a thing ſo much the more to be admired in ſo delicate a complexion.

A certaine Father one day inuited him to warme himſelfe at the fyre, and not being able to be brought vnto it, he felt his hand, and finding it to be benumm'd through cold, he cryed out: Great is the ardour O Sonne, thou haſt within thee ſince thou feeleſt not the extremity of cold without. But what great wonder is it, that he approached not to the fyre, who neuer went as it were into the garden likewiſe, being the only recreation, and ordinary diſport of the Monks? At diuine offices he would ſtand bolt vpright, without leaning a whit eyther on the right or left hand. He would ſecretly make moſt cruell diſciplines; as teſtifyed the many ſtripes all black and blew, through his whole body, with the frequent ſtaynes of bloud thereon appearing.

In the dolours of infirmityes, he would ſhew incredible patience. Being yet a Nouice, his neck was full of ſwelling of the Kings euill. The Phiſitians for a laſt and only remedy threatned him firſt cuppings, then launcings, and laſtly ſearing with fire. And the Fryars doubting, he would faynt vnder the cure, he couragiouſly anſwered: what feare you Brothers? Let come the raſor, bring in the burning irons; can not he happily giue me constancy in this daunger, who affoarded it to the three children in the furnace? So as he was cut and burned, without fetching the lest groane or sigh, or sending forth other voyce, then Iesus for once only.

Howbeit indeed, it is no great matter, he should shew such fortitude in the greener, who gaue such an example thereof in his latter age, and perhapps more memorable then it: Because, that being vnmeasurably sweld at that tyme in the throate, and being not able to resolue the corrupt humour thereof without incision of the knife, the Father being desirous to be rid of the trouble, to attend more freely to the care of soules, stood still at that launcing as quiet and vnmoueable as a stock, speaking to the timourous Chirurgeon: Cut on couragiously, for thy rasour can not exceed the burning hot irons of the Martyrs. In this sort, the flesh being vanquished quite, and subdued, and the noble Warrier, with full & perfect renunciation, quitting himselfe to his power, of al terrene charge, endeauours to conquer the other impietyes one by one; so much more powerfull and daungerous, as more inward and spirituall they be. But the principall fight which he tooke in hand, was against that horrible monster of Pride, taming it as well in the interiour as exteriour, with contrary, frequent, and intense actes. The garmentes that he wore were all torne; the more abiect offices, and more noysome of the Monastery (most manfully therein subduing his stomack for the loue of Christ) he would take to himselfe.

Besides, he stucke not to go forth a begging of almes, with a Wallet on his backe. And wholy to trample vnder foot the foolish reputation and vayne pride of the world, he would put himselfe of purpose into the thickest nobility, and where the greater concourse of the inhabitants was. He would come also sometimes to the very house, where he was borne, and remayning in the streets be crying aloud, *for Gods sake*. At which words and voyce of his, the motherly bowells being mooued, to cut off at least the walke or circuit of her deere bloud, she suddenly commanded the seruants to fill vp his wallet with victualls. But he contenting himselfe with two loaues of bread, and wishing peace to such as had done him the charity, would depart from thence as altogeather vnknowne, and so continuing his round from doore to doore, being tyred at last, with the burden, and sometymes ouer loaden with reproaches, he would returne

turne to S. *Georges* agayne.

Being further prouoked, though altogeather vniustly truly, with other occasions, or reprehended for some thing, he would force himselfe (in biting his tounge sometymes) to represse the naturall vehemency, which the Children of *Adam* haue to iustify and defend themselues. Through which exercise, by little and little he got such a power ouer himselfe, as that being once accused in the open Cõgregation, by a peruerse man, for hauing committed in gouernment something against the rule, though he knew the malignity of him, & could haue yielded a good accompt of himselfe; notwithstanding without opening his mouth, or changing his countenance, arising from his seate, with eyes cast downe to the earth, and with a moderate pace, he went into the midest of the Chapter, and there falling downe on his knees, craued humbly pennance, and pardon of all those Fathers: so as the accuser himselfe being quite confounded at so great a patience of his, could not hold from casting himselfe at the feet of that innocent, and in the presence of all to condemne his owne malignity. And as in publike acts, so likewise in priuate conuersation would *B. Laurence* most willingly yield to the iudgement and wills of others, and as much as he might without affectation, alwayes seeke the lowest place.

He bare all respect, and veneration to Superiours, he held their becks insteed of Oracles. Nor only in things at large, and indifferent, by cutting off all sensuall appetite, he purely followed their will; but euen also in things otherwise very lawfull and vertuous, captiuing his owne vnderstanding, would not dissent a whit from their rules and dictamens. Whence it happened (as all vertues are with a wonderfull harmony conioyned together) that the seruant of God, very perfectly acquiring a habit of Religion, became rich and adorned with many others at the same tyme. Whereby preparing in his hart, a cleane & gratefull chamber for the holy Ghost, in short tyme he obtayned so high a guift of teares, and so much familiarity with his Creatour and Lord, as that remayning with his body on earth, with his soule he conuersed in Heauen; and dealing with men by diuerse occurrences, he departed not at all from the presence of God; chasing away from himselfe with great dexterity, all importune and superfluous phantasmes. From this purity of conscience, soone after ensued such a light, as far surmonted all learning purchased otherwayes, and in the will so great an

ardour

ardour, as all the waters of the world had not beene able to extinguish it. But rather he sought allwayes, to aduance forwardes, according to the obligation of profession, and so much abhorred to turne himselfe, and looke back being (as they say) at the plough, or to reedify that which he had destroyed, or to resume agayne any thing which he had left and renounced in the world, as he could neuer be brought once, to put his foot in his Fathers howse, allthough he liued so neere vnto them, and his dearest freinds were of the best reputation, and of rare example of Christian vertue: Saue only at the death of his Mother, and Brothers, was he present to assist them with due piety in their last passage.

How B. Laurence *conuerted a kinsman of his from his euill purpose. And of the goodly saying he was wont to vse.* Chap. 3.

B. *Laurence*, had not beene yet many yeares in Religion, when a deere companion of his, in the world, who for this meane while had beene in the East, and but newly returned to *Venice* (so powerfull the instigation of the Diuell is) went presently to S. *Georges*, accompanyed with musique, loud and soft, to allure the new Monke to his former life, partly also with a band of men, to vse some violence with the Conuent, if need were. This Gentleman was a man of great employments, and of much respect, so as he obtayned very easily to speake with Blessed *Laurence*; but yet with farre different successe from his designes. Because at the first sight of the new Souldiour of Christ, beholding the modesty of his countenance, the grauity of his gestures, and composition of the whole person, he remayned astonished thereat. And notwithstanding vsing some violence with himselfe, and taking courage withall, he began the enterprise for which he came thither; but the seruant of God permitting that breast full of passion and youthfull errour to vent it selfe forth, with a cheerefull countenance and mild speaches, began first very dexterously to feele him: & then with the memory of Death, of Hell, and of the last Iudgement, and with liuely representing vnto him, the vanity and deceipts of the world, pressed him so hard, as the good man being now compunct, vpon a sudden yielded himselfe; & so yielded, as cutting of with the force of spirit, all transitory designes whatsoeuer, resolued to adhere to that Rule, which he had thought to haue violated

ted, and from henceforth offering himselfe to the diuine worship, he perseuered in the holy Cloyster, with like profit of his owne, and amazement of the whole Citty. In this manner the ancient aduersary departed, and he who had thought to haue had a prey, was himselfe caught in the net.

Nor with the seculars only, being free and dissolute, were the perswasions of the B. *Laurence* efficacious (especially his good example and feruent prayers to our Lord concurring withall) but euen also (a thing to my iudgement yet more hard) with the tepid and negligent Religious. Since he awaked some of them more then once from the deadly sleep of slouthfullnes, and withdrew them from a foolish and vnwary presumption, to a sollicitous and wise feare of Christ: others, being now weary with the spirituall warfare, or rather basely already put to flight, he caused on a sudden to turne head agayne, and beyond all hope, to stand stoutly in the front of the battayle. For the eminent Pulpit, and popular preachings he wanted strength of body: but yet in priuate assemblyes, he would make sweet homilyes and deuout discourses, to the great profit and consolation of the hearers. And also in his dayly speach, would often proceed very notable sentences from his mouth, whereof for example sake we shall put downe some.

He would say, It was not the part of a Religious man to fly only the greater synnes, since that behoued euery one to doe, but euen also, to keepe himselfe from the lesse, least Charity should wax cold. He was wont also to note concerning fastings, that they are not to be remitted wholy as soone as the body waxeth leane, for asmuch as the wished extenuation thereof, is conserued with that which procures it. Three things he iudged to be necessary for a Monke, to wit, feruour, discretion, and heauenly grace, because where any of these are fayling, there can be no perseuerance. He compared the vertue of Humility, to a riuer that swells with rayne: for that euen as a torrent is very low and stil in the sommer, and runs outragious and boystrous in winter; so the humble man, being slack and remisse in prosperity, in aduersity agayne appeares to be high and magnanimous. He added, that no man well comprehends, what the guift of Humility is, but he that hath receiued it from God, and that there is nothing wherein men are more deceiued, then in discerning this vertue, and how true science consists in knowing two things; that God is all, and man nothing.

In the greater troubles of his Country (which at that tyme was much infested with warrs) he stuck not to admonish the principall Senatours, that if they would obtayne mercy of God, they should hold for certaine they were nothing, nor could do any thing of themselues. He aduised that none should be receiued into Religion without mature examine, least by admitting the bad, the good might be hurt. Besides that, when the number of subiects, is too much increased, the Rule cannot long last in its rigour, because perfection is of few only.

A Gentlemans sonne being come to S. *Georges* for the habit, as soone as the Blessed *Laurence* heard that he was induced thither, through the artificious inticements of the Monkes, he renders him to the sollicitous Father with these wordes: Heer take him to you againe, for this renouncing of the world should proceed from the Holy Ghost, and not for human instigation, and much worse it is to fayle afterwards, then to haue neuer begun at all. From the day he was made Priest, he fayld not to celebrate euery day, vnles by occasion of infirmity; and concluded, that he who neglects when he may, to enioy his Lord, declares sufficiently that he maks little account of him. To goe about to keep chastity, amidst commodityes and ease, he protested to be as much as with fuell to extinguish the fire. In the matter of Christ his counsails, he resolued (among other thinges) that no man vnderstands, how great a good this Pouerty is, but he that loues, when tyme is, contemplation and his Cell; and that God of purpose keepes secret the felicity of the Religious state, because that if it were knowne, euery one would be running into it.

He often remembred, that we are neuer to loose our hope in God, since heerin consists the life of the soule. As for the rich he affirmed, that they cannot be saued, but by dealing of almes. He held the Pastorall care to be so much more greiuous and difficult then the gouernment of the state of warre is, as the rule of inuisible things is harder then that of the visible. He likened a good Prince to a head, especially for this reason, that euen as the head & tongue are sufficient to craue help for the whole person, though the rest of the body be quiet & stand still; so the feruent prayer of a Prince, sometymes is inough to appease the wrath of God, though the rest of the Citty apply not it selfe, or attend thereunto. These violent enterprizes, and such as meete with encounters euery foot, he

counsailed

counsayled to forbeare, as growing from an euill spirit, since to the good and holy, the diuine Prouidence it selfe, is wont to open the way, and quit the obstacles that hinder.

How B. Laurence *was chosen to gouerne the* Religion: *and how afterwards he was made Bishop of Venice.* Chap. 4.

BY these and other such like aduices, may well be discerned, what light the man of God had, not only in abstract & spirituall matters, but euen also in the morall and practique; yea and without euer hauing attended to Scholasticall doctrine, or subtile disputes, he would answere when need was to profound interrogations of Theology, with so much acumen and clarity, as euen the Doctours themselues would be amazed therat. With the same wisedome surely infused more from Heauen, then borrowed from bookes, he composed diuers workes, fraught as well with soueraigne conceits, as with amorous affects. Which labours being publiquely set forth, and put in print, doe walke and passe at this day through the handes of learned men with notable fruite and help of soules. Amidst these thinges, after the Blessed *Laurence* had giuen a long and sufficient proofe of himselfe, he was elected by the Monkes, full sore against his will, to the gouernement of the Religion, and he bare that burthen with singular approbation vnto the 51. yeare of his age.

At which tyme, the good odour of such vertues, being now spread into diuers parts, it seemed good to Pope *Eugenius* the IV. without doubt through diuine inspiration, to create him Bishop of *Venice*. At which tydinges, it may easily be imagined, how much the holy man was confounded and troubled. Twice he was ready to fly away and to hide himselfe: but the matter not succeeding so with him, he determined at last to remit himselfe to the iudgment of his Congregation. And first hauing made for that intent many fastes and prayers, the Fathers resolued at last to dispatch a man of purpose to the Pope, humbly beseeching his Holynes, not to depriue their Order of such and so great a Guide-maister, and Pastour. And being not heard the first tyme, they replyed the second with more instance, but al in vaine, as appeares by the two Briefs, writen by the same *Eugenius* to the sayd Congregation, with words very, amorous and consolatory withall.

The Blessed *Laurence* then being not able to resist the Pope without sinne, accepted the power in such sort, as he not only changed not his manners to the worse, as it happens, but continually made them more admirable and perfect then euer. One day about the euening, he tooke possession of the Bishopricke, so simply, and so without all pompe, as euen his nearest friendes had no knowledge therof, till he was entred therinto. Then all that night without shutting his eyes, he remayned in prayer, beseeching our Lord with many teares, since for the only seruice of his diuine Maiesty, so wholy against his owne inclination, he had condescended to that degree, he would not depriue him of his protection and clemency: that he knew very well, the importance of the charge, the greatnes of the Citty, the variety and multitude of the Orders and states, the forces of the secular power; and how great disgusts had passed heeretofore, betweene that Domination and the Bishops his Predecessours, and how poore a stacke he had for such a manage, and for such accidents, being so a sily wretch as he was, and euer shut vp in a Monastery. His deuout prayers, and feruent sighes, were not powred in vayn. Because they found the eares of the diuine goodnes to be opened to them. Whence, being illustrated with a sudden and new light, he tooke so much vigour and comfort thereat, as he afterwards gouerned the whole Diocesse, as easely as he had been but to rule some Conuent, as shall appeare in the next Chapter.

How B. Laurence *gouerned his House, and the Citty, with singular fruit and edification of all.* Chap. 5.

TO begin with domesticall matters, Blessed *Laurence* ordayned his family in this manner. He chose out two vertuous companions of his Congregation; one for diuine offices, the other for the more weighty cares of the Bishoprike. For the seruice of the house, he would haue but fiue assistants and no more. To this retinue of Courtiers was his Table and Wardrobe answerable. He had no plate but of earthen-glasse. Arras, or Tapistry were not there to be seene at any tyme. In his cloathing he neuer altered the purple habit. In the night he lay vpon a scanty bedde of straw, couering himselfe with a grosse and course rugge. His table by how much more exquisite it was for neatnes, so much the more was it purposely

purposely neglected in vyandes. He neuer had longing for any thing, nor had as little auersion from any, contenting himselfe euer with that which was set before him.

His family thus ordered, he gaue himselfe to the reformation of the Citty, beginning first from the Cathedrall Church, which through others default and carelesnesse, had great need thereof. He set the Chapter on foot agayne, & the Order of the Chanons, now brought almost to nothing, and increased it with Priests and petty Chanons and Quiristers. He reduced many other Churches to so good tearmes, where hardly any Masse was wont to be celebrated before, as they seemed to be Cathedrall and Pontificall. Applying himselfe afterwardes to the censure of the Clergy, he made very excellent Decrees & Constitutions in this nature, nor had he any great difficulty to procure them to be kept and obserued, such was the grace & benignity, wherewith he obliged the harts of his subiects, since he was helpfull to many, and neuer imposed burden vpon any, permitting them fully to enioy the fruites and their rents: howbeit on the other side, when the matter required, he spared not to vse due seuerity.

With the same care and loue he dealt with the Monasteryes, especially of Nunnes; not suffering the frayle sex to suffer any thing, neyther in the body, or spirit. He repayred the Parishes which were ruined, and erected so many a new, as that finding some 20. of them, with good obseruance he left no lesse then 30. behind him at his death, nor vsed he lesse diligence with all the rest of his flocke. It is incredible, what concourse there was euery day at his house of distressed persons, who resorted to him for counsayle & succour. Notwithstanding he was more particularly vigilant vpon Curates and Vicars, as they call them, reducing often into their memory, the strait accompt they are to make to our Lord God. But how shall we expresse his great liberality? He despised money as much as euer was despised of any. His gate, the dispense, his chests, stood euer open to all the poore. He could not be brought by any meanes to take accompt of the mayster of his house; while it seemed to him an vnworthy thing, that a superintendant for the care of gaining souls, shou'd set himselfe of purpose to cast for farthings. And tooke heed much more, least in the manage of Episcopall rents, flesh and bloud might haue place: knowing how much this imported for edificatiō, & for purchasing the minds of the Citty. And therfore endeauoured he alwayes, that the world might cleerely know, how in temporall or œconomicall matters, he had no manner of commerce at all with his adherents.

So as, a certayne poore man, being recommended to him, on behalfe of the *Magnifico Leonard* his brother: Go thy wayes (sayd he to him) and bid him from me, to do thee the fauour, since God hath afforded him the meanes. The good Bishop answered to a certaine kinsman of his, not very rich, who demaunded some succour to marry his daughter with: Consider I pray, good Syr, that if I giue you but a little, it is not that which you pretend: and if I giue you much, I shall wrong many to helpe one only. Besides, how litle or much soeuer I hap to giue you, hath been commended to me, by the Church for mayntenance of the poore, and not for iewells, & other ornaments of women. He more willingly gaue almes in bread, wine, wood, garments, and other such like, then in money, to take away (I beleiue) the occasion from many of spending it ill, and when indeed he gaue any mony, he would diuide it into many peeces, that the greater number of the needy and necessitous might participate thereof. Nor in examining their merits was he very scrupulous, or exact; but rather sometymes let himselfe be deceiued, as chosing rather to benefit some vnworthy person, then defraud in the least any well deseruing. True it is that for the bashfull and shame-fac't poore (towardes whom the holy man, had perticular compassion) he had certaine Matrons deputed of much confidence, and of eminent vertue; who by some good way or other, might take faythfull and exact information of the secret necessityes of ech, especially of those who from good degrees through diuine permission haue fallen into straits.

In summe, he was farre from all tenacity, as when with monyes he could not furnish others necessityes, he would supply with suretyships for them, or by charging himselfe with their debts. And being demanded by his neerest domestiques, vpon what foundation he layd vp his treasure? He would say, of my Lord, who will pay me well for it. Nor was he awhit deceaued of his hope, since when others least thought of it, there would come to him heere and there great quantityes of gold and siluer, that he might dispend them on the poore at his owne pleasure. With all these thinges went vnited togeather a peace and serenity of mind, not easily to be expressed with wordes; as seeming in a certaine manner, he held

held the Moone vnder his feet, and had his mind fixed and seated in a place, where the clouds of sadnes, or the winds, and tempests of other disordinate passions could not reach. And to this purpose I will not spare to touch some thinges, not so light in substance, as they will seeme perhaps at first, if it be true indeed that by sudden accidents habits are knowne.

Two notable examples of B. Laurence *his Patience: and how welcome he was to Pope* Eugenius. Chap. 6.

THe Blessed *Laurence* being one day set at the table, one of the wayters deceaued (as sometyms it happens) insteed of wine presented him with vinegar, when the good Bishop hauing tasted it, without altering his countenance, or speaking a word, went on with his dinner, and listened to the lesson read, vntill at last the poore seruant aware of the errour, craued pardon for his offence. The B. *Laurence* (as we haue sayd aboue) was exceedingly reuerenced and beloued of the Citty. And yet neuerthelesse sometyms he had potent aduersaries: One whereof, taking by occasion a great disdaine at certaine Canons published against pompes, assembling a great number of men togeather, for the most part very noble & honourable personages, laboured of purpose to make an Inuectiue against the seruant of God, tearing him (as he was wont) in his fame, and exhorting all to oppose themselues mainly to the too much seuerity, and the indiscreet feruours of the Monke. In the like tenour spake some few of them, but the others partly resented the same, and partly derided such arrogancy; nor was the conuenticle hardly dissolued, when as one deuoted to the holy Pastour, being exceedingly troubled at those blasphemies cast forth, went presently in great hast to acquaint him with what had happened, and that with words so liuely, and with such ardour of the eyes & gestures, as had beene inough to haue set any one on fire, though he had not beene sensible of the iniury. But the Blessed *Laurence*, not being willing to be further informed, eyther of the fact, or the persons, made answere with a cheerefull countenance: Doe not trouble your selfe, my Sonne, for God will haue care of his honour; and so indeed it fell out, since that wretched accuser with his followers was soone very grieuously punished by the Magistrates vpon other occasions. I will add another example like to this.

The

The vigilant Bishop, with great equity had condemned a certaine Clerke for ill life, not regarding much the protection which a seditious Lay-man gaue vnto him. Whence this other lewd cōpanion was so enraged against him for it, as the solemne Procession of *Corpus Christi* passing before his doors, at the approach of the Bishop who carryed that sacred Custody, with a loud voyce he vomited forth a number of vile reproaches & contumelies vpon him, calling him (among other thinges) a Cosener, an Hypocrite, and warning the people to beware of him. From which sacrilegious affront ensued so great a scandall, and choler of the standers by, that the Maiesty and reuerence of that great Feast could hardly hold them from running suddenly with their burning torches, to set his house on fire. But the Priest of God, what did he in this case? Holding his eyes fixed on the Venerable Sacrament, without altering his pace awhit, or changing his countenance, he went forwaard with great grauity on his way. Although indeed, without indeauour of the Saint, the vnbridled presumption of the Wretch was soone punished, because being constrained by the Senate, to recant publiquely, he was afterwardes miserably banished also. Nor amidst persecutions and trauailes likewise the B. *Laurence* would shew himselfe to be stoute and constant, but euen also (a thing much more rare and difficult) amidst fauours and greatnesses themselues.

He was more then once inuited by Pope *Eugenius* to *Rome*, but alwayes in vayne, since he finding out new excuses euery houre, eschewed honours, and pompe as much as others sought them. True it is, the same *Eugenius* being come afterwardes to *Bologna*, and renewing the inuitement, the Seruant of God could no more alleadge, as he was wont, eyther the weaknes of his complexion, or the difficulty and length of the way: so as recommending himselfe to our Lord, he went his wayes thither, and in the presence of many Cardinalls, was very graciously receaued by the Pope, and saluted with these wordes: *VVelcome the ornament, and splendour of the Episcopall order*. And frō henceforth his Holines with the rest of the Clergy and the Citty, held him in great veneration all the tyme that he remayned there, which was but short, through the care and sollicitude he had, to returne to his Diocesse as soone as might be. And howbeit the Pope much desired to haue him with him, with humble instance notwithstanding effectually ta-

king

king his leaue, he departed from Court, without the least rust of auarice, that could once take hold of the fine polish of his Charity.

How B. Laurence *was made Patriarke of* Venice: *and what testimony was giuen of him, by a holy Hermite.* Chap. 7.

AFter *Eugenius* the IV. succeeded *Nicolas* the V. who in a certaine manner, contending with his Predecessour to exalt B. *Laurence*, determined to create him Patriarke of *Venice*, translating the Primacy into that Citty, from another Citty and Iland of the Adriatiqne Sea, called *Gradus*, very famous & magnificent in tymes past, though now, as humane vicissitudes are, as it were forgot, & vtterly destroyed. This newes at the beginning, was not very gratefull to the States of *Venice*, fearing least in processe of tyme, with such augmentation and aduancement of the Prelacy and the Title, the troubles and factions againe, might come to increase, which had anciently growne between the Ecclesiastical & secular Court. As soone then as the Blessed *Laurence* had notice thereof, to shew himselfe in deedes to be no lesse a good Cittizen, then a good Religious man, and a good Bishop, he went to the Senate, and there publiquely declared his desire was to retire himselfe rather, and to lay downe the charge now borne for these eighteene yeares against his will, then now in old age to charge himselfe a new with such a burden. But for as much as the name and title of *Patriarcke* offered by his Holynesse, redounded not so much to his honour, as the reputation and Maiesty of the Commonwealth, he would by no meanes dispose of himselfe any thing in that case, without first comunicating the matter with the Superintendantes and Tutours thereof. Wherfore they should plainely signify in the meane tyme, their owne inclination; since he would wholy gouerne himselfe according therto, in a busynes of that importance, looking alwayes a great deale more into the common good, then to any particuler consolation, or disdaine of his.

These wordes and the like, sayd the B. *Laurence*, with such affect and candour withall, as the Duke himselfe, through tendernes, being not able to hold from teares, and the Senatours astonished at so great a height of courage, conioyned with Charity alike, by a common consent made answere; By all meanes, and without respectes he should accept the offer, as after he did, with the extraordinary iubily, and ioy of the whole people.

About the same tyme, to the new glory of the B. *Laurence*, fell out another thing of great wonder. There liued for more then 30. yeares, neare to *Corfù*, in a craggy and desart place, a Man very famous for continuall prayer, and strict abstinence, and that which men more esteeme of, for a notable spirit of Prophesy. Now the Venetian Republike at that tyme, being much oppressed and reduced to ill termes by the armyes of *Philip Duke* of *Millan*: It came into the mind of a certaine noble Venetian, who had then some busynesse at *Corfù* at that tyme (so curious and sollicitous are men about future things) to learne of that solitary man, whether true it were, as it was commonly spoken, that the Venetian Empyre was neere vpon ruyne? To which demaund the Prophet answeared without delay: You may all be thankefull to the bitter plaints, and earnest intercessions of your Bishop, without which take this for certayne you had now a good while since been quite vndone; & that which had of old happened to those fiue infamous Cittyes, had fallē vpon yours, since you haue so turned your backes to our Lord, and put his holy Law so quite in obliuion.

This testimony gaue the deuout Hermite of the blessed *Laurence*; not knowing the same by any humane way, nor vnderstanding, but by diuine inspiration, what passed in the world in those dayes. Which thing being suddenly diuulged, confirmed the vniuersall opinion which was then had of such a Patriarke. So as there arriued into the Citty of *Venice* no personage of quality, nor pilgrime, (who then for sundry deuotions came flocking from *Hungary*, *Germany*, *France*, and *Spayne*) who endeuoured not to enforme themselues exactly of his sharp and austere life; and of his most irreprehensible manners, to receiue his benediction, to reuerence his Reliques as holy, the lodging he dwelt in, the Couch where he lay in, and the clothes which he had worne. They neuer tooke vpon them any enterprize of moment, eyther in publike or priuate, without hauing recourse to the prayers of this great seruant of God.

Lastly, he neuer likely went forth of doores, but the people would runne to him, as to an Angell descended from heauen, while euery one held himselfe happy, but only to behould him, much more to treate with him, and to receaue answeres or aduices from that Oracle. All these and many other thing besides, which for breuityes sake are passed ouer, being apt to puff a man vp, how

wise

wise and wary soeuer, and to put him quite besides himselfe; yet were not able to disseuer the B. *Laurence* from the loue and feare of God, and from the knowledge and contempt of himselfe.

The great talents which B. Laurence *had, in deciding causes as Iudge: and of the blessed end which he made.* Chap. 8.

VVHat shall we say, of the manner, which B. *Laurence* held, in giuing audience, and dispatch of causes touching his tribunalls? Wherein he had such light & so great dexterity withall, as howbeit he gaue the most part of his tyme, to all other things, yet he seemed to be as borne only and created for this. He would stand amidst the cryes and clamours both of clients and pleaders, as firme as a rock: and after he had listned to the partyes what sufficed (discouering now and then, with more then human vnderstanding, the secret traces, and frauds which lay often hid) he would breifly then giue sentence, but with such iudgement and equity, as among other things in the Court of *Rome*, they were allwayes held in a high degree most iust and irrefragable. Nor left he those awhit lesse satisfyed, who came to visit him in priuate, since to be admitted to his presence, there was no need of wayting or attending more fit opportunityes. For whether he studyed, or wrote, or made his prayer, suddaynely cutting of the threed of the present occasion, he would receiue all with such peace and benignity, as he seemed not to be subiect to troubles, or clothed with flesh, but with all loue, all sweetenes, all spirit.

By these wayes now approaching to the terme of his pilgrimage, hardly had he finished the Treatise intituled, *The degrees of perfection*; when being now some 74. yeares of age, he was surprised by a burning pestilent feauer. Whereupon his domestikes preparing him a bed, according to his infirmity, the true imitatour of Christ, being troubled at it, sayd to them: What then, doe you make ready feathers for me? My Lord was not layd vpon feathers, but stretched on a hard and cruell bat. And doe you not remember that which S. *Martyn* protested in his last article, that a Christian should dye vpon ashes, and clad in cilices? Finally there was no meanes to lay him otherwise, then vpon his wonted straw. Perceyuing afterwards, to cure his malady, there was no neglect had of trauayle or costs, being angry as it were against himselfe. Ah (sayd he) what paynes is taken, and how much mony cast away vpon a vile sack, when the poore of Christ haue no food the while, nor fire, nor any remedy for their necessityes.

Heereupon presaging his owne death, he recollected himselfe more seriously; and the two contrary affects, Feare, and Hope (as it happened in the like case to the blessed *Hilarion*) began to goe & come with him. So as now with a cheerefull and smiling countenance, forbidding teares to the standers by, he exclaymed, Behold the spouse, let vs go, and meete him: and added with eyes cast vp to heauen: Good Iesus, loe I come. And now agayne with iust a ballance weighing the diuine iudgements, he would shew forth signes of Feare: insomuch as a freind of his saying to him, with tender eyes: How willingly, my Lord, may you goe to the palme which is now ready prepared for you? he answered with a graue countenance: this palme, my Sonne, is giuen to the valiant combatants of Christ, not to the base and cowards as I am. And yet taking courage at last from his owne conscience, & much more from the merits and Passion of our Sauiour, he goes about to declare his last will.

And heere now I could wish them present who do greedily amasse vp treasures and rents of the Church, conuerting the stocke of the poore vnto their priuate vse, and with diuers slights continuing the sacred benefices in the same family. The faythfull dispensour of Christ had not any thing to leaue, hauing allwayes been so great an enemy of all propriety, as that (being a person otherwise so addicted to learning) of purpose, not to seeme to possesse a booke, he had euer studyed in volumes stiched vp only. His Testamēt was then to exhort his followers to true vertue, and very often to ordayne expressely, he might be buryed at S. *Georges*, without any pompe, in the sepulcher of the Monks there.

In the meane while, the rumour was spread of his last extremes through the whole Citty. Whence hastened a world of people to behold him, vpon whome hauing for two continuall dayes togeather, most deerely stretched forth his handes, the doore being open to all, amidst holsome aduices and admonishments, which he gaue them, and the sweet colloquies he had with God, his strength fayling him by little and little, receauing the diuine Sacraments with great deuotion, he finally expired on the 8. of

Ianuary

Ianuary, in the morning being the third yeare of his Patriarkall dignity, and the twentith of his Bishopricke. The sacred body was put in the Church, and publiquely celebrated, not with mourning blacks and funerall exequyes, but with feasts and wonted processions as made for some notable victory, as shall appeare in the Chapter following.

A notable miracle wrought by B. Laurence *in his life tyme, with another that happened after his death.* Chap. 9.

THe Cōfraternityes which are there called the Great Schools, went to honour the body with lights, and festiuall garments, and guilt torches. There met also the whole Clergy with the Magistrates and persons of ech quality; and while the offices lasted, was heard from aboue by two *Celestine* Fryars, a sweete harmony of celestiall accents. Besides which miracle, are many recounted of the B. *Laurence*, as well at his death, as also in his life, as the deliuery of possessed persons of euill spirits, curing of the sick, and predictions of future or hidden things, and other like effects aboue nature. But we only for assay, shall touch but two of them.

The one was, that in the Feast of *Corpus Christi*, the virgins of a certaine Monastery neere to the Bishoprick, being not able to cōmunicate, by reason of some troubles which then happened, were all exceedingly grieued thereat, but particulerly one of rare deuotion, & of excellent vertue, who was of the opinion with others, to send to the Bishop in all hast, to beseech him in his high Masse he would dayne to remember them, that they remayning that day depriued of the feast of *Angells*, might not also be defrauded of the intercession of the Preist. The B. *Laurence* oftentymes did promise to doe so. When behold in the midst of Masse, after he had eleuated the sacred Hoast, being rauished quite besides himselfe, without departing awhit from the peoples eyes, he caryed the holy Cōmunion, and gaue it by diuine priuiledge, to the aforesaid Virgin alone; who, the other being distracted vpon sundry occasions, was euen at the selfe same hower, in secret in her Cell, rapt likewise in deep contemplation, and burning desire of receauing her Lord. From which office of Charity the Seruant of God returning immediatly againe into himselfe, so ended the Masse, as none of the standers by could beware of what had happened: the Confessour only of the Virgin had knowledge thereof, and told it to the Patriarke, who exhorting them both to yield thankes vnto God only for it, imposed vpon them a strict silence thereof, so long as he liued. And with this, came to be renewed the ancient miracles, which are recounted of some other Saints likewise in the same matter.

The other miracle was, that after the happy passage of the B. *Laurence*, there growing a contention betweene the Chanons of the Cathedrall, and the Monkes of S. *Georges*, about the custody of that sacred Treasure; and there wanting no reasons for eyther part, it was necessary while the strife was deciding, to keepe it *in deposito* aboue ground; and so being a day or two, not only without signe of corruption, but with yielding also a most sweet odour, on the third day, began moreouer the cheeks to looke red, and the bloud to come, with so much the greater astonishment of all, as they were certifyed, there was vsed no preseruatiue of Balmes, or of any other druggs about the same; and the Phisitian sincerely affirmed, the feauer to haue been malignant and pestilent, and of its nature apt inough to corrupt withall. Whereof the rumour, running through the Citty, there was agayne such a multitude and presse of people at the Gates, as from the Sacristy where he was kept, they were fayne to cary him to the Temple, to satisfy the peoples eyes, who not contended with a simple view, began with an audacious piety, to seize on his reliques, so as his shoes on a sudden were vanished, his garments were cut asunder, and perhaps the feruour had proceeded further, if betymes remedy had not been found by a Guard set vpon the body.

From thence, being conueighed backe againe into the Sacristy, it perseuered entire, vntill notwithstanding the Order left by him, sentence was giuen in fauour of the Chanons; while in the Cathedrall Church remayned a continuall concourse of people men and women, who being stirred vp at so great a newes, came running thither, not only from the neighbour-countreyes there about, but euen also from diuers partes of *Italy* and *Sclauony* it selfe, for the space of 65. dayes; at the end whereof still vntouched as at the first, in the same Cathedrall, it was reuerently layd in a Vault, which to this day also is visited by the faythfull with much deuotion, and not without fruit, since that Blessed spirit, being there inuoked, obtaynes them many graces from Heauen. And to speake some thing also of his exteriour person, the holy man was tall of staftature, of well knit ioyntes, of a pale coulour, of gracious eyes, and the whole aſpect both venerable and amiable; a thing truly not vſuall, becauſe indeed we do ſee many fayre ſoules to be encloſed by the mighty hand, and ſweet diſpoſition of the Higheſt in proportionable lodgings. To whom be all prayſe, power, and glory, for all Eternity.

FINIS.

Gentle Reader:

THE faults which haue eſcaped in printing (by reaſon of the vncorrected copy, and imploying of ſtrangers not skillfull in our language) I hope are not very many, nor yet ſuch, as may not eaſily be corrected, by thy iudicious Reading.